Praise for *The Journey of Soul*

"Once in a blue moon, a book appears that is so synchronistically aligned with the zeitgeist that it integrates the sacred with nature, and our individual life paths with our collective evolution. Informed by a lifetime of engaged experience, deep listening, and pattern seeking, and graced by beautiful language and storytelling, this book offers a map for those yearning to find their soul's purpose. Now, when we're called to act on behalf of what we love and to contribute our unique gifts to the maturation of our endangered species, Bill Plotkin offers lucid and grounded guidance, wisdom, and an illuminated pathway. I am in awe of this book. A rare and precious gift."

— **Nina Simons**, cofounder of Bioneers

"The people who gave me bones, flesh, and story — the Yoruba people of West Africa — knew how to see in dark times. In times of crisis, they encoded an ancient ritual in the ordinary act of greeting an elder with prostration. That ritual tells a story of descent, of generous libations, of lingering memory, and of creative moves in the wake of destruction and utter ruin. I am pleasantly shocked Bill Plotkin knows a version of this meta-story. This book glows at the interstitial matrixes between despair and cultural renewal; it is a trace of departures we must yet make into forbidden depths where — quite ironically — we might see ourselves as if for the first time. Read it."

— **Bayo Akomolafe, PhD**, author of *These Wilds Beyond Our Fences: Letters to My Daughter on Humanity's Search for Home*

"With this important book, Bill Plotkin continues his crucial work of teaching us how to live properly, and how to live properly on the living planet. Anyone who reads this book will forever be grateful to Plotkin for the gentle, informed, yet powerful guidance he provides."

— **Derrick Jensen**, author of *A Language Older Than Words* and *The Myth of Human Supremacy*

"For four decades Bill Plotkin has been coaxing the human psyche out of its self-enclosed cages, liberating the terrestrial imagination, inviting and empowering the human soul to remember its ancestral alliance with elk herds and dark woodlands, with rivers overflowing their banks and the improvisational riffs of garrulous ravens. His methods have steadily widened into a capacious toolkit for personal and cultural metamorphosis, laid out in these luminous pages strewn with poetry, mythology, and dreams. A remarkable guidebook."

— **David Abram**, author of *Becoming Animal* and *The Spell of the Sensuous*

"*The Journey of Soul Initiation* provides a detailed map of the journey toward real human maturity. Beginning with the reconnection of our soul with the web of life, Bill Plotkin guides us through the magical and visionary encounters that belong to our reengagement with the more-than-human world. Full of stories and lived examples, here is a rich tapestry of the personal exploration needed if we are to realize our soul's purpose and make a true contribution to the greater Earth community — if we are to learn to love and care for our common home."

— **Llewellyn Vaughan-Lee, PhD**, editor *Spiritual Ecology:*
The Cry of the Earth

"Bill Plotkin — and his teachings — are in a category all their own! He is a priest of the soul, a therapist of the heart, a stimulator of the mind, and a companion of the body. And then he works them all together! Plotkin is a theologian of no particular religion, but he creates a solid foundation for a truly natural religion — that still honors growth and transcendence. You must know this is a most rare and much-needed synthesis!"

— **Fr. Richard Rohr**, Center for Action and Contemplation,
Albuquerque, New Mexico

"Humans and other-than-humans alike ought to be grateful for Bill Plotkin's life's work of putting the wilderness, and with it the sacredness of the Earth, forward as our destiny in this perilous time of ecocide, matricide, and species narcissism. In *The Journey of Soul Initiation*, Plotkin, now as an elder, continues his important vocation to nurture and guide a spiritually famished society to greener pastures."

— **Matthew Fox**, author of *Original Blessing* and *Julian of Norwich*

"Bill Plotkin has created a fascinating and intelligent approach to deepening life and developing yourself to be in the world in an engaged and individual way. I haven't seen anything so original and solid. It is both contemporary and traditional, mapping out the soul's descent into a meaningful way of life. We need this kind of charting of depth more than ever before."

— **Thomas Moore**, author of *Care of the Soul*

"In this beautiful and fascinating book, Bill Plotkin brings a rare depth of thought, insight, and experience to elucidating the soul's journey to purpose and wholeness. *The Journey of Soul Initiation* offers both a practical and theoretical synthesis of his life's work, guiding others to reimagine the links between nature and the human soul, encouraging each of us to become 'a partner in the unfolding of Earth's story.' For those of us born into a culture whose prevailing mythology is on the point of collapse, who are suffocating from a dearth of meaning, Plotkin's grounded wisdom is more essential than ever."

— **Sharon Blackie, PhD,** author of *If Women Rose Rooted*
and *The Enchanted Life*

"*The Journey of Soul Initiation* has the feel of a life's work about it. It's ambitious: sweeping when it needs to be, forensic when required. It's a book to do with the complex work of cultural maturation, and there's no quick fix present in these pages. Bill Plotkin places something marvelous in our hands. A key. There are innumerable hours of experience in these lines, and a mythic underpinning to a world on fire."

— **Dr. Martin Shaw,** author of *Wolf Milk: Chthonic Memory in the Deep Wild*

"We all say we want to grow, to change, to become ourselves, but do we? In *The Journey of Soul Initiation*, Bill Plotkin synthesizes the wisdom and shamanic traditions of the millennia whose archetypal structure of death, initiation, and transformation, once found in tribal practice, must now be accessed from within. His work is a great gift, and a guide, to those who wish to undertake the journey set in motion when the gods brought us here."

— **James Hollis, PhD**, Jungian analyst and author of *Living Between Worlds:*
Finding Personal Resilience in Changing Times

"A provocative and pioneering answer to our slide, as individuals and a species, into deep species loneliness. Here is a challenge to the self-congratulatory and ultimately devastating Anthropocene."

— **Richard Louv,** author of *Our Wild Calling* and *Last Child in the Woods*

Praise for Bill Plotkin's *Soulcraft*

"As we enter a future where humans and the natural world are more intimate with each other, we will surely be powerfully influenced by this new guide into the mysteries of nature and psyche. In *Soulcraft*, Bill Plotkin gives us an authentic masterwork. In the substance of what he has written, in the clarity of his presentation, and in the historical urgency of the subject, he has guided us far into the new world that is opening up before us. We will not soon again receive a work of this significance."

— **Thomas Berry**, author of *The Dream of the Earth*
and *The Great Work*, from the foreword to *Soulcraft*

Praise for Bill Plotkin's *Nature and the Human Soul*

"Plotkin brings forth a new model for the whole of human life and spirituality in our world....An essential, weighty book for our perilous times."
— ***Publishers Weekly*** (starred review)

Praise for Bill Plotkin's *Wild Mind*

"Bill Plotkin's *Wild Mind* ushers in a new era of depth psychology....To study it is to pass through a magical gateway into one's unique role within the Great Work that Earth is calling us to."
— **Brian Thomas Swimme**, California Institute of Integral Studies, coauthor with Thomas Berry of *The Universe Story*

the
JOURNEY
of SOUL
INITIATION

Also by Bill Plotkin

Soulcraft: Crossing into the Mysteries of Nature and Psyche

Nature and the Human Soul: Cultivating Wholeness and Community in a Fragmented World

Wild Mind: A Field Guide to the Human Psyche

the
JOURNEY
of SOUL
INITIATION

A Field Guide for Visionaries, Evolutionaries, and Revolutionaries

Bill Plotkin

New World Library
Novato, California

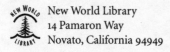 New World Library
14 Pamaron Way
Novato, California 94949

The material in this book is intended for education. It is not meant to take the place of diagnosis and treatment by a qualified medical practitioner or therapist. No expressed or implied guarantee of the effects of the use of the recommendations can be given or liabil-ity taken. The publisher advises such activities as fasting or wilderness excursions not be attempted or practiced without appropriate guidance and support.

Soulcraft is a registered trademark of Bill Plotkin.

Illustration on page 34 originally from *Nature and the Human Soul* by Bill Plotkin © 2008, published by New World Library.

Text design by Tona Pearce Myers

Library of Congress Cataloging-in-Publication Data

Names: Plotkin, Bill, date, author.
Title: The journey of soul initiation : a field guide for visionaries, evolutionaries, and rev-
olutionaries / Bill Plotkin.
Description: Novato, California : New World Library, [2021] | Includes bibliographical ref-
erences and index.
Identifiers: LCCN 2020039913 (print) | LCCN 2020039914 (ebook) | ISBN 9781608687015 |
ISBN 9781608687022 (ebook)
Subjects: LCSH: Spiritual life. | Vision quests. | Soul. | Psychology, Religious. | Jung, C. G.
(Carl Gustav), 1875-1961.
Classification: LCC BL624 .P56 2021 (print) | LCC BL624 (ebook) | DDC 204/.4--dc23
LC record available at https://lccn.loc.gov/2020039913
LC ebook record available at https://lccn.loc.gov/2020039914

First printing, January 2021
ISBN 978-1-60868-701-5
Ebook ISBN 978-1-60868-702-2
Printed in Canada on 100% postconsumer-waste recycled paper

 New World Library is proud to be a Gold Certified Environmentally Responsible Publisher. Publisher certification awarded by Green Press Initiative.

10   9   8   7   6   5   4

For the future ones.
And in loving memory of Betty and Bernie Plotkin.

If we will the future effectively it will be because the guidance and the powers of the Earth have been communicated to us, not because we have determined the future of the Earth simply with some rational faculty.

— THOMAS BERRY

Contents

Author's Note

When one makes a map, it's essential to be perfectly clear what one means by its symbols — otherwise, use of the map might increase the chance of getting lost. In this book, I use many common words and expressions in uncommon ways. I also use some not-so-common phrases and even personally coined neologisms. In the glossary, I specify my meanings. When I use a common word germane to the journey of soul initiation — like *Soul*, *Ego*, *Adolescence*, or *Adult* — I capitalize it simply as a way to remind you, throughout the book, that I mean it in a particular and often unconventional way. When I use the same term in a generic, common, or nonspecific way, I don't capitalize it. Some words, like *Muse*, *Confirmation*, or *Cocoon*, I capitalize for an additional reason: I use them as proper nouns — my name, for example, for an archetype, a life passage, or a life stage. Other words and phrases used with specific meanings — like *subpersonality*, *the journey of soul initiation*, *mythopoetic identity*, or *delivery system* — are uncommon enough that there's no need to capitalize them; you're not likely to mistake my meaning once you know what I mean. These, too, are defined in the glossary.

Death's Apprentice

A Personal Introduction

God speaks to each of us as he makes us,
then walks with us silently out of the night.

These are the words we dimly hear:

You, sent out beyond your recall,
go to the limits of your longing.
Embody me.

Flare up like flame
and make big shadows I can move in.

Let everything happen to you: beauty and terror.
Just keep going. No feeling is final.
Don't let yourself lose me.

Nearby is the country they call life.
You will know it by its seriousness.

Give me your hand.

— RAINER MARIA RILKE

When I was a child, I dreamed of a cemetery. Repeatedly. The same dream. I was only four or five at the time of my first visit to those holy grounds.

My nightworld cemetery was not like any I had seen in my dayworld life, with their flat expanses and well-ordered gray gravestones on manicured lawns beneath shade trees. My dream cemetery was populated with haphazardly sited tombstones and monuments of all sizes and shapes. It was in a hilly, craggy land, dry and dusty, nearly treeless, with rock walls and ramparts painted in shifting tones of reds and browns, streaked in places with black. It was a landscape wildly unlike anything I knew as a child in New England. From where do such dreams arise?

I'm standing on a road of soft coral-colored sand that winds its way in gentle curves between undulating earthen walls, draped here and there with green vegetation. There is no one else around. It is dusk. The low light rises from the ground itself — the land is softly glowing.

I am being summoned, called by a distant song, a high, haunting, wordless strain like a cathedral choir. The song radiates awe and holiness. It feels both dangerous and alluring.

I move slowly along the road toward the mysterious singing. I am not exactly walking; it's more like floating, like I am being pulled toward the song. I move like a disembodied spirit, like a breath of desert breeze.

I am aware there is a cemetery on the other side of the wall. I can't quite see it, but I can feel its mystery, its otherworldly song, as if the most holy things exist there. But this graveyard also feels strange, even alien, not of my people. I sense this must be a Christian cemetery, that it has something to do with Jesus. It feels as if there are secrets there — in the land and in the air.

I float-walk through an opening in the wall on my left. A long steep slope extends up to the right. Scattered tombstones loom everywhere on the parched, arid hillside. Some are quite large, most of odd shapes, and all fashioned from the same soft, buff-colored stone.

Now the singing emanates from all directions, but ahead I also hear a lower-toned chanting, a droning beneath the higher-pitched voices. I float-walk toward this new sound, winding through alleys and passageways, between small rectangular one-story stone buildings — windowless but with dark open doorways.

As I round a corner, the chanting grows louder. It seems to be coming from an underground vault. I move down a short flight of stone stairs toward the opening and stop on the threshold. I smell damp rock mixed with pungent incense. The small room is dimly lit, but I'm able to see four or five men in brown-and-green hooded robes standing around a high stone table. They are chanting in unison, in low wordless tones. It is too dark to see their faces. I am just tall enough to see that on the table before them is a body, a dead person draped in a thin pale cloth. The monks nod slightly, as if they had expected me, but they do not pause. They each hold brass-colored wands shaped like small barbells, and while they chant, they wave them slowly and methodically over the dead body. The wands are elaborately wrought with emblems and adorned with the characters of an alphabet unknown to me. I don't understand what is going on but I sense the monks are showing me something about death. This is not about the process of dying. It is about death. It does not feel morbid but, rather, of the holy or sacred. I am more fascinated than afraid.

A few years before puberty, my cemetery dreams vanished into a dark corner of my psyche, but sometime in my midteens I remembered them again. I didn't know what to do with them but I didn't ask anyone for advice. In most American families and communities at that time, people seldom spoke about dreams and never in any depth. But the dream cemetery and its mysteries lingered in the background of my awareness.

My understanding now, more than sixty years after my first visit to the night-world cemetery, is that these dreams were like initial lessons from Mentor preparing me for the odyssey that would be my life. They were like numinous breadcrumbs scattered over the suburban streets, backyards, and routines of my early school years. They were, as Rilke put it, like God speaking to me as he walked me into life: "Let everything happen to you: beauty and terror." I've come to think of my time in the nightworld cemetery as an early shaping of my psyche, a nudge in the direction desired by Soul.[1]

What *are* the mysteries of death that the crypt monks showed me? Why did the DreamMaker repeatedly place me in this particular dreamscape? What are the clues within the dream itself?

Although I'm inquiring here about my own psyche and although I've had decades to ponder these riddles, I can still only hypothesize, and humbly so, because, after all, I (the Ego) did not create or choose these dreams. A greater power was and is at work. That said, here are some speculations on what the DreamMaker was up to:

First is the spellbinding sense of awe I feel in this dreamscape — the holiness animating the cemetery and the magic emanating from death itself.

Second, while in the nightworld underground crypt, I, the dream Ego, am not at all repelled by death. Quite to the contrary. I'm allured, fascinated. It's as if Dream-Maker wanted me, in this life, to move toward death, not away — to learn what happens underground, in the tombs.

Since my early twenties, I have believed we are transformed and matured by living with a consciousness of death. When we ask what matters most in the light of our mortality, life becomes simpler, our values clearer. What will you offer the world if your life itself and the way you live it are the only meaningful and lasting gifts you can give? Death serves life in this way. Our greatest gifts to the world are engendered by the reality of mortality.

Third, in this dream I'm placed in the role of a student of death, an apprentice to the archetype of Death. Perhaps the dream was the commencement of this apprenticeship, one that I accepted while in the dream by responding to the song that drew me up that long desert road into the exotic graveyard and to the underground vault and the monks with their mysterious rituals and symbol-laden implements. But if it is true I agreed to apprentice during the dream, it was then only on the dream level. It was not till decades later that I consciously said yes to this apprenticeship.

Fourth, the dreams foretold an apprenticeship not just with Death but also with the monks. These monks are perhaps in the role of psychopomps, those who guide the dead to the underworld. But psychopomps are also those who guide living people in their underworld encounters with Soul — encounters that requires a type of dying along the way.

Last, for now, there is in this dream a strong attraction to a particular desert landscape, the redrock canyon country, a terrain I didn't know existed until my college years when I first visited southern Utah and was captivated and haunted by its magical shapes and hidden treasures, a land I have now lived on the edge of and through which I have wandered regularly for over forty years. On my first desert hike, I discovered that what in my dream I had thought was a road was actually a dry sand wash, iconic to and ubiquitous in the redrock country.

As a teenager, I was intrigued by the mysteries of life and death, but no one I knew talked about such things. The religious traditions of Judaism, at least as they were taught to me during six years of Hebrew school on Sunday mornings and on Tuesday and Thursday afternoons, were of no help whatsoever — not to me.

In college I began to find, off campus, some resonant pathways of spiritual study and practice: first, Zen Buddhism and Kundalini yoga; then, Sufism and the Fourth Way teachings of the Armenian mystic George Gurdjieff. In college courses, I was introduced to the work of Carl Jung and the contemporary Western field of depth psychology.

During graduate school in Boulder, Colorado, I continued my exploration of the mysteries, my mind filled with questions about consciousness and other worlds. My primary research area was nonordinary states — sleep and dreams, and worlds accessed through hypnosis, meditation, and biofeedback. I also personally explored nonordinary states through Tibetan Buddhism (as a summer student at Naropa Institute) as well as through entheogens, rock climbing, and wilderness immersions.

After graduate school, I took a position as an assistant professor at a state university in New York, teaching psychology and continuing to research nonordinary states. Two years later, age twenty-eight, in midwinter, I snowshoed up an

Adirondack mountain and, on the summit, received the terrifying and ecstatic revelation that a life of scholarly research and teaching was for me neither a path with
heart nor a pathway to soul. I descended (in more ways than one), went home, and
resigned from the university.

For a year I studied and practiced psychotherapy as a postdoctoral intern at a
community mental health center in Oregon. During that year, I learned of the work
of Steven Foster and Meredith Little of the School of Lost Borders in California,
providing my first glimpse of a portal into the realm of mysteries I had been seeking.
In the late seventies, Steven and Meredith had begun to reintroduce to the contemporary West the ancient pan-cultural ceremony of the vision fast. After written
correspondence with them that included their wise and generous guidance, I decided to enact a vision fast on my own, in the late summer of 1980. Provisioned with
little more than Steven and Meredith's early handbook and an ardent desire for self-
discovery, I backpacked several miles into a trailless corner of the Colorado Rockies
and fasted for four days and nights. That story is told in my first book, *Soulcraft*.
During that fast I met another monk:

> The monk, cleverly disguised as a majestic spruce tree, stands alone on the
> shore of a subalpine lake surrounded by soaring granite peaks of lumi-
> nous silver. I sit in my ceremonial circle of stones about thirty feet from
> the spruce and the lake. It's not until this fourth day of fasting that I at last
> truly see this tree, see him for who he really is: a monk clothed in a vivid
> blue-green hooded robe and brown leggings, a monk who, after decades of
> meditation upon the surface and into the depths of the lake, has achieved
> an understanding of both the nature of the world and his unique place in
> it. I watch him, his back to me, as he converses with the beavers of the lake.
> I'm inspired by his grace and serenity, his wildness and wisdom, the way he
> celebrates each dazzling moment of the mountain miracle in which we're
> mutually immersed.
>
> Then he turns ever so slightly toward me and, with a sweep of his left
> arm, calls my attention to a yellow-and-black butterfly floating in my di-
> rection. I watch as she dances ever closer, feel her wing brush my cheek like
> a kiss, and hear her say, *Cocoon Weaver.*
>
> After four days of fasting in vast mountain solitude, monk-trees and
> talking butterflies are not particularly surprising to me. And what the
> butterfly says is not at first more interesting to me than the other won-
> ders unfolding in and around that meadow. Like the little pikas gathering
> watercress for the coming winter. Or the red-tailed hawks circling above.
> But a few moments after the butterfly's flyby, something stirs in my belly,
> shoots up through my heart and out my mouth as a gasp or a cry, and I
> realize I've just been gifted with an image that is already opening a door,

revealing a way forward and deeper into the world. I don't have a clue what it means to weave cocoons, but I know with certainty this is what I was born to do. It feels utterly yet strangely familiar.

Following my vision fast, I learned, through trial and error, how to help others weave cocoons for their transformation from caterpillar to butterfly. By degrees, I came to understand the process of human maturation in a way that had virtually no relationship to anything I'd learned in mainstream Western psychology and, even more disturbingly, had little overlap with the array of spiritual traditions I had studied and practiced. Only after years of searching did I find a few world-views — some within the Western tradition and some beyond — that had resonance with what I came to understand about the weaving of cocoons for human transformation.

But that territory is covered in my earlier books and, in a different way, later in this one. Here I want to explore with you my numinous encounter with the monk and butterfly and the relationship between that experience and my cemetery dreams. My visionary encounter in the Colorado mountains ushered me into the next stage of my apprenticeship to Death. A Cocoon Weaver *is* an apprentice to Death.

For the caterpillar, the cocoon or chrysalis is, at the outset, a tomb. Within this crypt (for most moths, it's a cocoon spun from the caterpillar's silk; for butterflies, it's a chrysalis the caterpillar itself molts into), the caterpillar's body dissolves. The life of the caterpillar is over; this creature will never again be an earth crawler, will never again consume a caterpillar diet, will no longer have caterpillar dreams or longings.

As I began to help other humans weave cocoons for themselves, I soon understood I was supporting them to die in a sense, to abandon everything they had thought they were and everything they had thought life was supposed to be and what the world was. I was an agent of Death, and I could see in their faces that they saw me this way. This was startling and disturbing to me. I suspect most people wouldn't cheerily sign up for the role of agent for Death. But more and more it seemed this was the role for which Mystery had been preparing me since my earliest days.

After the caterpillar body dissolves in the chrysalis, the cells in that elixir begin to reassemble into a butterfly. The chrysalis shifts from being a tomb to a womb. The image of a womb is much easier for most people to embrace; the idea of rebirth resonates with positive possibilities. But at the start of the journey of soul initiation, it's the tomb and its ending we encounter first, not the womb and its promise. A Cocoon Weaver must portray the tomb as alluring — or at least necessary.

I find it interesting that the image of weaving cocoons was presented to me by a butterfly. Butterflies don't make cocoons (nor morph into chrysalises). Caterpillars do. The cocoon means death to the caterpillar, an ending. The creature who fully appreciates the purpose of the cocoon is the butterfly — the beneficiary of the caterpillar's demise. My vision fast shifted the accent from death, as in my cemetery dream, to birth — but a birth that retains death as an integral element.

Sixteen years after my first vision fast, I walked into the Cemetery itself and fasted there alone for four days and nights.

It had never occurred to me that the Cemetery might exist as an actual place on Earth — until the day in 1991 when I spotted it as I stood, astonished, on a high ridge in the southern Utah redrock country and gazed down a thousand vertical feet into a wildly convoluted maze of canyons. It then took five years and three attempts before I found a route into that maze. But the story of how I stumbled upon the Cemetery begins in the spring of 1981, during one of my early desert treks dedicated to finding suitable sites to guide vision fasts.

A friend and I have backpacked many miles into a rare desert oasis in a deep and labyrinthine canyon system. The next day, while exploring one of the many side canyons, we reach a spot near its head from which we gaze out over the redrock country to the west, into the main canyon and beyond. On the high western wall of the main fork, a mile or two distant, a large and striking rock formation dominates the landscape, roundly lit by the long light of morning, its profile unequivocally male and humanoid — and eerily familiar. A feeling of both doom and hope swirls up from my belly, almost toppling me — nausea interwoven with a sparkly giddiness.

The rock formation's head and neck form one of the higher points on the distant ridge. From shoulder to crown alone, he looks to be more than two hundred vertical feet. He stares back at us, his gaunt red visage topped by close-cropped brown hair, his eyes lost deep inside elongated sockets, his long nose casting a shadow across half his face. He has an intelligent and alien look, perhaps due to his large, thin ears with their extended upper edges. His blocky chin is solidly set in a gaze of great gravity. On his broad shoulders lie grayish-brown epaulets, giving him the look of a commanding officer of an unknown and inscrutable force.

I recognize him instantly. This is not our first meeting.

Ten years earlier, while in college in North Carolina, my two roommates and I swallowed sizable doses of mescaline, the primary psychoactive agent of the hallucinogenic peyote cactus native to Mexico and the American Southwest. During that trip, my psyche — or was it the world soul? — assaulted me with the image of a colossal humanoid figure, just the head and shoulders.

It didn't feel like a mere image; I felt like I was being accosted by a revelation. This being, holy and terrifying, would not let me go. It blasted me with rumbling sound, blinding colors, and a furious exhortation that I obey its command, of which I had no comprehension. For an eternity, it seemed, I sat trembling at the feet of an unknown power I could not escape. Desperate to respond in some way, I searched for something I could do with my hands. I found a set of multicolored sculpting clays.

I hoped I could somehow appease this god if I could shape its figure with my hands, as if I might convince it that I had received its message and that it would be alright to let me go. I worked the clay for what seemed like hours and fashioned a decent likeness of that mysterious being, the finished piece standing a mere four inches tall, from shoulders up. It had brown hair; a red face, neck, and shoulders; and grayish-brown epaulets.

For several years, that little sculpture lived on a windowsill or a bookshelf as it accompanied me through my twenties and a succession of rented apartments and homes that stretched from one side of North America to the other and back again. I suppose I thought of it as a souvenir from an anomalous experience and perhaps as a passable artistic creation. A couple of friends wondered if it was Spock from the original *Star Trek* series. The truth is I didn't have a clue what it was.

Until that day ten years later in that redrock canyon in Utah. The shape, colors, facial features, and expression of the rock formation were identical to both my vision and the replica I had sculpted. I felt the same overwhelming mystery and fear that took hold of me the first time — and once again had the feeling that some entity was calling me and demanding I do…something.

After that day in 1981, I returned multiple times to that canyon, mostly to guide vision fasts. During the long hike to base camp, there is one spot where you can see the giant rock-being on the western skyline. Pointing him out to the others in our group, I referred to him as the Rock Guardian because it seemed as if he watched over this complex of canyons and knew its secrets. I was determined to visit him one day.

But finding him in that tangled maze of canyons was anything but easy. Several years passed before I found the route.

When we at last come face to face, I am dumbstruck by his immensity. I stand at the feet, nay the toes, of a giant, Buddha-like being rising several hundred feet above me, a complete torso now visible beneath his shoulders. His feet rest in the sands of the wash and his head pierces the heavens. He presides over a court of solemn rock-ministers who tower above me in two long lines forming the walls at the head of the canyon.

For years, I had imagined myself climbing up to one of his shoulders to stand on an epaulet and shout my long-standing questions into his ear: *Who are you? Why did you call me? What might you teach me or show me? How might I serve you?* But, alas, his precipitous lower body is unscalable, nor is there any other realistic route by which to approach his shoulders from within his own canyon.

Another two years passed before I found a way up the western wall of the main canyon to his section of the ridge. When I did, I approached the Guardian's left ear with great anticipation. But when I reached him I no longer had questions, only wide-eyed wonder.

> From his shoulder, I look down for the first time into the canyon behind him. I had known from my maps another canyon was there, but I had no idea it would look like it does, no idea this is what he has been guarding all along.
>
> I stand transfixed by a canyon so remote and so difficult to access that there are no records of its exploration. The guidebooks do not make even passing reference to it. Yet this landscape is bewilderingly familiar, impossibly personal. I had seen and passed through this very terrain during my childhood cemetery dreams.
>
> Spread out below me is a surrealistic valley of grotesquely eroded rock formations populated by herds of mushroom-shaped knobs and domes, an army of sandstone spires and needles, a forest of collapsing monoliths, all in earthtone shades of reds, browns, and purples. The walls of the canyon are covered with a multitude of rock towers that look like a packed stadium of hushed aliens that have just risen to their feet in awe as the ultimate moment of a sacrificial rite plays out below. Through the center of the valley curves a dry streambed of coral-colored sand, like a tree-lined drive to nowhere, except this one is bordered not with stately conifers but with demonic stone monuments.

My psyche had been impeccably triangulated: a childhood dream, a psychedelic vision, and a wilderness landscape that now animated and amplified one another. Discovering the Cemetery in the dayworld was like finding a prophesized key, inserting it into an ancient lock — and the door swings open.

I believe that Mystery arranges such psyche-animating alignments for each one of us and that we find the doorway, if we ever do, only after we're psychospiritually prepared to enter a cocoon of transformation. Although for me the elements that opened the door were a dream, a vision, and a landscape, for others the strands might include a sign, an omen, an inner image received while awake, a close encounter with a nonhuman creature, a disembodied voice, a ceremony, a line of poetry, a storm or rainbow or meteor, a prophecy, a wound, a somatic awakening, or a sacred object such as a knife or a chalice. We're all guided by Mystery. When the time is right and if we offer our attention, we'll find the door and it will open.

Five years later, after several failed attempts to find a route, I at last hiked into the Cemetery:

A steep slope five hundred feet high is colonized by hundreds of sandstone minarets, cabin-sized mushroom rocks, and boulders shaped like tombstones. The hillside is enclosed on three sides by precipitous red ramparts topped with enormous monoliths.

As I climb up toward the ridge, I weep much of the way. I am finally entering a holy place that has called me since age four. This is an exceedingly remote spot with no obvious signs of previous human visitation. And now I've intentionally placed myself in the midst of a graveyard in which, I imagine, my death is as likely as any other outcome.

On a high, narrow pass overlooking both the Cemetery and an adjacent canyon, I make my solitary camp — not much more than a sleeping bag on a pad, three gallons of water, and a few ceremonial items.

A deep sadness claims me, a lament. I am filled with unbearable grief for a world embroiled in madness. I recall the heartrending hope I had harbored for so many years, hope fed by visions of a society that honors all life, visions invested with the greatest longing. As a young man, I had dared to want something passionately.

I am seized by a more personal sadness as well. As fulfilling as my life has been, I have felt in recent months that I've reached the end of the road I've been traveling. I'm in my midforties and have realized most of the dreams of my early adulthood — for meaningful work that might contribute to a more sane and just world; a fulfilling romantic relationship; a caring community of friends; an aesthetically pleasing and ecologically valid home; and joyful ways to explore and celebrate the natural world. Having achieved these things, I now find myself filled with melancholy. The prospect of sitting back and enjoying the fruits of my labors leaves me thoroughly downhearted. Will I listen to the inner voice that says there isn't any more to achieve in life, that anything else is a starry-eyed illusion? Or will I accept the risk of once again leaving the inner home I've built for myself?

During these four days, I live with heat and cold, blasting ridgetop winds, lizards, the staccato flutter of bat wings at dusk, stars and galaxies, blooming claret-cup cacti — and ever-present hunger. A canyon wren whistles her melodious aria of descent. Vultures circle silently.

A thought arrives that maybe I need to drop everything and find a master in some art or discipline, someone I can study with. Become an apprentice again. If I've gone as far as I can with my early-adulthood dreams, I reason, then it must be time to become a student again. It doesn't seem to matter so much what I become a student of.

At the time, it didn't occur to me that my strategic mind was incapable of devising any plan for my future that would be useful to my Soul. A vision fast is an opportunity to make oneself available to revelation, not a time to figure things out.

That night I dream of a large mining operation in the desert run by an attractive woman. Ore is successfully being extracted and moved on conveyor belts, but the mine hasn't made a profit yet. But there's still hope it will.

The next day, several people come to visit in my imagination. All of them dead. Dorothy Wergin, my first spiritual mentor; my oldest sibling, Ricky, who died as an infant before I was born; my friend Phil, who died in an avalanche while we skied in the backcountry; my friend Richard; my grandparents. With words on the wind, I send them my love and gratitude.

Each day, my ridgetop camp feels more like an as-yet-unlit funeral pyre or a sacrificial altar at the top of the colossal, high steps of an Aztec temple. I once again avow Death as my teacher and ally. And Death turns to me and asks, *Who are you? For what do you live? What will you bring your people?*

The wind blows all day, each day, driving me even crazier than I might have been anyway. I name my camp Windy Gap. My lament grows stronger. I weep. I feel extraordinarily weak. I moan, cry out.

Midmorning of the fourth day, a giant yellow-and-black swallowtail flutters by, her wingspan at least six inches. I've never seen a butterfly so large. Now she dances around my camp for several minutes before coming close to my left cheek. She says, *Cocoon Weaver, Impossible Dreamer of Windy Gap.*

That night I dream. I'm a teenager, not yet driving age. There's an exceptionally large yellow-and-black school bus. I decide to take it for a spin. I'm driving down the moderate slope of a broad avenue, scared and exhilarated, almost out of control (the brakes are shot), but I manage not to hit anything. I drive to the workplace of a man I know, perhaps to show off. He's a strong, wise, and kind man in his early mature-adulthood. He's a craftsman, what we would think of as a blue-collar artisan, and very much alive and able. He seems to feel I did well to get there in the big bus. He offers me a job loading heavy sacks of material on a cart and then delivering them to a factory where the material is used to make things. He shows me in detail how to balance the sacks on the cart, seven maximum, he cautions, or it will tip. As a special treat, he makes a run of sacks that have a drawing of me on them (like a logo) instead of the usual one. I'm thrilled.

My wish to study with a master has been granted in the nightworld.

I returned home ready to take the big, risky, yellow-and-black ride and to be guided by the mature craftsman (of me) toward a new task of carrying what is hidden as a gift to others. To truly become such a man myself, I understood I would have to remain faithful to a mining operation and the woman who runs it (the Muse) and to trust my impossible dreams, the ore from deeper layers of the psyche.

I began to design new programs, which I called "soulcraft journeys," distinct, in both intent and form, from what I had been doing during the first half of my Adulthood. I began to develop my own nature-based approaches to dreamwork, Shadow work, ecotherapy, Sacred Wound work, council, and self-designed ceremonies. Innovating in this way was a good deal riskier than seeking another human teacher. It felt as if I were going a long way out on a limb. (I was.) I stopped thinking of or labeling myself as a vision-fast guide or a psychotherapist and became a soulcraft guide who was creating, along with my colleagues, new forms for the ancient art of weaving cocoons of soul initiation.

In hindsight, it seems I had, in fact, begun mining that soulcraft ore a few years before my Cemetery fast. However, those early attempts at new forms had not yet been "profitable": I had not yet been ready or willing to fully trust I could manifest a mystery in my own way, that I could dream the impossible and create innovative forms. My psychospiritual center of gravity had not yet shifted from form to art, from tradition to renaissance.

Fasting in the Cemetery was a major step in my apprenticeship with Death, although far from the last. During those four days, I surrendered my young Adult identity. And then the Cemetery gave birth to me as an Impossible Dreamer of a contemporary, Western, nature-based approach to the perennial journey of soul initiation and of cultural transformation from an egocentric society to an ecocentric and soulcentric one.

The next phase in my apprenticeship with Death was to study the death-rebirth process not only for individuals but for the collective (shifting from a life-destroying society to a life-enhancing culture); to contribute whatever I could to the death-rebirth of the most common mode of Western psychotherapy (from a limiting fixation on wound healing and symptom relief to the cultivation of wholeness and the engendering of cultural revolutionaries); and to help provoke a death-rebirth shift for the contemporary idea of the soul.

I have often wondered if the transformation I experienced in the Cemetery could have happened anywhere else. I've wondered if it might have been the greatest good fortune (or some divine plan) that it would take me so many years to find the Cemetery and then a way into it. And I've wondered if my repeating childhood dream of the Cemetery made the whole journey possible.

The work to which I've been privileged to give myself sprouts from several seed ideas: That we are each born with what Carl Jung called a personal myth, or what I call a mythopoetic identity, through which we can find and occupy our destined place or niche in our cultural and ecological world, somewhat like the way monarch butterflies are born with the ability to find their way from Canada to the exact spot in Mexico that their ancestors left five generations earlier. That we can create our own contemporary practices through which we can discover and be initiated into that unique niche. That we are each conceived by Mystery as something like a singular poem, song, rhythm, or dance — one that the world needs in order to complete its own symphony, drama, or performance. That the universe is, in essence, an artist and each individual human has been shaped with the capacity to mature into one of its works of art, as has every other creature.

When the time comes for our soul initiation, our conscious self (our Ego) merges with and is reshaped by our innate mythopoetic motif or image — our original instructions — and we emerge as an Adult, in the way a caterpillar transforms into a chrysalis within which the butterfly is formed. The butterfly was always the caterpillar's potential, its nonguaranteed destiny.

The Ego cannot merge with the Soul until the Ego is ripe. When that time approaches, it is a great crisis for the Ego. The transformation won't happen without such a crisis, and the crisis is always severe enough that the outcome is uncertain.

Perhaps as a species — and a planet — we now find ourselves in an analogous moment: As a collective, humanity has entered a death-rebirth crisis, a crisis that perhaps needed to be wildly extreme in order to make our next evolutionary transformation even possible. Will we make it through as a species and as a planet? It may be that to do so we'll need to learn again how to prepare for and navigate our *individual* crises of initiation.

Some caterpillars perish in the cocoon or chrysalis, never to emerge as moths or butterflies. Others, miraculously, take flight.

Introduction

The Descent to Soul

An Overview of the Terrain

Tell a wise person or else keep silent
for those who do not understand
will mock it right away.
I praise what is truly alive
what longs to be burned to death....

...And so long as you have not experienced
this: to die and so to grow
you are only a troubled guest
on the dark earth.

— JOHANN WOLFGANG VON GOETHE

This is a field guide to an ecstatic and hazardous odyssey that most of the world has forgotten — or not yet discovered — an essential spiritual adventure for which you won't find clear or complete maps anywhere else in the contemporary Western world. This journey, which begins with a dying, enables you to grow whole and wild in a way that has become rare — and yet is vital for the future of our species and our planet.

I believe the root cause of the dire crises and challenges of our time — all of our currently cascading environmental and cultural collapses — is a widespread failure in individual human development. This has been true for so long and in so many societies that most people today (including most psychologists, educators,

1

and religious leaders) are unaware of this breakdown in the natural sequence of human maturation, a failure now plainly evident — as witnessed in the current epidemics of psychological dysfunction as well as social and ecological degradation. Vital threads in growing whole are missing from the cultural fabric. Too many of us are only troubled guests on this Earth.

Our developmental dilemma stems primarily from our disconnection from nature, from both our "outer" and "inner" natures: the loss of our experienced belonging to and entanglement within the natural world and the loss of our communion with the very core of our own individual human nature — our Soul.

What we have lost, in particular, is the journey of soul initiation — a psychospiritual undertaking that connects us in the most profound way to both the Earth community and the source of our deepest humanity. This journey, if revitalized and reclaimed, can transform everything for us, individually and collectively.

This loss is our single gravest human and planetary crisis because the journey of soul initiation is the path to true Adulthood — to becoming a cultural visionary and evolutionary — and true Adulthood is essential to a genuinely healthy, mature culture. This journey will be a core element of any future society capable of growing a flourishing culture in partnership with all other species and life processes of Earth.

The central and pivotal episode of the journey of soul initiation is the Descent to Soul (a phrase I capitalize to remind you I mean something specific and distinct). This book is a map of the terrain of the Descent, including its five phases.

Key words in these pages — *soul, descent, underworld, initiation, vision* — may be familiar, but their meanings have become obscure, exotic, often indecipherable. The meanings of other common words have become slippery, vague, or ambiguous — *ego, adolescent, adult, elder, purpose, wholeness.* I hope to offer some clarity by introducing intelligible definitions that, largely because they are unconventional, might be able to offer real support in our time for human maturation and cultural renaissance.

My greatest challenge in writing this book — and perhaps your first obstacle in reading and understanding it — is that its subject matter lies outside the worldview of most contemporary cultures. What I mean by the Descent to Soul is most likely not what you, dear reader, would imagine or guess. It might be hard to accept that there could be a dimension of human development you have not experienced and for which you might not yet have a reference point.

You might reasonably suspect the Descent to Soul to be a version of any number of familiar therapeutic or spiritual practices, methods, or endeavors — but, despite similarities, it is none of them. It is not, for example, some kind of self-help regimen or a form of psychotherapy. It is not a way to recover from addiction, stress, or trauma (although doing so, for some people, is an essential element in preparing for the Descent). It is not a way to heal anyone of anything in the usual ways meant by *healing.* It is not a method for improving your relationships. It's for sure not a way to better adapt your life to any culture or worldview currently destroying our biosphere; its actual result is the opposite. The Descent to Soul is not what most depth psychologists or Jungian analysts facilitate in their consulting rooms or explore in their books or articles. It is not a generic submersion into the personal or collective unconscious. It's not a trip into Wonderland or some new or old way of chasing rabbits. The Descent is obviously not an ascending path to enlightenment or nondual consciousness. It is not the hero's journey or a vision quest. It is not shamanism or a psychedelic trip. It is absolutely not a way to find your social or vocational "purpose." It is not a men's or women's or teenagers' initiation workshop or weekend. It is neither a "dark night of the soul" nor "hitting bottom" and then altering your routines so you can get back on your feet. It is not merely or primarily a psychospiritual encounter with death. It is not religion or mythology. Most emphatically, it is not a rite of passage (probably the single most common misperception). It is not even a rite of initiation.

Rather, the Descent to Soul is an extended *process* of initiation that takes place in a stage of human development most contemporary people never reach. It is a psychospiritual adventure that spans at least several months — and sometimes a few years or more.

As the central episode of the journey of soul initiation, the Descent results in visionary leaders, paradigm innovators, and evolutionary artisans. As such, its introduction into the contemporary world renders it a profound interrupter of culture as well as a necessary seed or catalyst for possible future Earth societies that will be not only life-sustaining but also life-*enhancing*.

The Descent to Soul — or something like it — is probably as old as humanity and has most likely been embodied in as many different forms as there have been thriving human cultures. The Descent as described in this book, however, is not a white person's adaptation, appropriation, or co-optation of any indigenous culture's practices or traditions. Rather, it's a contemporary Western process and experience that my colleagues and I have been tracking and guiding for forty years. This long and extensive field study, carefully documented, has gradually yielded the model presented here: a modern re-visioning and evolution of a timeless and archetypal path to true Adulthood and Elderhood.

However — and this is a vital point — the Descent to Soul as described in this book is not primarily a re-visioning of something old. As I'll explore with you later in this overview, this model of the Descent is innovative and emergent in ways that suggest an evolutionary shift in our species — one that has been unfolding for some time now, a movement into realms of human development that were not widely attainable in previous eras. The models and methods we've been developing at Animas Valley Institute might help our species embrace and realize an evolutionary opportunity on the threshold of which we now stand.

In some ways, then, the journey of soul initiation has been lost and is now simply being rediscovered, yet in other ways, the journey of soul initiation is itself in the process of evolving and a new developmental possibility for humanity is emerging. Either way, our species is clearly in the midst of an initiatory interlude — and consequently, our planet is as well.

The most innovative and original element in this book is not the set of practices for navigating the Descent to Soul but the model of what that journey actually is, a map sketched, drafted, and redrafted over the course of four decades of guiding thousands of people. At Animas, our goal has always been to honor the integrity and sheer mysteriousness of the journey — to track the patterns that reveal themselves — and to avoid placing our observations into earlier interpretive boxes. Although we've improvised many practices of our own and modified many long-established techniques, our methods are not radically new in the way the model is. A practice, however, can have very different results and can, in essence, become a different activity depending on the model or intention with which it is used.

To our knowledge, very few if any other guides are doing this kind of work with Western people. This includes vision-fast guides, rites-of-passage leaders, practitioners of neo-shamanism, facilitators of psychedelic journeys, and depth psychologists. I write this with humility but also with regret that we haven't yet discovered more guides developing kindred models and methods.

The ease of misconstruing the nature of the contemporary journey of soul initiation might be one reason its precursors have been lost for so long. Once lost, it's hard to find again. Here's why: Most people have felt an immeasurably deep longing for their life to be a passionate adventure and a meaningful and valuable contribution to the world. But few know how to make that real. For those of us who reach our midteens with this longing still alive in our hearts — not buried beneath the dross of the overculture — there arises an irrepressible desire to embark on a quest for our true life. And many of us do. But our longing is so strong we might believe we've found a path to that life when we haven't. Our yearning is so fierce we end up embracing a practice or method that seems to be the Holy Grail — but isn't. It's not that we consciously settle for less. It's just that it can take a while before we can admit to ourselves that the path we're on is not getting us closer to the passionate and meaningful life we yearn for.

As valuable as they are in their own right and for their own purposes, the familiar practices, methods, and endeavors noted above — from psychotherapy to psychedelics, from "purpose" workshops to shamanism — are examples of paths that Western people have explored in recent decades, but none are the Descent to Soul (although some can be components of it). You can, for example, undergo multiple healings of various kinds, even *invaluable* healings, but although you may emerge more whole, your longing for meaning — deep, life-fulfilling meaning — will remain untouched. You can go through a rite of passage and you may be healed, revitalized, and gain a new, more rewarding social status or role, but your longing for soul-stirring purpose will not be realized. You might experience satori or nirvana, but after the ecstasy, there will still be an emptiness at your core — the wrong kind of emptiness. You could for most of your life practice yoga, meditation, or contemplative prayer, but as invaluably enriched, centered, and resilient as you might become, you will not be satisfied if your original hunger was to know and inhabit the one unique life you can truly call your own.

I'll say it again and more emphatically: I am not hawking a new self-help fad, and the Descent to Soul is not therapy or a rite of passage. Rather, this book is something like a psychospiritual bomb placed as carefully as I'm able at the very heart of the techno-industrial civilization currently ruining our world. More importantly, the Descent is a generative seed-germinating wildfire indispensable for any human or planetary future worth inhabiting.

This is my first written presentation of the five phases of the Descent to Soul, a model that differs in significant ways from my own earlier attempts to map the journey and, to my knowledge, from any other model for initiatory odysseys. In these pages you'll find a thorough description of the most essential things I've learned over the past forty years about the trail to true Adulthood, including much of what I've discovered since writing *Soulcraft*.

I confess I've written this book for future human generations as much as for those living now. Today, in the early twenty-first century, we face unprecedented existential crises — environmentally and culturally. Our human and natural systems are collapsing due to our "success" at creating human systems (cultures) incompatible with the health of the greater natural systems within which we exist (Earth's ecosystems). If we are to survive and thrive as a species — and as an Earth community of innumerable life-forms — future human generations will need to know how to navigate the journey of soul initiation. This book is an exploration of what I understand to be the most important patterns, motifs, and symbols of the journey as well as a description of a contemporary, Western, nature-based version of it. It's also a treasury of stories of contemporary people who have experienced it. This book is an embodiment of my faith that there might *be* future human generations and that they might be vastly more capable than we have been of undertaking the journey to full maturity.

Although the Descent to Soul — the expedition across a vast plain, then down into the depths of what I call Soul Canyon, and eventually, with good fortune, up and out the other side — can be hazardous and harrowing, it is also joyful and engaging. If only the hypnotized masses of the mainstream contemporary world had some idea of the extraordinary riches, mysteries, and intricacies of the human psyche and of the daily dazzling miracles of the self-organizing, more-than-human world! If they did, whatever glimmer and glamour glimpsed in the flatland of conformist-consumer culture would swiftly fade and be seen for the sham it is. What waits on the other side of that vast plain is so much more interesting and inspiring. And those mysteries and treasures are no further than your nightly dreams, your wild love for this world, or for that matter, your deepest emotional wounds; no more remote than the rustling leaves outside your door, the every-moment miracles of your own body, the mycelium-webbed soil beneath your feet, or the waxing and waning of the Moon above; no harder to find than the myths that arise everywhere from the depths of the human psyche. These mysteries are not just of nature and of psyche, but of the inherent communion and dance of mutual enrichment between them.

Peter Pan, as it turns out, was wrong — dead wrong. Being a true Adult is a profoundly exhilarating and fulfilling experience!

Our Unique Ecological Niche

Each species has its unique ecological niche, a distinctive role it plays in sustaining and enhancing life on our planet. By fulfilling its role, each species does all it can to sustain, increase, and evolve its own kind. When Charles Darwin spoke of the survival of the fittest, he meant the flourishing of those who fit best — those who cooperate best with their environment and are best able to adapt to changing conditions.

Salmon, for example, carry vast amounts of marine nutrients from the ocean to river headwaters. These nutrients are incorporated into food webs in rivers and their surrounding landscapes by many species of mammals, birds, and fish that forage on salmon eggs, juveniles, and adults. Brown bears disperse these marine nutrients into surrounding forests, enhancing the growth of trees that protect stream banks from erosion. These trees eventually return the favor for salmon by falling into the streams and forming logjams that provide shelter for juvenile salmon and protect the gravels that adults use for spawning.

In addition to each species having its own unique niche, we might suppose this is also true for each individual. It is plausible — and probably necessary — that every creature is *born with* the capacity and desire to occupy its species' distinctive ecological role in its own individual way. Adolescent salmon, for example, without in-person guidance from their parents or anyone else, know how and when to migrate to the ocean and how, after several years, to locate the very river in which they were spawned and to make their way up that stream often to the exact spot in which they began life. Biologists have hypothesized what tools or mechanisms salmon use to return (*how* they do it) — such as being able to recognize the distinct scent of their home river — but they don't have a clue how salmon know to migrate at all, or when, or to where, or what motivates them (*why* they do it). We don't know, in other words, how it is that each salmon — or an individual of *any* species — is born with the capacity and desire to occupy its species' distinctive ecological role in its own way. But without a doubt, every living thing has this innate knowledge and desire. This is one of the astounding mysteries upon which all life depends. This is a mystery of psyche, not a mystery of eco-biological mechanisms.

The curious thing is that we seldom apply these insights to our own species — as if humanity might be an exception to the rule, as if we are purposeless visitors in a meaningless world or as if we can take any ecological role we want. But as a species, we, too, have a distinctive niche in the community of life, a particular potential, a role that evolution has shaped us to occupy. Most of us are just not at all sure what that might be. Or perhaps we don't even consider the question.

Given what is unfolding globally in the early twenty-first century, we might be tempted, in moments of despair, to conclude that our unique human niche must be to perpetrate the sixth mass extinction of life on our planet. This is, after all, what we are in fact doing and what is already well underway — the apocalyptic diminution of our planet's biodiversity, as if Earth is seeking to renew herself by first clearing the decks through the life-slaughtering genius of our own species. Could this be it? Could we have evolved so as to "cooperate best" with the rest of life by becoming the obliging eco-assassin that annihilates most present-day species, including our own? *Really?*

I don't think so. I believe that ecocide/suicide is not our destiny but, rather, our fate if we do not succeed at embracing and inhabiting our true niche (leaving aside for now the question of why we might be the only species capable of *not* fulfilling its true niche). Further, I believe we will not be able to inhabit our true niche as a species unless and until enough of us inhabit our true *individual* niches.

Let me tell you why:

In order to realize our evolutionary potential, most human cultures have to be healthy and mature enough to choose and support such a mission — "the great work" of our time, as Thomas Berry framed it in his visionary book of that title. In order to have such cultures, there must be humans mature and healthy enough to cocreate those cultures. Such humans (initiated Adults and Elders) are not people who are primarily looking out for themselves (their "small" selves), but rather people who are creatively crafting ways of inhabiting the life-enhancing individual niche they were born for. And *that* niche is what we discover and what we become able to occupy through the journey of soul initiation. Consequently, in order for humanity to take its true place in the world, enough individual humans must take *their* true places.

True Adults and Elders are people who know why they were born, who know who they are as unique individual participants in the web of life, and who, in most everything they do, creatively occupy their distinctive ecological niche as a life-enhancing gift to their people and to the greater Earth community.[1]

The primary reason ecocide could end up being our collective fate is due to a specific kind of cultural decay that is the inevitable result of the absence of the journey of soul initiation.

In other words, we industrialized humans are failing to occupy our true collective niche because we don't know how to find or occupy our individual roles in the greater web of life. *We don't know who we are as a species because we don't know who we are as individuals.*

But we can learn how to remember[2] who we were born to be as individuals, and we can collectively discover who we might yet become as a species.

Twenty-First-Century Practices for Soul Initiation

I want to explore with you the question raised earlier of whether the model of the Descent to Soul presented in this book is a contemporary form of what older, healthier cultures had and later lost or if this is a journey and a destination for which humanity was not ready until now. Or both.

One factor that makes our work at Animas new, relative to earlier, indigenous traditions, arises from the fact that we are addressing the journey of soul initiation with a very different consciousness and within a very different cultural context. This is simply by "virtue" of several cultural revolutions — agricultural, scientific, industrial, and digital. Humanity now operates with a significantly different mode of consciousness relative to the Neolithic; we exist in a radically transformed cultural context in terms of our knowledge, social structures, economies, technologies, spiritualities, and cosmology.

One of the consequences of these cultural revolutions is a degradation of our shared environment to such a degree that humanity as a whole now faces an unprecedented and ultimate dilemma, namely, accelerating ecocide and possible self-extinction. Because of the cataclysmic events now playing out (mass extinctions, deforestation, ecological poisoning and degradation, overpopulation, climate disruption), we find ourselves having to make an evolutionary leap of a magnitude we may not have needed since we climbed down from our homes in the trees some four million years ago. This leap might not have been possible without our having unwittingly created the conditions in which it is necessary. This is the way evolution works: The species that survive are the ones able to adapt to changing conditions. In this case, we, ourselves, have created, unintentionally, the conditions that require us to evolve. Although this leap might now be both possible and crucial, it is in no way guaranteed. We are traversing a knife-edge ridge, and the outcome is unknown.

We now find ourselves in an initiatory crisis of our own making that will result in either our demise or our metamorphosis. We cannot continue on our current course and we cannot remain as the humans we've been. This is a collective circumstance akin to what is faced individually on the Descent to Soul. Not all people or species — or planets — survive their initiations.

Our contemporary industrialized cultures, though in the process of destroying our Earth home, have in many ways achieved great advances in personal development, well-being, and human potential. In addition to the life-enhancing accomplishments of our arts and sciences, we now enjoy unprecedented degrees of freedom in individual exploration and flourishing. We have a much more differentiated and expanded set of possible social roles and identities. This expansion of roles is quite new — and another factor that likely requires a novel approach to the journey of soul initiation. We have vastly more ways of being human than ever before, a surge in role diversity likely due to the evolution of the relatively new life stage of Adolescence (as I explore later). Many of these new ways are deadly to self, community, and world: Ponder the modern assortment of addictions from which to choose, the proliferation of self-serving political strategies, and military leaders armed with a mind-boggling variety of life-destroying weapons. Yet many other innovations have opened doors to wholesome, new human possibilities: Consider the modern array of scientific specialties, life-enhancing technologies, and medical interventions; the diversification of the arts and of religious and spiritual paths; and the rainbow variety of gender orientations and roles. As with all new capacities, our aptitude for dreaming up new roles and possibilities brings both opportunities and risks. Gender roles are a good example: Compared to the traditions of some indigenous peoples, there is now much less of a divide between women and men in terms of available social and vocational roles. This is also true when we compare current times with our own Western Middle Ages — or even, for that matter, with 1950s America. Most of us consider this progress, a positive sign of consciousness change and cultural evolution, but it also necessitates challenging societal adjustments.

Greater role differentiation is true not only of contemporary societies compared with earlier ones but also of our species compared with others. The variety of niches individual humans can occupy seems immeasurably greater than the niches available to individuals of other species. This is our forte as well as our flaw. One of the distinctive attributes of the human psyche is that it takes wildly diverse and creative shapes. But the capacity of most earlier human cultures to support that diversity and autonomy seems limited compared to contemporary options.

More generally, I suspect there are no older *or* existing cultures with practices or worldviews that are unambiguously relevant to what we need to navigate our current planetary moment, none that are wholly adequate to enable us to face what we now must as a species. This, indeed, was the conclusion of geologian and Earth Elder Thomas Berry after a long life studying cultures all over the world:

> We must go far beyond any transformation of contemporary culture.... None of our existing cultures can deal with this situation [namely, the loss of what Thomas termed our cultural "survival capacity"] out of its own resources. We must invent, or reinvent, a sustainable human culture by a descent into our prerational, our instinctive resources. Our cultural resources have lost their integrity. They cannot be trusted. What is needed is not transcendence but "inscendence."[3]

This book presents a contemporary, Western, nature-based map and set of methods for what Thomas, coining his own word for the Descent, called "inscendence."[4] Thomas, by distinguishing inscendence from transcendence, was declaring that we live in a time in which the spiritual descent has become essential — and more vital than the spiritual ascent, which, alone, too often amounts to a spiritual "bypass" of our individual and collective needs for healing, wholing, and tending to our crises and opportunities.

There are additional indicators of an emerging human paradigm that might require a new approach to the journey of soul initiation, a new way to understand the Descent to Soul. I explored some of these in *Nature and the Human Soul* (see the section on "*Homo Imaginens*"). These include our modern awareness (astonishingly, in just the last 150 years) of a one-way, nonrepeating evolutionary arc to the unfolding world (not just ever-repeating cycles); the determining role humanity now has in the evolution of life on our planet; the relatively recent universal cultivation of the deep imagination, bestowing every person of every culture with the potential for visionary achievement (not just the rare prophet or shaman); and modern Adolescence as a potential evolutionary advance — as yet unfulfilled.

These perspectives suggest that the journey of soul initiation is itself in the process of evolving, that a new developmental possibility for humanity is emerging, and that our species is in the midst of an initiatory journey. We are entering uncharted waters.

For these reasons, I believe we will not find what we need now by returning to the initiatory practices of earlier cultures. Although we might employ some universal techniques and strategies (like dreamwork, fasting, and trance dance) and embrace certain arts of the older Western mystery schools (like deep-imagery journeys, symbolic artwork, and the Mandorla), we primarily must invent never-before-seen maps and methods to navigate our never-before-seen circumstances and courageously accept a destination we can only partially understand.

It's not simply that we must not appropriate from or co-opt indigenous traditions. It's not simply that we must invent our own ways of doing what earlier cultures might have done. More fundamentally, we must envision methods for a journey no previous cultures had even attempted — or were ready for. And we must do this not only to prevent horrific things from happening — like ecocide — but also to enable a human possibility not previously seen in this world.

We must now collectively weave a cocoon for the metamorphosis of our own species.[5]

The Lost Journey

Although I believe we now stand on an evolutionary threshold, that we must envision maps and methods for an unprecedented planetary voyage, we might still wonder why earlier variants of the journey of soul initiation — where they existed — disappeared from most cultures. See appendix 1, "The Lost Journey," for an exploration of this question as well as examples of cultures in which these earlier variants once existed or perhaps still do.

The Scarcity of True Adults, Not Just Elders

It's become a common observation that contemporary societies have very few real elders — plenty of "olders" but not many people of wisdom capable of effectively caring for the greater Earth community. However, a much more devastating and incisive cultural critique is to observe that the modern world has very few true *adults* — and that this is precisely the root cause of our current crises. Lest we get ahead of ourselves by lamenting the scarcity of elders, we would do well to reflect upon the scarcity of Adults, the consequences of this, and how a true Adult is made (as well as a true Elder).

When too many of us don't grow into true Adults, our cultures deteriorate into immature collectives and dysfunctional societies. Instead of engendering healthy communities that contribute to life and evolution, we end up harming each other and ourselves and destroying the very world that conceived and sustains us — and ecocide is also anthropocide. Contemporary industrialized societies are clear examples.

What do I mean by a true Adult? My comprehensive answer is the book you hold in your hands. But I've already offered a short sketch, namely: someone who knows why they were born, who knows who they are as a unique individual participant in the web of life, and who creatively occupies their distinctive eco-niche in their everyday life as a gift to their people and the greater Earth community. Here's another version, this one in three parts: someone who experiences themselves, first and foremost, as a member of the Earth community, and has had one or more revelatory experiences of their unique place in that ecological community, and embodies that unique place as a gift to their people and the Earth community. Doing so makes them a visionary agent of evolution — and in an egocentric, patho-adolescent society like ours, an agent of *revolution*.

These definitions have virtually no relationship to contemporary understandings of adulthood, but they're probably close to those of some healthier, earlier cultures. The superficiality of our conventional Western definitions of adulthood — such as reaching age eighteen or twenty-one; or, slightly better, becoming a parent and raising children; and/or contributing to the economy, safety, or governance of the community — suggests a root cause of our cultural immaturity: a lack of depth.

"Very few true adults" is such a radical cultural critique that almost no one has been able to bring themselves to plainly say it, mean it, and spell out its implications.[6] But when we consider it impartially and carefully, we see that the scarcity of true Adults is, naturally, the explanation for why there are so few real Elders. It is the passage from psychological Adolescence to true Adulthood that has become so challenging and so rarely traversed — not the passage from Adult to Elder.

It's not as if we are seeing hordes of Adults piling up like frenzied sports fans against the entrance gates to Elderhood — and just somehow not being able to break through. No. The bottleneck is with the psychological Adolescents (whether in their teens, twenties, forties, or later), who are getting stuck in their development long before they reach the entrance gates to Adulthood. The reality is that most contemporary people are lost and languishing in a Village on the edge of a vast deserted plain on the far side of which arise the gates to Adulthood — and few of them find their way across that plain. There are at least four reasons they don't: They're not psychospiritually prepared for the journey. They don't have the skills to navigate the crossing. They wouldn't know how to get through the gates even if they found them. And there are very few Adults and real Elders to help them navigate the rigorous passage. Indeed, this last reality is precisely why the land between the Village and the gates to Adulthood has become a barren and eroded district and not the lush and alluring wilderness it might once have been in certain places — or that it might be in the future.

The journey does take significant preparation. Our conformist-consumer cultures[7] do not help psychological Adolescents with this. Quite to the contrary. And most people do need support with both the preparation and the journey itself. In a healthy society, this support takes the form of initiation processes and practices conserved and overseen by Adults and Elders. This is what we've lost — not only our initiation rites but also most of the Adults and Elders who could guide those rites.

This loss results in societies filled with immature Adolescents, which is why there are so few true Adults — mature Adolescents being the raw material for making Adults. And the reason we have so few psychologically and ecologically mature Adolescents is due to the modern degradation of childhood, resulting, in turn, from cultural deterioration, including too many immature parents and educators whose developmental challenges are due to the loss of the journey of soul initiation, and so on. Each loss compounds all the others.

To meaningfully address our current cultural and environmental collapses, the most essential initiative is to reclaim, redesign, and revitalize practices for the journey of soul initiation. Of the many strategies proposed for creating a sane and sustainable world, this is not one you're likely to have come across. Consult even the most progressive culture-change activists and you'll get the usual list: reductions in human population and pollution, transformations in energy and food production, and new models of and practices for social justice, equality, governance, business, community, and healthcare. All of these changes are necessary and urgent, but few activists or futurists include what lies at the root of all of these dilemmas — the vital need to restore or enhance the process of human development. And virtually no one notes the nearly absent journey of soul initiation as the fundamental and core necessity. Maybe this has been lost so long that few now are capable of seeing it. Perhaps for some it's the elephant in the room — too troublesome to discuss. Others might intuit this as the crumbling foundation under our cultural house of cards but don't want to be the one to name it.

The breakdown in human development does not have to be addressed before our other more urgent dilemmas can be, but enhancing how we grow is the ultimate path to a healthy, mature culture. It would be good to get started sooner rather than later.

Soul-initiated Adults and Elders are the most potent agents of cultural regeneration. And children and Adolescents are the younger people those initiated Adults emerge from — especially if those children and Adolescents are nurtured and supported by true Adults and Elders.

The nature-based journey of soul initiation is the way to personal revelation, visionary leadership, and cultural renaissance.[8]

It's the journey from early Adolescence to Adulthood — not from Adulthood to Elderhood — that once inspired and necessitated complex, arduous, and often lengthy initiation ordeals and practices.[9] There's good reason for this: The features of our psyche and of the world that we must claim and incorporate in order to become an Adult are precisely what we had to ignore earlier in our life in order to first become viably human — that is, in order to become an authentic and socially accepted member of our human community, which is the developmental goal of childhood and early Adolescence. This book is, from one perspective, an exploration of what those essential features are and why our Ego had to resist their assimilation until the time was right. The journey of soul initiation brings about the death of our Adolescent Ego and of our Adolescent worldview — and the Adolescent Ego does not go gently into that good night. Only a very mature Adolescent would want and be able to.

The Possibility of Extraordinary Lives

We all know or have at least heard about true Adults, people who have followed an inner compass and made our world a better place, people whose lives are foundational to our own. Some of these people are well known.

Martha Graham, for example, broke the rules of traditional ballet and created a new language of dance. Nelson Mandela gave his people freedom, democracy, and the foundations for racial reconciliation — and inspired cultural revolutionaries around the world. Carl Jung gave us our first Western depth psychology with real depth. Rachel Carson launched the global environmental movement. Thomas Berry introduced us to the dream of the Earth. Mardy Murie, one of our fiercest guardians of wilderness, helped write and pass the 1964 US Wilderness Act and was instrumental in the creation of the Arctic National Wildlife Refuge. Wangari Maathai gifted the world with the Green Belt movement — and over fifty million new trees. Joanna

Macy has given us the Work That Reconnects. Steven Foster and Meredith Little have gifted us the contemporary Western expression of the panhuman vision-fast ceremony.[10]

Our own lives can be as fulfilled, fruitful, and inspiring as theirs.

These women and men brought forth a boon for their people, something unique and priceless, something that transformed human societies. And they did so despite living, as we do, in damaged cultures. We all know of people like this, those who are following something we can't see. What makes them different? They followed a feeling, a hunch, an image, a possibility, a golden thread. What drove them was not the directions of the Ego or the directives of the culture. They might not all have been aware of what I call the journey of soul initiation or the Descent to Soul by these or any other names, but it's likely they navigated their way through this very terrain. Their lives are extraordinary because they discovered their unique ways to embody universal archetypes. "Dedicated spirits," as Wordsworth would say.

Rites of Passage versus the Journey of Soul Initiation

What the contemporary world has lost is much more than effective rites of passage.

In their original or traditional forms, rites of passage support people in their transition from the end of one life stage into the start of the next. The rite does not bring about the passage; rather, the rite formally marks, announces, celebrates, and supports the passage. The developmental successes throughout the previous life stage are what give rise to the passage. Without those successes, there is no developmental progress, no passage, and no real grounds for a rite. Attending to the developmental tasks of the life stages is even more important than ceremonially observing the passages.[11]

Rites of passage are a relatively small piece of what we're missing. The voyage from what contemporary society thinks of as adolescence to what I think of as true Adulthood — the journey of soul initiation — involves three distinct life stages, two major passages, and a great number and variety of initiatory rites and practices utilized throughout those three stages (which is to say, *between* the passages; see *Nature and the Human Soul*). This takes several years at least. A weekend or multiday rite of passage does not come even close to providing what is needed to become a true Adult.

My perspective that there are many kinds of developmental processes that are not rites of passage should not seem so radical. Rites of passage, as invaluable as they are, are actually infrequent and minor elements of human development. The journey of soul initiation and navigating through any stage of life are the primary examples of developmental processes that are not passage rites, but there are many others, such as the changes we go through as we develop any major skill or important relationship. Consider, for instance, an apprenticeship to a master pianist. This is an extended developmental process, not a rite of passage. The apprenticeship might last many years; then, if proficiency has been attained, there might be a social rite of passage, perhaps in the form of a public debut concert. Same with marriage: Ideally the rite of passage (the wedding) takes place only after acquiring the basic skills of romance and the successful navigation of several months of intimate relationship. A bar mitzvah (the rite of passage) ought to occur only after years of study of Judaism. Other developmental processes that may or may not be followed by a rite of passage include a meditation practice, a martial art discipline, or the study of poetry.

In recent decades, many organizations around the world have crafted new and very creative rites of passage in a good-faith effort to address our compounding crises of psychological, societal, and ecological collapse. But this might in some ways be a Band-Aid on a mortal wound. Rites of passage are an inadequate substitute for the knowledge and practices needed for tending the gradual multiyear development of Adolescents into Adults. Rites-of-passage weekends and experiential journeys can provide invaluable benefits — nature connection, for example, or the deepening and differentiation of social identity, the cultivation of self-care skills, the healing of emotional wounds, recovery from addiction or trauma, and the development of relational literacy. Yet without sufficient success with the developmental tasks of childhood and Adolescence, and without a successful navigation of the journey of soul initiation, no rite of passage can bring about true Adulthood.[12]

An Ecological Definition of Soul

In my work — and in this book — I use the word *soul* in a way that diverges from and is sometimes irreconcilable with its more familiar uses. I have found this re-visioning of *soul* necessary to enable us in the Western world to once again understand ourselves, experience ourselves, and treat ourselves as native participants in our animate Earth. This re-visioning is equally necessary in order to make sense of the journey from psychological Adolescence to initiated Adulthood.

Foundationally, *Soul*, for me, is an ecological concept, not a psychological one nor a spiritual or religious one.

Specifically, by *Soul* I mean a person or thing's unique ecological niche in the Earth community.

By this definition, *all* creatures have Souls, not just humans. And not just creatures, but every naturally occurring thing: every flower and stone; every river, mountain, forest; every cloud, storm, rainbow; every season; every species. Even every human language, community, and culture — which is to say, all human creations that evolve organically, those that we do not fabricate solely with our strategic minds. Each natural thing, in other words, has its own unique position or role in the larger web of Earthly life. A niche, in essence, consists of a thing's unique set of relationships with every other thing in its ecosystem. A thing's eco-niche — its Soul — is what makes it what it is on the deepest, widest, and most natural level of identity.

This foundational relationship between eco-niche and identity is why I believe "unique eco-niche" is the best definition for *soul*. Notice, too, that this definition is completely resonant with how we commonly use the word *soul* in everyday speech: We're most often referring to the deepest meaning, significance, distinctiveness, place, or purpose of a thing — its original essence, independent of how we might interpret it. This is implied, for example, in phrases like "his soul work," "she searched her soul," and even "she is the soul of discretion." "Soul" has always implied "that which is most true and real." What could be more true or real than a thing's unique place in creation?

When it comes to our own species, the individual human Soul is, by this definition, the particular ecological niche a person is born to occupy *whether or not that niche is ever consciously discovered or embodied*. This caveat must be added because we humans might be the only creature capable of never discovering the individual niche we were born for — or refusing it if we do. This has consequences.

To reduce the chance of being misunderstood, I'll be even more explicit because the following point is the hardest for most people to grasp: By *human Soul*, I mean a person's unique place, *not* in human culture, but in the greater Earth community, the more-than-human world.[13] The human Soul, when understood as unique eco-niche, is an identity much deeper than our personality, social-vocational role, or political or religious affiliations. Although we express ourselves *through* human culture by way of our social roles, our Soul is of and belongs to the larger, natural, not-only-human world. Each human Soul is first and foremost an element of the Soul of the world, the *anima mundi*. We, like individuals of all species, are creatures that emerge from and are shaped by Earth and by our relationships with all her other inhabitants and environments.

This concept of eco-niche returns the idea of soul, at long last, to its original home and context — the greater web of life. This is the only definition of soul I know that can support culturally exiled humans to return to Earth.[14] With this definition, Soul becomes the missing link between ecology and psychology: Soul — the ecological niche we were born to occupy — is precisely what connects our human psyche to ecology (where *psyche* refers to our capacity to experience, both consciously and unconsciously — including dreams, thoughts, perceptions, imaginings, memories, and feelings). The way we experience both the world and ourselves has everything to do with our innate eco-niche.[15]

This ecological definition of *Soul* is itself one of the core features that distinguishes this book's model of the Descent to Soul from other models.

Although we're born to fill a particular ecological niche, we aren't capable of comprehending such a niche (nor should we attempt to) during childhood and early Adolescence. To discover our eco-niche, we must go through an initiatory process — the journey of soul initiation — if and when we're developmentally prepared for it.

From the perspective of Soul as eco-niche, no one is born to have a particular job or role in a human community. Rather, like members of all other species, we're each born to take a specific place within the *Earth* community, to fill an individual ecological niche in the greater web of life, to provide a suite of unique ecological functions. *That* place is what I mean by Soul, and occupying *that* psycho-ecological niche and providing *those* functions is what I mean by soul purpose. This most essential realm of purpose is nearly absent from contemporary discussions and from most contemporary practices and methods for uncovering and embodying purpose.[16]

Soul and Mythopoetic Identity

Because knowledge of our place in the greater web of life is something we're born with, it is necessarily precultural and prelinguistic. As a consequence, our unique place in the world cannot be identified, described, understood, or experienced in conventional cultural terms; it can't be equated with an everyday social or vocational role or identity — such as physician, pianist, priest, president, or parent, or even the more generic categories of healer, artist, or leader. So how on Earth do we identify or name our Soul's place?

Here's an additional way to appreciate the difficulty: We humans possess a special realm or veneer of consciousness — our Ego's conscious self-awareness — that rides on top of the more extensive consciousness we have in common with all other species. Our human Ego is both a great boon and a great barrier.[17] For example, because each individual Ego, unlike the Soul, is a child of culture and language, we at first — in our childhood and teen years — come to understand our place culturally and linguistically, in terms of social roles. This is unavoidable, necessary, and a good thing. But we're also born with an entirely different kind of knowledge, a felt-sense about our ecological place or niche in the world. This knowledge exists only within the deeper realm of consciousness that all species share, knowledge that is not linguistic but imaginal, knowledge that an immature, egocentric human Ego cannot access.

So the questions become: What is the nature of this innate, imagery-based, and mysterious knowledge about our ecological place in the world? How do we access this knowledge when it exists at a deeper level than the ego-consciousness that dominates our experience and sense of self by the time we're in our early teens? How do we linguistically identify our Soul to ourselves and others once we experience it consciously?

In a word: metaphor.

When it comes to identifying Soul, we can only point or allude to it using metaphor — in the manner of poetry or myth. We can linguistically understand our Souls only indirectly, only mythopoetically. Not coincidentally, this is precisely how we learn about our Souls in the first place: We discover (or remember) our innate place, our true home, when the world mirrors it to us by way of nature-based metaphors, human archetypes, or other mythic or poetic images or symbols. We don't choose these metaphors or figure them out with our strategic minds. Rather, we're shown them in a moment of numinous vision or mystical revelation. They are shown to us by…what? "Mystery" is as good a way as any to name our benefactor, our guide, our initiator.

This is to say that when we begin to fathom and appreciate our unique eco-niche, we do so in the form of our *mythopoetic identity,* a phrase that Geneen Marie Haugen and I coined many years ago to name the way that human consciousness experiences and embraces Soul — through symbol and metaphor, image and dream, archetype and myth. So although *Soul* for me is an ecological concept, the process of coming to know our Soul is not ecological but psychological — and spiritual as well.

It's important to keep in mind that Soul is not the *same* as mythopoetic identity. Soul is our unique eco-niche, while mythopoetic identity is how Soul is communicated to and represented by our human consciousness.

The embodiment of our Soul — the manifestation of our unique eco-niche — is our mature, Adult life purpose, our singular destiny.

Although numinous visions or mystical revelations themselves do not specify a particular social or vocational role, we eventually need to identify and choose such a role *as a delivery system for Soul.* We need that delivery system in order to incarnate our mythopoetic identity and offer our unique gift to the world. But the delivery system is not our mythopoetic identity. Our job or task is not who we are.

What I mean by *Soul,* then, is something mystical but not upperworld mystical and not any more mystical (or less) than salmon or monarch migrations. It corresponds to what poet David Whyte refers to as "the largest conversation you can have with the world," a conversation you were born to have and that only you can have and that the world needs you to have for it to be whole. This conversation — and the niche, role, function, identity, meaning, and purpose associated with it — is not cultural or even merely human; rather, it is ecological and mythopoetic, which is to say clothed and communicated in the metaphors, symbols, images, dreams, and archetypes of the wild world and of your own wild mind. As Diane di Prima reminds us: "you have a poetics: you step into the world / like a suit of readymade clothes."[18]

This is actually true of all creatures, not just humans: Every being has its own innate poetics, and there's no better way than poetry to identify a unique ecological niche. Try describing the niche of an individual fox, for example. You can point to some of the primary relationships she has with other species in a particular habitat and perhaps the way her uncommon cunning allows her to carry out her distinctive calling, but her niche is something more than that and categorically different. Her unique niche is the sum of all the relationships she has with everything else on Earth, especially the things in her ecosystem, something we can't even get close to fully describing. The best way to understand a fox's niche is to live for several years as a native in her neighborhood while offering your daily reverent attention to her wanderings and ways. Then you'll know something of her niche but still not be able to describe it precisely or systematically. Your best option, really, for portraying her niche would be to recite fox stories, preferably outside at night around a fire or in the dark beneath blazing stars. Or fox poetry. Or vixen myth. And that of course is precisely how nature-based people have always done it.

It's no different when it comes to linguistically portraying an individual human's Soul.

Through the journey of soul initiation, we come to understand that we each were born as something like a poem, as a unique dance, as a story in conversation with other stories, as an essential and utterly singular episode in the unfolding story of Earth, of Cosmos. As Gary Snyder writes:

> The world is made of stories. Good stories are hard to come by, and a good story that you can honestly call your own is an incredible gift. These stories are part of a bigger story that connects us all.[19]

On the Soul level, we are each like a story or a poem that was part of the world even before we were born or conceived. And this poem, this mythopoetic identity, remains a feature of the world even after we die. This poem might be "about" the way a cocoon is woven. Or "about" the way stone can anchor feather and feather reveal the secrets of stone. Before we consciously encounter it, we might imagine this poem to be hanging on a certain branch of a tree in a forest, or waiting in a hollow spot on the land beneath leaf litter, or hovering between two standing waves in a river. And we might imagine it calling to us — it wants us to find it. The journey of soul initiation is, in essence, a long wander in the "forest" in search of that poem. When we find it, it claims us — our Ego — and we are changed by it. In that moment, our Ego begins to be shaped into a handmaiden for that poem, a way to embody and celebrate it. To seek the Soul is to wander ever deeper into the world searching for the poem you're destined to be a vehicle for. That poem has always been calling you. The day you're ready to embark on the journey of soul initiation is the day you first hear that call. When you do, any life project that would have interfered with that journey falls away as vanishingly insignificant.

A few brief examples of mythopoetic identity might be helpful before we get to the more intricate and elaborate stories later in this book. Although it's impossible to communicate the numinosity of the human Soul in a few words, here are five linguistic sketches, five exceedingly brief word portraits, that embody the wild mysteries of soul encounter and how they have been communicated mythopoetically to five individuals:

- The overseer who guides others into the oceanic depths of the psyche
- She who dances the Earth and dreams song to feed the longing
- Spark heart on bear path
- She who generates perception-expanding images and identity-destabilizing questions
- The impossible dreamer who weaves cocoons of transformation

Despite their brevity, you can tell that these soul-infused identities and purposes contrast with middleworld cultural roles. These are not job descriptions you'll ever see advertised. They are not careers a vocational guidance counselor is going to recommend to you. They are of the dreamtime or the mythic. And they are the kinds of purposes utterly core to our deepest, innate human identities.

Soul as What Earth Asks of Us

Thomas Berry counseled that in order to take our destined human place on this planet, we must listen to and understand what Earth herself asks of us: "The guidance and power of the Earth [must be] communicated to us." It is through the journey of soul initiation that we receive this guidance. Our unique individual ecological niche — our Soul — is itself a power granted us by the animate planet we call Earth. Each individual Soul is a participant in Earth's Soul. The discovery of our eco-niche provides the most essential guidance we need in order to take our individual place in not only the sustaining of life but its enhancement. If we humans, as a species, end up truly contributing to life, it will be, as Thomas says, "not because we have determined the future of the Earth simply from some rational faculty," but because we have learned once again how to listen to what Earth is asking from each of us individually as well as from all of us collectively. This is the ultimate goal of the journey of soul initiation — not individual self-discovery and fulfillment, but cultural renaissance and the evolution of our species and our planet.

With good fortune, an ecological "soul revolution" will be the heir of the industrial and digital revolutions.

The Journey of Soul Initiation versus the Descent to Soul

The journey of soul initiation is a long developmental process that takes us from the end of one particular life stage (early Adolescence, which I call the Oasis), across the passage I call Confirmation into a second multiyear stage (late Adolescence, or the Cocoon), and then across the next passage (Soul Initiation), which is the start of early Adulthood (the life stage I call the Wellspring). In this sense, the journey of soul initiation is named after its finish line. The elements of the journey — the three stages of the Oasis, Cocoon, and Wellspring, and the two passages of Confirmation and Soul Initiation — are described in detail in *Nature and the Human Soul* and can be seen in the diagram on page 34. In a psychosocially healthier culture, this initiatory process would take place for most people in the teen years. In most contemporary societies, it seldom occurs at all (because the Cocoon stage is rarely reached), but when it does, it generally begins, at the earliest, in our twenties.

In contrast to the journey of soul initiation, the Descent to Soul is a particular kind of initiatory experience, a sojourn in Soul Canyon. The key feature of any Descent is an encounter with Soul, the vision or revelation of mythopoetic identity. The Descent, which begins with a plunge into the shadows of our psychological depths, is named after its starting block.

The journey of soul initiation is an extended developmental process with several major elements. It happens only once in life. The Descent to Soul, in contrast, is a type of numinous odyssey that is a core element of that journey, and it often takes place more than once during and after that journey. Any given Descent might take place over a few weeks or several months — or even longer.

Structurally, the journey of soul initiation encompasses three *stages* and two *passages*. The Descent to Soul, in contrast, has five *phases*.

The Five Phases of the Descent to Soul

The Descent to Soul is a psychospiritual expedition into one particular precinct of the underworld, Soul Canyon, and, if one is fortunate, the eventual emergence from those depths having been radically transformed by an encounter with Soul. As a field guide, this book introduces you to — and can accompany you through — the five phases of the Descent to Soul, which I name Preparation, Dissolution, Soul Encounter, Metamorphosis, and Enactment.[20]

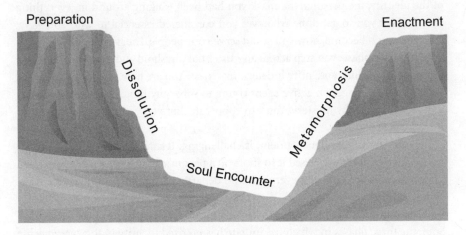

The Five Phases of the Descent to Soul

The first phase of the Descent, Preparation, readies you developmentally and psychospiritually for the journey and supports you to ultimately arrive, for the first time, at the rim of the Canyon, from where you can gaze down toward the intimidating and alluring mysteries that await below. There are several realms and dimensions of personal development that, if you engage them, will support you to arrive at the rim and be able to descend with a good chance not only of surviving but of being blessed with an encounter with Soul. In a healthy (ecocentric and soulcentric) culture, much of this preparation would occur as a matter of course during everyday living, learning, and loving, but this kind of personal development is at best absent from contemporary egocentric societies and, at worst, actively suppressed.

For this reason, the preparation needed for the Descent usually entails something quite different from and much more than whatever life experiences you've had in our current cultural context. The Preparation phase, for example, is not a matter of psychotherapy or the healing of emotional wounds, although this sometimes supplements Preparation. It's not something you would have gained through even years of meditation, contemplative prayer, yoga, healthy diets, or nonviolent communication — as valuable as these and many other practices are. It's not a matter of journal work, ceremony design, or physical conditioning. It's something entirely distinct: the cultivation of several dimensions of our innate human wholeness that are generally neglected or undermined in the contemporary world. The Preparation phase can last several months or more.

The second phase, Dissolution, comprises the psychospiritual descent itself into Soul Canyon. Dissolution is not merely severance from your everyday community and social roles. Rather, this phase is the conclusive dismemberment of who you believed you were, the unconditional disintegration of what you understood the world to be, the definitive end of the story you had been living, the unqualified dissolution of the identity, the persona, the mask you had been walking around in, everything that enabled you to get done whatever you considered essential to who you were, who you could become, how you could serve your people. Everything.

With this phase, you step across an existential threshold and enter a ritual space of liminality, a kind of identity indeterminateness. You are now in a state of suspension. You're no longer an active agent trying to solve anything. Rather, your goal is to be *dissolved* — by Mystery. You can cooperate, but you cannot make it happen. It happens *to* you.

Dissolution, in understatement, is challenging. It may last only a week or two (although I've never witnessed it so short on a person's first Descent), or it might go on for months or years. Not everyone who departs reaches the bottom of the Canyon — or even very far down.

Dissolution is the first of the three central and liminal phases of the Descent to Soul, the three phases in which the initiate has no fixed identity in the everyday life of the Village (and, in many traditional contexts, is separated physically and socially from the Village).

The third phase, Soul Encounter, is what happens when you reach the depths — namely, visions and/or revelations of your unique ecological niche in the greater web of life. But the experience is not anything like receiving a textbook description of species, habitats, food sources, and ecosystems. Rather, it's a glimpse of a pattern or image that metaphorically characterizes or connotes that niche. It is more like a poem, a myth, or a dream. It is the revelation of your mythopoetic identity. What this vision or revelation does is root your Ego in the mysterious soil of Soul. The seed of you cracks open and you begin to draw your life from a realm much deeper than you had previously imagined possible.

How long must you be in these hazardous and often frightening depths? How long, that is, do you get to enjoy these peculiar and rare ecstasies? Maybe a day. Maybe a few weeks. Maybe years. In a healthy cultural setting — one that had prepared you well for the Descent and provided you with the psychospiritual tools to go deep quickly — alas, probably not as long as you might wish. But let's be clear: Although the Soul Encounter phase is the time when something of your mythopoetic identity is revealed and activated, you'll hopefully be drawing on and living this revelation the rest of your life.

The fourth phase, Metamorphosis, is the shape-shifting of your Ego in light of and in accordance with the revelation or vision. To become an initiated Adult, the Ego needs much more than a vision, a cognitive revelation, or a blueprint for a mature human. The Ego needs to be reshaped, reconfigured, metamorphosed. The dismembered Adolescent Ego must be re-membered into its Adult form. This re-memberment takes place in part as a result of your efforts to embody your mythopoetic identity by showing up in the world as the person who occupies your unique eco-niche; which is to say, by cultivating relationships with people, other-than-humans, and communities *as that person*. Metamorphosis, however, does not require you to engage in acts of service (which is the *sine qua non* of the next phase). There are many practices from which you can choose that support and intensify the refashioning of your Ego. But this shape-shifting can take place even without your cooperation — possibly even in the face of your active resistance.

Metamorphosis can take a while. You wouldn't want to rush it. Plan on a few years, though it might be quite a bit less.

The fifth and final phase, Enactment, is when you learn to embody your mythopoetic identity in acts of service to your community. It's when you activate your giveaway, when you begin to perform your vision for your people to see, when you first discover how to deliver your gift of love-service to your world. As you embody your mythopoetic identity for others, you receive feedback that allows you to continuously deepen and develop your soul-infused conversation with the world. The primary way you come to understand your gift, after all, is through the lifelong journey of embodying it.

With the metaphor-image of Soul Canyon in mind, we could say that a Descent to Soul ends with an ascent from the depths, but in a certain sense we never really leave the Canyon. Our everyday lives in the Village world above the Canyon become expressions of those depths. As our lives unfold — as we continue to individuate — our Ego is rooted ever deeper in the mysteries of Soul.

The five phases of the Descent are both more in number and different in kind and name than the more familiar three phases of rites of passage popularized by the ethnographer Arnold van Gennep or the three phases of the hero's journey as described by the comparative mythologist Joseph Campbell. This is in part because the Descent is neither a rite of passage nor a hero's journey. For more on these differences, see appendix 2, "The Descent to Soul Compared to Rites of Passage, the Hero's Journey, and Indigenous Practices," which will be of special interest to rites-of-passage guides and students of cultural or social ecology, anthropology, mythology, ethnology, or depth psychology.

The five phases of the Descent to Soul are not necessarily or always experienced in a linear sequence as described above — except on our first Descent. It's hard to imagine a successful first descent into Soul Canyon without adequate preparation; or a first soul encounter without having experienced identity dissolution (our old identity would make it impossible to receive the new); or a first metamorphosis without a first soul encounter (morph into *what?*); or a first enactment without having first become a vehicle for that enactment. Even on our first Descent, however, once we reach a given phase, we can also be, simultaneously, in one or more of the previous phases. We can, for instance, be undergoing ego-metamorphosis from our first soul encounter while also, at the same time, experiencing a deeper unraveling of our identity (Dissolution) — perhaps due to that very metamorphosis — and this deeper unraveling could set the stage for another soul encounter.

During a later Descent, on the other hand, we can find ourselves in any phase at any given time. Toward the end of our first Descent, we shift permanently from a cultural-role-based identity to an ecopoetic identity, and consequently, after that first Descent, we don't need another dissolution experience before having another soul encounter or in order for our Ego to still be shape-shifting. In other words, after a first Descent, the five phases are less phase-like and more like facets or panes of experience. Once the way has been opened, any facet of a Descent can occur or intensify whenever the conditions are right, and we can experience one or more of these facets simultaneously. We now have the capacity, the Soul-infused fluency, to navigate and assimilate our encounters with the numinous. Our soulful ripening enables us to be continuously responsive to the depths.

The Metaphor of the Cocoon

The five phases of the Descent to Soul correspond to the five developmental phases of the butterfly — in particular, from adolescent caterpillar to adult butterfly. The first phase, Preparation, is comparable to the period during which the caterpillar sheds its skin several times ("molts"), each time growing a larger and more able body — eventually becoming capable of weaving a cocoon for its own transformation (strictly speaking, for the butterfly, it's not a cocoon, but a chrysalis that the caterpillar itself molts into). Dissolution is what happens after the caterpillar enters that cocoon — the literal dissolution of its body into an amorphous fluid, the loss of its caterpillar form and its caterpillar life.[21] Soul Encounter corresponds to the awakening of what biologists call the imaginal cells that have existed all along within the caterpillar body but do not become activated until this phase. The imaginal cells have been, from the beginning, imagining the form of the adult creature, the butterfly, which biologists call the imago — hence the term "imaginal cells." Once awakened, these cells get busy reconfiguring the elements of the former caterpillar into the shape of a butterfly. This shape-shifting work is the Metamorphosis phase. Once the butterfly body is complete, the cocoon cracks open and the butterfly first stretches its wings. This is the commencement of Enactment, which reaches fullness when the butterfly takes flight and begins its adult life of pollination and reproduction.

The caterpillar is to the butterfly as an uninitiated human Ego is to an initiated one. The imaginal cells are to the caterpillar as a Soul-infused vision is to the uninitiated Ego.

A Book of Stories

This book is filled with stories of women and men who have been through the journey of soul initiation, stories that illustrate how this spiritual adventure has transformed their lives and enhanced the well-being of their people and the larger Earth community. Because these stories arise from realms far beyond the borders of mainstream society and conventional consciousness, they can be difficult for the strategic mind to understand, or maybe hard to believe — but the mythopoetic imagination trembles in recognition. These true spiritual adventures emerge from the wellspring that is at the heart of our human relationship to the world.

To me, these stories are some of the most extraordinary ever told in the contemporary West — the kind of stories that have become exceedingly rare. Numinous stories. Initiatory sagas. Radiant stories of modern men and women entering the dreamtime, emerging with personal myths expressed in the language of ancient and timeless archetypes, and then embodying those myths in ways that engender healthy, ecocentric, life-enhancing cultures. These stories are rare and precious jewels. It's been a singular privilege to receive them, work with them, and attempt to tell them in a manner equal to their splendor.

This book — and the work of Animas Valley Institute — would not have been possible without what my colleagues and I have learned from these contemporary people undergoing the Descent to Soul. What I offer here are field notes from four decades of guiding real people. What you'll find in these pages is not an abstract theory about the Descent but rather a report on the common patterns (and their variations) found in the experiences of thousands of people. Each pattern is illustrated with true stories.

Carl Jung is one of the people whose story I've included, though I obviously didn't work with him directly, being born a hundred years too late. But with a careful reading of his personal journal — his *Red Book*, which records in elaborate detail his journey of soul initiation — and his memoir, *Memories, Dreams, Reflections*, I was able to track Jung's experience through the five phases of the Descent. The result is an understanding of the *Red Book* that contrasts in significant ways with contemporary Jungian perspectives.

I have been especially intrigued by Jung's story for several reasons. First, unlike most of the other people in this book, he is well known. Second, his professional work can be understood as Western society's first attempt to comprehend the very realm of human experience I'm mapping in this book. Third, he was self-guided on his Descent and, at the time, had no map to help him grasp what was happening to him or where he was going; his journey, consequently, was navigated by his own intuitions and instincts, not influenced by anyone else's compass or map. Fourth, his entire body of work (his depth psychology) is, as he makes clear, derived from what he discovered on his Descent. Fifth, the experiences that make up his journey of soul initiation were impeccably self-documented. Sixth, Jung's experiences readily fit the model presented in this book even though the model was developed long before I read his *Red Book*. And finally, I believe the model illuminates Jung's experience better than does his own psychology. Jung had the *experience* of the Descent and developed a few practices that can support it, but he didn't have a map of the terrain that would have enabled him to fully understand the Descent or to guide it.

Soul Purpose versus Social Purpose

It's essential to emphasize, here at the start, one final distinction: Our Soul purpose is categorically different from our social or vocational purpose. This is one of the most common misunderstandings of the map presented in this book — and the most regrettable and consequential.

Soul purpose is what we're born to accomplish in our lifetime — the numinous gift we are here to offer to the Earth community. It can be identified only in metaphoric, poetic, or mythic terms, which is why I refer to it as our mythopoetic identity. Mine, as I've noted, is, in part, the weaving of cocoons of transformation from psychological Adolescence to psychospiritual Adulthood.

Social or vocational purpose is an Adolescent perspective on personal meaning. It identifies us in terms of our social roles, our job descriptions, or the intended outcomes of our creative projects. Although a social or vocational perspective on purpose is necessary, appropriate, and healthy in Adolescence, it doesn't derive from the depths of the psyche or go to the depths of the world, and it is not enough to build a full life on. Yet, tragically, in the contemporary world, it's very rare to find anything beyond this Adolescent perspective on purpose. It can be late in life before we discover, if we ever do, that our true selves are not related to the roles we've played within our family or society.

Within our psyches we each have what I call "inner protectors" who, before Soul Initiation, are constantly trying to convince us that a social or vocational purpose is our raison d'être. (I describe these in "Our Inner Protectors," pages 58–59.) They do not want us to embark on the journey of soul initiation because they know it will entail dismemberment, loss, risk, and radical change. They want us to settle. Guides and coaches who would support people in the Cocoon stage to find their purpose in the form of a social role, job, or creative project are in cahoots with those inner protectors.

After our initiation into our Soul purpose, we no longer have what might be called a middleworld purpose — a purpose defined in terms of social or vocational roles. After the life passage of Soul Initiation, there's only a middleworld *delivery system* for our true purpose. Our social roles and vocational endeavors are no longer purposes; they are, rather, means to an end. Following my Soul Initiation, for example, I have occupied the roles of psychologist, vision-fast guide, author, and soulcraft facilitator, among others, but none of these roles constitute my purpose. Rather, they have been, for me, delivery systems for the weaving of cocoons.

From the perspective of our middleworld lives, the Soul is a dream. From the perspective of our Soul's purpose, our middleworld lives are illusions or phantasms.

But our middleworld lives are not incidental to the Soul. Far from it. In fact, it's entirely to the contrary. The healthy, mature Ego is our means for making real our Soul's desires. This is why it's often said there's a love affair between the Ego and the Soul, and that when they come together in partnership, they form a Sacred Marriage. Each has what the other lacks and what the other longs for and is deeply allured by. The Soul holds the knowledge of our true, destined place in the world, of what is truly worth doing with our lives. But the Soul has no means — no head or hands — to manifest that purpose. It is the healthy, mature Ego that can construct things and accomplish things in the world. The Soul is spellbound by the Ego's capacity to manifest. The Ego is moonstruck by the Soul's visions and passions. The mature Ego wants, more than anything in life, to make real the dreams the Soul has been weaving since before our birth.

The central message of this book is that there is indeed a way to uncover and realize our Soul's purpose. It is the journey of soul initiation — in particular, the Descent to Soul. And we can engage this journey in a contemporary way that does not require us to adopt, co-opt, or appropriate methods from any other culture or to first become someone we are not already. It requires no particular belief or faith, religious or otherwise, only a willingness to dive in.

In the following pages you'll find a description of the journey — to the extent it's possible to put into words. To truly understand the journey, however, you must embark upon it.

Chapter One

PHASE ONE

Preparation for the Descent

Part 1: Attending to the Foundations of Human Development

**Prospective Immigrants
Please Note**

Either you will
go through this door
or you will not go through.

If you go through
there is always the risk
of remembering your name.

Things look at you doubly
and you must look back
and let them happen.

If you do not go through
it is possible
to live worthily

to maintain your attitudes
to hold your position
to die bravely

but much will blind you,
much will evade you,
at what cost who knows?

The door itself
makes no promises.
It is only a door.

— ADRIENNE RICH

The Descent to Soul is an epic personal odyssey, a spiritual adventure that has been metaphorically compared with a solo sea crossing in a rowboat or a prolonged trek through a trackless jungle. As you've seen, I prefer to imagine it as a descent into a sheer-walled desert gorge, an expedition into the unknown labyrinthine depths of Soul Canyon.

In whatever way you conceive of the journey, it is arduous, and preparing for it takes time, possibly years. But the preparation itself can be an extraordinarily rich spell. There are many opportunities of several kinds.

Sadly, few in the contemporary world ever discover Adrienne Rich's door to the mysteries of identity or locate the lost trail to Soul Canyon and one day find themselves standing with their toes edged up to the vertiginous precipice, prepared to descend into mist and tangled darkness. For the most part, this is not due to a lack of longing or courage. The primary obstacle is insufficient psychospiritual preparation, which, in turn, is the result of living in communities entirely unaware of the existence of Soul Canyon somewhere out beyond the gates of the Village. Most societies today have no awareness of Soul itself — that we each are born to occupy a unique ecological niche — let alone encourage the journey of soul initiation. Even worse, the paths of human development that would prepare us for an encounter with Soul are actively thwarted by the global conformist-consumer culture and its major institutions — including education, religion, medicine, and "mental health."

But with an adequate understanding of the terrain that lies between the civilized and the wild, a map to help you navigate, an irrepressible longing to wander into the mysteries, and a set of practices that support you to cultivate the necessary personal resources, it's not so difficult to find your way to the edge. Besides, the preparation itself affords invaluable benefits for your everyday life — as well as resources and necessities during the actual descent and after.

The primary work of Preparation is psychological and spiritual, but not of the kinds commonly considered or engaged in the contemporary world; it is not principally, for example, a matter of psychotherapy or of meditation or yoga. The Preparation phase is also not primarily about clarifying your intentions for the journey.

The essential preparation is not physical conditioning or gearing up for wilderness travel, although at times you might need to do this, too.

The crucial preparation is to attend to the foundations of human development — honing these to a level far beyond what you'd need to get by in the mainstream contemporary world. This chapter and the next present a condensed summary of the nonnegotiables — the dimensions of personal development you need in order to descend with a good chance of survival (both physical and psychospiritual) and to encounter the mystery that awaits you in the twilight depths of Soul Canyon. (For more elaborate and detailed guidance, see my previous books *Nature and the Human Soul* and *Wild Mind*.)

As the counterpart to the very real dangers of embarking on the journey unprepared, there is also the rare but conceivable hazard of *over*preparing — of placing so much emphasis on groundwork that you end up with a perpetual excuse for never actually walking through the door. It's possible to survive and benefit from a Descent to Soul without preparation beyond what your life has already afforded you — if, that is, you are that rare individual already ripened in the ways discussed in this chapter and the next. The timing of your Descent, after all, is not entirely up to you. What you *can* choose is to prepare yourself adequately so that you're ready when the call arrives. This chapter and the next, then, are not a compulsory checklist but a set of invaluable preparations until that beckoning threshold appears or until, without warning, a gnarled hand reaches up through the soil and grabs your unsuspecting ankle. At some point, in other words, Mystery deems you ready and down you go.

Most Westerners who have descended into Soul Canyon in recent centuries probably didn't prepare specifically for this journey. They were abducted. But most who survived the journey *and* benefited from it were prepared by virtue of their prior life experiences, even though their adventures with personal development were undertaken for reasons other than the Descent. But prepared they were nonetheless. Unlike them, you have the opportunity to prepare consciously.

The two conclusions about the journey of soul initiation that have been personally hardest for me to assimilate and have been most challenging for others to understand and accept are (1) that a particular developmental stage must be achieved before a person is ready to embark on the journey and (2) that relatively few contemporary people achieve this stage. Most people, including psychologists and educators, don't think this way about human development. The common assumption is that if you've reached a certain age and are neurologically normal, you're eligible for any kind of personal development you'd like — you only have to get the training or engage in the practices. Everything about our view changes, however, when we begin to think about life stages as personally achieved — not simply reached by virtue of age, neurology, or genetics — and when we realize that attaining a new stage is the necessary portal to further development. This view radically shifts the way we understand and approach education and psychological or spiritual growth. It's no longer one size fits all. What you're capable of depends on your life stage. When it comes to the search for life purpose, for example, even the meanings of "search" and "purpose" are entirely dependent on your developmental stage.

There are three primary realms within which to ready yourself: The first concerns this matter of developmental stage, the second is the cultivation of your innate human wholeness, and the third is Self-healing. Then there is a fourth realm of final preparations when you've reached that moment in life when you are soon to slip over the edge into the beckoning unknown. This chapter considers the first of these four realms of preparation.

Developmental Stages

If it's true that most contemporary crises, individual and collective, are due to a widespread human failure to grow whole, then our most fundamental long-term agenda must be the enhancement of how we understand and support human development. We must create new practices for helping people fully mature. The preparation for the Descent begins with such practices.

In the contemporary mainstream West, we tend to think of the human life journey in terms of only three or four loosely and poorly defined stages — childhood, adolescence, and adulthood, and sometimes elderhood, too. But I believe there are actually eight distinct stages in a full human life. The problem is that most contemporary people get only as far as the third. One of the great challenges of living in an egocentric culture is that we believe, and act as if, a person is "grown up" simply by virtue of having reached a certain age or of having completed school, gotten married, or achieved economic independence. Although some psychologists recognize elective opportunities for human maturation beyond the attainment of the nominal status of "adult," very few consider the possibility that there are culturally unrecognized stages of human development that are necessary before reaching true maturity.

The journey of soul initiation, as a case in point, does not commence in earnest until one enters a stage of development that is, psychospiritually, what a mature culture would consider simply a healthy late Adolescence. This is the stage I call the Cocoon, the fourth of eight optimal or "ecocentric" life stages in the Eco-Soulcentric Developmental Wheel, as described in *Nature and the Human Soul*.

The Wheel

The Eco-Soulcentric Developmental Wheel is a model of human development that diverges radically from mainstream Western ideas of maturation. It's a blueprint for individuation rooted in the cycles and qualities of the natural world. It describes what the stages of human development look like when we grow with nature and Soul as our primary guides: We take root in a childhood of innocence and wonder;

sprout into an Adolescence of creative fire and mystery-probing adventures; blossom into an authentic Adulthood of visionary leadership and cultural artistry; and finally ripen into a seed-scattering Elderhood of wisdom, grace, and the holistic tending of the more-than-human world.

The Wheel asks us to think in a new way about life stages: The timing of the transitions between soulcentric stages is independent of chronological age and social role and, for the most part, independent of biological and cognitive development. Individuals don't pass from one stage to the next just because they reach a certain age (thirteen, twenty-one, or sixty-five), obtain a certain social status (schoolchild, eligible for dating, married, breadwinner, parent, or grandparent), or have certain hormonal releases begin or end. Rather, the movement from one stage to the next is spurred by success with the specific developmental tasks encountered at each stage. Life passages occur when (and if) an individual's center of psychospiritual gravity shifts by virtue of success with these tasks.

The developmental tasks that characterize each stage of the Wheel have a nature-oriented dimension as well as a more familiar (to Westerners) culture-oriented dimension. Healthy human development requires a constant balancing of the influences and demands of both nature and culture. For example, in middle childhood, the nature task is learning the enchantment of the natural world through experiential outdoor immersions, while the culture task is learning the social practices, values, knowledge, history, mythology, and cosmology of one's family and culture.

In contemporary society, however, we have for centuries minimized, suppressed, or entirely ignored the nature task in the first three life stages of early childhood through early Adolescence. This results in an Adolescence so out of sync with nature that most people never mature further and are unable to imagine a life beyond consumerism and soul-suppressing jobs.

The diagram on the next page shows the most essential elements of the Wheel. The design is based on the universal template of the four cardinal directions. The cycle of life begins and ends in the East (with sunrise) and moves sunwise (clockwise in the Northern Hemisphere, as shown here). Each of the eight life stages is characterized by a number, a conventional name (like "early Adolescence"), an archetypal name consisting of a human archetype (the Thespian) and an Earth archetype (the Oasis), a developmental task (creating a secure and authentic social self), the gift that people in that stage provide their community simply by being a healthy person (fire), and the psychospiritual center of gravity of people in that stage (peer group, sex, and society). In the center of the diagram, arrayed around the cardinal directions, are the passages between the stages. It's important to emphasize that this Wheel consists of the optimal (ecocentric and soulcentric) stages of human development, not the egocentric stages more commonly experienced in contemporary societies.[1] If you would like to download the diagram, go to https://animas.org/wp-content/uploads/Eight-Stages-diagram_3-3_hi-res.png.

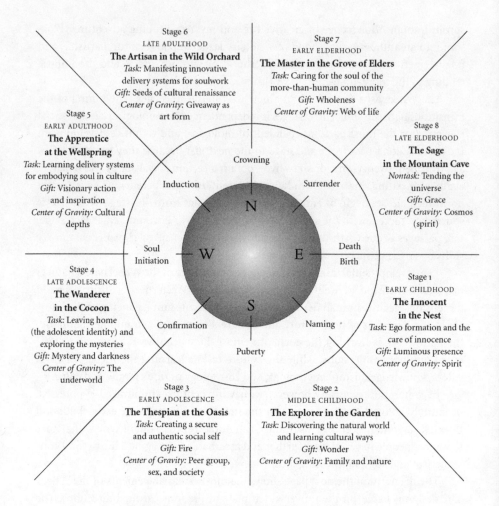

Stage 6
LATE ADULTHOOD
The Artisan in the Wild Orchard
Task: Manifesting innovative
delivery systems for soulwork
Gift: Seeds of cultural renaissance
Center of Gravity: Giveaway as
art form

Stage 7
EARLY ELDERHOOD
The Master in the Grove of Elders
Task: Caring for the soul of the
more-than-human community
Gift: Wholeness
Center of Gravity: Web of life

Stage 5
EARLY ADULTHOOD
**The Apprentice
at the Wellspring**
Task: Learning delivery systems
for embodying soul in culture
Gift: Visionary action
and inspiration
Center of Gravity: Cultural
depths

Stage 8
LATE ELDERHOOD
**The Sage
in the Mountain Cave**
Nontask: Tending the
universe
Gift: Grace
Center of Gravity: Cosmos
(spirit)

Crowning

Induction

Surrender

Soul
Initiation

Death
Birth

Stage 4
LATE ADOLESCENCE
**The Wanderer
in the Cocoon**
Task: Leaving home
(the adolescent identity) and
exploring the mysteries
Gift: Mystery and darkness
Center of Gravity: The
underworld

Stage 1
EARLY CHILDHOOD
**The Innocent
in the Nest**
Task: Ego formation and the
care of innocence
Gift: Luminous presence
Center of Gravity: Spirit

Confirmation

Naming

Puberty

Stage 3
EARLY ADOLESCENCE
The Thespian at the Oasis
Task: Creating a secure
and authentic social self
Gift: Fire
Center of Gravity: Peer group,
sex, and society

Stage 2
MIDDLE CHILDHOOD
The Explorer in the Garden
Task: Discovering the natural world
and learning cultural ways
Gift: Wonder
Center of Gravity: Family and nature

The Eco-Soulcentric Developmental Wheel

The Cocoon

The Cocoon stage (late Adolescence) begins after the life passage of Confirmation —
that propitious and turbulent turning point in life when a person has had sufficient
success with the tasks of early Adolescence: They have achieved a personality and
a way of showing up in the world that is not only socially accepted and admired
but also fully authentic. As a consequence of this achievement, they find themselves
asking the deeper questions about life and identity, and they find themselves longing
to stride into the great wilderness of life with the grail-goal of intimate encounters

with the perennial mysteries of nature and psyche. In the Cocoon, the archetype of the Wanderer becomes dominant and central in the human psyche.

The reason why the Cocoon stage is rarely attained in the contemporary world is straightforward: failures with the developmental tasks of the previous three life stages. Widespread developmental arrest is the unsurprising result of shortcomings in family life, education, religion, psychotherapy, and community.[2]

It's important to keep in mind that I use the word *Adolescence* to refer, not to a chronological age range (our teen years), but to a psychospiritual life stage. This stage of life and the two childhood stages preceding it are navigated so poorly in egocentric cultures that the outcome is too often heartbreaking and tragic: chronic anxiety, depression, and addiction leading to cruelty to self and others, violence, or suicide. In contrast, healthy *eco*centric Adolescence affords enormous opportunities for individuation and maturation and provides invaluable benefits and blessings for the community.

In egocentric cultures like ours, the passage of Confirmation into psychological late Adolescence (the Cocoon stage), if reached at all, most often occurs many years after we obtain the nominal status of "adult." It's helpful to make the distinction, as does Jungian analyst James Hollis, between a "first adulthood" of vocational, social, and civic responsibilities and a "second adulthood" of visionary cultural artistry.[3]

My estimate is that approximately 10 percent of contemporary Western people reach the Cocoon stage *and* manage to descend into Soul Canyon. What enables them to do this despite the lack of cultural support? Two things: First, they have made the transition from egocentrism to ecocentrism. On the Wheel, this means they have crossed from the egocentric version of early Adolescence (Conforming and Rebelling) to the ecocentric version (the Thespian at the Oasis). Although both these stages are early Adolescent, there's a world of difference between them. Second, by achieving sufficient success with the developmental tasks of the Oasis, they reach the life passage of Confirmation, ushering them into the Cocoon. Let's explore these two transformations one at a time — and what you can do to bring them about if you have not already experienced them, or to help others if you have.

Eco-Awakening

The shift from egocentrism to ecocentrism is what I call Eco-awakening, a major life passage (but not described in my previous books).

Eco-awakening occurs when we have our first conscious and embodied ex- perience of our innate membership in the Earth community. All other affiliations then become secondary and, in fact, derivative of our inherent participation in the larger, more-than-human world (which is to say, the not *merely* human world, the world that includes the human realm as one element). A romantic partnership and memberships in family, social or ethnic groups, and perhaps a religious community will continue to provide great riches and lend abundant color to our life, but these will forever after be experienced as secondary. The vitality of the Earth community, of which we have always been part, is now our first concern and first gladness and commands our greatest loyalty. What would our world be like if all humans experienced Earth as sacred?

Dan, a Presbyterian pastor, described his Eco-awakening, at age fifty, in a summer, high-altitude, Rocky Mountain forest:

> I was sitting by a small stream on a starry, moonlit night. I felt a strong, sentinel-like presence from a stand of large pine trees above the stream. For the first time in my life I didn't feel like a tourist in nature. The forest was alive, and I was in communion with her. When I heard the trees clearly say with one voice, *Now you belong to us!* I was shaken. At that moment a great tectonic shift took place within me. I felt a sense of belonging to the whole cosmos, not just a church or denomination. I looked up in the sky full of stars and began to weep, overwhelmed by joy in the admission that I no longer felt the need to save the world. I just wanted to belong more fully to it.

Eco-awakening is a somatic, emotional, and spiritual experience, not a (mere) cognitive one. It is the embodied, heart-stretching, and world-shifting experience of oneself as being as natural, as wild, as interconnected and related, and as magical as anything else on our planet — as much as a fox, a chanterelle, a wild desert stream, or an old-growth forest. People with a general knowledge of ecology might understand this intellectually but relatively few have located and passed through the unseen veil that exiles most contemporary people from an everyday conscious communion with the animate world.

Eco-awakening rocks your world. You now realize you had previously been a kind of refugee, existentially and ecologically homeless. The restlessness, anxiety, alienation, and displacement you had experienced all your life disperses like mist in morning sunshine. You feel at home in the world in a deep, rich, and unprecedented way, a way you hadn't known was missing, hadn't even known was possible. Each natural thing is no longer an object but a subject to whom you are related and have always been related. Separation has ended. You've escaped the conformist-consumer "matrix" and returned consciously to the world into which you had been born, an animate world in which everything is alive, everything speaks, everything is related to everything else.[4]

Eco-awakening is an essential developmental milestone in preparation for the Descent to Soul. Discovering your own Soul — your unique eco-niche in the more-than-human world — cannot happen without it.

Eco-awakening terminates the egocentric early-Adolescent stage of Conforming and Rebelling and initiates the ecocentric early-Adolescent stage of the Thespian at the Oasis.[5] In the Oasis, people experience themselves as fully eligible participants in the more-than-human world, enabling them to take a variety of social and vocational roles that are both authentic and useful to their communities. They are social and ecological actors (authentic thespians) in a self-organizing gathering of many clans and species in a fertile and fruitful place (an "oasis").

Before Eco-awakening, we feel disconnected from the larger web of life. This experience of existential homelessness results in a compensatory craving for social acceptance as our be-all and end-all, and we act out this craving by socially conforming and rebelling. After Eco-awakening, when we are rooted in our greater and deeper belonging, we feel relatively little need or desire to conform or rebel. Instead, we're drawn to wander deeper into the mysteries of our original more-than-human home.

Eco-awakening is an artifact of egocentric culture. In healthy, ecocentric cultures, no one ever goes through the passage of Eco-awakening. Children never lose their innate communion with the wild self-organizing world. They have no need to be awakened from a culture-imposed slumber or trance. They are raised in families and communities where wild kinship is a daily reality. Never having found themselves in the egocentric early-Adolescent stage of Conforming and Rebelling, they have no need to be liberated from it.

Although an artifact of egocentric culture, Eco-awakening is nonetheless among the greatest blessings imaginable when it occurs. And it's a *necessary* transition for any further maturation, including your eventual arrival at the rim of Soul Canyon.

How to Eco-Awaken: Attend to the Nature-Oriented Tasks of Childhood

How do you bring about the life passage of Eco-awakening in yourself or others? You devote yourself to the nature-oriented developmental tasks of the two stages of healthy (ecocentric) childhood. These two nature-oriented tasks are the ones most neglected and often in fact suppressed in egocentric culture.[6] Once we're in psychological Adolescence, we cannot return to childhood itself, but we can (and must) return to the neglected developmental *tasks* of childhood.[7] Most psychotherapists neglect to support their clients in these two tasks despite how essential they are to our psychological, social, and cultural well-being.

CULTIVATION OF INNOCENCE, PRESENT-CENTEREDNESS, AND RELATIONALITY

The nature-oriented task of early childhood (birth to approximately age four) is the preservation of innocence, which is, in essence, the capacity for present-centeredness. It is the responsibility and opportunity of parents and other family members to address this task on behalf of the preschool child — by, for example, encouraging the child's natural curiosity, their full-bodied emotionality, their unfettered sensuality, and their thrill of wild movement, and by recognizing their daily need for nurturing touch and for play, both indoors and in outdoor natural settings.[8] If your family did poorly with this, it might be challenging for you to be fully (and innocently) present to the here and now, a capacity essential to human development. In particular, presence is foundational to relationality and to the skills of empathy and compassion. Without some degree of presence and innocence, it's impossible to feel connected to anyone or anything.

If you are preparing for a Descent to Soul but your capacity for present-centeredness is only fair to middling, it's vital to address this unfinished business from childhood. Present-centeredness can be cultivated in a number of ways, including through a meditation practice (such as mindfulness, contemplative prayer, yoga, or qigong), transpersonal psychotherapies that incorporate such practices, regular periods of attentive solitude in wild or semi-wild places, devoted play with any of the expressive arts, psychotherapies (like Gestalt) that emphasize present-centeredness, the practice of presence and innocence in social settings, and last but not least, apprenticing yourself to infants.[9]

NATURE CONNECTION

The nature-oriented task of middle childhood (approximately age four until puberty) is to learn the enchantment of nature through intimate contact with the wild, other-than-human world — the world found in a backyard and in nearby woods, mountains, and seashores. Through outdoor play, children discover that their innate membership in this greater, wilder world is the other half of their birthright beyond family, school, and market.[10]

If, in childhood, you had not fully immersed yourself in the boundless enchantments of the natural world — and still have not — begin now. You can do this on your own or you can enroll in nature-connection programs, which now exist in a great variety in many places in the Western world, or you can seek support from an ecotherapist skilled in nature-connection practices.[11]

Perhaps the single most effective (and intoxicating) practice is to wander alone, for several days at a time, in the least tame places you can get yourself to. This assumes that you have adequate gear, knowledge, and skill, that you have the socioeconomic privilege that makes this possible and safe enough, that you're willing and able to take the time, and that you have a way to get there. Extended wilderness immersions have a profound impact on your psyche, your consciousness, your worldview, and your readiness for the encounter with Soul.

The wilderness odyssey, most often in solitude, has been pursued in all places and times by the archetypal Wanderer, including Moses, Christ, and Muhammad in their desert lands, the eponymous Odysseus on the high seas, Alexandra David-Néel in forbidden Tibet, John Muir in the California Sierras, Beryl Markham in the cross-continental air, and Jack Kerouac by way of the American roads. In this book, you'll read of many solo wilderness sojourns that were pivotal elements of contemporary soul journeys.

Innumerable commentators have decried the loss of (and great need for) the foundational experiences of both social interconnectedness and nature connection. It's not a coincidence, then, that these are precisely the core experiences cultivated in the two stages of a healthy childhood and the two experiences most needed and lacking among contemporary people. This underscores that the great crises of our time stem from breakdowns in natural human development, and that the long-term, deepest solutions are psychological, spiritual, and communal. What we most need in order to deeply respond to our current global crises — and to adapt to the extreme and compounding changes we will not be able to prevent — is also what each individual needs to be most fully prepared for the journey of soul initiation and, in particular, for the Descent to Soul. Individual maturation and real cultural development are not separate.

Success with the Two Tasks of the Oasis

Preparation for the Descent includes two developmental passages that must be reached and navigated. The first, explored above, is Eco-awakening, the transition from egocentric early Adolescence to ecocentric early Adolescence. The second passage is Confirmation, the transition from the ecocentric early-Adolescent stage of the Oasis to the late-Adolescent stage of the Cocoon.

Confirmation is set in motion by success with the two tasks of the Oasis.

The nature-oriented task is the cultivation of authenticity, the capacity to know who you are psychologically and to express and embody this identity in your social life with friends, family, and coworkers. The culture-oriented task of the Oasis is to obtain social acceptance from and belonging in at least one desired peer group.

This doesn't sound so difficult, does it? Well, it is. This is, in fact, precisely where the majority of contemporary people get stuck in their personal development. Either task of the Oasis is not so hard by itself: Authenticity is a piece of cake if you don't mind alienating others and possibly being friendless. And social acceptance is a snap if you're okay with being an impostor, willing to act in whatever ways are necessary to be accepted. But succeeding simultaneously with the two tasks of the Oasis can be immensely challenging. This is due in part to how formidable it has become in the contemporary world to be authentic — to even *know* who you are, let alone be able to embody the real you in your choices and relationships. In our advertisement-saturated and fear-infused society with its emphasis on looking good (or even merely acceptable), driving us to act within narrow prescribed bandwidths, most people have lost the ability to identify their bedrock values, needs, desires, and limits, or their genuine opinions, attitudes, and personal styles.[12]

Social self-design is a foundational skill with which few contemporary people receive guidance in childhood or teen years.[13]

Because psychological authenticity and social belonging have become rare, they are perhaps the greatest and most pervasive longings in the contemporary world. This is what most people mean when they say they yearn for greater meaning or purpose in their lives or for the opportunity to participate meaningfully in the world. They want to feel more real and more in communion with the web of life. They want their lives to make a difference. This, indeed, is the ultimate goal of the journey of soul initiation. But the necessary foundation for the Descent to Soul is an achieved sense of *psychological* belonging (knowing who you are, a feeling of personal authenticity), *social* belonging (acceptance in a peer group or human community), and *ecological* belonging (communion with the more-than-human world, what you experience after Eco-awakening).

When most contemporary people say they want more "soul" in their lives, they usually mean they want to experience more psychological and social belonging. For those who are Eco-awakened, they also mean greater ecological belonging.[14] For those in the Cocoon stage, they usually mean the kind of mystical belonging to the world implied by the way I use the word *Soul.*

For people in either egocentric or ecocentric early Adolescence, it's difficult to truly understand what *Soul* means in the ecological, underworld, or mystical sense of the word. This would be like a caterpillar fully understanding flight.

We might imagine some caterpillars have fantasies about flight, but they may not be aware that achieving it requires that they first go through the chrysalis stage during which they'll experience a definitive death of their caterpillar form. Likewise, Adolescent humans might have fantasies about adult freedoms, but they're not likely to fathom the psychospiritual death they'll have to face along the way or what true Adult freedom really entails.

How to Address the Developmental Task of the Oasis

The task of creating a socially acceptable and authentic self can be divided into (at least) eight subtasks:

- Value exploration, which entails asking and living big questions like: What is worth striving for? What genuinely brings me alive? What has heart for me and what doesn't? Who are my people? What principles will I fight to uphold? To whom and what will I be faithful? What is necessary for a decent life? What is the meaning of human existence? What, to me, is God? Death?
- Learning to distinguish between authenticity (your own) and self-deception.

- Cultivating emotional skills. This includes the capacity for the full somatic experience of your emotions; the skill of insight into their meaning and significance; and the ability to compassionately express and act on your emotions in a way that honors both yourself and any others involved.
- Learning the art of conflict resolution.
- Developing the ability to define yourself culturally and to cocreate your social world.
- Cultivating dexterity and sensitivity in sex and sexual relationships.
- Developing the ability to take care of yourself and earn a living.
- The practice of human-nature reciprocity and ecological responsibility for the well-being of the greater Earth community.

How would you rate your level of development with each of these subtasks of creating a socially acceptable and authentic self? For support in addressing these subtasks, see *Nature and the Human Soul*, chapter 6, where they are explored in some detail, including suggestions for finding assistance.

You might presume that the quickest way to reach the Cocoon is to address that stage's developmental tasks. But it isn't really possible to address those tasks until one is *in* the Cocoon. The only way to reach the Cocoon is to attend to the tasks of the Oasis, as explored above. When sufficient success is realized, Mystery shifts our psychospiritual center of gravity to the Cocoon. This is the shift from a life centered in peer group, sex, and social style to a life focused on the mysteries of nature and psyche. Attempts to be in a later stage are likely to result in an indefinite stay in the stage you're in. Conversely (and both ironically and paradoxically), loving the stage you're in (and its tasks) shortens your time there.[15]

Confirmation

Success with the developmental tasks of the Oasis moves you toward Confirmation, the passage into the Cocoon, which, in turn, ushers you into your first Descent to Soul when the time is right. Confirmation is an even more profound life transition than Eco-awakening. While Eco-awakening brings about the shift from one early-Adolescent stage to another, healthier one, Confirmation ushers you into an ecocentric *late* Adolescence, a stage reached by probably less than 20 percent of contemporary Westerners.

Two things are confirmed at this passage: First, that you have succeeded at fashioning a social presence that is both authentic and socially successful — a healthy, Adolescent personality. In a soulcentric community, people would celebrate your debut as a socially individuated person with a distinctive, even if provisional, identity, a person with a particular set of skills, ideas, sensitivities, styles, and values, an individual with a salient social cachet. This celebration could be a component of a rite of passage — not into Adulthood but into late Adolescence.

But on this auspicious occasion, a second thing is confirmed, something with a dark as well as a joyful implication: You are now psychospiritually prepared to explore the mysteries of nature and psyche. Your psychosocial success in the previous three stages qualifies you for the formidable initiatory journey in search of Soul and destiny. A trapdoor will soon enough open in the floor of your life, and whether you desire it or not, you will be headed for the depths, which is to say, the greater significance of your life. You'll be introduced to life's verticality, its third dimension. A rite of passage at this time, if you were to have one, would include preparations for the Descent, and it would inform your community that you will soon "disappear." The Cocoon, after all, entails a long period of withdrawal from the everyday social world — which your life had been all about for almost as long as you can remember — as you leave behind your early-Adolescent beliefs about self and world and seek your unique gift for your people and for the greater, more-than-human world to which you and your people belong.

Molting versus Dissolution: A Caterpillar Tale

The transformation that takes place in the Cocoon is categorically distinct from even the most profound changes in social or vocational identity. Contemporary people who long for their soul journey often think they are on a Descent when they might actually be undergoing an Adolescent shift in social role, relationships, vocation, social scene, or spiritual practice. It's important to distinguish one from the other.

Caterpillars, the larvae of the order Lepidoptera, can be thought of as the early adolescents of moths and butterflies. Caterpillars go through a series of transformations called instars or molts, between four and seven depending on the species. With each molt, the caterpillar sheds its exoskeleton in order to grow another larger one. Each molting, we might imagine, is a profound event for the caterpillar, but the caterpillar nonetheless remains a caterpillar (a larva) after molting.

When the caterpillar reaches its limit of skin shedding, this ends its early-adolescent road. Now it faces an entirely new frontier. At its next passage (corresponding to Confirmation), the caterpillar enters its pupa or chrysalis stage, during which it transforms into a butterfly.

A key thing to note about the chrysalis stage is that it involves a radical change in bodily structure, not just from one caterpillar physique to a larger one, but a transition into something utterly different — from a crawling to a flying creature.

For a caterpillar during its caterpillar days, transformation is all about molting — shedding and growing exoskeletons. For a chrysalis, in contrast, it's all about sprouting wings. These are very different sorts of transformations!

Likewise with humans. In psychological early Adolescence (the Oasis), we experience "moltings" when we go through a significant transformation in our social, vocational, geographical, religious, therapeutic, or other circumstances. Maybe we leave one romantic partnership and enter another. Perhaps we move from Midwest Catholicism to California Buddhism. Or from a Buddhist who has never experienced *kenshō* to one who has. Or we change careers from corporate management to life coaching. Or perhaps we make the transition from addiction to recovery. These are profound changes, but they are all moltings nevertheless, from one version of early Adolescence to another. The chrysalis stage — the Cocoon — is categorically different. *This* is when the journey of soul initiation begins in earnest.

During our early-Adolescent moltings, we identify ourselves first and foremost as social beings — on both sides of these transitions. Upon entering the Cocoon, in contrast, we leave behind forever our primary self-identification in terms of social roles. While in the Cocoon, we gradually come to understand ourselves in mythic or poetic terms. When we emerge from the Cocoon and commence initiated Adulthood, we henceforth experience ourselves as an embodiment of a mystical image or archetype, as a kind of poem or dream, as someone who's living a unique myth whether or not we're also living a unique social or vocational role.

When people in psychological early Adolescence learn about what I call the Cocoon or about soul initiation, they often believe their most recent molting must have been a chrysalis experience or a soul encounter. This misinterpretation is unavoidable because, before we reach the Cocoon, moltings are the only kind of major personal transformation within our experience. That's our only frame of reference. Even if it is carefully described to us, we can't yet clearly conceive a psychospiritual metamorphosis that is utterly different from a molting, even though we might believe we can.

With this distinction between an Adolescent molting and the Cocoon, we can now understand that Eco-awakening, as absolutely essential as it is to human maturation in our contemporary egocentric world, is a type of early-Adolescent molting; it is not a late-Adolescent chrysalis experience.

Before Eco-awakening, the Ego is the center of our world; it anchors our experience of everything. After Eco-awakening, we find ourselves at home in a world that is as ecological as it is social, a world rooted in the greater Earth community. Then, after Confirmation, our world is primarily mystical and mythic, embedded in the mysteries of both nature and psyche.

Consuming versus Pollinating

The caterpillar's primary task in life is to eat, to consume as much as it can in the interest of its own growth and maturation. Caterpillars are, in one sense, pests from the perspective of the plants they voraciously feed on. But this is an acceptable arrangement for the plant world because the butterfly (or moth) that the caterpillar becomes does a world of good for the local ecosystem. Feeding only on nectar, the butterfly provides the essential ecological service of pollination, an indispensable element in the sex lives of plants. (It also has a great interest in its own sex life — it's going to mate and conceive a new batch of its own kind.) If caterpillars never transformed into pollinators, they would be solely destructive to plants.

Consider this an analogy for the dilemma facing our own species — and our entire planet. As early Adolescents (whether in our teens or later, possibly the entire rest of our lives), we do a lot of consuming (in the form of acquiring stuff), and this is well and good as long as this sort of consuming goes on for only a few years and as long as it truly supports our growth and eventual maturation into Adult humans — soulcentric pollinators. But if too many of us fail to grow beyond early Adolescence, humanity becomes an Earth plague, a swarm of locusts, a horde of out-of-control consumers eating our world down to its bones, with scant left for the rest of the Earth community, not even for our own human descendants. We forever remain "takers" — to use Daniel Quinn's elegantly blunt and unambiguous term from *Ishmael* — consumers in a dead-end materialistic society. This is precisely our Earth predicament today: too many egocentric consumers, not enough soulcentric pollinators.

I believe our destiny is not to be ecocidal consumers but, rather, (r)evolutionary and visionary enhancers of life on Earth. With the rediscovery, re-visioning, and contemporary embodiment of the journey of soul initiation, we can engender whole generations of pollinators. Imagine every human community populated with visionary changemakers and artisans of cultural renaissance.

Chapter Two

PHASE ONE

Preparation for the Descent

Part 2: Wholing and Self-Healing

The Healing Time

Finally on my way to yes
I bump into
all the places
where I said no
to my life
all the untended wounds
the red and purple scars
those hieroglyphs of pain,
carved into my skin, my bones,
those coded messages
that send me down
the wrong street
again and again
where I find them
the old wounds
the old misdirections
and I lift them
one by one
close to my heart
and I say   holy
     holy.

— PESHA JOYCE GERTLER

The previous chapter explores the first realm of Preparation, which catalyzes, deepens, and extends two major shifts in developmental stage: the life passages of Eco-awakening and Confirmation. The latter ushers you from the Oasis to the Cocoon, the stage in which the Descent first becomes possible. This groundwork can take a year or more. Sometimes less. Or perhaps you're already in the Cocoon. But even after Confirmation, you still have the opportunity to enhance your readiness for the Descent through additional work on the tasks of the first three life stages.

In this chapter, we look not at life stages but at elements or dimensions of the psyche you possess through all stages but probably haven't fleshed out to the level needed for the rigors of the journey ahead. And you'll want to. Actually, you'll need to. This preparatory work can be done before, during, and/or after what's described in the previous chapter. The realms of Preparation explored here are the cultivation of your innate human wholeness and the practice of Self-healing. This personal development work, too, could keep you busy for several months or more. You want to be adequately resourced for the journey — your psychospiritual "gear" being more essential than your boots and backpack.

Cultivating Our Innate Human Wholeness

By "our innate human wholeness," I mean four realms of fundamental human potentials with which we are each born. In the course of our lives, however, we're not able to competently embody or benefit from these potentials unless we cultivate them using practices crafted for that purpose. These hidden, unrealized personal resources must be gradually honed. The conformist-consumer mainstream, as a rule, has little awareness of and few practices for developing these vital dimensions of our humanity — in fact, it actively suppresses them — but support and methods for "wholing" exist abundantly at our cultural margins and beyond.

The fact that we're born with exceptional human potentials and the opportunity to cultivate them is recognized in all mature cultures and spiritual traditions, but the psychospiritual development systems I was able to find during my early adulthood all seemed to encompass only a partial range of the full spectrum of potentials. As a consequence, I began, in the late eighties, to create my own contemporary Western map of human wholeness, employing the perennial pan-cultural template of the four cardinal directions.[1] The result is what I call the Nature-Based Map of the Human Psyche, the subject of my book *Wild Mind: A Field Guide to the Human Psyche*. With this map, we can identify and distinguish the full set of our innate psychospiritual resources and their relationships to one another and to our wounded parts. In this way, the Nature-Based Map of the Human Psyche provides a comprehensive inventory of what can be right about a person — a "positive shadow" version of mainstream psychology's Diagnostic and Statistical Manual (DSM), the latter being a disparaging, misanthropic list of what can go wrong with human beings. This chapter is, in part, a condensed summary of what you'll find in *Wild Mind*.

As mapped onto the cardinal directions, our human potentials can be grouped into what I call the four facets of human wholeness. Before embarking upon the Descent, you'll want a decent level of cultivation of all four. Most people find one of their facets easiest to develop, one quite challenging, and the other two of intermediate difficulty or ease. Naturally, you'll want to focus on the facets that feel most foreign or unexplored, the facets that depth psychology would refer to as your "inferior functions." Our weakest facet is always an essential resource for our healing and well-being as well as for the Descent and for the eventual manifestation of our soul work.

The four facets of wholeness together constitute what I call the Self. This is similar to Carl Jung's concept of the "self" but with some distinct differences (see the glossary). The cultivation of the Self is the necessary foundation for healthy relationships, spiritual development, and mature cultures. It's also the dimension of our psyches by which we're able to heal our own psychological woundedness. And most important here, having excellent access to the fourfold Self is vital for the Descent to Soul — as well as the rest of your life.

Although the Self is a single dimension of the psyche, an integral whole, it can best be described in terms of its four facets. Here's a brief introduction:

NORTH: THE NURTURING GENERATIVE ADULT

This facet is empathic, compassionate, courageous, competent, knowledgeable, productive, and able to provide genuine loving care and service to others and ourselves. With the resources of our North facet, we contribute our best and most creative parenting, leading, teaching, directing, producing, and healing. The Nurturing Generative Adult is a version of and draws from universal archetypes such as the Leader, the benevolent King or Queen, the spiritual or peaceful Warrior, and the mature and caring Mother and Father.

SOUTH: THE WILD INDIGENOUS ONE

This facet is emotive, sensuous, instinctive, playful, erotic-sexual, and fully at home in the human body and in the more-than-human world. It embraces and is enlivened by all emotions. This South facet of the Self is indigenous *to Earth* in the sense of directly and deeply experiencing its original belonging in the greater community of life on our planet. This dimension of indigeneity is a feature of all human psyches because all of us are from people who once were indigenous to a particular watershed somewhere on Earth. The South facet is every bit as wild and natural as any undomesticated animal or flower, or as an undammed river — and experiences an instinctive and intuitive kinship with all species and habitats. The Wild Indigenous One is resonant with archetypes such as Pan, Artemis/Diana (Lady of the Beasts), and the Green Man (Wild Man).

EAST: THE INNOCENT/SAGE

Innocent, wise, clear-minded, lighthearted, wily, and extroverted, the East facet of the Self is fully at home with big-picture consciousness, light, enlightenment, laughter, paradox, eternity, and the mysteries of the Divine and the upperworld. The Innocent/Sage wants to lead us up to the realm of pure consciousness beyond distinctions and striving. I place a slash rather than a hyphen between the two parts of this facet's name because paradox is the Innocent/Sage's friend and ally — "both/ and" its stock in trade, its modus operandi. The Innocent/Sage sometimes appears naive and uncomplicated, and sometimes seasoned and sagacious, but it's unfailingly both. The Innocent/Sage is always having a good time, and that twinkle in its eye — is this naiveté or wisdom? This facet also draws from the archetypes of the Fool, Trickster, Priest, Priestess, and Guide to Spirit.

WEST: THE DARK MUSE-BELOVED

This facet is imaginative, erotic-romantic, idealistic, visionary, adventurous, darkness savoring (shadow loving), meaning attuned, and introverted. The West facet of the Self revels in night, dreams, destiny, death, and the mysteries and qualities of the underworld. The Dark Muse-Beloved wants to lead us down to Soul and wants us to be continuously dying to our old ways while giving birth to the never-before-seen. In addition to the Muse and the Beloved, this facet is resonant with archetypes such as Anima/Animus, Magician, Wanderer, Hermit, Psychopomp, and Guide to Soul.

These four facets of wholeness are not just somebody's (my) selection of favorite archetypes to recommend to contemporary people, but rather a map intended to represent the full spectrum of what it means to be a human being. The cultivation of each of these four facets of the Self ought to be a core dimension of education and personal developmental in any human culture that wishes to support its members to grow whole and wild — and eventually uncover their unique mythos, their particular ways to serve their people and the greater Earth community.

The Four Windows of Knowing

Related to the four facets of wholeness are what depth psychologist Eligio Stephen Gallegos calls the "four windows of knowing": feeling, imagination, sensing, and thinking.[2] These are the four human faculties needed to fully understand and appreciate anything about ourselves or our world. Each of the four is of equal power and importance in living a balanced and creative life. Each is a distinct faculty not reducible to any of the other three. Agility and artfulness with all four windows is somewhere between invaluable and essential on the Descent.

Each of the four windows of knowing has a special resonance with one of the four facets of the Self, although each facet utilizes all four windows. The four natural pairings are North and thinking, South and feeling, East and sensing, and West and imagination. But the kind of thinking employed by the Self is not just any kind of thinking but specifically *heart-centered* thinking. Likewise, the other three windows of knowing, as utilized by the Self, are *full-bodied* feeling, *full-presence* sensing, and *deep* imagination.

NORTH: HEART-CENTERED THINKING

This is not the logical, analytical, deductive mode of thinking endemic to the contemporary Western world; rather, it is thinking that is independent, critical, creative, moral, and compassionate. It is "critical" in the sense that it reflectively questions assumptions, discerns hidden values, and considers the larger social and ecological context. Entirely distinct from the rote memorization and parroting commonly stressed in mainstream Western schools and society, heart-centered thinking overflows with an animated curiosity that leads to a constantly adjusting and in-depth knowledge of human culture and the wider environment. The Self is a compassionate systems thinker, understanding the patterns and dynamics that connect the interdependent members of the more-than-human community. The Self intuitively comprehends how our actions ripple across space and time to other places and future generations.

SOUTH: FULL-BODIED FEELING

This includes our emotions but also several other kinds of feelings: premonitions and hunches ("gut feelings" or "the feeling in my bones") about particular social gatherings, city neighborhoods, or natural habitats; interpersonal vibes; sexual passion; our general sense of corporeal well-being, malaise, or dis-ease; and our bodily feelings — our awareness of our internal organs (interoception) and the positioning of our limbs (proprioception and kinesthesia, or "muscle sense"). To have heartfelt and gratifying relationships with our fellow humans and with the other creatures and places of our world, we must proceed, first and foremost, by way of full-bodied feeling. True communion is impossible without feeling. Although the other beings indigenous to our world do not speak a human language, we can nevertheless come to know them through feeling, through a kind of nonphysical touching.[3] By way of feeling, we can instinctively translate what's being "said" by the nonhuman flora and fauna (and stones, rivers, and forests). When it comes to communion with others of our own kind, we must remember that we're at least as much feeling-infused as we are linguistically inclined. What on Earth would our relationships be like if we couldn't sense social vibes, read the emotional field, or discern the bodily states of our friends and family? Certainly our sexuality is founded on our capacity to feel, in all senses of the word. To be fully human we must fully feel.

EAST: FULL-PRESENCE SENSING

I mean the way we can learn to reside in the five senses of vision, hearing, taste, smell, and touch. The sharp and nuanced sensing we're capable of with a well-developed Self contrasts with the diminished perception typical of people in egocentric cultures. In the mainstream Western world, for example, the senses are often dulled by disinterest, disuse, and stultifying cultural activities that take place indoors and in denatured outdoor environments with a woeful constriction in the diversity of things that can be seen, heard, touched, smelled, and tasted. Too few contemporary people are intoxicated by the songs of birds and bowled over by their colored plumage. Can we feel the delicacy of a cool breeze jostling the hair on our sunbaked arms? Do we linger with the perfume of peonies?[4] Keen sensing is a talent, one that must be cultivated and practiced in order to be maintained and honed. The Self is a connoisseur of full-presence sensing, a devotee of the rainbow spectrum, a maven of music (including the songs of creatures, wind, and waters), an epicure of food and drink, an aficionado of texture and textiles, and quite frankly, a fanatic of floral fragrances.

WEST: DEEP IMAGINATION

By "deep," I'm signifying the images, symbols, dreams, visions, and revelations that we do not command or control but that arise unbidden and possess the immediate ring of truth. In egocentric cultures, the imagination has been contrasted with and pitted against truth and reality: "It was just my imagination." "Leave the dull, everyday world behind, and escape to the land of imagination." But in fact the deep imagination is an indispensable faculty for discovering the truth about everyday life, no less essential than sensing, thinking, and feeling. Our deep imagination not only shows us what might be but also illuminates what already is. Without deep imagination, we would have only the most superficial experience of another person, a relationship, a song or painting, a bird or flower, a meal, or the design of a book or a business. Our deep imagination also reveals things we may never have detected with only our senses or emotions or by deduction. The nineteenth-century German chemist August Kekulé discovered the ring shape of the benzene molecule after having a reverie of a snake seizing its own tail. A psychotherapist, by way of an image that suddenly appears to her inner eye, might grasp — accurately — her client's long-standing conundrum. The deep imagination is also our primary resource for recognizing the emerging future, for "seeing" the visionary possibilities of what we can create right now — individually and collectively — and consequently for creating a better world. Deep imagination is the essential resource for all genuine human creativity. The Muse or Dreamer waits within everyone to be reclaimed as an indispensable resource for liberating ourselves from the flatlands and wastelands of the mainstream and for designing and building new, life-enhancing societies.

A Closer Look at the South and the West

Although conformist-consumer societies neglect all four facets of the Self, the South and West are often actively suppressed because they are the most dangerous to such societies, which is, tragically, the majority in the twenty-first century. These are the two facets most needed in ourselves, our children, and our youth in order to interrupt and subvert the life-destroying features of contemporary cultures and to invent and shape new, ecocentric cultures. Not coincidentally, the South and West facets are deemed the most "feminine" by egocentric, patho-adolescent cultures, especially their patriarchal varieties.

People who have cultivated their South facet — their Wild Indigenous One — experience, somatically, every hour of every day, the magic and wonder of creation, the sacredness of each aspect and element of the more-than-human world; enjoy a communion with all flora, fauna, and habitats; and naturally celebrate and defend the diversity of life. They would never treat the Earth as a gravel pit or lumberyard, a mere resource for human use. Which is to say: They are naturally subversive to mainstream conformist-consumer culture. Revolutionaries. (Not mere Rebels.)

People who have cultivated their West facet — their Dark Muse-Beloved — possess a wildly prolific imagination; experience every day the extravagant creativity and hidden meanings of each thing; hear and respond to what Joseph Campbell referred to as the call to spiritual adventure; experience their own life to be the unfolding of a poem, dance, dream, or sacred story; and naturally celebrate and defend the mysteries and ineffable depths of our world. They're not in the least attracted to the dull and offensive social and vocational roles of the conformist-consumer flatland. Which is to say: They are imaginatively subversive to the mainstream overculture. Revolutionaries. (Not mere Rebels.)

What is true for the South and West facets is also true for the South and West windows of knowing: Many in the Western world believe that women are more emotional and imaginative than men. If there is any truth to this, it's due only to the cultural suppression of these faculties in men. This suppression is the result of a tragic breakdown of Western culture that began millennia ago and has persisted and deepened ever since: Immature, uninitiated men, especially those in positions of social or economic dominance, fear what is for them the Ego-destabilizing powers of deep imagination and full-bodied feeling. But instead of acknowledging this to themselves and others, they name these windows, these powers, as "not me" — which is to say, they are of and for women. In so doing, they defend themselves from powers, both within themselves and in others, that would threaten their dominance. Historically, some of these uninitiated men have gone a step or two further: In addition to denying the value of these powers for themselves, they have disempowered, oppressed, harassed, abused, raped, and murdered women, especially those who honor, preserve, hone, and wield their powers of feeling and imagination. This foundational form of terrorism is perhaps at the root of all other varieties, including environmental destruction (resulting in mass extinction and climate disruption), racism, genocide, and the state-perpetrated terrorisms of war and economic sabotage of other nations. These forms of violence constitute self-destruction as well as other-destruction: Uninitiated men in dominator roles suppress or conquer in themselves and others the precise human powers they most need in order to grow up. This is truly and literally a king-sized tragedy, one that, as a species, we might now be ready to recover from. And must.

In our egocentric world, the reclaiming and cultivation of full-bodied feeling and deep imagination, especially by men, are acts of revolution — and ecstasy.

Cultivating the Four Facets of Wholeness

Although most contemporary people need to attend especially to their South and West facets, odds are that further cultivation of all four facets of the Self would serve you well on your journey toward Soul Canyon and before stepping over the edge. If you suspect this might be true for you, I recommend the practices you'll find in in *Wild Mind*. These include several ways of employing four timeless, cross-cultural practices for cultivating each of the facets: voice dialogue, four directions circles on the land, dreamwork, and deep-imagery journeys. You'll also find several other practices unique to particular facets.

Plus here is an essential tip: Because the four facets of the Self are innate resources existing in latent form within each of us, we can partially cultivate them simply by choosing to embody or enact them the best we can in any moment. Just conjure an archetypal image of one of your facets, feel its presence in your body, and then invite it to act through you.

Beyond that tip and the practices described in *Wild Mind*, there are many places in Western and other societies where you can get support in cultivating the four facets of your innate human wholeness. For example, you can get help developing your North facet, your Nurturing Generative Adult, through courses or trainings in leadership, nonviolent communication, parenting, conscious loving and intimacy, social artistry, sustainability, participatory democracy, group facilitation, community organizing, and social justice and environmental activism. Or you can cultivate your North facet through what amounts to in-service training: Offer yourself to your community as a volunteer; help families in need; act in support of oppressed people or endangered species; restore a ruined place such as a clear-cut forest or a polluted river; speak truth to power; assert your community's right to local self-determination (and protect it from corporations or state and federal governments); occupy public space in support of true democracy; or join a nonviolent environmental movement using civil disobedience to compel government action on biodiversity loss, social and ecological collapse, and the climate emergency.[5] Psychologist James Hillman proposed that offering yourself in service to the world can be more therapeutic than anything that could happen in a therapist's office.[6]

To get help cultivating your South facet of wholeness, your Wild Indigenous One, you might enroll in a wilderness program that travels by foot through untamed lands. You might take experiential courses in nature connection, animal tracking, gardening, or permaculture. Study massage or other somatic practices such as Feldenkrais. Sign up for courses in emotional intelligence and expression, sensory awakening, sacred sexuality, yoga, or dance.

To awaken or ripen your East facet, your Innocent/Sage, you might seek training and practice in meditation or contemplative prayer. The study and practice of standup comedy, clowning, or miming are also excellent options because they support you to embody your Sacred Fool or Trickster. Movement-based meditation practices such as tai chi or qigong support the cultivation of simplicity and present-centeredness.

Last but not least, you can find cultural support in developing the West facet of the Self, your Dark Muse-Beloved, in many places: Take courses in dreamwork, deep-imagery journeys, or the artistic or creative process; study myth, ritual, mystery traditions, death and dying, or depth and archetypal psychology; or apprentice yourself to poetry, dance, music-making, and (of course!) soulcraft.

The Four Facets on the Descent to Soul

The Descent to Soul offers some of the most harrowing challenges of a lifetime. We encounter dangerous opportunities that range from the physical to the psychological to the spiritual. Here's a summary of the ways each of the four facets of wholeness is essential on the journey.

NORTH: THE NURTURING GENERATIVE ADULT

On the way to Soul, we might be compelled by our initiation guide or by our own psyche to wander into wilderness (remote mountain ranges, claustrophobic caves, or searing deserts) or into our own psychospiritual wilds (core emotional wounds, Shadow realms, nightmares, memories of personal or collective trauma, or confrontations with our own mortality) that demand a well-honed capacity for self-care, self-reliance, and creative response if we are to benefit from these experiences — or even survive them.

In *Soulcraft* (in "Practices for Leaving Home"), I explore the many North capacities that must be honed for a fruitful Descent. These skills include the abilities to relinquish attachment to our former identity, welcome home our Loyal Soldiers (our inner critics and flatterers), explore our Core Wounds, choose authenticity over social acceptance, and make peace with our past. The complementary set of generative skills that support your capacity for soul encounter includes those of soulcentric dreamwork, deep-imagery journeying, talking across the species boundaries, self-designed ceremony, symbolic artwork, journaling, and the arts of wandering, Shadow work, soulful romance, and mindfulness. Cultivating and deploying these two sets of underworld-relevant skills require a well-developed Nurturing Generative Adult.

SOUTH: THE WILD INDIGENOUS ONE

Soul Canyon is a wilderness — an outback defined not by a particular ecology or topography but by a state of consciousness, a frame of mind, a realm of the psyche in which meaning, metaphor, and symbol percolate from their generally invisible depths and flow through our moment-to-moment experience like creatures from another world. Sometimes it seems to be a circus world, but it's always a sacred one, a heaven or hell exuding eloquent signs of portent or promise. Here, denizens of our personal unconscious mingle, strangely, with archetypes of the collective human unconscious and creatures of the terrestrial wild. To our astonishment or bafflement, our own Souls might appear in a great variety of shapes and guises. Characters from dreams and nightmares materialize out of nowhere. We find ourselves faced with unavoidable and seemingly fated tasks and trials — supremely challenging adventures, perhaps impossible but nonetheless necessary ones — and we recognize that how well we engage with these quandaries determines whether or how fully we will realize our destiny in this lifetime. Every move we make seems critical and fraught with significance.

In order to thrive in such circumstances — and certainly to benefit psychospiritually — we require an instinctive aliveness, an ability to respond without thinking, or prior to thinking, like an animal with corporeal faith in its natural embeddedness in the world, an animal equipped with instincts not merely for survival or defense but for imaginative response and enchanted play. We need to feel our belonging to place so profoundly that it seems as if the place itself thinks and feels for us, that it opens the way for us to proceed simply by virtue of the fact that it knows us and recognizes the way in which we are meant to be there.

In other words, on a Descent to Soul, you need to be rooted in your human wildness and your indigenous belonging.

You need to be emotionally alive, too, because your emotions provide you with invaluable clues to how well you're currently adjusted or acclimatized to Soul Canyon and to the others you encounter while in that state of mind, and clues to what to do if you're not. You want to be able to trust your embodied emotions.

Beyond the ability to access, appreciate, express, and otherwise act on your emotions, you also need a highly cultivated capacity for *feeling* — your ability to feel the vibes of people and places, your felt-sense of the world. Among other things, a well-honed feeling-sense is needed for you to commune deeply with your fellow humans and to communicate in even a minimal way with other-than-humans.

And you want to be able, more generally, to trust your animal body. You want to be confident your body will react and move you toward your true place in the world without having to first (or ever) rationally analyze your situation. You want to have faith in your faculty of allurement, your gift of feeling the more-than-human relational possibilities in the shimmering, interactive field within which you find yourself while in the depths.

An excursion into Soul Canyon is one hell of an adventure, and your Wild Indigenous One knows and loves sacred adventures of all kinds. You wouldn't want to embark on the Descent without considerable cultivation of the South facet of your innate human wholeness.

EAST: THE INNOCENT/SAGE

The state of consciousness I call Soul Canyon can get pretty wild. To the Ego, it often seems like a madhouse of maelstroms or a precarious precinct of pandemonium. Your underworld hours can sweep you from your feet so surely you might never again right yourself. And yet keeping your wits about you means everything. Your potential for creating meaning, for discerning your way toward your destiny, depends utterly on your capacity to be fully present with the chaos of your underworld encounters.

You want to be sure you won't shut down when things get interesting. While in Soul Canyon, you must be as open and receptive as you've ever been — an Innocent. You don't want to be analyzing underworld events while they're happening — that can wait for another time. You want to absorb everything that's unfolding. To enter underworld consciousness and fully benefit from your encounters there, you need the East's capacities for presence and equanimity.

And you don't want to be defensive, trying to save your life at all costs, when, after all, Soul Canyon is the "place" into which you've descended in order to transform that very life. Surely you understand transformation as a death-rebirth experience, and you know it's not possible to just skip over the first half, as much as you might want to.

While in Soul Canyon, you need a cultivated capacity for present-centeredness and receptiveness, as well as a certain nonattachment to your own life, at least as it's been — the sort of transpersonal perspective embodied by the Fool.

Equally essential during underworld journeys is the wisdom of the Sage, enabling the big-picture perspective that allows you to remember what's most important and to choose well.

When faced with choices during underworld encounters with personal demons, Shadow figures, or traumatic memories, you also need the perspective-shifting tactics of the Trickster. You'll never benefit from these encounters if you approach them from the restricted perspective you retreated to long ago to keep yourself safe from them. For real transformation, you must be able to see how your demons are actually your partners in the individuation process, how they hold the missing segments of your path to wholeness. This psycho-perceptual shift is precisely the domain of the Trickster, who knows how to lure you out of defensive positions (your caves and fortresses) to glimpse at last, from a vast perspective, the terrific and terrifying terrain of your unfolding personal mythos.

Even though it sits opposite the West (the direction most resonant with Soul Canyon), the East facet of the Self is essential on the Descent.

West: The Dark Muse-Beloved

To successfully enter Soul Canyon and return with a mythopoetic boon for your people, you need, as we've seen, the well-honed capacities and sensibilities of the North, South, and East facets of your Self. But this leaves the question, Who in the world would want to embark on such a Descent in the first place? And why?

Enter the Dark Muse-Beloved, who knows precisely why, and is, quite frankly, immoderately enthusiastic about it. This explains why one of the Muse's nicknames is the Guide to Soul. She's a lover of mystery, a devotee of the fecund dark, an aficionado of profound change, a freakish fan of fearsome affairs, and an enthusiast of symbolic significance. The West Self loves nothing more than to wander, hopelessly lost, in the romantic and alluring (to her) dark waters of Soul Canyon. There a person can undergo a transformation considerably more profound than what the West can work in the middleworld, and this is something the Muse-Beloved loves.

There, in Soul Canyon, you can glimpse and be shattered by the revelation of the myth, story, name, poem, or song you are meant to live in this lifetime. This shattering — this "decisive defeat," as Rilke frames it — enables your reconfiguration, your reshaping, into a means of expression for your true identity. This reshaping allows you to make, as David Whyte says, "a promise it will kill you to break," a vow to manifest the mysterious, metaphoric truth at the center of your psyche, to carry this truth, as a gift to others, in what you do and how you be.

It's the Dark Muse-Beloved, then — the Anima or Animus, the Wanderer, the Magician, the Psychopomp, the Guide to Soul, by these or other names or images — it's this West facet of the Self that most desires to descend to Soul…when, that is, the Ego is ready for the journey.

Along with the desire to descend, this facet of Self also possesses the knowledge and the skills to do so. Your Guide to Soul has an innate understanding of what Soul Canyon is and how to maneuver in it, like a seasoned wilderness guide always prepared for the unexpected — indeed, one who lives for it — and has the instincts to adapt to almost anything that shows up. Your Guide to Soul comprehends what is being sought — the largest conversation you're capable of having with the world — and how to track such a treasure in the wilderness of Soul Canyon. Your West Self will not be appalled or repelled should you stumble into one of your Core Wounds, personal demons (Shadow figures), unacknowledged addictions, or inner critics. These are all welcome and honored guests, grist for the mill of soul encounter. And your Guide to Soul is entirely comfortable with states of nonordinary consciousness (in fact, craves them); knows how to operate when the rules, norms, and frames are incessantly shifting; and knows how to recognize symbols encountered and how to surrender to and be changed by them. Your Guide to Soul loves to deconstruct, to disassemble things, even to help you (your Ego) disintegrate, which, of course, is the necessary precursor to imaginative reassembly.

During your journeys beneath the rim, having a well-honed capacity for communication with nonhuman others is essential, and your deep imagination (your Muse) is central to this capacity (in addition to the South's full-bodied feeling). To encounter the Soul is to cross into the mysteries of not only your own psyche but those of the greater world. The deep dreaming of your psyche is one strand of the dreaming of the Earth.

In short, when venturing down, the Dark Muse-Beloved is your most indispensable facet of the Self.

Self-Healing

The third realm of preparation for the Descent is Self-healing.

Relative to what's available in mainstream contemporary psychotherapy, Self-healing is a radical approach to psychological betterment. If embraced by the mainstream, it would revolutionize psychology — and conformist-consumer culture more generally. Why? First, Self-healing enhances our autonomy, self-reliance, and sense of self-efficacy. We heal ourselves rather than depend on "experts" to do it for us — or even with us. Second, with Self-healing, we don't struggle against any parts of ourselves but cooperate fully with all of them; we don't attempt to get rid of or quarantine any elements of our psyche, but instead love them all, even any parts previously involved in self-harm. Third, Self-healing emphasizes the positive rather than the negative: It cultivates our wholeness rather than merely reducing or eliminating our symptoms or struggles, our depressions or anxieties. Self-healing is not pathology-conquering; it is wholeness-enhancing. The goal of Self-healing is not to get rid of our woundedness but to enlist our wholeness to *hold* our woundedness. Self-healing does not merely reduce our suffering; it enhances our well-being and incites our magnificence.

A first step to understanding Self-healing is to recognize that the elements of our psyches that cause us distress, such as our inner critics, victims, or addicts, are actually our inner protectors — each doing its best to help us, to keep us safe, each having been forged or fashioned by our psyches when we were very young, as early as our first months. These subpersonalities (or "subs," for short) are constellations of feelings, images, and behaviors that operate more or less independently from one another and often independently of our conscious selves (Egos). They first formed and came into service very early in our lives when we needed to be protected from being harmed (physically, psychologically, or socially) — mostly by other people. Our subs brilliantly created and implemented the childhood survival strategies we needed at that time. (If yours hadn't, you'd be dead or so debilitated psychologically and socially that you wouldn't be reading a book like this, nor preparing for a Descent to Soul). The problem is that their survival strategies also limited us — and still do. We continue to use these strategies far beyond the time they are the most effective ways to protect ourselves. Our inner protectors are the primary source or cause of what contemporary psychology understands to be our psychological symptoms and illnesses.

Self-healing is a matter of cultivating a compassionate relationship with our inner protectors, a relationship possible only by using the fourfold resources of the Self.

Our Inner Protectors

As with the four facets of wholeness, I've mapped our inner protectors or subs onto the four cardinal directions. This is one of the layers of the Nature-Based Map of the Human Psyche as presented in *Wild Mind*. We all have the same sort of protective strategies. The four categories of subpersonalities are distinguished by the general ways in which they protect us (physically, psychologically, socially, and economically) or at least how they *attempt* to keep us safe. Here's a brief description of the four sets of subs:

NORTH: LOYAL SOLDIERS

Our Loyal Soldiers try to keep us safe by inciting us to act small (either beneath our potential or one-dimensionally) in order to secure a place of belonging in the world. They achieve this by avoiding risk, by rendering us nonthreatening, useful, or pleasing to others, or by urging us into positions of immature power over others (dominator power). Versions include Rescuers, Codependents, Enablers, Pleasers, and Giving Trees; Inner Critics and Inner Flatterers (the kind of flattery that motivates us to be useful and nonthreatening to others); Tyrants and Robber Barons; and Critics and Flatterers of others.

SOUTH: WOUNDED CHILDREN

Our Wounded Children try to keep us safe by attempting to get our basic needs met using the immature, emotion-fueled strategies available to them. They do this by appearing to be in need of rescue (Victims); being harmless and socially acceptable (Conformists); being coercive or aggressive (Rebels); or being arrogant or condescending (Princes or Princesses).

EAST: ESCAPISTS AND ADDICTS

Our Escapists and Addicts try to keep us safe through evasion — rising above traumatic emotions and circumstances and sidestepping distressing challenges and responsibilities. They do this through strategies such as addictions, obsessions, dissociations, vanishing acts, and delinquency. Versions include the *puer aeternus* and *puella aeternus* (Latin for "eternal boy" and "eternal girl"), Blissheads, and Spiritual Materialists.

WEST: SHADOW SELVES

The Shadow and Shadow Selves try to keep us safe through the repression (making unconscious) of our characteristics and desires that are unacceptable or inconceivable to our Ego. Shadow characteristics can be either "negative" or "sinister" (what the Ego would consider morally "beneath" it) or "positive" or "golden" (what the Ego would consider "above" it and out of reach). The Shadow is not what we know about ourselves and don't like (or like but keep hidden) but rather what we don't know about ourselves and, if accused of it, would adamantly and sincerely deny. Our Shadow Selves attempt to maintain psychological stability by briefly acting out Shadow characteristics and doing so flamboyantly or scandalously, but without our being conscious of what we're doing — letting off steam as the only available alternative to complete self-destruction.

The Practice of Self-Healing

In the prevailing paradigm of Western psychotherapy, the therapist acts as the agent of the client's healing. The mature therapist accomplishes this by being present to the client utilizing the resources of the therapist's Self. It's the therapist, in other words, who supplies the wholeness. This Western mode of psychological healing provides a great service — especially when the client has little access to their own Self — but this is not the sort of in-depth healing from which we most benefit. It's more of a temporary fix or a relatively shallow healing that might later reveal deeper problems. The more in-depth healing occurs when we learn to use our own wholeness to embrace our woundedness.

Self-healing entails five steps: (1) becoming conscious of our inner protectors when they spring into action with their childhood survival strategies; (2) thanking them for attempting to protect us and for having protected us in the past; (3) letting them know we no longer need their strategies (but only if this is actually true); (4) telling them about our more mature strategies, if we have developed them, for engaging the world (not merely for protecting ourselves); and (5) *using* those more mature strategies. To do these things is to love our inner protectors. By doing these things, we heal ourselves. The specific strategies for Self-healing vary depending on a number of considerations including which kinds of inner protectors are involved. See *Wild Mind* for a full description of the four sets of inner protectors and for a comprehensive exploration of Self-healing and its practices.

Meanwhile, the inner resources we possess for healing ourselves are — ta da! — precisely our four facets of wholeness, which together constitute the Self. Hence the term *Self-healing*. The fact that we need access to the Self to be able to heal ourselves is an additional reason why wholing is essential to personal development. And once we're in the Cocoon, and especially after a Descent to Soul begins, we might very well have a greater need for Self-healing than ever before. We are, after all, risking everything our subpersonalities have succeeded in protecting — our self-concept, our relationships, our job, our community standing. Everything. Consequently, our inner protectors are going to show up with a vengeance. We need much greater levels of wholeness than in the past. This is an essential dimension of our preparation for the Descent.

If you don't possess the capacity to Self-heal, you won't get far on the Descent to Soul. You can't take your psychotherapist with you to bail you out when your woundedness shows up along the way, which it will. You need to recognize your inner protectors when they kick in so that you can immediately begin the process of Self-healing.

Liberation from Lifetimes of Conditioning

Early in her journey of soul initiation, Kate Joyner found herself with a need for deeper layers of Self-healing. She had previously had a year of guided wholing practices, which prepared her to Self-heal when her subpersonalities became activated. Such an activation was sparked when she began to remember the ways, throughout her life, that she had neglected, suppressed, and dishonored her femininity — in particular, what she calls her "wild feminine," including her instinctive capacity to speak truth, her sensuality and sexuality, and her embodied connection to Mystery:

> I had to meet the places in me where instead of embodying a whole-mother energy, I was smothering or abandoning my own self. Instead of speaking with clarity and truth, I had adopted a more passive-aggressive approach or had lashed out in righteous anger. Instead of honoring my sensuality and sexuality, I was objectifying myself — or had made myself unreachable for fear of being hurt. Instead of walking with an embodied connection to the mystery, I had adopted a transcending holier-than-thou attitude to life and spirituality.

Although Kate was starting to see the protective strategies she had used in the past and was awakening to and embracing her wild feminine, she also unearthed a particular subpersonality, an inner critic, who was still very much active:

> There was still a huge part of me that was massively skeptical, a part I came to call the "inner patriarch." This one didn't believe or trust that any of the inner work I was doing was real. This one wanted to make sure the wild feminine was not in any way awakened. I was discovering that the part I had so feared and projected outside of myself — this repressing force — was inside me, too.

For her Self-healing, Kate engaged and embraced her protectors, including her inner patriarch and her wounded child. She undertook this healing not from a wounded victim consciousness but with an Ego resourced in the wholeness of the Self, in particular her Nurturing Generative Adult. She was compassionate with herself as well as with her family and cultural history:

> By engaging with my inner critic [a North sub], I saw how much pressure I put on myself to do everything "perfectly." By meeting my wounded child [a South sub], I realized how hard it was to really express my feelings and what was true for me, how hard it was for me to embrace my vulnerability. I met the deeply ingrained beliefs I had carried about myself: I wasn't worthy, I was unlovable. I also saw that I was living a story that didn't belong to me; it had been passed down through generations and through my cultural conditioning. I saw that what had happened to my own wild feminine had happened to the collective wild feminine. This wasn't just about me; it's what has happened to all of us, throughout history. As I started to peel away the layers, I began to see that all this wasn't really me, it wasn't who I was at my core; it was a box I was encased in. It wasn't who I came here to be. Working in this way was the real alchemy. Through a daily practice

of meeting with my subpersonalities, I liberated myself from lifetimes of conditioning around what it means to be a woman.

Through this self-exploration and Self-healing, Kate reclaimed personal resources that had been repressed and lost — and that she needed on the next phase of her Descent:

> In the beginning I met with the part of me who felt like she was unworthy of love, that she was "bad" [her Wounded Child]. I did this in a relational embodied way — not just a notion in my mind, but a lived experience of touching this part of me. She gradually revealed to me more and more about herself, things I had not known [Shadow]: the way she had been unseen, neglected, shunned, banished to the shadowlands (by me as well as others). I saw how some of my qualities had been cut off so that I could be safe and accepted, the qualities others deemed powerful and consequently threatening and therefore unacceptable for a woman to incarnate. As I sat in her place, I picked up more of her story through the subtleties of my energy body, deep feeling, and imagination. I discovered that she held so much of the unspoken mystery, the unspoken shadow, the essence of soul itself. Because these things were so destabilizing to the status quo, others rejected her, and then I rejected her myself. I began to relive memories of both this lifetime and past lifetimes: times I had been rejected for my ability to see, memories of being persecuted. I saw how I made these core beliefs from real-life experiences as a child. I saw, for example, that my parents, through no fault of their own, were unable to accept and assimilate their own shadows, which I had a particular sensitivity to. Because my parents and culture were unable to acknowledge the unseen, she/I believed that I was bad for seeing, mentioning, or wanting to acknowledge the darker aspects of our existence.

Kate's Self-healing work dramatically changed her relationship with some of her subpersonalities, who became true allies of her psychospiritual growth, not mere protectors of her social safety. This work shifted her understanding of herself and her personal and cultural history in a way that enabled her greater participation in the world — ultimately, as an agent of cultural regeneration.

Trauma and the Descent to Soul

In resonance with Canadian physician Gabor Maté, I've come to understand psychological trauma as *not* the experience of deeply distressing or overwhelming events but, rather, what we do within our psyches — mostly unconsciously — to protect ourselves from the psychological, social, and physical impact of those experiences.[7]

From my perspective, these protective measures are specifically our subpersonality survival strategies. The trauma is created and sustained not by the original disturbing experience but by our subpersonalities — most often without our awareness of what they're up to or why. The primary way we protect ourselves is the Escapist (East) strategy of disconnecting our awareness from the affective and somatic dimensions of these experiences (our emotions, body feelings, and gut instincts). We numb out and tune out. In addition, our Inner Critics (North) might tell us, endlessly, that we're flawed and unworthy — experienced as self-hate — to deter us from actions or situations that could result in additional distressing experiences. Our Wounded Children (South) might blame other people for our condition and/ or become terrified of catastrophe — to keep us from examining or assimilating the original disturbing events. Our Shadow elements (West) might project evil on those who could be blamed for our condition while projecting godliness on those who might be seen as agents of our liberation, in both cases to distract us from the unassimilated experiences themselves.

When our inner protectors come to our rescue following an intense and disturbing experience, we end up disconnected from other people, our surroundings, and ourselves. This can become a chronic condition. We lose access to our inner resources (the Self) and to our outer resources (our social network and potential guides and caregivers) that could have interrupted the downward spiral. We might feel like we're losing our mind and have no safe harbor. This kind of isolation is what craziness feels like, and it can result in extreme solutions, like substance abuse or suicide. In their attempts to protect us, our subpersonalities can make things a whole lot worse.

If you're suffering from a trauma condition, your optimal response is Self-healing: utilizing the skills and perspectives of your fourfold Self to enact the five-step process outlined above, which includes a grateful embrace of your inner protectors. But with trauma reactions, it's also essential, once you're stabilized (re-centered in the Self), to begin the process of metabolizing the distressing experiences that resulted in the inner trauma response in the first place. This is easier said than done.

Many people are not able to heal from a trauma condition without help from others, usually professional caregivers, people who support them to return to their stable center (the Self), guide them through the steps of Self-healing, and when they're ready, help them revisit the original disturbing experiences in order to assimilate and integrate them. Once they are assimilated, there is no longer a need to defend against those experiences with subpersonality strategies. We can even directly benefit from the conscious incorporation of the original experience. Bodywork or somatic psychotherapy is often a vital component of this healing.

Unresolved trauma can make it challenging to make developmental progress in early Adolescence because succeeding at the authenticity task of that stage becomes difficult if not impossible: When our inner protectors have cut us off from our direct and immediate experience of self and world, there's no way for us to know what's real or authentic.

To be human in today's world, however, is to live with various layers of un-resolved trauma — if not personal, then cultural, ancestral, and/or ecological. Most contemporary people who reach the Cocoon still have unresolved trauma, and much of this will need to be addressed during this life stage. One principle of human development is that the later our life stage, the more inner resources we need to succeed at our developmental challenges and tasks. Each successive stage asks more of us. A corollary is this: The later our stage, the deeper the healing or Self-healing that's needed. You might have suspected the opposite. Developmental successes eventually lead to the next life stage, but they can also bring into con-sciousness previously unsuspected trauma experiences.

When unresolved trauma shows up during a Descent, the best practice is to press the pause button until you've addressed your current wholing and healing needs and you're once again adequately resourced to continue the journey. I'll elab-orate in later chapters.

The Fourth Realm of Preparation: Some Comprehension of the Terrain Ahead

Ideally, before submerging into Soul Canyon, you will have regained or deepened your connection to self, others, your human community, and the animate world (Eco-awakening and Confirmation); you will have cultivated the resources of your Self (wholing); and you will have learned to embrace your inner protectors (Self-healing). Those are the first three realms of the Preparation phase.

One last strand of preparation remains: Some comprehension of the terrain ahead and of the sorts of practices and ceremonies that will support you during the next four phases of the Descent. This, of course, is what you'll garner from the rest of this book. A map of the journey and a general sense of the kinds of experiences you can anticipate can make all the difference in how deep you're able to go and how much you're able to benefit.

And one last word of general advice for the trail — for whenever your actual descent into Soul Canyon might begin, and whether or not you feel fully prepared in that moment: Please remember you are not undergoing this journey alone, even if you don't have the support of a soul-initiation guide. You always have an indis-pensable partner — your Soul! You're not wandering in the dark unaided, left to your own devices, your own wits — even if at times you feel this way. Your Soul is constantly reaching out to you and offering support. But you must make yourself available to Soul, and you must make your own choices while wandering through the mysteries of nature and psyche.

With any luck, you'll have other guides in addition to your Soul. Perhaps you'll have human mentors. You might also have guides in the form of animals, wind, or rivers. For sure you have inner guides, including your Guide to Soul (your West facet).

On your journey, it might be comforting to keep in mind that your destination is already determined. Your goal is to become who you were born to be. This frees you up because you don't need to decide where you're going — and can't. What you *can* choose to do — and this makes all the difference — is to observe carefully, to offer your attention mindfully, to stay tuned to signs and omens, and to move in the direction and in the way they suggest.

Chapter Three

PHASE TWO

Dissolution

Part 1: The Descent into Soul Canyon

You are not surprised at the force of the storm —
you have seen it growing.
The trees flee. Their flight
sets the boulevards streaming. And you know:
he whom they flee is the one
you move toward. All your senses
sing him, as you stand at the window.

The weeks stood still in summer.
The trees' blood rose. Now you feel
it wants to sink back
into the source of everything. You thought
you could trust that power
when you plucked the fruit;
now it becomes a riddle again,
and you again a stranger.

Summer was like your house: you knew
where each thing stood.
Now you must go out into your heart
as onto a vast plain. Now
the immense loneliness begins.
The days go numb, the wind
sucks the world from your senses like withered leaves.

Through the empty branches the sky remains.
It is what you have.
Be earth now, and evensong.
Be the ground lying under that sky.
Be modest now, like a thing
ripened until it is real,
so that he who began it all
can feel you when he reaches for you.

— RAINER MARIA RILKE

Sinking Back into the Source of Everything

I don't know a more accurate, daunting, or electrifying evocation of the Descent to Soul, especially at its outset, than Rilke's poem, in which he envelops us in death-doused images of wild weather, autumn, descent, loneliness, withering, and empti-ness. This is what Dissolution feels like. Not by chance is this the opening poem in Rilke's "Book of Pilgrimage," the second section or chapter of his *Book of Hours*. This, indeed, is how the pilgrimage into Soul Canyon begins — with a tempest sweeping away everything you thought was yours, including and especially your very identity. Dissolution. The force of this storm might shock everyone else, but not you. Indeed, your lack of surprise is what tips you off that it's time to descend. You find yourself moving toward this storm, not away from it. It has your name written on it, and you welcome your immersion.

When at last you enter Soul Canyon, you are forever leaving behind what Rilke portrays as the summer of your life — an evocative and telling image for psycholog-ical early Adolescence (not just our teen years, but the life stage of the Oasis[1]). Now your life energy is no longer rising but, like the sap of trees, "sink[ing] back into the source of everything" — back to your mystical beginnings so that you might retrieve your original instructions for this lifetime.

During this journey into the underworld, you will no longer be recognizable to others or to yourself; you will again be "a stranger." This will be your social and existential reality throughout the middle three phases of the Descent, the liminal phases. You must "go out into your heart as onto a vast plain." You must start over with learning what you really love. At first, there appears to be nothing, just an open expanse, but one that is somehow filled with possibility and promise. You can hear the emptiness singing, like a single unceasing violin note or a distant chorus of an-gels. You're alone in a way you've never been before; the only world you had known to be real has vanished. You are both bereft and free.

Rilke ushers you into emptiness but he does not leave you empty-handed. He has some spare but invaluable advice: Having left your summerhouse and begun the Descent, you must now rely on the sacred simplicities and clarities of the sky, the Earth, and your evensong — the prayers you hear emerging from your own lips at sunset as you face the west and the impending darkness. Your goal, your grail, is nothing less than the moment when Mystery ("he who began it all") might reach out and bless you with vision.

Dissolution is the phase when you undergo the actual descent into Soul Canyon. The Descent to Soul is named after this one phase because the way you get to Soul is by going down. As you approach the edge of the Canyon, all you know is that the journey is a plunge into the unknown. What you are saying yes to is a descent. And the return (the ascent) is, at the start, a hypothetical proposition at best.

Free Fall

The Dissolution phase may or may not be pleasant. Although sometimes and in some ways joyous, it can be terrifying and agonizing as well. At the beginning of his own Descent, Carl Jung experienced some "joy" at the prospect of making contact with his soul, but mainly he was seized by "terror," "horror," "torment," and "fear and doubt." He noted "the terrible sacrifice that the depths demand" and how his descent into those depths "completely burnt up my innards" and "forced the bitter drink between my lips."[2] Strong words, these, but an accurate portrayal of how Dissolution is experienced by many.

Jung makes Dissolution sound like dying. Psychospiritually, it *is* dying. Consider what death is: Beyond the stark fact that your body stops functioning and soon begins to decompose, what is at the core of this transition? It is the termination — for both you and others — of your embodiment of the social, vocational, and community roles you've been occupying. All of them. Others might soon fill some of those roles, but no longer will you. You will no longer dwell within or through them. Even if, as James Hillman suggests,[3] you might continue as an enduring imaginal presence among your people, you will no longer be embodied among them.

Likewise with the Dissolution phase of the Descent: As you approach the threshold, you are, ideally, stripped of all the roles you've been occupying. Or you voluntarily relinquish these roles. In some nature-based societies, you physically depart your village for an extended spell. A funeral might be held for you, for the person you have been. The place you formally occupied in your village is now vacated, and if ever filled again, it will not be by you. As a kind of dead person, you now have a different, although indeterminate, relationship to the village; you are "betwixt and between." This is why, in healthier cultures, the journey of soul initiation — or its forerunner — is begun before marriage and before becoming a parent or accepting a central role in village life. (This might leave you wondering if the Descent to Soul is possible for you if you're in a romantic partnership, have dependent children, or are unable to leave a full-time job. I've witnessed many people manage this, but their Descent is often slower or less deep than it might have been otherwise. Descending while parenting is a special circumstance we'll explore later in this chapter.)

In some nature-based cultures, initiates on the Descent to Soul are unconditionally relieved of their everyday responsibilities and are banished, or voluntarily wander off, far from their village — for example, the walkabout of the Australian Aborigines, the initiation camps of the Dagara of west Africa, or the year of solo wandering in the Pyrenees as practiced by the Basque. Such traditions separate initiates from relationships and routines that anchor their old identity, allowing them to drop that much deeper on their Descent.

There are several other factors that might support indigenous initiates during Dissolution. First is their culture's holistic and animate worldview, which fosters the instinctive human experience that everything is alive and interconnected and that the Descent to Soul for the purpose of discovering their unique ecological niche is normal, essential, and sacred. Second is their prior psychospiritual preparation: all the ordinary skills and knowledge they gathered simply as part of growing up in an ecocentric culture (which might include their version of cultivating the four facets of the Self) as well as the specialized trainings provided by Elders and initiators as the time of the Descent nears. A third kind of support is, of course, the presence of flesh-and-blood human guides during the Descent. A fourth is the guidance provided by "inner" or imaginal figures from both the nightworld and waking life, including the archetypes or facets of the Self I call the Muse, Magician, Wanderer, Warrior, Martyr, Sage, Innocent, Trickster, Fool, Wild Woman, and Green Man. Fifth is the wild world itself and its multitude of forms and forces: This is the world in which the initiates are constantly immersed — the other-than-human, self-organizing world that offers continual inspiration, natural metaphors, psyche-enlivening challenges, immersions in a web of interconnectivity, numinous encounters and conversations with the Others, and the blessings of sunrise and sunset, mountain and river, storm and mist and night. The wild world also offers "plant allies" or "sacred medicines" (aka psychedelics or entheogens), which, in many traditions, serve as significant catalysts for the Descent.[4]

Severance, temporary or permanent, from your Village — or from the Village roles you've been playing — is a significant dimension of Dissolution. But much more is happening here than a mere leave-taking. Dissolution precipitates a complete meltdown of your prior identity, the definitive end of the story you've been living, the unconditional disintegration of your former prospects and of what you believed the world was. You shed your former identity and do not receive a new one for quite some time. You are neither who you have been nor who you will become. If you have an identity at all now, it is a nameless embodiment of the archetype of the Wanderer.

You exist outside and beyond the benefits and limitations of selfhood, social role, and cultural norms. Your capacity and eligibility to make things happen is minimal. You're more a passenger than a driver. You are a seeker but you cannot decipher. You can cooperate but you cannot make it happen. You are not a solver but that which gets dissolved.

As you slip over the rim of Soul Canyon, it's the end not only of the particular social and vocational roles you've been living through but — especially if this is your first Descent — of your entire conception of what a life role is. It is the end of the way you've understood identity. It's the utter loss of your faith that there's anything essential or intrinsic to any social or vocational role. It's the end of your capacity to pretend that anyone's true identity could be defined by frameworks as prosaic, pedestrian, and unpoetic as a job description, career trajectory, Facebook presence, social group, or political affiliation. If you ever again live in the Village, you might choose to be fully engaged in its life, but you'll never again be fundamentally *of* it — your roots will draw sustenance from the deeper and wider web of life.

As you drop below the rim of the Canyon, the sky diminishing and the crumbling crags converging around you like a cocoon, you leave behind, forever, all Adolescent roles and caterpillar aspirations and, whether you know it or not, tumble toward the mere possibility — the promise and/or threat — of a butterfly or moth existence, the life of a winged Adult. And you do this by way of an intermediate status of a chrysalis, which is an existential realm that has no place in the everyday routines of the Village. In Village life, you're an egg, a caterpillar, or a butterfly. Or dead. To Village people, a chrysalis is a variety of being dead. While in Soul Canyon, you have no social reality to those in the Village, other than being a person who has slipped into the underworld seeking vision — something of inestimable value to the Village, should you succeed. And they know this. Your loved ones are praying for you and might even offer tangible support, but for a time you exist in a different existential realm.

The Hazel Wood

In his celebrated poem "The Song of Wandering Aengus," William Butler Yeats offers us a brief, lyrical account, written in his mid- to late twenties, of his encounter with Soul, a tale that's equal parts poetry, Irish myth, personal mythology, biography, and an exquisitely accurate and concise foretelling of how his life would unfold from the perspective of his Soul. This short story in verse illuminates much of what you, too, can expect to experience while wandering. Yeats ascribes his poem to Aengus, the Irish god of love, beauty, and youth, whose destiny is to become a ceaseless wanderer. Here is the first of the poem's three stanzas, corresponding to the phase of Dissolution:

I went out to the hazel wood,
Because a fire was in my head,
And cut and peeled a hazel wand,
And hooked a berry to a thread;
And when white moths were on the wing,
And moth-like stars were flickering out,
I dropped the berry in a stream
And caught a little silver trout.[5]

As a young man, Yeats, like all Wanderers, finds himself one day at a total loss about himself and his life. His identity and his understanding of the world have gone up in flames — there's a "fire" in his head. Everyone who reaches the Cocoon stage soon enough experiences this inferno. What do you do? In one form or another, you get yourself posthaste to a place of magic and mystery, a zone of transformation where anything can happen. For the Irish, such a place is symbolized by — and literally embodied in — a hazel forest. In Celtic lore, the hazel stands at the center of the underworld, where nine hazels grow over the Well of Wisdom, into which the hazelnuts drop, imparting their mystical qualities to the waters. The salmon who eat these nuts become incarnations of the Salmon of Knowledge and Inspiration. Those who eat the salmon gain "poetic and prophetic powers."[6]

Having descended into the underworld courtesy of cephalic fire, Yeats prepares to fish in the enigmatic waters, perhaps with the hope of finding something unfathomable, something that doesn't exist in his everyday Village world, something he needs. He fashions a fishing rod, but the poet nimbly names it a wand, a hazel wand being a Druidic implement with considerable magical spark. He selects a "berry" as bait, but we might imagine this a hazelnut, a food fancied by the Salmon of Knowledge and Inspiration. Yeats is courting here some major underworld and mythic players. During the Dissolution phase, this is your goal as well. Although Yeats uses berry bait, he is, in essence, making *himself* bait — for Soul. If he succeeds, he will be eaten, digested, and utterly altered. As must happen for you. At first you go fishing, keeping yourself safely above the surface, not yet understanding that soon enough you'll have to wholly submerge in those dark holy waters.

To further enhance his chances of initiatory self-demolition, Yeats, as Wanderer, chooses his timing shrewdly. When he drops his berry into the underworld waters, it is dawn, one of the two quotidian moments of heightened liminality (along with dusk), a moment of transition between dark and light when shapes shift recklessly and magic is afoot on the land. He is, in other words, asking for psychospiritual trouble, just the kind of trouble (and help) necessary for soul encounter, for his own radical transformation.

Take a tip from a William or two: You'll want to conduct certain of your Dissolution practices and ceremonies at dawn and dusk.

Notice, furthermore, how the poet informs us it is dawn: "when white moths were on the wing, / And moth-like stars were flickering out." Moths are well known for their fatal attraction to flame. This first stanza, then, contains two images of dying by way of the transformational agency of combustion (three if you count stars "flickering out"). Like fire, the Descent to Soul promises nothing less than a radical alteration of form and substance, a definitive ending to one state of being and the release of essence into another. Perhaps the poet's choice of moth as metaphor also anticipates a transformation of form to come, from adolescent caterpillar to adult moth (or sometimes butterfly).

Does the fishing Wanderer catch something? Indeed he does: "a little silver trout." The Wanderer has lured a magical being from the depths — surely a propitious sign of his preparedness for the journey. He doesn't yet understand the nature of what he has caught (or what, in truth, has caught him). But given the mythic relationship between the hazel and the Salmon of Knowledge and Inspiration — and the fact that a trout is a member of the salmon family — we might suspect our ignited (and benighted) Wanderer is about to be changed forever. On the Descent to Soul, this is true for all of us...if we shall be so fortunate.

The Fall to Freedom and the Mythology of Descent

Dissolution is a beginning (of our time in Soul Canyon), but whether by fire or otherwise, it's also an ending. As such, we might experience it as a blunt termination or, from another angle, as a consummation that affords liberation — again, like death. Dissolution is both a free fall and a fall to freedom.

Many myths of the Descent speak of this free(dom) fall, but they don't tell us much about how it is personally experienced in the emotional body or in the dissolving or disintegrating psyche. But we might be able to imagine what it would be like to be the Olympian goddess Persephone, the daughter of Zeus and Demeter, abducted into the underworld by Hades. Or to be Inanna, the Sumerian Queen of Heaven, on her way down to the underworld with the intention to conquer that domain, being progressively stripped of her seven layers of raiment as she descends, and then upon arrival, naked, is slain, her corpse hung upon a hook. We might be able to empathize with Beowulf, the Anglo-Saxon hero, plunging into the depths of a swamp for an underwater/underworld confrontation with the enraged mother of the monster Grendel, previously slain by Beowulf. Or with Little Mouse, of the Native American teaching story, risking everything by leaving his Village and venturing down to the River on his quest to find the source of the roaring in his ears. Perhaps we can relate to Parzival, leaving King Arthur's court as a megaflop of a question-asker and wandering in the chthonic wilderness for five years while seeking the Holy Grail. Or we might imagine being in the position of the young Prince Siddhartha Gautama, the Buddha-to-be, renouncing his life of royalty in the midst of his first Saturn return (age twenty-nine), leaving his palace and descending into the commoners' world unaccompanied, penniless, in search of enlightenment. Or perhaps we can feel what it would be like to be in the sandals of Jesus of Nazareth, just baptized (also at the time of his Saturn return), wandering alone into the wilds of the desert to fast for forty days and nights and cry for a vision.

In this chapter, we'll reflect on the stories of several contemporary people whose tumbles to psychospiritual death and freedom embody and exemplify the archetypal themes, symbols, and patterns of these mythologies.

The Crisis and the Call

As explored in the Preparation chapters, in order to descend into Soul Canyon and benefit from the journey, we need to have reached the Cocoon, the fourth life stage as described in the Eco-Soulcentric Developmental Wheel, and we must have achieved adequate levels of wholing and Self-healing. But there are additional conditions: There must, for example, be a life crisis and a call to spiritual adventure.

It seems we're rarely willing — or able — to leave the comfort and predictability of our familiar early-Adolescent life stories without the supportive intervention of a major life crisis, like a fire in the head or an immense storm with your name on it, some event or condition that destabilizes the Ego, that disrupts the Ego's current adaptation to the world — a shift in consciousness resulting in a profound and prolonged nonordinary state. This could be a significant personal loss such as the ending of a primary relationship, a job, or a career. Or it could be a crisis sparked by one or more intense and life-disturbing dreams or nightmares, a Kundalini awakening, or a disaster of some sort — some major dislocation from what you had previously considered "normal life" or the "real world." Or the dislocation might begin with a seemingly minor nonordinary state, perhaps an unsettling and unshakable feeling that you are living too small and/or that your house of cards is about to collapse, or an acute existential boredom, and then, when you attempt to address your inner disturbance, whatever you do ends up triggering a major crisis. Although some sort of crisis seems to be necessary, it will precipitate a Descent only if it occurs when you're in the Cocoon stage (or later).

Most often the crisis is not sought and arrives without warning. At other times, however, the destabilization arrives courtesy of a chosen initiatory ceremony or practice, such as a psychedelic trip, a vision fast, a dreamwork practice, a hundred-mile wilderness run, or a month living with a tribe of nature-based people. The initiatory ceremony or practice, although chosen, may or may not have been elected specifically as a means of ego-destabilization, but if it precipitates a crisis and you're in the Cocoon stage, a soul-activating ego-destabilization is what happens.

The kinds of crises that initiate a Descent to Soul are of a different order than the crises of psychological early Adolescence. The latter revolve around social acceptance, authenticity, and belonging — and the fear of losing relationships or social standing. The crises of the Cocoon, in contrast, are existential or ontological. Even if the crisis within the Cocoon is precipitated by a social event, such as the ending of a romance, the resulting dislocation is not so much about the loss of social belonging; rather, it mostly concerns uncertainty about one's place in the larger web of life and perhaps even about one's sanity. In that we are never completely finished with the tasks of previous life stages, we can and do have social crises while in the Cocoon, but the initiatory crisis that triggers the Descent is a different creature entirely.

In addition to a life crisis, there must be a call from the depths, such as from the enigmatic waters in a hazel wood or from the alluring and sensuous power of a storm; some condition or circumstance must pull the altered Ego down toward one or more bewitching mysteries of nature or psyche. This call to spiritual adventure can show up by way of a big dream, overpowering emotion, mystical encounter, uncontainable longing, or numinous event. But we must be irresistibly pulled down toward *something* — even if at the time we have no idea what that something really is.

What *is* pulling us down? The call is from our Soul, which is to say from both nature and psyche. As the unique ecological niche we were born to occupy, Soul is a feature of the natural world. But because the psyche understands and experiences Soul in terms of metaphor, myth, and symbol, the call is also from the depths or core of our own psyches. The feeling-sound we hear murmuring from the bottom of Soul Canyon is our unique call from the wild, which is also our call from our own hidden depths — the unique way we are each summoned into life by the *anima mundi*, the Soul of the world.

In sum, for a Descent to begin, there must be both a crisis and a call. Some life event unmoors us from the conventional world while at the same time something pulls us down. Without a downward lure, it's easy enough to reorient and restabilize in a crisis; without a life-disrupting event, it's easy enough to ignore or resist an enticement from below. In order for the Dissolution phase to begin, we need to fall apart *and* fall toward.

Dan's Descent into Hell

Dan — the fifty-year-old pastor we met earlier (see "Eco-Awakening," pages 35–39), who awoke to his native belonging to the animate world while in a high-altitude mountain forest — began his Descent courtesy of a crisis whose precipitating dimensions were spiritual, psychological, and social, a not-uncommon mix:

> Before my "call to adventure," I was answering another call as the senior
> pastor of a Presbyterian church in Colorado. I enjoyed many aspects of my

vocation, such as walking alongside people in their spiritual journey and being present to them during times of great joy and sadness. My faith community gave me a defined sense of identity and purpose. However, during the last few years I felt a growing sense of discontent. It seemed that, in spite of the good things that came from our [Christian] tradition, it was being used for self-deception. The practices of our Western consumer culture were colonizing us much more than the resources of our faith.

Another disturbing realization was that, while we were seeking to form authentic spiritual community, what we had done in reality — along with many Christian traditions in the West — was create a small belonging system with clearly defined boundaries to identify the insiders and outsiders. It is easy to feel good about yourself when you know you are God's chosen and it is the rest of the world that needs redemption.

These realizations, combined with my longing for something more wild and organic, sparked a crisis. I experienced a sense of "lostness" where the old familiar road signs of meaning and belonging no longer had power to direct me. I felt I did not belong to my faith community like I did before; increasingly, I felt like a stranger in a foreign land.

I realized how much I had been schooled in conformity rather than in innate wholeness. I realized that conforming to certain moral and spiritual practices and ideas about the Divine may have actually served to cut me off from my innate wholeness and wildness. If I did only the ascent half of the spiritual journey, without the descent, the shadow within would just grow larger.

I began to grieve. The grief cracked me open in ways I had never dreamed possible — an unexpected gift. I discovered that much of the anger in men (including me) was the result of depression from unresolved grief turned inward. I became less concerned about programs and appearances and more focused on the present moment. Learning how to grieve and be with people who are grieving deepened my longing for community and spiritual wholeness.

This gift of grief was the tipping point. Without it I might have remained numb to my longing and been content with my comfortable and secure life. I had been trained to believe that Jesus did the underworld work for all of us, the "descent into hell," and therefore this was already accomplished for everyone. But now I was feeling the pull "down" myself.[7]

For Dan, the crisis that destabilized him began with doubts about his religious tradition and culminated in feeling that he no longer belonged to the community he served as a religious leader. The call from below came in the form of his longing for his own "innate wholeness and wildness" and, as we shall see, from an ensuing series of life-shifting dreams. What enabled him to hear the call was the doorway to grief and his ability and willingness to walk through it.

Going In for the Kill: Amplifying the Crisis

Knowing that an existential crisis is the necessary precursor to radical transformation, a soul-initiation guide, if you're fortunate enough to have one, looks for opportunities to be a catalyst for such a crisis — if, that is, the guide believes you're ready for the Descent. The guide doesn't create the crisis but, rather, considers how your Soul is already brewing one — and for people ripe for a Descent, the Soul always is. Then the guide suggests an action, practice, or ceremony that might amplify the crisis, or she tells you a story or frames your dilemma in a way that pulls the rug out from under you.

One way the guide spots your crisis is by noticing what your subpersonalities (or inner protectors) are doing their best to resist. By aligning with your Soul, the guide intends to make enough of a difference to enable the crisis-and-call combo to propel you over the edge. In most instances, the guide enlists your conscious help to intensify the crisis. In others, the guide directly deepens your predicament with or without your permission — not by adding fuel to the fire but by nudging you closer to the flames. There's an element of the Trickster in every soul-initiation guide.

Keep in mind, everyone has an *inner* Guide to Soul (our West facet), who sometimes is in cahoots with our Trickster (our East facet). It's not uncommon for people on a Descent to discover after the fact that they have played tricks on themselves — of the self-disintegration variety.

During Dissolution, your guide's goal — whether an inner or outer guide — is the compassionate amplification of your existential crisis. Compassionate, yes, but a soul-initiation guide is not what you would normally consider a friend.

For example, when Dan began to doubt his church and ministry, a guide supporting his Descent might suggest he write a sermon about those doubts — pointing out that it would be Dan's choice, of course, whether or not to actually preach that sermon to his congregation. Or the guide might advise Dan (who is well-experienced in wilderness travel) to wander alone in a wild place for a few days, letting himself feel utterly lost and enacting there a ceremony confirming his loss of bearings by, for example, ritually burning symbols of his "old familiar road signs of meaning and belonging." The guide might suggest that Dan review Jesus's teachings, ask himself how he might follow Jesus on his Descent, and then design ways to do just that. Most likely the guide would also support Dan to cultivate his four facets of wholeness, especially his weakest ones, as well as suggesting grief rituals and practices. The guide would not go so far as to advise Dan to leave his ministry — this would be taking too causal a role in his crisis — but if Dan made this choice on his own, the guide would not be surprised. On the other hand, it's possible Dan could remain a pastor and fully experience his Descent nonetheless, but there is no chance he could remain *the same sort* of pastor and ever reach very deep into Soul Canyon. The old familiar life must change in fundamental ways.

Soul-initiation guides sometimes refer to this crisis-amplification business as "going in for the kill." After all, it's clear that the Wanderer's Ego, in its current configuration, must die. The Wanderer might understand this intellectually but not fully grasp its implications or understand what it will feel like when it actually happens. The guide, on the other hand, has no illusions in this realm. The Wanderer must lose conviction in and devotion to the story he had been living. The guide understands that the places where people are most vulnerable are the places where they can be shifted toward their depths. The Wanderer must in fact be shifted by life toward his depths, must find himself tumbling headlong into Soul Canyon, a descent that always feels like a death.

Intensifying the Experience of the Call

In addition to amplifying a crisis, soul-initiation guides (as well as inner Guides to Soul) often aim to intensify the experience of the call. They might do this by suggesting or leading practices that enable the Wanderer to hear the call more loudly or feel it more emphatically or decisively — like a quake demolishing the Wanderer's old house of belonging.

A guide, for example, might suggest activities that intensify the longing for the encounter with the Soul as beloved. This might include a daily practice in which the Wanderer sings songs of longing or praise — preexisting songs or original ones composed by the Wanderer. Or the Wanderer might be invited to write love letters to Soul, to dance her experience of the call, or to paint or draw the summons. The guide might give the Wanderer a sheaf of poems to read and suggest the most resonant be committed to memory. Or the Wanderer might be encouraged to write his own poems that emerge from his depths like wildflowers watered by the call.

Guides also utilize active imagination (aka guided interactive deep imagery) to intensify the experience of the call. Dan, for example, might be guided into a trance state in which he experiences himself in a wilderness setting, wandering in search of "something more wild and organic." Whatever Dan encounters on his inner wandering, the guide would support him to experience it fully with his (imaginal) senses and his embodied feelings and to cultivate a relationship with the beings and places encountered.

Here are some ways you can intensify a call for yourself or make yourself more vulnerable to the experience of a call:

• Design and enact ceremonies by which you say a wholehearted yes to the call.

- Engage in activities or practices that weaken your resistance to a call that has already occurred, such as extended wilderness time, intense physical exertion, holotropic breathwork,[8] prayer, trance dance, a vision fast, or the use of entheogens in ceremonies led by an experienced guide.
- Redesign or simplify your current life logistics so as to enable a fuller yielding to a call.
- Do Self-healing work with any subs who are resisting a call. (See "The Practice of Self-Healing," pages 59–62.)

A soul-initiation guide can support you in all of the above practices and can also help you discern if you're in the Cocoon, if what you're experiencing is in fact a call, and with how to respond from your depths.

Soulcentric Dreamwork

One of the most effective ways to intensify a call is dreamwork. The call from Soul, after all, often arrives when the everyday Ego is asleep or otherwise distracted. Soul-initiation guides use a form of dreamwork I call soulcentric, an approach that does not interpret dream images but, rather, ushers the Wanderer back into the full experience of the dream so that the dream — in this case, the call — can do its disintegrative work on the Wanderer's Ego.

Soulcentric dreamwork diverges from almost all other contemporary Western methods for working with our nightworld experiences. Most Western approaches seek to mine the dream, extracting information, messages, or guidance that the dreamer can use in their everyday middleworld life. (How do I mend a relationship, jump-start a creative project, or climb the corporate ladder?) In other words, the dream is conscripted to work for the Ego. In contrast, soulcentric dreamwork supports the dream itself to do its work on the Ego — to shift the shape of the conscious self. Soulcentric dreamwork amplifies the dream's power to transform the dreamer's psyche in the same way a profound waking experience does, the way we can be deconstructed and remade by, for example, an immense storm, a fire in the head, the death of a parent, a divorce, a transpersonal encounter with the divine, or a mystical immersion in the natural world. Dreams possess precisely this sort and magnitude of power. But when we do our own egoic work on our dreams (or on someone else's), that power is dissipated or squandered; the Ego is protected from the work the dream itself wants to perform on the Ego.[9]

Marty and the Scarified Woman

Marty Miller is a fifty-one-year-old writer, naturalist, soul activist, and leader of one of the first and oldest mythopoetic men's conferences in the world. A few months before his first vision fast, he dreamed of a beautiful woman:

I'm walking around a city at night with people — revelers — I do not know. I see a beautiful and enchanting woman with ritual scarring on her cheekbones and wearing a flowing dress and headscarf. The Scarified Woman is crossing a large cobblestone circular town square. I leave my party and follow her. She disappears. Dejectedly I step into a nightclub. I sit down just as the Scarified Woman steps up on the small stage and begins to sing. It is a high haunting lament, Middle Eastern sounding, almost like a call to prayer of the muezzins in the Islamic faith, which I have always loved.

A soul-initiation guide, acting as a soulcentric dreamwork facilitator, might invite Marty to close his eyes, become keenly aware of his body, and tell the dream again, slowly, letting himself fully reenter the particular dreamworld of that nightcity and that nightclub. The guide would invite him to linger in those moments in which the Scarified Woman is singing, encouraging Marty to allow her song to pierce his heart, to seep into his depths, to have its way with him. As this unfolds, the dreamworker/guide might encourage Marty to notice what happens in his body, what emotions arise, and what images those emotions evoke or morph into. The guide would continue inviting Marty to gently lean into these experiences. Both the guide and Marty would allow themselves to be infinitely curious about what happens when he does, where the song takes him, and the effect on him of the melody and the voice.

After this dyadic phase of the dreamwork, the guide might suggest that Marty allow himself to hear the Scarified Woman's song as often as possible, throughout the day and especially at certain moments that he intuitively recognizes as just the right ones to surrender to the Scarified Woman and her song. Marty might even learn to sing her song himself — this lament, this call to prayer — and then do so regularly until his vision fast, and during it as well.

All the practices discussed above for amplifying the crisis and intensifying the call are ways you can participate in your own Descent. You do not want to be a passive passenger. The way you participate matters, especially in the throes of an existential crisis.

Silver Moon's Crisis and Call: Into the Tunnel of Darkness

Kate Joyner, a thirty-something woman "of English origin," as she says, now goes by Silver Moon and self-identifies as a "poetic revolutionary" and "sacred activist." In the last chapter, you read a bit about her wholing and Self-healing work in preparation for her first Descent (see "Liberation from Lifetimes of Conditioning," pages 60–62). She first felt the call to her depths in her early teen years, a call that arose from her inchoate awareness that something essential about the human psyche was being neglected or suppressed by mainstream Western culture, something she could not name at the time. This apprehension of a vital omission, in addition to being a call to spiritual adventure, was a core element of the crisis that initiated her journey to Soul. A second element was her father's death when she was nineteen.

Silver Moon had the good fortune to begin her Wandering when she was only twenty-one, relatively young for contemporary Westerners. But without conscious knowledge of the Descent to Soul, and without a guide to support her, her journey was hazardous and circuitous. Incited by crisis and sustained by a call from her depths, she embarked on a post-university wander to "dance with the unseen":

> I went out into the world in search of meaning. I lived in South America for seven years, studied circus and, eventually, psychology. At age twenty-eight, I returned to England with a renewed faith in the larger picture of which I was a part. I knew then there was something more to life than surface appearances. I had experienced synchronicities, been guided beyond my own plans, and met people along the way who led me down all sorts of rabbit holes. At such a young age and with no real ties in the world, I was open and vulnerable to something other than me. I began to dance with the unseen, and I also began to trust it, to believe wholeheartedly in the unknown, and to let myself go into it. Back in England, I was awakened but didn't know what to do with my expanded consciousness. I tried for a while to establish a normal life: get a job, get married, and start thinking about kids. I wanted to build something, to serve, to put to work the professional training and life experience I had gathered. But something didn't feel right. I was trying to mold myself back to a way of being that was too small for everything I had experienced in those seven years of wandering.

These yearnings and her sense of confinement ripened into the crisis that sent Silver Moon over the edge into Soul Canyon:

> As quickly as I was married, I was then divorced, I left my job, and I lost touch with my few friends. Still only twenty-eight, I was being called to let go of what I thought was meant to happen, my ego ideas of what my life should look like. This became the initial part of the necessary death process. Something else was calling me as my world crumbled. It felt like I was entering a tunnel of darkness. I had nothing to hold on to. I didn't know where any of this was going. But I trusted. It was painful.

Silver Moon had become unanchored to the conventional world courtesy of the intertwined crises of cultural collapse, father-loss, and the implosion of her young-adult social-vocational life. And she felt a call — from a mysterious and suppressed dimension of the human psyche and from the possibilities and freedom tasted during seven years of wandering.[10]

Matt's Crisis and Call: A Profound Longing for the Other

Sometimes the crisis that opens the portal to the underworld arrives in the form of an ecstatic *upper*world experience of mystical union. At age twenty-three, Matt Syrdal, a young, stable, upwardly mobile Seattle software professional, had a numinous vision he describes as "a transcendental encounter with God/Spirit/Mystery that nearly ruined me." This was a spontaneous encounter with no forewarning, induced without drugs or other consciousness-shifting practices.

It began while riding in the passenger seat in my cousin's SUV, in traffic down the 405 on the east side of Seattle. I was watching the evergreen trees and the sunlight playing through the shapes and shadows sprinting past. I was filled with a deep tenderness, strangely familiar, nurturing yet sorrowful, like the rising tide of some forgotten memory. Tears came to my eyes as we drove, and I asked my cousin to pull off the freeway. The next exit led us to a park in Bellevue. Stumbling out of the car, I staggered, sobbing, into an open field surrounded by trees, gardens, and an open beachfront down to Lake Washington. As I stood, rooted in the middle of the field, my sense of time shifted or stopped, and my conscious self ceased to be. "I" somehow merged with every movement, sound, and sensation around me — not exactly in the body or even out of the body, but *this* body had become a small aspect of the *greater* Body. My consciousness merged with everything around me — as if I was the bee and butterfly loping playfully past my face, as if I was the breeze that seemed to whisper through me, as if I was the bending grass and the leaves in the gently moving arms of the trees, expanding with the breath of the clouds. All was alive, all was suffused with mystery, all was one ultimately inexpressible reality. It was as if I had suddenly awakened after being asleep for twenty-three years. The world itself was alive, permeated by a mysterious Presence.

Afterward, I felt profoundly calm. I felt both full and empty. I felt both a deep sense of belonging, of being at home, as well as a painful longing left by this mysterious encounter. This numinous "other" had touched something so deep within me that my life as I had known and enjoyed it had come to an end. Seeing everything again for the first time, I felt like a newborn — the world alive, resonant, and full of enchantment and meaning. And in this reborn state of innocence, a wound was revealed and unearthed, a place of deep tenderness and grief that had been buried under layers and strata of life even beyond my own.

Over the course of the next year, Matt found himself weeping every couple of days, sometimes even sobbing, "as if some underground glacier was melting." He had been a successful director for a software company, single, the life of the party. Now, what he had once valued, what had previously affirmed him and provided him security, was empty of meaning.

> I lost the desire for recognition, achievement, success, power, or control. Something shifted so dramatically that my life was disorienting at times, difficult, even painful. Trying to make sense of what was happening to me, I struggled with how to live with this newfound freedom. I could no longer live the life I had been living; that much I knew. I made the mistake of sharing the experience with a couple of friends, even a couple of pastors. They didn't really understand what I was talking about. I lost many of my closest friends who had become family to me. I struggled to find a community or even a single friend or mentor from whom I could get support or guidance as to what to do with this new awareness. I felt like some sort of stranger in a world that once felt so familiar, now dissolving. It was the first time in my life I didn't feel lonely, yet I was acutely aware that I was totally alone. My longing was to be with none other than this One who had pierced me, and the call brought with it the pain of vulnerability and my need to trust without qualification, without holding anything back.

An experience like this — at once an upperworld taste of oneness, a mystical immersion in the animate nature of all things, and an experience of intimate connection with, or even identity with, everything — radically destabilizes the Ego and irreversibly alters one's experience of life. But the descent to the *underworld* of Soul might not begin for quite a while after such a theophany, perhaps not for years, as in Matt's case. Or it might never occur at all.

Although Matt's transcendental encounter did not immediately precipitate his Descent, it did bring about his Confirmation — the end of his early Adolescence and that stage's embrace of social and vocational success as a primary motivator. The passage of Confirmation delivered him — as it does everyone — into the late-Adolescent stage of the Cocoon, but he had no mentors or initiators to guide him, no one to help him understand or deepen into what had happened to him in that field above Lake Washington, no one to introduce him to the new world and altered consciousness of the Cocoon or to help him prepare for the Descent. In the aftermath of his experience, Matt was left with only an ineradicable call, "a profound longing for this One, a painful longing for this Other." By following his longing, Matt eventually arrived at the rim of Soul Canyon. He was one of the fortunate few. Most contemporary people who've had mystical encounters never discover what to do with them. More often than not, these experiences are misunderstood or even pathologized by self or others.

The Call from the Depths

Following his "divine wounding," as he calls it, Matt began to read the mystics and to practice meditation and centering prayer. He entered seminary, got his master of divinity, and became a Presbyterian pastor. Meanwhile, his longing for the Other grew ever stronger and became "almost unbearable": "It felt as if I was not living in the world I was meant to live in, a mysterious world that was calling me, inviting me in some sense to die." In hindsight, we can understand this invitation as a call from Soul.

Not knowing what else to do, Matt entered therapy and began to unearth his unassimilated anger and grief, something he needed to do in any case. He became aware that so many of his peers — new ministers and therapists — were psychologically wounded, like him. He has since come to see that through their studies they had all been seeking their own wholing and healing as much as preparing for a career through which they could serve others. Even at the time, he felt, "there were entire expressions and experiences of our deepest humanity that were missing, a willful ignorance of the values, beliefs, and experiences of entire cultures, and a psychospiritual alienation from the living, wild, and natural world." This short list of developmental deficits is a decent summary of what must be addressed during the Preparation phase of the Descent to Soul.

Matt, by then in his early thirties, had already been in the Cocoon stage for several years. He searched the Christian tradition for language for the "call from the depths." The closest he could find were mystics like St. Francis, St. John of the Cross, and the anonymous author of *The Cloud of Unknowing*, but "there was something missing." That something was an understanding of the Descent, a journey most likely experienced by Jesus himself during his solo desert time but not discussed as such by mainstream Christianity, nor commended by its priests to their congregants, nor virtually ever experienced by those priests before, during, or after seminary.

The Great Wave

When he was thirty-six, Matt found his way to a four-day experiential immersion exploring the Eco-Soulcentric Developmental Wheel. This intensive, with more than a thousand participants, was held at a conference center in New Mexico along the Rio Grande. I co-led this intensive with the visionary and great-hearted Franciscan priest Richard Rohr. During those four days, Matt began to cultivate underdeveloped facets of his wholeness. He also learned the differences between spiritual underworld journeys and upperworld journeys, as well as how they complement and supplement one another. But something else happened for Matt, something profound and life-changing — an experience rooted in a recurring dream from childhood, which he calls his Great Wave Dream:

I am standing alone at night on a boardwalk in an empty beach town. It is dead calm as if time itself is holding its breath. I look out into the dense blackness of night. As I climb down the steps to the sand, I am searching for the horizon. Suddenly, I see it. I can just make out a faint, thin, white, horizontal line in the darkness. By now I am standing thigh-deep in the ocean. I feel the pull of cold white froth rush past my legs, out into the sea. The silent undertow of the black water seems to pull my heart into my stomach as I look up into the darkness again with a shooting pang of both awe and dread. I make out the foam crest of a massive wave rapidly approaching the shore, sixty to a hundred feet high, and it dawns on me — there is absolutely no escape! It is then that I feel it pull me, pulling something deep within me, as powerful as destiny itself. And without hesitation, as if everything in the universe hinged on this moment, I dive into the dark water and swim straight out into the black night toward the great wave. Now there is no fear, simply a naked clarity of awareness. I feel my heart pound in my chest with an exhilaration of a complete surrender that I do not understand, but I know one thing — this is it, this is the end. And as I am drawn up into the crest of the wave, all my senses set aflame, my whole life up to this moment, my existence itself, converges into this single point — and I wake up.

DreamMaker had gifted Matt, early in his life, a full-bodied experience of complete surrender to something vast and unimaginable. What was DreamMaker preparing him for?

At the intensive along the Rio Grande (the Great River), Matt, without intending to, ended up enacting his Great Wave Dream. It was the third day. At the midmorning break, Matt walked out of the conference room and into the lobby for coffee but was instead drawn to the large windows facing the cottonwood trees growing along the distant river.

It was a very windy morning. In front of the trees, tall grass blew in radiant ripples and lustrous swells like a golden sea. As I stood transfixed by this wavelike pattern, it seemed like something beyond the trees was pulling the grass and the wind, like an undercurrent. My consciousness shifted into dreamtime. The band of dark gnarled trees became the Great Wave. The fence just before the trees became a threshold I was going to cross. Tears were streaming down my face as the glass doors opened and I was pulled across the brick terrace and down the steps. I plunged into the golden grass, the wind pushing me from behind and a mysterious force pulling me toward the trees. This was it — I was being swept up into the Great Wave.

I started sobbing. I became part of something much greater than me, merged into something I had never experienced before. And I was absolutely under its power. As I floated on the wind through the field, my sobs became louder and louder, my tears, mixed with wind, stung and burned my face and neck. I lost my ordinary state of awareness and became immersed in a greater, much older consciousness that felt as if it came up from the earth itself — a deep sorrow, a lament that transcended my own lifetime. I howled with an ancient grief, my cries rising up in the cacophony of the wind, movement, and light. The closer I came to the tree line — the Great Wave — the harder and louder I cried. It felt like a very real death.

Then, as I crossed the threshold of the gated path and entered the looming, dark trees, my weeping turned into laughter, like giggling at first. As I strode deeper into the trees — the destructive Wave — I broke into howling laughter. What was happening to me? A kind of peace came over me, enough to trust whatever was happening was not only not crazy but absolutely necessary. So I just let it happen — wild laughter deeper than I had ever experienced. A power and aliveness surged through my body — as if the Earth herself was laughing through me, a warrior's laughter. I stumbled as if drunk, laughing through the trees. I felt nauseous and started dry heaving. I felt like something came out of me, but not in a frightening way, in a liberating way. As if nature herself had extracted something from me, as a doctor would extract poison from a wound, as if I had surrendered some old unconscious wound or emotion that had been trapped in my body a long time.

I returned to an ordinary state and began to make my way back. I tried to reflect on what had just happened. Was I crazy? Was this a God thing, or was it a weird transpersonal experience? I didn't know what to make of it, but one thing I knew: I was more energized than I had felt in a long time. I felt fully awake and alive as if my body was radiating and some new awareness or instincts had switched on. I walked through the trees, still laughing sporadically in a new voice, a warrior's voice. I knew in my heart I had completed something significant, that it was now time. But time for what?

In addition to a healing experience, this was Matt's entry into Soul Canyon, the start of his Dissolution. The Great Wave began to transform Matt — somatically, psychologically, and spiritually — shifting his center of gravity from his former social and vocational identity toward one rooted in the much wilder and deeper mysteries of nature and Soul, "a greater, much older consciousness that...came up from the earth itself." Since childhood, his DreamMaker had been preparing his Ego for just such a moment. The Great Wave Dream had created something like a trapdoor in his psyche; when the conditions were right, the door opened and Matt plummeted toward Soul.

The Necessity of Risking Everything

Once on your way down, you risk losing everything, including your social and vocational standing, your home and possessions, your most precious relationships, even your sanity. Or perhaps the pattern is this: The more you're willing to risk, the deeper you're able to descend into Soul Canyon. As you tumble over the edge, you don't know which elements of your former life will be there to greet you upon your return — if you do return — and which will be lost forever. Whatever you're not willing to risk will act as an encumbrance on your way down, like a buoy tied to a diver.

This is in part because your acceptance of risk correlates with the depth of your longing. When your longing to encounter Soul is sufficient, nothing else really matters. But it's also because your readiness for an encounter with Soul is measured by your conviction that a life defined by any social or vocational conventions is no longer a life that holds allure. The caterpillars most ready for their cocoons are those who've had enough of crawling around, consuming, and molting.

When embarking upon your Descent, you are giving over your life to what T. S. Eliot named "a condition of complete simplicity / (costing not less than everything)."[11]

What if, when you hear the call to descend, you happen to be a parent to preteen children? This can be a real dilemma. If parenting is for you a sacred contract, is soul work, then you might choose to postpone your Descent, if you can, so you don't betray this contract or risk harming your children or your relationship to them. Some parents, however, are able to do both, but this requires a bold and uncommon honesty with themselves and their family. Can you truly and adequately be present to your children while wandering in the depths of Soul Canyon? You might be in nonordinary states of consciousness for hours at a time, if not days or weeks. During other periods, Mystery might call you to wander far from home. Will it compromise your Descent if you limit how far or deep you wander — or for how long? For most it would; others, perhaps not. Jung, for instance, navigated his Descent while living and working at home. He saw his patients during the day and then plunged into the depths of his imagination each evening. He did have young children at the time, but most of the childcare fell to his wife, Emma — most likely a customary arrangement in early-twentieth-century Switzerland. For single parents, the Descent to Soul might be especially challenging if not impossible without significant support.

Transpersonal Dedication

What motivates a person to risk everything?

It might be an irresistible pull toward a felt possibility. Or it might simply be that you've lost belief in the old life and no other choice can be imagined. Others risk everything because they've dedicated their journey — and their lives — to something greater than themselves. These Wanderers don't embark upon the journey solely or primarily for their own personal reward. They seek a vision or revelation, a bestowal of knowledge or ability, with which they can serve their people, their more-than-human community, or the beings of the future — the children of all species for many generations to come.

Jung, for instance, ardently desired to provide greater service to his patients and also to contribute more meaningfully to the development of the then-incipient field of depth psychology. Barbara Hannah, a close associate of Jung's, describes what motivated his "confrontation with the unconscious," begun when he was thirty-eight:

> It was [Jung's] conviction that he could not help his patients with the fantasies they were bringing him without first knowing where his own were leading which was often his strongest motive for persevering with his inner work. How could he ask them to do something he did not dare to do himself? And he realized then that all he had to help them with were "a few theoretical prejudices of dubious value." He added: "This idea — that I was committing myself to a dangerous enterprise not for myself alone, but also for the sake of my patients — helped me over several critical phases."[12]

We see a similar dedication in Pastor Dan, who descended with the goal of better serving his congregants, and in Silver Moon, who "wanted to build something, to serve, to put to work the professional training and life experience I had gathered along the way."

A transpersonal dedication, while not universal, is unsurprising because, after all, the goal of the journey of soul initiation is the fulfillment that springs from a life of true service to the Earth community, a life of engaged participation in the evolutionary unfolding of the world. Choosing to embark on the journey in order to obtain something merely for oneself can be a sign of someone unprepared for the Descent. This contrasts with someone longing to be more fully part of the world by discovering how to serve it in an ecocentric and soulcentric manner.

Those who are abducted, who descend involuntarily, might not have a transpersonal dedication before the Descent begins, but if so, such a dedication usually develops along the way.

Sabina's Crisis and Call: The Last-Minute Ticket Agency

One July morning in Switzerland when she was twenty-four, Sabina fell into Soul Canyon and made a deal with the universe. She had been in the Cocoon stage for a few years, but this was the first time the Earth opened up and swallowed her. Still in bed, Sabina was trying to fall back asleep so she wouldn't have to face the fact that her life had fallen apart. Her spiritual teacher and guide had banished her for not conforming to his wishes. Her best friend had abandoned her. She and her boyfriend had broken up. A whole chapter of her life was in ruins. And she had just recently moved to Basel, where she knew very few people.

Sabina felt lost, desperate, disillusioned, at a dead end. Her life was in full crisis. Then, that morning, still in bed, she heard and felt the call:

> While my tears pooled on my bedsheets, something much grander, deeper, and overwhelmingly large came rolling in. Like thunder. Like a roaring fire in my depth. A very clear and calm feeling-thought emerged: *Learn to follow Soul and everything else will be easier.* Bammm. There it was. Like a detonation. It changed my life — forever. Such truth. Such a *yes* in me, even as fear crept in. I had done many years of inner work, looking for what we humans and this life on Earth are really about — because I knew it could not be what others said. It just couldn't. Such emptiness, such meaninglessness, such cruelty — there's *got* to be something else. And then this simple truth arrived.
>
> I said, "Okay, I am going to learn to follow Soul. I will step over the threshold into what seems like nothing but air, and just fall. I will allow the not-knowing, the mystery, the abyss to swallow me and take me fully and wholly. I will let myself be led by Soul."

Like all Wanderers who fully say yes to the call, Sabina walked out the door of her existing story and radically simplified her life. She quit her job, gave away most of her belongings, vacated her apartment, parted with her few friends and former boyfriend, and left behind her treasured means of music-making: her piano and violin. It was time to leave "home" — her Adolescent house of belonging. She told her parents and friends, "I am going away. I do not know for how long and I do not know where to. All I know is that I will not contact you. I need to be on my own." It was 1993.

Sabina gave Mystery complete control over her life:

> I said to Soul, "Okay, on July 25, I will go to the last-minute ticket agency and I will take whatever flight you direct me to book."
>
> I went there on that specific day, my heart pounding so loud everybody across the city must have heard it. Much to my horror, there were only two flights available. One was a week in Mallorca. Nope, this was certainly not it. Then my eyes wandered to the only other last-minute ticket: Los Angeles. I just about lost it. *The USA!?*
>
> At that point in my life I hated the US — the huge waste of natural resources, the arrogant conviction of what is best for other countries, and the stupidity and superficiality of TV shows like *Dallas*.

I stood there, in shock. America? No! But it quickly dawned on me that this was already Soul's first lesson. If I really wanted to follow Soul, then I had to let go of preconceived notions, prejudices, and thinking, *We are better* or *I know better*. Bang...got it. Thanks. I booked the ticket to Los Angeles, the epitome of superficiality, new-age fluff, and waste. *Of course* Soul would send me there! And it was a one-way ticket. Having very little money, I thought, *How in the world will I ever get back home?* even while noticing my Soul snickering at the phrase "back home."

I stepped over the cliff, into the abyss. I had no idea what was going to happen, where I would go once I got to LA, what I would do.

These conditions, as challenging as they might sound, are actually close to ideal for the Wanderer in Soul Canyon: a definitive and thorough leave-taking combined with a radical faith and resolve to follow the signs of Mystery. What was not so ideal for Sabina — but entirely common now in the Western world — was the absence of initiatory guides or Elders and her being underprepared, psychospiritually, for the journey. Like most contemporary Wanderers, she was in the difficult position of needing to address much of her Preparation during the Dissolution phase of her Descent.

Both scared and thrilled, Sabina strode over the irreversible, one-way threshold, letting go of everything and everyone. On her flight to LA, she wept, grieving the loss of all she had been — or had thought she was. She had brought with her only a backpack with a few basic items and a small amount of cash. She had no credit card, no computer, no cell phone. She was on her way to a country and continent she knew next to nothing about, where they spoke a language she barely knew, and with no plan whatsoever.

Upon arrival in LA, she took a shuttle to a cheap hotel and slept. When she awoke, she went out and bought a used car, which cost nearly everything she had. For the next nine months, she wandered through the American Southwest, Mexico, Guatemala, and Belize. More importantly, she wandered off the script of her old story and explored new ways to be in the world.

I started to get to know me apart from all the identifications I previously had. Lots of tears. Lots of relief. Lots of pain. Lots of joy. As deeply as I could, I consciously shed my old ways of being so as to see what new would emerge, a tip I got from Soul/Mystery. More and more I listened/felt for these tips, the leading feelings, the signs and omens.

No one knew me, so no one could hold me to my old ways of being. I could invent new, more authentic ways. For countless days and nights, I wandered landscapes and soulscapes in a timeless way, nowhere to go from an egocentric standpoint, and everything to learn and be immersed in as I apprenticed to Mystery/Soul.

Here we see many of the archetypal themes common to the Wanderer during the Dissolution phase — spontaneity, faith, acceptance, wanderlust, intimacy, solitude, adventure, risk, invisible guidance:

> Soul led, I followed — into inner sanctuaries and hells, outer paradises and moments of acute danger of losing my life. I was protected. I was led. I was formed, kneaded, thrown into a heap of bones — only to be reshaped again and again.

In addition to supporting her severance from her old life and identity (the primary effect of Dissolution), her experiences while wandering supported her to cultivate her four facets of wholeness to the higher levels needed for the journey of soul initiation — her capacity for self-nurturance and self-reliance (North); her ability to embrace and fully feel her emotions (South); her capacity to acquire knowledge through her deep imagination (West); her leadership capacities (North); her innate innocence, which for her meant gradually losing self- and culturally imposed beliefs that she was "not good" and could get on "God's good side" only by earning it (East); and her kinship with nonhuman beings, which she cultivated through long stretches of solo time in wild places (South). Other experiences afforded opportunities for Self-healing.

> What shaped me most while I was wandering was being in nature. With so little money, motels were out of the question. Wherever Soul guided me, that's where I slept. Somehow this young, blond, blue-eyed woman traveling alone was protected from harm. People told me I was crazy, but I knew I wasn't. I thought, rather, *they* were crazy — for not following the promptings of Soul. Life made sense to me for the first time. I started to fill with a deep trust, deeper than anything I knew before, a trust I would need and rely on with all that was to come.

Kevin's Crisis and Call: A Very Wild Mind

In the Cocoon stage, sometimes the crisis that precipitates a Descent to Soul consists of — or is amplified by — an alteration in neurochemistry, perhaps brought about by entheogenic substances or by high stress that exacerbates a preexisting neurological vulnerability. For Kevin Lloyd Fetherston, an American river-restoration ecologist, it was both. When our human neurochemistry wanders outside its normal range, our consciousness likewise wanders across borders into nonordinary perception, realities, and abilities. When this happens for people in the Cocoon — archetypal Wanderers — the resulting altered consciousness can initiate a Descent.

Kevin grew up in Milwaukee, on the western shore of Lake Michigan. In 1972, in the spring of his senior year of high school, he accompanied his surgeon father on a medical mission to a remote region of Nicaragua. There he met a Peace Corp worker who invited Kevin to travel with him by dugout canoe two hundred miles up the Rio Coco to build a medical clinic. For the next five weeks, Kevin was immersed in a journey of wandering that permanently transformed his felt-sense about the world and the possibilities it held for him. This experience touched off his passage of Confirmation — his entrance into the Cocoon. Upon his return to Milwaukee, all Kevin wanted was to "experience this larger, amazing world." He was no longer interested in college but made an agreement with his parents to go for a year.

After his freshman year, Kevin did in fact set off wandering, his inner life "focused deeply on mysteries, the occult, my dreamworld." He followed signs and omens. For four years, he hitchhiked around North America, planted trees in Idaho, attended hippie gatherings in the Colorado mountains, backpacked in Wyoming and Montana, and worked on ships as a longshoreman on the Great Lakes. He sampled a variety of Western mystical practices and explored nonordinary states by way of entheogens, fasting, and long-distance running.

When he was twenty-three, seeking psychological stability, a vocational trajectory, and a scientific grounding to his mystical experiences, Kevin returned to college as a premed student at the University of Wisconsin at Milwaukee:

> The underworld was continuing to pull at me, and I was having experiences of nonordinary realities, some destabilizing, some quite ecstatic. I thought a rigorous training in the sciences would help me hold the reins of my very wild mind. So I jumped back into university, became enthralled with a scientific understanding of the cosmos, and began my scientific career.

One night that autumn, Kevin had a harrowing experience that initiated his Descent, the irreversible unraveling of his Adolescent identity. This crisis was set in motion by his preexisting neurological malleability now inflamed by academic stress and the cumulative effect of his years of exploring mystical states:

> At 10:30 on a Saturday night, while studying intensely at the university library for an organic chemistry exam, a large man floated into my view and over my head, whereupon he burst into flames and continued, engulfed in fire, to float out the library windows. This scared the daylights out of me. I grabbed my books and fled into the night. Shaken, I made my way along the dark elm-lined streets of Milwaukee, where I came upon a block of forest from which hundreds of different-shaped eyes looked at me. The trees swayed wavelike against the night sky, as in Van Gogh's *Starry Night*. The eyes were alive, watching me, inquiring. I could not collect myself to engage with them, and I hurried home all the while thinking that something was not right with my mind at a depth I simply did not understand. I was finding myself thrust into realms way outside my upbringing and cultural understanding.

Kevin has a type of neurological sensitivity or mutability that can give rise to either a disabling psychological condition or an invaluable psychological and spiritual gift, or both. In the contemporary Western world, neuromercuriality is most often diagnosed as a "mental illness," a perspective that results in a tragic misunderstanding and mislabeling, with devastating consequences for the individual — and an immense loss for the community. In a mature society — one with a genuine appreciation for individual differences, including neurodiversity — Kevin would have been recognized in childhood as someone with an innate gift that rendered him able to perceive much more readily than most the hidden world behind the everyday world. In his youth, he would have been taught to understand his gift, to use it, and how to turn it off and on. He would have learned how to keep himself grounded in the everyday world while maintaining communication with that other, invisible realm that reveals relationships and dynamics difficult or impossible to detect with everyday consciousness, knowledge of inestimable value to the human and greater Earth communities. Much of the failings and pathology of contemporary societies can be diagnosed as an inability to form a viable relationship with the depths and significance of the visible world, let alone the invisible. Instead, conformist-consumer society oppresses and marginalizes people born with these gifts — whether in premeditated self-defense or as a consequence of simple ignorance. Kevin eventually discovered how to manage, use, and offer his particular genius, but it took many years and an assortment of pharmacological and institutional detours along the way. He very nearly didn't survive it.

Kevin's vision of the burning man led to his eventual internment in the psychiatric enterprise, but it also constituted the crisis that precipitated his Descent to Soul and the Dissolution of his Adolescent identity. As we'll see later, Kevin's first encounter with Soul — his first revelation of mythopoetic identity — took place within the year. Although he had no soul-initiation guides until many years later, he was blessed with several numinous encounters, likely facilitated in part by his neurological mutability, which bestowed him with a greater-than-average capacity with his West facet, the Dark Muse-Beloved (see "Cultivating Our Innate Human Wholeness," pages 46–48). His vulnerability in one domain of life constituted a great boon in another.

Abduction versus Conscious Descent

In Greek mythology, the god of the underworld, Hades, falls in love one day with his niece, the goddess Persephone, and decides to kidnap her and make her his wife. Not exactly chivalrous. But this myth contains both a crisis and an allurement, both of which precede the abduction. Earlier on the fateful day, on an outing from Olympus, young Persephone is playing on Earth with some of her nymph friends (the daughters of Ocean), but she is lured away by the sight of the enchanting yellow narcissus flower. In one version of the myth, the narcissus is planted there by the goddess Gaia, as requested by her grandson, Zeus — Persephone's father — so as to lure her away from her friends so that Hades can snatch her. Persephone's call or longing, in this myth, is for the enchanting flower. (In Greek, this flower is *narkissos,* suggesting its narcotic effects.) The crisis, on one level, is her social isolation, the severance from her friends, even if brief. The allurement (the call) and the resulting isolation (the crisis) together make possible the abduction by Hades. As Persephone goes to pluck the narcissus, the ground splits open and out of the chasm leaps Hades on his golden chariot. And the rest is…mythology.

But there's an additional background crisis, one that Persephone isn't aware of till later. Hades has previously gone to see his brother Zeus to propose that Persephone become Hades's queen. Zeus not only agrees but even conspires with him by arranging for the narcissus, which Zeus knows will allure Persephone. This is, of course, a terrible father betrayal, but one that ends up engendering a soul-fomenting crisis for Persephone. Some middleworld tribulations provide underworld benefits.

Persephone's abduction may or may not be necessary for her to eventually take her true (destined, ultimate) place in the world as Queen of the Underworld. Whether through abduction or otherwise, she first has to be shorn of her previous (maiden/Adolescent) identity as an innocent Olympian goddess. Before her abduction, Persephone's name is Kore, which means "maiden." "Persephone," on the other hand, means "to bring destruction," a name with considerably more gravitas, a name that reveals a core dimension of her mythopoetic identity.

Dissolution — sometimes by abduction — is always and everywhere necessary for the initiation into our soul lives. Why are abductions so common? As much as we long for an encounter with Soul, the prospect also terrifies us. We understand at some level that our lives will be forever, irreversibly changed. No one descends to the underworld, to Hades, without some resistance — if not complete refusal. As often as not, we must be abducted.

However, it *is* possible, despite our natural resistance, to consciously choose Dissolution and to voluntarily step over the edge into Soul Canyon (like Inanna or Orpheus). Or we might choose to embark on an epic journey but not realize one of our initial stops is the underworld (like Beowulf, Parzival, Jesus, or Buddha). We also can simply refuse the call (and perhaps evade any attempted abductions).

Dan, the Presbyterian pastor, was abducted — successfully:

> Right after my first Animas intensive, it was as if the underworld reached up, grabbed me by the ankles, and dragged me down.
>
> My dream life exploded. I started remembering as many as three a night. There were thieves chasing me. Animals regularly appeared — roaring bears, fierce badgers, running elk, magnificent steelhead, and invisible jaguars stalking me. Many times I awoke in the night terrified of these

creatures. But as I began working with the dreams with the help of guides, I learned to talk to the animals, to befriend and merge with them. I realized that rather than something sinister, they were actually my allies on the inner journey. There were pieces of my wholeness that needed to come together before I was ready for the next phase of the descent.

After a year and a half of this work, the persona and identity I had developed throughout my adult life was unraveling. It was terrifying. I felt alone. My sense of religious faith was radically morphing. I was having amazing experiences in nature and in my dreams, but I felt like if I shared them with anyone, people would suggest I see a doctor immediately.

It was at the same time beautiful because the world came alive in wondrous ways. I no longer felt like a tourist passing through on my way to a better place. I was a part of this magnificent, enthralling, and alluring natural world. All I wanted to do was fall more deeply in love with it.

Although the details vary from one person to the next, Dan's experience of Dissolution reveals a common pattern: The journey down into the underworld is both terrifying and beautiful — the disintegration of the only identity and life story we have, and yet the opening into a more alive, liberating, wondrous, connected, meaningful, and alluring realm of destiny.

The Necessity to Relinquish Control

Whether abducted or a voluntary *plutonaut* — the Roman name for Hades is Pluto — one thing for sure is that we have limited control during the journey. Something calls and draws us down, but we don't really know what it is. It's possible to resist the call, but this might not forestall our Descent; resistance itself could lead to a further destabilization or dissolution of our current identity.

We have to get used to an existential state that is the reverse of the everyday conditions and requirements of life for most people, especially in the mainstream West: We must come to terms with not being in control — even of our own life. We must surrender Ego jurisdiction and let ourselves be acted upon by wild and mysterious figures and forces within and around us. This contrasts with what we had progressively been getting better at our whole life up to this point: being the fashioner of our fate, the determiner, the decider. Now, on the Descent, the Ego is the clay that gets shaped, not the shaper. After Metamorphosis, our Ego will be a shaper again, but in a very different way.

The Descent can feel unbearable at times. We must learn how to be nonattached to outcome. Until our arrival in the depths of Soul Canyon, it's not possible to know what waits for us there. We must let our old story fall away, neither clinging to it nor angrily pushing it away. Our greatest need during Dissolution is to access our fourfold Self, to live and experience from this place of wholeness, and to return to the present moment whenever we realize we've drifted somewhere else. Any moment might include grief, but there is also wonder and joy and the celebration of the miracle and magic of life and of our participation in it. Our Ego is growing roots in the underworld, but the green shoots of our Soul life won't appear above ground for a while yet, the blossoms even later. Dissolution means being in deep, uncharted waters for a time. We're being tested, strengthened, readied.

While in this phase, you'll want to attend to your nightworld dreams and your dayworld fantasies and images. Record them in your journal; allow them to do their work on you. Quit your tent and stride ever deeper into the mysteries of the self-organized, more-than-human world, without a predetermined destination. Every moment in your life up to now has been preparing you for this pilgrimage. Embrace being lost for the time being.

> I said to my soul, be still, and wait without hope
> For hope would be hope for the wrong thing; wait without love
> For love would be love of the wrong thing; there is yet faith
> But the faith and love and the hope are all in the waiting.
> Wait without thought, for you are not ready for thought:
> So the darkness shall be the light, and the stillness the dancing.

> — T. S. ELIOT[13]

Chapter Four

PHASE TWO
Dissolution

Part 2: A Bundle of Practices and Ceremonies for Descending

> ...Farther down this tangled trail
> love will crack the guardhouse
> of your heart until you wail
> with Earth's pain — or weep
> with the ecstasy of angels.
> In the least presence you will find
> unspeakable cosmic glory.
> In the night sky you will
> recognize ancestors.
> The dead will come in dreams.
> The living are everywhere,
> wearing the faces of clouds,
> water, sequoia, granite....

— GENEEN MARIE HAUGEN

If you are psychospiritually prepared for the Descent, have heard the call, and have surrendered to the tug from the depths, it would be good to have at hand a variety of practices and ceremonies that accelerate your descent into Soul Canyon and enable you to drop deeper than you might have otherwise. Or, if you suddenly wake up after an abduction and have the good fortune to realize you're now in the underworld, you can choose from these same practices in order to amplify the effects. Be grateful for the abduction and make good decompositional use of it.

There are many practices and ceremonies for initiating and amplifying Dissolution. What they have in common is that they destabilize our everyday Village consciousness and assist us to die to who we thought we were. They support the unraveling of identity, the dismemberment of the familiar life, the deconstruction of the old story, and the cessation of belief in or reliance on any core story with roots in social or vocational realms. They help us courageously cross into the unknown.

In this chapter, I introduce ten practices to use when engaged in self-vanishing. Appendix 3 lists many additional Dissolution methods, including those described in my previous books.

You'll know the Dissolution phase of the Descent has sufficiently shifted your identity — that you have arrived at a deep enough layer of Soul Canyon for the next phase to commence — when your fear of the descent abates, when the uncanny sensation of falling ceases, or when you find yourself feeling wholly fortunate to have entered this other world, a world that feels bathed in moonlight even at noon.

Grief Work

We long for the encounter with Soul, but we're also terrified due to what must be risked, even abandoned. Great anxieties arise…and often great resistance.

Our anxiety is invariably accompanied by grief, even engendered by grief. We're saying goodbye to life as we've known it. This is not the "mere" loss of a romantic relationship, a job, a home, a community, or a secure or comfortable social role. It is the irreversible end of a way of being. It is forever leaving home — our Adolescent, first house of belonging.

Such an immense loss can be metabolized only through active grieving. We must allow the grief to have its way with our body and our psyche. We must take care that this grief not be impeded by our inner protectors, who might be terrified by tumultuous emotion or radical change. By consciously and ceremonially taking our leave from our prior life and by emotionally embracing the reality of what has been set in motion, our descent is accelerated and deepened.

Our grief during Dissolution, especially at this time in the world, is not simply personal. We also mourn the interconnected losses of mass extinction, habitat destruction, climate chaos, social injustice, and cultural collapse. We grieve because of the suffering of so many humans and nonhumans and earthly places. On the Descent, we become much more open and vulnerable to this transpersonal suffering because, after all, we've embarked on this journey with the intention of becoming more useful to the world. The losses and suffering we witness everywhere shatter our hearts, unravel us further, and intensify our Dissolution. On our way down, our grief and dismemberment amplify each other.

If grieving is not easy for you, seek help from those who are gifted in breaching emotional dams. You might consider, for example, the brilliant approaches to group/community grief work developed by Francis Weller and by Joanna Macy and Molly Brown.[1]

Full-Bodied Experience of All Emotions

During Dissolution, there will be — in addition to grief — fear, joy, guilt, anger, hurt, love, and other emotions. "Entertain them all!" as Rumi recommends. Once we've embarked on the Descent, the full-bodied experience of any feeling accelerates Dissolution. The more we open to our emotions, the more we open to the world.

If your emotions are not flowing fully and freely, nothing else on the Descent will flow easily for you. The capacity to allow your emotions to move through you, to allow each passion to have its way with your body and psyche, is one of the distinctive gifts of the South facet of the Self, the Wild Indigenous One, which is one reason why cultivating this facet is an essential element of Preparation (see "Cultivating the Four Facets of Wholeness," pages 52–53).

During Dissolution, then, allow ample time to sink into your feelings, like an unclad and unarmed diver in a dark, lush swamp. To amplify your full-bodied emotional experience, use a variety of methods such as inspirational and stirring poetry and music, heartfelt conversation with compassionate friends and mentors, love letters you write to the world or to God, letters to intimate others who will fully understand what you're feeling (and also to those you suspect would not understand you at all), extended time in solitude, journal writing, body-centered therapeutic practices, holotropic breathwork, dance, expressive artwork, sacred sweat ceremonies, aerobic activities, and wandering in wild places.

Surrendering to Your Deepest Longing

If you consciously choose to embark upon the Descent, it's because you've experienced a mystical yearning, a call to merge with Soul. This longing may be unlike anything you've felt before. You may be unsure what to do with it. Actually, what you may suspect (accurately) is that this longing will have its way with *you*. Your opportunity is to fling open the doors as wide as you can and let your longing be the cauldron into which you cast yourself. The Indian mystic and poet Kabir tells us that it's the intensity of the longing that does all the work.

Your longing may be so great at times it may feel like it will break you open and alter you beyond recognition. At times you may fear you won't survive. Exactly. This is indeed the goal — that your early-Adolescent Ego does not make it through intact.

During Dissolution, surrender to your longing in as many ways as you can. Give it free rein. Write letters about how you yearn for Soul. Address one such letter directly to your Soul, and others to the world, to your Self, to Mystery, to a trusted friend or mentor. Dance your longing, passionately. Draw it. Shape it in clay.

Allow it to flow through you as poetry or song. Make love offerings to your Soul, to Mystery.

Your longing is intertwined with your grief, so let both streams flow together, and wildly. A poignant sense of lack leads to deeper longing, which, eventually, leads to deeper *be*longing — a deeper belonging to the world, the intent of the journey of soul initiation.

Your not-yet-met desire to fully participate in the world will burn so strongly it will be unbearable at times. Allow it to hurt beyond what you believe you can endure. The longing and the grief, together, will break you open in just the right way.

Relinquishing Attachment to Outcomes

The Dissolution phase is not the time to decide on a social or vocational role by which you might share your gifts with the world. It's not the time to plan how you'll make a living (or a better one) or where you'll live after the journey — or with whom. This is what your inner protectors would like you to do, especially your Escapists and Conformists. This sort of planning during Dissolution might abort your Descent. But if you proactively relinquish your attachment to outcomes, you can turn a potential diversion into an intensifier of the Dissolution phase.

I suggest, then, that you abandon any attempts to find "the answer." What you seek — your Soul — can never be found by the part of you currently looking. Actually, you can never find your Soul at all. Rather, it is your Soul that finds you (your Ego) — if, that is, you become still enough. Instead of striving for an answer, allow yourself to be undone by opening wide the doors to your longing and grief.

During Dissolution, you don't want to be thinking about your future social or vocational roles because your Soul — your unique genius, destiny, or ecological niche — cannot be defined in these terms. Its substance is ecological and mystical. Your Soul can be understood by your Ego only as mythopoetic identity. During this second of the five phases of the Descent, your aim is simply to be unmade.

During Dissolution, it's true you're not yet embodying your full potential or fulfilling your destiny. Actually, most people in the Western world *never* do. You, however, by virtue of the journey you're on, have the opportunity to do so. You have the possibility of unearthing your unique eco-niche and learning to get out of its way. But that comes later. In this phase, you're learning to get comfortable living in limbo.

Romancing the World and Dwelling in the Wild

One of the most potent and indispensable Dissolution practices is romancing the world — the wild, animate world. If we understand the human Soul as our unique ecological identity, in contrast to our cultural or social identity, then in order to encounter our Souls, we must fully immerse ourselves in the more-than-human world — the world our species did not invent, the world we were born into, the world that evolved *us*.

To romance the world, hone your capacity to swoon over sunrises and sunsets, to be utterly fascinated by rabbit tracks in snow and the way lichen glows green and gold on stone after rainfall, to be endlessly curious about the variations in character, style, and embodiment of your fellow human animals, and to wonder about the dreams of hibernating bears, skin-shedding snakes, and spadefoot toads aroused by a desert rainstorm after months of underground slumber.

You have the opportunity now to cleanse your doors of perception so that once again, as in early childhood, you can experience the world as fully animated and yourself as fully participating in a world in which everything is alive and everything speaks in its own way, a world of relatives because everything is interconnected and co-arising with everything else, a world in which every thing has its own story.

For most Westerners, treating (and experiencing) the world as animate and enchanted undermines and transmutes consumer-industrial consciousness, leaving us more vulnerable to alterations of our psyche that support Dissolution. Romancing the world erodes our old worldview by way of ecstasy and rapture, by way of seductions, allurements, and fascinations.

As often as you can, then, wander alone in wild or semi-wild places — especially during dawn and dusk — and tend the mystery of your relationship with the larger psyche of Earth and cosmos. In wild precincts, the veil grows thinner between our Egos and the mysteries of the land, and between our Egos and the mysteries of our own Souls.

The breathtaking magnificence of this world assures us that we, as human creatures who have been formed by this very world, are as enchanted as anything else. To fully take in this fact can be devastating in just the right ways. Perhaps a fear of our own magnificence is, in part, why so many people unconsciously block out the grandeur of the world and why, as a culture, we desecrate it. It can be unbearable to wholly open to beauty and mystery, including our own; to do so makes it nigh impossible to live a conventional Western life. The conformist-consumer society numbs and distracts its members so effectively that most are unable to experience the world's splendor or endure its beauty.

Rilke was one of the exceptions:

If I cried out, who
in the hierarchies of angels
would hear me?

And if one of them should suddenly
take me to his heart,

I would perish in the power of his being.
For beauty is but the beginning of terror.
We can barely endure it
and are awed
when it declines to destroy us....[2]

Rilke gave himself fully to a love affair with Earth and allowed this love to arise in him and as him:

Earth, isn't this what you want? To arise in us, invisible?
Is it not your dream, to enter us so wholly
there's nothing left outside us to see?
What, if not transformation,
is your deepest purpose? Earth, my love,
I want that too. Believe me,
no more of your springtimes are needed
to win me over — even one flower
is more than enough. Before I was named
I belonged to you. I seek no other law
but yours, and know I can trust
the death you will bring....[3]

To romance the world, follow your fascinations and allurements. Let yourself be undone by the spectacle of storms, bones, birdsong and bird flight, mountain cascades, and the way the light falls upon a delicate spring bloom, a decaying fall leaf, or even a roadkill squirrel. Falling in love with the miracle of the world is a way to crack yourself open, enabling you to fall into the Soul's terrain. This also triggers grief — your heartache from the losses our world suffers at the hands of our mostly asleep species and your sorrow over how much beauty you failed to notice before.

Here are some additional romancing-the-world practices Geneen Marie Haugen and I have used:

- Experience and embrace each moment in nature as if the world is seducing you. (It is.)
- Live Geneen's question: "If Earth is romancing us for her own purposes — very much the way the nectar lust of bees serves the desires of flowers — what wild child, what honey, will we create from this joining?"
- Keep a journal of Earth seductions, including your own poetry inspired by wild creatures and places and by dreams featuring them.
- While in wild and semi-wild places, hold in your awareness your biggest questions, doubts, longings, fears, and the places your faith is most shaky.

- Introduce yourself to the Others by announcing out loud, "I am the One who…" Complete the sentence as mythopoetically as you can. For example, "I am the One who dreams of cemeteries," or "I am the One who has been called into the wild by the Rock Guardian."
- Find an alluring "sit spot" in wild or semi-wild terrain and visit it regularly, year-round. Sit quietly, with no distractions, for an hour or more each time, especially at dawn and dusk. Get to know the nonhuman residents and the place's rhythms (and vice versa); cultivate relationships with individual Others.[4]
- While romancing the world, call upon the support of your Wild Indigenous One (South) and your Dark Muse-Beloved (West), and use all four of your windows of knowing (see "The Four Windows of Knowing," pages 48–51).
- During any of these practices, shift and deepen your consciousness with techniques such as rhythm (using a drum or shaker, for example), breathwork, chanting, or "smudging" yourself with burning sage, cedar, or sweetgrass.
- Right before these practices, find a natural border (a creek, a forest edge, a space between two rocks or trees, a road or trail, or even a stick on the ground) and make a conscious threshold crossing there. Before crossing, linger at the threshold; clarify your intentions for the practice. Then cross. After completing the practice, recross the threshold in the other direction.

The Most Difficult Letter

Who are the most important people in your life, past and present, but especially over the last several years? These may include those now dead or even those not yet born. You've probably told some of them about what you're going through, this Descent to Soul. Perhaps with others, you've mentioned nothing — or said something misleading, soft-pedaled, or whitewashed.

Of all these people, which ones would it be emotionally challenging for you to tell the full, uncensored truth? Maybe you'd be afraid of hurting them, worrying them, or disappointing them. Maybe you fear they'd criticize or ridicule you. Perhaps you wonder — if you told them what this is truly about for you — whether you'd be able to endure the immensity of feeling you might let loose (both theirs and yours).

After making a list of such people, choose just one, the one who'd be the single-most-challenging person to tell the full truth. Now write that person a letter and tell them. Don't hold back. Tell everything. Provide the full context. As you do, let all arising emotions and feelings happen to you. Take your time.

After completing the letter, I encourage you to read it aloud to someone you trust, someone who will be able to hear it and get it. This step is very important (take my word for it; you'll see why). Consider also the possibility of reading it to the very person to whom it is addressed.

The One-Way Portal Ceremony

Soul speaks to us by way of feeling-infused symbol and image, which is also how we, in turn, communicate with Soul when we enact ceremony. During the Descent, both listening and speaking in Soul's language provide great benefits. Say, for example, you want to let your Soul know you've made a commitment to encounter her mysteries. You can design and enact a ceremony to tell her.

A one-way portal ceremony is one way to tell your Soul that you've left behind, irreversibly, the identity and life story you've been living and that you are striding toward the great unknown of your destiny. It's not that your Soul doesn't know you're on a downward trajectory toward her; your ceremony isn't meant as a news flash. Rather, it's intended to deepen your commitment and to accelerate your rate of descent.

When we say yes with ceremony, our whole being co-responds with an even greater yes. We might generate a momentum impossible to stop — or even slow down. This is both the power and the danger of ceremony. *Caveat emptor.*

A one-way portal ceremony can be designed ahead of time or be spontaneous.

On my first vision fast, I performed a spontaneous portal ceremony, a crossing of an irreversible threshold. On the second day, I was walking back to my high-altitude, early-fall mountain camp after a short wander higher up in the alpine basin. I ambled down a sunlit slope through lush wildflowers enfolded by subalpine conifers. On my right, a stone's throw away, a sheer granite wall several hundred feet high formed the southern boundary of the basin. Between me and the wall ran a snowbank ten to fifteen feet high and perhaps six feet wide at its base, paralleling the granite scarp for a half mile. A shadowy gap a few feet wide separated the snow wall from the granite. As I strode down the slope, immersed in troubled feelings as well as buoyant wonder about the world and my place in it, I found myself giving serious consideration to walking away from the brief but flourishing university career I had spent most of my early adulthood preparing for. I had no clue what I would do instead, but I had grave doubts as to whether the life of a research psychologist and college professor was something I could call my own.

As I walked along, something caught my attention: a tunnel running through the snow wall, an oval portal five feet high and three feet wide. I stopped, on the edge of sun, bewildered, as if this were the entrance to an unknown and unsuspected dimension of the cosmos, some kind of existential black hole from which return was impossible. This snowdoor felt like the threshold between everything I had known and whatever lay ahead. I had a choice either to enter the unknown or to say, "No,

I'm not ready to leave my promising life and career. Maybe some other time." I knew, too, that if I walked through, it would also physically be a one-way portal. My only option would be to continue toward camp by way of the narrow sloping hallway, between rock and hard snow, with only the hope it would not dead end.

I stood, transfixed. I let my awareness settle as the consequences of crossing became clear...and the consequences of not. It seemed everything in my life till that moment — every road taken, every ally with whom I'd been blessed — had ushered me to this choice point, where all my life possibilities neatly divided themselves into two sets. Which would I choose? The safer, known, and predictable? Or the undetermined, mysterious, and unguaranteed possibilities that began on the other side of this snow portal?

I looked away from the shadowed wall and into the immense, sun-drenched alpine basin. Glistening peaks soared above. A yawning river gorge fell away into hidden depths. Addressing the assembled massifs, I spoke aloud my gratitude for the people and opportunities that had ushered me to this point in my life and to all the indeterminate future possibilities I might realize if I were to continue the story I had been living. I bowed deeply to that life and those possibilities. I turned back toward the portal. I said yes out loud to the shadowed unknown and walked through.

If you perform a one-way portal ceremony, you, too, will walk through. You can design a ceremony in advance, or yours might be as spontaneous as mine: a threshold suddenly materializing, a creek crossing, a hidden passageway in an exotic city, a one-way plane ticket to an unknown country.

Unplugging from the Matrix and Entering the Wild

Ideally, during the Dissolution and Soul Encounter phases of a Descent, you withdraw entirely from the Village and from your everyday social life. You are searching for something that can't be found in the Village nor in your Village consciousness. Those are not the native habitats of the mystery you seek. What you hope (and fear) to encounter lives in wild places, places where the rules, norms, and ontological assumptions of everyday life don't apply.

A wild place can be a wilderness precinct seldom visited by humans, or it might be a remote hermitage. Maybe you'll wander, like Yeats, through "hollow lands and hilly lands," rarely encountering other humans — or only exotic ones who do not abide within conventional consciousness. But a wild place could also be a social, cultural, or spiritual setting unfamiliar to you and that does not support your former identity. The unraveling of that identity — your goal during Dissolution — is not likely to happen if you spend much of your time in settings that switch on, require, or reinforce it.

During Dissolution and Soul Encounter, maybe you'll be blessed with a human guide who accompanies you or with whom you rendezvous from time to time, or maybe you'll be in a group of Wanderers who support each other with or without a guide.

In the contemporary world, most people would find it difficult or impossible to withdraw entirely from everyday social and vocational life for extended periods, especially if they live with children or others who depend on them or if they have a nine-to-five requiring conventional interactions. If you are at the start of the Dissolution phase of a Descent and are unable to withdraw from everyday life, it might be best to postpone your Descent — if you can. Or perhaps you can arrange for a month or longer retreat. Or it might be possible — although tricky — for you to remain in the Village but not of it, utilizing as many Dissolution practices and ceremonies as you can and minimizing your conventional interactions. I've witnessed Wanderers who, with careful planning, managed to function at the margins of the Village while essentially disappearing socially. As noted earlier, Carl Jung navigated his Descent while living with his wife and children and seeing his patients five days a week.

However you do it, you'll want, during Dissolution, to unplug from "the Matrix" of conformist-consumer culture — its everyday activities, priorities, and conversations. As you begin, in this way, to weave a cocoon for yourself, it might at first feel something like a tentative and exploratory art project, but then one day, if you're fortunate, the floor drops out, everything shifts, and you find yourself completely enclosed within your cocoon, your former story already dissolving. Suddenly your Descent is very real and it's too late to change your mind.

Whatever form your Dissolution takes, the objective is to release your attachment to the social-cultural world as you have known it. Live in ways and places that afford minimal support for your old identity. Offer yourself to a mysterious journey of unknown duration, character, and significance — an amped-up version of what life truly is anyway. You might create and enact a ceremony in which you ask to be worked on, to be shaped into an agent for Mystery, for your Soul, for the Soul of the world. Such a ceremony might be of the irreversible threshold type.

Undoubtedly there will be demons awaiting you, perhaps taking the form of grief over the loss of a predictable life trajectory or fear of suffering, social isolation, poverty, madness, or death. There *will* be tests and trials. The field in which you're at play is much bigger than the human world, the possibilities much grander and more potent than anything you alone could summon, and certainly more than you could predict or control.

And now, truth in advertising and fair warning from a psychologist gone wild: At most times in life, a meaningful and wholehearted experience of social belonging is the single most essential factor in attaining and maintaining psychological health. This is especially true through the first three stages of life (childhood and early Adolescence). What I am encouraging you to do with this practice of unplugging from the Matrix is to undermine and vacate that very sense of belonging. This is risky. You wouldn't want to do this unless you're in the Dissolution phase of a Descent and are thoroughly prepared for it. If you unplug from the Matrix and your psyche becomes unbearably or suicidally wobbly, you must reverse course, reestablish your social network, and then cultivate your fourfold Self and tend to your Self-healing — in essence, you must return to the Preparation phase. Do not continue with Dissolution practices until your Ego is solidly anchored in the more-than-human world and you have reliable access to your four facets of wholeness.

The Mandorla: Amplifying the Tension between Opposites

Most people know what a mandala is: an image or symbol of wholeness, usually circular and quadrated. A mandorla is something else. It's the almond shape formed at the center of two partly overlapping circles — *mandorla* being Italian for "almond." As used in this book, a Mandorla symbolizes the interplay of opposites, the inherent tension between them, the interaction and interdependence between apparent contraries.[5]

This is the way it is with us humans: Our psyches contain — are even made up of — innumerable sets of opposites, like divine/human, introvert/extrovert, feminine/masculine, good/evil. Most of the time, we experience ourselves as if we reside exclusively within one pole or the other: I am an introvert, not an extrovert; masculine, not feminine; this, not that. But occasionally we find ourselves unnervingly pulled by or even occupying both poles: I am this but somehow, inexplicably, also that — *and I cannot be both.* I know who I am and I don't have a clue who I am. At such times, the tension between opposites destabilizes us and renders us vulnerable to an identity collapse. At the first sign of such tension, most people in conventional mainstream consciousness do whatever they can to escape it by fleeing to one pole or the other.

This is not what we do if and when we're on a Descent to Soul.

During Dissolution, when we detect a set of opposites agitating within our psyches, we leap into the fray. This is a first-class opportunity for the destabilization of our familiar story. Our goal in this phase is not a resolution or a compromise between opposites, but rather...the opposite: the amplification of the tension so that it can do its full work on us.

There are many oppositional pairs you might discover within you, and any given pair might feel like a couple of madmen with crowbars trying to break you in half. Your specific intrapsychic opposition might be one of the more universal ones noted above. Or it might be something more particular to you, such as meaning/meaninglessness ("each thing and event in the world is utterly infused with meaning" versus "it's a random universe of colliding molecules with no significance whatsoever"); rule-following/authenticity; being right/being compassionate; self-serving/whole-serving; control/surrender; hope/hopelessness.

If, during Dissolution, you find an active pair of opposites within, you have the opportunity to crack yourself open and quicken your plummet toward Soul using the Mandorla Practice.

Here's how it works: Go to a place where other humans will not disturb you. Ideally this would be outside in a place of relative wildness, but it could, if necessary, be in your backyard or even in your house. Imagine two overlapping circles on the ground, each eight feet or so in diameter. Make the circles visible if you want — perhaps with a temporary placement of stones, pinecones, or tree bark — but seeing these circles with your mind's eye is all that's really necessary. Let the place know why you've come and ask for permission to be there. If you receive a "no," go elsewhere. If you feel welcomed, express your gratitude and make an offering — a blessing, some berries or herbs you've brought with you, a poem, a handful of your breath.

Stand in one circle, face the other circle, and embody as fully as you can one pole of your opposition. Say, for example, your opposites are joy/accomplishment — exultation in the moment versus dedication to purpose. You feel a great pull toward each, but you can't imagine having both at the same time. (This experienced incompatibility is an essential dimension of a Mandorla. If you can imagine having both, it's not a true opposition for you, though it may be for others.)

Let's say you begin with accomplishment (or ambition). As fully and outrageously as you can, embody the value and benefit of achievement. Sing its praises. Tell Joy, in the other circle, that you have a fervent and undeniable life purpose that is invaluable to the world — even if you don't yet have a clue what it is. Express this with your body, using gestures or postures, as well as with your voice. It's essential you feel the truth of it — deeply and vibrantly. Let yourself be surprised by what you say, how you feel, and how your body expresses it. (If it's a real opposition you're experiencing — and not just two poles on a continuum — you can be sure there are forces within you, beyond your conscious mind, that are fueling the tension. Your goal in this practice is to hand the "microphone" over to those forces.) You might find yourself telling Joy, for example, that you're willing to never experience her again if that's the price you must pay; that your true fulfillment lies in delivering the sacred goods that only you carry. Strive to be utterly convincing, to feel the absolute rightness and necessity of accomplishment. Amp it up.

When you feel you've compellingly embodied the first pole, step into the center of the other circle — in this example, Joy. Move, dance, and speak effusively about how joy is the most important quality in your life — or *anyone's* life, for that matter — that whatever brings you bliss or ecstasy is the way to be. Life, you might find yourself shouting, is about being, not doing. Show Accomplishment how empty he is in comparison, that life is not about achievement and progress but about being fully present to the every-moment miracles. Pull out all the stops, not to convince Accomplishment of anything but to demonstrate the utterly undeniable ontological superiority of a life of joy.

In this way, continue moving back and forth between the two circles. Your goal is to increase the experienced tension until it becomes unbearable. When, for instance, you feel the allure of Joy much stronger and more compellingly than the pull of Accomplishment, go back to Accomplishment and embody him even more vigorously — until Accomplishment again feels bigger than Joy, and then go back to Joy, and so on.

While in the midst of a Mandorla Practice, you might, from time to time, choose to stand or sit in the Mandorla itself, in that almond-shaped space where the two circles overlap. Do this when the tension feels exquisite. While in the Mandorla, simply feel the formidable pull from both directions and let the tension have its way with you. Be curious and attentive to what happens in your psyche and to alterations in energy or sensations taking place in your body. *Your goal in the Mandorla is not to learn something, but to be changed.*

A Mandorla Practice with any particular opposition is rarely a one-time event. You'll want to return to the practice at least a few times over a period of days or weeks. You know a Mandorla Practice is working when your former identity is crumbling or when you have the bodily sensation of falling.

It's essential to understand that the Mandorla Practice is not intended as a way to choose between two incompatible behavioral choices, such as between two job offers, two possible romantic relationships, two potential places to live, two vacations. The Mandorla Practice is not for helping you make a choice. It's not about finding compromises or solutions to situational dilemmas or quandaries. The goal is the opposite of a solution: You hope to trigger a *dis*solution of your identity, courtesy of intrapsychic tension.

The Obstacle Threshold: The Wall That's Actually a Door

From our very earliest days, our subpersonalities — our inner protectors — have the job of keeping us as safe as possible and minimizing our exposure to emotional or physical harm. For the most part, they do an admirable job. One of their strategies is to steer us away from personal development opportunities they deem too risky, that might shake up and overturn our comfortable routines and relationships. They believe this is the case for many *spiritual* development opportunities, especially those that are Soul-related. So when a door swings open inviting us toward Soul, our subpersonalities want us to see not an entryway but a brick wall or a dead end.

During Dissolution, we might run into lots of brick walls. When we do, we'll be tempted to give up and go home, or we'll try to climb over or find a way around or beneath. These Walls are various life circumstances that seem to impede our progress and keep us from our destiny. But some are actually doorways to Soul.

Your Wall might be, for example, the many people who want something from you. You've been doing your best to avoid them because otherwise, you imagine, you'd have no time for yourself. But perhaps if you selectively open the door to some, allow them into your world, you'd be off on adventures impossible to predict, experiences that could change everything.

How do you determine which apparent Walls in your life are actually Portals to Soul? Perhaps you just have an intuition that tells you so.

Or you could use this exercise: Gather drawing paper and an assortment of pastels, crayons, or colored pencils. Then use your favorite process for inducing a state of deep relaxation. Engaging your deep imagination, enter a temple, cave, or sacred grove, carrying with you an offering for Soul in the form of a question, something like: "On the Descent to Soul, what will I encounter that will at first seem like an obstacle but is something I must engage and allow myself to be changed by?" Slowly repeat your own version of this question several times within yourself, offering it as a gift to an unseen presence. Be attentive for a response, which might arrive in the form of an image, shape, or color, or in the form of an emotion, an intuition, a memory, a bodily sensation, a sound, or a thought-out-of-nowhere. You're not seeking an answer so much as a response from your depths, something that moves or disturbs you. It would be better, in fact, if the response does *not* feel like an answer. Let go of any solutions your strategic mind might construct and, instead, continue to simply offer the gift of your question, waiting until you're surprised by a response. Then represent that response with a drawing. Don't interpret it; just stay as true as you can to the image and the inner response that is its source. When the drawing is complete, write about the image, not explaining it but describing what it feels like, what it reminds you of, what emotions or memories it stirs. Let yourself be surprised where this leads you.

Place your drawing somewhere you'll see it often. Let this Obstacle image work on you for a few days. Notice what it evokes in you. Observe how it lives in your body. Move it or dance it. Write more about it. Continue until you become clear about the life circumstance that this image represents — something you had thought was a Wall but might turn out to be a Doorway.

Then, the most important step: *Walk through the Door.*

For one woman, a cultural change agent but a rather shy one, her Wall was represented by an image of a microphone. Her work had mostly involved helping movement leaders network with one another, but she avoided the spotlight herself. Through this deep-imagination and drawing process, she came to realize that entering the spotlight — grabbing the mic — might undermine much of what she had thought was true about herself, and that it might be time to do just that.

A not-uncommon "obstacle" is grief. One woman's drawing was "deep black emptiness." As she sat with the image, she realized she had been concealing from herself immense grief over the dire circumstances of the natural world and a great fear and bewilderment about where humanity was collectively heading. She began a regular practice of lamenting. Grief opened her door to Soul.

If it's not obvious to you how your Obstacle image — your Wall — might be a Portal, you might enact what I call an Obstacle Walk, a solo outing of an hour or more, perhaps a full day, in a wild or semi-wild place. Bring your Obstacle image with you — at least in your imagination and as it lives in your body. Move onto the land with the felt-sense that everything is alive and everything is aware of you — not just the birds and other creatures, but each stone, stream, flower, cloud, and gust of wind. Be aware you move amidst immeasurable mysteries of both nature and psyche — and that you are one as well. Without using your strategic mind, allow yourself to be found by a place that either feels in some way like your Obstacle (a place that evokes a similar feeling, whether or not it looks like your drawn image) or is in fact a physical obstacle to the direction you're heading. Let yourself be surprised. When you find yourself at an obstacle of either kind, tell it why you've come. Explore it. Speak to it. Listen to it. Allow yourself to be in relationship, simultaneously, with both the image you drew and this place on the land. When the moment feels right, use your imagination to fill this place with a question — "How does my Obstacle want to change me?" or "What does my Obstacle make possible for me?" Do not seek — or accept — an answer. Instead continue filling the space with your question until you receive a *response* — until, that is, you are moved by something that occurs in your inner world or in the world around you. Record this in your journal.

On your Obstacle Walk, it might seem as if you have happened onto an unseen trapdoor and suddenly you're in free fall.

The founder of a nonprofit that serves inner-city youth drew an Obstacle image of a hydra — a many-headed snake — with lightning bolts emanating from each head. This man went out onto the land and walked with this unsettling image. After a while, he came upon a stick in the same shape as the hydra. He stopped. Sat. He gazed carefully at the stick. He "heard" a female voice say, "Blood flows through this space." He asked who she was. A Kali-like presence responded, "You must be devoted to me, first and foremost. Learn from me. I require fierce devotion. There is beauty in death and destruction. You are *not* following your heart. You are part of the system you condemn. You must devote yourself to *me*. I am the Queen. You must come to know a deeper, eternal love." This man had never devoted himself to anything or anyone in the way the Queen demanded. But he had no doubt her charismatic authority warranted his reverence. He told her that everything he did from that moment would be enacted in service to her. She gave him a long list of the attachments he was to release; these included his job and his beliefs about Western culture. He did — through a ceremony in which he felt and imagined his identity as no longer anchored to most elements of his current life. Through this release and surrender, a process of self-emptying, he encountered his Obstacle and moved through it as a Doorway. Several days later, he received a life-shifting revelation during a four-day vision fast in the depths of a redrock canyon on the Colorado Plateau.

Chapter Five

Jung's Preparation and Dissolution

The years when I was pursuing my inner images were the most important in my life — in them everything essential was decided. It all began then; the later details are only supplements and clarifications of the material that burst forth from the unconscious, and at first swamped me. It was the *prima materia* for a lifetime's work.

— C. G. JUNG

Carl Jung's Descent to Soul — which he called his "confrontation with the unconscious" — is perhaps the most thoroughly documented and carefully examined underworld experience in the modern Western era. But how well it is understood, even by Jungians and other depth psychologists, is another question.

Jung's engagement with the depths of his psyche, from age thirty-eight to forty-two, as recorded in his *Red Book*, was not a "nervous breakdown." Nor was it a healing experience. It was not some form of self-administered psychotherapy, nor a generic submersion into the personal or collective unconscious. It was not shamanism or a dark night of the soul. It was not the creation of a new psychology (whether or not it was later used that way by Jung or others), nor was it the conscious creation of a new religion. It was something else entirely. It was, to be specific, a Descent to Soul — but mostly only its first two phases: Preparation (primarily a discovery, recovery, and cultivation of his least-developed facets of wholeness) and Dissolution (a thoroughgoing process of destabilizing and dismembering of his Ego). Jung's first glimpse of his mythopoetic identity (Soul Encounter, the third phase) did not take place until very near the end of the experiences recorded in the *Red Book*, more than two years into his journey.

Even while it was happening, Jung knew he was engaged in a quest that was not definable by the medicine or psychology of his time. His own understanding was that he was searching for what he called his "personal myth" — close enough to what

I mean by the journey of soul initiation. And his personal myth is what he found, and this encounter is what transformed him into someone capable of creating a new psychology.

Jung's confrontation with his unconscious is also a great example of an initiatory experience that was neither a rite of passage as van Gennep described them nor a hero's journey in Joseph Campbell's rendering — these twentieth-century templates being the two best known and most widely used for understanding transformative human odysseys (see appendix 2).

Jung appears to have entered the Cocoon stage in 1909, when he was thirty-four.[1] This was when his relationship with Freud began to rupture. His Descent began no later than October 1913, with his first soul encounter taking place in January 1916. This chapter explores the Preparation and Dissolution phases of Jung's first Descent; chapter 7 explores his soul encounters.

What I've found most astonishing about Jung's Descent is that he was able to guide himself without a map of the terrain and with relatively few psychospiritual tools for navigation, that he did so without support from anyone who knew the territory (beyond the *dramatis personae* accessed through his deep imagination), that he didn't go permanently mad, and that he survived and benefited despite being quite unprepared at its start.

Jung was abducted into the underworld without advance notice. Consequently, he had to do much of what normally would be phase-one Preparation during the second phase, Dissolution. In the contemporary world, this better-late-than-never preparation is the more common pattern for the relative few who reach the Cocoon and begin their Descent. There is much we can learn from Jung's courageous, trailblazing experience.

In his memoir/biography, *Memories, Dreams, Reflections* (first published in 1961, the year of his death), Jung dedicated a lengthy chapter to his confrontation with the unconscious — primarily a long series of deep-imagination journeys he called "fantasies." He carefully recorded these journeys in his personal journals (his six "black books"), which he later transcribed, illustrated, lightly edited, and extensively annotated in his folio-sized *Red Book*. Jung began work on the *Red Book* in 1915 and continued for sixteen years, adding long commentaries to his accounts of his deep-imagination journeys from those seminal years of 1913 to 1916. Yet he never chose to publish it — apparently because it was not a scholarly work, and it had always been paramount to Jung that he appear to the world as a credible and respected scientist (even if he himself had lost his belief in science). Decades later, Sonu Shamdasani, a historian of psychology, persuaded Jung's heirs to make this invaluable work public. Under Shamdasani's editorial direction, it was published in 2009, almost fifty years after Jung's death and exactly one hundred years after he entered the Cocoon.

Confirmation

Near the start of the *Red Book,* Jung confesses something that is as clear an expression as you could want of the experience of Confirmation, the passage from the Oasis to the Cocoon:

> I had achieved everything that I had wished for myself. I had achieved honor, power, wealth, knowledge, and every human happiness. Then my desire for the increase of these trappings ceased, the desire ebbed from me and horror came over me....I felt the spirit of the depths, but I did not understand him. Yet he drove me on with unbearable inner longing.[2]

This is exactly how and when the Oasis ends: Our early-Adolescent wish list has been accomplished. Our first house of belonging is complete. Suddenly, we're psychospiritually homeless and headed for the depths. The inscrutable way ahead is both terrifying and enthralling. Danger and allurement. The crisis and the call. Thus begins the stage of the Cocoon — and soon enough thereafter the first Descent.[3]

Jung was emphatic that his real work — all he accomplished in the second half of his life — was rooted entirely in the experiences recorded in the *Red Book.* These experiences comprised, in addition to his Descent to Soul, the visionary source of his groundbreaking psychology, what came to be called analytical psychology or, more casually, Jungian psychology, as well as its later offshoots in depth psychology, anthropology, mythology, film, and literature. In other words, these are the experiences through which Jung became Jung, when his Ego began its Soul-infused transformation, through which he came to understand his calling, his unique place in the world.

The Three Worlds

Upon first reading the *Red Book,* I was startled to discover just how well Jung's experience resonated with the three-worlds model I had then been developing for many years. In particular, Jung's experiences closely match the ways in which I understand the underworld as well as the journey to those depths for the initiation of the Ego into the world of — and in service to — the Soul. Reciprocally, I found that my model of the human psyche helped me understand many features of Jung's experiences I might have found baffling otherwise.

In the *Red Book,* Jung uses different terms than I for the three worlds, but he appears to be making the same distinctions. My *middleworld* (the Village world of everyday domestic life, business, and politics) corresponds to Jung's "the spirit of this time." The way I use the words *underworld* and *Soul* parallels Jung's "spirit of the depths." And what I refer to as the *upperworld* — and to Spirit, in particular — Jung encompasses with a cluster of terms, including "God," "the image of God," and "the supreme meaning."[4]

The following excerpt from the first few pages of the *Red Book* describes the dissolution of Jung's worldview and self-concept as he struggles to grasp what is happening to him, the shift of his center of gravity from the middleworld to the underworld. Here you can see the resonance between what Jung calls "the spirit of the depths" and what I refer to as the underworld and, in particular, the Soul.

> I have learned that in addition to the spirit of this time there is still another spirit at work, namely that which rules the depths of everything contemporary. The spirit of this time would like to hear about use and value. I also thought this way, and my humanity still thinks this way. But that other spirit forces me nevertheless to speak, beyond justification, use, and meaning. Filled with human pride and blinded by the presumptuous spirit of the times, I long sought to hold that other spirit away from me. But I did not consider that the spirit of the depths from time immemorial and for all the future possesses a greater power than the spirit of this time, who changes with the generations. The spirit of the depths has subjugated all pride and arrogance to the power of judgment. He took away my belief in science, he robbed me of the joy of explaining and ordering things, and he let devotion to the ideals of this time die out in me. He forced me down to the last and simplest things.
>
> The spirit of the depths took my understanding and all my knowledge and placed them at the service of the inexplicable and the paradoxical.[5]

The fierceness and fervor of this passage is characteristic of the experience of the Descent, especially early on when the Ego is being stripped of its former "pride and arrogance," two traits common in psychological Adolescence, especially among white men in the contemporary West. Here Jung is experiencing the erosion of identity and the radical simplification that arrives with the passage of Confirmation and especially with the commencement of the Dissolution phase of the Descent. We could say that this is the day (November 13, 1913) the younger Jung, as true-believer scientist, died, the day that Jung forever left behind the home of his early-Adolescent story.

Jung's first Descent to Soul was not intentional. He was abducted while at home with his wife and children in the village of Küsnacht, Switzerland. A consciously chosen Descent must have been an extremely rare event in mainstream early-twentieth-century Western culture. It is seldom intended or desired even today. This fact renders all the more remarkable Jung's courage to submit to such a harrowing experience as well as his persistence and diligence.

The Crisis

What crisis opened the trapdoor beneath Jung's everyday life and "forced [him] down to the last and simplest things"? There seems to be more than one, but the most central was his break with Freud, his mentor and friend of several years. The fault line of this rupture first became visible — at least to Jung — in 1909, when he was thirty-four, following a disagreement about the reality of parapsychological phenomena. Jung at times experienced synchronicities, automatic writing, poltergeists, and other "occult phenomena." Freud, on the other hand, was a complete skeptic about such things, a scientific materialist, and dismissed the paranormal as nonsense. Jung, by standing up for his beliefs despite the enormous social and vocational costs, revealed and embodied the success he had achieved with the nature-oriented task of the early-Adolescent Oasis stage (the cultivation of social authenticity). In so doing, he placed himself directly above that trapdoor to the depths.

For Jung, the breakdown of this relationship was a great loss, an enormously destabilizing event. Freud, after all, had named Jung his successor, his "crown prince," a great honor, but a position in which Jung gradually lost interest as the differences between them became increasingly apparent. By late 1909, Jung and Freud's falling out was in full evidence while they returned, by ship, from their transatlantic journey to the United States. It became clear to Jung that he could no longer accept Freud's claim of authority over him nor some of the most central tenets of Freud's theories, including his perspectives on sex and dreams.

The crisis gave rise to an unbearable tension within Jung's psyche. We might consider this a Mandorla — his rejection of Freud's authority being in direct opposition to his continued projection of paternal power onto Freud:

> At the time Freud had lost much of his authority for me. But he still meant to me a superior personality, upon whom I projected the father.
>
> I had, as far as possible, cast aside my own judgments and repressed my criticisms. That was the prerequisite for collaborating with him. I had told myself, "Freud is far wiser and more experienced than you. For the present you must simply listen to what he says and learn from him." And then, to my surprise, I found myself dreaming of him as a peevish official of the Imperial Austrian monarchy, as a defunct and still walking ghost of a customs inspector....I wanted at all costs to be able to work with Freud, and, in a frankly egotistic manner, to partake of his wealth of experience. His friendship meant a great deal to me.[6]

It's easy to imagine how this opposition shredded the very fabric of Jung's first-adulthood (early-Adolescent) identity. Jung's "egotistic" and ambitious Conformist subpersonality insisted on deferring to and venerating "the master," while his

DreamMaker (a close cousin of the Muse and the Soul), and perhaps his Rebel as well, impelled him in the opposite direction. This inner discord eroded Jung's psyche to its foundations and opened the way to his first Descent. (Intrapsychic oppositions and the effects on the Ego of their collision-in-consciousness are parts of a process Jung later named "the transcendent function," a core element of his psychology.)

In order to maintain any semblance of authenticity and personal integrity, Jung found himself in the unenviable position of having to turn his back on the story he had been living — the heir apparent of the new empire of psychoanalysis — the story that had defined and given promise to his life. This was the moment in which Jung, as Wanderer, left the "home" of his first adulthood, betrayed his mentor, and struck out on his own.

Jung's pivotal move of self-declaration was in 1912 when he published his views on incest, which differed decisively from Freud's. But before he did, he wavered on the edge of the cliff:

> For two months I was unable to touch my pen, so tormented was I by the conflict. Should I keep my thoughts to myself, or should I risk the loss of so important a friendship? At last I resolved to go ahead with the writing — and it did indeed cost me Freud's friendship.
>
> After the break with Freud, all my friends and acquaintances dropped away. My book [*Symbols of Transformation*] was declared to be rubbish; I was a mystic and that settled the matter....I had known that everything was at stake, and that I had to take a stand for my convictions. I realized that the chapter, "The Sacrifice," meant my own sacrifice. Having reached this insight, I was able to write again, even though I knew my ideas would go uncomprehended.[7]

Jung could write again, but the sacrifice of his old life had been accomplished and his Dissolution had begun:

> After the parting of the ways with Freud, a period of inner uncertainty began for me. It would be no exaggeration to call it a state of disorientation. I felt totally suspended in midair, for I had not yet found my own footing.[8]

This is the experience of someone tumbling over the edge into the abyss of Soul Canyon, someone whose Adolescent life story and identity are dissolving.

Dante begins his epic poem, *The Divine Comedy*, with the line, "In the middle of our journey of life, I came to myself within a dark wood where the straight way was lost" — a compelling image for the experience of Dissolution. At age thirty-seven, Jung realized that he, too, was lost in the middle of his life, that he knew nothing about his true identity, his "personal myth," and that everything depended upon finding it:

> About this time [1912] I experienced a moment of unusual clarity in which
> I looked back over the way I had traveled so far.... And promptly the ques-
> tion arose of what, after all, I had accomplished. I had explained the myths
> of peoples of the past; I had written a book about the hero, the myth in
> which man has always lived. But in what myth does man live nowadays. In
> the Christian myth, the answer might be. "Do *you* live in it?" I asked myself.
> To be honest, the answer was no. "For me, it is not what I live by." "Then do
> we no longer have a myth?" "No, evidently we no longer have a myth." "But
> then what is your myth — the myth in which you do live?" At this point
> the dialogue with myself became uncomfortable, and I stopped thinking. I
> had reached a dead end.[9]

A dead end — this is the way Dissolution at first feels. An existential crisis. The
great, open thoroughfare of preinitiated life, of "the first adulthood" — the road you
felt would go on forever, opening endlessly into ever-greater and more-inspiring vis-
tas, ever-greater opportunities for personal triumph — turns out to be a cul-de-sac.
The old, familiar story is over. You realize, like Jung, that the story you've been living
is not yours — and that this is not another segue from one social-vocational scene
to the next, not another early-Adolescent molting. You no longer have a myth to live
by. Now your only option is to search for your *real* myth.

On October 27, 1913, Jung wrote to Freud, formally and definitively breaking off
relations and resigning as editor of the psychoanalytic journal. Seventeen days later,
on November 13, Jung was in free fall.

Although Jung's break with Freud was the primary precipitant of the ego-destabilization necessary for his Descent, there was an additional crisis at that time.

Toni Wolff was twenty-two and Jung thirty-four when she became his patient
in 1911. As an element of her treatment, Jung invited her to be his research assistant — to provide her "a new goal to reawaken her interest in life."[10] By the time his
Descent began, in 1913, Jung felt that Toni was the only person able to "accompany
him intrepidly on his Nekyia to the underworld," as Jung's colleague and biogra-
pher, Barbara Hannah, put it.[11] Toni became his closest companion — and his outer
anima, the feminine dimension of his psyche. This intimate relationship was naturally a crisis for Jung's marriage to Emma.[12] Both relationships were essential to
Jung — his marriage (and family) for its normalcy, its "joyful reality," and the way
it grounded him, and his relationship with Toni to help him bridge between his Ego
and his unconscious. Hannah comments that Jung had "to deal with perhaps the
most difficult problem a married man has ever to face: the fact that he can love his
wife and another woman simultaneously."

Although the three of them eventually settled on an arrangement that worked well enough, Jung's romance with Toni added more inner and outer chaos to what he was already navigating with Freud.

In addition to amplifying the ego-destabilization that is the core of Dissolution, Jung's relationship with Toni became one of the most significant factors enabling him to survive and benefit from his Descent. Although Toni was not his guide — she, after all, had not yet made the journey herself — she was his invaluable companion.

The Call

The call is always both an allurement and an additional destabilizing event. During the period in which his relationship with Freud was unraveling and his affair with Toni commencing, Jung felt powerfully pulled toward some inchoate mystery. One facet of this enigma arrived as a dream in 1911: In a modern European city at noon, in the midst of a streaming crowd, he is astonished to see a twelfth-century knight in full armor walking toward him. No one other than Jung seems to notice the knight, who is "full of life and completely real." Following the dream, Jung "did a great deal of thinking about the mysterious figure of the knight,"[13] which triggered a memory of his early fascination with the myths and legends of King Arthur's court and the quest for the Holy Grail, an enchantment that first gripped Jung's conscious mind at the time in life when the Cocoon, in ideal cultural circumstances, would have begun:

> The stories of the Grail had been of the greatest importance to me ever since I read them, at the age of fifteen, for the first time. I had an inkling that a great secret still lay behind those stories. Therefore it seemed quite natural that the dream should conjure up the world of the Knights of the Grail and their quest — for that was, in the deepest sense, my own world, which had scarcely anything to do with Freud's. My whole being was seeking for something still unknown which might confer meaning upon the banality of life.[14]

Jung's knight dream was a call from his depths. In its aftermath, he knew his life, "in the deepest sense," was now all about a quest for something numinous, something secret, "something still unknown which might confer meaning upon the banality of life." Exactly.[15]

The call from Soul is usually transpersonal (prosocial and/or environmentally enhancing) as well as personal. Concurrent with his dream of the knight and its association with the Grail myth, Jung was longing to better understand the mysteries of the human psyche in order to better serve his patients and to contribute to the field of psychology. This call was especially strong following his break with Freud, so strong he was willing to risk everything: "I was prepared to sacrifice a good deal in order to obtain the answer."[16]

The Arrival of the Guide to Soul

One or more guides to Soul appear during the Dissolution phase — and, with good fortune, we notice. One of Jung's first guides arrived in a dream, in the form of a white dove:

> [A]round Christmas of 1912, I had a dream. In the dream I found myself in a magnificent Italian loggia with pillars, a marble floor, and a marble balustrade. I was sitting on a gold Renaissance chair; in front of me was a table of rare beauty. It was made of green stone, like emerald. There I sat, looking out into the distance, for the loggia was set high up on the tower of a castle. My children were sitting at the table too.
>
> Suddenly a white bird descended, a small seagull or a dove. Gracefully, it came to rest on the table, and I signed to the children to be still so that they would not frighten away the pretty white bird. Immediately, the dove was transformed into a little girl, about eight years old, with golden blond hair. She ran off with the children and played with them among the colonnades of the castle.
>
> I remained lost in thought, musing about what I had just experienced. The little girl returned and tenderly placed her arms around my neck. Then she suddenly vanished; the dove was back and spoke slowly in a human voice. "Only in the first hours of the night can I transform myself into a human being, while the male dove is busy with the twelve dead." Then she flew off into the blue air, and I awoke.[17]

The White Dove / Little Girl, like a guide, nudged him toward Soul — by evoking the mysteries of shape-shifting and of death and through the effect of her embodied presence on his consciousness. Jung's propensity, however, was to attempt to interpret his own dream — something depth psychologists did in his day, and still do — rather than to simply, and with much greater risk and potential, allow the dream to do its work on his Ego. James Hillman, himself a student of Jung's, maintains that when we interpret a dream, we lose the dream in exchange for what we get from it: "Interpretation turns the dream into its meaning. Dream is replaced with translation."[18]

> Dreams can be killed by interpreters, so that the direct application of the dream as a message for the ego is probably less effective in actually changing consciousness and affecting life than is the dream still kept alive as an enigmatic image.... For a dream image to work in life it must, like a mystery, be experienced as fully real.[19]

If Jung had utilized a soulcentric approach to dreamwork — or if he had a soul-initiation guide to help him — he might have returned several times, in his imagination, to sit in that Renaissance chair in front of that beautiful emerald stone table and feel the little girl's arms around his neck, being intensely curious about the effect on his emotions and imagination of everything in that moment and how all this might move within his somatic experience, how it might shift his experience of himself. Likewise, he might have dwelled reverently with the feeling of that white dove transforming herself into a human being while the male dove is busy with the twelve dead — not using his strategic thinking mind to understand what she might mean but allowing the poetry of that moment and of those words to have their full effect on his awareness.

Soul-initiation guides want to maximize this sort of shift in identity and consciousness during Dissolution, in part by supporting the initiate to surrender to the power and magic of the dream images. Interpretations too often prop up the pre-Descent identity and can be diversions from the journey. Our Escapists and other inner protectors are big supporters of dream interpretation.

Instead of deepening into the images, however, Jung tried to figure out who the twelve dead were and what business of the male dove they might be. He also tried to interpret the emerald table in terms of alchemical legends. Fortunately, he failed:

> Finally I had to give it up. All I knew with any certainty was that the dream indicated an unusual activation of the unconscious. But I knew no technique whereby I might get to the bottom of my inner processes, and so there remained nothing for me to do but wait, go on with my life, and pay close attention to my fantasies.[20]

Because he made the effort to record his dream and to wonder deeply about it, the White Dove most likely had her effect on Jung's Ego despite his efforts to interpret her. Meanwhile, Jung waited and kept his "fantasies" — his deep-imagery journeys — close to his awareness.

As we'll see, other imaginal guides to Soul arrived for Jung, including the one he named his "soul" (by which he meant his anima), as well as Elijah and Salome, the serpent, and ultimately, Philemon and Ka.

Jung's Dissolution Practices

At the time — late 1912 and early 1913 — Jung "knew no technique whereby I might get to the bottom of my inner processes." He had not yet discovered what he would later call "active imagination," a method he would rely upon during his Descent (and also a principal technique of what would become Jungian analysis). Jung also began to experiment with dreamwork, journal work, and expressive arts — three of the core techniques of what I call "soulcraft," a set of practices found in traditions around the world for facilitating the Descent.

After his encounter with the White Dove, Jung's dreams and waking images were filled with human corpses that turned out to be still living. In one dream, he sees mummified dead people lying with clasped hands, like sarcophagi; occasionally they move a little, but only when Jung is looking at them. These sarcophagi are not unlike "dead" caterpillars beginning to stir and "come alive" in their chrysalis coffins. It's as if Jung's unconscious was preparing him for the death of his Adolescent self and the possibility of some kind of shape-shifting and rebirth. His Muse or Dream-Maker was, in this way, continuing her Dissolution work on his Ego and aligning his consciousness with the transformative mythic images of death and resurrection. These dreams and images also foreshadowed what Jung would ultimately discover to be his mythopoetic relationship to the dead.

But Jung did not understand what was happening to him with these dreams. He thought the goal was to become *less* disoriented — rather than the full loss of bearings the Descent requires:

> The dreams, however, could not help me over my feeling of disorientation. On the contrary, I lived as if under constant inner pressure. At times this became so strong that I suspected there was some psychic disturbance in myself.[21]

Being a psychiatrist, Jung attempted to diagnose himself and twice reviewed "all the details of my life, with particular attention to childhood memories."[22] But he found nothing. It's a good thing he came up empty-handed. His self-diagnosis might otherwise have derailed his Descent, substituting a therapeutic intervention, a healing opportunity, for a soul encounter. This is the way many contemporary psychotherapists — as well as friends and family — tend to respond to people as they plunge into Soul Canyon. They might attempt to rescue would-be initiates by framing the Descent as a kind of pathology, and then advising or administering "treatment." Jung's "disturbance" was not an illness nor a problem to be solved. It was the necessary dismemberment of an old story and identity — the liquefaction, in the cocoon, of the caterpillar body. Mercifully, Jung recognized this on some inchoate level:

> Thereupon I said to myself, "Since I know nothing at all, I shall simply do whatever occurs to me." Thus I consciously submitted myself to the impulses of the unconscious.[23]

Truly brilliant and daring! Without any (outer) guidance from Western culture or beyond it, this courageous man — accustomed to being in charge with others as well as within his own psyche — chose to submit himself to the control of powerful and mysterious forces. To let unraveling happen to him. To let himself (his Ego) be reshaped by Soul. In "The Man Watching," Rainer Maria Rilke wrote of this dynamic in his own life just a few years earlier:

...What we choose to fight is so tiny!
What fights with us is so great!
If only we would let ourselves be dominated
as things do by some immense storm,
we would become strong too, and not need names.[24]

While letting himself be dominated, Jung found himself remembering his child-hood experience of passionate play with building blocks, during which he would form little houses and castles. So, with the intent of reclaiming the creative life of the little boy he once was, he began every day to play outside with stones, gradually building an entire miniature village. This, in addition to dreamwork, was a second Dissolution practice Jung devised.

[I] asked myself, "Now, really, what are you about? You are building a small town, and doing it as if it were a rite!" I had no answer to my question, only the inner certainty that I was on the way to discovering my own myth. For the building game was only a beginning. It released a stream of fantasies which I later carefully wrote down.[25]

This "stream of fantasies" is none other than the three years' worth of deep-imagery journeys he recorded in his *Red Book.* Jung's personal *katabasis* (the ancient Greek term for the underworld journey) to the depths of the human psyche and, for that matter, the entire project of modern Western depth psychology were set in motion by child's play! All the elaborate and tangled machinations of Western medicine and psychology of Jung's time were of no use to him. He found his portal to the depths by abandoning his strategic mind, his analytic proclivity, his scientific rationalism, his need to figure it out or be in control. He surrendered to a process his peers would have regarded as utterly crazy — and that *felt* crazy to him (and that many psychologists, over the years, have in fact unimaginatively framed as a "mental illness"). This required immense courage. Jung allowed the natural wisdom of his psyche to guide him. It's no wonder that one of his first dream guides appeared in the form of an eight-year-old girl, a wild child — not "adult" nor male nor do-mesticated, like him — who, at first, ran off to play with Jung's own inner (dream) children in his own inner castle.

On the Descent to Soul, the initiate might engage in any number of practices and ceremonies for commencing or accelerating Dissolution (Jung's "rites" and those described in chapter 4). Often these practices involve what are now known as "expressive arts," employed for the purpose of submitting oneself to the images arising from the depths by way of dreams, waking imagery, or encounters with mys-terious others, human or otherwise. Jung, self-guided, accelerated his Dissolution by playing with stones. Later, he painted pictures, drew mandalas, hewed stone, and built a hermitage he called the Tower.

Expressive arts can be used to amplify the Ego-altering effects of a dream. The dreamer might be invited, for example, to draw a dream image, shape it with clay, embody it through movement, or express it in poetry or song. Jung used this approach. One of his inner guides, Philemon, for example, first appeared to him in a dream as an old man with the horns of a bull and the wings of a kingfisher. "Since I did not understand this dream-image, I painted it in order to impress it upon memory."[26] I suspect that Jung's artwork not only impressed the image on memory but deepened its impact on his psyche, on his Ego in particular, allowing the experience to dominate his conscious self.

Using the framework of the Nature-Based Map of the Human Psyche, we might say that the West and South facets of the Self are essential for finding the route and opening the door to Soul Canyon — the Dark Muse-Beloved's West capacity and proclivity for deep imagination, symbolic expression, art, and the shadowed corners of the psyche; and the Wild Indigenous One's South embrace of play, full-bodied feeling, and our innate kinship with all of life. All the more reason for you to cultivate these two facets of the Self in the Preparation phase of your Descent.

Intensification of the Crisis and Acceleration of the Fall

In addition to his break with Freud and the start of his romance with Toni Wolff, another crisis amplified and quickened Jung's Dissolution. This occurred when Jung was alone on travels, in October 1913, the same month his relationship with Freud ended. For a full hour, he was...

> ...suddenly seized by an overpowering vision: I saw a monstrous flood covering all the northern and low-lying lands between the North Sea and the Alps....I saw the mighty yellow waves, the floating rubble of civilization, and the drowned bodies of uncounted thousands. Then the whole sea turned to blood.[27]

Two weeks later the vision recurred, this time even more vividly. Jung was deeply disturbed and confused by these and additional disaster visions the following spring. He concluded he "was menaced by a psychosis."

Then on August 1, 1914, while Jung was in Scotland to deliver a lecture, World War I began. On one level, Jung now suspected his visions of blood had been auguries of impending war, but he also understood them as disturbances in his own psyche. It's likely that, in his state of disarray, he was unusually sensitive to the psychological tensions of the world, a sensitivity we can consider an additional catalyst of his unraveling. In any case, he regarded the coordinated crises of his visions and of world war as presenting him with an "obligation...to probe the depths of my own psyche."[28] He continued recording his deep-imagery journeys, a project that "took precedence over everything else."

By now, Jung knew he was in free fall and that everything depended on his staying conscious and remaining faithful to the journey his psyche was taking him on:

> An incessant stream of fantasies had been released, and I did my best not to lose my head but to find some way to understand these strange things. I stood helpless before an alien world; everything in it seemed difficult and incomprehensible. I was living in a constant state of tension; often I felt as if gigantic blocks of stone were tumbling down upon me. One thunderstorm followed another. My enduring these storms was a question of brute strength. Others have been shattered by them — Nietzsche, and Hölderlin, and many others. But there was a demonic strength in me, and from the beginning there was no doubt in my mind that I must find the meaning of what I was experiencing in these fantasies. When I endured these assaults of the unconscious I had an unswerving conviction that I was obeying a higher will, and that feeling continued to uphold me until I had mastered the task.[29]

This is an extraordinary phenomenological account of the Dissolution phase of the Descent, during which one's Ego, the former identity, is being shattered: one storm or avalanche after another. ("You are not surprised at the force of the storm.") Does one resist or submit? Jung's approach was an amalgamation: He dove into the imaginal journeys and let them happen to him, but he also tried to maintain cognitive control through attempts at interpretation.

I can't help but wonder what would have happened if Jung had wholly submitted: Perhaps he would have lost his mind and, in a sense, not have returned, in which case we would never have received his pioneering body of psychological depth work. Or perhaps he would have gone even deeper than he did. Or both. We can only speculate. We might wonder, too, what would have happened if Jung had wholly submitted and also had a flesh-and-blood soul-initiation guide. Such a blend of full submission and experienced guidance is of course the ideal arrangement on the Descent to Soul.

The Severance Dimension of Jung's Dissolution

Severance from the social roles and vocational identities of our Adolescent life is, as we've seen, one dimension of Dissolution — not the only dimension, but an essential one. The more we can withdraw from everyday Village routines, the better for the Descent. Instinctively, Jung knew this and bravely gave himself to the task. In the spring of 1913, as the pull from the depths became increasingly fierce, he resigned from his position as lecturer at Zurich University, where he had taught for eight years:

> I was confronted with the choice of either continuing my academic career, whose road lay smooth before me, or following the laws of my inner

personality, of a higher reason, and forging ahead with this curious task of mine, this experiment in confrontation with the unconscious. But until it was completed, I could not appear before the public.

Consciously, deliberately, then, I abandoned my academic career. For I felt that something great was happening to me, and I put my trust in the thing which I felt to be more important *sub specie aeternitatis*. I knew that it would fill my life, and for the sake of that goal I was ready to take any kind of risk.[30]

Also in the spring of 1913, Jung resigned as president of the International Psychoanalytical Association (Freud's circle). These two exits marked a near-complete separation from his social and professional world beyond his family and his private practice conducted at home. The result, he writes, was "an extreme loneliness."

I was going about laden with thoughts of which I could speak to no one: they would only have been misunderstood. I felt the gulf between the external world and the interior world of images in its most painful form.[31]

The chrysalis is indeed and necessarily a world set apart. Some initiates might be in the company of other Wanderers from time to time, but their days unfold far from everyday Village life, at least psychospiritually if not also geographically.

Guidance and Support during the Descent

In addition to his imaginal mentors (such as the White Dove / Little Girl, Elijah, Salome, Philemon, and Ka), Jung, in some ways, served as his own guide:

I was frequently so wrought up that I had to do certain yoga exercises in order to hold my emotions in check. But since it was my purpose to know what was going on within myself, I would do these exercises only until I had calmed myself enough to resume my work with the unconscious. As soon as I had the feeling that I was myself again, I abandoned this restraint upon the emotions and allowed the images and inner voices to speak afresh.[32]

Jung's method — keeping himself together only enough to enable the journey to continue — amounts to staying grounded in what I call the Self (our fourfold wholeness) while the process of Dissolution proceeds. I suspect that Jung's yoga practice was a way for his North facet, his Nurturing Generative Adult, to support him during his time of psychological disintegration, so that the journey would not be aborted.

Other ways Jung maintained a modicum of stability during Dissolution were his sessions with his patients, his family life, and reminding himself regularly of his middleworld identity — again, evoking the presence and support of his North facet:

My family and my profession remained the base to which I could always return, assuring me that I was an actually existing, ordinary person. The unconscious contents could have driven me out of my wits.[33]

There are many reasons why Jung, in order to descend into Soul Canyon at all, may have needed to anchor himself in his everyday family and professional life, reasons why he might not have done well if he, like initiates in nature-based societies, had wandered off alone into the wilds for weeks on end. The absence of embodied human guides and Elders and the lack of a psychospiritual framework for understanding what was happening to him or how to embrace it are just two of these reasons. Jung's Descent was conducted entirely in the Village and through his emotions and imagination. He did not have the benefit of encounters with other-than-human creatures in wilderness settings or with the forms and forces of the self-organizing world. It's extraordinary he did so well.

The Dangers and Opportunities of the Descent

Jung fully submitted himself to his emotions in order to allow associated images to emerge in consciousness. This work constituted the primary catalyst or driving force of his Descent:

> To the extent that I managed to translate the emotions into images — that is to say, to find the images which were concealed in the emotions — I was inwardly calmed and reassured. Had I left those images hidden in the emotions, I might have been torn to pieces by them.[34]

Here Jung depicts both the dangers and opportunities of the Descent. The goal of Dissolution is precisely to be torn apart, to be dismembered so that we can be subsequently reconfigured in a never-before-seen pattern — as an initiated person with a particular mythopoetic role to embody for our more-than-human community. This underscores the danger of the life passage of Confirmation, the grave risk, that is, of succeeding with the stage-three task of balancing authenticity with social acceptance and, as a result, leaving (or being expelled from) the Oasis. Once we pass through Confirmation and move into the Cocoon, we find ourselves on something like a knife-edged alpine ridge with a fall to our psychospiritual death on one side (in the form of the Descent) and a fall to a very different sort of psychospiritual death on the other side (in the form of a life of banality and meaninglessness). In healthy cultures, the parents of young initiates would rather have their children risk the former death than the latter.

When people get stuck in an egocentric version of early Adolescence, theirs will be a life of meaninglessness — because the Descent will not be an option, at least not one with any benefit. Healthy (ecocentric) early Adolescence, in contrast, is not meaningless. Thespians (ecocentric early Adolescents) enjoy a rich life of social innovation, sexual fire, and community involvement — one that eventually propels them into the Cocoon.

In Jung's preceding words, we witness the initiate finding himself existentially between a rock and a hard place. If he descends, he could lose his mind — or his life. If, on the other hand, he refuses the call and abandons the Descent, he could be assigning himself to a life of quiet desperation, preyed upon by a dominator culture — while at the same time being an agent of that very culture.

Jung's Use of Active Imagination: Elijah, Salome, and the Serpent

As developed by Jung, active imagination is the technique by which the conscious Ego actively engages and interacts with the contents of the personal and/or collective unconscious — images that emerge unbidden from the depths of the psyche through imagination, visions, or dreams. Essential to the technique is that the person (their Ego) does not attempt to change the images to their own liking or comfort but treats these depth images as entirely real and allows them to remain autonomous beings with which the Ego can sincerely interact.

Jung's personal use of active imagination resulted in elaborate dreamlike mythic encounters by which he was utterly captivated, entranced, and afflicted and which he recorded with great care and detail. He described his specific technique of imaginal descent as follows:

> In order to seize hold of the fantasies, I frequently imagined a steep descent. I even made several attempts to get to [the] very bottom. The first time I reached, as it were, a depth of about a thousand feet; the next time I found myself at the edge of a cosmic abyss. It was like a voyage to the moon, or a descent into empty space.[35]

Here is his description of one of these early descents, on the longest night of winter solstice, December 21, 1913:

> I had the feeling that I was in the land of the dead. The atmosphere was that of the other world. Near the steep slope of a rock I caught sight of two figures, an old man with a white beard and a beautiful young girl. I summoned up my courage and approached them as though they were real people, and listened attentively to what they told me. The old man explained that he was Elijah, and that gave me a shock. But the girl staggered me even more, for she called herself Salome! She was blind. What a strange couple: Salome and Elijah. But Elijah assured me that he and Salome had belonged together from all eternity, which completely astounded me....They had a black serpent living with them which displayed an unmistakable fondness for me. I stuck close to Elijah because he seemed to be the most reasonable of the three, and to have a clear intelligence. Of Salome I was distinctly

suspicious. Elijah and I had a long conversation which, however, I did not understand.[36]

This deep-imagery journey with Elijah, Salome, and the serpent — the first of three — was, like most everything in the *Red Book*, not an encounter with Soul (in the sense of a revelation of mythopoetic identity) but both a wholing experience and an intensification of his Ego dissolution, thereby paving the way for a later encounter with Soul.

Let's consider, first, the wholing dimension: Elijah, Salome, and the serpent can be seen as features of Jung's psyche, features that had, many years earlier, been cast out from the realm of his conscious awareness and held captive in his Shadow. (They can also be seen, without contradiction, as Jung's personal experiences of three universal archetypes.) Through these imaginal encounters, Jung had one of his earliest conscious experiences of inner resources that were vital elements of his wholeness or Self, resources that had been repressed and consequently underdeveloped and that now needed to be cultivated in preparation for soul encounter. The fact that our psyches know things like this and create these opportunities is one of the everyday miracles of human development.

Of these three biblical/mythic figures, Jung was most comfortable with Elijah, who "seemed to be the most reasonable, and to have a clear intelligence" — in other words, most like the way Jung experienced himself.

However, Jung was shocked and revolted that Elijah was allied with Salome. She, after all, was the one who coerced King Herod to behead John the Baptist. Jung, in his *Red Book* commentary, refers to her, in no uncertain terms, as "devilish," "engendered from heinous seed," and evincing "vain greed and criminal lust." Yikes. Elijah, on the other hand, was a Hebrew prophet and miracle worker who defended the worship of the Hebrew God over that of the Canaanite deity Baal.

But Elijah and Salome tell Jung that Salome *loved* "the holy man" John the Baptist. This utterly confounds and outrages Jung, who sees Elijah and Salome as an "extreme contradiction" — a "prophet, the mouth of God" united with a "bloodthirsty horror."[37] Jung, in other words, has been flung into a Mandorla.

Elijah, as embodied in Jung's imaginal encounters, possesses qualities of both the Sage (East) and the Nurturing Generative Adult (North). Jung notes, for example, that Elijah is "the figure of a wise old prophet,"[38] sees the future, and knows the deepest mysteries (all East qualities) and that he also is a "thinker" and "his wells hold healing waters" (both North). Salome, in contrast, combines qualities of both the Wild Indigenous One (South) and the Dark Muse-Beloved or Anima (West), but more the former. She, for example, is portrayed as a "beautiful maiden"[39] and "the erotic element,"[40] which is commonly how Western cisgender men experience their own South and West facets, and which they project onto women they find attractive. We also learn that Salome's way of knowing is, explicitly, feeling in contrast to thinking; there's even the intimation she might be *anti*-thinking — after all, she had John the Baptist decapitated. This feature portrays Salome as South. (West is aligned more with imagination than feeling.)

In the contemporary mainstream Western world, the qualities of North and East are considered masculine, whereas the qualities of the South and West are typically thought of as feminine.[41] With this in mind, we might say that Jung's visions of Elijah and Salome were imaginal embodiments of the masculine and feminine dimensions of his own psyche and that they embodied the great tension or "contradiction" Jung experienced within himself between these two dimensions — between thinking and feeling, observation and imagination, fact and myth, wisdom and eros. As with many Western men, much of Jung's feminine qualities had been rejected and repressed when he was a boy, banished to his Shadow. One feature of this banishment is the mislabeling of the feminine. Consequently, as his feminine nature emerged from his Shadow in the form of Salome, he initially saw her as evil and sinful. This mislabeling is why Jung was so confounded that Salome could possibly be partnered in any way with Elijah, the virtuous prophet, the man of God.

Through the course of three deep-imagination journeys involving these figures, this internal tension did its work on Jung's Ego, and in three ways: It transformed his conscious attitudes about the feminine, the world, and himself; it directly transformed his Ego itself, through the experience of dismemberment or Dissolution; and it enabled him to access and cultivate the psychospiritual resources (all four of the facets of wholeness) he would need for his further individuation — for his Descent, in particular.

Jung's experience of Salome, for example, progresses from disdain in the first encounter to acceptance in the second to embrace in the third. At first, Jung's reaction to Salome (his own South and West facets) is "horror" and righteous indignation ("I dread you, you beast," he actually says to her). His mood is "gloomy," "doubtful," "afraid." Jung, who identified himself primarily as a "thinker," wrote in his *Red Book* commentary on this encounter, "A thinker should fear Salome, since she wants his head, especially if he is a holy man," but then he went on to comment, "He who prefers to think than to feel, leaves his feeling to rot in the darkness,"[42] which is to say in the Shadow.

Then, on the very next evening, December 22, at the outset of the second encounter, Jung's experience of Salome has already shifted to acceptance, empathy, and contrition. Seeing her this time, he wrote, "She is like someone suffering. I cannot detect any sacrilege in her nature."[43] Now what he's uncertain about is not Salome but himself: "I am lost in my ignorance." To Elijah, he admits, "It seems to me as if I were more real here. And yet I do not like being here," a common theme during Dissolution. This time, he confesses that Salome "is my soul," by which, as we've seen, he means his anima or what I refer to as the Dark Muse-Beloved or the *Guide* to Soul — in short, his West facet of wholeness. Now he's no longer critical of Salome or Elijah, but of himself:

"I am inflicted by fatal weakness." Jung lets himself be instructed by Elijah, including about the objective nature of thoughts, as well as by Salome, who says she and Jung are siblings, children of Elijah and Mary, "the mother of our Savior." This wild contention, that he is somehow related to Jesus, once again plunges Jung into a "terrible confusion," an intensification of his Ego-dismemberment.

By the third encounter, three nights later (Christmas night, as it happens), Jung's relationship to Elijah and Salome has developed further, and he is much more open to the mysteries these two figures represent and mediate. His struggle now is between doubt and desire. He desires to be with Elijah and Salome, to learn more, but doubts his capacity to bear it. (Danger and allurement comprise the recurrent pattern on the Descent.) This encounter culminates when Elijah shows him a scene on a mountain: Christ on the cross and a stream of blood flowing from the summit. At this point, Jung has progressed from his habitual stance of skeptical and judgmental thinking (seen in the first encounter) to full, empathic feeling as he experiences Christ "in his last hour and torment." Then this episode makes the final turn from empathy to identification: Jung experiences *himself* on the cross and the black serpent wound around his body! If this weren't enough, Salome implies again that Mary, Jesus's mother, is also Jung's. Jung responds, "I see that a terrible and incomprehensible power forces me to imitate the Lord in his final torment. But how can I presume to call Mary my mother?"[44] Salome, now delivering the final blow, says, "You are Christ." By the end of this episode, Jung is enraptured and filled with tears in the face of "the glory."

We can see, then, that what took place over the course of three deep-imagination journeys — in a matter of just four days — was a transformative experience: the dissolution of Jung's Adolescent identity, a profound transition in worldview, and a reclaiming of some facets of his wholeness. Jung progressed from projecting sinister qualities onto Salome (his own feminine nature) to acceptance and love for her, his anima, to an initial assimilation and integration within his conscious self of her capacity for feeling, and finally, to a profound experience of self-sacrifice through an empathic identification with the crucified Jesus. "Through the self-sacrifice," he commented, "my pleasure is changed and goes above into its higher principle," namely "love."[45] Indeed. He also explicitly recognized the necessity to claim and accept the opposites within himself: "You need your wholeness to live onward." Here he primarily means what I would call the North and South facets or, alternately, two of the four windows of knowing — heart-centered thinking and full-bodied feeling:

> If you go to thinking, take your heart with you. If you go to love, take your head with you. Love is empty without thinking, thinking hollow without love.[46]

These profound integral experiences confounded Jung's existing attitudes and beliefs, leading to a shift in his world and in his consciousness, a kind of identity shift necessary to eventually be able to approach the ultimately mysterious realm of the Soul. In this way, these deep-imagination journeys contributed decisively to his Dissolution as well as to his Preparation. And let's keep in mind the astonishing fact that these experiences came about neither through Jung's conscious intention nor the expertise of an outer soul guide's facilitation, but through the innate brilliance of the deeper human psyche.

Although Jung later used his strategic mind to interpret the significance and meaning of Elijah, Salome, and the serpent, it was his underworld experiential encounters and distressing interactions with these figures, not his subsequent interpretations, that altered Jung's consciousness and contributed to his shift of identity from egocentric to soulcentric. Jung tells us as much in the *Red Book* itself, in which he refers to his imaginal interactions with Elijah and Salome as a "mystery play":

> You have to bear this in mind, it is also a world and its reality is large and frightening. You cry and laugh and tremble and sometimes you break out in a cold sweat for fear of death. The mystery play represents my self and through me the world to which I belong is represented.[47]

Jung goes on to describe his underworld experience and the dissolution of form that took place:

> The scene of the mystery play is a deep place like the crater of a volcano. My deep interior is a volcano, that pushes out the fiery-molten mass of the unformed and the undifferentiated. Thus my interior gives birth to the children of chaos, of the primordial mother. He who enters the crater also becomes chaotic matter, he melts.[48]

Another stunning depiction of the experience of the Dissolution phase of the Descent! Being in the depths of a volcano is akin to being in a cocoon. Becoming "chaotic matter" and "melting" is what we might suspect a caterpillar would experience while dissolving. Jung's very next sentence, in fact, refers explicitly to dissolution: "The formed in him dissolves and binds itself anew with the children of chaos, the powers of darkness" which "stretch beyond my certainties and limits on all sides." Exactly, poetically. This is the experience of dying to an old, familiar identity and being unable to see what comes next.

Shadow Work

Much of this Dissolution-phase alteration of consciousness and shift in identity — not only for Jung, but for all initiates — is brought about by the cultivation of our least-developed facets of wholeness. Often, as with the Salome encounters, this is a matter of Shadow work. One of the reasons our facets are underdeveloped in the first place is because our Ego, when younger, experienced aspects of our facets as a threat to its integrity. Consequently, some features of those facets were repressed — denied and locked up in the intrapsychic dungeon Jung named the Shadow. The Shadow is at once a prison for what the Ego considers unacceptable and also a storeroom for preserving and safeguarding the inestimable psychological treasures that the Ego is not yet mature enough to embrace. Ultimately, *all* these unacceptables turn out to be treasures. To prepare for the encounter with Soul, we need to retrieve and reclaim some of these elements of our Shadow — which, as often as not, are aspects of our facets of wholeness. But when elements of the Shadow — I call each element a "shade" — first become visible to our Ego, they appear to be either demonic or divine because these are the ways our psyches labeled them at the time of repression in order to keep the Ego at a safe psychological distance from them. Experiencing something as demonic or divine enables most Egos to perceive it as "absolutely not me." So, upon first coming face to face with a shade — whether in a dream, deep imagination, or projected onto something or someone in our dayworld — the Ego experiences it as either "divine" or "devilish," as Jung put it. Then, as the Ego gets to know the shade, the experience gradually moves from "not me" to "part of me," and eventually to "indispensable in order to be the *real* me."

As we've seen, Jung's imaginal encounters with Elijah and Salome can be understood as Shadow work — Shadow work in service to the Soul, which is to say in preparation for Soul Encounter. In order to proceed with the journey of soul initiation, Jung needed to reclaim some aspects of Self that had been banished to his Shadow when he was a child and that he had subsequently projected onto dayworld people and onto imaginal figures.

Absolutely-not-me was Jung's initial experience with both Elijah (a "prophet, the mouth of God" and thus divine) and Salome (a "bloodthirsty horror" and thus devilish). From the depths, Jung's psyche (via his Self? his Muse/anima? his Soul?) made a brilliant and risky move in generating these imaginal encounters that combined a golden projection with one so sinister. His psyche could have generated encounters with just Elijah or just Salome, and these might have been beneficial enough. But appearing together, these two figures placed Jung's Ego in an impossible position of intolerable tension — a Mandorla. Something had to break — to break open. And something did: his Ego, in a way that prepared him for his later encounter with Soul.

These two shades (three, counting the serpent) are at first akin to "the children of chaos." This is one of the ways the Ego experiences shades when they first appear to consciousness. But then, through the encounter, Jung's Ego itself becomes "chaotic matter" and he "melts" and merges with these shades, integrating some of their qualities the Ego had formerly refused and repressed. The goal of Shadow work — this particular way of wholing — is for *both* the shade and the Ego to transform as they are revealed to each other and begin to merge, to be bound together anew. What had once been whole — the human psyche at birth — and was soon enough torn asunder (to enable viable Ego development in a particular family and cultural environment) is eventually restored, so that Mystery may be served. This is the key dimension of the process Jung came to call "individuation."

Merging with the Archetype of the Wanderer, the Self-Sacrificing Hero

By way of the Elijah-Salome-serpent encounters, Jung (his Ego) was adeptly maneuvered into the position and role of the archetypal Wanderer, the initiate who yields to the call and surrenders to the longing to merge with Soul regardless of the costs. At the start of these imaginal encounters, Jung had no clue what was happening to him — he had only a gutsy resolve to descend — but eventually he realized that Elijah, Salome, and the serpent were three of his guides or initiators. By the end of the third encounter, he had surrendered to the inevitable self-sacrifice.

Why self-sacrifice? This is the core difference between the egocentric early-Adolescent hero (of any chronological age) and the mature hero or heroine. Egocentric heroes stride boldly into danger in order to defeat the enemy, save the world, or rescue the child or the damsel in distress. They are usually successful, suffer a few superficial wounds, are greatly admired and celebrated, and emerge from their adventure basically unchanged — other than, often, a more-inflated Ego. Mature heroes and heroines, in contrast, descend into the shadowy depths, sacrifice who they have been, including their early-Adolescent achievements and their desire for more of the same, and offer themselves to the numinous forms and forces of the underworld as raw material to be dismembered and then reconfigured in a way that might enable them to return to their people humbly bearing a never-before-seen gift and contribute to their community's survival, if not its renaissance or evolution. Mature heroes and heroines, then, are not only willing to die but know on some level that their *psychospiritual* death is both inevitable and necessary. Even desired. Like the butterfly drawn to flame in Goethe's "The Holy Longing" (see page 1).

Given Jung's Christian background — and perhaps also the fact that this imagery journey took place on Christmas — Jesus would have been the most compelling example available to his psyche of the mature, self-sacrificing hero. So it's no surprise that in the third Elijah-Salome-serpent encounter, Mystery or Soul maneuvered Jung to experience himself as Jesus in his supreme moment of self-sacrifice. This informed Jung — somatically, emotionally, imaginatively, and cognitively — of this essential feature of the journey upon which he was now embarked. But it not only informed him, it *trans*formed him, radically altering his experience of himself and of the nature of his journey.

This transformation was engendered by what Jung referred to as "the objective psyche." He means there are *dramatis personae* within our human psyches who are real and autonomous intelligences quite distinct from our Egos — not mere subjective characters under our conscious control or whom we intentionally conjure.

As threatening as it may be to our worldviews, as it was to Jung's, we must concede that Elijah and Salome knew things about Jung and about human development and transformation that Jung (his Ego) did not. This fact profoundly rearranged the furniture in Jung's mind — as it should for us as well. Elijah and Salome also knew how to do things Jung did not, such as transforming him, in three impeccably devised steps, from a self-aggrandizing early-Adolescent hero to a self-sacrificing mature hero, a Wanderer. This was a major conversion, a significant shift in his psychospiritual center of gravity.

Let us note, however, that this was not a soul encounter, not a revelation of unique mythopoetic identity. The Wanderer is an archetype that exists universally in each human psyche. To consciously embody this archetype is to achieve something that all people must during the journey of soul initiation. There is nothing unique about this. In contrast, a soul encounter is the revelation of an identity that is entirely unique to the individual. Embodying the Wanderer is one element of the journey that eventually leads to soul encounter and then to the metamorphosis of the Ego into a form capable of embodying its unique eco-niche.

While figures like Elijah and Salome exist independently of our Egos, this is equally true of many other elements of our psyches — our DreamMakers, for example, and the dreamworlds they make, and also all four facets of our wholeness and, for that matter, our inner protectors, including our shades. The realization that such intelligences exist within our psyches (and within the world more generally), and that they profoundly influence and guide us through our lives, was mind-blowing and world-changing for Jung. Is this any more surprising, really, or any more incomprehensible than adolescent salmon somehow being guided as to the timing and destination of their migration — or butterflies somehow knowing, and knowing *how*, to begin their multigenerational journey from Canada to Mexico?

Our human Ego is not nearly so much in control as we like to imagine. And we have sources of support and guidance in life that the mainstream Western world is still, in the twenty-first century, just beginning to recognize and understand.

Only a few days before his Elijah and Salome encounters, for example, in a dream the night of December 18, 1913, the DreamMaker placed Jung in the role of the one who kills the Adolescent hero. And not just any Adolescent hero. The murdered one is none other than Siegfried, the dragon-slaying, chariot-riding prince of old German and Norse epics, which is to say the culture hero of Jung's own ancestral and intrapsychic heritage. With a rifle, from some distance, Jung, like a sniper, assassinates one of the greatest Adolescent heroes of his people's legends. The DreamMaker could have had Jung vanquish Siegfried in something like an epic, face-to-face, swashbuckling swordfight. But no, that would have made Jung into an Adolescent hero himself. Instead, DreamMaker had Jung play a role something more like a scoundrel, a cowardly modern gunman — decidedly nonheroic.

Jung wrote that "the dream showed that the attitude embodied by Siegfried, the hero, no longer suited me. Therefore it had to be killed." Jung recognized, in other words, his "secret identity with Siegfried," and felt "the grief a man feels when he is forced to sacrifice his ideal and his conscious attitudes."[49] Precisely. But keep in mind that Jung did not consciously choose to make this sacrifice; he was "forced" into it by an element of the "objective psyche," the DreamMaker.

We might understand this dream as something like a warm-up for the experience of being the one who is slain. Here, too, Jung was being shepherded through a sequence, this time from the one who murders the Adolescent hero to the Adolescent hero who is slain (Jung's Dissolution), and finally to the mature hero who accepts his own inevitable sacrifice. The *Red Book*'s first of three sections (*Liber Primus*) ends with Jung's heroic-Adolescent Ego having been sacrificed (with the conclusion of the third Elijah-Ṣalome encounter) and now consciously merged with the archetype of the Wanderer. Then the second section (*Liber Secundus*) opens with the arrival of another Wanderer — in the guise of a red horseman, as we shall see. I found it of great interest that in his first draft of the *Red Book*, Jung had actually titled the opening paragraphs of *Liber Secundus* "The Adventures of the Wandering."[50]

Who Maneuvers? Who's in Control?

If Jung was maneuvered into the role of the archetypal Wanderer, we might ask, "Who or what did the maneuvering?" Or, "Who's in control during the Descent to Soul?" For sure it's not the initiate's Ego. Some say it is Mystery who orchestrates things, where "Mystery" might refer to Spirit or God or, in less religious terms, to life itself, or as Taoists would have it, to *the way of* life. Others prefer to say that the primary initiator is more specific to the individual and identify it as the person's "soul." What I mean by Soul, as noted earlier, seems close to what Jung meant by "the spirit of the depths." Jung, for example, referred to "a terrible and incomprehensible power [that] forces me to imitate the Lord in his final torment." This power might be what I call the Soul (but not what Jung means by "soul"), or it might be some other aspect of the psyche: assistants or colleagues of the Soul, such as the DreamMaker or the Muse.

On the Descent to Soul, the initiate's Ego is more in the position of a passenger, the one who is guided, or the raw material for a metamorphosis, or even the sacrificial offering. The Ego is not the agent of transformation but rather that which is transformed. The Ego that survives the journey (if it does) is not the Ego that chose to embark. But once the journey has begun, the Ego can actively cooperate with Soul or Mystery. The Ego, for example, can choose and engage in Dissolution practices, can hone its skill in using these practices, can depart from the Village or at least choose solitude during the Descent, and can follow the instructions or advice of guides, initiators, and Elders.

On the other hand, the Ego can actively resist the journey, and often does. It can refuse the call. It can abort the Descent. It can cooperate with others who want the journey to be abandoned, terminated, or reversed — a psychiatrist, psychotherapist, friend, parent, spouse, or child.

Jung's success with Dissolution was made possible by his willingness and ability to allow his Ego to be worked on by other parts of his psyche and by the world's psyche: the pull of Soul itself, the guidance of Elijah and Salome, the effect on him of the serpent, and the use of consciousness-shifting techniques such as active imagination, dreamwork, and expressive arts.

The surrender of control is particularly difficult for most contemporary Western people, not just for people of privilege with Adolescent masculine Egos. Relinquishing power is un-American, un-Western, unmodern — and certainly unwhite. Un-Adolescent, quite frankly. Most American men, for instance, have been taught they ought to be and, really, *need* to be in charge. If something has to happen, they need to "figure out" how to do it — using their strategic thinking minds, not their intuition, imagination, feeling-sense, or heart-centered thinking — and they should never give over their fate to anyone or anything beyond their Egos. Even when they feel called to the journey of soul initiation, their initial fallback position is to try to figure it out and maintain control (and "dignity") at all times. This is the first hurdle: submitting, surrendering, self-sacrificing, allowing, cooperating. "If only we would let ourselves be dominated / as things do by some immense storm," Rilke advises.

Liber Secundus

There are at least thirty-three deep-imagination journeys in the *Red Book*. Each journey appears to be an experience created by Soul or Mystery to accomplish one or more of the following three things in preparation for Jung's first soul encounter:

- They intensify the Dissolution phase of his Descent (by supporting and amplifying the dismemberment of his former identity and life story).
- They support the wholing of his Ego (the cultivation of the mature resources of his psyche as embodied in the four facets of the Self).
- They facilitate his Self-healing (his embrace of his inner protectors, using the resources of the fourfold Self, and the retirement of his childhood survival strategies).

Jung's psyche, in other words, provided him with a multidimensional preparation for his discovery of and his capacity to eventually live within his unique ecological niche. The methods used by Jung's psyche are all instances of the Preparation and Dissolution practices described in this book.

Liber Secundus, the second section of the *Red Book*, opens with a wandering horseman, "the Red One," who in essence is a masculine embodiment of Jung's South facet, especially of Jung's capacity for experiencing full-bodied joy. Due to the fact that Jung's joy had been mostly repressed up to this point in his life, he first experiences the Red One as a "pagan" and a "devil." This again illustrates the Shadow dynamic in which sinister valuations are projected onto a repressed personal quality in order to keep the Ego distant from a feature of its own psyche that its subpersonalities deem unsafe.

In this imaginal encounter, Jung is a lonely and isolated guard who is posted on the tower of a castle, a very unjoyful job and life indeed. He is dressed in green. The Red One rides up to the castle, passes through the gate, dismounts, and walks up the stairs to where Jung waits in his tower. They converse. The Red One experiences Jung as "unbelievably ponderous and serious," as "too German," as a solemn Christian "fanatic" — and straight-out tells him so.[51]

Through his interaction with the Red One, Jung begins to reconnect with his joy, in particular what he calls his "joy before God that one can call dancing."[52] In the moment when Jung realizes that the Red One embodies Jung's own abandoned joy, Jung's green garments, "Oh miracle — everywhere burst into leaf," as if Jung shape-shifts into a Green Man, an archetypal embodiment of the Wild Indigenous One, the South facet of the Self. This is once again an instance of wholing as well as further Dissolution of his former Adolescent identity of the solemn scholar and scientist. With this encounter, Jung began to consciously and somatically integrate "that strange joy of the world that comes unsuspected like a warm southerly wind with swelling fragrant blossoms and the ease of living" — a glorious South-facet image. Jung commented that a joy like this "knocks you down, and you must grope for a new path." This experience, in other words, helped dissolve his old identity and supported his search for a new one, a more fleshed-out experience of self and world. By reclaiming and cultivating his South facet, Jung enhanced his chances of one day discovering his personal myth.

In a later imagery journey in *Liber Secundus*, Jung is a well-to-do "gentleman" wandering in a snow-covered land. He finds himself in the company of a one-eyed tramp, "one of the lowly," a poor soul who had been imprisoned, had recently lost his job, and now had a serious lung infection. That night, in a country inn, the tramp dies in his bed after a bloody coughing fit while Jung, who had heard the commotion from the next room, holds him as he expires.

For Jung this was a profound and disturbing encounter with another person's destitution and death and with his own eventual death and the destitution inherent in the life he had been living, an impoverishment he had not previously recognized. Following this imagery journey, Jung realized he must embrace "the bottommost for my renewal."[53] He must acknowledge and integrate his own mortality and commonness if he was ever to encounter his Soul. He must surrender his sense of being special or entitled, "no longer an individual on a high mountain, but a fish among fish, a frog among frogs." This cultivation of humility is a common Dissolution practice. For Jung it was also a catalyst enabling him to grieve as the unraveling of his old story quickened. And it was a Self-healing of his Prince subpersonality, the entitled one who had been protecting him from the psychospiritual dangers of his Soul by separating him from "the holy stream of common life."

In yet another imaginal journey, Jung suddenly comes fully alive while in a stunning redrock desert, a wild place that becomes wholly animate and real for him, likely an experience he had not had since childhood.

> And a wondrous life arises in things. What you thought was dead and in-animate betrays a secret life and silent, inexorable intent.... Even the stones speak to you, and magical threads spin from you to things and from things to you....Nothing happens in which you are not entangled in a secret man-ner....The stars whisper your deepest mysteries to you, and the soft valleys of the earth rescue you in a motherly womb.[54]

This is what the mainstream contemporary world might think of as a "nature mystic" experience and what a healthy ecocentric culture would call everyday aware-ness. For Jung, it further enlivened his South facet with its sensuous experience of the animate world and of an embodied kinship with all things. It seems to have expanded his ecocentric awareness and deepened his romance with the world. The encounter with Soul is unlikely for people who do not feel fully at home in a living, breathing world where each thing — each stone, tree, creature — is a relative who speaks and who desires.

During his next imagery journey, Jung finds himself in a remote, desolate, and cold spot on the edge of the sea. There he meets Death embodied as a man in a wrinkled black coat. Through this encounter, Jung learned more fully that he must accept Death in order to embrace life and to experience joy. He must accept Death as his advisor during his Descent to Soul.

Through his imagery journeys over the next several days, Jung experienced in a number of ways that each element of his psyche is balanced by its opposite, and he learned that he must find a way to embrace both poles. "Whatever I reject is nev-ertheless in my nature."[55] In one of these journeys, for example, he (his Ego) wants to move east, toward light, to rise toward personal power, while another part of his psyche (personified as the Babylonian hero-king Gilgamesh) journeys west, toward night, to sink toward rebirth. They meet on a narrow path on a mountain pass and each blocks the other's way. This is an instance of the Mandorla Practice (see pages 107–109), in which the tension between intrapsychic opposites is deliberately am-plified for the purpose of dissolving the Ego's current identity and its familiar story. "My hope for the fullness of the light shatters, just as his longing for boundless conquered life shatters."[56] In this series, Jung allows additional oppositions to shat-ter him, including: science versus religion, science versus belief, outer truth versus inner truth, knowledge versus wisdom, science versus nature, Ego versus Shadow, words versus Gods. Each of these oppositions is embodied in an imaginal encounter brilliantly choreographed by some dimension of Jung's psyche for the apparent purpose of dismembering Jung's former identity. His willingness and capacity to submit to these experiences is nearly as astonishing as his psyche's power to generate them.

The rest of *Liber Secundus* features what I would call advanced Dissolution experiences, in which Jung's former identity was further shredded. Here are just three examples, in which he is confronted with his culture's and his own misogyny, beliefs about sanity, and attitude toward magic. In one encounter, Jung's anima (his "soul") insists that he, as a man, accept his shared guilt in his (our) culture's femicide. His anima forces him to atone by compelling him to eat a piece of the liver of a murdered and mutilated girl.[57] In another, because he is reading Thomas à Kempis's *The Imitation of Christ*, he is diagnosed by doctors as suffering from "religious madness." He tells the doctors he feels "perfectly well," but unmoved, they confine him to a hospital ward. He understands that he is seen as having a type of "madness that cannot be integrated into present-day society," which is to say he is left with no option but to define himself outside the pale of the mainstream.[58] His anima then encourages him to recognize and accept his madness — the dissolution of his old story and identity. She asks:

> Have you noticed that all your foundations are completely mired in madness? Do you not want to recognize your madness and welcome it in a friendly manner?...Madness is not to be despised and not to be feared, but instead you should give it life....If you want to find paths, you should not spurn madness, since it makes up such a great part of your nature....Life itself has no rules. That is its mystery and its unknown law. What you call knowledge is an attempt to impose something comprehensible on life.[59]

In this way, Jung was led to question everything he had believed about life and sanity. He writes, "Everything inside me is in utter disarray. Matters are becoming serious, and chaos is approaching....I believe that I have gone crazy."[60] Dissolution.

Later his anima gives him a black rod formed like a serpent. She tells him it is a magical rod that will do "a lot" for him, but to possess it requires him to sacrifice his solace, "the solace you give and the solace you receive."[61] He doesn't know what magic is but confesses he doesn't believe in it, *can't* believe in it, because to do so would require him to set aside his "science." In the end, he takes the magic rod. This leaves him with "unbearable tension." Mandorla.

Philemon and Ka: Later Stages of Wholing and Guidance

On January 27, 1914, a few weeks after the Elijah-Salome-serpent encounters, an imaginal character appeared, someone who "developed out of the Elijah figure," an old, semiretired magician named Philemon.[62]

Philemon can be seen as the template or archetype for the next stage of Jung's wholing. Whereas Elijah possesses qualities of the East facet ("a wise old prophet," "the mouth of God," "superior insight") and the North (a thinker and healer), Philemon incorporates these same qualities but now adds the West: He's a magician, and Jung refers to him as his "psychagogue,"[63] someone who calls up the spirits of the dead — a very West enterprise.

Four years later, Philemon morphs into yet another guru-like figure, whom Jung calls Ka. Ka, too, has striking West qualities (for example, he is "Mephisto-phelian," an agent of the devil or of the underworld depths), but unlike Elijah or Philemon, Ka also brings in the South facet — he's "a kind of earth demon," "a spirit of nature," and is Dionysian (sensual and emotional).[64]

By interacting with and accepting guidance from Philemon and Ka, Jung was being led yet further into his wholeness — into the cultivation and embodiment of his South and West facets (the more "feminine" ones) as well as his East and North facets (the more "masculine"). Jung had previously been introduced to and incor-porated some of his South and West qualities through his imaginal interactions with Salome, a female character. Now he is incorporating additional dimensions of his South and West through mentorships with male guides. Elijah, Philemon, and Ka constitute a deepening series of male role models for Jung's mature Self.

During the Descent to Soul, characters from our deep imagination become as real as the people of our dayworld lives. This was true for Jung:

> Psychologically, Philemon represented superior insight. He was a mysteri-ous figure to me. At times he seemed to me quite real, as if he were a living personality. I went walking up and down the garden with him, and to me he was what the Indians call a guru.[65]

A guru is, among other things, a role model for our own individuation, some-one on whom we initially project, in a golden way, our not-yet-reclaimed wholeness. As long as we continue this projection — and consequently see the guru as better or more enlightened than us — we remain fragmented and "protected" from our own potential. Projection is a form of subpersonality protection.

Jung's encounter with these "quite real" figures of his unconscious had a pro-found impact on his conscious self, his Ego. But still, so far, the result was ego-dissolution plus wholing and Self-healing, not soul encounter. As in Rilke's poem, "The Man Watching," Jung's interactions with these figures were like wrestling with an angel, being "decisively defeated," having his "shape shifted."

> Whenever the outlines of a new personification appeared, I felt it almost as a personal defeat. It meant: "Here is something else you didn't know until now!" Fear crept over me that the succession of such figures might be end-less, that I might lose myself in bottomless abysses of ignorance. My ego felt devalued — although the successes I had been having in worldly affairs might have reassured me."[66]

Such fears of endless undoing, insanity, or loss of worldly identity are common during the Descent, probably unavoidable. In the midst of the tumultuous transition from egocentric human caterpillar to soulcentric butterfly, the Ego is utterly destabilized for a time, sometimes for months or years. The Ego for sure feels "devalued." An entire structure of consciousness, a worldview, is ending and another slowly gelling. It is in fact entirely possible, as Jung feared, to irrevocably lose one's mind in the process. During such crises, a soul-initiation guide or Elder can make all the difference.

Jung *did* have soul-initiation guides, masterful ones — they just weren't the kind anyone else could see or interact with. They were provided by Mystery in the form of characters of "the objective psyche." When we embrace this reality for ourselves — that our psyches possess sources of vast perspective and wisdom independent of our Egos — the world changes; we must reconsider everything.

The Serpent Returns

Late in *Liber Secundus*, immediately after his first meeting with Philemon, the serpent reappears — the very serpent Jung had met, along with Elijah and Salome, at the start of the *Red Book*, the serpent who had "displayed an unmistakable fondness" for Jung and with whom Jung was profoundly uncomfortable. But Jung has now been sufficiently altered by his Dissolution experiences that he no longer fears serpents. He notes, in fact, that he has become "fond" of them — although, during his imaginal journeys, he also captures them and decorates his cave with their "dazzling skins." On one journey, he befriends a large iridescent female serpent. He enchants her by playing his flute and calls her "my sister, my soul" (his anima). They have a long conversation and he is entirely content when she wraps herself around his feet. He suspects she has a close connection with the underworld and he wants to partake in her serpentine wisdom. She offers it in a variety of ways. And she confirms and commends the dissolution of his former identity: "You deny everything that you believed. You've completely forgotten who you are."[67]

So the creature who once terrified Jung now becomes his ally. During the ensuing imaginal journeys, Jung merges with her and incorporates some of her powers, a common pattern on the journey of soul initiation: The Ego is transformed and initiated by confronting and then uniting with a shade. For example, Jung asks the serpent to go to the underworld ("Hades") to obtain counsel for him. She returns with none other than Satan. Through a series of interactions, it becomes clear that Satan, the serpent, and Jung's soul/anima are all aligned with one another and are, in essence, three faces of the same being. Jung asserts that Satan no longer has influence over him because Jung has united himself with the serpent. Satan, he declares, is "the quintessence of everything serpentlike" and "the quintessence of evil."[68] Jung is reclaiming these features of his Shadow, which he refers to as "one's own serpenthood, which one commonly assigns to the devil instead of oneself." Through this Shadow work, Jung profoundly deepened his wholeness as well as his Dissolution. (No wonder he so feared the serpent when he first met her!)

By befriending the serpent, Jung says, he also accepted "the demands" of the dead and was consequently "no longer threatened by the dead." And by satisfying the demands of the dead, "I gave up my earlier personal striving and the world had to take me for a dead man."[69] His identity, in other words, was no longer centered in the social life of the middleworld Village but in the Soul-oriented life of the underworld — a further measure of Jung's Dissolution and his shift in identity.

By the end of *Liber Secundus*, Jung has incorporated many of the serpent's qualities he had initially experienced as utterly "not me": her embrace of opposites, her feminine traits, and her "hardness, wisdom, and magical powers."[70]

What, Then, Is the *Red Book*?

I hope to have demonstrated that the *Red Book* is, before anything else, Jung's journal of his first Descent to Soul (at least its first two phases). But the *Red Book* can be explored and appreciated in at least three ways: as the narratives of Jung's imaginal journeys, his commentaries on them, and the psychospiritual impact of these journeys on Jung the person. Only the latter perspective reveals Jung's Descent. If you focus on the narratives or commentaries, the *Red Book* can read as a work of psychology, literature, theology, prophecy, or cosmology, and it might seem that Jung's primary intention was to communicate something about the psyche, the world, or God. For example, Sonu Shamdasani, the *Red Book*'s editor, writes, "whereas Zarathustra proclaimed the death of God, *Liber Novus* depicts the rebirth of God in the soul."[71] Whether this is true or not, Jung himself makes it clear he did not undertake his confrontation with the unconscious for the purpose of proclaiming or depicting *anything*. Indeed, he didn't really choose these experiences at all. They happened to him, like someone standing on a beach when a tsunami arrives. This is clear when we focus on the actual experiences recorded in the *Red Book* — Jung's deep-imagination journeys — and how they affected him.

To interpret the content of an experience is a categorically different enterprise than attempting to understand the effects of that experience on the experiencer, or to appreciate the structure of the experience (its phases). A useful analogy is the difference between the more common forms of Western dreamwork, in which the content is interpreted, and soulcentric dreamwork, in which the dream is supported to have its way with the psyche of the dreamer. With his commentaries, Jung later interpreted his imaginal experiences — a hermeneutic experiment overlaid upon the original experiential encounters. Much the same might be said about the hermeneutic experiments conducted by others following the *Red Book*'s publication.

If it's true that the nature of the *Red Book* has been misunderstood, this might be due in part to the unavailability of Western models that illuminate the Descent to Soul.

Psychotherapy versus the Descent

Jungian (and other) psychotherapists are trained in some of the practices that are useful in guiding the Descent, but they rarely use these practices for that purpose[72] and they don't possess a functional map of the journey, including of the developmental and psychospiritual preparation needed before Dissolution can begin or be beneficial.

There are at least three distinct kinds of individuation processes that might be guided by a psychotherapist — if they possess the skills to do so: (1) addressing everyday problems in living (what I call the healing of subpersonalities, which Jung called "ego complexes"); (2) the cultivation of wholeness (what I call the four facets of the Self, and what Jungians might call "tending the whole psyche"); and (3) the Descent to Soul (what Jung referred to as the search for a personal myth). These three processes have different and often divergent outcomes. Most psychotherapists are not trained in the second process, and virtually none in the third.

The fact that a therapist might have an avid fascination with the unconscious, a devoted interest in myths and dreams, and a finely honed set of tools for probing the depths of the psyche does not by itself enable them to guide a Descent or to even realize one is happening. As we've seen, the Descent won't commence until the Cocoon stage has been attained and a Descent-provoking crisis has occurred along with a call from Soul. Depth-oriented psychotherapists and their clients are not necessarily more likely to have had these experiences than other people. They're not even more likely to have undergone the developmentally earlier life passage of Eco-awakening (see "Eco-Awakening," pages 35–39).[73]

These comments illustrate two principles of human development at the heart of the model presented in this book: Developmental stage makes all the difference when it comes to what kind or level of individuation is possible. And a set of practices, while valuable and perhaps necessary, is not the same as a map of human development or a map of the Descent.

Without a map, you can use whatever practices you like but you may never reach the destination you have in mind or even be aware that certain kinds of nonordinary destinations are possible. You might have the canoe and the paddle and be able to make your way down the river but you'll never find the wellspring hidden in the dense forest a mile up the mountain. You might stumble upon the general location of the wellspring but not have the awareness to see it — especially if it's the sort of spring that can't be detected without a mode of consciousness accessible only after having achieved a certain stage of development. Without a map, you may not even know if you're in the river or on the mountain. You might not even know that you don't know where you are.

Jung himself had the experience of the Descent but not such a map. Whether he had one sometime later is a matter of debate. He did eventually adopt the map of the sixteenth-century alchemists, but he used the alchemists' texts not to map the *structure* of the Descent (its phases) but to understand the *content* of the experiences. Also, the alchemical map has not been an easy one for contemporary people to decipher or to agree upon its meanings.

Jung deftly developed practices — such as active imagination, dreamwork, and expressive arts — but he didn't show us how (or when or with whom) to use these practices specifically to facilitate the Descent. And yet he did clearly distinguish the Descent from what he understood psychotherapy to be.[74]

Jung's set of clinical practices was limited in number — whether used for healing, wholing, or the Descent. They worked for him on his own Descent, but they are not the most effective approaches for many people. The bundle of practices described in this and my previous books — some of which we've developed at Animas but most of which are common to many traditions — is a much more extensive and varied set.

One conclusion we might make from Jung's confrontation with his unconscious is that if an early-twentieth-century, overly cerebral, socially conventional, Swiss physician — married with five kids — could undergo the Descent to Soul without the support of outer guides or guidebooks, with essentially no understanding of what was happening to him, and with no methods other than those he could cobble together on his own, then surely you can. You might even find it quite a bit easier than did Jung — you who are blessed with postmodern consciousness, a map of the terrain, a guidebook, perhaps even a guide, and access to all sorts of twenty-first-century perspectives and multicultural psychospiritual practices that can support you in your Preparation for the journey. What are you whining about?

In chapter 7, we return to Jung's Descent to Soul as he entered its next phase, Soul Encounter, when he uncovered the primary images, symbols, and roles of his mythopoetic identity.

Chapter Six

PHASE THREE
Soul Encounter

Part 1: Numinous Awakenings in the Underworld

> ...When I had laid it on the floor
> I went to blow the fire aflame,
> But something rustled on the floor,
> And some one called me by my name:
> It had become a glimmering girl
> With apple blossom in her hair
> Who called me by my name and ran
> And faded through the brightening air....
>
> — W. B. YEATS

Soul Encounter is the pivotal phase of the Descent to Soul — the climactic nadir of the odyssey. During this phase, you are blessed or blasted by a conscious encounter with the chthonic mysteries of your Soul, and this confrontation radically shifts your experience of yourself, your life, your world, your possibilities. Your Ego begins to deepen and mature as it takes root in something much larger and greater than itself — namely, in Soul, which is to say in your singular place in the greater web of life. What's more, because your Soul is your particular strand of Mystery or Spirit, your Ego now forms a second bond with Mystery: Not only are you joined with Mystery in the nonspecific, universal way that all things are, but now you're being guided into the individual, unique place you were born to take in the evolution of Mystery itself. This is the onset of your conscious cocreative partnership with evolution. It doesn't get much better than that.

This phase of the Descent begins when, after wandering ever deeper into the world — our unfathomably complex and enchanted world — you at long last reach the outer limit of your former, Adolescent identity, pass through that veil, and gain access to a realm beyond the pale of everyday society and beyond your former understanding of who you were and what the world is. At this portentous turning of the trail, you sense, with both joy and dread, that you are being changed irrevocably and you feel both the promise and the consequences. Once you enter this third phase, the experience of soul encounter will happen soon.

The eventual outcome of soul encounter is the major life passage of Soul *Initiation*, when your center of psychospiritual gravity completes its shift to your mythopoetic identity, which is the start of true Adulthood. But that passage won't take place until after you've been through the Soul Encounter, Metamorphosis, and Enactment phases of the Descent — likely months or years in the future.

Some One Called Me by My Name

Yeats's "The Song of Wandering Aengus" offers us an intimate inside look at, and a vicarious feel for, the experience of soul encounter. In the first stanza of the poem (see "The Hazel Wood," pages 71–73), the Wanderer, at dawn, ventures out from his home and — on account of his inflamed head — out from his former, "caterpillar" identity, and enters the enchanted domain of the hazel wood. He then descends further yet into the mysteries by fishing in the numinous waters beneath the hazels. There he catches a "little silver trout," a magical being — mythically, the Salmon of Knowledge and Inspiration itself. With this encounter, his Dissolution is complete.

Now, in the poem's second stanza (previous page), the central phase of the journey unfolds. The Wanderer has returned home with his catch, unwittingly creating the conditions for an irreversible transformation in consciousness. He lays the trout on the floor and intends to revive his home fire — perhaps to cook breakfast — but as it turns out, he is the one who gets cooked. The existential tables turn. This is the moment of soul encounter, which, for Yeats, takes the form of a numinous interaction with his anima (or Muse or Guide to Soul). The little silver trout shape-shifts into a "glimmering girl," transforms herself from a "something" into a "some one," a fully conscious presence. More astonishing yet, she calls him by his name. She *knows* him. Indeed, she knows him better than he knows himself. We understand from the context — and the fact that the poet tells us twice — that the name she calls him is one he had never before heard but one he instantly recognizes as his true name, one that points to his deeper identity. I understand this to be his Soul identity, his place in the greater web of life.

Hearing his true name for the first time — and perhaps having a nascent feeling for its far-reaching implications and repercussions — is Yeats's experience of soul encounter, along with the shift that begins in his psyche in that moment, a shift that leaves him forever changed.

The poet doesn't explicitly tell us the name by which the glimmering girl calls him, but we can be certain it's not something familiar or commonplace, like William or Bill. Perhaps the name — or something related to it — is in the poem's title. Aengus is just the sort of name you'd expect from the Soul: something mythic, in this case the name of the Irish god of love, youth, and poetic inspiration. In the realm of Soul — in our chthonic depths — we're each named after gods and goddesses, the archetypes of the collective unconscious.

In Irish lore, Aengus wanders endlessly in search of a girl he falls in love with after seeing her once in a dream. Yeats had a similar fate. At age twenty-three, he fell in love with a brilliant young woman, Maud Gonne, who later became an actress, Irish revolutionary, and suffragette. Over a ten-year period, he proposed marriage to her at least four times. She never accepted. In some ways, Yeats spent the rest of his life in pursuit of Maud, or we might say, in search of what she represented to him, his Muse or anima. As we'll see, this is just what the poet tells us in the third stanza.

Why "apple blossom in her hair"? This is, in part, a reference to the springtime moment when Yeats first met and fell in love with Maud.[1] But those blossoms appear in the poem for an additional reason: They will bear fruit in the third stanza (in the Enactment phase), as will his meeting with Maud — and the glimmering girl.

During this encounter with Soul, Yeats's anima reveals to him his Soul's resonance with the mysteries of love, youth, and poetic inspiration. But what is essential here is that this encounter with the glimmering girl — this experiential moment — initiates a radical change in Yeats before he could have any deep understanding of the meaning of the name she calls him, long before he could know how he might live that name, long before any insight as to how (or if) he will embody it. The experience itself initiates the transformation, like the penetration of egg by sperm, but in this case, it's the piercing of Ego by Soul. In "Aengus," we can feel the electricity of this encounter in the magic of Yeats's word painting — the glimmering girl's sudden appearance by way of transfiguration and her equally sudden vanishing by way of daylight.

Resonances between Yeats and Jung

Carl Jung's encounter with his depths includes themes similar to Yeats's. One theme is the shift from being in control — the active agent — to being the one who is acted upon and changed, as in Yeats's conversion from the one who catches a fish to the one who is caught. Jung writes in his memoir:

> From the beginning I had conceived my voluntary confrontation with the unconscious as a scientific experiment which I myself was conducting and

in whose outcome I was vitally interested. Today I might equally well say that it was an experiment which was being conducted on *me*.[2]

Indeed. We might also say that the outcome of interest to Jung's Soul was not some intellectual discovery by Jung or his interpretation of one or more symbols. Rather, his Soul — like all Souls — desired a direct change in or conversion of consciousness: from an Ego persevering on its own agenda (egocentric) to an Ego illuminated by and dedicated to the Soul's agenda (soulcentric). For Jung, this was a shift from the ambitious young psychiatrist singled out to be Freud's intellectual heir to an apostate pioneer, a plucky explorer of the mysteries of the human mind.

In his memoir, written in his eighties, Jung seems to appreciate that the primary outcome of the Descent is a direct shift in how we experience what it is to be alive and human. His metamorphosis was not brought about by a mere compilation of meanings but by earth-shattering experiences. His later intellectual insights were a result of the transformation of his Ego, not the other way around. After recounting one of his dreams from this time, Jung writes:

> Although at the time I was not able to understand the meaning of the dream beyond [a] few hints, new forces were released in me which helped me to carry the experiment with the unconscious to a conclusion."[3]

These "new forces" were the significant aftermath of the dream, not his interpretations of the dream.

Another astonishing resonance with Yeats involves a dream Jung's nine-year-old son had shortly before Jung's first encounter with Soul. Jung was at home during these days, with his wife and children, and the house was filled with "an ominous atmosphere."

> [One] night my nine-year-old son had an anxiety dream. In the morning he asked his mother for crayons, and he, who ordinarily never drew, now made a picture of his dream. He called it "The Picture of the Fisherman." Through the middle of the picture ran a river, and a fisherman with a rod was standing on the shore. He had caught a fish. On the fisherman's head was a chimney from which flames were leaping and smoke rising.[4]

Jung had no doubt he was the fisherman in his son's dream.[5] And clearly this was at a time in Jung's life when, like Yeats, there was "a fire in his head." This might lead us to wonder, as it did Jung, about the "objectivity" of the psyche. The image of a fisherman undergoing cranial conflagration appeared not to Jung but to his son. The image was apparently in the collective air, in the psychic space of Jung's home, as if the image was objectively present and waiting for Jung to find it — or more to the point, be transformed by it whether he himself found it or not.

Later that same day, Jung did, as it happens, go "fishing" in the mysterious waters of his psyche and caught a kind of fish that turned out to be his first soul encounter.

Flames and fishing — delving into mysterious waters when your psyche is coming apart and then retrieving something sacred from those depths — this is an archetypal pattern that characterizes the Descent, not only for Jung and Yeats.

Elisabeth: She Who Dances the Earth
and Dreams Song to Feed the Longing

Elisabeth Nicolson is an Australian whose Soul Initiation took place in her late thirties. But she first heard the call from Soul when she was only sixteen. At the time she
had few words to describe that summons nor any guidance as to how to respond.
She was simply aware of an intense longing to drop out of school and go to a place
both on the land and within herself that felt like "a large, vast open plain."[6] But she
succumbed to pressure from parents, friends, and teachers, a common experience
of contemporary youth who approach the life passage of Confirmation and are,
tragically, deterred and redirected. By the time she completed college, she had been
captured by the mainstream socioeconomic system and was falling into a deep depression, a frequent outcome when the call is refused. "It all felt so incredibly mediocre and boring, so known, controlled, and contrived. There was nothing to want
except a career progression that looked like an offensive straight line. I felt trapped
and compromised."

But Elisabeth is one of the few who managed to free themselves. At age twenty-
one she traveled overseas for nearly a year, including several months working on a
trail construction crew in a remote area of Alaska, an experience that afforded her
vast expanses of solitude and a communion with wild land and creatures. This was
the start of her Cocoon time of wandering.

At twenty-four, the breakup of a romantic relationship brought about the end
of her life as she had known it. She left her job, friends, and community and embarked on a second year of wandering. "Many miles, many countries, and many
tears later," Elisabeth says, she was in Nepal in the midst of a twenty-three-day solo
trek when the Dissolution phase of her first Descent began. Her psychospiritual
center of gravity began to shift from Ego toward Soul:

> The physical pain, the solitude, and the sheer brilliance and expansiveness
> of the place saw me completely "break down." At this turning point of the
> hike, at the edge of an icy lake, I emerged naked and freezing from the wa-
> ters and knew to my core that I would never be the same. I had heard/felt
> something that would always guide me. I now know that voice to have a
> name — my soul — and as dark and terrifying as the things it periodically
> shouts at me, and as painful as the "trauma" it sometimes heralds into my
> life, I know it will never lead me astray. By following it, I know I will live a
> life that is deeply my own.

After Nepal, Elisabeth embarked upon a full ten years of off-and-on wandering. She would work for a year or two in the field of environmental management and then take off for a year. She was drawn to remote cultures vastly different than her own. "I wanted to be in places I could not understand, that filled me with a deep sense of being lost, being immersed in a strange mysterious world that changed me in ways I could not comprehend." To be lost and changed is the yearning that is emblematic of Wanderers in the stage of the Cocoon.

Earth Dancer

In the midst of her ten years of wandering, at age thirty-two, Elisabeth enacted her first vision fast — unguided, just herself and a friend in the Australian bush. During this fast, she had her first soul encounter and returned with a name that she did not at first embrace, "Earth Dancer":

> It sounded so cliché that I automatically wanted to reject it, but I couldn't reject the circumstances of it being told to me. It was on my last day of my fast. Each morning I had watched a sea eagle fly up my little valley past me. This day it stopped and flew a few circles before flying off. The name then "appeared" in my head. Moments later I heard a rustling. I watched a wallaby bound through the river toward me. I sat so still it got within a foot or two of me. It suddenly saw me and then bounded off. A wallaby is an Earth Dancer.

This was Elisabeth's first revelation of mythopoetic identity.[7] For the next three years, she "lived with" this name "rather than into it." She mostly tried to interpret it, and only in superficial ways — for example, because of her love of travel, "that I was meant to 'Earth Dance' my way around the world." A shallow response to soul encounter can abort the journey. But the Soul doesn't give up easily. The Soul uses our resistance in an attempt to undermine the Ego in a way that supports the journey. Elisabeth, for example, fell into a Mandorla, in which, as we've seen, the growing intrapsychic tension generated by a pair of opposites weakens the Ego until it breaks open. For Elisabeth, the tension was between purpose and purposelessness: "The same question kept arising, 'What is the purpose of my life?' combined with a sickening feeling that perhaps there was no purpose. If this was true, it seemed to me a fate worse than death."

Stand Up for What Is Wrong with Your People

When she was thirty-four, Elisabeth wandered off again for a year, this time into the vast, wide-open spaces of Western Australia.

> For the first time in my adult life, I started to "hear" the landscape speaking to me. She told me things that were beyond my cultural knowing. I was working

on a farm at the time. We had planted Blue Hopi corn, a whole field of it. I had come across a song recording of a corn prayer. We planted the corn with this prayer. Once the corn had grown large I would lie on the ground beside it listening to it moving in the breeze. There seemed to be some kind of message or instruction for me in that corn. I started to remember me when I was about ten years old. I remembered my deep love of indigenous peoples, particularly Native Americans, which was fueled by a family trip to Diné (Navajo) country. I started to remember me when I was a late teen, her darkness and depth. I started feeling like there were parts of her that were now really important to me. That she had some "knowing" that I no longer had.

The parts of herself that Elisabeth was remembering and reclaiming were the facets of her wholeness she needed to progress on her journey of soul initiation. Her South facet — her Wild Indigenous One — was being reanimated by her remembered allurement to the cultures of native peoples and by the relationship she was developing with the corn plants and her emerging ability to understand their speech. Her West facet — her Dark Muse-Beloved — was reawakening by virtue of recalling her teenage "darkness and depth" and also of her deepening embrace of her dream life:

Just before we harvested the corn, I had a dream: A Cornman appears in firelight before me wearing a robe of cornhusks and a headdress of corn. He looks me square in the face, maybe a foot away, and says, "You must stand up for what is wrong with your people."

Although she didn't know what Cornman meant, she accepted that she must somehow do what he asked. This perplexing dream-delivered command was Elisabeth's second soul encounter. It revealed another strand of her mythopoetic identity — she who stands up for what is wrong with her people.

A Song That Is Me

When she was thirty-five, Elisabeth enacted a second vision fast, this time in the redrock canyons of the southern Utah desert, with Geneen Marie Haugen and me as her guides, our first time meeting her. During the five preparation days before the solo, she found herself in an existential crisis:

I had hit a new kind of rock bottom where I repulsed myself. I felt confined by my language. I felt intensely fake/fraudulent and could not trust who I thought I was anymore, someone who felt horribly empty and bogus.

When our old way of being is dying, everything about us might feel wrong, and our subpersonalities — our inner protectors — might viciously attack us in an attempt to divert us from radical change. Elisabeth's crisis revealed that she was in the midst of a Dissolution deeper and more extensive than any previously.

One of the Dissolution practices we enact on Animas Quests before the fast is a fire ceremony during which initiates sacrifice a symbol they have fashioned in the preceding weeks, something that represents the life story that is ending. For Elisabeth, the fire ceremony was quite disturbing — in just the right way. She had made an effigy of herself as a globetrotting wanderer, the identity she had been living most fully and passionately for almost fifteen years:

> I burnt her. It was one of the hardest things I have ever done, to let her go into the fire, and yet I knew that I had to if I was going to get any sense of why I was alive. Afterward I felt so empty and sad. "I" was gone, was dead, was no more. I also remember having an intense sense that I was actually dying. I was so sure of death being nearby and wanting me that later, during the solo, I tied myself to a tree at night to prevent my being lured over the edge of the nearby cliff by some kind of spirit.

To open the way to a first or later soul encounter, we must sacrifice our attachment to the story we've lived up to that point. When we do, it's quite common to feel like we're actually dying. On their vision fasts, people often believe they will physically die.

Another group ceremony we enact in base camp before the solo is an evening trance dance, accompanied by our own drums, shakers, and voices. For Elisabeth, the trance dance, despite her conscious resistance to it, ended up confirming and deepening her first soul encounter — Earth Dancer — and introduced the possibility of another mythopoetic strand involving the ability to sense other people's "songs."

> The trance dance was an unwanted confirmation of an aspect of my name. Just before the dance started, I stood there thinking, *This is so stupid, I am not even going to really participate. I am just going to kind of stand here.* But then the drumming began and I got lost in rhythm. I ended up being consumed by the rhythm and feeling like my dance and voice were somehow taking me and all of us somewhere else. I could sense other people's "songs" somehow. That night I dreamed of being a part of a dance in a dancehall with three Black jazz musicians and many dancers. I was filled with so much joy as I danced with a billboard that advertised the dances.

Elisabeth's trance dance experience and her subsequent dream illustrate a few recurrent patterns of the Descent to Soul:

- Our subpersonalities' resistance to the journey itself and to what is revealed during it. A soul encounter often violates our existing beliefs about ourself and our world, so it's common for our subs to reject our Soul identity or attempt to evade it.
- The motif of not being in control, of being "taken" on a journey and transported to an unfamiliar, strange, or exotic place — a "somewhere else."

- The fact that later experiences often confirm, deepen, or extend earlier soul encounters.
- The way that dreams resonate with and amplify soul encounters — as if the mystery that is afoot in our shared world is in cahoots with our Dream-Maker. (It is.)

For her fasting site, Elisabeth chose — or was chosen by — a place several hundred vertical feet above base camp on a narrow and miles-long, bare-rock sandstone ridge, an ancient petrified sand dune, mottled beige and red, with virtually no vegetation, only an occasional cactus or small juniper tree. During her four-day-and-night solo, she sang and danced almost constantly. Before the end of her fast, Elisabeth experienced her third soul encounter, her most profound yet:

> On the third night an electrical storm sat with us all night. I was terrified, as I am afraid of storms, and my spot was so exposed. The electricity was everywhere. I just had to run my hand over my bivouac bag and static could be seen in the darkness. I thought I was going to get struck and die. I was certain and I was intensely afraid. In the early morning, lightning struck very close — the flash and the thunder were simultaneous. All I could do was wait to die. Then the storm left and I lived. I rested all day. I was exhausted, but I was alive. I had this strong sense of being deeply fortified by that storm. I lived! That evening, as I watched the sunset and sang praises to her, the wind came and touched my face. She cupped my cheek and said, *Song Dreamer.* My first thought was, *Oh now I have two useless, stupid names.* But another part of me wept with joy at finally coming home. After years of wandering and longing, I was home. I belonged to the world in the only way that I could.

This experience illustrates several additional common features of soul encounters:

- Intense fear — often of the nearness of death — preceding revelation. Getting shook up loosens our grip on our old life, opening the way for a vision of a deeper calling.[8]
- The link between visions and storms: tempests signaling the imminent arrival of mystery; storms as shape-shifters; a storm we freely walk into; being fortified and readied by a storm.
- The arrival of a soul name communicated by an other-than-human being — in Elisabeth's case, the wind. For me, it was a butterfly. In both cases, our cheeks were touched as our names were spoken: "She touches your face / and says your name / in the same moment," David Whyte writes.[9]
- Our subpersonalities' immediate attempts to "protect" us from being radically altered by revelation. Some subs will simply try to distract us, while

other subs will immediately go on the offensive, as with Elisabeth's swift inner critic.

- Soul revelations occurring during the two quotidian moments of liminality: sunset and sunrise.
- The deeply moving nature of soul encounter: We feel it holds the truth we were born with, that we're destined to embody.
- The direct and irreversible shift in our Egos that begins immediately after the experience, as when Elisabeth says: "After years of wandering and longing, I was home."

But Mystery had more for Elisabeth on this vision fast, two additional and coordinated encounters with Soul, one an aural vision at dawn, the other in the form of an instruction received out of nowhere and "heard" inside:

> The last night of the solo I enacted an all-night vigil. I sat facing west, drifting in and out of sleep. Very early in the morning whilst it was dark, I woke to a woman's beautiful voice singing a song in an unfamiliar language. She was not far away, maybe fifty feet. I could not see her, but I could hear her, she was hiding in her song. Her voice was so clear and beautiful. She sang a song that somehow lives in me still, a song that *is* me and what I must do in this lifetime. I was moved by the beauty but also terrified and frozen with fear.
>
> I must have fallen asleep again as the next thing I knew it was day. I packed my things to prepare for the reunion with the group. As I was doing so the following phrase entered my head: *Dance the earth and dream song to feed the longing.*

Hearing a song is a not-uncommon form of soul encounter. But not just any song; it's a song that we instantly recognize as our own and one that somehow expresses the deepest secrets of our Soul. Although Elisabeth didn't recognize the language of the song, she for sure recognized its feeling-meaning. This numinous encounter again illustrates how the transformation of the Ego begins in the moment of the experience and how the encounter is both a blessing and a burden, an inspiration and a violation.

Another frequent feature of a soul encounter is that soon after, in a moment of distraction, Mystery or Soul follows up and amplifies the encounter by whispering a mythopoetic directive or command both utterly mystifying and undeniably the way forward for the embodiment of our singular gift. Elisabeth heard this directive as, essentially, a soul name: She Who Dances the Earth and Dreams Song to Feed the Longing:

> For me, this name is an instruction on how to do what Cornman told me to do: *Stand up for what is wrong with your people.* My people have forgotten

the sacred and thus forgotten how to belong to the world. Songs and their physical manifestation through dance are a way of embodying the sacred and communing with the world. They help the great song and dance of life to continue. Their vibration creates form. The songs create the field, and the form follows on from there. When people sing those kinds of songs, they are literally playing with reality. My role, my home, is to somehow help people, places, and things dance in their song.

The answer to Cornman's riddle (received in a dream a year or two earlier) arrived on Elisabeth's vision fast by way of the revelation of a Soul name. Soul encounters often explain or amplify one or more previous numinous experiences.

Both Blessing and Burden

It bears repeating that a soul encounter is a burden and a violation as well as a blessing and a joy. Witness Elisabeth's description of the aftermath of this second vision fast, written three years later:

Coming off the mountain, it felt like my life had been ruined and made. In naming me, the world had claimed me. My life was no longer my own. This was a devastating revelation and I still am torn between feeling great joy at knowing who I am/my place in the great dance and also wanting a simple life. I feel like the role of Earth Dancer is too big. It requires and demands so much. It is a big role to grow into. I have been literally bamboozled with images and information from the muse since my return. I often have no idea of what to do with it all. Sometimes I want it all to stop or at least slow down. I often feel overwhelmed by the task of being Earth Dancer.

The other hard thing about returning was feeling utterly alone and unguided. I felt like I had seen the other side of something that completely altered me forever. My culture and people now felt devastatingly shallow and young, small. I still feel this at times. I have even doubted my sanity at times. The joy has been finally feeling like I am living my life! This is a paradox because I no longer feel like my life is of my choosing, but I am living the only life that can be called my own; my unique, sacred, gifted way of being here and being a part of the great song and dance. Since this second vision fast, I have never again wondered, *What is the purpose of my life?* This has provided great stability, strength, and presence. Now I live with the question, *How am I being asked to be Earth Dancer, and in what ways is she being asked to show up through me?*

Later, we'll explore some of Elisabeth's answers to that question. Here, the focus is the primary change in a person after soul encounter: They are not necessarily happier, less stressed or busy, wealthier, more famous or fertile, or less prone to illness or injury — the most common standards of "success" in egocentric cultures. Rather, the primary change is that they no longer wonder about the meaning of their life. They know who they are at a depth far below any of the social or vocational details of everyday existence. They no longer ask what the point of life is, whether of their particular life or of life generally — even if they do not yet know the specific ways they will embody their mythopoetic identity. They have been blessed with a mission bigger than themselves, one that stretches far beyond the temporal horizon of their own life. This one gift makes all the difference. It's of greater value than all the material riches of the world. Now they know how they belong not only to their social group or to the organizations they work with but, more significantly, to the greater Earth community and to the unfolding of the cosmos. They know what they were made for. They no longer experience the existential doubt and unrest that emanate from the core of most contemporary human psyches. It's like falling in love but longer lasting and bigger; this is, after all, falling in love with the world and all of life.

Dreaming Song

A couple of weeks after her vision fast in the redrock desert of Utah, and before returning home to Australia, Elisabeth traveled, as previously arranged, to Peru. There she experienced yet another soul encounter, this one facilitated by a ceremony in the Amazon jungle in which participants drank a brew of the entheogenic vine ayahuasca. The ceremony was guided by a native shaman (an ayahuascero):

> I had periodically dreamed of ayahuasca for some years but had no desire to use plant allies. I was terrified of them. Whilst in Peru, I started having dreams of ayahuasca every night. So I went to the Amazon and drank. It felt like my life was almost claimed that night. The imagery was of me sitting in the jaws of a giant snake, of endless death, and of lines of intergenerational trauma caused by centuries of colonization that damaged the bodies and psyches of both the colonized and the colonizers. When I opened my eyes all I could see were songs, thousands and thousands of shamanic songs of the sort the ayahuascero was singing. I could literally see the song forms, everywhere, like patterns or waves of sand. Hours went by like this. I realized the power of song. And I sang and sang along with the Shaman as though I knew those songs from another time. I felt myself become the songs.

This journey with ayahuasca was a confirmation of her name, She Who Dances the Earth and Dreams Song to Feed the Longing. Elisabeth was in fact dreaming song while awake. Perhaps this experience was also an amplification of her name: She was able to *see* songs — more than just "sensing" them as she did during the trance dance before her second vision fast. We might suspect this as one of her soul powers. As with all soul encounters, Elisabeth was directly shifted by this experience, as if ayahuasca directly bestowed on her an existential and ontological initiation.[10]

Advanced Wholing and Self-Healing during the Descent

Elisabeth, like most psychospiritual Wanderers, experienced some very intense and destabilizing moments on her Descent. At times, she felt lost and feared she was losing her sanity or that she might not physically survive. Often her inner protectors (her subpersonalities) were doing all they could to divert her from the journey — by telling her to abandon the whole undertaking, harshly criticizing her, or causing her to doubt her authenticity, trustworthiness, or readiness. These are some of the challenges you can expect to face on your own journey. At some point during your Descent, you'll probably need to do some advanced wholing and Self-healing work, as described in chapter 2.

Keep in mind that just because your subpersonalities are doing their best to protect you does not necessarily mean you don't need their protection. This is true at any time in life — just all the more so during a Descent. Let's dig further into this: Our beloved subs took care of us in childhood when we didn't have mature and resourced adults available to help us. After childhood, our subs have done their best to protect us when we haven't had access to our own mature resources (our facets of wholeness). Thank god, then, for our subs! Even after we outgrow the need for their survival strategies most of the time, there are still spells in life when the challenges are so great or unfamiliar that we need our subs more than usual. The journey of soul initiation is one of those spells. This is why it's essential both before and during a Descent to cultivate a more advanced degree of wholeness and maybe, if necessary, to allow your subs to protect you from intense experiences for which you are not yet sufficiently resourced — like, for example, the experience of fully embracing your mythopoetic identity as you begin to become conscious of it.

Your mythopoetic identity is, by definition and origin, a threat to your Ego when you first encounter it. If it weren't, you would've uncovered it long ago. It's one of the realities your subs have most wanted to protect you from, since uncovering and embracing it means the end of your former (Adolescent) identity and the life, story, and world implied by and anchored by that identity. As that identity crumbles, as you begin to slip away from that mooring and out into the open sea, your subs will naturally rush in and attempt to save you. When they do, if you're not sufficiently resourced to be able to gratefully embrace and love your subs, then you really do need their help.

During your Descent, your subs might try to protect you from an experience you're actually ready for, something for which you're sufficiently resourced. If this happens, do the Self-healing work of embracing your subs (see chapter 2) — and then walk through the very doorways they're trying to block you from, because those are the ones that will take you to Soul.

On the other hand, your subs might try to protect you from an experience for which you really are not sufficiently resourced at a time when you don't have access to your Self for more mature protection. In this case, let your subs protect you, and deepen your wholing work. If necessary, seek help from a soulcentric psychotherapist and begin or deepen a centering or stress-reduction practice (meditation, centering prayer, yoga, tai chi, or qigong, for example). At times during a Descent, you might need a break from the intensity of your numinous encounters. Sometimes you can choose to step out of that river or into an eddy; sometimes you can't and need help from a guide.

Fear is common during a Descent. You might hear yourself thinking or saying it's your "ego" that's afraid, but what part(s) of your psyche are you referring to? If it's one or more subs, this might suggest you're not yet sufficiently resourced for the Descent. Or you might be adequately resourced but your subs don't believe it. (They virtually never believe it; their motto is better safe than sorry.) It could also be that your Ego — even if highly resourced, with good access to all four facets — is afraid because, let's face it, the Descent *is* hazardous, especially to your former identity. This kind of fear is healthy and helpful — it summons your resources for the hazards ahead. Courage, of course, doesn't mean the absence of fear.

The well-resourced Wanderer roams through our enchanted world and actively submits to Mystery (by using Descent practices), remains wide awake and present to Mystery, romances the world, and follows the lead of Soul (especially when her subs resist). Supported by inner and outer guides, she trusts her own unknowing. This Wanderer might enact ceremonies of gratitude for her subs — her Rebel, for example, or her Skeptic, Curmudgeon, Victim, or Prince — to reassure them of the inner and outer resources she possess should she run into difficulties.

Soul Encounter: Sinking the Roots of Ego More Deeply into Soul

The primary feature that distinguishes soul encounters from all other experiences is that they root the Ego (the conscious self) more deeply into the psychic substratum that is the Soul. They shift Ego further away from being an agent for itself and further toward being an agent for Soul. This is the shift from egocentric to soulcentric — for example, from environmental management to dancing the Earth and dreaming song, or from psychologist to cocoon weaving.

Soul — our unique eco-niche — can be imagined, metaphorically, as psychic soil. It is as if the human Ego, in order to be formed and viable at all, must begin its life in the constructed and protective environment of a human culture, somewhat like a seedling in an indoor plant nursery. Then, if and when ready, it is transplanted outside (outside human culture) in the Earth soil of Soul. This amounts to a second birth for the Ego: The first occurs at age three or four, when the Ego is birthed from the womb of human culture,[11] while the second takes place at the time of soul encounter, when the Ego is reborn from the womb of the natural, more-than-human world.[12] The development and maturation of the human Ego, then, is necessarily a two-step project: First, it is shaped and clothed with familial, cultural, and linguistic fundamentals and garments, and second, this fragile sprout undergoes the delicate and dangerous initiatory procedure of being extracted from its native habitat of human culture (Dissolution) and planted into what at first is experienced as an entirely unfamiliar and exotic medium (Soul). Most transplants thrive but some do not survive the shock. The risk is unavoidable, even necessary. Adequate preparation of the seedlings can make all the difference. This is what healthy childhood and Adolescence is for. Although the psychological life of a human Ego can begin only in a cultural nursery, remaining in that nursery beyond a certain point is not a real life at all.

Given the etymological relationship between *human* and *humus* (Latin, for earth, soil, ground), perhaps we've always known that to become fully human, one must at some point be rooted in earth, in soil, in Soul. The contemporary mainstream world has forgotten how this is done; indeed, it has forgotten that it ever *has* been done. Most humans now live their entire lives disconnected from humus, literally and figuratively. The result is a world of immature humans, green in the wrong way, a world that neglects and is potentially destroying the humus on which it depends, both psychically and physically.

The transformation of psyche that begins with soul encounter alters our world, not just our consciousness. Our consciousness changes because how we experience *ourselves* changes. But soul encounter also transforms our experience of the world itself, of what it is to be alive and human: not, for example, a cognizant cog in an immutable machine nor a would-be survivor (or winner) on a dog-eat-dog planet, but a visionary partner in an ever-unfolding and evolving story. As our identity undergoes the transition from fundamentally egoic and social to fundamentally ecological and soulful, we cross a threshold into a different world. Now we are aware that life is, first and foremost, something like a mystery play — to borrow Jung's image — or a dream, a poem, a story, a song.

David Byrne, founding member of the Talking Heads, says something similar:

> I sense the world might be more dreamlike, metaphorical, and poetic than we currently believe — but just as irrational as sympathetic magic when looked at in a typically scientific way. I wouldn't be surprised if poetry — poetry in the broadest sense, in the sense of a world filled with metaphor, rhyme, and recurring patterns, shapes, and designs — is how the world works. The world isn't logical, it's a song.[13]

Our first soul encounter is a particularly distinctive life experience because this is when our conscious identity shifts from the social realm of the human community to the psycho-ecological realm of the more-than-human community, the greater and wider web of life. We no longer experience ourselves primarily in terms of our relationships, social roles, or means of earning a living. Now we know ourselves as an individual with a particular place in and relationship to the larger, natural world within which our human village is only one realm.

This is the shift into our fourth way of consciously participating in the world. When we're children, family is our primary experienced context; our world is centered in our home life. Then, at puberty, our center of gravity undergoes its first conscious shift — into our second way of participation: from family to peer group and the wider human community. Later, if we reach the Cocoon, our center of gravity shifts again, this time to a third realm, the mysteries of the more-than-human world. And then, at the moment of our first soul encounter, our center of gravity moves vertically, downward for the first time, rooting itself in Soul, our fourth way of participating in the world. This last shift is not complete until the life passage of Soul Initiation, the commencement of true Adulthood.

Your soul encounter is an experience of a soul image, symbol, or story — something numinous or sacred at the very core of your individual life, and which mythopoetically communicates something of your unique, innate ecological niche. A soul image can be multifaceted and complex, like an elaborate tapestry with many smaller component images. A single soul encounter might be a glimpse of only one facet of your soul image. At times in your life, you could be simultaneously drawing on several soul-infused images, and you might not yet be able to understand their relationships to one another. Eventually, the puzzle comes together, perhaps when you experience a deeper image — one more central to your Soul — that holds all the others as specific facets. The value of less-deep images is that they are easier to access and easier to understand and act on. The value of deeper ones is that they embrace more of your mythopoetic potentials, are closer to the essence of the mystery that is your Soul, and have more power once you're able to embody them.

Common Qualities of Soul Encounters

How can you tell if a profound experience — even a mystical one — is an encounter with Soul? How do you distinguish a soul encounter from, say, the voice of your Muse (creative epiphanies); an eruption of your Shadow (an encounter with repressed elements of your psyche); an experience of Spirit or God (a theophany, or a mystical union); or an insight or revelation of something you must do, described in everyday middleworld terms? In addition to the primary and defining feature of soul encounters — that they sink the roots of Ego more deeply into Soul — there are a dozen additional attributes I've found to be common qualities of soul encounters.

These are neither definitional elements nor "requirements" for an experience to count; rather, the more of these qualities an experience exemplifies, the more likely it's a soul encounter:

1. It reveals your foremost ecological contribution in the great scheme of things: your soul-infused life purpose understood mythopoetically, not in terms of social or vocational role.

2. It is profoundly moving in the moment: the feeling, for example, that an image or declaration holds the truth you were born with, the truth you were born to embody.

3. You feel ecstatic, beyond reason and the Ego's control, rapturous, lifted out of yourself; it renders you an agent for Mystery (via Soul).

4. It is uncanny, eerie, or wildly mysterious: numinous, as if wrapped in sacred cloth: you feel you're in the presence of the holy or a great mystery.

5. It shakes your whole world to its foundations, upsets the applecart of your life.

6. It is accompanied by synchronicities between outer and inner experiences (for example, being touched by the wind or a butterfly wing and, in the same moment, hearing your name).

7. It is experienced during nonordinary states, such as dreams, deep imagery, trance, fasting, and illness, or it is induced by plant allies or other entheogens.

8. It evokes a second wave of profound emotional reaction: of hope, desire, gratitude, joy — as well as grief (for the years living without it) and fear (for the immense changes it will mean and the demands it will make on you).

9. You feel a boundless desire to embody it in your life plus an equal terror to do so; you feel equally blessed and burdened; it feels way too big to live; it feels like both a violation and an inspiration.

10. You have the conviction that its embodiment will serve a whole community, not just yourself and a few others.

11. It resonates with other numinous events both before and after it; it explains something significant about your past and eventually confirms and amplifies future events.

12. It is ultimately confirmed both by your joy in living it and by the fact that it serves the world.

Matt: Compost Bridger of Worlds

Earlier, you learned about Matt's crisis at age twenty-three that precipitated his Confirmation (passage into the Cocoon), a crisis provoked by an ecstatic and unnerving experience in a field above a lake near Seattle. Many years later, at age thirty-six,

Matt's first Descent began when he enacted his Great Wave Dream along the Rio Grande (see "Matt's Crisis and Call," pages 82–86).

Old Man Compost

Several months after his Great Wave experience, during a summer vision fast in the mountains of western Colorado, Matt experienced his first soul encounter, his first revelation of mythopoetic identity. It unfolded in a number of phases over several days, starting before his solo time, continuing during his fast, and culminating the day after.[14]

On the first morning after backpacking into the group base camp, Matt got up out of his sleeping bag and felt drawn by "some mysterious pull" into a grove of aspen saplings that seemed "enshrouded in some mystical quality."

> Dew-laden ferns carpeted everything up to my waist and chest as I strode cautiously and silently through a thick morning mist. I saw a lone dark figure — standing, half-hidden, calling to me. As I drew closer, the dark shape took the form of a large stump, old and ominous, surrounded by hundreds of young aspens. He was hunched forward and dead, yet radiating a dark animate wisdom. It felt as if everything in my life had conspired to bring me to this encounter, as if the old stump had been waiting for *me*, as if he held some key to my life, my identity, and my destiny.

It's common during a Descent to experience something like this — a sense of having passed through a veil into a strange and unfamiliar realm, yet one that feels intimate and personal, a sense of having finally entered the real world and uncovering a truth at the very heart of your life.

The next morning, two days before the start of his fast, Matt returned to the tree stump — "Old Man" — and knelt before him in the mud and the morning mist, up to his neck in shimmering green ferns.

> Suddenly I was swarmed by hundreds of flies. I became uncomfortable to the point of being a little scared, but I endured the discomfort of the flies all over my body and face, biting me. I introduced myself to Old Man and I felt him say he already knew me and, to my fear, that he was tasting me. It was as if he tasted decay on me, something decomposing on my body or in my life. A perceptual shift came over me: He was in the flies. It was as if he was checking me out, getting to know me by tasting me.
>
> I came to realize I was enacting my own decomposition, like a rotting carcass. I asked Old Man Compost to teach me how to decompose and he said he already was. I walked behind him and looked out over the aspen grove and saw that his realm is the dying, decay, and decomposition that feeds all these trees, the damp, rotting world out of which this new life and

energy emerges. I understood that the old ways in my life that no longer work must somehow become food for the new.

Meeting Old Man Compost accelerated and amplified the Dissolution phase of Matt's Descent — the decomposition and composting of his previous identity.

By his third day in base camp, Matt felt he had entered into an apprenticeship with Old Man Compost. He returned to the young aspen grove and once again knelt before the stump.

What is decomposing in me? I wondered, a question pregnant with both grief and longing. My way of relating with others in my life had been draining me for far too long. The many strategies I would employ to keep myself small and unthreatening, the thousands of small capitulations to those voices demanding that I edit what I really want to say so as not to offend. The countless ways I avert my eyes in ordinary conversation to limit exposing who I really am. There was a surprising tenderness in these small revelations. I began to sob. An image began to emerge of who I really am, what I most value, and how I need to be in the world. I began to recognize the truth that *I am* Compost, that there are mysterious microbial decomposing energies at work within me and that somehow these energies also work *through* me, that in some way I myself am an agent of psychospiritual decomposition. Through my encounter with Old Man, I felt mirrored in depths I had not before experienced.

This was Matt's first glimpse of mythopoetic identity — "an agent of psychospiritual decomposition." Soul encounter often emerges out of a great grief that derives in part from the loss of an earlier identity and in part from a longing for something deeper and more real. It's as if the vision or revelation hatches from an egg that must be incubated by a lament.

Bridging between Worlds

While in base camp, Matt was designing ceremonies to enact during his solo time. One, which he called "a Childhood Portal," was a way of returning, in his imagination, to a magical place in the woods behind his childhood house, a world of moss-covered trees and rotting stumps where he would play nearly every day with friends or alone, a place and time in which he sensed he had lost something essential.

Matt's Childhood Portal ceremony, enacted on his first solo day, was perhaps the most important event on his actual fast:

I gathered leaves and moss-covered sticks to create a diorama of the magical place in the woods behind my house. Strong memories surfaced of the creek at the bottom of the steep hill and of the woods beyond, a place with fallen trees that became a refuge for my imaginal worlds. I began to feel pangs of grief. I had a strange and haunting feeling that I had lost something back there, that I had *known* something or was *known by* something — a mysterious relationship with the place itself that was natural and ordinary to my childhood self. I had a particularly vivid memory of a small split-log bridge covered in moss that I used to cross with a wheelbarrow to dump grass clippings in a compost bin on the other side of the creek. This threshold — the bridge and the compost bin, together, a threshold between my given childhood life and my created imaginal world — hit me at a cellular level.

The gateway to soul encounter is often found in just such a numinous childhood memory, as if a portal to Soul had been constructed early in life by Mystery and had been waiting ever since for the right moment to open. In this case, the portal was a waking experience from childhood. Earlier we saw how a dream from childhood — Matt's Great Wave Dream — served a similar function. His Childhood Portal ceremony opened a magical door — and he walked through. What he found on the other side was a second element of his mythopoetic identity: a Bridge image that was now merging with the image of Compost.

On the second night of his solo, Matt ritually created a small compost bin out of sticks in order to enact a "composting ceremony." As he trance danced into the night while filling the bin with mulch, he entered an altered state and the ceremony spontaneously morphed into a "Seed Ceremony": He found himself planting "seeds" (carved sticks) in the mulch, thrusting them into the compost with loud cries.

> The ceremony reached a frenzied crescendo; it felt like I had surrendered to something in my deepest nature, like it was a way of Bridging worlds. By the end, I very much expected something to grow or emerge out of the compost of my life.

The Stone Column

After Matt returned to base camp, one of the guides led the group on a deep-imagination journey — a way to consciously access images that arise unbidden from the depths of the psyche, in contrast to those that might be suggested by a guide or consciously generated by the journeyer. (This is essentially the same method as Jung's self-guided use of active imagination.) During this imagery journey, Matt returns to the young aspen grove. There Old Man Compost asks Matt to push him over headlong into the Earth. He does.

> As I look at Old Man Compost, now lying flat on the earth, he elongates into an enormous fallen tree covered in moss. I climb up on this tree and walk across it and realize it is a bridge going through the Earth into a massive underground chasm or fissure. The bridge leads toward a large stone

column in the center of the chasm. The column of stone feels like the underground center of my existence and of all existence. I feel completely in awe of it.

But this was not Matt's first encounter with this stone column. About a year earlier he had one of the most numinous dreams of his life:

> I am in an art exhibit indoors, alone. It is a sacred, creative space. Suddenly, I am drawn right through the wall of the museum into a dark inner chamber, a deep cavernous space. I am floating in this vertical fissure that seems to go up and down forever. In the center is a massive column of stone that shimmers in ambient light. It's sinuous, sensual, erotic, and profoundly strong. I silently float up the chamber, transfixed in awe by the sheer beauty and magnitude of this encounter.

Immediately upon awakening, Matt knew this dream was somehow key to his mythopoetic identity, but he didn't understand how. By the end of his vision fast, however, he was discovering the resonances and connections between the images of a stone column, a bridge across a chasm, compost, and the planting of seeds.

Compost Bridger of Worlds

What we are witnessing here is Matt's mythopoetic identity forming out of a bundle of mutually amplifying experiences from a variety of times, settings, and states of consciousness, including childhood memories, dreams, experiences in the wild, self-designed ceremonies, and deep-imagination journeys. Many of these events took place before or after the solo time of his vision fast.

The alchemical interaction of these experiences bestowed Matt with the psyche-shifting and life-clarifying mythopoetic image he calls Compost Bridger of Worlds:

> I am both a decomposing bridge that spans worlds and the one who leads others across this bridge. Beholding this image of Compost Bridge, I am both enlivened and troubled. I am enlivened because I have discovered a treasure hidden long in the depths of my psyche but also because the world itself has revealed one of its mysteries in a very intimate and personal way. It is troubling for the same reasons and also because it demands a response from me, a change that will affect my worldview, my lifestyle, and my way of expressing my faith. The stakes are high.

Matt's story demonstrates several patterns, including the way numinous waking experiences, such as with Old Man Compost, connect with and are amplified by dreams, memories, and deep-imagery journeys. Another is how magical childhood experiences can become portals to soul encounters later in life.

Matt is not the only one who lost something back in childhood. We all have. We're born with a connection to our Souls and then inevitably lose that connection during the necessary busyness of learning a particular language, family, culture, and landscape. The goal of the journey of soul initiation is to reclaim that connection utilizing our deepened and more individuated consciousness achieved in the Cocoon.

Matt's consciousness and life were thoroughly shifted by his soul encounters. His Ego began to grow roots in the fertile soil of his mythopoetic identity. He understood that the mythos of Compost Bridger of Worlds would change "my worldview, my lifestyle, and my way of expressing my faith." It did.

Sabina: Spark Heart on Bear Path

Somewhere in the middle of her nine months of wandering in Central America and the western United States, Sabina, the young Swiss woman who left home on a one-way flight to LA (see "Sabina's Crisis and Call," pages 88–91), found herself, by wild chance, in the high Sierra Nevadas of California's Yosemite National Park. The navigational method that brought her there was the same one she had been using since leaving Switzerland: "Follow soul's input." She was twenty-five.

A Gaze Both Wild and Refined

Soon after arriving in Yosemite, Sabina loaded up her backpack and walked off, alone, into the wilderness, not in the famous valley but high above it in the remote Tuolumne subalpine world of granite peaks, conifer forests, lush meadows, lakes, and cascading streams. She wanted to be alone in the wild and far from other humans — to "open myself even more to Soul/Universe/Guidance." And she wanted to be in the company of bears. She had loved bears since her childhood — even though the living variety was long gone from the Swiss Alps, and she had never actually seen one in the wild.

Before her hike, Sabina had dutifully obtained a backcountry permit. The ranger had given her a quick lecture on wilderness etiquette, rented her a bear-proof canister for the small amount of food she was bringing, conveyed the standard cautions about bears and how to minimize the chance of encounters, and portentously made a point of mentioning that a bear had injured a Yosemite hiker just a few days before.

At the time, Sabina knew nothing about vision fasts, but she wanted to be alone in a wild place and knew that fasting, in the more common sense, was a "powerful opener" for her. But because she planned on hiking the whole time — and hiking alone — she ate lightly, reasoning that a complete fast would be too risky. She wandered in this way for four days, following her felt-sense and intuition. She would stop and listen for a while and then wander farther. Not having brought a tent, she slept under the stars.

On her third night, she awoke out of a sound sleep, her eyes instantly open. She was lying on her side. In the moonlight, five inches from her nose, was a bear paw, stationary. Before her body knew to panic, she looked up and was spellbound by the magnificent animal towering above her — the shaggy, matted fur of his leg, his claws directly in front of her face, his overpowering scent. He stood parallel to her sleeping bag, looking toward her backpack by her feet. She lay perfectly still, feeling "blessed and incredibly lucky to be so close to a wild creature." Then, remembering the ranger lecture, a wave of fear washed over her, soon followed by a calm willingness to die should this be her time. Bear was so close, his body heat and scent engulfed her.

Bear moved a few paces to Sabina's backpack and pawed at it. She knew that without her pack and its contents, she would not survive. Without conscious intent, Sabina lifted up slightly on her elbow and heard a soft warning sound emerge from her own throat, a sound that alarmed her as much as it did Bear, who dropped into a crouching, attack position. Sabina, her heart now beating wildly, assumed this was her last moment.

As we stared into each other's eyes, two feet apart, time stood still and we entered something way beyond time. Bear penetrated the very core of my being with his eyes. I had never felt seen like this — a gaze that was primal, instinctive, and wild, and at the same time, refined, soul-piercing, and gentle, utterly beautiful as well as terrifying. In his eyes, I saw a deep curiosity and a readiness-to-kill-if-need-be — not aggressive or ego-driven as with us humans, just a matter-of-factness, a beingness beyond what we humans ever get to feel or see. I felt no discord in him — the way we humans so often live in discord with ourselves and everything and everyone around us — only "rightness."

This moment of soul contact between Bear and Sabina endures independent of time, alive forever in Sabina's psyche, and perhaps in Bear's as well. But at some point, maybe after only seconds in the ordinary unfolding of time, Bear turned on his heels, wheeled away from Sabina, and disappeared into the forest. Something of Bear, however, remained behind.

What a gift: to experience a wholeness in this bear beyond what I had thought possible. Something came to peace in me I hadn't known could find peace on Earth. Something awoke in me that was primal, wild, and hugely refined and delicate. It never went back to sleep.

Nor did Sabina that night.

Sabina's midnight meeting with Bear began the rooting of her Ego in Soul. Ever since, Sabina has experienced Bear as a palpable presence walking beside her. "He guides me into my true, innate power and how to live that power in the world." One of her soul powers is her exceptional capacity to be "steadfast, unafraid, calm, determined," even in the midst of turmoil or danger.

Sabina's exchange with Bear was her first soul encounter: It established the image-feeling of Bear at the center of her soul path. The fabric of this encounter with Soul is woven of the sensory experience of Bear (sight, scent, sound), the extraordinary emotions of the encounter (awe, terror, deep gratitude), and the numinous image-feeling of Bear as spiritual ally. This encounter granted her the courage "to walk my own path," not that of any teacher, and awoke her capacity to "walk toward it" rather than to run away, hide, or wait for "it" to come to her. Bear mirrored a part of her she had previously projected onto others, the part of her that "is powerful, clear, steadfast, reliable, and knows what she wants." At the time Sabina could not have told you more about the relationship between Bear and her mythopoetic identity, but this encounter changed her irreversibly and fundamentally.

Bring Your People Here

Several years later, when she was thirty-one, Sabina experienced another soul encounter during a group vision-fast ceremony in the Colorado Rockies. I was one of her guides. Our base camp at treeline, at an altitude of 11,500 feet, was four miles from and two thousand vertical feet above our trailhead. Directly over us towered the 14,017-foot summit of a mountain known to the native Ute people as Shandoka — "Storm Maker." It was early August.

> The weather was fierce: freezing cold, thunderstorms, rain, and hail — storms not only outside but also inside. It took me to my knees. Literally. During my solo, I got so weak from all that was happening to me and in me, including fasting, that I could barely walk.

On the third night of her solo, Sabina "dragged" herself to a nearby boulder on the steep mountain slope. There she enacted a Death Lodge ceremony, to which she invited, in her emotionally and somatically charged imagination, anyone who wished to be in conversation with her and to say goodbye to her before she released the story and identity she had lived up to this point. The ceremony lasted hours and was extremely intense emotionally — full of tears, both of sadness and joy. When the ceremony was complete, she stayed at her Death Lodge in the dark beneath the summit and the cold and now crystal-clear night sky.

> Then it happened. The universe opened. The darkness took me in with its piercing spark of stars crashing into my being while driving me at lightning speed out of my known reality. The stars were exploding/imploding, dying and at the same time being reborn. At first I felt fear of the immensity that I might lose myself in, forever wandering the vast blackness without ever again finding another human or a path back to Earth. At the same time, it

felt *so* much like home, more than anything before or after. The stars crashing and at the same time being reborn pierced my heart, tore it open, like the abyss in the universe I was seeing. I did not know if my physical body would survive it, but I did not care because what was happening was way bigger than this one earthly life in this physical body.

And then I received clear, straightforward instructions of what I was to do in my life. I heard — like a booming demand but also a gentle whisper — *BRING YOUR PEOPLE HERE*. I felt/heard it, but it was simultaneously "translated" into clear English.

I was so startled, it took me right out of the deep state I had been in. *What?? What did you say? Could you repeat this, please?* Silence. The curtains were drawn closed again, and the universal explosion/abyss looked again like the starry sky as I had known it before. *Could you at least tell me what you mean by this?* Silence. *Anything?* Silence. Then, in the same whisper/booming "voice" ringing inside me and throughout the universe — although a bit less demanding, a bit softer — I heard, *Spark Heart, you are Spark Heart.*

The "spark," it seemed, referred to the gigantic tearing open into the abyss/universe that I had just experienced. *You are Spark Heart.* Immediately I felt, deep in my bones, that this does describe me and my task in the world.

Sabina's experience under the stars exhibits most of the common qualities of soul encounters (see "Common Qualities of Soul Encounters," pages 162–63). Interestingly, it begins with a transpersonal opening into an ego-subverting and awe-filled beholding of Spirit — for Sabina, her witnessing of "the universal explosion/abyss." Then the experience segues into a revelation of individual mythopoetic identity — for Sabina, "Spark Heart" and "bring your people here." It's as if her conscious self was first brought into the presence of the infinite, so that Spirit could reveal Sabina's unique, exclusive, and ultimate place within that ultimate context of Spirit.

But Sabina received one more vital insight that night: "I realized that Spark Heart is only half my name. I just knew. I asked for a dream to let me know about the second part of my name." A few months later, the dream arrived:

> I am walking in a spiraling, Earth-wise direction [counterclockwise], and Bear is on my left. My hand is on his furry back, and he leads me on my spiral path in life, turning ever deeper into Soul-land. When I awake, I realize my name is Spark Heart on Bear Path.

Like everyone who experiences an encounter with Soul, Sabina found herself now entrusted with a task she rightly called "larger than life" — as Spark Heart on Bear Path, bring your people here — with little understanding of what it might mean to be or do this and no clue whatsoever how to go about manifesting it. But this ecopoetic mission and her soul name now lived in her body and in her psyche, and they began their work of reshaping her. Like all soul initiates, she had been blessed and cursed by a vision without yet having a way to perform it.

Joanna Macy: The Great Turning Wheel and the Stone in the Bridge

Ecophilosopher, author, and Earth elder Joanna Macy is a scholar of Buddhism, general systems theory, and deep ecology. She interweaves her scholarship with six decades of activism in international movements for peace, justice, and a healthy environment. She is the originator of the Work That Reconnects, a paradigm-shifting model and methodology for both personal and social transformation. Also known as Despair and Empowerment Work or Deep Ecology Work, this is a body of practices for groups that is designed, as Joanna writes, "to foster the desire and ability to take part in the healing of our world."

In her memoir *Widening Circles*, Joanna recounts two soul encounters that occurred nine years apart. The first was at the noteworthy age of twenty-eight,[15] at the birth of her second child, Jack. Joanna's physician gave her ether before closing her birthing tear with stitches. In the resulting trance, woven of the anesthetic, the ordeal of labor, and the mysteries of childbirth, she had an ego-shifting and life-changing vision:

> I am lifted up, high over the world, which is so far below that I cannot see it. Yet I am also at the heart of the world, and a giant wheel is turning — and the manner of its turning is the secret of all things. I am on it, spread-eagled across its spokes, my head near its open center. Sometimes it seems I could *be* the wheel, I'm so inseparable from it. I feel the spokes shudder through my body with alternating and intensifying sensations.[16]

At first she feels warmth, and it is very pleasant. But then the warmth slowly increases until it reaches intolerable heat. Then the heat slowly turns to its opposite — a relieving coolness, which gradually deepens into a terrifying frigidity. Then it's slowly back to warmth. Next the warmth turns into slow movement that gradually grows to an agonizing frenzy followed by a gradual slide to its extreme opposite of stasis. The wheel keeps turning, each sensation giving birth to its opposite. Additional pairs are freedom and order, then reason and passion.

> Each of the opposites becomes intolerable without the other. Each, when clung to, gives rise to its antipode. Bearable life occurs only at the point of balance between opposites, and that point, so fleeting and fragile, is won only through a terrible openness, through allowing the pain to pass through. Other than that, no god, no self, no safety. There is only the turning of the wheel, and the hole in the center that allows it to turn. I accept, as if I have always known, the inevitability and accuracy of what now is revealed. But I am frightened and pray for ignorance.[17]

This ecstatic and terrible vision is an instance of soul encounter that directly and permanently alters the psyche, sinking the Ego's roots into the depths of Soul. Although it did not itself reveal mythopoetic identity in an obvious way, it changed Joanna at her core:

> In a way that I could not explain, even to myself, the turning wheel betokened an order at the heart of reality. It erased my fear of the hole inside me....If a hole appears, just walk through it, see what's on the other side.[18]

In 2019, as she was about to turn ninety, I asked Joanna what was the hole inside her that she had feared in her twenties. She said it was "what I experienced after I walked out of Christianity. It was the hole where God and Jesus had been, the hole where something solid had been that I could trust." Christianity had been her faith and passion through her youth. But while in college, she discovered that "whole dimensions of life had been left out." She could no longer "commune with what God had become for me...a jealous, righteous judge...breathing down my neck, crowding me, sealing me in."[19] After her Wheel vision, the hole inside her became a kind of opportunity, a portal into mystery — something all Wanderers seek. As she said during our 2019 conversation:

> The hole is at the center. It's why the Wheel can turn. You have to have a hole. If we try to fill it up the way corporate capitalist consumer society would, it doesn't let the hole be there; it fills it up with its vulgarity and its crassness and its certainty and its peddling of certainty and "we are the best" and "we know." It fills up. You see, the necessity of not knowing. We have to leave space for not knowing. And I think the indigenous world always did. It's a very ancient apprehension of reality.

Three years earlier, in March 2016, I asked Joanna to what extent the Wheel had lived with her during the almost sixty years since she first encountered it. I asked her if, for example, this vision had frequently returned to her awareness, if it revealed to her something essential about her identity, and if it had helped her make major life decisions. Or in contrast, if it was more that the experience itself changed her alchemically, in every cell of her body, so that she had become a different person because of it and she didn't need to do anything more with it to interpret it or understand it. She said it was much more the latter. What follows are some portions of that conversation:

Joanna: I love your phrasing, Bill, when you said [the vision of the Wheel] just entered my body. It's the barest and in a way the most scalding encounter with truth I ever experienced — because it went through me so physically.

Bill: Have you ever said to yourself, "Well, I may never know how that vision came about, but it was as if Mystery was trying to, or even succeeded at, doing *something* to my psyche"?

J: "To"?

B: Or with. Or initiating you in some kind of way.

J: I think so. It felt like that. And for the weeks afterward, it was quite strong, but still, even if I think about it today, everything looked [after the vision] as if it were made out of paper, or as if I could put my finger through this reality at any moment, that it's just a fleeting thing — thrown together at this historical moment by forces so big.

At this point in the conversation, it seems that although Joanna's vision of the Wheel changed her directly and indelibly, it was only in a general, transcendent, or archetypal way. It left her with an everyday felt-sense that her reality — any reality — is insubstantial and ephemeral, that there is a greater truth behind it, a truth embodied in the universal opposites giving birth to one another.

But it turns out that her vision also changed her in a specific, soul-rooted way, a vital way that bore fruit years later in the development of her work. It's as if Mystery or Soul wanted her to have an early, foundational experience, deep in her bones, of a universal and archetypal dynamic that would later blossom at the heart of her vocation — as if, with her vision of the Wheel, Mystery was preparing her psyche to one day develop the innovative work for which she is now so well known, the Work That Reconnects. Continuing from our 2016 conversation:

B: Joanna, I wonder if your Despair and Empowerment Work is an example of your vision of the Wheel put into action. Because you've let yourself go into — and you've guided people into — some rather extreme places of despair in order to help them come through to empowerment, something almost opposite. As far as I know, you discovered this through your own experience.

J: Yeah. For example, that first workshop I did back in 1980 had been called "*from* despair *to* empowerment." And I realized instantly, almost, by the time I came out of it, that that was wrong. I can't use those prepositions: *from* and *to*. It was despair *and* empowerment. I realized that they have a mutually facilitating relationship. For one thing, you're never free of despair. And if you think you are, then you're going forward into the world in a hypnotic state, you know, a deluded state. Because there's still tremendous reason for despair, and there's still tremendous suffering. But they dance together, sort of yin and yang. And you discover that the despair or the grief — the great grief, also the great anger and fear and the overwhelm — that these enable you to discover what appears to be a tremendous belonging, something better than you could have imagined. It's better than being optimistic. It also builds trust. Because you can see people experiencing despair and you don't have to rescue them. You don't have to make them feel better. Because you know what they are going through is generative of the popcorn popping.

B: As we're talking, I've noticed myself making up a story: It's as if, through your
vision of the Wheel, Mystery was preparing your psyche to be able to say yes to
some really extreme features of the human experience.
J: Oh, how interesting. And not to be afraid of any intensity.
B: Yes.
J: Oh, thank you! That feels right. I could put on *that* pair of gloves.

When I've thought about Joanna's development of the Despair and Empowerment Work, sometimes I've asked myself how she managed to create that body
of practices when there was nothing like it in her experience. It seems that Mystery or Soul has a hand in such manifestations of genius. And it seems we can
see that inscrutable hand at work in Joanna's vision of the Wheel and its turning:
the way this vision prepared her psyche in the deepest manner imaginable to appreciate that every experience is relative to its opposite, is made possible by its
opposite, that empowerment and despair, for example, have a mutually facilitating relationship.[20]

Joanna's appreciation of the relationship between her vision and her life's work
is an example of recognizing, at some point in our lives, that there's something moving through us, something greater than us, a soul power or genius for which we are
merely the vehicle. We realize that if we try to own that power, egoistically, we end
up making it small and we risk making ourselves crazy.

In addition to directly changing Joanna at her core, both noetically and somatically, and enabling her psyche to embrace, without fear, intense and even harsh
dimensions of the human experience, there's a third way in which her vision of the
Wheel profoundly influenced her life and calling. Several years after her vision of the
Wheel, Joanna, while living in India, had a brief audience with the Dalai Lama. This
meeting was before she became a Buddhist. There, in the room in which they met,
she saw a painting of an eight-spoke wheel, the sacred Buddhist symbol of the Wheel
of the Dharma, which immediately recalled her vision.

The memory of the great wheel on which I had hung and turned had never
dimmed in the seven years since the ether experience at Jack's birth. It let
me glimpse a vast, underlying order that connected and made sense of all
things, and left me with the hope that I might someday be able to understand. Now in India, among the Tibetans, I encountered it again. Had the
Dharma been in store for me all along? This time, instead of fear, I felt only
awe and promise.[21]

As we've seen, a soul encounter can reveal a symbol or a thread of meaning that
runs through a life like an underground stream. For Joanna, one such thread is the
Buddha Dharma, with which her psyche strongly resonated and which became a
central theme, pillar, and partner in her soul work.

A Stone in the Bridge

In contrast to her vision of the Wheel, Joanna's second soul encounter, nine years after the first and two years after meeting the Dalai Lama, was of the sort that reveals mythopoetic identity. She was thirty-seven and still living in India, in Dalhousie. She had recently begun a meditation practice under the guidance of a Buddhist elder, and during her first weeklong retreat of intensive practice, she was experiencing the disorienting yet exhilarating sensation of no solid "I" that she could hold on to:

> This was scary; it was like the everlasting turning of the ether wheel. With no solid place to stand, to call my "own," I felt almost seasick. But it was also exhilarating, like skiing a steep slope, when you throw your weight away from the mountain.[22]

It's of great interest that her memory of her first soul encounter helped create the conditions for her second, which occurred during this week of meditation practice:

> To my inner eye appeared a bridge, slightly arching, made of stone. I could see the separate rocks of which it was built, and I wanted to be one of them. Just one, that was enough, if only I could be part of that bridge between the thought-worlds of East and West, connecting the insights of the Buddha Dharma with the modern Western mind. What my role might be — at the podium of a college classroom? at a desk in a library tower? — was less clear to me than the conviction possessing me now: I would be a stone in the building of that bridge.[23]

The Stone in the Bridge became a core soul image for Joanna, a bridge she might become part of and to which she might contribute in acts of service. At the time of this vision, she was not able to identify the nature of her delivery system — a professor? a librarian? — but she had no doubt she would become a stone in that bridge.

During our 2016 conversation, she told me:

> I remember it was stone, and I just wanted to be *one* stone in a stone bridge between East and West. And I *think* that in my mind it was about bringing Buddhism to the Western mind....But as I think about it, I see that it is a two-way bridge, and that my role has been — and my appetite has been — to bring Western thought into Buddhism, particularly by using one other body of thought that is basically, fundamentally, thoroughly nonlinear — mutual causality. I brought that through systems theory, and that has been extremely useful for me in unpacking the beauty of and relevance of the Dharma in our time. And it has for others, as well, who've read the more scholarly of my books, *Mutual Causality in Buddhism and General Systems Theory*, which is the intellectual grounding of all the work I do.

Comparing her experience of her two soul encounters, Joanna told me that the image of the Bridge "had a sense of mission" while her vision of the Wheel "felt far more esoteric and elusive of easy meaning." In my terms, I would say the Stone in the Bridge revealed a core image of her mythopoetic identity, her unique ecological niche. In contrast, the Great Turning Wheel vision was more a direct shifting of her psyche, a sinking of the roots of her Ego into the mysterious depths of Soul. In particular, it imprinted on her psyche a universal and archetypal dynamic — the dance between opposites — that would later blossom at the heart of her soul work, and without which her soul work might not have been possible.

There are a few last things to note about Joanna's soul encounters. She was not, either time, seeking or expecting any kind of numinous revelation of her individual destiny. And she was not using any consciousness-shifting practices commonly associated with soul-revealing visions. In the contemporary world, it's not uncommon for visionary moments, as rare as they are, to occur without warning or purposeful preparation — when the conditions are right. We might suspect the right conditions for Joanna included that she was in the Cocoon stage during both experiences, that she was adequately resourced psychologically, and that she was in a nonordinary state both times.

Chapter Seven

Jung's Soul Encounters

It was then that I ceased to belong to myself alone, ceased to have the right to do so. From then on, my life belonged to the generality....It was then that I dedicated myself to service of the psyche. I loved it and hated it, but it was my greatest wealth. My delivering myself over to it, as it were, was the only way by which I could endure my existence and live it as fully as possible.

— CARL JUNG, writing about his first soul encounter

> ...To be human
> is to become visible
> while carrying
> what is hidden
> as a gift to others.
>
> To remember
> the other world
> in this world
> is to live in your
> true inheritance....
>
> — DAVID WHYTE

Carl Jung had two soul encounters — *only* two, as far as I can tell. They took place relatively late in life (ages forty and fifty-two). We might have thought the founder of analytic psychology, an intrepid explorer of the psyche, would have had more than two, but let's place this in perspective: This is two more than most Western people *ever* have, it's one more than anyone needs, and the fact that he, a mainstream Western psychiatrist at the time of his first, with a family and an active professional life and a whole lot to lose — and no knowledge of or guidance on the journey — was able to descend into Soul Canyon at all and surrender to such a radical experience is a modern miracle of which we all are the beneficiaries. Jung himself made it clear that these two experiences revealed the meaning of his life and provided the needed orientation for his work.

Jung's first soul encounter arrived by way of active imagination; the second, courtesy of a dream. Both occurred while he was indoors at home — not in circumstances one would think of as nature-connected.

The Seven Sermons to the Dead

Jung's first soul encounter, described in both *Memories, Dreams, Reflections* and the *Red Book*, began on January 30, 1916, almost two and a half years after the start of his "confrontation with the unconscious" (his first Descent). The experience itself lasted several days. This wild ride of a visionary encounter began when Jung felt accosted by a mostly invisible throng of the dead who showed up at his house in the Swiss village of Küsnacht and announced that they were on their way back from Jerusalem. This confrontation resulted in Jung's writing his seven sermons to the dead, one of the final episodes in the *Red Book*. Jung's first soul encounter was the apex — actually, the nadir — of his intrapsychic journey that had begun in the fall of 1913. Two and a half years in the Dissolution phase of a Descent might seem like a long time, but given Jung's lack of preparation and guidance, it's not unusually long.

This first soul encounter began on the same day Jung's nine-year-old son awoke with his "anxiety dream" of the Fisherman (see "Resonances between Yeats and Jung," pages 149–51). On that "ominous" Sunday, Jung writes, "the atmosphere was thick," as if his house was "haunted," as if "the air was filled with ghostly entities." One of his daughters saw "a white figure passing through the room."[1] If all that wasn't weird enough, late that afternoon the front doorbell began ringing "frantically" but no one was at the door. (This doorbell was the older, mechanical kind with an actual physical bell.) Everyone in the house — his wife, five children, and two maids — heard it. Through a window, Jung could see the doorbell and watch it move.

> The whole house was filled as if there were a crowd present, crammed full of spirits. They were packed deep right up to the door, and the air was so thick it was scarcely possible to breathe. As for myself, I was all a-quiver with the question: "For God's sake, what in the world is this?" Then they cried out in a chorus, "We have come back from Jerusalem where we found not what we sought."[2]

That last sentence is essentially the first in Jung's thirteen-page booklet, *Septem Sermones ad Mortuos (Seven Sermons to the Dead)*, which he began writing on that

Sunday afternoon and completed in just ten evenings.[3] The dead had come to consult with him, and in order to retain his sanity and regain peace within his home, he knew he had to acknowledge them and respond. He was correct: "As soon as I took up the pen, the whole ghostly assemblage evaporated. The room quieted and the atmosphere cleared. The haunting was over."[4]

Such an abrupt shift upon saying yes to Soul is not uncommon. It's as if an immense psychic pressure has been building behind a dam and then at last the waters break through and a flood pours forth from the deep imagination, from the unconscious, from the underworld. Our subpersonalities constructed that dam to protect us from a psychological swamping, a worldview disruption they believed we would not survive (sometimes they are correct). These efforts of our subs are bolstered by the covert influence of people in our lives who also don't want us to change. If and when the dam bursts, the pressure subsides and the transformations begin.

Jung published his booklet, *Septem Sermones ad Mortuos*, privately and pseudonymously later that same year, 1916. In that version, Jung presented the sermons as if they had been written in the second century CE by the Gnostic author Basilides, who lived in Alexandria, Egypt.[5] (This version also appears as an appendix in *Memories, Dreams, Reflections.*) In the later-drafted *Red Book* version, however, Jung presents the sermons as delivered by Jung's inner guide, Philemon.[6]

To get the full effect of the *Seven Sermons*, you'll want to read them yourself — either version or both. But to summarize ever so briefly, the *Sermons* amount to an entire cosmology, a set of fundamental revelations about God, the unconscious, the human psyche, and the complex relationships between the three. Jung recorded these revelations as he received them. They were, in essence, channeled. ("It began to flow out of me."[7]) We might say that the *Sermons* were downloads from Jung's Soul (or Mystery) about vital psychospiritual dynamics, such as the principle of individuation, about pairs of opposites as qualities of the divine mystery, about gods and devils, about Eros and the Tree of Life, and about spirituality and sexuality as manifestations of the world of the gods.

The *Seven Sermons* were imparted directly to Jung in a way that both mystified his conscious mind as well as provided him with a lifetime's worth of material to unravel and offer as his primary contribution to our world. We might say that Jung's Soul forced the *Sermons* out of him, or *through* him, by aggressively confronting him (his Ego) with the dead and the burning questions they brought to him — questions such as: Where is god? Is god dead? What is the devil? What is holy communion? What is humanity?

But as with Jung's Dissolution experiences, the most important feature of the sermons, for Jung's journey of soul initiation, was not their content — his answers to the questions of the dead — but the mythopoetic or psycho-ecological position in which his Ego was placed as he channeled those sermons. What makes the *Seven*

Sermons a soul encounter is that Jung's transmission of them compelled him to experience himself and the world from the position and perspective of his unique psycho-ecological niche. He was placed in the psychological, social, and ecological role of a teacher, a preacher, a psychopomp with a particular relationship to the dead — and to all people who one day *will be* dead. As the sermons flowed out of him, his Ego began to be reshaped by his Soul into someone born to communicate certain dimensions of psyche and world to the modern era. On the level of Soul, Jung, to his surprise and perhaps horror, discovered himself to be destined to identify and articulate some realities about the dead and their relationship to the human unconscious. As he later wrote, "The unconscious corresponds to the mythic land of the dead, the land of the ancestors."[8]

To have such a relationship with the dead is not what we would normally consider a vocation or a profession. Rather, it's a psycho-ecological role expressed in mythopoetic images, a role that might have been largely vacant from Western culture for centuries, one that might be terrifying and sobering to discover as one's own. But this was precisely Jung's understanding of the role he had been assigned by Mystery. His channeling of the *Seven Sermons* was how he discovered this and how he began to take the necessary shape to fulfill that role.

Notice that, with the *Seven Sermons*, Soul did not advise Jung to be a psychiatrist, psychoanalyst, mythologist, alchemist, author, or the founder of a school of psychology — all these being among the middleworld delivery systems for Soul that Jung ended up utilizing, not the actual underworld gift that was to be delivered. Rather, Soul revealed that Jung's destiny and genius was to make conscious to others the enduring reality of the dead and the nature of the unconscious. This is the difference between socio-vocational role and psycho-ecological niche. Here's how Jung expressed it:

> From that time on, the dead have become ever more distinct for me as the voices of the Unanswered, Unresolved, and Unredeemed....These conversations with the dead formed a kind of prelude to what I had to communicate to the world about the unconscious: a kind of pattern of order and interpretation of its general contents.... [I]t seems as though a message had come to me with overwhelming force.[9]

The *Seven Sermons* initiated a permanent shift in Jung's consciousness. Unlike the other events in the *Red Book*, this was neither a wholing or healing of his psyche nor a Dissolution of his old story and identity, but rather an embodiment of his ultimate place in the world, an initiatory transformation of identity.

When cultivating a facet of wholeness (see "Cultivating Our Innate Human Wholeness," pages 46–48), what we learn about who we are is by and large what anyone would learn by cultivating that same facet. The facets are aspects of the human psyche we all have in common. In contrast, a soul encounter is the discovery of something unique about us: what is ours alone to do and be in life — our singular place to stand in this world, our identity from the Soul's perspective. Two people might possess the same set of skills and deploy them with equal talent but, in doing so, provide entirely different services. Soul encounters reveal our particular place in the larger Earth community — and the deep structure of how we are destined to participate in the world. Our four facets of wholeness, on the other hand, are the core resources we employ at any time in life to accomplish anything in a life-enhancing manner. After Soul Initiation, our facets of wholeness are what we use to embody or manifest our mythopoetic identities.

With the *Seven Sermons*, Jung's Soul impressed upon him the experience of his mythopoetic place in the world by planting him precisely in that place. He began to be rooted there by the psychospiritual impact of the dead forcing their way into his home — both his material home and his psychological home (his Ego).

With his transmission of the *Seven Sermons*, Jung's consciousness — his Ego, his psychospiritual center of gravity — began its shift from egocentric to soul-centric, from his Ego being an agent for itself to being an agent for Soul:

> It was then that I ceased to belong to myself alone, ceased to have the right to do so. From then on, my life belonged to the generality.... It was then that I dedicated myself to service of the psyche.[10]

This is precisely how soul encounter sets in motion the transformation of the Ego: We cease to belong to ourselves alone. Our Ego becomes rooted in Soul. We dedicate ourselves to the service of the Soul. We take a major step in our long passage from egocentric to soulcentric.

Jung's channeling of the *Seven Sermons* was the core event of his first Descent. It's no wonder this was the only part of the *Red Book* Jung included in his memoir. Soon thereafter, he entered his first Metamorphosis. And not long after, he entered the Enactment phase as he began to "plant the results of my experience in the soil of reality."[11]

The Flowering Tree and the Sunlit Island at the Center

Jung's second and last soul encounter arrived by way of a dream on January 2, 1927, eleven years after his channeling of the *Sermons*. He was fifty-two.

In this dream, Jung found himself walking through the dark and grungy streets of Liverpool, England, on a rainy winter night. In the very center of the city, he came to a round pool with a small island in its middle:

> While everything round about was obscured by rain, fog, smoke, and dimly lit darkness, the little island blazed with sunlight. On it stood a single tree, a

magnolia, in a shower of reddish blossoms. It was as though the tree stood in the sunlight and were at the same time the source of light....I was carried away by the beauty of the flowering tree and the sunlit island.[12]

In his memoir, Jung commented on this life-changing dream:

I had a vision of unearthly beauty, and that was why I was able to live at all. Liverpool is the "pool of life."...This dream brought with it a sense of finality. I saw that here the goal had been revealed. One could not go beyond the center. The center is the goal, and everything is directed toward that center. Through this dream I understood that the self is the principle and archetype of orientation and meaning. Therein lies its healing function. For me, this insight signified an approach to the center and therefore to the goal. Out of it emerged a first inkling of my personal myth.[13]

As a result of this dream, Jung understood his life task was to introduce people to the concept, image, and reality of the self "as the principle and archetype of orientation and meaning." Jung expanded on the dream's significance for him:

Without such a vision I might perhaps have lost my orientation and been compelled to abandon my undertaking. But here the meaning had been made clear. When I parted from Freud, I knew that I was plunging into the unknown. Beyond Freud, after all, I knew nothing; but I had taken the step into darkness. When that happens, and then such a dream comes, one feels it as an act of grace.[14]

This is a stunning way for Jung to frame his experience. He is saying that, in parting with Freud in 1912, he had entered "the unknown," and that he had remained in that "darkness" until this dream-vision arrived — *fifteen years later!* Jung had entered the Cocoon in 1912 and was still in it in 1927. The Cocoon is indeed a place of the unknown, of darkness — a fruitful, psychospiritual darkness.

Jung's Liverpool dream was a soul encounter because it revealed to him, for the first time, his personal myth. The dream afforded him "a sense of finality" to his quest. This second soul encounter went deeper and was more conclusive than the *Seven Sermons*; it further focused his mythopoetic identity. With the *Sermons*, his eco-niche was revealed as the one who communicates the dynamics of the unconscious, including the desires and laments of the dead. Now his eco-niche was identified as something more specific: the one who illuminates the particular dimension of the unconscious Jung called the self, the one who explores and expresses the reality of the self as the center of the psyche and as "the goal of psychic development."[15] Jung's Liverpool dream revealed his destiny as what we might call the Illuminator of the Self — one who casts a Western light on our innate human wholeness. He might have been the first to do so.

Notice that Jung's eco-niche was not the Illuminator of the Search for a Personal

Myth — the one who communicates the nature of the Descent to Soul. This is likely the reason the Descent to Soul, by any name, did not end up as an explicit element of the psychology he developed, even though it was a vital element of his own individuation journey. He understood his task in life was to support the cultivation of psychological wholeness, the "self" — "the undeveloped and neglected aspects of the personality."[16] As we've seen, this is an aspect of the psyche that all people have in common, not a person's unique personal myth.

Jung made it clear, however, that his Liverpool dream was the culmination of his own search for a personal myth, his own process of Soul discovery:

> After this dream I gave up drawing or painting mandalas. The dream depicted the climax of the whole process of development of consciousness. It satisfied me completely, for it gave a total picture of my situation. I had known, to be sure, that I was occupied with something important, but I still lacked understanding, and there had been no one among my associates who could have understood. The clarification brought about by the dream made it possible for me to take an objective view of the things that filled my being.[17]

This dream, in other words, conclusively shifted Jung's Ego: It enabled him to take that "objective view." It completed the rooting of his Ego in Soul.

I am fascinated that Jung drew his first mandala soon after his first soul encounter[18] and completed his last immediately after his second. It's as if his Muse (or his Soul or Mystery) had been preparing his Ego for its climactic shift (through his Liverpool dream) by providing him with eleven years of wholeness images, images in fact of the "self." His first mandala appeared in imagery as his Ego began its rooting in Soul, and the last arrived as that rooting reached completion.

Endowed with his "objective view of the things that filled my being," Jung was at last, at age fifty-two, able to give himself fully to his soul calling. As it turns out, he had thirty-four more years to manifest his mature work.

Chapter Eight

PHASE THREE

Soul Encounter

Part 2: Practices and Ceremonies for Discovering Your One True Life

...What shape
waits in the seed
of you to grow
and spread
its branches
against a future sky?...

— DAVID WHYTE

Silver Moon: "Do Something More Taboo with It"

Silver Moon, as we learned earlier, entered the Cocoon at age twenty-one and soon after began seven years of wandering through the world and her "dance with the unseen." At the end of this period and following a brief marriage, she "entered a tunnel of darkness," her first Descent to Soul (see "Silver Moon's Crisis and Call," pages 80–81).

Cultivating Wholeness, Especially the Feminine

Like Carl Jung (and most contemporary initiates), Silver Moon was under-resourced at the start of her first Descent, but she was able to cultivate her facets of wholeness during the Dissolution phase. But whereas Jung accomplished his wholing without outer human guides and primarily through one method (active imagination), Silver

Moon had a full year of support from a guide named Elisabeth Serra, who used a variety of methods including dance, bodywork, archetypal imagery, tantric practice, and shadow work. Under Elisabeth's guidance, Silver Moon developed all four facets of wholeness (see "Cultivating Our Innate Human Wholeness," pages 46–48) but especially the two that, in the contemporary world, most need tending, those often considered more feminine: the South (the Wild Indigenous One) and the West (the Dark Muse-Beloved). Her South work, for example, included an enhancement of emotional capacity and a deepening of her connection with the land, all of life, and her own body:

> I began to see and experience my innate and intimate connection to the Earth through my body as a woman. I began to honor my blood cycles. I began to reclaim the wisdom and authority of my feelings. I was awakening to ancient memories of my connection to the land. By engaging with my energetic body, I was able to retrieve memories of sisterhood, of brother-hood, the deep reciprocity with life.

Her West work included the further cultivation of her imagination and erotic sensibilities, her deepening appreciation of psychological woundedness as a portal to the sacred, and a retrieval of collective memories:

> I began to trust more deeply my imagination, intuition, my inner know-ing. I became conscious of a whole other field of reality, one that I had been taught to ignore or mistrust: the deep erotic connection to life, the beauty and the mystery of what it means to be alive. I saw the holiness in my humanness, that all of the broken places of my being were in fact doorways to something mysterious and sacred. That each emotion was an invitation into a deeper layer of myself, layers that traversed time and space and tapped into the ancient memories of my soul.
>
> I also retrieved memories of terror, ridicule, and shame for carrying this divinity and my deep knowing of the sacred. I saw what had happened to the feminine; I reexperienced it through my energetic field, memories that had been stored there lifetimes waiting to be remembered, reclaimed, made whole and sacred.

Silver Moon's preparatory "inner work" of gathering intrapsychic resources likely made all the difference on her journey into Soul Canyon, including its first stop: her Core Wound.

The Core Wound: How the Light Gets In

The Core Wound, deeper and more painful than the hurts and injuries of everyday life, is a psychological torment so distressing we form our primary subpersonality survival strategies in reaction to it, so hurtful that much of our personal style and sensitivities have their roots there. For many contemporary people, these wounds originate in family dysfunction, in emotional abuse or neglect. But a Core Wound is at least as likely to stem from afflictions with no human perpetrators, like birth trauma, the early death of a mother, a father's absence due to illness, or guilt from surviving a car wreck that claimed a younger sibling. The Core Wound, however, rarely stems from a single traumatic incident. More often it consists of a pattern of hurtful events or a disturbing dynamic in one or more important relationships. We all have a Core Wound. From a spiritual perspective, this isn't an accident. Nor is it unfortunate.

Our Core Wounds arise from the convergence of two factors that are categorically distinct: a preexisting innate sensitivity or core vulnerability, and one or more wounding events — that is, an inner quality and an outer incident. Core Wounds, in other words, are not mere woundings. Each one of us is born with a physical, psychological, and/or spiritual vulnerability — a susceptibility perhaps arranged by Soul itself. This core vulnerability renders us woundable in a particularly painful way by a certain variety of wounding events that penetrate all the way to the core of our psyche.

Without the wounding events, we might never know or experience our core vulnerability. The wounding events expose that vulnerability. If we hadn't been born with that particular vulnerability, we wouldn't be so disturbed by those particular events; maybe we would hardly notice them.

Our experiential encounter with Soul would be unlikely or impossible without a Core Wound. An impeccably assembled Ego, one that never encountered a moment of supreme self-doubt, would be invulnerable to falling apart, would never be motivated to leave the "home" of its Adolescent story, would never second-guess its conventional life trajectory, would never wander off into the mysteries of nature and psyche, and would, consequently, never reach true Adulthood. Mystery, then, sees to it that we are born with a core vulnerability, one that will be actuated or precipitated by certain kinds of wounding events.

As Leonard Cohen sings in "Anthem," "There's a crack in everything; that's how the light gets in." The Diné people (Navajo) of the American Southwest say that perfection keeps Spirit from entering a thing. In their masterful weavings, they incorporate a deliberate irregularity, an errant line or color that looks like an unintended flaw but is actually a purposeful deviation called a "spirit line," the place where Mystery might enter. Our core vulnerability — and by extension, our Core Wound — is the spirit line in the work of art called a human psyche or a human life.

Our core vulnerability virtually assures that we'll experience, usually in childhood, one or more events that will be exceptionally traumatic or damaging.

We ourselves, then — or our Souls — have a certain kind of responsibility, in a transpersonal or spiritual sense, for our Core Wounds. Responsibility, not blame. Yes, we will innocently suffer one or more wounding events in the form of an accident, a disease, a loss, or abuse, but the effect on us of those events is amplified by our own core vulnerability. As much as the Core Wound is a liability for the Ego, it is an opportunity for the Soul.

In Core Wound work, a person consciously and experientially reenters the wound, not in order to heal it — which is neither possible nor desired — but rather to be changed *by* it, to be initiated by it. The initiatory intention of Core Wound work is for the Soul gift hidden in the wound to be revealed, reclaimed, and reintegrated. When this happens, the Core Wound becomes what psychologist Jean Houston calls a Sacred Wound.[1]

If you're in the Cocoon stage or later and have good access to the fourfold resources of your Self, you can experientially dive into your Core Wound, revisit your memories of the wounding events, and discover how they affected your psyche, your relationships, and your life. You can experience, in a way you never have before, the vulnerability built into the core of your psyche — and what this might reveal about your Soul. By courageously and patiently allowing the associated suffering to do its work, neither indulging nor repressing the pain, you might reach the bedrock of your psyche, where the most profound truths of this lifetime await.[2]

Our core vulnerability is at the same time our core *sensitivity* — our capacity to deeply feel the world in a particular way, a way that has everything to do with our soul powers and our Soul's calling. Core Wound work results in the animation or quickening of a soul power and/or the discovery or deepening of mythopoetic identity. Through Core Wound work, our understanding of our wounding event(s) is transformed via mythologization, the revelation of the larger or deeper story, the sacred myth of our lives. In many myths, there's a wounding that turns out to be an essential ingredient that later enables the god or mortal to embody their true identity (as in Persephone's abduction, Inanna's torture, Jacob's broken hip, or Jesus's crucifixion).[3]

For Silver Moon, her wounding events were countless social interactions and dynamics, from early childhood on, in which what she calls "the wild feminine" was shamed, restrained, or unseen — by her family and community, by the contemporary world more generally, and by self-inflicted emotional bruising. Her core vulnerability is an exceptional, innate sensitivity to both the wild feminine and its repression. As it turns out, this is also one of her soul powers.

EXPERIENTIALLY EXPLORING THE WOUND

There are at least four phases of Core Wound work, though some may be combined or skipped. In the first phase, the wound is explored experientially, through somatic and emotional feeling, in order to reexperience the wound as fully as possible. This should not be attempted if you're not adequately resourced in all four facets of wholeness. Core Wound work is not meant to be a therapeutic experience but rather soulcraft: a method for encountering Soul. Experientially reentering this wound is psychologically risky, even for well-resourced people, and potentially devastating for those with significant unhealed trauma.

Silver Moon's conscious work with her Core Wound began during her year of guided group support, when she was twenty-eight. With courage, self-compassion, and fierce tenderness, she consciously entered the vault of her most vulnerable experiences (see "Liberation from Lifetimes of Conditioning," pages 60–62). There, she became aware, for the first time, of the ways her subpersonalities (her inner protectors) had neglected, blocked, suppressed, and dishonored the wild feminine within her — including her instinctive capacity to speak truth, her sensuality and sexuality, and her embodied connection to Mystery. A key to the success with this self-exploration was that she approached it — and experienced it — with her wholeness (in particular her Nurturing Generative Adult), not through her woundedness (by way of her subpersonalities). During this exploration, Silver Moon discovered, to her astonishment, a subpersonality — a Loyal Soldier self-critic — that she calls her Inner Patriarch, who was dead-set against her awakening the wild feminine.

SELF-HEALING

This troubling insight led to the second phase of her Core Wound work: her devoted Self-healing, in which she engaged and embraced her wounded parts (her protectors, including her Inner Patriarch and her Wounded Child). This resulted in significant changes in her relationships with these subpersonalities and in her understanding of herself and of her personal and cultural history. She became aware that all her life she had been living a false story about what it is to be a woman, a story passed down through millennia of customs and conventions. She saw that what had happened to her own wild feminine had happened to the collective wild feminine. Gradually, she liberated herself from these lifetimes of conditioning.

RECLAIMING THE GIFT IN THE WOUND

Although Silver Moon Self-healed in this way, she also accomplished something even more valuable: She paved the way for the third phase of her Core Wound work — discovering and reclaiming the *gift in the wound*, that which had been repressed and buried there. Silver Moon unearthed this gift through a type of Shadow work: By starting with aspects of herself she already knew, she eventually uncovered repressed parts of her psyche whose existence she would have previously denied. She began with her Wounded Child (a South subpersonality), and this led to her wild feminine (mostly aspects of her South and West facets) that had been neglected, shunned, and buried in the Shadow (her West subpersonality) in order to keep herself safe and socially accepted. Her wild feminine held her ability to see, as she says, "the unspoken mysteries, the unspoken shadow, the essence of soul itself...the darker aspects of our existence." This ability and these qualities were threatening to the powers that be and so had been repressed.

These personal discoveries opened Silver Moon's awareness to the collective, transpersonal, and archetypal dimensions of the wild feminine that had been banished to the Shadow: "I began to see that this is what had happened to the witches. They had been burnt at the stake for their relationship to the unseen."

UNEARTHING THE WITCH, THE WILD WOMAN OF THE WOODS

As Silver Moon, while grounded in her wholeness (Self), submitted to her Core Wound and embraced the emotions, bodily feelings, and memories embedded there, the wound did its direct work on her Ego. In this, the fourth phase, the Core Wound work can precipitate a soul encounter. The fact that it's the wound that does its work on the Ego — not the other way around — is what I mean when I say the Core Wound is not for healing: It is not for us to heal, nor is it healable, nor does it heal us. Rather, when reentered, deeply experienced, and loved, the Core Wound can bring about an encounter with Soul, as it did for Silver Moon, her first:

> A soul image began to emerge. I began to see a witch, a mangled, one-eyed creature, full of the dark of night. Slowly out of the quagmire of the wound came this crone, this wild woman of the woods. She was dirty, ugly, imperfect in all of the usually imagined ways. She didn't care about convention — she was untamable. By pouring my love, divine love, into my wound, the wild woman/the witch started to show herself to me. First her gift came through, namely the ability to see the unseen. I saw how the very things she had been shamed for, unloved for, were in fact her powers, her gifts. She showed me that her capacity to see the things people weren't willing to acknowledge for themselves — their shadow, their unrealized potential, their deep vulnerability, their wounds — that this capacity was in fact *my* gift as well. Her sacred task, the gift of her wound, was to embrace her deep connection to the unseen realms of our existence and to hand it back. This was my sacred task as well. I began to see that her/my ability to see the shadow meant that she/I had an alternative way of thinking; she/I was able to offer the promise of a new paradigm.

Having earlier uncovered the innate, core vulnerability at the heart of her Core Wound — her exceptional, innate sensitivity to both the wild feminine and its repression — and having allowed that vulnerability to open up and rearrange her psyche, Silver Moon was able to recover and reclaim one of her soul powers: the ability to bring "the deeper mysteries of existence to consciousness" and to help others "reclaim their shadow as a source of their empowerment."

Silver Moon's Core Wound work revealed one of the archetypes or mythopoetic images that informs her soul identity: the Witch — the Wild Woman of the Woods.

> The Witch had been shunned from the collective field in order to create a subordinate version of the feminine, submissive to patriarchal values and life-destroying systems. Her image had been unloved, banished to the dark shadow, much like she had been physically hung and burnt at the stake.

Silver Moon's Core Wound was now a Sacred Wound. By remembering and redeeming the Witch, she reclaimed what she names as "the divine essence of the feminine" — "the essence of love, the capacity to be in deep intimacy with life, the capacity for deep feeling and emotion, and a relationship with the inner world, the imaginal realm of our existence." Over the next several months, this process of reclamation deepened as Silver Moon merged her images and somatic experience of the Witch with time in outdoor wild settings, in this way rooting her Sacred Wound story in Earth's story. This culminated in a second soul encounter:

> One day, while wandering in mountain foothills, I had an uncontrollable urge to let out a giant roar, a scream that was being stoked up like a furnace. With this came an equal urge to squash down this scream for fear of being heard or causing trouble. In that moment the land lent its imagination to me and I had a vision of women running naked through the woods, screaming hysterically, loose and wild, free hair flapping in the wind, falling into laughter and tears, into dance and song. I saw that the force that wanted to keep down my impulse to scream was the patriarchal rule that had violently tamed the wild out of the woman for the past few centuries. Deep in my psyche, this wild woman still existed untamed by centuries of repression. In that moment I knew I had to do something ceremonial; so I gathered what I could find from the earth beneath my feet and started to sculpt a figure. It became clear that I was sculpting a witch. I was blown away by her beauty and began to say over and over, "I see you, I see you, I see you." I wanted this witch to know I saw her beauty. I saw the majesty in all the things for which she had been wronged, shunned, exiled. In that moment I realized I was talking to my Core Wound. I saw the witch of my wound and all of the beauty I had been exiled for.

In this second encounter with Soul, Silver Moon glimpsed more fully the particular qualities and gifts of the Witch. This is an example of a soul encounter brought about by a mixture of deep imagination and an interaction with the natural world — in this instance, through a spontaneous ceremonial process incorporating expressive art.

The Chalice of Menstrual Blood

Silver Moon's third soul encounter arrived by way of a dream she had while preparing for her second vision fast. She was thirty-one at the time. This dream was perhaps the single most numinous of her life. It revealed another vital strand of her mythopoetic identity — that, in addition to being a contemporary version of the Witch archetype, she has a particular soul-directed task in this lifetime:

> I am standing in the center of a circle of men at the edge of a canyon, and I am holding up to the sky a chalice of menstrual blood. This feels like a witch's gesture of grounding and casting a circle, one hand to the sky and the other to the earth. It is a gathering of energy: The blood is being charged, but I too am being charged. There is a sense of immense and innate power. Meanwhile, some of the men are producing sperm to place into the moon blood. When they have done this, I move from the circle to the edge of the canyon to offer the blood (with the sperm in it). I kneel down and pour the blood on the earth. Then, with the backdrop of a stormy sky, the crash of thunder, and the flash of lightning, Elisabeth [Silver Moon's guide and teacher] appears and tells me to "do something more taboo with it." She looks at me with wild cat eyes that look otherworldly, powerful, dangerous, as if there's an instinctual, uncompromising reality to the task ahead. She doesn't tell me *what* I'm supposed to do with the blood.

Silver Moon experienced this dream as a marriage of her masculine and feminine, and she came to understand the key to her soul work as doing "something more taboo with it" — with that infusion of menstrual blood and sperm. The menstrual blood was obviously connected to the feminine, but she was not yet clear about the role of the masculine, of the "sperm donors." She awoke from the dream asking, "What is my seed?"

On her fast, she came to understand the sperm as the seed of consciousness, the masculine seed of consciousness in partnership with the feminine wisdom that embraces "our human connection to Mother Earth and the deeper, hidden mysteries of love and of soul." Feminine wisdom infused with masculine consciousness. This revelation emerged through a sequence of spontaneous ceremonies, including one in which she placed flower seeds into a bowl of moon blood on her altar. She realized that, within humans of all genders, the mature masculine seed of consciousness escorts the suppressed and repressed feminine from the dark to the light. In this way, we remember what has been hidden: the wild woman, "the one who trusts her inner knowing, the one who communes with the mysteries of the underworld, of soul; the untamable feminine."

Silver Moon came away with the understanding that the suppression of the wild feminine in everyone is what enabled the distortion of the masculine in everyone, and that the distorted masculine perpetuates the suppression of the wild feminine.

The Point of No Return

On this second vision fast, Silver Moon had a fourth encounter with Soul: a series of insights in which several of her previous numinous experiences arranged themselves into a pattern that made her mythopoetic identity clearer and more undeniable. With this encounter, she reached what she called "the point of no return." The trail there began the moment she arrived at her solo spot, at the start of her fast, and saw, in a tree directly opposite her, her soul image, the Witch.

Over the next four days, through continuous conversation with Witch, Silver Moon fully embraced the truth she could no longer turn away from:

I have always had the burden of seeing the shadow, a burden that was my gift. I had denied myself this knowing, too scared to accept the task. But now I knew this was my calling: to bring the shadow to the light, to name the things that can't be seen, to speak the unwanted and suppressed voices of the wild feminine and call out of the shadow these repressed voices and show they are part of divinity. In our culture, the capacity for deep feeling, a gift from nature, has been shunned, and in that deep feeling is our erotic life force. The Witch knew this. She knew the power of her deep imagination and trusted her seeing. Due to this deep wound in the feminine collective, there exists a split whereby the more beautiful, nurturing aspects of the feminine are deemed acceptable, but the ugly, dirty, wild aspects have been deemed unacceptable. In reality, there is no split; they are all part of one whole. It was shown to me that my sacred task is to help reconcile this split, to reveal all parts of the feminine as love.

Become Your Blood

At thirty-three, Silver Moon received the answer to the dream-given riddle-command she had been living with for two years: "Do something more taboo with it." During a five-day Animas intensive in the Scottish Highlands, while sitting by a stream and "deep in the soul stream," she remembered her dream of the menstrual blood and she found herself writing a poem, wherein the answer emerged. This was her fifth soul encounter, one that further extended and amplified her understanding of what she was born to do.

The answer: "*Become* your Blood. Your Blood is your Poetry, your Poetry is your Blood." Poetry is the language of the Soul. The Soul speaks in tongues, images, metaphor, sensation, raw and wild feeling — a language that lies just beneath the surface of things. Poets, mystics, and lovers know this language. You have to tap into an altered state of consciousness to hear it. To become your blood is to become your poetry, which is to say, your Soul.

A woman's blood holds the magic keys that allow her to tap into her mystical connection to the sacred, to her Soul, to her innate capacity for Love. When we bleed, we enter the consciousness of the dreamtime. When we bleed, we are closest to the Earth, the *anima mundi*. When we bleed, we are pulled down into the underworld. If we get really still and listen closely, we come back with gifts and visions to embody. To become your blood is to become your love, the sacred essence of the feminine, the erotic pulse of life itself. To become your blood: This is a bold revolution just waiting to happen, a revolution stored in the matrix of every woman's womb.

I asked Silver Moon how becoming your blood is more taboo than simply pouring it on the ground (as she did in her dream):

To Become Your Blood is a public affair; it's to become visibly embodied as the feminine force of love, mystery, and soul. It's to walk as the erotic force of life itself — in deep reciprocity to life. Pouring the blood on the earth is to make an offering, whereas when you Become Your Blood you become the offering itself; you offer yourself up to Mystery as the Mystery.

I also asked Silver Moon if there was a relationship between her name and her soul image or task. She said that silver moonlight is feminine consciousness and that this silver light is what illuminates the Dark — what's hidden, what's underneath the appearance of things. Her soul task is to shine her moonlight on the Dark Feminine — on the repressed, unconscious, and unknown aspects, revealing the full nature of the wild feminine, so that these can be seen for the magic and mystery they hold.

Practices and Ceremonies for Discovering Your One True Life

Once you're in the third phase of a Descent, you might not actually need any specific methods for eliciting soul encounters. In that you're now ripe for revelation, soul encounters might simply happen in the course of whatever else you're doing — as with Joanna Macy's Great Turning Wheel vision following childbirth, or her Stone in the Bridge vision while meditating; Sabina's encounter with Bear while camping; Elisabeth's dream exchange with the Cornman; Matt's deep-imagination encounter with the stone column; or Jung's confrontation with the dead while at home and minding his own business. By the time you're in the Soul Encounter phase of a

Descent, you have for the most part surrendered control over your journey. You're being guided by other forces, such as your Muse, your other facets of wholeness, your Soul, the animate world (including creatures, plants, landforms, waterways, and your own body), and Mystery — forces that can precipitate a soul encounter without the Ego's active participation. That said, you can use certain practices and ceremonies to amplify the likelihood of an encounter with Soul or to deepen or amplify one that you're already in the midst of.

All the practices listed or described below can be used alone. Many can be combined. Many can be used during vision fasts. Most are described in more detail in *Soulcraft* and *Wild Mind*, but I include here two additional soul-encounter practices — filling your space with a question and the Empty Vessel — not described in my earlier books.

Any of the techniques described or listed below can, of course, be used by people who are not in the Soul Encounter phase of a Descent and even by people who are not yet in the Cocoon. In such circumstances, these practices will often yield interesting and valuable results, but soul encounter will not be among them.

The Vision Fast

If you're in the Cocoon stage or later, a wilderness-based vision fast is perhaps the single most effective method for evoking a soul encounter, especially if your vision fast is guided by others who have extensive experience designing and enacting this ceremony as a Descent to Soul (a relatively rare approach).

Having written at some length in *Soulcraft* about my perspective on and approach to vision fasts, I'll not offer, in this book, descriptions of how to structure them as a Descent to Soul, other than what you can pick up from some of the stories in these pages. Besides, as noted, I believe it would be best (deeper and more effective, and also safer, both physically and psychospiritually) if you were guided by people with a long track record with this ceremony. But some contextualizing comments might be of value:

Vision fasts, especially as enacted in the contemporary Western context, have many purposes and potential benefits other than soul encounter. These include healing; grieving a loss; Eco-awakening; deepening of or recommitment to middleworld life purpose; marking a significant life passage; precipitating, intensifying, concluding, or celebrating a molt (a significant change in social or vocational life — see "Molting versus Dissolution," pages 42–43); cultivating one or more facets of wholeness; and enabling a conversation with Spirit or a direct experience of the divine.

My understanding — based on having guided thousands of people on vision fasts, having read a wide range of literature on contemporary forms of these ceremonies, and having had many conversations with guides and participants from a variety of traditions — is that perhaps only 10 percent of contemporary people who enact vision fasts have encounters with Soul. Quite possibly less. But my Animas colleagues and I have discovered that this proportion can be increased to as much as 100 percent by carefully screening participants for life stage and psychospiritual readiness (phase one of the Descent), by employing effective Dissolution practices (phase two), and by including as part of the vision-fast ceremony many of the soul-encounter methods noted below (phase three).

Although vision fasts are one of the most powerful methods for evoking soul encounter, there are numerous other methods. For many people, the other practices noted below might be more effective.

Soul-Encounter Practices Described in Soulcraft

Soulcraft describes dozens of methods that can spark a soul encounter — for people who are in the Cocoon stage or later. All of these can be used on their own. Many can also be incorporated into a vision-fast ceremony. A few of these practices, as noted with cross-references below, are also explained or illustrated in this book. *Soulcraft*, however, describes all of these methods and often more thoroughly. (In *Soulcraft*, see "Soulcraft Practices," on pages xi and xii.)

- Soulcentric dreamwork (in this book, see "Soulcentric Dreamwork," pages 79–80; "The Arrival of the Guide to Soul," pages 121–22; "Becoming the Jegermeister," page 270; and "Soulcentric Dreamwork," pages 274–75).
- Deep-imagery journeys or active imagination (in this book, see "Jung's Use of Active Imagination," pages 129–35; and "The Stone Column," pages 166–67).
- Self-designed ceremony: a means of conversing with Soul in Soul's own language of embodied symbol and image (in this book, see "Bridging between Worlds," pages 165–66; and "Self-Designed Ceremonies," page 276).
- Symbolic artwork or expressive arts (in this book, see "Jung's Dissolution Practices," pages 122–25; and "Unearthing the Witch," pages 192–94).
- The art of Shadow work (in this book, see "Shadow Work," pages 133–35; and see the Shadow work sections in *Nature and the Human Soul* and *Wild Mind*).
- Talking across the species boundaries: dialogues with other-than-human beings and places (in this book, see "The Obstacle Threshold," pages 109–11; "Old Man Compost," pages 164–65; "The Point of No Return," page 195; "Christie: A Dedicated Spirit," pages 222–33; "Let Me Be Your Feast," pages 283–86; and "FeatherStone: A Tether between Dream and Earth," pages 319–23).
- Animal tracking and other methods of skillful observation of the other-than-human world: In addition to learning about and from the Others and enhancing our own wildness and ecocentricity, this can be a means to explore the mysteries of nature and psyche and to evoke soul encounter.

- The practice of lamenting: our passionate expression of grief, not just or primarily for our personal losses but for the world's, for the ways our communities, including the other-than-humans, are suffering and for our felt limitations to help as much as we'd like; surrendering to our most difficult truths of loss and crisis and to our deepest longings for ourselves, our people, and our world; gazing into the bottom of our unprotected heart and wrestling with our demons, with what is most unsettled and troubling in our lives (in this book, see "Old Man Compost," pages 164–65).
- Discovering, fashioning, and using symbols and ceremonial objects: as a way to attract Soul images.
- Journal work: creative writing as a way to connect with our own depths and to cultivate a relationship with Soul.
- Apprehending and responding to signs and omens.
- Body practices for altering consciousness, including the following:
  - Trance drumming and rhythms: for entering trance states, opening the door to the depths, and unearthing the mysteries or numina beneath our surface lives.
  - Ecstatic trance dance: surrendering to the images and entities, inside and out, that want to move us and be danced by us.
  - Fasting (not necessarily in the context of a vision-fast ceremony).
  - Breathwork: consciousness-altering breathing techniques.
  - Practices involving extreme physical exertion.
  - Yoga postures and movement.
- Ceremonial sweats and saunas: for altering consciousness, communing with the Others, and evoking visions and revelations.
- Depth council work: the specific use of council for supporting the Descent to Soul.[4]
- Telling, retelling, and study of myths and other sacred stories: deepening our awareness of the archetypal and numinous.
- Composing a personal myth: understanding the events of our own lives from a larger, deeper, symbolic perspective.
- Sacred speech: conversation that deepens our presence with other people, self, and place.
- Ritual silence during initiatory group processes.
- Sacred sexuality: a doorway to the mysteries of Soul.
- Skillful and/or guided use of entheogens (aka plant allies or medicines, hallucinogens, or psychedelics) as one component of ceremonial explorations of the underworld of Soul.
- Soul poetry, music, and chanting: altering consciousness and aligning it with Soul.
- The art of solitude.

- Practices for discovering the natural world as a mirror of the Soul.
- Wandering in wilderness.
- The art of being lost.
- Befriending the Dark.
- Living the questions of Soul.
- Confronting your own death.
- The art of romance.
- Mindfulness practice.
- Developing a personal relationship with Spirit.

The last ten practices are also described in *Nature and the Human Soul*, which includes two more: service work and praising the world.

Advanced Subpersonality Work

In *Wild Mind*, I explore a set of soul-encounter practices I call *advanced subpersonality work*. Cultivating a relationship with your inner protectors is not merely an exceptional means for everyday healing and wholing; it can also provide a path to soul discovery and initiation, an underworld way to be with your woundedness. This work is "advanced" in two respects. First, it's rarely possible and certainly not recommended until you've reached the stage of the Cocoon and have achieved a solid foundation of wholing and Self-healing. Second, the goal is not healing but something nearly opposite and often counter-therapeutic: the intentional destabilization of the Ego, which supports the encounter with the worldview-shifting mysteries of nature and psyche.

The central principle of advanced subpersonality work is that our childhood survival strategies can provide portals into the depths of our psyches. During a Descent to Soul, we can invite our wounds to do their work on us, as with Core Wound work. We can seek not to be healed but rather to be torn open so that we may remember who we really are. Employing the resources of the Self, we invite Ego-death or psychospiritual dismemberment in order to discover what remains when we are unprotected.

There are four realms of advanced subpersonality work, one for each of the four groups of subpersonalities as mapped onto the four cardinal directions of the Nature-Based Map of the Human Psyche (see "Cultivating Our Innate Human Wholeness," pages 46–48). See *Wild Mind* for more complete explanations and the associated soul-encounter practices, but here are brief descriptions:

- **North:** Deliberately enter the very fires from which your Loyal Soldiers have attempted to keep you safe, the fires behind the Loyal Soldiers' backs. For some people, this might be taking a certain kind of social risk, like singing onstage for the first time, or publicly announcing your expertise and availability in a new (for you) arena that will test everything you're made of. It might mean an "inner" psychological risk, like fully feeling a grief you've managed until now to keep a lid on (or maybe it's a longing); or a spiritual risk, like cultivating your own relationship with God regardless of whether this fits the template offered by your church, or questioning, for that matter, whether there's one god or many gods — or any gods at all.[5]

- **South:** This is Core/Sacred Wound work, in which you choose, as Silver Moon did, to experientially reenter and explore your Core Wound, surrendering to the grief, fears, and somatic traces you encounter, allowing your psyche to be torn open so you might find the treasure within the wound (see "The Core Wound," pages 188–94).
- **East:** Addictions can be a path to Soul. *After* achieving a stable recovery, consciously enter the passion-pain your inner addicts or escapists have been avoiding or failing to find, living the question, "What is the deeper longing from which I protected myself through my addiction, or that I thought I was satisfying through my addiction?" One person discovered in this way her wild and exuberant freedom of expression; she eventually unearthed her talent for dance, one of her soul powers.
- **West:** This is advanced Shadow work — cultivating an intimate relationship with a Shadow element (a shade) in order to discover and reclaim, not what you have projected onto others (that's the more "basic" Shadow work), but the hidden resource and gift that await you in the depths of the shade, living the question, "What is the resource within the shade?" This is what Silver Moon experienced when she recovered her Wild Woman from the Shadow.

Filling Your Space with a Question

In the contemporary Western world, we're constantly encouraged to be in control — at least of ourselves, our lives, our outcomes: Make a five-year plan. Choose the right mate. Get genetic testing. Be proactive. Buy insurance. Achieve the American dream.

Being in control is not all bad, but it's also emblematic of egocentric Adolescence: Look out for number one. Get what's yours, what you deserve.

If you're not careful, being in control can become a significant theme even during a Descent into Soul Canyon: Cultivate your wholeness, Self-heal, develop your soulcraft skills, choose the best vision-fast guide, and especially this — do everything you can to figure out what your Soul wants for your life.

We're on the journey of soul initiation to find answers to our biggest life questions. We can't be blamed for wanting to figure out how we can be of greatest use to our endangered world. But just because we want to be of service doesn't mean we aren't trying to control the journey.

The problem with our being in control on the Descent to Soul is that it would be our Ego in control, and our beloved Ego, with its familiar way of understanding itself and its world, would sabotage the journey if it succeeded at controlling it.

What to do? Use your (Egoic) control to undermine your control, to disintegrate yourself (your Ego). All the Dissolution and Soul-Encounter practices in this book are ways of doing just that.

One of the best general practices is to stop trying to figure it out, to totally surrender even your desire to generate answers to your greatest life questions about purpose and meaning. Instead, let the questions do their work on you rather than you doing your work on them.

One way to do this is what I call *filling your space with a question*. During a Descent, when you find yourself bedeviled by a big question about your life, yourself, or the journey, go out onto the land, hold your question in your awareness as fully and intensely as you can, and wander until you find yourself called to or allured by a particular place (a forest clearing, a stretch of creek, a mud bog) or a particular thing (a boulder, anthill, rotting critter corpse). Most importantly, don't consciously *choose* a place or thing; wander until one chooses *you*. You might experience where you end up as pleasant or find it disturbing or even repulsive. Sit there. Bring all your senses alive. Look around with care. What do you hear? What scents are detectable? What do you taste on the breeze? What emotions are stirring? What do you feel about this place or thing? What images or memories arise? Take your time to fully arrive. Then, using your imagination, fill the space you're in with your question as if you're pumping air into a balloon. Repeat your question with each pump stroke. Speak it out loud. Maybe your question is your counterpart to: What can I do with this Chalice, something that would be more taboo? Or: How can I stand up for what's wrong with my people? Or: What exactly were the Dead seeking in Jerusalem, anyway?

Once you have your space amply filled with your question, stop and let the space itself have its effect on you. Notice what happens to your awareness, your somatic experience, your emotions, memories, imagination. What happens around you? Do birds or animals appear? What do you hear? What images or feelings arise? Let all of it happen to you. You're not in control. There's nothing to figure out, but there's everything to experience. *You're not looking for an answer, and you must not accept or entertain one should one arrive.* You're not seeking a meaning. The only reason you brought your big question with you and filled your space with it was to help shift your consciousness — which is what will happen if it really is one of your biggest questions. Now that you're totally immersed inside your question, you're hoping to be changed by the way that space responds to you. You're tracking responses (not answers!) from within and from the land, air, and waters.

If, when engaging this practice, a cognitively kindled answer appears, do not give in to it; it was probably generated by a subpersonality attempting to protect you from the journey. Instead, imagine a wall behind you with a shelf labeled "Some of the World's Best Answers": Place the answer on this shelf of honor and then turn your attention back to the place you're in and to whatever is being offered to you there.

Whatever happens while you're in that question-infused place, don't call on your strategic mind to analyze or interpret it; rather, call on your Muse to imagine or remember, on your Wild Indigenous One to feel, on your Innocent to notice without thinking, on your Nurturing Generative Adult to think with its heart. In this way, let it happen to you.

When Silver Moon, one day, filled the space she was in with her question about the Chalice ("What would be more taboo?"), a hummingbird shot toward her, loudly hovered inches from her face, and she experienced herself as a rose, exuding floral radiance and scent; she felt both her transience and the way she allured other creatures. Then, in the next moment, she received an image of a bowl of moon blood with flower seeds in it. This image was the genesis of the ceremony, during her vision fast, that resulted in her revelation of the relationship between the masculine seed of consciousness and the wild feminine (see "The Chalice of Menstrual Blood," pages 194–95).

The Empty Vessel

This is a practice I designed for vision fasts, but you can use it as a stand-alone soul-encounter ceremony or adapt it for use with other practices.

One way to approach a vision fast or other soul-encounter ceremony is to make yourself as psychospiritually empty as you can before and during the ceremony. The emptier you are, the more you can be filled — by Mystery. To support yourself in this, you might fashion a small Empty Vessel in the days or weeks prior to the ceremony. The shaping and crafting of the Vessel is a ceremony in its own right. Most likely you'll be surprised by what you experience during the hours or days you're crafting it.

Your Empty Vessel represents your intention to get out of the way of Mystery so that you become an Empty Vessel yourself, available to be filled. Your Vessel will receive and hold experiences offered by Mystery.

You might construct your Empty Vessel out of fiber, leather, clay, paper, bark, leaves, and so on. Once your Vessel is formed, weave into it a number of symbolic items that represent your prior numinous experiences — encounters with the sacred, human or Earth archetypes, and/or your previous encounters with Soul. In this way, your Vessel resonates with the part of you (your Muse or Guide to Soul) that already knows how to seek vision and receive it. As you create your Vessel, you're further cultivating your West facet as well as aligning your consciousness with the intentions of your upcoming ceremony — or with the Soul Encounter phase, more generally.

Your Empty Vessel embodies your longing for something beyond the domain of your Ego, a vision of how you might best serve your people and contribute to a life-enhancing society. It's also an expression of your gratitude to Mystery for shaping this world, you, and your place in it.

One or more of the symbols you weave into your Vessel might represent the great longings and passions of your life — your longing-pains, as Rumi says:

> God picks up the reed flute world and blows.
> Each note is a need coming through one of us,
> a passion, a longing-pain....[6]

If you enact a vision fast, you will sit with your Empty Vessel through those long days and nights and make yourself as empty as possible. Primarily, you'll fast from food, human company, and all but the most basic shelter (a tarp or small tent). But you might use other self-emptying practices, such as — a short list — offering your reverent attention outward to our breathtaking world, praising aloud the Others, drum or shaker rhythms, prayer, and especially this: lamenting (see "Soul-Encounter Practices Described in *Soulcraft*," pages 198–200). You'll make offerings to Mystery and pray that Mystery might pour something into your Empty Vessel. Each succeeding day, you'll become emptier physically (no food) but also spiritually (receptive to the interventions of Mystery). You'll become an Empty Vessel yourself.

Dan: Keeper of the Underground River

The Dissolution experiences of Dan, the Presbyterian pastor, included his crisis of belief arising from qualms about the practices of his church, the ensuing time of feeling lost, an extended submersion in the dark waters of grief, and an unraveling of his identity and roles (see "Dan's Descent into Hell," pages 75–77). This was eventually followed by a sensation of being abducted, a sudden increase in the frequency and intensity of his dream life, and his falling in love with the world in a way and to a degree he had never imagined possible (see "Abduction versus Conscious Descent," pages 93–95). With this, Dan entered the depths of Soul Canyon, the third phase of the Descent: "I felt like I was walking between two worlds. On the one hand, I remained in the middleworld as a father and pastor. On the other hand, I inhabited the underworld of soul and dreams."

Dan was also cultivating his access to the four facets of Self; he was developing his capacity to recognize, embrace, and heal his subpersonalities; and he was learning to dialogue with his dream figures.

Then Dan had a particularly powerful and life-shifting dream that was "vibrant and full of energy," suffused with mystery and holiness. This was his first encounter with Soul:

I am in a large underground cavern with a river running through it. This is where people come to be initiated. I am walking upstream in the river and examining the golden shrimp underwater on the riverbed to make sure they are plentiful and healthy. I am the "river keeper." My job is to tend to the river and to the golden shrimp because both are necessary when people come here for their initiations.

Dan awoke with the feeling that this was a vision of his place in the world, a vision of his future.

A month later, an Animas guide led Dan on a deep-imagery journey:

A man in a white robe and wearing what looks like an African mask walks toward me. I am sitting. I sense that he has come for me. He reaches down and gently grabs my forearms, inviting me to stand up. We start walking together. There is a great flash of light and we emerge in the underground cavern with the river from my dream. We are standing on the bank. He puts his arms around my shoulders and starts to wrestle with me. I am scared, not knowing what to do next or why we are here. He is fierce but playful at the same time. We are locked head to head, aggressively moving side to side, when the man stops, closes the fingers of his left hand into a fist, rears back, and strikes me in the face. I flinch at the blow. I am shocked he hit me. It is more a surprise than painful.

After the imagery journey, I remembered that in some ancient initiation rites, the initiator would slap the initiate in the face to remind them of or make them attentive to the travails and hardships of their initiation.

All dreams are initiatory in one sense or another. In every dream, after all, the Ego has been ushered, or perhaps abducted, into the underworld to be granted an experience that might make the Ego (and, in that way, the person) more useful to the world. This can also be true of deep-imagery journeys. Like a biblical angel, the masked man wrestled with Dan and gave him an initiatory blow — perhaps a strike that shifted his psychospiritual center of gravity, as in Rilke's image:

> ...When we win, it's with small things,
> and the triumph itself makes us small.
> What is extraordinary and eternal
> does not want to be bent by us.
> I mean the Angel who appeared
> to the wrestlers of the Old Testament:
> when the wrestler's sinews
> grew long like metal strings,
> he felt them under his fingers
> like chords of deep music.

> Whoever was beaten by this Angel
> (who often simply declined the fight)
> went away proud and strengthened
> and great from that harsh hand,
> that kneaded him as if to change his shape.
> Winning does not tempt that man.
> This is how he grows: by being defeated, decisively,
> by constantly greater beings.[7]

Following his dream and imagery journey, Dan felt called to the role of "Keeper of the Underground River." He longed to be in service to this river on behalf of the Earth community, not only in service to the humans who were there for initiation. In his dayworld, he suspended his pastime of fly-fishing and took up the practice of simply being with rivers. He also began cultivating a relationship with the mysterious humans and animals who appeared in his dreams and his deep imagination: When on solitary outings in wild or semi-wild places, he walked alongside these figures and asked what they might want to say to him.

Dan's evolving relationship with his Muse (his West facet) gradually enabled a deeper understanding of his underground river dream and of his mythopoetic calling:

> My role as Keeper of the Underground River is to nurture and be a steward to the flow of the river, with special attention to the shrimp, which I understand as imaginal beings that appear during initiatory encounters. Wrestling with the man in the mask is an ongoing courtship of underworld images that might lead to my own soul initiation.

Where Do We Look for Clues to Mythopoetic Identity?

Where do we look for the golden threads that might help us unearth the unique, mystical relationship we have with this world? What are the various realms of life experience that might reveal themes or patterns related to our particular psycho-ecological niche?

Once we've reached the Cocoon, it's common to find clues to mythopoetic identity not only in our current adventures but also in our past experiences, including those of childhood and early Adolescence. Earlier numinous experiences when recalled during a Descent to Soul often have consciousness-shifting effects they did not have and could not have had when they originally occurred.

The reason that conscious revelations of mythopoetic identity are rare in childhood is because our Ego is still forming and we have little interest in or capacity for the deeper questions about identity, meaning, and purpose.[8] Then, in psychological early Adolescence, we're primarily interested in social belonging and authenticity, which makes the existential soul questions mostly irrelevant and potentially dangerous to our psychosocial development. If clues to mythopoetic identity appear, we might find them mildly disturbing or somewhat entertaining, but we wouldn't be inclined to explore them in this stage or pursue their implications — or be able to.

It's in the Cocoon, especially during the third phase of a Descent, that our Ego is most penetrable by mythopoetic memories and experiences; at these times, our Ego is already destabilized from Dissolution and so can be more easily moved and reconfigured by the mythic, including numinous memories now recalled somatically and emotionally.

During this third phase, when we want to increase the likelihood, frequency, or intensity of soul encounters, we might direct our attention to the following domains of experience, past and present. Not coincidentally, these most promising locations for finding mythopoetic clues are precisely those that most people in contemporary Western culture rarely visit or explore to any depth.

- Our dreams — especially repeating dreams and recurring dream themes, symbols, or figures — including the earliest dreams we can remember and our somatic experiences within those dreams
- Experiences when profoundly moved or inspired by the untamed/wild world
- Experiences when wandering solo, especially for three days or more in places rarely visited by humans
- The particular ways we experience the world (not primarily or only our beloved) when we fall in love
- Synchronicities we notice
- Experiences during nonordinary states (fever, trance, coma, sexual ecstasy, use of plant allies or other entheogens, extreme physical exertion, deep-imagery journeys, breathwork, fasting, dance, chanting, contemplative arts)
- Our deepest wounds (Core or Sacred Wound; the South form of advanced subpersonality work; see "Advanced Subpersonality Work," pages 200–201)
- The realms of experience our inner critics and other Loyal Soldiers have tried to keep us from (the North form of advanced subpersonality work)
- The spiritual longings that lie beneath our addictions (the East form of advanced subpersonality work)
- Our Shadows — explored by way of our projections, transferences, dreams, extreme emotional reactions, and so on (the West form of advanced subpersonality work)
- The common denominator in the effects we seem to have on others, especially when we're not trying to have an effect
- Our natural talents — those we know and those noted by others

- What we most loved to do or be when we were children
- Our own poems, songs, dances, and other art forms that arise from our deepest feelings about the more-than-human world
- Insights that arise out of our greatest heartbreaks, disappointments, and despairs — as well as our ecstatic moments of joy
- The significance or origin of our obsessions or the situations we repeatedly find ourselves in
- Symbols or images that regularly appear to us
- Odd or perplexing events that seem to occur often in our presence
- The qualities of the landscapes, animals, birds, flowers that most move us
- The archetypes, symbols, and myths that most inspire and trouble us
- The essence of the longing that lives within the greatest hopes and dreams we hold for our lives
- Haunting memories from previous lives (or future lives)
- Experiences during vision fasts
- Numinous experiences at any time, especially the common themes or symbols among them

Keep in mind, however, that clues to mythopoetic identity are not the same thing as profound experiences that reshape the Ego. The clues we gather from earlier life events are simply places to begin an exploration. Searching for clues and thoroughly exploring them can, however, precipitate a soul encounter. This is what happened for Silver Moon during her Core Wound explorations of childhood experiences in which the wild feminine had been shamed or restrained.

The review and exploration of the realms of experiences listed above is a fruitful supplement to whatever else is happening during the Soul Encounter phase of a Descent. There are times during this phase, however, when we don't need to actively look for mythopoetic clues because we're already getting flooded with enigmatic memories or having current experiences that overflow with transformational potential. Our Ego is least defended from the mysteries during the destabilized psychospiritual state of this phase. Numinous experiences simply assert themselves. We might even find ourselves praying for a respite.

We might also want to look for clues to mythopoetic identity after this phase — during Metamorphosis and Enactment, or even following our Descent. Earlier life experiences can confirm more recent revelations or reveal additional dimensions of mythopoetic identity. Conversely, our Soul Encounter experiences can illuminate strands of our mythos that might have been in plain sight during childhood and early Adolescence but are only now fathomed.

One of the most extraordinary features of the journey of soul initiation is that, during it, the strangest and most astonishing events of our life start to sync up. Events or images from our dreams begin to correlate with our experiences in the natural world. Our recent numinous moments resonate with motifs in the lives of our ancestors — or their names. Symbols and myths show up in the midst of remarkable conversations with strangers. Childhood illnesses or traumas are revealed as initiatory catalysts. Moments of madness are exposed as brilliant flashes of illumination. An entheogenic journey provides the key to understanding a childhood dream, which unlocks the mystery encountered in an ancient ruin. Deep-imagination journeys foreshadow magical encounters with wild creatures. What had once been experienced as a defect or weakness is unveiled as a soul power. The mythopoetic pattern is laid bare and amplified. We remember who we've always been, who we were destined to become. It all lines up or spirals together. The journey becomes mytho*poeic* — myth-making. Our life makes sense in a way we had never imagined possible. The way forward becomes clear — but seldom easy.

FeatherStone: The Tethered Feather and the Fire Sand Mandala

The first Descent to Soul experienced by Kevin, the river ecologist, was precipitated, as we saw, by a psychospiritual crisis when he was a twenty-three-year-old undergraduate at the University of Wisconsin, a crisis that culminated in his library apparition of a floating man bursting into flames, followed by Kevin's night flight (see "Kevin's Crisis and Call," pages 91–93). Because he was already in the Cocoon at the time, this crisis provoked Kevin's first Dissolution and, within a year, his first soul encounter.

Although Kevin managed to find better psychospiritual support than do most contemporary Wanderers, it was not what it might have been if he had crossed paths with a soul-initiation guide. First he requested guidance from a psychiatrist friend, but this was of little help. Then, he sought refuge with the Trappist monks and the silence of Gethsemane Monastery in Kentucky, the home of Thomas Merton, whose writings on war, social justice, and Western mysticism had deeply influenced Kevin. There he found a book on creation-centered spirituality by the theologian and priest Matthew Fox. Profoundly moved and inspired, Kevin took this as a sign and drove up to Mundelein College, in Chicago, where Fox was teaching.

Kevin's study with Fox led, indirectly, to his first soul encounter:

At one of Father Matthew's gatherings at the edge of Lake Michigan, I met a Diné (Navajo) Catholic priest. It was a beautiful, sunny, windy autumn day atop a bluff overlooking the Great Lake, and as we spoke, he asked me my name. I told him Kevin Lloyd Fetherston, whereupon he pulled out a small leather pouch from which he removed a beautiful piece of turquoise tethered with a fine thread to a small feather. He held up the turquoise and feather in the palm of his hand, and the wind caught the feather and it fluttered in the sunlight. We both gazed upon the feather and stone, in the sun and wind, neither of us saying a word, and I began to see my name Fetherston connected to my ancestors, and to heaven and earth.

The moment the Diné priest put the turquoise and tethered feather in the palm of his hand and held it up at face level between us, *all time stood still.* Space was extremely clear. The wind was blowing off Lake Michigan and the autumn sun was shining down brightly, and the wind lifted the feather off the stone, suspending it in the air and sun between us. There was a deeply kinesthetic feeling of expansiveness. It was like a lucid dream, but I was very much consciously awake.

And the priest and I never said a word to each other about it! I felt a depth of connection to the Feather and the Stone, to who I was, to the wind and the sun, to my ecocosmological place on Earth, and to my ancestors.

The fact that this occurred along the bluff of Lake Michigan was significant because I had had many awakening experiences along the shores and bluffs of this same lake near my childhood home in Milwaukee. I already felt I was part of that land, part of those waters, part of the Great Lake storms and waves and migrating flocks of birds.

This encounter with Soul is of special interest for several reasons, including its spontaneity: Kevin was not on that day utilizing any practices or ceremonies for soul encounter; he was not seeking or expecting a numinous experience. But for a Wanderer who has been through the Dissolution phase of a Descent, the right combination of circumstances elicits an encounter with Soul even without the use of any initiatory (soulcraft) practices. Carl Jung's experience at his home when he channeled his *Seven Sermons to the Dead* is another example.

In addition to life stage and Descent phase, several other elements contributed to Kevin's first soul encounter, including the location on the bluff above the lake he grew up near, the light and the wind, and the astonishing synchronicity between his surname and what the priest pulled from his pouch. But we would do well to suspect an additional and undoubtedly indispensable element: his Soul. Even if we would reject the notion that his Soul helped to orchestrate this meeting with the priest, we might at least suspect that Kevin's Soul had been waiting for just such an opportunity to indelibly impress upon his consciousness the unique psycho-ecological niche he had been born to occupy. This might be akin to the mathematical concept of a "strange attractor." The relationship between feather and stone, the various layers of meaning held in that relationship, the embeddedness of that relationship in his surname, and the hidden resonances within his ancestral lineage — these together formed something like a psychospiritual vortex that Kevin would be ineluctably drawn into sooner or later. Or these mythic threads created something akin to a gravitational field that had been tugging on his consciousness, perhaps for years, but that would not be able to capture him until he got close enough. We might imagine that the social, psychological, ancestral, spiritual, geographic, and meteorological circumstances of that moment on the bluff brought all the needed strands of fate together. Kevin fell in…and experienced himself for the first time as FeatherStone — even though the name itself had always been in plain sight.

At the time of this writing, Kevin is in his sixties. At age twenty-six on the bluff above Lake Michigan, he had only a beginning sense of how the image of Feather and Stone would be a guiding template or blueprint for his life. But the transformational reshaping of his psyche began that day, rooting his Ego into the depths of Soul. "The experience began to work on me immediately such that there was Kevin Fetherston before, and then after, there was FeatherStone with a deep connection to my ancestors."

This first soul encounter formed the foundation for Kevin's eventual understanding of his mythopoetic identity as "a conduit," as he now says, "between heaven and earth — a thread through which energies flow." He began his conscious exploration of his destiny to connect two worlds, one symbolized by the feather, the other by the stone, he being the thread joining or bridging the two.

It would be some years before Kevin would be able to keenly understand the meaning of FeatherStone or be able to embody this identity as a gift to his people. At age twenty-six, the Feather of his own psyche was not yet adequately tethered to the Stone of his body or to the Stone of the world.

The Cosmic Web of Life

About a year later, in 1980, Kevin transferred from the University of Wisconsin to Boston University. There, he studied ecology with the evolutionary microbiologist Lynn Margulis, who became one of Kevin's most important mentors. The study of ecology was profound for Kevin, in part because it coalesced a number of earlier numinous experiences that are foundational to who FeatherStone is mythopoetically. The first of these experiences took place when Kevin was just fourteen:

> One midsummer afternoon during my freshman year of high school, while I lay immobile on my bed in darkness, Mystery cracked me open. I saw and felt everything in the universe as a vast spiderweb extending infinitely outward from me. Stunned and amazed, I discovered I was physically and psychically a thread in this infinite web, interconnected with everything.

This deeply kinesthetic experience of interconnectivity — a fundamental principle of ecology — gave Kevin a first golden thread that he has followed ever since, resulting in his capacity to perceive or intuit "the jeweled web" in many dimensions of life. This experience at age fourteen was both his Eco-awakening and a spiritual

glimpse of the unity of the world. Although not a soul encounter — it did not identify his unique ecological niche — it was a pivotal revelation, a clue that became an
essential foundation for his later discoveries of mythopoetic identity.

> The web vision became for me a "search image," like the image a birder,
> botanist, or hunter has of different species when walking in a landscape; a
> search image, once acquired, enables a person to more easily spot individu-
> als of a particular species and to recognize natural landscape patterns. After
> my web vision, I began to consciously see and kinesthetically experience
> the web of life in many different contexts. It led me to become a natural-
> ist and ecologist, one who studies the network of relationships within the
> Earth community.

This early vision of the web was amplified and extended by Kevin's later somatic
experiences on the land during his teen years:

> It was through early "shape-shifting" experiences along the shore of Lake
> Michigan that I began to realize that the external boundary of my body was
> really not so bound; that actually my body's boundaries were fluid. This led
> to the conclusion that I did not "end" at my skin. I was having these experi-
> ences somewhat regularly, often during storms, along the bluffs and shore of
> the lake. These were classic "flow experiences" where all of my senses became
> heightened and acutely alive to my surroundings. My sensate body would
> begin to tingle, and I felt unbroken connections with the energies of the great
> weather, the migrating flocks, the deep cold of northern Wisconsin. These
> experiences awakened me to the profound beauty of the web of life.

This is a magnificent example of how soul-encounter experiences enable a person to understand and contextualize key life experiences that took place many years
earlier, even (or especially) in childhood. Conversely, these formative experiences
can build the foundation for later encounters with Soul. We might say that Soul
itself is the pattern that connects the most meaningful events of a person's life[9] — or
that Soul is the deep structure of a living being, its "primary organizing, sustaining,
and guiding principle," as geologian Thomas Berry puts it.[10] Or we might say that
the human Soul is the "morphic field" (biologist Rupert Sheldrake's term) of a person, a field of influence that shapes a person's life and guides their development. Or
consider the "implicate order" of physicist David Bohm, the generative field underlying specific manifest forms, from atoms to humans to galaxies; the "pattern integrity" of systems theorist Buckminster Fuller; or the "blueprint" or "primal pattern"
of Jungian analyst Robert Johnson. The "cosmic web of life" is a blueprint image
that has shaped FeatherStone's life and guided his development.

In college and graduate school, Kevin came to intellectually understand the web
of life through the lens of ecological science: the flows of energies through ecosystems, the natural elemental cycling processes. His studies with Lynn Margulis

opened the door for him "to a framework that encompassed organismic deep time and space, Gaian coevolutionary symbiogenesis, the micro- and macrocosmos," a framework that completely rearranged his conscious comprehension of the world.

Grandfather of the Desert Night and the Fire Sand Mandala

In the midst of his undergraduate studies at Boston University, Kevin had his second soul encounter at age twenty-eight, this time by way of a life-shifting dream-vision in which he met a second essential mentor and received a vital ecology lesson:

> It is a dark, fall evening. I am walking down an elm-lined street. I see a two-story 1920s Milwaukee bungalow, similar to the homes in the neighborhood I grew up in. I stride up the front steps, across the wooden porch, and through the front doorway. Inside, the house is dark. As my eyes focus I see the home has been ransacked: bookshelves overturned, a mirror broken, curtains torn down. In front of me looms a staircase and I am drawn upward. As I ascend I become aware I am dreaming. I open the second-story door and step through into the cool air of a Southwest high-desert night with the Milky Way and billions of stars overhead. Before me an elder is seated on the scrub desert floor gazing into a large, spiraling river of yellow, orange, and violet-green currents of fire and sand flowing counterclockwise down into the ground. Silently, without motion, he beckons me forth. I kneel next to him and we gaze into the living mandala. Together we study the currents and eddies. Slowly, carefully, he picks up small sticks and rocks from the desert floor and places them into the river. The streaming currents shift and change with each set object. And we spend the entire evening watching as the river pours down into the interior of the Earth.

Kevin refers to this visionary experience as "the dream of Grandfather of the Desert Night and the Fire Sand Mandala." The profundity and lucidity of the experience shook him and further ransacked the Adolescent life story he had been living, resulting in a psychological version of the interior shambles of that Milwaukee bungalow. It also gifted him with a dreamworld elder and teacher, a luminous vision of a natural mystery, and a template for "how to observe and study wild, flowing nature through the teachings of the fire sand mandala." Although he didn't know it at the time, this template turned out to be a dream-bestowed vision that, like an oracle, prefigured the deep pattern of his later visionary work as a river restoration ecologist, a vocation he would not begin for several years:

> In my dream of the fire sand mandala, Grandfather taught me how to patiently observe the ecocosmological powers that sustain specific landscapes and then act with them by placing rocks and sticks into the river, both literally and figuratively, exactly what I do now as a river restorationist.

Kevin understands Grandfather to be a variation on the Taoist Sage, both a facet of his own psyche and an archetype of the collective unconscious or *anima mundi*. At times, in his work as an ecologist and in the way he trains and mentors young ecologists, Kevin notices that what he is doing is, in essence, an embodiment of Grandfather.

Fiery, Spiraling Mandalas

The renowned Jungian analyst Robert Johnson recounts an intriguingly similar event as a young man, a soul encounter that took place in the wilds of the Pacific Northwest, "a visionary experience," he writes, "that demanded my attention, uninvited, one day when I was occupied with some mundane task."[11]

> One evening I made a campfire on the side of Mount Saint Helens, where I had spent many happy summers in childhood before the volcano erupted. I squatted on my heels looking into my campfire at dusk. Even today I can remember the vivid colors of that evening and how they thrilled me. The orange of the campfire, the dark blue color of the evening sky, the purple-gray shadows on the mountain. I felt a great sense of joy, beauty, peacefulness — but also expectancy.
>
> A young man, about my own age, came walking up and stood just on the other side of the fire. I was on my heels by the fire; he was standing quietly; and we just looked at each other for a long time. I was still in a sort of ecstasy over the colors of the fire.
>
> Then, to my astonishment, the fire moved and transported itself down into Spirit Lake, way at the bottom, and burned there as a tiny orange speck in the midst of that indigo blue water. Then the fire came back and burned before me. The young man took one step, into the middle of the fire. He absorbed the fire into his bloodstream so that he had fire circulating in his veins rather than blood. We stood there for some time, I looking in awe at these events, and then he said: "Come, I'm going to show you how the world was made."

The young man took Robert far out into space and directed his gaze toward a spiral nebula spinning ever so slowly, gradually concentrating itself until it became a huge, multifaceted diamond emanating its own light. As they watched, the diamond transformed, erupting from its north pole and reabsorbing the current into its south pole. Then it split itself down the middle, the two halves rotating in opposite directions and radiating great sparks of light and color. These images "were etched forever on my memory and had almost entered into the physical cells of my body."

Robert writes that "visionary experiences" like this "change us": "They form our character in very deep places. They determine what kind of people we will be in five, ten, or twenty years after the experience, when all its power has worked its way back to the surface of our lives." This was certainly true for Robert, who became a lifelong student of both the transformative fires met in the depths of the psyche and of the grand motifs of the cosmic drama. This was true as well for Joanna Macy, who was forever changed by her interstellar vision of the Great Turning Wheel; and for Sabina, who was transformed by her middle-of-the-night encounter with the explosive and piercing "spark of stars."

In a fascinating resonance, both Kevin and Robert, when they were young men, encountered the poetic mysteries of their Souls through an enigmatic encounter at night in the wilds with a mysterious teacher directing the initiate's attention to fiery, spiraling, mandala-like flows on Earth or in the Cosmos. Such dream-visions have a profound effect on the human psyche. For both men, the experience initiated them into an inscrutable mystery at the very core of their soul lives.

FeatherStone's Descent to Hell: Learning to Ride the Wind Horse

After Boston University, Kevin began graduate studies in forest ecology at Harvard.

Then, at age thirty, two years after his Fire Sand Mandala vision, Kevin's neuro-psychological instability increased as he moved further into his life without yet knowing how to tether the Feather of his psyche to the Stone of his body and the world. His turmoil peaked one evening when, after days of insomnia and agitation, he again fled into the night and drove aimlessly for hours, awakening in a roadside motel far from home. A few days later, he found himself at Harvard Medical School, where a kind psychiatrist, after a medical workup, diagnosed him as having manic depression — bipolar illness — and opined that this would be a lifelong journey for him. The psychiatrist also gave him the "good news" that his "symptoms" could be controlled with lithium and other psychotropic drugs.

Kevin was not entirely surprised to be psychiatrically diagnosed. His father, an obstetrician beloved in their community, was prone to unpredictable outbursts and deep depressions. Kevin's older brother was born with profound autism and at the age of five was institutionalized. His sister took her life at twenty-five, his first cousin at forty-two, and his younger brother was an alcoholic. "All good people," he says, "caring and kind, yet fate had dealt us a very difficult hand."

That day at Harvard Medical School, desperate to understand his own fate and the constellation of "mental illness" in his family, he "accepted with some sense of relief the idea I was living with a broken brain."

During the next fourteen years, in addition to completing his master's in ecology and starting his work as a restoration ecologist, Kevin "journeyed through the pharmacopeia of Western psychotropic medicine." When he was forty-six and fed up with being drugged, he stopped using his meds and had two "relatively calm years." But then his "overwhelming energetic experiences" recurred along with insomnia and the wild swings between highs and lows. This time, newly prescribed meds didn't help.

> I was suffocating. It was beyond bearable. One night, after obsessing for weeks about suicide, I took my life. Mystery, however, had another version of my story, for my wife found me and I awoke a day later in an intensive care unit under full life support and four-point leather restraints.
>
> Over the following four months, I lived mostly alone, encountering again very real malevolent presences, demons arising from other worlds that beckoned me to leave this life. Finally, in a hell I could not find my way out of, I again succumbed to the voices, and was legally committed to the locked wards of the state psychiatric hospital for two and a half weeks. I then spent six weeks in a recovery center and began a new life.

Three years after leaving the hospital, at age forty-nine, Kevin was divorced, still on psychotropic meds, but stable. After nearly dying, he became committed to learning how to live within his particular body and mind. He had accepted that he was "simply energetically different than most people." He also had the great fortune to meet a woman, Kim, a qigong teacher. They began dating and he began practicing qigong, which he describes as "embodied moving meditation practices that align one's body/mind with the natural energetic pathways in nature." Qigong turned out to be a highly effective means for Kevin to manage his neurological mutability, eventually without drugs, "a way of grounding my highly sensitive sensory gating systems." He experienced the benefits of qigong almost immediately and, as his practice deepened, cultivated an energetic equilibrium he had never before known. The qigong, along with tai chi and yoga, was transforming his nervous system, enabling him to "ride the wind horse without falling off." The Wind Horse, a Tibetan Buddhist symbol, combines the speed of the wind with the strength of the horse to carry prayers from earth (as in stone) to heaven (as in feather). "Learning to find my 'seat' on my wind horse is a metaphor for the transformation of my nervous system. Learning to ride my wind horse is another way of describing how I am now tethered to the ground."

Within three years, Kevin felt confident enough, psychologically, to taper off his medications. His maturing psychospiritual balance was also deeply supported by his marriage with Kim, by his caring family, and by his completion, at age fifty, of his doctorate in forest and river ecology. By 2019, Kevin had been free of all psychopharmacological drugs for eight years. He says, "I have learned to rewire and heal my nervous system such that when these heightened energetic encounters occur — and they still do occur — I am able to breathe into them and open fully to them while remaining physically and emotionally grounded."

> During my healing, I found Animas Valley Institute, through the intermediary of Thomas Berry. In the stories told by kindred spirits in circles

throughout the beautiful, wild American West, I found a place to celebrate the voices, dreams, and visions that kept breaking through into my world. These wild sojourners — along with river, salmon, beaver, and cotton-wood — taught me to embrace my visionary life as a gift, not as pathology. I learned how to make a healthy descent into, and back from, the under-world, and how to creatively navigate my visionary and dream worlds within the context of wild nature, my lifelong refuge and healing ground. I have come to fully own my gifts as a visionary student and teacher of Earth mysteries and science, and as a caregiver to the land.

Salmon Woman and the Dreaming of the Earth

At age fifty-eight, FeatherStone was gifted with another life-changing lucid dream, a third soul encounter that confirmed and extended his mythopoetic identity. He holds this dream as a blessing from his mother, from Mystery, and from the spirits of the place he has made his home, the coastal Pacific Northwest — and as a blessing of his ecological restoration work and of the fact that his dreams and visions are an essential dimension of that work. In this dream he met a third vital mentor:

I am hiking at night through an ancient rain forest on the Olympic Penin-sula, beneath a dark canopy of Sitka spruce, Western red cedar, and big leaf maple. As I walk I realize I am dreaming, which I find exhilarating. As I hike to the crest of a hill, I look down into a roundish embayment off the coast with a central tidal slough opening to the ocean. The slough has a dendritic network of tributaries that extend up into tidal marshlands ending at the edge of the forest. I see an altar-like structure to my right along the edge of the high marsh adjacent to a lean-to. The altar table is glowing, casting light down into the marsh and up into the gallery forest behind. Turning back to the marshland sloughs, I see hundreds of dark fusiform shapes of salmon streaming in from the sea into the marsh. I stroll over to the altar and realize it is an ancient fish-cleaning table that has been used by many generations of Indians to prepare the salmon. As I am taking this in, I find myself walking with my dear mother, who is holding my arm. We are walk-ing along the bank of a dark river coursing down through the ancient rain forest. The river is twenty to thirty yards wide and rushing, pouring down the channel into the dark forest, with conifer trees 150 to 200 feet tall lining its banks. Mother and I are tremendously enjoying each other's company. As we gaze into the river and the darkened forest, we begin to see the dark forms of salmon streaming upriver in schools of twelve to twenty fish. And as we look on, amazingly the salmon begin to glow in mixed colors of yel-low, orange, green, red, and violet. Set against the dark rushing river, they are spectacular to behold. Mother and I are delighted at this display and

laugh together, enjoying each other and the beauty and mystery of the returning salmon.

As we continue to walk, the riverbank becomes steeper and too challenging for Mother to negotiate. She lets go of my arm, encouraging me to
go on, to walk down to the river's edge without her. I do, and when I reach
the river I sit back on the bank and find myself awash in salmon slime, all
around and under me. I look up to the right, and sitting on the riverbank
is a woman, dressed in the rain gear and boots of a field biologist, but also
wearing a traditional Salish Indian cedar hat. She has long black hair and
is looking intently at the school of salmon passing by. She turns to me
and says, "You can tell the species of salmon by the shape of their bodies
and dorsal fins. I am Salmon Woman and I come here every year to welcome the salmon home." I can see by her nature, her descriptions of the
salmon, and her dress that this woman is very much at home here and has
a deep knowledge of the river, the salmon, and the forest. I am deeply impressed by her presence and am attracted to her.

There are several extraordinary features of this dream. First and foremost,
DreamMaker placed Kevin *in the experiential position, the niche,* of someone who
is a caregiver for the salmon, the rivers, and the forests of the Pacific Northwest,
a person who is an apprentice to this ecosystem and all its creatures, habitats, and
natural processes. (This is akin to how Jung's first soul encounter placed him in the
experiential position of a bridge or channel between the dead and the living.) Another way to say this is that Kevin was placed in an apprentice position to Salmon
Woman herself, the archetypal or mythic being who "welcome[s] the salmon
home."

As I've been maintaining, the primary effect or power of a dream is not its
meaning but the direct way it shifts the Ego's perspective or worldview, often in a
healing or wholing way, but at other times, especially when the person is in the Cocoon or the Wellspring, in a way that initiates the Ego into an experience of self and
world in accordance with the person's soul destiny. Kevin's Salmon Woman dream
is of the latter sort. It afforded him an immediate, somatic experience of what it is
to be an apprentice caregiver to the Pacific Northwest ecosystem. And ever since the
dream, by returning regularly to both its images and its embodied experience, Kevin
has been cooperating with the DreamMaker to steadily shift his consciousness in a
way resonant with his mythopoetic identity as FeatherStone.

Another astonishment is that, at the time of this dream, Kevin knew nothing
about the mythic-archetypal figure of Salmon Woman and very little about the traditions or lifeways of the Salish people of the coastal Pacific Northwest. He had
known about their fish-cleaning tables but, in his dayworld, had never thought of
them as "altars" in the religious or spiritual way they appeared in his dream, in which
the altar tables are part of "an ancient ritual." He had not known that the Salish had

forever been telling stories of Salmon Woman, who greets her children, the salmon, as they come home to their natal spawning grounds at the headwaters of the coastal rivers. He did not know that his dream paralleled a story given to the people who have lived in that place since time before memory. Once he learned of this stunning correspondence, Kevin embraced the dream as, in part, an invitation to learn the stories of the traditional people of his adopted homeland and to understand Salmon Woman's place in those stories.

Kevin also experienced this dream as a blessing of his work as a restoration ecologist, as a caregiver to salmon, rivers, and forests. Salmon Woman's appearance in this dream felt to Kevin like a blessing by the spirits of his homeland that acknowledged his ecological niche and mythopoetic role. He experienced the dream itself as a blessing from Mystery of the delivery system he had chosen. Further, the implication is that his delivery system, as an ecologist, is and should be conducted in a sacred way, as suggested not only in Salmon Woman's presence but also in the fish-cleaning tables that the dream-ego sees as glowing altars.

Kevin had been gradually learning that his dreams, spontaneous images, and visions could support and inform his soul work. As Kevin explains, "My work is to listen to the dreaming of the Earth of my homeland and waters and then to act in concert with the communiqués I receive." As an ecologist, he experiences the unique "dreaming stories" of each ecosystem he works in or travels through. This is essentially the same understanding of the "dreamtime" held by the Aboriginal peoples of Australia. More generally, this ability to enter the imaginal to discern the dreaming of particular places is found worldwide among, for example, shamans, herbalists who consult plants about medicines, land caregivers, people who hunt in a sacred way, Taoist farmers, spiritual ecologists, river stewards, and the founders of ecospiritual communities like Findhorn in Scotland.

Dreams and myths emerge from the same realm, one that might be called the underworld or the world behind the world, the collective unconscious, or the dreamtime. Salmon Woman came to Kevin from the same place from which she has been coming to the Salish people from the beginning of time. The land — the Pacific Northwest ecosystem — was calling to Kevin through his dreams.

> The dreaming of the Earth comes to me literally in dreams, arising from the spirits, elementals, and creatures of a particular place. With the dream of Salmon Woman, Thomas Berry's "dreaming of the Earth" became profoundly real to me.

FeatherStone is one of the gifted people to whom the Earth speaks frequently and directly through dreams and visions. He has come to understand himself as a conduit between worlds, a thread between feather and stone, between dream and Earth. By "tethering" or "grounding" something etheric or invisible, something of the dreamtime, he serves as a channel between invisible beings or processes and his people or place. *This* is what FeatherStone does; this is who he is.

The Feather represents things that are invisible, ineffable. This could be a feeling, a sensation, a flow of energy coming from a tree, river, or storm, or simply an intuition. There is a sudden change in the quality of my normal experience where my sensations become heightened, light becomes exceptionally clear around things, my kinesthetic body begins to tingle lightly, and auras are more visible. I become acutely alive in my animal body.

As FeatherStone, I open myself to wild energies that flow between heaven and earth, between the world-behind-this-world and this world, and translate these experiences into a cocreative, regenerative Gaian ecological story of relationships. I am, in other words, a forest ecosystem scientist who happens to operate on a regular basis through realms of human experience generally not acknowledged in the world of science.

His Salmon Woman dream deepened and focused FeatherStone's apprenticeship to his soul work — from a more general student of the web of life to someone who apprentices specifically to the rivers and forests of the coastal Pacific Northwest. His apprenticeship ties together the mythopoetic meaning of FeatherStone and the ancestral origins of his family name: Kevin, as it turns out, is a descendant of a people of the salmon, people from Ireland, Wales, and England. He has ancestral roots with the forests and natural processes that cocreate the conditions for the coflourishing of salmon and people.

There are two final features to note about FeatherStone's dream. First, his attraction to Salmon Woman suggests she is an anima figure, an embodiment of his West facet, his Guide to Soul. Given the nature of what she teaches him in the dream, we can see her in the additional West-facet role of his Muse, his guide to his soul *work*. Second, Kevin soon understood the dream as a farewell blessing from his beloved mother, who, unexpectedly, died just two weeks later. If we keep in mind that his mother let him know that she could not accompany him down to the river but clearly encouraged him to go, we might imagine this dream, in part, as something like a "handoff" from Mother to Muse. We might wonder if a shift of this sort is an initiatory feature of many people's passage into true Adulthood.

Marty: Singing Death Back into Life

During his Dissolution phase, Marty, the writer and men's conference leader, dreamed of a beautiful Scarified Woman who sings a high haunting lament (see "Marty and the Scarified Woman," pages 79–80). A few weeks later, Marty was preparing for a vision fast. The group was guided in a deep-imagination process in which people offer a question to the Muse: "On the Descent to Soul, what will I encounter that will at first feel like an obstacle but is something I must engage and allow myself to be changed by?" (see "The Obstacle Threshold," pages 109–11). The image Marty received was of a small blue pool of water holding at its rim a reflection of a new moon. He called this pool the Well of Tears.

A couple of months later, Marty was on his vision fast, out in a remote tangle of redrock canyons and petrified sand dunes in southern Utah. Next to his solo spot was a large pool of water in a bedrock basin. The Well of Tears. On the third of his four nights…

> I sit at the edge of the pool and wait for the water to do its work. I see many faces appear in that pool. Some of the faces I have grieved over: My father, who died of cancer three years ago. My best friend, Barry, who committed suicide four years earlier after his wife's death by cancer. And my own wife, who died just a few months ago from a brain tumor. Grandparents long gone. Ancestral presences that I do not recognize except by some vague familiarity.
>
> I am in tears by the time she arrives, the Scarified Woman — ritual scarring on her cheekbones, flowing dress and headscarf.
>
> As I stare into the dark pool, I hear her song, her lament — like a call to prayer. She appears in the pool. Her face is close to mine. I can almost touch her but I dare not disturb the reflection. She leans in and asks, "Will you promise to bear God's heart?" She asks again. I nod. She tells me that before I can truly be wed to my "Beloved," I must promise to bear God's heart. To do this I must "sing Death back into Life." I say in a loud clear voice, "Forgive me. I don't know yet how to sing Death back into Life. But I promise to do my best to learn. I will bear God's heart." She gives me an image of a crescent moon rising over a crack in the altar rocks just before sunrise. I am made to understand that should I see this, I will be wed with my Beloved. She slowly disappears, singing, into the dark night of the pool.

The next day, the last of his fast, Marty prepared for his wedding.

> Near dusk I take a ceremonial bath and change into my wedding garb, a blue silk embroidered shirt and white silk pants. I enter the circle at dusk, barefoot, drum in hand. I dance and sing in an earth-wise circle [counter-clockwise] as the stars gradually become visible. The wind howls. After two hours I put on more layers. I stop occasionally and kneel in the center repeating some prayers, never stopping my drumming. In the early morning hours it has become so cold I am shaking. I have brought my sleeping bag. I pull it to the center of my circle and climb in. Soon the shivering stops and I drift off.
>
> I awake with a start and leap out of my bag. There's a hint of light over the east stone. In a crack in the altar wall, the slim cat's claw of the new moon slides up the face of the rock. I have a sense of vertigo. I drum and dance and shout and soon the Sun comes up with the Moon.

Several months later, I asked Marty to tell me what it was like when the Sun came up that last morning:

> I experienced for several minutes, maybe longer, the feeling of what the world looks and *feels* like from a vastly enlarged perspective. I hesitate to say it, but it felt like what Death and Life might feel like to God, or at least to some minor deity. It was as though the human part of me became infinitesimally small, and I felt something of the scale of this dance of the creation and destruction of worlds, the rising Moon, the advent of tides, and great swaths of joyous birdsong circling the Earth for millennia at the orange event horizon of traveling daybreak. And it was not of my human scale. It was a glimpse of the great whirring insides of the engines of existence, and it was terrifying. And it was absolutely stunningly beautiful.
>
> This is what I am being asked to do: somehow bear God's heart, sing Death back into Life, reveal the vertigo-inducing Mystery that lives in the bone cave of the human heart, mine and others'.

Christie: A Dedicated Spirit

Christie is a clinician, educator, and leader in healthcare — and an occasional harp player. She lives on Vancouver Island, British Columbia, where she was born and raised — and formed, as she says, by cedar and moss; sea and mountain; salmon and orca; wolf, bear, and cougar; deer and elk; and heron and eagle. Christie is most often quiet, compassionate, and gentle; some would say guarded. When I met her, at her first Animas intensive, she looked a bit frightened most of the time, like a prey animal in constant vigilance. She wrote that she made her way in life "mostly by hunkering — aligning myself with what is small and delicate; participating, loving, and observing from the intricate spaces between things; avoiding the open spaces that beckon full height and visibility."

Preparation: A Search for Something Else

Between the ages of twenty-seven and thirty-four, while in the Oasis (stage three), Christie went through a number of moltings, each one significantly shifting her understanding of herself. These moltings were set in motion by sudden deaths of friends and family members and also by serious injuries of her own. Over time, she lost her capacity to recover from these losses by simply returning to her former life. She began to question her beliefs about death and about the meaning and purpose of life. Why, she wondered, did the lives of her loved ones come to an end while hers had not? She began to live this question — and others:

Is there a reason for my life, an agreement I need to honor, a contribution that only I can make? These questions and experiences of loss combined to launch me into a search for something else. The two questions that most haunted my heart were: *Who am I? What is my purpose?*

These questions are indicative of the passage of Confirmation. But Christie's full experience of the Cocoon was delayed because even though she was feeling and intuiting these questions on the mythopoetic level of Soul, she was understanding and engaging them in a middleworld way — as if the answers might arrive in the form of a conventionally identified career or social role. Nevertheless, Christie was now in the Cocoon.

When she was thirty-nine, Christie participated in her first Animas immersion, a five-day intensive. There, she began to consciously cultivate her facets of wholeness by, for example, "sensing the distinctions and connections between Divine Masculine and Divine Feminine energies" and by beginning "a study to transform my understanding of beauty." Even more importantly, she first heard the call from her depths:

> I met Hummingbird at the edge of the forest and she called me back into the garden. There she asked me to drink the sweet nectar. I heard her say I am someone who *belongs* to Life. Also during the week, I began to feel a strong presence of Orca and had a sense of Orca being in some way connected to the harp. I received an image of Orca coming near to shore and my resting my hand upon him and also an image of the harp as a hidden resource within me. One night as I stood at the edge of the garden, I found myself mesmerized by a chorus of frogs, and I remembered an encounter two years earlier in which Frog had suddenly hopped onto my chest as if he was anointing me. The chorus and the memory together created a certain sense of potency and significance. I listened for what was being called for but couldn't quite catch it. For some reason, this prompted me to recite aloud, in a whisper, a few lines from Wordsworth's "The Prelude": "I made no vow, but vows / Were then made for me: bond unknown to me / Was given, that I should be — else sinning greatly — A dedicated spirit." At the edge of that night garden, I was brought to a place of accepting that there is a purpose and calling in my life that was yet to be discovered, and a need to be a dedicated spirit to that process of discovery. I left carrying this call and response:
>
> Universe to me: *Please serve something good for the others.*
>
> Me to Universe: *I am willing to reveal my heart, that I might offer something good.*

In this passage, we can recognize the Preparation theme of cultivating wholeness as well as the familiar Dissolution motifs of crisis (existential questions about life, death, and purpose), the call (by way of Hummingbird, Orca, and Frog), and transpersonal dedication.

Dissolution: Severance Ceremony for Mo Inion Dilis

Four years later, at age forty-three, during her second Animas five-day immersion, Christie more fully entered Dissolution, her psychospiritual dying quickened by an encounter on the land:

> I am startled to see a gorgeous yellow bird lying near where I had slept the night before, her life force just leaving her body. Part of me wants to flee, part of me deeply hopes she will recover and fly away, part of me is terrified of not knowing what to do, and another part recognizes I have arrived in this moment and must honor it accordingly. I cradle the bird in my palm, her exquisite gray wings stretched across my outstretched fingers, as if in flight. I admire every aspect of her magnificence, from the depths of her dark eye, to her bright feathers, to her miraculous wings, to the undersides of her ancient yellow feet. Eventually, I tenderly release her, and when I look down, there is a trail of blood across my palm.
>
> I feel deeply moved to be the one who happened upon her and was given the opportunity to honor and respect her life as it was ending. I have never done anything like this before, in the past letting fear and uncertainty turn me away from the truth of such moments. At first I wonder if this is an opportunity to learn how to honor the endings of the ones I love, when their time comes, with greater sincerity and simple beauty. But then I consider it may also signify recognition of a part of *me* that is dying — perhaps the part my dad has always referred to, in soothing Irish, as Mo Inion Dilis, My Sweet Daughter.

A few weeks later, Christie went to the nearby mountains to enact a severance ceremony, to honor and say goodbye to her previous identity as Mo Inion Dilis. The exceptional self-compassion exhibited here is rare — but perhaps essential during the Dissolution phase of the Descent.

> Though I would not have chosen for her to go, I recognize her sudden departure, and honor all she has offered, protected, and served. I acknowledge her and mourn her loss with these words:
>
> "With gentle acumen, you learned what was needed and adjusted yourself to seek the greatest harmony. With miraculous self-healing, you learned what was in your quiver:[12] intellect, joy, humor, kindness. You brightened hearts simply with your presence.
>
> "Your years of protection have served their purpose. Now I am ready to handle the implications of visibility, desire, sensation, passion, energy — to undam the river, let the current carry me.
>
> "You were scared to release your star-cords — your connection to and

affection for the celestial realm — lest your longing to be back among the stars be too great without them. But it is time now for you to release these cords; they have prevented my full immersion in this Earth journey. I am here for a reason! It is time to discover what I am meant to experience and contribute here."

When I am finished, I find a place in the sun and discover I am sitting beside a fully intact snakeskin. I jump a little, realizing that by honoring Mo Inion Dilis, I have stepped out of a skin that has become too small for me. I recognize that a doorway is now open to learn how to be in the world in a new way, to move beyond the embodiment of the Sweet Daughter, to discover the unique place only I can inhabit.

Telegraph Cove: The Calling Song

A few months later, Christie began a yearlong immersion with two Animas guides and twelve other participants; this was comprised of four weeklong sessions, one in each season, each in a different wilderness setting in the American West. The third session would include a four-day vision fast. At the end of the first session, Christie received a dream with mysterious but specific instructions as to how to proceed with her journey. Such a dream is of the greatest value on the Descent to Soul, even though the opportunity it offers is always dangerous to the Wanderer's current identity. In this dream...

A companion in our group says he and I should go to our next session by bicycle and that we should start our journey from Telegraph Cove. I answer, "Because who wants to start in the middle?" By which I mean yes, good idea, let's do that. But I am also worried how long this will take and whether or not I will be able to get enough time off work to start the trip from Telegraph Cove.

Telegraph Cove, as it turns out, is an actual dayworld place near the north end of Vancouver Island, about a five-hour drive from Christie's home. She had never been there but had always wanted to go. She resolved to visit Telegraph Cove before the second session, but she procrastinated for weeks ("What is the point? What will I do when I get there?"). Then one evening her Muse showed up with a call from the depths, a compelling and startlingly clear image of herself at Telegraph Cove playing her harp for the orcas.

So, I do go. At twilight, I play my harp to the sea. I feel slightly ridiculous but also a little exquisite, like I have entered into the painting of the image I had seen in my mind. I play Irish folk songs, some ancient and some modern, including love songs. Nothing dramatic seems to happen; no whales appear. But I feel a bit mischievous, and something in me delights in the idea that perhaps whales have been experiencing a strange longing for the sounds that can only be made by human hands and carried across the clarity of air, and that maybe my hesitant tunes have been heard in the depths below.

"Nothing dramatic seems to happen," she claimed, but unbeknownst to Christie, she had just enacted a motif found around the world in myths and stories of the Descent to Soul, in which the initiate and the Soul call longingly to each other, the one on the surface of the world, the other in the depths. Like destined lover and beloved, each sings a "calling song" to the other, the Ego yearning for the visionary wisdom of the Soul, the Soul hoping for a human partner with the capacities to embody the Soul's dream. And Christie's Muse, playing the role of the bow-and-arrow-wielding Cupid (the Roman version of the Greek god Eros), sets this up with a twofold piercing, first the beckoning and ensnaring dream of Telegraph Cove and then, as further bait, the irresistible image of her playing her harp for Orca (the Ego calling to Soul with harp chords, the Soul answering with whale song). The harpist on the shore and the waiting whale in the depths of the dark waters — Christie had turned loose these chthonic images and they began their delaminating work on her psyche. The early results became evident the next day....

The Hunter and the Hunted

As Christie drove home, something curious happened. She saw a sign, not far from Telegraph Cove, that said, "No black bear hunting area." This puzzled and bothered her. She hadn't known bear hunting was allowed *anywhere*. When she got home, she searched the web and discovered that not only is bear hunting legal at certain times in certain places in Canada but that the Telegraph Cove region hosts a thriving industry serving trophy hunters. As she looked at photos of slaughtered bears and read posts of the hunters and their sometimes dishonoring and dishonorable methods, she was deeply disturbed that she had no awareness bears were being hunted. She became frightened and heartbroken by the attitudes of dominance being proudly shared and displayed online. Christie may not have realized the striking contrast between these hunters' attitudes and the way she had reverently honored the death of the little yellow bird and the passing of Mo Inion Dilis.

Although she was immediately unsettled by her new awareness of bear hunting, it wasn't until late February, during the second session of the yearlong immersion, that she felt the full impact of this grief. There, in a cactus-studded desert canyon in the American Southwest, she was brought to her knees with uncontrollable sobbing.

Why did Christie's DreamMaker and her Muse — her inner Guide to Soul — send her explicitly to Telegraph Cove? Perhaps it was to experience precisely this grief in order to accelerate and amplify the dismembering effects of Dissolution, as grieving always does. No doubt it was also invaluable for her to enact the ceremony of playing her harp for the whales, which set in motion two additional Ego-sabotaging influences. First was the mutual calling between Ego and Soul, an otherworldly romantic alliance that is profoundly destabilizing to the Adolescent worldview. Second, by playing her harp for the orcas, she strengthened a relationship with the non-human Others, a relationship that was in stark contrast to the way she thought and felt about the relationship between hunter and hunted. The tension between these two kinds of relationships (partnership and dominance) laid the groundwork for a Mandorla dynamic, one that would help finish off Christie's Adolescent identity.

Soul or Mystery seemed to be brilliantly orchestrating Christie's experiences, providing her with just the right set of opportunities for her soul initiation. But keep in mind that the Soul needs a willing partner, a mature Ego able and willing to say yes to the opportunities.

While in the desert on the second session, two additional events occurred that amplified and accelerated Christie's Dissolution. First, a companion in her group — the same man who appeared in her dream and suggested they start their journey from Telegraph Cove — gave her a book of poetry by Lorna Crozier. One of the poems asks that we reconsider the words we use when referring to the Others: "How about / A magnificence, a blessing of bears. / If we say a *blessing of bears* / Over and over again / will we come to believe it?"[13] As Christie read, a light turned on: "It lodged in my heart that it might matter to offer attention, praise, holy language to the Wild Others — as an act of Love." Her resolve to do so further intensified her developing romance with the world.

Later that day, something happened that had the opposite effect: It increased her ambivalence about being in this world at all. One of the men in the group spoke about how his recent dreams seemed to suggest that he had a mythopoetic resonance with the archetype of the hunter. Being somewhat uncomfortable with hunting, he exclaimed, "I have *no idea* what it feels like to be hunted." Hearing this one remark had an earth-shattering impact on Christie, triggering memories of wounding events from her late teens and early twenties:

> With a *whoosh* I understood my whole life in a new way, because *I* know *exactly* what it feels like to be hunted. I had never before held that frame of reference, but it fit precisely. I know intimately the perpetual vigilance of the one who is hunted: how to make endless minute choices to minimize the likelihood of being caught. I know the internal sensations of fear that come with being followed maliciously and perpetually by an individual; to have them wait outside where I live, sit in the place where I work, or walk behind me as I go to work or school or the bus or to the store — to feel the hairs on my neck stand up and have alertness spark through my being. I know the behaviors I learned to make myself more difficult to track: never

disclose where I live, keep to the back of a crowd, always have an eye on an exit and all surroundings, notice everything, trust judiciously, vary my routes and routines, choose work with unpredictable schedules, do not count on what is rational, the police, or the law to protect me.

Christie's grief over the hunting of bears was now getting entangled with and amplified by her memories of being hunted herself. And a bedrock tension within her psyche — between her love for this world and her fear of it — was increasing as well. The Adolescent structures of her psyche were crumbling. Although Christie knew what it was like to be hunted in an abusive and oppressive way, in a way that lacks integrity, she did not yet know what it was like to hunt in a sacred way; she did not yet understand the sacred dance between hunter and hunted.

Soul Encounter: Beautiful Huntress with a Loving Heart

What we discover about our mythopoetic identity is often the last thing we could have imagined — and sometimes the exact *opposite* of what we *would* have imagined. It's as if our inner protectors (our subpersonalities) have been trying to obstruct our encounter with Soul because they know something of our destiny, our genius or daimon, and what that destiny would demand of us, how it would change us. Or perhaps on some level beneath conscious awareness we have glimpsed our destiny and, because it terrified us, we gravitated toward the opposite of the image. A common theme of soul initiation is this: You become what you (most) fear.

Although many women share Christie's history of being hunted, we might wonder if something in her particular experience provided a fissure in her psyche — a "spirit line" — that Soul could later use as an entry point.

As Christie slid ever closer to her first soul encounter — that for which she most longed — she also, like most everyone, tried to protect herself from it. After Christie's shocking recognition that she knew intimately the experience of being hunted, one of her guides suggested she spend the next day embodying the archetype of the hunter while walking on the desert. Being immensely uncomfortable with this proposal, she was greatly relieved when the next day's schedule shifted and there was no time for this existential experiment.

But Mystery offered her other nudges to look into the hidden heart of the hunter. Before coming to the desert, she had been feeling a need for guidance concerning this second session, so she consulted an oracle deck and drew a single card. The card read, "Be the hunter, not the hunted." This is the only card in this forty-four-card deck that makes any reference to hunting. She immediately disliked the card.

Later on the day that she first saw her life from the perspective of being hunted, Christie had an encounter with Frog. This is the creature who often appears in myths at the threshold of magical realms, usually as an ally, and who was enchantingly present for her in that night garden, four years earlier, when she first heard the call from the depths. This time, Frog tricked her into the role of hunter, anointing her once again, and had some advice for her:

> During a break in our group process, I sat by the creek on a boulder, my left heel resting on the rock. Frog came out of the water and hopped toward me, tucking himself into the space between my heel and where the rest of my foot hovered above the rock. I was surprised and sat very still. Eventually I shifted and he returned to the water's edge. But then he did it a second time! He hopped directly to me and sat in the space under my foot. If I were to suddenly lower my foot, deliberately or just in the act of standing, I might harm or even kill him. It was as if he was pointing to my innate power to either harm or protect him. When again he returned to the water's edge, he turned back toward me and we sat looking at one another. As I stared into the fierce eyes of Frog, his message was clear: *Embody the Huntress!* When I walked back to the group, I said, "Apparently it's Hunt-ress, not Hunter, that I need to familiarize myself with."

Later, two of the other women in the group separately asked Christie if she knew about Artemis, which she didn't beyond a vague recollection of school lessons on the Greek pantheon.

Over the following months, between the second and third sessions of the year-long immersion, Christie made courageous, if "skeptical," efforts to follow up on the mythopoetic clues she received in the desert. She read about Artemis. And bears. And bow hunting. She even took archery lessons. And for each step toward Mystery, Mystery took a step or two toward her. There was, for example, the knife episode:

> One morning I awake with a sinking feeling in my stomach, knowing I would need to own a hunting knife before my vision fast in May, more for symbolic than functional purposes. I am quite averse to the idea; I do not want to be associated with any mechanism for causing harm. I take weeks slowly circling my way toward it: I go to an outdoor store that sells knives and locate the knife cabinet. On another visit I look in the cabinet and a staff member asks if I am interested; I leave.
>
> Within a day or two, I am out hiking on a mountain trail. I notice Slug in front of me starting to cross the trail. I stop to watch Slug with a certain fondness because he had previously been a harbinger of healing for me. I tell Slug about my angst and uncertainty about the vision fast and about owning a knife and am eased just by watching his steady motion as he moves from relative safety into the exposed path — exactly what I have been reluctant to do. I pour some water onto the dry trail and wait for him to cross. I am noticing the contrast between his soft gentleness and the sharp edge of the knife I do not want to own when Slug suggests I consider the knife as a necessity in order to be a "Protectress of the Vulnerable." I

receive this as an initiation, an invitation that I accept by stepping across the trail that Slug has left on the path as if I am crossing a one-way threshold before it disappears.

I go back to the outdoor store and take a closer look at the knives, and I see one that seems like it could be mine. But it has a name, *Jegermeister*, and I don't know what it means, so again I leave. At home I discover that *Jegermeister* is Norwegian for "Hunt Master," a title given to an official in charge of matters related to hunting.

The next day, Christie returned to the store and, as she put it, "acquired the knife — and its power."

A few weeks later, in May, on our third session, this time in the southern Utah redrock desert, each member of the group enacted a four-day vision fast. Christie chose a solo spot in the upper reaches of a sheer-walled, narrow canyon. The raging battle within her — between her longing for soul encounter and her terror of it — unfolded into its final two acts of decisive Ego defeat followed by revelation:

By the afternoon of the third day of my fast, I'm not sure what I'm supposed to be doing. I am drowsy and listless and vaguely recall that I'm here for a reason, but I can't quite muster enough focus or energy to do anything. So I spend much of the day just lying down and watching the crescent moon cross the daytime sky. At some point, a part of my brain remembers that Artemis is connected with the crescent moon and I get squinty-eyed and suspicious. I tell Artemis (via the Moon) that she would be mistaken to be considering me for any further apprenticeship. I build quite a strong case, listing my sensitivities, lack of experience, and overall aversion to her realm. There is no apparent response. As the hours pass and the Moon has not gone away, I begin to change my pitch. Now I am beseeching: *Why would you choose me? Surely you have better options!*

When the Moon disappears in the night, I am left feeling uneasy that things are not going how they are meant to. After all, I am here to discover my unique gift to offer, and I can't see how Artemis and the Moon are connected to that.

By the afternoon of the final day, I am starting to panic. What if nothing happens? What if I do not receive any clues about my gift? The very thought is unbearable. I cannot go back without some hint. I cannot go back at all to the life I was living. I need some sign, anything, to help me know who I am.

I curl into the shade of a juniper tree and begin sobbing. I feel a desperate longing in every cell of my body: I want to live as someone who is guided by love, who loves generously and receives love graciously. I let the force of my longing take over my body, and a torrent of tears douses the stones beneath me.

As darkness descends, I know I am running out of time. I walk the perimeter of the small ceremonial circle I made. I tell the story of Skeleton Woman to the setting sun, for it is a hunting story about love. I gather my blankets and settle into the middle of the circle. It has come to this. I am so humbled now that, before the Moon disappears in the West, I stretch out my arms. "I am willing," I say. "If it is meant in some way, even though I cannot understand, I will accept that it is so." The night is clear. The Great Bear constellation seems to dominate the sky and I can scarcely look away even though it is usually the Seven Sisters, the Pleiades, that draws my eye. All I am able to do is send out to the stars my repeated pleas: *I came to find out what I don't know. Please. Help me see what is mine to carry! How can my life be in service?* I say all this over and over again, hours passing in the night, my urgency growing. The sky begins to lighten in the east. I keep my gaze on the Great Bear constellation. My pleas are whispers now. I slowly exhale and begin to accept that I may not receive any signs. I close my eyes. Then, suddenly, it arrives with a *whoosh* (perhaps like receiving a telegraph): *Beautiful Huntress with a Loving Heart, the one who attends to and appreciates all things!* This comes as a declaration, as if spoken by an audible voice — feminine, commanding, and kind. I am so startled I repeat it back as a question: Beautiful Huntress with a Loving Heart? In that moment, a shooting star blazes right through the Great Bear constellation. I take this as an affirmation. Doubt follows closely behind. But then something brings me to my knees, tears soak the Earth, and some part of me recognizes and understands this is my true name.

As I watch the Sun rise in the east, I feel a new certainty in my being. It might be relief. But it also might be confidence. I feel I am standing for the first time in a way that occupies the full height of my being. Remembering what I had learned during my archery lessons, I pick up my imaginary bow and shoot an arrow toward the rising Sun. Today is a new beginning.

This numinous experience — Christie's first soul encounter, her first revelation of mythopoetic identity — was an incontestable announcement of her essential place in the world, her psycho-ecological niche. Mystery expressed this place to her as a variation on the archetype of Artemis, the Huntress. By then, this was not at all a surprise to Christie, but the particular variation — *Beautiful Huntress with a Loving Heart, the one who attends to and appreciates all things* — is not something she had seen coming. More importantly, it arrived on the wings of a certain feeling-tone and with a meaning that fused two images that had previously been irreconcilable opposites for Christie — the hunter and the heart — and in the process transformed both images within her. Previously for her, the hunter was always and only the irreverent, threatening, trophy-seeking predator, and the heart was always and only the sweet daughter caregiver. The polarization of these two symbols had served her well by keeping her developing Ego safe from an awareness of her destiny until she was ready to behold and embrace her soul image, and by sensitizing her to the preciousness of all life. Now the two symbols had merged, transformed each other, and began their transformation of her. Now she had both the blessing and the burden of learning to embody, simultaneously, the Huntress and the Lover. It would be a great fortune for anyone to be called to live either archetype; Christie had been bestowed with the dangerous opportunity to live both. To be the Huntress-Protectress.

The Huntress who loves all things: Christie was only beginning to sense how this could even be possible. The transformation of her Ego was in its early stages. The completion and fulfillment of this transformation depended on her cooperation. By holding true to both powers — hunting, on the one hand, and honoring and loving, on the other — and letting their collision in consciousness do its work on her psyche, she would be transformed. As we've seen, this process is what Jung referred to as the "transcendent function," in which the tension of opposites produces a new, uniting function that transcends both. This is the Mandorla process.

Although Christie, like every person, is entirely unique, her Soul, like everyone's, can be understood as a particular variation on one or more universal archetypes. The Huntress, obviously, is most significant for her. Each culture has its own way of representing this archetype. Artemis, for example, is the Greek version of the virgin huntress. Among other things, Artemis embodies a few distinctive oppositions or contradictions, some of which we also see within Christie: Artemis both hunts animals and protects them; she is both the goddess of wildlife and patroness of hunters. She both brings and relieves diseases in women. She is the goddess of both virginity and childbirth. The opposition between the poles is what allows each to exist.

A few other things about Artemis ought to catch our attention here: She arms herself with a bow and arrows. She is associated with the Moon. The bear and the deer are sacred to her. As a goddess of maiden dances and songs, Artemis is often portrayed with a lyre — essentially a small, U-shaped harp.

Is it just a wild coincidence that there are so many correspondences between Christie's life and that of a Greek goddess? We wouldn't think so if we embraced the reality of the archetypes — common patterns and images that have existed in all times and places within the collective human unconscious. Christie, from this perspective, was formed as a unique variation of the Artemis archetype (and others).

Is it possible that part of the reason Christie had been so reactive to bear hunting was because she was destined to be a hunter? I asked her if this felt true. "Well," she replied, "it makes me cry, hearing it. I think this emotion is in recognition of the resonance of it. If I travel back into that period of my life when I suffered and made sacrifices in order to survive, there is something powerful in coming to understand that it might also have been preparing me to live into my soul identity."

The Varieties of Soul Encounters

Soul encounters come in a variety of colors. There are, for example, three ways they appear in consciousness: visions while awake, dream or trance visions, and soul-infused insights.

Silver Moon's five soul encounters exemplify all three varieties (see "Silver Moon: 'Do Something More Taboo with It,'" pages 187–96). She had visions while awake (the somatically animated image of the Witch — first in imagery during her Core Wound work, and then later during ceremony and expressive artwork on the land), visions while asleep (her dream of the chalice of menstrual blood), and soul-infused or soul-fueled insights (her task to "speak the unwanted and suppressed voices of the feminine," and more specifically, "Become Your Blood").

With all three varieties, deep imagination is always a key element. We need our Muse (the Guide to Soul) to assist or mediate the experience.[14] Deep feeling is also a universal dimension of soul encounter. We might wonder which comes first, the emotion or the image; which is cause, which effect? We are invariably moved by the experience, yes, but it might be that the image-saturated encounter blossoms out of a powerful emotional state.[15]

Visions While Awake

The first variety of mythopoetic revelation is waking encounters or interactions with other beings, whether human or otherwise.

Sometimes our mythopoetic identity is revealed in what the Other says to or tells us, perhaps a name we're given — our true name or soul name. Sometimes this soul-disclosing Other is a tangible presence — a butterfly, a wallaby, or the wind. At other times, it's a nonembodied voice or a thought appearing out of nowhere — as with Christie's *Beautiful Huntress with a Loving Heart*. Sometimes the Other shows us who we are, perhaps demonstrating this through a symbolic enactment such as a song we hear or a sculpture we find ourselves forming (a witch, for instance). Or the Other might take us on a physical journey, perhaps, like the Rock Guardian, through a maze of redrock canyons, on which we learn something of our mythopoetic identity.

Sometimes the Other might maneuver us into — even force us into — a role that embodies our true identity. Jung, during his first soul encounter, was maneuvered into such a role, the role of someone whose destiny was to bring awareness to the dead and to the human unconscious more generally. Was this experience imaginal only? Or did it involve his perceptual world as well? His verbal engagement with the dead, including the sermons themselves, certainly came through his deep imagination, but what of the other events: the doorbell ringing furiously, the "thick atmosphere," his children seeing ghosts in the house?

Elisabeth's first mythopoetic revelation was a combination of perceivable visionary events while awake (a sea eagle flying circles above, a wallaby nearly colliding with her) and an intrapsychic event — a name, Earth Dancer, mysteriously appearing in her awareness. A later soul encounter also arrived as a waking vision in which a tangible Other — the wind — makes contact and calls her by her soul name, Song Dreamer. Then, the next morning, she had another waking auditory "vision" of an unseen woman singing an alluring song in an unknown language.

My own first soul encounter took place within the context of an awake interaction with two beings, a Zen monk embodied as a spruce tree and a yellow butterfly who touched my face and called me by my (true) name.

Yeats's encounter with a silver trout is a poetic rendering of an awake interaction with a numinous other, a silver trout, who shape-shifts into a "glimmering girl" and calls him by his (true) name.

Matt's interactions with Old Man Compost were waking experiences with perceivable things of our shared world, and FeatherStone's first soul encounter occurred during a dayworld interaction with a Diné Catholic priest and a feather tethered to a stone.

Sabina's midnight encounter with Bear was a conscious interaction with a large flesh-and-blood critter. A later soul encounter was a waking vision of a "piercing spark of stars" followed by her hearing her (true) name: "You are Spark Heart."

Dream or Trance Visions

A second variety of soul encounter occurs when we are asleep or in some kind of deep trance state. We've seen many examples:

One of FeatherStone's revelations of mythopoetic identity arrived as a dream of Grandfather of the Desert Night and the Fire Sand Mandala. Another was a dream of Salmon Woman.

Elisabeth's second soul encounter came through her dream of the Cornman. A later soul encounter was catalyzed by an entheogen, ayahuasca — an aural vision of songs that she was able to literally see and become. Was this a waking vision, a dream, or both?

Joanna Macy's vision of the Great Wheel took place while in a deep trance evoked by childbirth and ether. Jung's second soul encounter arrived by way of his Liverpool dream of the inner-lit magnolia on the island at the center of the city.

Sabina had a soul encounter that took the form of a dream of walking a spiral path with Bear. Dreams were the source of mythopoetic revelations for both Silver Moon (the Chalice of Blood) and Dan (the underground river).

Soul-Infused or Soul-Fueled Insights

My last category of soul encounter consists of those that show up through heart-centered thinking, which is to say through thinking infused with imagination and feeling. They arrive as sudden thoughts out of nowhere or as insights into a life pattern that had been in plain sight all along but only now is seen.

Upon waking from her dream of walking with Bear, Sabina had the crystal-clear realization that her soul name was Spark Heart on Bear Path.

When Elisabeth was packing up her vision-fast camp at dawn, a bewitching phrase enigmatically and indelibly entered her awareness: *Dance the earth and dream song to feed the longing.*

Matt's first revelation of his mythopoetic identity arrived as a sudden insight about himself as Compost Bridger of Worlds, a revelation that followed a series of mutually amplifying experiences, including embodied encounters with Old Man Compost; a deep-imagery journey in which a fallen tree became a bridge; and childhood memories of crossing a bridge to a compost pile.

Silver Moon, on her vision fast, received a series of insights about how qualities of the Witch live within her, and several of her previous numinous experiences arranged themselves into a pattern that clarified her mythopoetic identity.

A soul encounter can change us radically, which is to say, to our roots. If it does, it's not because it gives us information but because we give ourselves so fully to the encounter; we surrender to it so wholeheartedly and vulnerably that a door opens and we step through into an astonishing realm from which we never return. It's something like finding ourselves in a forest in which the trees sing and we sing back or communing at night with enchanted creatures in a mountain meadow. The world changes. *We* change. Consciousness shifts. We might overhear ourselves saying things we hadn't known. We become someone we don't recall having met.

By giving ourselves to such experiences fully, we are changed forever, shifting closer to our ultimate place in the world, from which we are enabled to "carry what is hidden as a gift to others."[16] As depth psychologist Robert Johnson told us, visionary experiences "form our character in very deep places." This character-forming activity is the work of Metamorphosis, the next phase of the Descent to Soul.

Chapter Nine

PHASE FOUR

Metamorphosis

Part 1: Goals and Dangers

...As if your place in the world mattered
and the world could
neither speak nor hear the fullness of
its own bitter and beautiful cry
without the deep well
of your body resonating in the echo.

Knowing that it takes only
that one, terrible
word to make the circle complete,

revelation must be terrible
knowing you can
never hide your voice again.

— DAVID WHYTE

Submitting Yourself to Being Reshaped by the Dream of the Earth

Your encounter with Soul — your initiating revelation of mythopoetic identity —
takes place in the middle of your Descent to Soul, not at its end. It's not as if your
soul encounter wraps up your Descent and then you go home and offer your gift to
your community. No, your experiential encounter with Soul takes place in the dark

bottomlands of the psychospiritual underworld (see diagram, page 21), and in the wake of your vision, *while still in the depths,* the decisive formative work of the Co-coon commences — the work of the fourth phase of the Descent, when the dream of the Earth begins to reshape the raw material that is you.

Recall that in the second phase, Dissolution, the caterpillar body dissolves into a goo that includes those imaginal cells that, like secret-agent metamorphic stow-aways, have been waiting all along within the caterpillar. Then, in the third phase, Soul Encounter, these imaginal cells awake and something in the cocoon — the con-sciousness of the chrysalis, let's say — envisions flight as it beholds the far-fetched blueprint for, the possibility of, a butterfly. But there is not yet a butterfly or any solid thing at all. What happens next — in the fourth phase, Metamorphosis — is the actual fashioning of a flying creature out of the recyclable materials of the former caterpillar. The butterfly will not break out of the cocoon and take wing until the fifth and final phase, Enactment — and it will do so only to the extent that the work of butterfly formation is accomplished successfully.

So it's like this: In phase three you receive a vision of your destiny, and then in the fourth phase, the vision begins to do its work on you, on your psyche — on your Ego in particular, your vulnerable yet well-resourced human Ego. This is the work of shape-shifting or metamorphosis. Now your Adolescent Ego must be refashioned into an Adult Ego, an Ego able, in time, to hold, nurture, and embody your vision as a gift to others. The Ego cannot do this for itself — at least not *by* itself — any more than we could have given birth to ourselves. The monumental metamorphic ma-neuver of phase four is essential — and it is not easy. Expect several months of labor. This is the task of actively submitting yourself to being worked on — reshaped — by your vision, by your Soul, by Mystery, by the world, by the Dream of the Earth. Indeed, this could take a few years. Please be patient...but *actively* patient.

For decades, I called this shape-shifting phase of the Descent "the Return," in keeping with Joseph Campbell's monomyth of "the hero with a thousand faces" with its three-phase rhythm of departure-initiation-return. Campbell describes the Re-turn this way: "The full round, the norm of the monomyth, requires that the hero shall now begin the labor of bringing the runes of wisdom, the Golden Fleece, or his sleeping princess back into the kingdom of humanity, where the boon may re-dound to the renewing of the community, the nation, the planet, or the ten thou-sand worlds."[1]

I came to see, however, that "the Return" is entirely the wrong name for the fourth phase of the Descent to Soul (nor does it suit the fifth and final phase), even if it's exactly right for the final phase of the hero's journey. Immediately following your encounter with Soul, you are anything but ready to bring the runes of wisdom back to your community. You really don't yet *have* any runes of wisdom — not to mention a sleeping princess. After your soul encounter, you might return promptly to your community, in the geographical sense, but you would not return as a person prepared to embody your vision as a gift to your world. You're not yet ready to choose and cultivate a delivery system for your mythopoetic identity. What must happen first is the reshaping of your Ego into a form capable of carrying that formidable vision. Only after this fourth phase of the Descent will you be prepared to deliver that Golden-Fleeced boon.

As a consequence, I now call this phase "Metamorphosis," from the Greek word that literally means "change of shape." But unlike the butterfly, this is not a change in the shape of our body; it's a change in the shape of our psyche — in particular, of our Ego (our conscious self). This chapter and the next are dedicated to identifying the goals of that shape-shifting, its dynamics, its challenges, and its methods and practices, while recounting illustrative stories of how such a transfiguration is experienced.

Metamorphosis is the phase of the Descent that has been least well understood in the Western world, yet it is an absolutely essential phase. Consider what happens if the caterpillar's cocoon breaks open too soon, while it still contains only soup: A formless glop spills out onto the earth and the transformative journey is over. There will be no flight, no creature capable of the adult work of pollination and reproduction. Likewise with us humans: If we attempt to leave the Cocoon too early — to move too soon into choosing and cultivating a delivery system, to act as if we are in the Wellspring stage of Adulthood before we truly are — then we are sure to crumple or crash, perhaps never to become a creature capable of Adult visionary artistry and contributions to cultural renaissance. At best this will delay our passage to the Wellspring. Using a different metaphor: If we ascend too quickly from the oceanic depths of Soul Canyon, we'll get the bends and emerge infirm and unformed.

There's a great danger we'll neglect or attempt to skip over the necessary and difficult work of Metamorphosis. After all, we want to get on with the bestowal of the boon. From the start of the journey, we longed for a vision. Now we long to make that vision real. Perhaps we imagined that after revelation we would be instantly transformed and, practically in the very next moment, arrive back in the Village bearing a priceless pearl for the people. It might not occur to us that between the vision and its enactment lie the crucial labors of Metamorphosis, the sometimes-excruciating transmogrification of our psyche. As David Whyte gravely advises, "Revelation must be terrible / knowing you can / never hide your voice again."

My Mind Stopped and the World Began to Move Again

Looking back, it's evident I was in the Metamorphosis phase for a few years following my first soul encounter. During that time, my Ego was gradually shape-shifted into a form capable of weaving cocoons for others. I was not yet ready or able to embody my soul work.

The primary catalytic agent for the shape-shifting of my Ego was the vision itself — or, you could say, the bearer of that vision, my Soul — and my foremost guides during Metamorphosis were the imaginal presences of the monk-tree and the butterfly, the guides I had met during my fast. (See the preface for the story of my soul encounter on my vision fast on the shore of a mountain lake in Colorado.) After the butterfly called me by my true name, it flew off, and then, as I wrote in *Soulcraft*:

> My first thought was, *That's interesting*. I think I just received a spiritual name. Hmmm. Cocoon Weaver. Not bad. Well, at least it has possibilities. But it doesn't sound quite right, perhaps a bit archaic, but maybe we could change it to Cocoon Spinner or Cocoon Maker or...
>
> Nonplussed, my mind went on with this internal dialogue for several seconds, almost losing the unspeakable preciousness of the moment. Then something broke through my throat — a gasp or a moan. My heart swelled and burst open. I wept tears of gratitude. My mind stopped, and the world began to move again.[2]

Visionary moments have a profound effect on the psyche. It's as if our minds have been primed from birth — or before — to open and unfold in an expansive and unimaginable way when we are gifted with an experience that fits like a key into the lock of a concealed door in a dusty corner of our psyche. In that unnerving moment of personal genesis, our "imaginal cells" begin the process of reshaping our Ego, perhaps the way a fortuitously found fragment of poetry can forge new pathways within the psyche. Now the Soul at last begins to take its proper seat at the center of our life.

The moment that butterfly called me by my name was the start of my metamorphosis.

But our inner protectors, in the tsunami wake of an encounter with Soul, might panic and attempt to deflect or block the revelation, as mine almost succeeded in doing. Even if the process of Metamorphosis begins, our protectors can terminate or dull it. Ideally, the Ego receives the seed of vision and embraces the incipient change.

I was fortunate this first vision arrived when I was unencumbered by a job, a career, a romantic partnership, children, a mortgage, or any major obligations to anyone. Which is to say, it was relatively easy for me to allow the image of cocoon weaving to do its work on my psyche; there was little to distract me. Over the next several months, I cooperated with the shape-shifting of my Ego by holding this numinous image close in, at the front of my awareness or its near edge. This wasn't difficult because it resonated with my primary life project at that time: simply finding the right place to live. I was wandering the American Southwest, seeking a landscape and a community, the right sort of place for someone called to weave cocoons. The image was working its magic on me.

I also stayed in imaginal communion with the monk-tree and the butterfly. This, too, had its effect on my psyche. As I wrote in *Soulcraft*:

Like an embrace, the butterfly's vibrant touch and the monk's sturdy presence began to teach me, in a language older and far deeper than words. They said it was both my opportunity and obligation this lifetime to weave cocoons....

The monk and butterfly have faithfully remained with me as complementary teachers. The monk has advocated the Zen-like qualities of centeredness, nonattachment, and patience, while the butterfly has sung the praises of playfulness, alacrity, and spontaneity. And they have insisted I learn to weave together these contrasting qualities.[3]

The butterfly and the monk-tree supported my Metamorphosis in two ways: They helped keep the image of cocoon weaving in consciousness where it could do its transformative work on my Ego. And they helped me cultivate those two sets of qualities I needed in order to weave cocoons — Zen and alacrity. Years later, I came to understand these qualities as features of my weakest facets of wholeness — the East and South, respectively. This is a theme we'll encounter repeatedly in the stories in this and the next chapter — the "advanced" cultivation of our fourfold wholeness as one of the needs and goals of Metamorphosis.

During this phase of the Descent, we do whatever feels most resonant to make a living (our "survival dance"). It will be a while before we truly begin our soul work (our "sacred dance"). During my three or four years in Metamorphosis, I worked primarily as a psychologist in a community mental health center. This had little or nothing to do with weaving cocoons. And even though I also began guiding vision fasts, I knew so little at first about weaving cocoons, and was so psychospiritually unprepared to do so, that it's safe to say this wasn't happening at all. I was primarily functioning as a rites-of-passage guide.

My guide work at that time, however, accomplished two things. It served others by providing a ceremonial container for undergoing and celebrating significant life transitions. And it served me by reshaping my Ego into a form that would someday be capable of weaving cocoons. I cooperated with my own Metamorphosis by engaging in activities that felt resonant with my sense of calling, actions that felt like occupying my true place in the world, a certain somatic sense of expanded identity or amplified presence, of homecoming or joy.

At the time, I wasn't aware that, by guiding vision fasts, I was making myself — my Ego — vulnerable to the metamorphic interventions of Soul. But the settings and circumstances were ideal: In remote redrock canyons and on wild mountain ridges, I lived intimately on the land for several days at a time with small groups, each person risking everything to enable a profound life passage or to traverse one. And, rightly or wrongly, these people regarded me as someone who could and would guide them into the entangled mysteries of nature and psyche. My relationships with them placed me in a position of both power and vulnerability. I had the power to help or to harm, but I was also made vulnerable by the power of their projections onto me, projections that met and often matched my Soul's desire to help them weave cocoons for their own passages. My Ego was transformed in part by the way the archetype most alive in my psyche found resonance with the archetypes projected onto me, each amplifying the effects of the other. I was getting cooked from both inside and outside. This supported me to show up as a guide as fully and authentically as I could, with transformational consequences for me as well as for those I guided.

I felt thoroughly alive while guiding, in part because of the risks. I was fully engaged with participants, the place, and the ceremony, but I was also aware that everything could suddenly collapse if, for example, I were to make a terribly wrong guide move or if a participant's subpersonality — or my own — were to be triggered, or if there were a serious injury, or if the weather turned violent. Even before I was really weaving cocoons, I regularly asked myself who I was showing up as — Bill or Cocoon Weaver? A key part of my task seemed to be creating a space in which Cocoon Weaver *could* show up.

The social roles we inhabit — such as vision-fast guide — affect us at least as much as they affect others. When those roles align with our Soul's intentions, we are radically reshaped, like soft and supple clay in a potter's hands.

Many times in those early years of guiding, a strange disturbance, always unanticipated, would engulf me, the origin and nature of which I didn't understand. These moments would begin when I found myself envisioning a certain guide move I could make, a risky one that might succeed by toppling us all further into the depths…or might backfire spectacularly, perhaps psychologically or spiritually harming someone, or losing my credibility with the whole group. At those choice points, to my surprise and alarm, I'd physically tremble, and yet my vision and hearing would become exceptionally keen and my focus sharp, similar to psychedelic awareness or while on a technical rock climb. I could sense a transformative shift that was possible for someone in the group or for the whole group, and I could see exactly what I needed to do as a catalyst for this shift. When I then enacted my part in the mystery play, although I could immediately feel its effect on the others — and having that catalytic effect was my sole intended focus — it also felt like *I* was being rearranged, like I was being deconstructed cell by cell and reconfigured, as if my psyche was being reorganized. Something profound was happening to me, as if a hidden door had swung open and I was being ushered into a strange landscape that somehow felt completely familiar. In those moments, it seemed like Mystery or Soul was doing its work *through* me, as if I was being played or enacted by the world, by life. At the same time, it felt like Mystery or Soul was doing its work *on* me.

In hindsight, it seems that, during these events, my "imaginal cells" were being especially active in their work of forming my butterfly body, the psyche of Cocoon Weaver. It was as if Mystery had placed me in the role of Cocoon Weaver and was showing me how to manifest this role so that Soul could reshape my Ego accordingly. Whether the actions I took in those moments were "successes" or "failures" (from the perspective of vision-fast guiding), the simple fact of being in that role or that niche changed me.

By guiding vision fasts, I unknowingly wove a cocoon for my own Metamorphosis. Or more accurately, Mystery wove it for me.

The experience was as difficult as it was blissful. On the one hand, I got to do what I was passionate about and fulfilled by: to show up fully as myself in wild and bewitching landscapes and in intimate communion with people wrestling with the biggest questions of life and undergoing dramatic and meaningful passages. On the other hand, the work stretched me beyond anything I had previously experienced. Despite my rather shy nature, I needed to be fully present with people all day for several days in a row. And the responsibilities I had taken on were so great (for the physical and spiritual well-being of others) that, by the time people went out on their three-day solos, I was wholly depleted from fatigue and stress. Often I would spend most of those three days confined to my sleeping bag, recuperating and preparing myself for the fasters' return. I was getting wildly shape-shifted through my work of guiding others.

A second example of my imaginal cells in action took place at times I was not guiding but wandering on wild lands in search of potential sites to bring groups. Some of my criteria were practical, like distance from a trailhead, the difficulty or danger of the terrain, and the availability of water. But other criteria concerned the mystical qualities of a mountain ridge or desert canyon — my felt-sense of the spiritual "field" or "dreaming" of the place and how facilitative or diminishing this might be for a vision fast. These expeditions felt like ceremonies — sacred undertakings to which I completely gave myself. The effect was similar to a full day of meditation but even better because I was in the wild and engaged in a task meaningful to me. On those search days, exquisitely focused on my mission for several hours at a stretch, my doors of perception opened wide to the subtle and imaginal, leaving my Ego vulnerable to the reshaping forces of the image I was born with. Whether or not I found a suitable site on any given search day, it felt as if the land found *me* and further aligned my consciousness with my Soul. I returned home, each time, feeling more like myself. Although I was not yet weaving cocoons, I was getting transformed into Cocoon Weaver.

Metamorphosis: A Bridge and a Direct Transformation

The phase of Metamorphosis is the indispensable bridge between Soul Encounter (vision) and the Enactment of vision, the bridge from the dream to its manifestation, from our former social-cultural-vocational identity to our soul-rooted identity. This bridge is the only path to the life passage of Soul Initiation. Metamorphosis, after all, is when the Cocoon, which had been a tomb for the Adolescent Ego, becomes a womb for the Adult Ego-under-construction. This is when the Ego, which had been an agent for itself (even if in a healthy and socially beneficial way) metamorphoses into an agent for Soul. We must incubate and gestate in the Cocoon for as long as it takes — and also not longer than it takes. During Metamorphosis, our Ego is soul-crafted — recrafted by Soul, reshaped by our new and greater love for the world, a love made possible by one or more encounters with Soul.

The most common mistake with Metamorphosis is to think of it as a time when you interpret or analyze your soul encounter, when you try to decipher its meaning (with or without help from others), when you rationally decide what you're going to do with it, how you'll perform it for your people. It's actually none of those things. In fact, a strategic or analytic approach to your vision will interrupt or undermine the whole Descent. The Ego gets transformed directly by making itself vulnerable to the vision, by inviting the holy thing, the revelation, to do its alchemical work on it. How this happens and how the Ego cooperates with and amplifies the process are what we are exploring in this and the next chapter.

Entering the Real World

As noted earlier, the primary feature that distinguishes soul encounters from all other experiences is that they sink the roots of Ego deeper into Soul. If Metamorphosis goes well, it gradually changes our consciousness, who we experience ourselves to be, which is to say the place we experience ourselves to occupy in the world. It transforms our experience of what it is to be alive and human.

Our first soul encounter is a particularly distinctive life experience because it's the first time the primary place we occupy shifts from the social realm of the human community to the psycho-ecological realm of the *more*-than-human community, the greater and wider web of life. In the metamorphic aftermath of that encounter, we no longer identify ourselves or experience ourselves primarily in terms of our social roles, gender identity, political or religious affiliation, or our means of earning a living. We now experience ourselves first and foremost as someone with a particular place in and relationship to the larger world within which our human village is only one element — although, for us, an essential one.

When our consciousness shifts, the world changes. As our identity undergoes the transition from fundamentally social to fundamentally ecological and soulful, we experience the world as a different kind of place. This is not merely a change in our experience of the world. The world itself changes. The world becomes something like a mystery play — to once more borrow Jung's image — a world we've been born into so we can take our unique place in the evolution of life in this cosmos. We die to an old, familiar identity and are shape-shifted into something previously unimaginable to the Ego. The Ego is utterly destabilized for a time, sometimes for months or years. An entire frame of consciousness, a worldview, is ending and another is slowly gelling. The revelatory worldview and transformed identity give rise to moments of intense aliveness and a sense of having passed through a veil into a strange and unfamiliar world, yet one that feels more intimate and personal than any previous moment in life. There's a feeling of having finally entered the *real* world and of experiencing a truth at the very heart of life.

The Journey of Soul Initiation as a Love Story

In the first stanza of Yeats's poem "The Song of Wandering Aengus," the Wanderer undergoes Dissolution (a fire in his head) and descends into Soul Canyon by way of a hazel wood and a stream, and there catches a little silver trout. In the second stanza, he has his encounter with Soul when the trout transforms into a glimmering girl and she calls him by his true name. (For these first two stanzas, see pages 71–73 and 147.) Now the final stanza:

> Though I am old with wandering
> Through hollow lands and hilly lands,
> I will find out where she has gone,
> And kiss her lips and take her hands;
> And walk among long dappled grass,
> And pluck till time and times are done
> The silver apples of the moon,
> The golden apples of the sun.

This might get us to wondering if Yeats anticipated for himself a rather extended Cocoon stage — "though I am old with wandering." He was, after all, only in his midtwenties when he penned these lines, and to the extent he was being autobiographical, he seems to have imagined that even when old he would not yet have tracked down the glimmering girl. Maybe he knew he wasn't meant to find her; that when it came to his being metamorphosed into the artist he was destined to be, it would be the intensity of his longing, as Kabir puts it, that would do the work.

Or, if we hear the poem through Aengus's voice, we might say that he — the Irish god of love, beauty, and youth — realizes and embodies his destiny by becoming the ceaseless wanderer, the one whose fathomless longing enables him to enter myth ("till time and times are done") as the one who forever plucks silver and golden apples.

Either way — as Yeats's imagined future or Aengus's timeless archetype — there's a lesson: If Metamorphosis goes well, we fall in love in a way and to a depth we could never have imagined possible, and we shape-shift into someone we never suspected but were always destined to be, just as Yeats was destined to reap, throughout his life and eternity, the fruitful symbols of the Moon and Sun.

Lovemaking and soulcrafting: This is the vital work of the Cocoon. Our romance with the world is what soulcrafts our Ego into a visionary artisan of cultural evolution. When we fall in love with the world deeply enough — when we have wandered far enough into the world that we can't remember who we're supposed to be[4] — then we discover who we were *born* to be, the very place or niche we took life in order to occupy. This grand love affair with the world is what makes it possible for us to embody our Souls.

The journey of soul initiation, then, is actually a three-way love story — between the Ego, the Soul, and the world. During Metamorphosis, the Ego is recrafted by Soul and reshaped by its new and greater love for this world.

Metamorphosis is, in effect, your mythic trek from the depths of Soul Canyon back up to the rim. It's the ascent module within the larger journey of Descent. During this ascent, you get shape-shifted whether or not you geographically and socially return to the Village during Metamorphosis. Although returning "home" during this phase is more common than not (at least in the contemporary world), it's possible your guides (inner or outer) will keep you in relative solitude through all or most of this phase.

Also keep in mind that, mythically speaking, the rim up to which you journey is not the same rim from which you descended. At the conclusion of Metamorphosis, you will have crossed from one side of the Canyon to the other. This unfamiliar rim is the threshold of a very different world. And you will be a very different person.

Five Goals of Metamorphosis

First, it's important to note that the goals and practices suggested in this chapter are intended only for people in the Metamorphosis phase of a Descent, people who have recently had a soul encounter. They are not generic recommendations for personal development or for just anyone coming off a vision fast.

The overarching goal of Metamorphosis is the rearrangement of your psyche, your consciousness, and your world — a transformation that enables you to enact your vision, to "carry what is hidden as a gift to others." This principal goal can be divided into several more-specific ones. Here are the five I've found most important, in more or less sequential order:

1.   The conscious gathering of your soul-encounter experiences
2.   The *preservation* and *embrace* of these experiences, especially in the face of social disinterest, incomprehension, or criticism — or your own subpersonality static
3.   The reshaping of your Ego by your vision
4.   The advanced cultivation of your facets of wholeness needed for the core work of Metamorphosis (goal three) and for the next phase of Enactment

5.   Developing the skills and acquiring the knowledge resonant with your mythopoetic identity

Goal 1: Conscious Gathering of Your Soul-Encounter Experiences

Gather your numinous experiences and keep them close to you, accessible to consciousness. This is essential whether you immediately return to your everyday life or whether (ideally) you can first savor some additional liminal days, weeks, or months dwelling in a wild place, or dedicated to further wandering, or perhaps in an encampment with mentors and other initiates. You'll want to do all you can to be in settings that support Metamorphosis more effectively than what is possible within the limits and distractions of the everyday routine.

To gather your numinous experiences, you need to appreciate what actually happened during the Soul Encounter phase of your Descent. This is akin to the challenges of dream recall: You can't support your dreams to do their work on your Ego unless you remember them. Don't underestimate the capacity of your inner protectors to inflict a complete or partial amnesia for what to them are the applecart-upsetting experiences of Soul Encounter.

To keep these experiences close, you might regularly review your journal entries; use deep imagination and somatic memory to reexperience the encounters; record in your journal any additional features of these experiences you might recall; and use expressive arts to embody them — draw or paint them, sculpt them, dance or sing them, describe them poetically or mythically. A soul-initiation guide, if you have one, will offer additional suggestions customized for you.

In order to gather your bundle of Soul Encounter experiences, you need good access to your Self — to all four facets of your wholeness (see "Cultivating Our Innate Human Wholeness," pages 46–48). This underscores the importance of adequate wholing and Self-healing work during the Preparation phase, as well as the additional and more advanced work needed after you begin your descent into Soul Canyon (see goal four below). You also need the resources of the Self to keep items from "falling out" of your bundle during your physical and social return to your community. These "spills" take the form of forgetting, rejecting, renouncing, or denigrating your soul encounters out of fear or embarrassment.

Without a well-cultivated Self, there's a danger you might toss your bundle in the trash as you arrive home — if, for example, your Wounded Children or Loyal Soldiers fear you'll be ridiculed or criticized. Your inner protectors don't want you to rock any relationship boats; they want to be sure you'll still be accepted socially.

You must also sidestep the opposite but not-uncommon conviction, for which your subs might be lobbying, that your soul-encounter experiences are so profound that everything about you and your life has already permanently changed and consequently there's no need to do anything special before, during, or after your geographical return to the Village. You might tell yourself (or hear a clever sub whispering) that there's absolutely no way you could forget a single detail of your numinous encounters. Many people who have believed such things found themselves empty-handed by the time they reached home, the contents of their bundle vanished into thin air.

You need the resolve to *thoroughly examine and explore the contents of your bundle,* enabling them to sprout as seeds of your soul-infused conversations with the world — in contrast to merely placing your bundle on an altar and allowing it to collect dust as a decorative piece.

Goal 2: Preserving and Embracing Your Soul-Encounter Experiences

In addition to consciously gathering your soul-encounter experiences, you must also preserve and embrace them, especially in the face of social disinterest, incomprehension, or criticism, but also in the face of your subpersonalities. Your subs might feel overwhelmed, confused, or threatened by your encounters with Soul; they might try to protect you (your Ego) with strategies such as repression, denial, escape, self-criticism, and/or superficial flattery (for more, see "Challenges and Dangers of Metamorphosis," below).

In a healthy culture, a major feature of a Descent is to be ceremonially received back into your human community by Elders, initiators, and mentors as well as by family and friends. This is an enormous boon in helping you preserve and embrace your experiences in the depths of Soul Canyon. In contemporary, mainstream Western culture, it's rare to be received home in a good and useful way. This depends on, among other things, whether there actually *are* true Elders, initiators, and mentors in your community. If not — sadly, most common — it's best not to tell anyone "back home" about your soul-encounter experiences. After all, your goal in Metamorphosis is to be shape-shifted by your experiences, not to receive social approval or admiration for them, or even empathic or compassionate regard. If people ask you about your time away, you might tell them in general terms about the practices or ceremonies you enacted, but it's probably best not to reveal anything about your actual soul encounters. If they insist, remind them (and yourself) that the most important thing to do with experiences like these is to learn how to embody them — and that speaking about them can weaken or undermine that intention.

If you were in the company of other Wanderers during your Soul Encounter time, you can provide invaluable support for one another upon your return to the Village. Whether in person or virtually, you can hold a Council of Elders, a ceremony in which you recount your soul-encounter experiences, and then the others, drawing on their Elder wisdom, celebrate and amplify the elements and themes of your encounters.[5] You might also compose in writing the story of your soul encounters and share it with your fellow Wanderers.

During Metamorphosis, most contemporary people do return to the Village —
in both its mythic and geographic dimensions. Few can postpone their return until
Enactment. But this return is often a minefield. The present-day Village holds many
dangers for the Wanderer while in the process of shape-shifting. But there's a flip
side to this vulnerability: Although others may be limited in how much they can
support you, there are ways you can support *them*. If you stay faithful to the ways
you are changing, you can be a transformative catalyst in your community even
while still in the Cocoon. Poet and soul guide Geneen Marie Haugen portrays both
the dangers and opportunities:

The Return

Some day, if you are lucky,
you'll return from a thunderous journey
trailing snake scales, wing fragments
and the musk of Earth and Moon.

Eyes will examine you for signs
of damage, or change
and you, too, will wonder
if your skin shows traces

of fur, or leaves,
if thrushes have built a nest
of your hair, if Andromeda
burns from your eyes.

Do not be surprised by prickly questions
from those who barely inhabit
their own fleeting lives, who barely taste
their own possibility, who barely dream.

If your hands are empty, treasureless,
if your toes have not grown claws,
if your obedient voice has not
become a wild cry, a howl,

you will reassure them. *We warned you,*
they might declare, *there is nothing else,*
no point, no meaning, no mystery at all,
just this frantic waiting to die.

And yet, they tremble, mute,
afraid you've returned without sweet
elixir for unspeakable thirst, without
a fluent dance or holy language

to teach them, without a compass
bearing to a forgotten border where
no one crosses without weeping
for the terrible beauty of galaxies

and granite and bone. They tremble,
hoping your lips hold a secret,
that the song your body now sings
will redeem them, yet they fear

your secret is dangerous, shattering,
and once it flies from your astonished
mouth, they — like you — must disintegrate
before unfolding tremulous wings.[6]

In our current cultural contexts, if you return to the Village during Metamorphosis, you'll most likely encounter the interpersonal dynamics Geneen portrays: egocentric people — even beloved friends and family — reacting with both fear of and longing for liberation and transformation. They will detect something about you — something both dangerous and alluring. Although few will admit it, you'll feel their longing beneath their fear, and this will move you, frighten you, enthrall you. If you're not careful, you could abandon your journey right there — or if you know how to hold their longing, deepen it.

So, intensify your journey by tuning in to "the song your body now sings," the song emanating from your bundle, whether you intended for it to sing or not. Focus on the effect this song is having, both on you and those around you. The power of your body-song, your soul-song, is reflected in the way others tremble in your presence, the way they hope for redemption, the way they fear your secret.

Deepen your Metamorphosis by inhabiting the facets of your psyche that have compassion for and can love those who are saying, in one way or another, there is "no point, no meaning, no mystery at all." These are the voices, within you as well as around you, who are understandably terrified of living in the real world, the world of "thunderous journeys," the world that overflows with "the terrible beauty of galaxies." Their fear and longing, if you let yourself fully feel them and be moved by them, will intensify and quicken your shape-shifting, the metamorphosis underway in your psyche.

Many who return to the Village during Metamorphosis feel a bone-deep and naturally human longing for a soulcentric community of fellow initiates, mentors, and elders. But too often they're met by the pathologies, tragedies, and dangers of an egocentric community. Do not mistake one community for the other. Do all you can to be in the physical or virtual company of those who understand where you've been and can offer real support. Otherwise, dwell in your solitude as much as possible and keep your bundle quietly to yourself. Your time to "perform your vision for the people to see" will arrive soon enough.

How *do* you preserve and embrace your soul-encounter experiences? Use the same practices suggested in goal one: Review your journal, do additional journaling, use your deep imagination to journey back to your soul encounters, use expressive arts, and spend time with soul-initiation guides or companions. And engage in the practices of goal three, which support the shape-shifting of your Ego.

Goal 3: The Reshaping of Your Ego by Your Vision

This is the central and primary goal of Metamorphosis — for your Ego to be shape-shifted by the numinous powers alive within your soul encounters, by the images, feelings, sensations, and insights at the heart of your revelations. Your Ego is not the agent of this metamorphosis; rather, Soul itself is, or Mystery. Your task during this phase is simply to make yourself available to this reshaping, this renovation or overhaul of your conscious self, of the very fabric of your psyche as you experience it day to day.

Imagine yourself standing on the rim of a pool of boiling, alchemical waters. Your task, your opportunity, is to dive into that transformative brew. It's that simple. The waters will take over from there. You're an active agent only while at the edge of that pool, from which you can dive in or walk away. Once in, you're the raw material, the passive element of the transmutation.

The paradox is this: The person who says yes to Metamorphosis is not the one who survives it. The understandings, capacities, and desires of the one who emerges are not those of the one who chooses to submerge. It may be up to you to decide to jump in or not, but if you do jump, you'll no longer be running the show. Caterpillars may or may not dream of flight, but we might suspect they don't understand what will happen to their body and psyche while that winged creature forms — or what the changes will feel like or how much they might end up missing the form and life of a caterpillar.

An ample measure of faith is needed for Metamorphosis.

Just as, in the way Rilke advised, you can "live the questions" until your life becomes an answer, you can, if you so choose, submit yourself to a soul image until you fully resemble it; you can live a soul story until one day you find you've grown into it, that you inhabit it.

The primary practices that support the shape-shifting of your Ego are what I call Experimental Threshold Crossings. I'll introduce you to these as well as other Metamorphosis practices in the next chapter.

Goal 4: *The Advanced Cultivation of Your Facets of Wholeness*

The need to cultivate your wholeness, all four facets, never ends. When you're in the Oasis (ecocentric early Adolescence), you need a foundational cultivation of your facets, as well as a good amount of Self-healing, just to succeed at the tasks of that stage: to create a social presence that's both socially accepted and authentic. Your wholing and Self-healing work during the Oasis supports you to make the passage into the Cocoon. Later, additional layers of wholing are needed to prepare yourself for your first Descent, especially during Dissolution when you surrender your early-Adolescent identity and social scene.

Now, having entered the agonies and ecstasies of Metamorphosis, you require even more advanced levels of wholeness. You need, for example, the self-care capacities of your Nurturing Generative Adult honed to levels sufficient to calm and center yourself while your very experience of yourself and your life bends, dissolves, vanishes, and re-forms multiple times and in unpredictable ways over weeks, months, or longer. You need even more dependable access to your Wild Indigenous One in order to embrace all the emotions that arise for you in the cauldron — to enable you to hold on to, not the solid rim, but the tempestuous emotions themselves, the way a shipwrecked sailor clings to a scrap of shattered boat. You also need to further cultivate the capacities of this South facet so that you can sink your roots of belonging into the Earth and the greater web of life rather than deeper into your social networks, where they had once been. In order for your West facet, your Dark Muse-Beloved, to guide you on this foray into the unknown — your deepest yet — you need to radically hone your wild love for the dark and the cryptic. And because, during Metamorphosis, things can get (ahem) rather heavy at times, you for sure need a super-reliable connection with your Innocent/Sage, who helps you lighten up and see the big picture in difficult circumstances, the likes of which you have not previously negotiated.

These are just examples. As you dive ever deeper into the wild alchemical waters of Metamorphosis, it becomes clear what previously untapped intrapsychic resources you'll need. Here's my advice: Continuously monitor what inner resources your Metamorphosis experiences are requiring, and take pauses as needed from your shape-shifting practices in order to devote yourself to these advanced levels of wholing. And please keep in mind that one dimension of wholing is Self-healing — because the capacities of your wholeness are what you need to heal yourself. During Metamorphosis, the ghosts of previously unremembered wounds are likely to appear, and your inner protectors, freaked out by your ongoing shape-shifting, will act out in ways or to degrees they hadn't before considered — or needed. You're going to require greater capacities for embracing and loving those subpersonalities when they flip out and for avoiding being hijacked by them. If you get hijacked long enough, this will derail your journey of soul initiation.

Goal 5: Developing Skills and Knowledge Resonant with Your Mythopoetic Identity

Metamorphosis is not the time to learn a delivery system. In fact, the next phase, En-actment, isn't either. You won't be doing that until your Descent is over and you've entered the next life *stage* (the Wellspring). A delivery system is an aqueduct, a process or service or way of being that delivers your soul gifts to the world. In Metamorphosis, in contrast, by developing skills and acquiring knowledge resonant with your mytho-poetic identity, you're primarily contributing to the transformation of your Ego (and your psyche, more generally) — whether or not those skills and knowledge turn out to be directly useful in your future delivery system(s). During Metamorphosis, your focus is on becoming someone who will later be *capable* of a delivery system.

Christie, for example, returned from her vision fast with the sacred task to ap-preciate and love all things — "as the Beautiful Huntress," she said, "who has vowed to protect and hold reverence for all life." During Metamorphosis, she engaged in a wide range of activities she felt to be relevant to the embodiment of the arche-type of the Huntress. To acquire germane knowledge, she researched Artemis and related topics, including other Artemis-like goddesses across eras and cultures, women's hunting stories, the art of storytelling, and feminine and masculine ex-pressions, including "where there has been an imbalance in our culture, what my own natural inclinations are, where the imbalance is in me." She cultivated a vari-ety of Huntress-relevant skills through such activities as archery lessons, animal-tracking class and practice, wilderness skills, a practicum in home-death assistance, additional harp lessons, a canine rehabilitation course, and an experiential intensive in cross-species conversation. "Each of these skills," she wrote, "is an arrow in the quiver." She explained further:

> I sense that the need in my village will materialize suddenly, and that there will come a moment in which I am called upon. And in that moment, I will need to act from a place of readiness that will only be possible through extensive and careful preparation.

None of these realms of knowledge or activities are delivery systems in them-selves, and any given skill developed may or may not end up as an element of her delivery system.

Art That Transforms Us

As I've been emphasizing, to bridge from a vision to a delivery system, we must first allow our soul image to do its direct work of transformation on our conscious self, our Ego. This is the effect of art on consciousness. A soul encounter is an especially potent form of art, one designed specifically for you, created by Soul (or Mystery) to have a particular metamorphic effect, namely to transform your Ego into a middleworld agent for Soul.

Remind yourself how you've been moved by certain works of art — a painting, a symphony, a great book, a powerful film, a dance performance. They seize your awareness. The images and sounds — and the feelings and memories evoked — keep working you for hours, sometimes days, occasionally a lifetime. You're altered in some fundamental way. Perhaps remade.

Your own visionary experiences — your encounters with Soul — have the same effect; they directly alter your psyche, but even more so because this art was made specifically for you.

Another kind of experience that affects us in this way is the full, undefended, aesthetic engagement with the natural world — a dazzling sunset or sunrise, a snowstorm, a close encounter with a mountain lion, a rainbow, or standing in the sun and wind on a far-flung mountain summit. These moments of beauty, too, are works of art designed for us collectively, as members of the Earth community. Or, better: *We* were designed to be transported into rapture or ecstasy by these everyday miracles of this world.

For most people, an encounter with Soul merges both kinds of art. They are numinous engagements with the wild world — like Sabina's shared midnight moongaze with Bear or, years later, her alpine piercing by a "spark of stars"; or Elisabeth, high on a desert redrock ridge, bewitched by the dawn song of the unseen woman; or Feather-Stone, in blufftop wind, entranced by a dancing feather tethered to turquoise.

We can say, then, that visionary experiences — encounters with Soul — have three dimensions that profoundly impact our Egos:

1. They are works of art.
2. They are designed specifically for us.
3. They are often revelations informed by the natural world.

We — our Egos — hardly stand a chance in the face of such experiences. Our identities do not survive intact. We are remade by soul encounters, especially if we cooperate by keeping their numinous images in awareness.

Challenges and Dangers of Metamorphosis

Some of the challenges and dangers of this fourth phase of the Descent have already been noted, but here we'll take a closer look.

The foremost hazard of Metamorphosis is trying to skip over it entirely, believing you can go directly and near instantly from a vision to a fully articulated delivery system. It's not the mere download of information or even a "soul blueprint" that enables the enactment of a vision. The primary need is for the metamorphosis of the Ego into a handmaiden for Soul, a transformation of our consciousness and our world.

Trying to figure out, choose, or manifest a delivery system while you're in Metamorphosis can be a sure way to get stuck in this phase — it can even abort your Descent. Your inner protectors, in order to sabotage your journey, might try to manipulate you into a premature delivery system. They might, for example, flatter you into believing you're already primed for a delivery system, with the hope you'll make the attempt and end up with one of two outcomes: You crash, give up, and return to your previous life. Or you succeed — in the social sense that others are moved and inspired — but you know what you did was inauthentic and not at all a true expression of your mythopoetic identity; you feel like a fraud, and this "success" results in the abandonment of your vision.

Your inner protectors are terrified that one day you'll authentically manifest your vision. They know that, if you do, everything about your life will change, and they believe you would not survive such a change. They're wrong about that, but they're right about something else: The Metamorphosis phase is not the time to manifest a vision. But they may or may not be right about a second thing: the question of whether you've cultivated sufficient wholeness to manifest your vision even after the Ego reshaping of this fourth phase is complete. In other words, at least two kinds of psychospiritual changes must take place in Metamorphosis: the reshaping of your Ego so you're able to inhabit your mythopoetic identity and the cultivation of your four facets sufficient for the embodiment of that soul-infused identity.

If you in fact have insufficient wholeness to embody your vision, then your subs would be serving you well to keep you from attempting it. Ideally, however, you wouldn't rely on your subs for this. You would, rather, employ your fourfold wholeness (the Self) to delay the Enactment phase (and even Metamorphosis) until you're adequately prepared. Rather than let your subs apply the brakes through self-criticism, self-flattery, addictions, or emotional meltdowns, you, as your Nurturing Generative Adult, would instead sit yourself down, consider things carefully, and choose to pause your initiatory journey while attending to your wholing, Self-healing, and developmental tasks.

How do you know if you're adequately prepared? You perform a self-assessment (see "Cultivating Our Innate Human Wholeness," pages 46–48; "The Four Windows of Knowing," pages 48–51; and "Self-Healing," pages 57–62) or ask a soul-initiation guide to help you.

Another challenge of Metamorphosis is that, early in this phase, it's often difficult to see how your soul encounter could be rendered into a useful offering for your people. This is not surprising. You've recently received a vision in the form of a mythopoetic image. This image is beautiful poetry but it's not yet much more than that. And it's poetry you do not yet understand in any depth. Besides, the goal in Metamorphosis is not so much to understand it as to become it. It's one thing to be moved by an image of weaving cocoons, for example, and it's another to understand how such an image could be manifested, and yet another thing to be shape-shifted in such a way that weaving cocoons becomes actionable.

A related and common experience early in Metamorphosis is to feel like your vision is way too big, that you couldn't possibly embody it or live up to it — ever. You might even believe it's a great vision but that Mystery mistakenly bestowed it on the wrong person, that it would be great if someone were to manifest such a thing but surely it isn't meant to be you. Must have been a mix-up. A vehement denial can be considered a sign of your qualifications. The best approach, should this happen to you, is to sincerely thank your inner protectors and assure them you won't attempt to deliver your gifts until you're adequately prepared.

People in Metamorphosis are in a great dilemma: They have a vision but aren't yet capable of performing it. They might feel an overwhelming urge to get out there and serve their community, but they're not yet able. This tension — between desire and wherewithal — can be excruciating, and yet it's the tension itself that does much of the work of Metamorphosis. This is, in essence, a Mandorla, in which the growing intrapsychic tension generated by a pair of opposites softens the Ego so that it is more easily reshapeable.

The gravest danger of Metamorphosis is suicide. This is an actual risk if you mistakenly believe you must manifest your vision while in this phase and then you either make the attempt and crash or don't make the attempt and feel like you've abandoned the journey and renounced your destiny. To my knowledge, no one I've guided on the Descent has attempted suicide — during any phase — but I do know a few who've had suicidal thoughts during Metamorphosis. Should this happen to you, it's crucial you seek support immediately — ideally from someone who is both a soul-initiation guide and a psychotherapist or, if that's not possible, from someone who's one or the other.

Elisabeth's Formidable Metamorphosis

Elisabeth's discovery of her mythopoetic identity is encapsulated in the somatic image of She Who Dances the Earth and Dreams Song to Feed the Longing (see the eponymous section, pages 151–59). Her six or seven encounters with Soul unfolded over a three-year span that included two vision fasts. It was on her second fast that she was blessed and burdened with the aural vision of a woman singing a bewitching song, "a song that *is* me and what I must do in this lifetime."

Elisabeth's numinous encounters with Soul were not only astonishing and life-changing, they epitomized all twelve of the most common qualities of soul encounters (see "Common Qualities of Soul Encounters," pages 162–63). A person could not hope for a more profound revelation of mythopoetic identity. But Elisabeth had one of the most difficult Metamorphosis stretches I've witnessed. Her inner protectors launched several valiant strategies to keep her safe from the reshaping of her Ego as she had known it. Also, she was at the same time faced with significant life crises. Elisabeth had not yet cultivated her facets of wholeness to the degree needed to respond well to these extraordinary psyche-destabilizing trials. (Few people *ever* do.) What's more, her guides (including me) failed her by not recognizing the early signs of difficulty.

For most people, Metamorphosis is not nearly so difficult, but a close examination of Elisabeth's experience might help you avoid the worst pitfalls and identify ways for you and the world to be best served by this phase of your Descent.

The trouble began soon after Elisabeth's Amazon jungle night with ayahuasca, the entheogenic tea she drank just five weeks after her second vision fast. Combined, the two experiences sent Elisabeth tumbling into the wild depths of Soul Canyon. This abyss, by itself, is exceptionally challenging for anyone to navigate, but Elisabeth had two additional, significant stressors: Her mother had recently suffered a serious injury, and Elisabeth had just returned home to Australia after traveling for two years. All this gave rise to a psychospiritual crisis that Elisabeth was unable to navigate with grace — at least not for a couple of years. Her integration of these experiences might have been much swifter if there had been soul guides or elders in her community to support her.

The result was that Elisabeth got hijacked by her subpersonalities in their best attempts to protect her from radical change. In addition, her friends and family, along with her Animas guides in America, were unaware of her plight for quite some time, in part because she is one of those highly competent people who rarely appear in need of help. Elisabeth herself was unaware she needed support — until it was almost too late.

She began to have overwhelming and disturbing dreams; they became frequent and terrifying in the intensity of their emotions and images — snakes and serpents, shamans, horses, and tigers. Despite their intensity, she became obsessed with the images and the meaningful patterns she felt they formed. The implications of her nightworld became at least as engaging and relevant to Elisabeth as her dayworld. Sometimes it was hard for her to differentiate between the two worlds. And she was not tending well to her Wounded Child subs, who were flipping out over these dreams and images, nor to the escalating troubles in her relationships with friends, housemates, and employers. Two and a half years into her Metamorphosis phase, she wrote:

Since my vision fast, I have been bamboozled, swamped, and saturated in images and dreams of the underworld. I have felt like a deer in the head-lights. It has been extremely hard to act because I have felt like I have so much information to try to make sense of. I have what seems like enough imagery to last a lifetime — and still more coming!

Despite Elisabeth's extended time in the depths of Soul Canyon, her Ego was not yet undergoing the kind of transformation needed to effectively embody her vision. She was not making progress toward the far rim. Instead, one of her Escapists — the one she calls her Meaning Maker with its obsession to make sense of "data" — was doing all it could to protect her from change by staying on the analytic level, thereby disconnecting her from the intense emotional and somatic dimensions of her nu-minous encounters. These two dimensions of the South facet — emotions and so-matic awareness — are domains of experience vital to the integration of visionary experiences. In better circumstances, Elisabeth would have been able to surrender to the process of Metamorphosis, but with all the inner and outer chaos, her Meaning Maker seized control of her psyche. In cahoots with this Escapist, one of her Inner Flatterers (a North sub she calls her Super Achiever, who believes she has to be the best in order to be merely acceptable) kept telling her that her soul encounters were exceptionally special and unique. At the same time, another North sub, an Inner Critic, was telling her she was flawed and unworthy. Meanwhile, her Wounded Chil-dren were in panic mode, freaked out by the intensity stirred up by her other subs and terrified of imminent catastrophe. And her Shadow elements (West) were pro-jecting evil on some people (those who could be blamed for her condition) while projecting goodness on others (those who could be seen as agents of liberation), in both cases distracting her from the need to assimilate her dreams and soul encoun-ters — and to be metamorphosed by them.

Working together, Elisabeth's Meaning Maker and Super Achiever launched her prematurely into a myriad of elaborate and ambitious manifestations of her visions — long before her Ego was prepared for choosing or implementing a de-livery system. This tumult of activity kept her too busy to tend to her wholing and Self-healing — or even to recognize the need. She applied to three graduate-school doctoral programs — each application centered on song, dance, and dream. She began an apprenticeship in song and dance with an Aboriginal elder. She formed networks with local people involved with nature-based and indigenous song and dance. She wrote an elaborate "job description" — plans for cultivating her delivery systems — based on the themes of her visions. She designed and ran a yearlong program with the theme of Dreaming Song to Feed the Longing. These were all bril-liant and admirable projects, but they were too soon and too many, and they weren't always chosen for the right reasons.

Another way to describe Elisabeth's state is to say she was having traumatic reactions to her dreams, her soul encounters, and the ayahuasca ceremony. This was not because there was anything inherently traumatic about these experiences, as intense as they were. Rather, Elisabeth's Ego was overwhelmed because she didn't have access to the resources needed to incorporate and metabolize these experiences — neither the inner resources of her fourfold wholeness nor the outer resources of guides or Elders. So her subpersonalities swooped in to protect her, and it was her subs' survival strategies that generated her trauma (see "Trauma and the Descent to Soul," pages 62–64).

Meanwhile, yet another dynamic within Elisabeth's psyche left her even more vulnerable. Emotionally and somatically intense experiences during the Descent often stir up memories of overwhelming experiences from childhood and teen years that have not been adequately assimilated. This was happening to Elisabeth. It's likely most people in the contemporary world have some degree of unresolved trauma — due to the pervasiveness of emotional dysfunction and our cultural histories of racism, sexism, colonialism, and other forms of oppression. When the effects of these unassimilated earlier experiences combine with the psychospiritual challenges of the Descent, the Wanderer's subs find themselves faced with not one but two sets of threats to the Ego. The result is an army of subs with double motivation for deploying self-protection strategies.

Elisabeth was hijacked for days on end without access to the inner or outer resources that could have interrupted her downward spiral. At times she feared she was losing her mind. In a certain sense, that's exactly what was happening — she was losing her access to her wholeness (her Self) as well as to the care of her social network and to the comfort and shelter of her previous Adolescent identity. She had no safe harbor. She lost friends and three jobs (twice by being fired).

This all came to a head when, at age thirty-eight, Elisabeth launched herself into the most ambitious of her premature delivery-system projects, which she called Her Temple, a series of monthly gatherings for women. From the perspective of her participants, the first session was an enormous success, but it was a disaster for Elisabeth because she was not yet sufficiently healed and wholed and her Ego had not yet shape-shifted enough to authentically embody the role of a guide with deep Soul-roots. She crashed. She emailed me a distress signal:

> I have been thrown a real curveball and have needed some deep time out. From the underworld of things, I mean. I thought the Muse spoke to me and told me to "build Her Temple." I even dreamed about it. Part of it was to host "moonthly" gatherings of women. Another part was to bring back initiations for young women. I found another keen woman guide, and together we built Her Temple. We held the first gathering on a full moon. Twenty-six women showed up. They loved it. It was a huge success. But overnight I got sick. I mean sick in the heart. I was doing this massive

project but it just felt wrong, like it was taking over my whole life. It led me to almost three weeks in bed, suffering the way the king did in the story of the Holy Grail. I just lay there, overwhelmed. I began to feel the grief I had been holding inside, a grief around the loss of the life I wanted to live: a cookie-cutter life, something poetically mediocre and NORMAL! I began to grieve for the children I never had because I never let myself fall into the longing of wanting them. I felt empty and finished. I regretted love I have held back and all of the ways I have avoided living wholeheartedly. It felt like I had used the underworld as another way to escape actually being here and present to my humanity.

This email made evident that Elisabeth had attempted too soon to embody her vision and that she was getting hijacked by subpersonalities, especially a Wounded Child who wanted Elisabeth to redefine herself in the early-Adolescent terms of mainstream conformist society ("a cookie-cutter life"). She was like a partially dissolved caterpillar trying to back her way out of the cocoon and return to her former life.

But something else was also apparent: She was belatedly grieving genuine losses, such as never having children. This grief work was important, natural, and wholesome; it was not a diversion from her Metamorphosis. She had made choices in life that inevitably precluded others. If not fully grieved, such losses act as anchors that limit aliveness. A "deep voice of wholeness," as she said, was revealing a truth she needed to embrace. She really *had* used the Descent as a way to escape some dimensions of her humanity. Not that she had to choose between her heart and her Soul. But her wholehearted grief work enabled her to pull out of her downward spiral and to eventually say yes to both.

Elisabeth took a break from her soul-embodiment projects. The Soul, after all, is only one of three levels of identity, and they're all important. She needed to tend to her middleworld life and to her upperworld spirituality.

To get back on her middleworld feet, financially and psychologically, she took a "regular" job in her profession of environmental science. This enabled her to regain confidence in herself and a sense of effectiveness and everyday purpose.

She also devoted herself to cultivating her wholeness. Her strongest facet was her West, her Dark Muse-Beloved, as embodied in her vibrant imagination, her romance with the world, and her sensitivity to "information" or "data." But a strong West often suggests a weak or undeveloped East (on the opposite side of the circle): the Innocent/Sage. Naturally adept West people need to cultivate their East facet — in particular the capacity for nonattachment (not to be confused with detachment). West people, when they enter Soul Canyon, are at risk of going so deep they get lost there. They're prone to taking their visions too earnestly and themselves too seriously. They get overly attached to their mythopoetic images. The Ego (the conscious self) can become a slave to those images. This is where the East facet is needed — with its capacity to lighten up, to laugh at oneself, to see the big picture and how the Soul's passions fit within it. We must be able to keep from identifying with Soul. To believe "I *am* my Soul; my Soul's powers are my Ego's powers" is mistaken and dangerous. This is one of the many reasons Elders are essential, with their deep embodiment of the East facet.

As part of her wholing, Elisabeth focused on embodying her Innocent/Sage. She practiced simple, open awareness to the everyday miracles. She began a regular meditation practice, developing her capacity for stillness in the midst of the storms of her life and her wildly creative mind. For people who get overwhelmed in the depths of Soul Canyon, it's best to balance soulcraft with upperworld spiritual practices, and to balance West with East.

For Elisabeth, cultivating her South facet, her Wild Indigenous One, was equally essential. The capacity to be in her centered wholeness while fully feeling her emotions and body was vital to the resolution of her trauma syndrome. Conscious, loving presence enables us to metabolize and reintegrate exiled experiences — for Elisabeth, her experiences with ayahuasca, her vision fast, her disturbing dreams, and her intergenerational trauma. Elisabeth needed to reinhabit her instinctual self, return to her body. Wholeness, for her, is primarily a somatic experience, as it is for many.

Cultivating her South facet was also key to Elisabeth's in-depth, full-bodied reconnection with her soul encounters — and this was, in turn, vital to the Metamorphosis of her Ego. Only through her body and her feelings is Elisabeth able to access the enchanting song of the unseen woman, a soul encounter that *arrived* through sound and feeling. The sound of Her Song *is* Elisabeth's unique eco-niche. Elisabeth adroitly describes this way of connecting to her Soul as "mythosomatic": "How her song feels in my body/memory, *that's* my place."

Advanced cultivation of her North facet, her Nurturing Generative Adult, was also indispensable. This resource enabled her to recognize when her subs were stirring, to engage in Self-healing, to attend to her wholing, to protect herself with mature strategies, and to pace herself during the remainder of her Descent. One way she strengthened this facet was by returning to her previous career in environmental science.

Elisabeth dedicated a year and a half to her wholing and healing, including some work with a psychotherapist. Although she put on hold the Metamorphosis work of embodying her mythopoetic identity, her wholing and healing work itself continued to transform her Ego into the shape needed to eventually embody that identity. "Did I put the brakes on my journey after Her Temple," Elisabeth has wondered, "or did Her Temple and the subsequent breaking of me actually brilliantly usher me through Metamorphosis?"

In hindsight, what is most remarkable is the creative and resourceful manner in which Elisabeth eventually navigated her Metamorphosis crisis and the rich harvest she draws from it today.

The journey of soul initiation is wildly intense and hazardous more often than not. Often it is counter-therapeutic. Elisabeth's story is a reminder that adequate preparation for the journey, especially with wholing and Self-healing, cannot be overemphasized or oversupported.

However, we shouldn't conclude from Elisabeth's story that the goal during Metamorphosis is to avoid disorientation, confusion, challenges, or pain. These states — as well as joy and ecstasy — are to be expected. Rather, *the question is whether your inner protectors are hijacking you.* If they are, you must put aside all else until you have regained your center in your fourfold Self. Whether this takes weeks, months, or years, that is what you must do.

Once you embrace with your wholeness the disorientation and other difficulties of Metamorphosis, these become additional helpful agents to shape-shift you into your Adult psyche-body. Elisabeth's troubles arose not from her doubts, fears, and confusion, but from getting hijacked by her inner protectors and not knowing how to self-arrest — and from not having guides, including me, who recognized soon enough what was happening.

Elisabeth has now emerged in great form from her Metamorphosis. Looking back, she writes:

> The hardest part of the journey was taking a series of experiences that were literally "from another world" and finding a place for them in a culture — my culture — that does not value, let alone believe in, the immaterial, that sees humans as cogs in a machine, that seeks parts rather than wholes, and that would view "visions," nonordinary states of knowing, and conversations with other-than-humans as folkloric at best, if not delusional and insane. To have come home to this culture in the state that I was in, in the depth that I was at, was frankly hazardous to me. My greatest task was finding a meaningful way to bring the gifts of my soul into the tragedy of my people and our way of being here — without true elders at close grasp watching me, guiding me, helping me navigate the perils of the return. In retrospect, it felt as stupendous and stupid as trying to plant a rose garden in an active combat zone.

Although such an arduous phase four is rare in my experience, it constellates an invaluable cautionary tale — for guides and initiates alike. Elisabeth's story illustrates the profundity of soul encounter, the ways the Descent can be immensely challenging, and methods to recover and benefit from the hardships.

Chapter Ten

PHASE FOUR

Metamorphosis

Part 2: Practices and Ceremonies for Shape-Shifting

You walking, your footprints are
the road, and nothing else;
there is no road, walker,
you make the road by walking.
By walking you make the road,
And when you look backward,
You see the path that you
Never will step on again.
Walker, there is no road,
Only wind trails in the sea.

— ANTONIO MACHADO

Christie's Metamorphosis: Eating the Bear

Christie, the Canadian whose Descent began with heartbreak over the hunting of bears, returned from her vision fast with both a yearning to embody the archetype at the center of her encounter with Soul — the Huntress — and a felt obligation to do so (see "Christie: A Dedicated Spirit," pages 222–33). But she had no idea how this image could be shaped into an actual life, how she could embody it in a way that would actually be valuable to anyone. Like many people following revelation, she resisted her calling; the holy thing received seemed too big and impossible to embody. And too risky. "Revelation must be terrible."

But Christie chose to press on. She started with what she had in front of her, and what she had was a single poem, Mary Oliver's "Hunter's Moon — Eating the Bear." This is a heartrending portrait of a hunter who holds Bear as sacred, as friend — a hunter who knows she herself will be radically transformed by the hunt, by a merging with Bear. A hunter caught in a Mandorla — like Christie.

Something about the poem pierced Christie's now-undefended heart. So she learned it by heart and recited it out loud, when alone, most everywhere she went. Often she'd be overcome with a jumble of emotions when reciting these particular lines:

> …Good friend,
> when I crouch beside the blades of fire,
> holding a piece of your life on a knife-tip,
>
> I will be leaning in like a spoke to the hub —
> the dense orb that is all of us.…[1]

All she knew at first was that the poem wove a web connecting Moon, Bear, hunting, and a knife — all key elements of her soul encounters — and that she was especially moved by the line, "I will be leaning in like a spoke to the hub." So she did. She recited the poem "to the forest and the sea and the Moon, letting the words embed themselves in my being." Metamorphosis in action. Her Ego was being reshaped by a recital practice and its emotional shock waves. Christie's conscious contribution was simply to surrender to the images and feelings.

The first goal of Metamorphosis is doing all you can to hold the revelation close — so it can do its work on you. This is not the time for you to work on your revelation — by trying, for example, to figure out a way to fashion it into a career. During Soul Encounter, your Ego takes root in the fertile soil of Soul; now, during Metamorphosis, your Ego begins to sprout above ground into its Adult form. You cooperate by proactively offering yourself to the image, as Christie did.

Experimental Threshold Crossings

Experimental Threshold Crossings (ETCs) are practices for embodying your mytho-poetic identity before you're ready to choose or develop a delivery system — practices that reshape your Ego to be a channel for that identity. They are your primary activities during Metamorphosis for bridging between the experience of soul encounter and the eventual cultivation of a method to embody your Soul as a gift to others. ETCs are your ways to ensure that the flower of revelation does not die on the vine before it becomes fruit. Engaging in ETCs is the most effective way to transform your Ego from an agent for itself to an agent for Soul. That transformation is precisely what must happen before you'll be ready to develop a delivery system.

The idea of ETCs sprang to mind some years ago when I noticed a common pattern in the way people struggled after their soul encounters: Many assumed they had to immediately return to their community and embody their vision — as if knowing their "soul blueprint" was all they needed. At last it dawned on me that we were neglecting an essential step — the reshaping of the Ego. The Muse whispered that what we lacked were practices designed to support the vision (and hence the Soul) to forge an Adult Ego. Initiates, she said, needed a way to bridge from vision to manifestation without the pressure of developing a delivery system, a set of practices that would take them halfway. They needed "Experimental Threshold Crossings." That's the phrase she used. They needed to show up in the world creatively clothed in their mythopoetic identity. Each time they show up in that way, they cross a threshold between merely having a vision and experimentally embodying it.

The Method

Here's how to create and use ETCs: Begin by experiencing yourself as occupying the mythopoetic place or niche that has been revealed to you. Call on your emotions, your feeling-sense, and your deep imagination — which is to say, the alliance of your South and West facets. Wherever you are in the moment — at home or out in the world — imagine and feel yourself as the person who has that unique role in the web of life. What's your bodily experience, your felt-sense, of being that person? What emotions arise? How do you, as this person, move in the world — physically and socially? What's your image of yourself? Then, when this embodied feeling has come thoroughly alive — and only if and when it has — ask yourself this: Today, what are some things I might do to express myself *as this person*, things I probably wouldn't have done before my encounter with Soul? Where do I notice opportunities, novel possibilities, whispered invitations — no matter how small or subtle, no matter how nonguaranteed to be fruitful?

To receive artful and useful answers, you must allow yourself to be led by your Dreamer — aka your Muse, Magician, or Poet. This means: Forget about figuring it out. Forget about your big plans. As often as you can, shift your awareness into the consciousness of the one who's been blessed with holy encounters. How? Just do it. It really can be that simple. If you need more support, reread your journal notes of your soul encounters until the feelings are flowing again and you're there. Or use your imagery to see, hear, and feel yourself as you were in the Canyon depths. Trance drumming or other consciousness-shifting practices can help.

Then, ask: What actions, activities, conversations, or projects — available to me in my life as it is now — would be expressions of who I am within this identity or consciousness? Rather than trying to puzzle it out, simply notice where the doors open, even if just a crack. The question is not: What would I do as my big project for the rest of my life — the project that might save the world or at least contribute to its healing? Rather, this: What would I do right now, *as this person*, whether or not it would ever be in service to anyone or anything? Ask several times a day. Each time, wait until you feel a response. Some responses will invite small actions. Others will urge elaborate projects. Some will fall in between. The most important thing is that you do what your Muse or Dreamer suggests.

At first and for a while (maybe a long time), your ETCs will probably have no apparent relation to your eventual Big Life Project. No worries. Remember: The only way to live into that Big Life Project is through a regular, ongoing Soul-infused Conversation with the World. ETCs are the best way to initiate that conversation while in Metamorphosis. *It's this active, engaged Conversation with the World — not your mere understanding of what that conversation is — that decisively shape-shifts your Ego.*

Please remember that no one receives a vision that reveals what their delivery system is. Your vision is a metaphorical, mystical, mythopoetic revelation, an experience that is unavoidably enigmatic at first. The way you discover what it wants from you, how it lives in you, the way in which it calls you to stride deeper into the world, is by pursuing your Conversation with the World. To summarize:

1. Shift your consciousness to your mythopoetic identity.
2. Ask: What shall I do today (or this week, or soon)?
3. Do it. (And be it.)

"It" might be something like: Start a conversation with that stranger sitting across from you. Or: Say yes to the invitation you recently received from a particular person, place, or feeling. Or: Memorize *this* poem and recite it to the wild world or to your friends. Or: Quit your job. Or: Take a nap and dream while holding a certain specific question in awareness. Or: Attend that community meeting and offer your voice. Or: Climb *that* mountain and notice, in particular, the lichen on the rocks above treeline. Or: Walk into that swamp...now. Or: Dedicate your day to helping the teenager who lives across the street, or invite him to help you. Or: Enter the forest in front of you and allow yourself to weep for the pervasive suffering and loss of life most everywhere in our world.

Most essential is that these actions feel like genuine ways of expressing and embodying your mythopoetic identity. Allow this identity — your "being" — to inform your doing. Let yourself be guided by the images and emotions that arise from your experiences in Soul Canyon. Then do whatever you feel prompted to do — specific and concrete things, imaginative and wild things. Trust your impulses. Sometimes it will feel completely ridiculous. Doing it might take great courage. Sometimes you'll fall flat on your face or make a fool of yourself. Sometimes it'll be wildly enriching.

The middleworld outcome is not so important. The opportunity and intention is for your Ego to be reshaped.

The point of an ETC is to experience your mythos "from the inside" — by living it, by feeling what it's like to be in that place, what it's like to occupy that niche, to walk around in that role (or at the very least, in its wardrobe), and to allow the experience of being in that place to have its effect on both your body and your psyche.

Consider Christie's Jegermeister knife. As an ETC, she simply began to carry it, often wearing it visibly on her belt despite the great discomfort of being seen with it. She had always kept her distance from weapons, from anything devised to harm. For Christie, her knife was what she called "a sacred, symbolic marker" of the "magnitude" of her archetypal role as the Huntress. But what she didn't see at first was that wearing her knife also allowed the magnitude of that role to do its transformative work *on her*. This is how ETCs work. Wearing the Jegermeister was not a service project, not a delivery system. It was an ETC that enabled the archetype of the Huntress to sculpt her Ego in its likeness.

It's like this: You've received a revelation. Great. But this is only a seed. Now plant the darn thing and water it. ETCs are your way of doing this. When planted and watered, your vision can sprout in your body, your psyche, your life, and the life of your community. It sprouts in your community when other people see it and you see and feel those others' reactions and responses to your sprouting, which feeds the sprouting, and so on. A positive feedback loop.

The best ETCs are usually not the ones you perform privately. Generally more effective are acts that entail outrageous middleworld visibility and audacious social initiatives — including your inevitable authentic failures, which are as valuable as the successes when it comes to shifting your Ego in the direction of Soul.

How Experimental Threshold Crossings Work

ETCs have their effect, in part, by the way the world responds to you while you're enacting them and how this response moves you, disturbs you, messes you up, rearranges the furniture of your psyche. This is what happened for me while guiding vision fasts during the early years after my own first fast. These were ETCs for me, as were my rambles into wild places in search of ceremonial sites.

When you enact ETCs — experiments often spontaneous or whimsical — you place yourself in circumstances you wouldn't have been in otherwise, and whatever happens and whatever beings you meet there will provide your next opportunity to converse with the world from and with your mythopoetic identity. One ETC leads directly into the next. You go through the first door, encounter something, and while there, you ask yourself again what someone with your particular ecological niche would do now, and then you go through the next door and continue in this way as you wander ever deeper into the world. The more you can compound ETCs in this way, the more your Ego shifts in the direction of your mythopoetic identity. You enable this shift by *being* that person, not by sitting around and merely imagining it.

A vital reminder and caution: *ETCs work only if you're in the consciousness of your mythopoetic identity when you ask, What shall I do now?*

These pre-delivery-system opportunities to embody your mythopoetic identity are "thresholds" awaiting you. They don't benefit you unless you cross them. What you'll experience on the other side is unpredictable. You'll meet people, have outlandish encounters, be struck by thunderous insights that course through your psyche like ground currents, each of these experiences offering you additional experimental thresholds. The momentum builds. With each ETC, your Ego shifts further into the shape of an agent for your Soul. When you step toward Mystery, Mystery steps toward you. The first steps might be the most difficult to identify, but simple enough to enact if you're willing.

The only way to discover what Soul is asking of you is to become the poet of your everyday life, not primarily in what you write, if anything, but in how you act.

Keep in mind that the intent of ETCs is not the crafting of delivery systems but, rather, the reshaping of the Ego by Soul and its images, by Mystery, by the land or the Others. When you embody your vision, this changes you (your Ego), and then the way people and the world respond to you further changes you, confirms your mythopoetic identity, and enables you to more easily and fully embody that identity. Sometimes the world's response is sweet, sometimes bitter, but both increasingly shape you into an agent for Soul.

The general principle in life is this: Whatever identity you embody — true or false, deep or superficial — *that* is the direction in which your psyche shifts. So speak and act from the part of your psyche you want to cultivate or strengthen.

Christie's Metamorphosis Practices, Part 1

Reciting aloud "Hunter's Moon — Eating the Bear" was Christie's first Experimental Threshold Crossing, her first answer to the question, "As Beautiful Huntress, what would I do now and here in my life?" Soon enough, a second threshold appeared and she said yes, crossed it, and discovered additional ETCs on the other side.

The Making of Tairseach

In the following story, you'll notice three themes: Christie would never have done these things before her soul encounter; these ETCs, while grounded in commonplace actions, had immense symbolic significance for her; and they had profound effects on her experience of self and world.

The same troublemaking companion who appeared in a dream and said I should start my journey from Telegraph Cove and who later, in waking life, gave me the book of poetry about praising the wild ones — now sends me a notice for a bow-making workshop, something in which I would previously not have had the remotest interest.

As August arrives I find myself camping in the bowyer's woods, committed to eight days. I opt to make a long bow. We begin with the yew-wood staves, and I allow myself to choose one with my eyes closed, letting my body listen and be drawn to the one that offers itself. When I open my eyes and see that the top of it is scarred by two claw marks of bear, and the handle area holds the imprints of antlers [the bear and the stag are both sacred to Artemis], I feel affirmed in the rightness of what I am doing — somehow this bow-making must be a part of my journey.

There are long days of effort, learning the tools, listening to the wood, shaping it into what is waiting within. At night, I borrow books from the library and learn about yew, instinctive archery, primitive skills. In the process of making the bow, there is something about actively having to choose and create each feature that helps to transform the bow from something that belongs to others into something that is unquestionably mine. I make some choices that go against tradition but that I seem to have a strong opinion about, such as selecting the style and material for the bow tips. The bowyer kindly humors me as we rummage through multiple options but none seem right until we come to the whalebone. He is doubtful, but I am certain. [Recall that Christie might never have gone to Telegraph Cove had she not had a lucid image of herself playing her harp for the whales.] It is most amazing to work with the whalebone and have the whole workshop fill with the scent of the sea. Like the bear claw scars at the top, having whalebone hold the string at both ends creates a deep resonance within me that this is indeed my bow.

One night, I sit by the sea with Moon overhead and Sun setting. I feel peaceful, relaxed, and connected to everything around me, my heart full. I listen for the right name for my bow. As I watch Heron silhouetted against the sea, I review everything that has happened to bring my bow into being. Then the name arrives: *Tairseach*, Irish for Threshold. The next morning, by the time I burn its name into the yew wood, we are deeply connected.

In addition to bearing elements that confirmed Beautiful Huntress's mythopoetic revelation (claw marks of bear, antler imprints of deer, bone of whale), this bow-making served as an Experimental Threshold Crossing, a way of stepping toward her soul identity. The making of the bow, as well as her handling it and using it, afforded the opportunity to step across an invisible threshold and *be* Beautiful Huntress, allowing her soul image to further shape her Ego. As with wearing her knife, the simple act of holding the bow compelled her to personify and accept the paradoxes of her soul identity. It is precisely this sort of consciously endured tension that soulcrafts the Ego.

Becoming the Jegermeister: Soulcentric Dreamwork

The bow-making was instigated by a friend's suggestion, but ETCs might also be proposed by the Muse, a mentor, or a dream.

While she was at the workshop, the fashioning of the bow was not the only way Mystery nudged Christie into the role of Artemis. DreamMaker did this, too — and not only into an Artemis-like role, but brazenly in the actual capacity of a Jegermeister:

> I dream I am administering a contract for how hunting would be con-
> ducted, the way weapons are made, the methods for hunting. I am signing
> the papers quite matter-of-factly, although I am aware my signature will
> significantly change the laws.

Christie told her dream to one of her soul-initiation guides. After a good shared laugh over DreamMaker's rascally brilliance, her guide suggested she help DreamMaker amplify the work of the dream by regularly returning, in her waking awareness, to the dreamworld Jegermeister HQ and, while there, experiencing herself — somatically, emotionally, and culturally — in the role of Jegermeister, precisely in the ways it unfolded in the dream.

By this point in her journey of soul initiation, Mystery (or Soul) had ushered Christie's Ego across an entire continent of self-image, from one coast to the other, from a hunting hater to a hunting overseer and administrator. She was surely not heading back to the canyon rim from which she descended, but to an exotic landscape on the far side.

Drawing the Hunter Card

In something like the way a hunter stalks and corners her prey, Mystery had been weaving around Christie an ever-tighter net of experiences, oppositions, and symbols drawn from both her dayworld and her nightworld: the knife, Telegraph Cove, harp, Orca, Frog, Slug, the Huntress, Artemis, bow and arrows, Bear, Ursula Major, Deer, Moon, "Hunter's Moon," lyre, Heron, and now the nightworld Jegermeister, the "Hunt Master."

By the time of her Jegermeister dream, Christie had crossed the irreversible threshold into her own mythos, the myth she was born with — or as. There would be no turning back now, no matter how much she might be tempted. She had irrevocably offered her Ego — as prey — to the hunter, the Huntress who happens to be her own Soul, somewhat like Bear might offer himself to a Huntress who has pursued him in a sacred manner.

Notice that Christie's conscious, egoic cooperation was essential to these initiatory experiences of Metamorphosis. Although she might never have gotten this far if she hadn't been gifted with the Telegraph Cove dream, her cooperation made all the difference: She recorded the dream in her journal, shared it with her guides and fellow participants, and as the decisive step, acted on it by traveling to Telegraph Cove.

Mystery got her attention several times: the "No Bear Hunting" sign, the oracular card admonishing her to be the hunter, the Jegermeister knife, the meetings with Dead Bird and Frog and Slug, and the notice about the bow-making workshop. She could have easily ignored or brushed off any of these encounters. But each time, she acted on what was given — courageously, for sure, but also, relative to her old familiar life of comfort and predictability, maybe foolishly and fatally. Each response was an ETC. Mystery saw to it that she drew the hunter card, in more ways than one — and she ran with it.

Eight Additional Practices for Metamorphosis

In addition to Experimental Threshold Crossings, there are several other practices for shape-shifting the Ego — things you can do for yourself and ways you can cooperate with your Muse and your DreamMaker. These practices support your imaginal cells to act as the catalysts of your Metamorphosis.

Keeping Your Soul-Encounter Experiences Close with Imagery and Expressive Arts

Keeping your soul-encounter experiences alive in your awareness is the first of the five goals of Metamorphosis (see "Five Goals of Metamorphosis," pages 246–53). This assures that your revelations won't fade or disappear — but this is also a means to amplify the transformation of your Ego. You do this by holding in your awareness the image or the moment of revelation — your actual experience, including its somatic and emotional fibers.

You can use expressive arts, too. Write a story about how your soul encounters came about, with a detailed description of the actual encounters. Compose your personal mythos as if it were to be read for its wisdom many centuries from now. Use metaphor and richly descriptive, evocative language to capture the qualities and emotions of these encounters and their effects on you and your world. Maybe you'll draft several versions. Your perspective will shift as you shift. As you give yourself in this way to these experiences, they transform the one who experienced them.

You might also draw or paint your soul encounters. Or sculpt them. Fashion an image of your soul-infused life birthing itself into the world. Or express your vision through movement, gesture, or dance.

Once you've crafted something that embodies your mythopoetic identity, you might enact it for others: Recite your poetry, invite others to view your images or sculptures, perform the dance or song. Don't tell anyone what the original experiences "mean" and maybe not even what brought them about. What shape-shifts your Ego is not explanations but embodiment of your soul encounters and your being witnessed by others — and by yourself.

Performing for others your soul encounter is an ETC.

Making Yourself Vulnerable to the Impressions of Others

When you first embark upon the journey of soul initiation, you are someone different than who you are during Metamorphosis. Before the journey, you lived a different story, a different identity. Call that earlier version of you X and the current emerging version Y. The people closest to you are going to notice the differences between X and Y. Some are going to appreciate, enjoy, or admire the differences. Others are going to feel disturbed, intimidated, or threatened. Some people will react with a mix. You'll have to deal with the social fallout, yes, but from the point of view of your Soul, there's something much more important regardless of how your everyday life and relationships might change.

Your Soul is interested in how social reactions to Y can be harnessed to help guide your Ego into its mythopoetic shape. The mirroring of your Y-ness by your friends, family, and colleagues can support and amplify the alchemical process of your Ego shifting from X to Y. Notice, however, that receiving these impressions from others in no way requires you to reveal your own sense of these changes, nor how they came about, nor anything about your mythopoetic identity. Generally, it's best not to reveal these things.

Marty, as you may recall, is the writer, naturalist, and men's conference leader who dreamed of the Scarified Woman singing a haunting melody. Months later, on his vision fast, the singer reappeared to him in the Pool of Tears. She told him he must promise to bear God's heart by learning to "sing Death back into Life." He promised. (See "Marty: Singing Death Back into Life," pages 220–22.)

> When I arrived home, I began to notice changes in me reflected in the eyes of my friends. I was and still am a bit guarded of my time and only slowly and selectively began to meet a few old friends for coffee or occasional dinner. In light of their reactions to me, I began to feel that I had changed fundamentally. Nearly everyone I met has said something about how much I have changed, but none can say how. They look at me quizzically, bemused, and say things like, "I don't know, but it suits you."
>
> I have noticed a new level of authority in my poetry. And this in turn, I believe, rests on the back of some new level of honesty to myself, to my friends, and to my work. I feel like I have no choice anymore regarding my

voice or moving from a deeper well of vulnerability that goes beyond my mortal claims. There is no "figuring out" here but only a kind of faithfulness I can sheepishly muster up.

Faithfulness to what or to whom? There is a new dimension here that is not of a human scale or of a mortal timeframe. Rilke's "terrifying beauty" strikes a chord here. I know I must not shrink from the task I was given on my vision fast — the task of singing Death back into Life.

The impressions Marty received from others — and letting himself be vulnerable to those impressions — supported and amplified his shape-shifting, which then became manifest in his poetry and his direct experience of his metamorphosing self. His poetry became an ETC, a way to embody Y.

An effective accelerator of Metamorphosis is to embody Y in such a way that you are experienced as Y by people who knew and loved you as X. But it's perhaps of even greater value for you to be seen in your Y-ness by people who never met X. After returning to your "everyday" life, you're something like a Y in X soil (which is to say, in X's social and cultural milieu). That X environment could turn you back into X. But by venturing beyond X's ecosystem and proactively engaging the larger world as Y, you shape-shift your Ego even more effectively into Y. As you deepen into this practice, your Ego and consciousness become increasingly identified with Y, and the Y of you becomes increasingly more embodied in your actions.

Marty imagined that a good next step (an ETC) might be public readings of his new poetry to circles beyond his closest friends. Soon thereafter he accepted an invitation to read at a monthly showcase of poets and storytellers.

There was the challenge of what to read. I chose six poems I had written over the last year. There was the challenge of not having the curriculum vitae of the other writers — all of whom in their short bios spoke about their magazine publications and books. I wrote what was true for me: that I was inspired by my backcountry treks, soul work, and the "hum and buzz of the numinous against the backdrop of everyday life" and that this would be my first reading in my home state and city.

When I stepped up to the microphone, the fourth of four readers, I felt a calm come over me. (Goose bumps down my arms and legs now as I write this.) I felt like there was no pressure. In fact, it felt like I was giving these words away as little gifts. I am not overestimating their worth. But I was almost giddy at the joy in reading them. The packed house hung on each word.

After the reading, a woman, a local poetry editor, introduced herself. She told me that, during my reading, she nudged her companion with her elbow and said, nodding at me, "Now *there's* a poet."

By publicly bearing and baring his heart through his poetry, Marty was beginning to embody the one who bears *God's* heart. People felt this even if they wouldn't have named it this way, and Marty could feel them feeling it, and this shifted Marty further toward his mythopoetic identity.

There's an important general principle here: Metamorphosis largely happens through the crucible of relationship — our relationships within the Village and within the natural world, as well as our relationship to Soul. Relational and contextual forces shape us. An essential dimension of Metamorphosis is to be witnessed by others in our mythopoetic identity. Relationships are the alchemical retort for the reshaping of the Ego.

Soulcentric Dreamwork

You, of course, will continue dreaming in the wake of your soul encounters. Some of your dreams will extend, deepen, or amplify those numinous revelations, like bonus episodes of an unfolding myth-in-progress, or like nightworld guides who escort you to the inner sanctum of your destiny. Some of your dreams will serve like Sherlock spyglasses or psychedelic spotlights that zoom in on a detail that sends you tumbling further, as if you had just stepped onto a leaf-covered trapdoor in a formerly familiar forest. Your soul encounters are like ego-dissolving acid introduced at just the right moments and in just the right nexus within your psyche to begin a metamorphic process that takes time to ripen and complete. Your Soul will do all she can to complete the process. The DreamMaker and the Muse are two of your Soul's most trusted associates. A soul encounter merely gets you in the door of your soul life. Once in, there's a whole world to explore, an odyssey to unfold.

During Metamorphosis, offer your reverent attention to your nightworld. As at any other time in life, eschew all dreamwork methods that seek to interpret or find meaning or that want to apply your dreams to your everyday waking world like shadowy overlays on your surface existence or like advice-column consultants to a happy, shiny life. Instead, use soulcentric dreamwork methods to support the dream to continue its work on your Ego (see "Soulcentric Dreamwork," pages 79–80). This kind of dreamwork shifts your conscious self further in the direction of Soul.

Christie's Jegermeister dream placed her in the role of one who changes the laws that govern hunting. Christie supported her Metamorphosis by repeatedly returning, while awake, to this dreamworld and experiencing herself as the Jegermeister.

Dreamwork, in its later stages, can take the form of dream-inspired ETCs that have enormous ego-metamorphosing potential. Imagine what might happen, for example, if Christie were to recognize a dayworld occasion to embody the role of the Jegermeister. What if, say, she were to launch a public movement to change the laws that govern hunting in her province — so that hunting might once again be embraced as a sacred dance, a healing and stabilizing force in the community, the return of a genuine partnership between humans and the wild others? Imagine the effects on Christie's Ego as well as the potential effects on the social and ecological fabric of her province.

For Christie, organizing this campaign would be a dreamwork version of a Metamorphosis practice, specifically an ETC — and not a delivery system. As an ETC, her intent, in addition to serving her more-than-human community, would be to show up and be seen as Beautiful Huntress with a Loving Heart. This would not be a delivery system because launching a public movement is not a specialized skill or one that takes years to develop (as is generally true of delivery systems for Soul); nor is it a skill specific to the archetype of the Huntress. It's simply something a Huntress would do. Actually, it might be something most any ecocentric person would do if they had the time and skills.

It's also possible that one of your soul encounters came *through* a dream. If this is true, then by all means, a core element of your Metamorphosis ought to be soulcentric dreamwork with those psyche-shifting nightworld assignations — like FeatherStone's first meeting with Salmon Woman, Elisabeth's encounter with Corn-man, or Jung's discovery of the sunlit island in the center of Liverpool.

Deep Imagination

Our imagination is a fundamental human capacity essential for full engagement in anything we do and for full presence in any act of perception. During a Descent to Soul, your waking imagination also serves as a portal into your mythopoetic identity — similar to how your night dreams serve in this way. How might you keep alive the images of your soul encounters so that you are imaginally and imaginatively living in the world from which those images arise? Doing so is a Metamorphosis practice for Ego shape-shifting.

Kent, an author and teacher, had a soul encounter in a dream in which he has a face-to-face encounter with a figure he calls Buffalo Heart Warrior, "an Israeli man, shirtless, with a Buffalo head. He has a weapon strapped across his chest."

During his Metamorphosis, Kent offered himself to the image of Buffalo Heart Warrior, merged with him, and then followed the clues received from his Muse:

> In a deep-imagery journey, I see myself as Buffalo Heart Warrior, joining a band of other warriors, at once very ancient and very contemporary. It's like we are moving out into the world, together but separate, all of us hunting down what my Muse calls "the heart of the matter." In my imagery, I tie a red band on my arm. I'm joining these other warriors on the edge of the village, hunting people who are ready to go further, whose wounds are shining through a bit. Maybe I can help these people descend into the heart of their own matter. I know I must hunt with the very thing I am hunting: Tiny juniper seeds that crack open the heart a little further. A red stripe

across my chest, which feels the wounds of others. Arrows that pierce. Buffalo Heart Warrior on the warpath.

It feels like I am joining something rather that creating something out of nothing. I wonder now about this group of Buffalo Heart Warriors. Might a few people already in my life have this mysterious band on their arms?

Kent used this deep-imagery process as a Metamorphosis practice — nudging his Ego to shape itself more like Buffalo Heart Warrior. This led to a further Metamorphosis practice, an Experimental Threshold Crossing: Over the next several months, in his everyday waking life, Kent covertly sought out other members of his warrior group. Each time he found one, he acted as if the other was also hunting down "the heart of the matter," without explicitly naming it, but as if they both immediately recognized this in the other.

Self-Designed Ceremonies

I've already described several formats for self-designed ceremonies — like the one-way portal (see pages 104–5), the Mandorla (see pages 107–9), and the Empty Vessel (see pages 203–4). With self-designed ceremonies, we speak to Mystery with actions that embody the very symbols Mystery has already used to speak to us. Most commonly what we're saying through such a ceremony is *yes* — to an irreversible threshold, for example, or to an intrapsychic opposition, or to a possible vision.

When we're in Metamorphosis, it's always the case that Mystery has recently spoken to us. Most likely, we want to respond with, "Yes, I will embody the truth at the center of the image I was born with." Perhaps you'll design a ceremony to declare your version of this.

Don't take lightly the design and enactment of such a ceremony. You're entering into an irreversible commitment. In essence, you're saying to our enchanted world, "Shape-shift me in any way necessary to render me an effective vehicle for the image you've shown me." You wouldn't want to declare this until you feel psychospiritually prepared for the consequences — including how it will accelerate your transformation beyond your control to stop or steer. When you're ready, this ceremony might be an essential step during your Metamorphosis.

Due to the profound significance for you of this ceremony, it's inevitable that both its design and enactment will further shape-shift your Ego, will move your consciousness in the direction of your mythopoetic identity. Then, what you receive from Mystery in response (through subsequent dreams, images, feelings, somatic experiences, or dayworld encounters and synchronicities) will have a yet deeper impact on your experience of identity.

Self-designed ceremonies can be a type of ETC, although they often don't involve other people, as most ETCs do.

The Making of Vows

A self-designed ceremony is one way to make a vow — to say yes to what Mystery has asked of you by way of a soul encounter. There are other ways: Simply speak your vow to the world. Write it in your journal or in wet sand or on a slip of paper you'll feed to fire. Or simply accept and embrace the vow that, like Wordsworth, you hear the world make *for you*.

Your most important vow during Metamorphosis is not a list of specific actions or projects but rather a dedication to your mythopoetic identity, a way of being in the world.

You vow to live the truth you heard the wild world whisper to you — your original instructions. You vow, forevermore, to speak in your own true voice.

Christie, for example, vowed as Beautiful Huntress, to "protect and hold reverence for all life."

The simple act of making this sort of vow has a profound reshaping effect on your Ego — even if you don't follow through impeccably.

Embracing the Tensions and Paradoxes within Your Mythopoetic Identity

Odds are, your Soul has asked you to do something you believe to be impossible. Or that you couldn't do and be yourself. Exactly. Soul has in fact asked you to become somebody else — namely, the person you've been protecting yourself from being all your life without realizing it. Your subpersonalities, as we've seen, are terrified you might accept the invitation — the summons — and step forward to cross that threshold. Independent of your subpersonalities, your caterpillar self finds it profoundly challenging to truly imagine flight. The identity you've been called to is, perhaps necessarily, beyond what you can fully wrap your mind around. If you attempt it, your mind might crack open. When you sincerely submit yourself to a numinous revelation, your Ego freezes or glitches or begins to warp. Good. This is your vision doing its work — the work of enwilding your psyche. Should you allow this to happen? Absolutely.

Actually, take it a step further: Proactively cooperate by noticing, exploring, amplifying, and embracing any and all tensions or paradoxes you uncover within your mythopoetic identity or that are aroused by it. Seek out the contradictions and oppositions. Celebrate the absurdities and oxymora. Bathe in the enigmas and impossibilities. Clothe yourself in the conundrums, farcicalities, and riddles. Let them do their work on you.

Embracing these tensions and paradoxes is a Metamorphosis application of the Mandorla practice.

Christie embraced the tension inherent between the Hunter and the Hunted. She did this by, for example, buying and wearing a knife and by making a bow and simply holding it. Consciously enduring this tension soulcrafted her Ego, helped fashion her butterfly psyche from the wreckage of her caterpillar mind.

Marty had no good option other than to embrace the tension spawned by the maddening task Soul had given him, to "sing Death back into Life." He embraced the tension through ETCs of writing poetry and reciting his verses in public. These activities had profound and challenging effects on his Ego. He felt...

> cracked open, like waxy jack pine seed cones that only open in the blazing heat of fire, my resistance melting and my heart opening, so my gifts too could be released. I felt frustrated at the impossible nature of what was handed me (how can anyone "bear the heart of God"?), stymied, feelings of inadequacy and not being up to the challenge of singing Death back into Life. I keep going back to that time on the ridge and feeling that other-than-human-scale sense of time and the divine-at-play or galactic grandeur and scale of it all, and it has the effect of grinding away at me, at what I thought were the furthest bounds of the possible and the humanness of me. It is humbling, to say the least.

And yet Marty continued to embrace the tension and cooperated with Soul:

> The closest I have come so far to "singing Death back into Life" is when I write poetry. Sometimes I can get back to something that has a taste of that moment on the ridge, some fragrance wafting for a moment through an open window. I'll write a line that seems to buzz on the page long after it has been written and know that it has some of that whiff of Eternity in it. Poetry for me flows from that river, this too-short life, and that certain death that makes our place in this passion play both infinitesimally small and yet unique and invaluable to the story.

Such is the process of Metamorphosis, the experience of the Ego being reshaped on the way to Soul Initiation.

Seeking Metamorphic Support from a Guide

Many of the Metamorphosis practices that could be most devastatingly effective for you are those you would never conjure up on your own. Even if they're plainly obvious. You're just too close in to see the possibilities. Or your inner protectors are doing all they can to distract you. Or it's simply not the way your imagination works.

So I encourage you to seek support from others who can see what you're missing, who would incite you to risk the more radical practices and ceremonies and help hold your feet to the fire. But not just any others. It's unlikely, for instance, that close friends or family members could — or would — help deconstruct the beloved life-comrade you've been for them. Most psychotherapists would urge you in exactly the wrong direction at a metamorphic life moment like this. Virtually all mainstream religious leaders wouldn't have a clue what was happening for you or how to support you if they did. Yes, there are exceptions, but be wary of assuming you know any.

Instead, seek mentoring from a soul-initiation guide, if you can find one. Search for someone who would not take you on as their "client." That sounds paradoxical. But at a time like this, you don't want to be guided by someone who has any interest in helping you become happy or positive, effective or successful, rich or popular. You want a guide who sees you, essentially, as caterpillar soup, as raw material out of which a butterfly might be fashioned, a mentor who works not for your Ego but for your Soul or for the possibility of cultural renaissance. You want a guide who will help you stay in relationship with the imaginal cells that are the generative seeds of Metamorphosis, a guide who, at the drop of a hat, will gladly betray or undermine your old identity at the necessary crucial moments. Seek guidance only from someone who sees you as a potential arrow tip of evolution's trajectory. At this planet-time in particular, when you're in Metamorphosis, accept counsel only from people who are culture interrupters and who see you as potentially one of their kind.

Mentors like this know how to lure or trick you into practices, actions, or ceremonies that enable your Soul to do its metamorphic work on you. They probably have tools you don't, and they know how to use the tools you do have in ways that would never occur to you to use on yourself.

Whether or not you're able to find such a mentor, you can also seek support from your fellow initiates, if you have any — those who are in Metamorphosis or beyond. They know the territory. They appreciate what's at stake. They understand the goals of this phase of the Descent. They can help you be honest with yourself. They can suggest practices and perspectives you might not have considered.

Christie's Metamorphosis Practices, Part 2

Protectress of the Sacredness of All Life: Making a Vow

During the fourth and final session of Christie's yearlong immersion (see "Telegraph Cove," pages 225–26), the Animas guides asked the participants to listen to what the Earth Community's longing might be for them, individually. Beautiful Huntress vowed to be faithful to what she heard:

> I promise I will work to restore a real and right relationship between humans and the Wild Ones and Wild Places; that I will remind us how to hold them with the reverence and love equal to that which they hold for us. I vow to protect the sacredness of all life and ensure it is rightfully honored.

This vow is intriguing for a few reasons. One is that it had been foreshadowed nine months earlier during the first session of the yearlong immersion: Each participant was asked to write on a slip of paper their deepest longing in life. These were placed in a hat, and then each participant drew someone's vow and was invited to read it aloud as if it were their own. Christie drew this one: "To protect and preserve the people, creatures, and the planet." At the time, she thought this longing was "noble, but not mine." A couple of years later, she reflected on this:

> This is an example of my sense that "it has been written." How is it possible that this simple exercise of letting Mystery bring to me a deepest longing could so precisely mirror what later becomes my mythopoetic vow? This is beyond what can be explained or believed. *This* is what humbles me enough to proceed despite my small protestations.

This synchronicity illustrates the always present but unseen guidance supporting us to find our way, as well as the necessity of the journey itself if we're ever to understand our gifts, acknowledge their reality, and live them into the world through acts of life-enhancing service.

The Protectress of the sacredness of all life — this is an essential strand in what Beautiful Huntress understands as her psycho-ecological niche, a strand relatively easy for Christie to accept and live. The hunter strand, in contrast, has been more of a challenge.

The Hunting License: An ETC

Christie's vow did not specify actions she would take but a way of being in the world. But Beautiful Huntress began to take specific actions as well, including some that embraced the more challenging strand of her identity. As another Experimental Threshold Crossing, she made a careful Jegermeister-like study of the hunting regulations of her Canadian province in order to acquaint herself with current language and practices. And then she took the tests, passed, and obtained her hunting license "so that 'hunter' can no longer be the other; it is now me, too." In a striking example of becoming what we most fear, Christie began to take her place as Huntress, not only the hunted — and not only the Protectress.

What's more, as another ETC — an act of nearly unfathomable grit — she also obtained a species-specific license to hunt Bear with bow and arrow:

> Now, at least on paper, we could each be in the role of hunted and hunter. I am now experiencing what it is to carry the "permission" to end a life, what is required to hold this level of responsibility. I could now legally go out with the intention of hunting Bear, of listening for the one who is willing to meet me. But I am not yet ready to respond to such a call.

Not yet ready to respond to a call to hunt Bear, but ready to be worked on by the hunting license she now carried at all times, like a vial of imaginal cells in her pocket.

Apprenticing to Artemis

In support of the fifth goal of Metamorphosis — developing skills and acquiring knowledge resonant with your mythopoetic identity — Beautiful Huntress embarked upon several additional ETCs (which also supported the reforging of her Ego — the third goal). These are all Artemis-related skills and knowledge:

> I am studying the ways that Wild Ones communicate through their tracks and signs so that I might understand their stories a little better, but I am also just making myself available in wild places to see what happens and to reveal to these places a little more about what it is to be a human: I have rolled my spine on the Earth to let her feel each articulation, shared the peculiarities of a sneeze with a juniper, marveled at the similarities and contrasts in the abilities of a paw and human hand. I have hummed and spoken and listened and cried. I have tended to the ones I have happened upon whose lives were ending, to be the witness and appreciator of all they have been and will now become. Doing such things is what is implied in my vow "to restore a real and right relationship between humans and the Wild Ones and Wild Places," in which we come to understand our *true* place in the Earth Community, that we have responsibilities to both revere and love the Others and, in reciprocity, offer our uniquely human gifts. We can be more than a force of destruction — not saviors but equal partners. I find myself wondering about what might be possible, imagining futures where there is restoration of right relationship.

These actions also supported the fourth goal of Metamorphosis, the advanced cultivation of her facets of wholeness: They enhanced her empathic and compassionate kinship with the Others (South and North facets), refined her capacity for innocent and careful observation (East facet), developed her role as a death doula and psychopomp for the Others (West facet), and deepened her capacity to imagine possible futures (West facet again).

The Hunter and the Hunted: Transformed by a Mandorla

Christie felt overwhelmed by what seemed like an incompatibility between "respecting, protecting, honoring, and loving the miraculousness of Life" and "carrying the ability to end it." This tension manifested most distressingly in the process of getting her hunting license, which she did only because it seemed necessary in order to embrace the hunter dimension of the Artemis archetype. As it was, she took several months to get through the process, putting off each step as long as she could. But her foot-dragging provided plenty of time for the Mandorla tension to do its reshaping work:

I didn't want to be connected with anything dangerous. In the process of making the bow, it was easy to fall in love with it. But when I made the arrows, I lost my marbles because while the bow on its own is beautiful, the arrow makes it a weapon. The bow is okay; the arrows…we're still becoming friends.

Who would I be to decide to end another's life? That's not a role for a human to hold.

But Christie embraced these tensions between the Huntress and the Protectress, and between the Hunter and the Hunted:

In reflecting upon my experiences of having been stalked, I have collected what the hunted-one of me knows and paired it with what I'm learning about being the hunter. Both the hunted and the hunter have needs and knowledge that can only be met by the other. Somehow it is essential that each understands and embodies both roles in order to return to a sacred balance — as in the following paired statements, which together express Love for the Sacred Other:

- The Huntress, in full reverence of life, hones her skills, sets an intention, and prays for a blessed meeting. She knows exactly the need she carries and what she is humbly asking of the Other.
- The Hunted, in full awareness of his ability to provide sustenance and life for another, willingly places himself in the path of the hunter. To be prey for the hunter is to offer a lifeline of hope for the hungry.

Gradually Christie came to experience the relationship between the Hunter and Hunted as an archetypal blood tie, a sacred dance. This change in perspective paralleled a shift in who she experienced herself to be — from Christie to Beautiful Huntress. More than learning new things about herself, she was being transformed directly; she was undergoing a change in form, in her nature. Metamorphosis.

Pairs of qualities that are inherent to an archetype — like Artemis being both Huntress and Protectress — are often Mandorlas for the preinitiated Ego. The Ego sees the two qualities as an opposition while the Soul holds them as natural complements. By embracing the tension, the Ego is reforged.

Christie's embrace of this existential tension resulted in essential progress with her Descent. And yet, like many Wanderers during Metamorphosis, her experience of shape-shifting was what she describes as a "spiral": As she lived her most difficult questions, she moved in and out of confidence about her identity as Beautiful Huntress — what it was asking of her, whether she was equal to the task, and whether it would have value for others.

But with each turn of the spiral, the doubt lessens and trust grows and the essence of my name is moving from something "out there" at arm's length to something that comes from within. My list of wonderings is long, including: Maybe I am hunting beauty. Maybe my arrows are harbingers of truth. Maybe my arrows are words.

Her wonderings became questions to live. Living these questions (a mode of ETC) further supported the reshaping of her Ego — her experience of self and world. As her Ego morphed, her understanding of her place in the world, her unique ecological niche, shifted and clarified.

One day, out of nowhere, a new more specific articulation of her vow "arrives intact," she wrote, "like a telegraph":

I, *Beautiful Huntress with a Loving Heart*, vow to myself and all Others:

- I will hunt what is real, the potential not yet realized, the beauty in everything.
- I will appreciate and attend to the wild within.
- I will send my arrows so swiftly, they will pierce to the deepest unclaimed territories of the heart.
- I recognize my need to experience the full essence of you, and that to ask this of you means you must be willing to surrender and die to all that is false — revealing a vulnerability so beautiful, the stars will dance across the heavens in response.

We can see, in this elegant rendering, an additional sign that Huntress and Protectress/Lover were merging. Christie was also coming to understand what her "arrows" were for: not (primarily) to pierce flesh and kill, but for the purpose of a psychospiritual death and rebirth.

Let Me Be Your Feast

Several months later, Christie was still getting worked by her questions of how to embody Beautiful Huntress. Was she really prepared and willing to take on such a daunting and hazardous mission, one so at odds with her Adolescent identity of My Sweet Daughter?

Her spiral path took her back to the bowyers to fix her bow. While there, she had a compelling feeling she must go back to Telegraph Cove — to ask her questions and to listen for direction, to look for a sign. She went. This was an Experimental Threshold Crossing:

This time, bow-only hunting season has just opened. As I near Telegraph Cove, it dawns on me that I am there not only with my hunting license but also with the specific tag to hunt Bear. I am aware of the contrast between my first visit with my harp and this visit with my bow.

That evening, I am down at the shore of a narrow, sheltered cove, and

I cannot take my eyes off a particular place in the woods. I am tempted to get my sleeping bag and spend the night there, in the woods, but I don't. Instead, I return back up the short trail to my tent. During the night I cannot sleep because I have a strong, vivid, and insistent sense of a very old male Bear. He is coming down the mountain to the shore. He senses my arrival with a certain relief. He feels his time has come. He is ready to go and has been longing to depart in a sacred way.

In the early dawn, I go back to the shore. I find a place to nestle in among driftwood and stones. The air is still. The sea is green and smooth and clear with a mist resting gently upon it. I am noticing and reveling in both the peace and expectation that fills a stillness such as this. My gaze softens, as if in response to the texture of the mist, as if the mist itself can only be seen by eyes that can dissolve the edges of things. The hairs on my neck begin to stand. Something is about to happen. Then there is a small sound — the slightest, tiniest rustle of salal that belies the magnificent appearance of Bear. From the place in the woods that had drawn me the night before, maybe thirty feet away, he steps from the forest and onto the mostly rocky shore. I notice the size and shape of his head, the way it blends into his neck and shoulders, the way his massive torso makes his legs seem tiny, the lumbering but graceful way he moves. I stifle an urge to wave or exclaim a greeting, so delighted at the arrival of what seems to be a mature male black bear. I am full of awe and attuned to the wonder of the moment. He continues in my direction, turning over stones the way bears do when looking for food, and I see his body carry the words about his body from the Mary Oliver poem I've been carrying, "Hunter's Moon — Eating the Bear"[2] [lines from Mary Oliver poem are italicized]:

> *holding your vast power, your grace,*
>
> I imagine it would take you only three bounds to reach me.
>
> *your breath, your hairiness,*
>
> And then my body shifts on the stones and you see me seeing you.
>
> *in the small sinews of my prayers.*

Bear and I look at each other. And an eternity passes between us. A part of me remembers guidance on encountering bears — do not make eye contact. I am aware my very gaze could be taken as a provocation. But I cannot look away. Strangely, I am not scared, though we are alone in this faraway place and I have brought nothing with me. I am mindful that I may be disturbing his morning outing, but it is as if we are in a dream and there is magic in the mist that surrounds us.

Eventually, Bear and I look away. He turns and continues down toward the sea edge, and I slowly rise and return up to the edge of the forest, where I watch him until he rounds the bend and disappears from sight.

Later, when Christie thought and felt about being held in the gaze of Bear, she imagined several possibilities:

It is as if Bear looked at me in recognition of the persistent steps I have taken so far to faithfully live into my soul purpose, as if to say, *You are not yet done, you must keep going.* And I know now that I will.

This was a mature bear, but not old like the one I sensed sensing me in the night. Maybe the Bear-of-the-Mist will call to me when he knows it is his time. As if neither of us are quite ready, but this meeting has set our fates.

Maybe in that moment, myself and this Bear, each carrying a need, willingly placed ourselves in the path of the other, and in this way simultaneously and equally fulfilled the roles of both Hunter and Hunted, together expressing a love for the sacred Other.

Perhaps Bear came to catch a glimpse of one who is trying to live into a new way of being in relationship with the Others, to see proof of a story that has been foretold.

Maybe both Bear and I are simply drawn to, and nourished by, the stillness of the shore at dawn.

Some people believe that if they have an encounter with a glamorous critter — even a distant glimpse — this is to be taken as an affirmation of whatever they were hoping to have affirmed. This perspective — often superficial and self-centered — mocks the real mystery and interdependence of Earthly life. There's a vital difference between interpreting an isolated encounter as a personal sign for us — as if the Other's presence in that moment or even their entire existence was solely for our individual benefit — and a more nuanced, equitable, and ecologically sensitive worldview. Often a human and an Other just happen to be sharing the same terrain. But, sometimes, autonomous beings are attracted to each other when there is a meaningful resonance between them. (The mystical relationship between Hunter and Hunted is one instance.) When wholeheartedly and vulnerably embraced, such an encounter is invariably a challenge to or a stretching of our self-image, not a comforting corroboration of a wished-for identity or role.

Christie's seashore encounter with Bear was hardly an isolated encounter. Here we have a creature whose slaughter and suffering Christie has deeply mourned; who is a familiar of her archetypal kin, Artemis; whose astral constellation had atypically called to Christie on her vision fast; whose claw marks are on the bow stave she chose with closed eyes; for whom she now improbably carries a license to hunt with bow and arrows; and who, the night before, came to her in a vision to offer himself. The next morning Bear walks directly to her out of the forest and the mist in the very place, Telegraph Cove, to which she had been called by DreamMaker two years earlier, and this second visit was for the purpose of asking if it is really her calling to embody Beautiful Huntress with a Loving Heart. Given what transpired that morning in that cove, we might wonder if Christie was as much a sign for Bear as the converse — a sign, perhaps, that, when his days run out, he will be hunted in a sacred way by a human who honors him, his land, and his kin. This event in these circumstances is not something you could make up, and if you did, no one would believe you. A numinous encounter such as this, under these circumstances, is usually reserved for myth. Or we could say that this meeting in the mist confirmed Christie's living mythos as Beautiful Huntress — and contributed in a major way to reshaping her Ego to accord with that mythos.

As a ceremonial response to her dawn encounter with Bear, Beautiful Huntress offered herself to Mystery as prayer and prey, to be the one who is Hunted by her destiny:

> I am praying to be equal to this privileged task of embodying Beautiful Huntress with a Loving Heart.

> I do not yet know what else will be asked of me, only that I must continue, following the clues that are offered, and in turn, offering myself to the longings of Mystery, Soul, the Earth community, and all its members. As I deepen my relationship with Mystery, I offer this plea:

> I want my life to be a prayer.
> Pray me.
> Prey upon me, Beloved Mystery.
> Let me be your feast.

> I see and sense that my future cannot be shaped only by what has come before; it must also be invited by Mystery, by dreams, and by stars.

This recognition that her future must be invited by Mystery is at the core of what I mean by a Conversation with the World. This is a two-way conversation, not a mere monologue that we speak *at* the world. We must listen to the world, receive what is "spoken," and respond.

Dancing with Mystery

A few months later, in late winter, during a mentoring session with a soul-initiation guide, Christie discussed her relationship with her bow. While listening, the guide had an image of Christie dancing with her bow at night in the forest and using her hands in a Huntress way — the bow as a dance partner. The guide offered the image to Christie and invited her, if it resonated, to use the image in any way she'd like.

Christie's perspective that bows are primarily weapons for killing, for taking life, was a kind of Obstacle in her Metamorphosis, blocking or inhibiting her embodiment of Beautiful Huntress. This is the kind of Obstacle discussed earlier, the kind that can become a transformational doorway — if we bravely encounter it, step through it, and let it have its way with us (see "The Obstacle Threshold," pages 109–11).

Over the next few days, Christie designed a ceremony of saying yes to Huntress more fully than she had yet been able.

One day in May, Christie drove to her childhood home. There, up the hill behind the house was "a lovely maple I've known all my life. It was always a special tree, a destination, held with a certain reverence in our family." Just before sunset, Christie walked up the hill:

> I carry my bow, one arrow, an exquisite dress, deerskin shoes, and my moon headpiece. As I move toward the high-arched branch of the maple, I see Stag stride off toward the southwest. I put the deerskin on my feet. I put. on the dress, then the moon circlet, remove the bow and arrow from their sleeve. I begin to dance with my bow, letting my hands run freely along the length of it, falling into a movement of feminine spiraled curves with my hands, a gentle sway through torso and hips, the solidness of ground supporting the fluidity above.
>
> Watching the setting Sun, facing West, I recall all my connections with Mystery, and it occurs to me that perhaps tonight Mystery — in the form of an alluring and dangerous Beloved — may have manifested itself as my bow, as a dance partner. I offer myself to this partnership. When we connect, there is a third thing that emerges. And it is this third thing that gifts the world's dreaming.
>
> I have a sensation of rightness, of healing energy, of potential running through my hands. It is possible this is the frequency of love coursing through my body, emanating from my fingers.
>
> I pick up my arrow and, for the first time ever, place the notch on the string. I align the arrow with the yew symbol I've burned into the bow. I rest the arrow in the nook between thumb and forefinger. I aim, pull back the string, and release. The arrow flies — fast and straight. The whoosh of it coursing through the air blends with the soft thud as it sinks into the decaying stump.
>
> So. It is like this: The image of my arrow lodged into the tree trunk, etched now always in my mind's eye. I walk up to collect it and am surprised by how far it has traveled into the stump. I repeat this twice more. I now know why it has taken me so long to get here: I have the potential to be accurate with the bow. And I now have the discernment to carry it wisely.

I now have enough love to tend the Other with care, the one I am hunting. I now feel wholly that I am Beautiful Huntress with a Loving Heart, and I can feel what it is like to move through the world in this way.

Later I am told that two days after my ceremony a neighbor spotted a bear near the maple. In the fifty years my family had lived there, we had never seen one. I like imagining I was drawn there because Bear was already near, or that Bear was drawn to the dance floor because there was a residual fragrance from the dance, like honey.

Christie's viewpoint on bows as primarily weapons for taking life turned out to be the kind of Obstacle that can turn into a transformational doorway. Through her ceremony, she discovered that her bow enables her to take the role of the Beautiful Huntress who is both Protectress of the Vulnerable and Emperor of Death. Christie's dance with her bow was a watershed moment in her Metamorphosis:

The thing about the dance with my bow was that I actually *felt* it: I felt in every cell of my body that I was showing up in the world that night as Beautiful Huntress, and that this alone was enough. I sensed a welcoming and participatory response from my surroundings — from the forest, the stag, the old maple, the bear. I felt that my being able to connect to the sacred dance of the hunt could be a healing and stabilizing force in that community, aiding in the return of a genuine partnership between humans and the wild others.

I think more than anything I have been able to carry with me that felt-sense of rightness in my being, of what it is to be authentic in my identity, without censorship, and that I experienced it as incredibly peaceful and somehow aligned with what is good, and beautiful and true. The feelings of being ashamed, troubled, and mystified about my soul's niche started to dissolve that night; the imagined fear no longer matched my experienced reality. I cannot know for certain that the feeling in my hands, during my bow ceremony, was the energy of love, but this was the only explanation that felt true. Perhaps all the practices and ceremonies that led to that moment made it possible for me to receive the frequency of love that is available in the world and offer it out again from my being.

It had been two years since Christie's vision fast — two years in Metamorphosis.

Jung's Metamorphosis: Carried Along by the Current

After Jung's first soul encounter, when he channeled the *Seven Sermons to the Dead*, what did he do to support his Metamorphosis? Two things: He "worked with" the images of his inner journeys and he drew mandalas. Later, he built his Tower.

Working with the Images

Jung, during his *Red Book* years, took great pains to keep the images of his inner journeys — his "fantasies" — alive in his awareness. In this way he assured that they continued to work on him, reshaping his Ego, his sense of self. After the dead burst into his home, he bravely allowed the *Sermons* to rise up from the depths and into his consciousness, and he conscientiously recorded them in his journal over several long evenings. He even published them privately as a booklet and gave copies to friends, in this way making himself vulnerable to the impressions of others. At the time, he believed he was acting as a scientist. Perhaps in some sense he was, but the important consideration here, for Metamorphosis, is that he kept his *Red Book* images — all of them, not just the *Sermons* — alive in his awareness by closely examining and acting on them:

> I took great care to try to understand every single image...and to classify them scientifically — so far as this was possible — and, above all, to realize them in actual life. That is what we usually neglect to do. We allow the images to rise up, and maybe we wonder about them, but that is all. We do not take the trouble to understand them, let alone draw ethical conclusions from them....Insight into them must be converted into an ethical obligation....The images of the unconscious place a great responsibility upon a man.[3]

Over a period of several years, Jung worked with his images — his imaginal cells — in ways I would consider an extended Experimental Threshold Crossing: This was not an act of service for others (at least not intended as such), but it did spring from his mythopoetic identity — namely, someone who communicates the dynamics of the unconscious and the desires and lament of the dead. This ETC included the careful documenting of his imagery journeys; his attempts to understand them "scientifically"; his "embellishments" of many of them with paintings or drawings; and transferring his notes from his original "black books" into his "red book" (which would become the *Red Book*) — and, in the process, redrafting them, adding long commentaries, "estheticizing" them, and setting the text in "calligraphic Gothic script, in the manner of medieval manuscripts."[4] In short, during his Metamorphosis, Jung filled an intrapsychic grotto with his unnerving images and enigmatic underworld encounters, and he submerged himself in those waters every day. After several years of this regimen, his Ego was more of the otherworld than of this one: He was no longer the young doctor, the ascending star of the new psychoanalytic movement; rather, he was becoming, more and more, "the shaman, the medicine man, of the West,...[the] ferryman to the underworld and back."[5]

The Mandalas

Found all over the world and in all ages, mandalas are geometric symbols, circular or square, for wholeness. They represent the totality of the human psyche — or of life, more generally, or even of the cosmos.

Jung's mandalas appeared suddenly and spontaneously. He painted his first in January 1916. Significantly, this took place right after his first soul encounter, his channeling of the *Seven Sermons*. ETCs are, of course, irrelevant before a soul encounter — and best initiated immediately after them. Later, in 1918–19, when he was serving in the Swiss military, Jung would sketch a mandala every morning.

These complex, multicolored, richly symbolic, and stunning images were unbidden creations of his deep imagination, images that presented themselves, fully formed, to his inner eye. "With the help of these drawings I could observe my psychic transformations from day to day."[6] And maybe not just *observe* his psychic transformations, but enable, inspire, and amplify them. He didn't understand the "meaning" of his mandalas at the time, but he kept at it because "they seemed to be highly significant, and I guarded them like precious pearls."

Jung's mandala drawings were invaluable in the post-soul-encounter reshaping of his Ego. Although a mystery to him, he knew they were forming him in a necessary manner:

> I knew by now that I could not presume to choose a goal which would seem trustworthy to me. It had been proved to me that I had to abandon the idea of a superordinate position of the ego. After all, I had been brought up short when I had attempted to maintain it....I was being compelled to go through this process of the unconscious. I had to let myself be carried along by the current, without a notion of where it would lead me.[7]

By surrendering to his mandala images, Jung was indeed carried along by that current and reshaped by those waters. A life-directing metamorphic conviction grew within him, one that was in accord with his personal mythos: "It became increasingly plain to me that the mandala was the center. It is the exponent of all paths. It is the path to the center, to individuation."[8]

The Tower: Reborn in Stone

Jung's building of his Tower served as an additional ETC supporting his Metamorphosis — a rather prolonged undertaking. The Tower is Jung's hand-built sanctuary in the village of Bollingen some thirty kilometers from his home in Küsnacht. He began construction in 1923 and did not complete it until 1955. The Tower was Jung's retreat from the world. More significantly, it was, as he put it, "a kind of representation in stone of my innermost thoughts and of the knowledge I had acquired...a confession of faith in stone."[9] Building the Tower, shaping the stone, was one way he shaped his Ego in resonance with his mythopoetic identity:

From the beginning I felt the Tower as in some way a place of maturation...in which I could become what I was, what I am and will be. It gave
me a feeling as if I were being reborn in stone. It is thus a concretization
of the individuation process, a memorial *aere perennius*....It might be said
that I built it in a kind of dream. Only afterward did I see how all the parts
fitted together and that a meaningful form had resulted: a symbol of psychic wholeness. At Bollingen I am in the midst of my true life, I am most
deeply myself."[10]

Jung said that his Tower, like his mandalas, represented his wholeness, the "self."
The self was what he was cultivating within his own psyche as well as the psychic reality his Soul wanted him to introduce to Western culture. In designing and building
his Tower, he was further shaping his Ego to be an effective agent for Soul.

This Stream of Lava

Jung experienced the depths of his psyche to be like a volcano "that pushes out the
fiery-molten mass of the unformed and the undifferentiated."[11] He referred to the
images he received in those years as a "stream of lava."

As a young man my goal had been to accomplish something in my science.
But then, I hit upon this stream of lava, and the heat of its fires reshaped
my life.[12]

Jung emphasized that it was the unconscious, not his strategic mind, that was
reshaping his psyche:

As I worked with my fantasies, I became aware that the unconscious undergoes or produces change. Only after I had familiarized myself with alchemy did I realize that the unconscious is a *process*, and that the psyche is
transformed or developed by the relationship of the ego to the contents of
the unconscious.[13]

I agree with Jung that the conscious self does not transform itself but is metamorphosed by the unconscious. Using my model and language, I'd say the Ego is
transformed primarily by that particular realm of the unconscious I call the Soul.
But because, in the course of this journey, the Ego becomes conscious of the Soul,
at that point the Soul is no longer (in the) unconscious. This transformation of the
Ego is the process of Metamorphosis.

What Good Is a Soul Name?

As we've seen, it's not uncommon to receive a soul name during a soul encounter,
as when Yeats was named by the glimmering girl, or Elisabeth (Song Dreamer) by
the wind, or Christie (Beautiful Huntress) by the Great Bear constellation, or me

(Cocoon Weaver) by a yellow butterfly. Or a soul name might be adopted from a dream, as with Kent (Buffalo Heart Warrior) or Dan (Keeper of the Underground River). Or an initiate might consciously generate their own soul name to summarize or encapsulate for themselves and others what they have learned about their mytho-poetic identity, as with Matt (Compost Bridger of Worlds) or Kate (Silver Moon). And sometimes our soul name turns out to be the same as or a variation of the name we were given by or inherited from our parents, as with Kevin (FeatherStone). Others might choose names with no obvious relationship to their mythopoetic identity but that serve as simple reminders that they have an identity bigger and deeper than their middleworld persona. Some soul-initiated people have no soul name at all and don't feel they're missing anything.

Soul names can be a great help in understanding, assimilating, and manifesting your mythopoetic identity, but a word of caution is in order. Soul names can also be a major encumbrance. The name by itself has little importance, can be inaccurate or misleading, and can end up being somewhere between worthless and a true obstacle or distraction from the hard work of manifesting your Soul identity. If you're not careful, soul names can result in ego inflation.

During Metamorphosis, the most valuable opportunity is to adopt a regular (daily, hourly) practice of somatically and psychically *feeling* your Soul identity (your unique place in the world) — which ideally your soul name, if you have one, points to as a kind of shorthand — and then to experience the world from that place and to act from that place. This is what an ETC is. Referring to yourself with a soul name or having others call you by that name is helpful only when it reminds you or supports you to step more fully into that identity, that unique place in the world, and to act from there. And if it works this way for you, your soul name is indeed of great value. It doesn't really matter if the name says anything meaningful in a denotative sense. It's useful to the extent that it ushers you through a noetic doorway into the underworld domain of the mythopoetic.

Besides, receiving a soul name from Mystery is at best the beginning of a unique conversation you can have with the world. The only way to discover what your soul name really means is through that conversation as it unfolds over many years. In any case, the important thing isn't what the name means but how that conversation changes you and makes you more useful to the world.

The real benefit of a soul name is to evoke the embodied experience of the eco-niche that has been calling you forever.

Some names that people receive or adopt early on the journey of soul initiation aren't soul names at all; they don't reflect mythopoetic identity. But they can have great value nonetheless. They might, for example, be Wanderer names, provisional names that serve to remind you how best to proceed while on the journey — names like Joy, Bridge, or Wanderer. Keep in mind, however, that they also could be names generated by one or more of your subpersonalities with the intention to distract or derail you from the journey.

Although soul names often appear during the Soul Encounter phase, sometimes they don't arrive until Metamorphosis. For Tracy Rekart, a somatic leadership guide in her forties, her soul name arrived a few weeks after her vision fast while she was on the phone with another participant in her group, an event she described in an email:

> I first heard my name while talking with LR the other day. I noticed it as the words came out of my mouth. LR said, "Did you hear what you said?" I knew instantly what he was talking about and I started to cry. It took my breath away to say it and to see that he knew, too.
>
> The name evokes both sadness and joy, both excitement and fear, all at the same time. I am not sure I am worthy of this name, but to not live into it would mean death. I feel as though I am being torn away from the life I once lived into the life I was meant to live. It is a good tearing, like ripping fabric along the grain after an initial cut in order to create something lovely. Yet the original fabric is forever altered. And it is really scary to live into the name for all that it opens me up to and means to me. My heart feels full and expansive.
>
> My name is Soul Traveler Between Worlds.

Tracy's story exemplifies the profound emotional and psychological impact of such a moment as well as its primary value and significance for the Descent to Soul — namely, how it immediately begins the metamorphic reshaping of the Ego.

Tracy's soul name, like all soul names and the mythopoetic identities they point to, does not reveal anything about her primary delivery system — somatic leadership guiding — but more importantly, the name connects her, somatically and intrapsychically, to that identity, to that place in the world: "In my work, I travel between the world of mystery and the everyday world and then find the language that helps my clients remember they, too, can live in both worlds."

The Metamorphosis of Matt: "Allowing Myself to Be Mulch"

Matt, the software professional turned Presbyterian pastor, encountered Old Man Compost on his vision fast and received the mythopoetic feeling-image of Compost Bridger of Worlds (see "Matt: Compost Bridger of Worlds," pages 163–68). When he returned home — to his everyday life — he had the conviction that he had to do something right away to embody his mythos.

There was a vow and a sense that if I didn't respond as fully as I could with a yes, it would feel like dying. I realized I couldn't go back. I couldn't pretend. I couldn't undo what happened.

Fortunately, Matt did not believe he needed to immediately choose and develop a delivery system for his soul image. Instead, he began the process of Metamorphosis by doing what he called "staying in the dreamtime" — the underworld consciousness he had entered on his vision fast. He let the dreamtime do its composting, transformative work on his Ego:

I stayed in the dreamtime for quite a while. I was being done unto, you could say. I wasn't planning things out strategically. I was allowing myself to be mulch, to continue to come undone and to feel that. I allowed the composting process to continue — to just let that happen to me.

During this time, Matt launched himself into two Experimental Threshold Crossings:

One of my small, immediate steps was to start a compost pile at my house and to start churning it right away. This was a whimsical, literal, physical, visible way of saying, "Yes, I'm here. You, Compost, are here. I want to be present to you."

Starting a compost pile was a kind of ceremony, a way for Matt to say yes to his soul image of Compost Bridge and to keep that image close so that it could continue its shape-shifting work on his Ego.

Matt's second ETC was more challenging and complicated:

Although my life journey so far had led me to the vocation of a pastor, this wasn't my real calling. I had an intuitive awareness that I was being asked to bridge from the institutional structures of faith to the wild, dark, luminosity of soul. As T. S. Eliot would say, institutional religion and culture has become a heap of broken images, an impoverished state that can no longer be metabolized into nutrient, but is now just frozen in a crystallized form. Part of what needs composting is the institutional religious system. Right after my vision fast, I had a corresponding premonition that my position as a pastor had to decompose and become something that was clearly in service to soul.

I needed to set a tangible goal to provide myself the space and the channel, to not only continue my own process but also to allow that vow and that seed to grow. My first project — without knowing what I was doing or what would happen or what people's reactions would be — was to dream up an offering, a three-day intensive, that would connect my fellow pastors and church leaders with the treasure of what I had experienced as

Compost Bridger of Worlds, to do something that felt authentic to my first budding relationship with my mythopoetic identity. This felt like sending out a network of mycelia into places where there might be nutrients.

In some ways this project was an early venture into Enactment, but its primary effect was to intensify the early work of Metamorphosis. By designing and offering the intensive, Matt showed up in the world as Compost Bridger, enabling his mythopoetic identity to have its way with him, allowing him to be seen by others in this role and identity and to receive feedback (not necessarily explicit or verbal) as to the ways in which he was seen — accurate and inaccurate perceptions being of equal value for metamorphosis. All this helped to reshape his Ego and amplify his experience of being Compost Bridger.

With this project, Matt tried on his mythopoetic identity and walked it out on a religious limb in a way that composted his former socio-vocational role as pastor while also enabling him to contribute to the decomposing of the religious institution that had largely defined his first adulthood (his post-teen Adolescence). With these actions, he crossed a threshold. He acted on his vow. And there was something else happening, something more difficult to articulate:

> I am beginning to feel something beyond synchronicities, something much more subtle, ordinary in a way, like barely felt shifts in people's responses to me, but even more importantly a budding awareness, like a curious calm in the air before something is about to happen.

Also during this Metamorphosis time, Matt employed practices for cultivating the facets of wholeness he needed in order to navigate the challenges of this phase of the Descent: meditation (for his East facet); intentionally embodying the "buffoonery" of the Sacred Fool (also East); writing prose and poetry that "feels alive and allows me to share through images and language" (West); and practicing somatic awareness to tap into his grief and longing (South).

Two years into his Metamorphosis, as another ETC, Matt returned to his childhood home for the first time in decades and met the people currently tending the house and the land. They shared stories of the place. Then Matt once again walked into the dark woods behind the house. There, by the little bridge where he, as a child, would cross over the creek on his way to the old compost bin, he enacted a "homecoming" ceremony that honored his "true place of birth":

> I introduced myself to the woods in the full potency and truth of my mythopoetic identity, which this place had dreamed, planting a wild seed all those years ago when I was a young child. I felt myself returning as a true adult to a mother who had given birth to me, or to a lover who had enraptured me — and who had awaited my return.

Now I return
Bearing the gift of a story
Birthed out of the dream
A new world-making, wearing new speech
Indigenous to this place
A native nectar on my tongue.

For Matt, the rhythm of Metamorphosis went like this:

Fail, get back on the horse, try something new, experiment, collaborate. It's that mycelial question of where is the food, where are things happening and coming alive?

The process of ego dismemberment and re-memberment inherent in Metamorphosis is at times excruciating:

It has felt like a pulling apart, a mandorla, really, like a grinding. There was a point where it was terrifying and painful and I'd want to shut it off or escape. But now it's more like the new normal. It's becoming richer and I'm able to let the tension and the whole mix of opposites have their way with me. In some ways it feels violent and violating, and in some ways tender and raw and alive. In some ways it feels like what's important is the journey, not the destination. It's not about me and it's not ultimately about my vision of success but really about staying fiercely true to what is happening and what wants to happen through my life — taking risks and being all in to the best of my ability but also having the grace and the humor of just not knowing and yet being fully in it. A level of trust.

This is an archetypal portrait of an initiate in the midst of Metamorphosis. As your Ego is being reshaped in the aftermath of soul encounter, you do indeed experience something like a Mandorla tension, perhaps the quintessential one — the natural opposition between your old identity and the new, both identities being true but in some ways incompatible. There is indeed something like a "grinding," and you might feel terrified and in pain at times, perhaps wanting to escape — especially as your East subs (your addicts and escapists) get activated. Your other subs, too, are likely to show up in an attempt to rescue you. Compost Bridger's advice is spot-on: Stay fiercely true to the metamorphosis and what Soul wants to happen through your life. Take the risk to show up in and as your mythopoetic identity, but also have the grace and humor to understand that you don't yet fully know what's happening to you.

The Metamorphosis phase enables the images and somatic experiences associated with your soul encounter(s) to do their work of reshaping your Ego. This reshaping by your imaginal cells is, as we've seen, analogous to caterpillar soup being formed into the body of a butterfly. This takes some time. The former caterpillar doesn't simply have a vision of a butterfly and then, presto, it has a butterfly body. The forming of the butterfly body requires some significant psycho-architectural engineering. The way we humans cooperate with this is not by engaging in delivery systems but through Experimental Threshold Crossings and other shape-shifting practices. When your psyche has become an adequate container for your mythopoetic identity, you'll then be ready to develop delivery systems...and doing *that* will hone your skills as an initiated Adult.

Chapter Eleven

PHASE FIVE

Enactment

Performing Your Vision for Your People to See

The Way It Is

There's a thread you follow. It goes among
things that change. But it doesn't change.
People wonder about what you are pursuing.
You have to explain about the thread.
But it is hard for others to see.
While you hold it you can't get lost.
Tragedies happen; people get hurt
or die; and you suffer and get old.
Nothing you do can stop time's unfolding.
You don't ever let go of the thread.

— WILLIAM STAFFORD

The start of the Enactment phase ends your long period of withdrawal or disengagement from the routine life of society while you journeyed through the three liminal phases of the Descent to Soul. From the start of Dissolution, when you descended into Soul Canyon, you had been physically, psychologically, and/or socially disconnected from ordinary Village life. You had been a kind of alien, a stranger. Now, as you commence Enactment, you rejoin society and begin to contribute to cultural evolution in ways and to depths you could not have dreamed. This is, of course, the whole point of the journey. You now offer your gifts to the world not because it might be the morally or culturally correct thing to do but because you can't help it. After your soul-orchestrated transformation, anything to which you devote yourself will play a part in the building and enhancement of healthy, mature culture — if, that is, you embody your mythopoetic identity, if you follow your thread.

When you enter the Enactment phase of your Descent, you become an active conscious agent for what Thomas Berry calls the dream of the Earth. You become a cultural visionary and evolutionary. One day, if and when most people on this planet undertake the journey of soul initiation, the dream of the Earth will be collectively embodied through humanity (as well as through all other species). This is what we were made for. We can be confident this is what Earth wants. Maybe we humans have accomplished such a thing in the distant past, maybe this would be our first time, but clearly it's not happening now. Not until we collectively join or rejoin the family of things will the dream of the Earth realize its full coherence and actualization.[1] This is not because our unique human aspect of the dream is more important than that of other species but because our *separation* from the dream has delayed its coalescence and indeed now threatens its fulfillment any time in the future foreseeable by us. But if enough of us impossible dreamers foresee and embody our individual destinies...

Silver and Golden Apples: Destiny Foreseen and Embodied

As we explored earlier, the final stanza of Yeats's "Aengus" evokes the Metamorphosis theme of the Adolescent Ego having been transformed into an Adult Ego (see "The Journey of Soul Initiation as a Love Story," pages 245–46). But in this same stanza we also see an Enactment theme. Yeats, the young poet in his twenties, proclaims the mythopoetic fountainhead of his future delivery systems when he declares he will...

> ...pluck till time and times are done
> The silver apples of the moon,
> The golden apples of the sun.

For the second time in the poem, Yeats evokes the image of apples. First it is apple blossom in the hair of the glimmering girl — his anima or Guide to Soul — who calls him by his true name, which enables his soul identity to first blossom in his awareness. Then, in this final stanza, these springtime blooms of Soul Encounter have matured into the autumn fruit of the Wild Orchard (late Adulthood), revealing the deep structure and soul-infused themes of his art as it would unfold over the coming decades of his life. Metaphorically speaking, plucking silver and golden apples is exactly what Yeats gave his life to, the thread he followed the rest of his days.

The Sun symbolizes the masculine principle, and the Moon the feminine — the masculine, for Yeats, corresponding to the will to express life ever more fully through meaningful achievement, and the feminine corresponding to the subconscious capacity to receive, absorb, and remember every experience, including dreams, images, instincts, and emotions. He considered the masculine and feminine to be the self-conscious and the subconscious, respectively. Much of Yeats's work can be seen as an exploration of the tensions and dynamics between these two poles of psycho-spiritual life, within individuals and between them, as well as two features of cultural life more generally.

Yeats's final book, *A Vision*, which he began in his midfifties and on which he labored more than fourteen years, was the culmination of his lifelong exploration of the Sun and Moon as symbols. It's a metaphysical treatise on the correspondences that the twenty-eight moon phases hold for personality type as well as for the stages of human development. The phases of the Moon are, of course, the expression of the eternal cyclical dance between the Sun and the Moon. *A Vision* offers an innovative and perhaps revolutionary perspective on life and human nature.[2] Yeats really did pluck those silver and golden apples throughout his life. And he considered *A Vision* to be his greatest gift to the world. He referred to it as "my book of books."

It might seem astounding that in his midtwenties — at the time he wrote "Aengus" — Yeats already knew, on some level, the deep themes that would hold together all the multifaceted strands of his long life of creative work in literature, theater, politics, and mysticism. But this is what happens for all initiated Adults: While in Soul Canyon, we glimpse the mythopoetic essence of the psycho-ecological niche we were born to occupy in this lifetime. Through this encounter with Soul, we are reshaped by the deep structure of our destiny long before we fully understand it, long before we decisively enact it, long before it becomes a dynamic thread in cultural enrichment. We don't deeply fathom our soul identity until we've been embodying it for some time. That's the way we learn — a kind of on-the-job training.

Soul Discovery, Enactment, Soul Initiation, and Delivery Systems

Discovering who you really are, in other words, doesn't end the moment you receive a vision. That's actually when the discovery *begins*. That's the first day you walk into the world in an engaged, soul-infused way. During the first few months or years of this walk, you're in Metamorphosis and your actions, especially your Experimental Threshold Crossings, gradually shift your Ego into a shape that eventually enables you to embody your vision — to "carry what is hidden as a gift to others."[3] Once you enter the Enactment phase, this embodiment begins. It will be a while, however, before you reach the Wellspring stage, during which you'll choose and cultivate a true delivery system. First are the fledgling exploratory implementations of soul embodiment that characterize Enactment. During this phase, three other things unfold: You may have additional soul encounters; the metamorphosis of your Ego continues;

and you are tending to your wholing and Self-healing — all three being the sorts of things one experiences and does toward the end of the Cocoon stage. Then, when you're at last ripened enough, you'll ecstatically suffer the major life passage of Soul Initiation — from the Cocoon (late Adolescence) to the Wellspring (early Adulthood) — when your primary motivation in life shifts from exploring the mysteries of nature and psyche to embodying those mysteries through your delivery system.

Soul Initiation takes place when we can no longer deny our calling, our original instructions, the unique nonseverable thread that connects us to Mystery. It's the moment we make a promise it will kill us to break — the promise to carry our distinctive offering as a gift to others, to help create another world, a life-enhancing Earth community.

But we can't make this supreme promise just because we want to. We must first be sufficiently metamorphosed. When we're ready, we know it because Mystery informs us. It will be like this: The promise happens *to* us. We surrender to it. We notice it rising from our belly and coursing up through our heart. It's more like giving birth than making a conscious decision.

After Soul Initiation, through a thousand experiments over many years, you will shape a delivery system or two for your Soul's passions. Your giveaway itself will gradually reveal — to both you and others — who you really are, what you were born for, what your Soul desires. The more you offer your human gift to our more-than-human world, the more you discover what that gift is and who that human is.

This process of soul-discovery-through-embodiment continues as long as you're breathing.

This has been true for me. It's been forty years since I was blessed with my first encounter with Soul, a vision of supporting others to weave cocoons of transformation. During the early years, I wasn't at all clear what that meant or how to do it. The meaning and methods became evident only gradually and only as I engaged the work wholeheartedly and persistently and only as I continued to follow the call from the depths. Not till about twenty years ago, for example, did it begin to occur to me that the models and methods my colleagues and I were creating might be a first contemporary, Western, nature-based approach to the journey of soul initiation — and that our work was not a version of what I had imagined, at one time or another, it might be: psychotherapy, ecotherapy, life coaching, shamanism, rites of passage, or "purpose" discovery.[4]

Two Metaphors for the Enactment Phase of the Descent to Soul

The butterfly metaphor: Enactment corresponds to the period when the cocoon opens and the imago, the recently formed butterfly, emerges and slowly, tenderly opens its damp, soft wings — but has not yet taken to the air. It is not yet capable of flight. It needs to sit a while and slowly flap those new wings to get the blood pumping and to fill out the wing structures. Although the former caterpillar is in its new form, it doesn't yet know what it can do. It is in the open air for the first time and fully experiencing its adult body, sensing its wings and their potential. Likewise, you, the human initiate, are still in the Cocoon stage but nearing its end while you're being initially seen and experienced by others in your Adult "form." You are "stretching your wings" as you show up culturally in your mythopoetic identity. Without a successful Enactment phase, you won't ever fly, won't fulfill your destiny.

The Soul Canyon metaphor: Your climb out of Soul Canyon is your Metamorphosis phase. When you reach the canyon rim, Enactment commences; you're no longer in the Canyon but are still on the journey — nearing its end — and still in the Cocoon stage. You'll remain in the Cocoon until you've traveled some distance from the rim while in your new mythopoetic form, conversing and interacting with the world from within your new identity and niche — until, somewhere down the trail, you cross a threshold into the Wellspring stage.

The butterfly metaphor is a bit limited because it seems to shrink the Enactment phase into the brief period between cocoon breaching and flight. The Soul Canyon metaphor allows for Enactment to stretch out from the recently gained rim of the Canyon, across the relatively horizontal landscape, to the eventual and possibly distant border crossing into the Wellspring. On the other hand, the butterfly metaphor spotlights the process and necessity of getting accustomed to a radical change in psychospiritual shape and capacities, while the Soul Canyon image does not.

Performing Your Vision for Your People to See

Embodying your vision is as difficult as anything you'll ever do, especially at the start. It's like beginning to write a book and all you have in front of you is a blank screen or sheet of paper. There's no reality to the vision yet.

Black Elk, the Lakota holy man, insisted there was an essential step between a vision and its use on behalf of others:

> A man [*sic*] who has had a vision is not able to use the power of it until after he has performed the vision on Earth for the people to see.[5]

Think of this "performance" of your vision as your task during the Enactment phase. Here's one possible way to paraphrase Black Elk's axiom: Being witnessed while embodying your vision is necessary in order to progress from the Cocoon to the Wellspring.

A second classic Enactment axiom:

> A vision without a task is only a dream.
> A task without a vision is only a job.
> A vision with a task can change the world.[6]

These two axioms are, in my experience, quite accurate, but neither one fully or clearly expresses what I feel is most important about Enactment. Namely this:

First, I understand Black Elk to be declaring that before you can serve the world with your vision, you must enact it in some way for your people — perhaps by way of a dance, a song, a dramatic performance, or oral or written storytelling. If you received your vision while participating in a group ceremony, such as a vision fast, you can perform your vision in this sense for your group. This might make all the difference. Or you can perform your vision in some way for your home community, perhaps without letting on that what you're enacting is a vision. Maybe, for example, you recite, at a public gathering, a poem that covertly portrays your mythopoetic identity. But it's essential you don't believe that once you've performed your vision "for the people to see" you've completed your contract with Soul. Rather, you must then move on to performing your vision *as your life* — not merely witnessed, but enacted in a way that actively engages the world and contributes to its evolutionary unfolding.

Second, it's not merely that the vision does something for a task — namely, transforms it from a job to a world changer. As true as this is, it's also the case that the task does something for the vision — two things, actually: The task completes the vision by manifesting it — by making it real — and equally important, your enactment of the task allows you to understand what the vision actually was in the first place — and what it may become.

Once you understand your vision and enact it with a task, the world might truly change and your consciousness might shift permanently.

The "task" referred to here — your way of embodying your vision — is what I mean by a delivery system for your Soul's desires.

When you were in the Dissolution phase, you had to learn to relinquish control of the journey. The Ego, as we saw, was the clay that got shaped, not the shaper. Now, in Enactment, the Ego becomes a shaper again — a shaper of forms for vision embodiment. But the Ego does not shape in just any way it wants, like a solitary Adolescent hero; rather, the Ego is now an assistant shaper in partnership with the Muse and in service to the Soul. By co-shaping delivery systems for vision embodiment, the Ego, in turn, gets steadily reshaped.

Silver Moon and Poetry:
Metamorphosis, Enactment, and Soul Initiation

When we last looked in on Silver Moon's Descent to Soul (see "Silver Moon: 'Do Something More Taboo with It,'" pages 187–96), we witnessed something of her five soul encounters: the recovery of a soul power hidden in her Core Wound (the ability to uncover mysteries hidden in Shadow); her embrace of the archetype of the Witch; her dream of the chalice of menstrual blood and sperm; her revelation that her soul task is "to speak the unwanted and suppressed voices of the feminine"; and her acceptance of her mission to "become your blood" and to guide other women to do so.

The Metamorphosis of Silver Moon: Becoming Her Poetry

Shortly after her second vision fast, with her four-day conversation with Witch (see "The Point of No Return," page 195), Silver Moon began to hear poetry, "like a mysterious voice speaking to me through the cracks of my soul." She transcribed what she heard. She had never thought of herself as a poet or even, particularly, a writer. Recording her poetry was an early ETC for her. In three months, she had a collection of fifty poems.

These poems — receiving them, recording them, and refining them — were reshaping her Ego in accordance with the images and archetypes of her soul encounters. By saying yes to the poems, she was showing up in the world as Silver Moon, as She Who Becomes Her Blood. Then she threw herself into an even riskier, more public ETC:

> It was clear to me that there was something important about my voice and my body in the delivery of these poems, so I began to create spoken-word performances, which is to say I began to let myself be seen in the dripping rawness of my uttermost vulnerability. This was a truly ego-destroying, soul-making task for me. In reciting these poems I was enacting my soul task of speaking the unspoken voices of the feminine, including embodiments of longing, despair, lust, desire, ecstasy, rage, grief, and the pain of unrequited love. And in doing so, my ego was being worked by coming face to face with my own insecurities, sabotage, fears, and shame to be seen in the true voice and essence of my soul, the very thing that I had kept hidden for...well, perhaps centuries.
>
> In enacting this bold and wild invitation from the Mystery to create spoken-word performances, I would memorize my poetry so that I didn't have to read from a sheet. In doing so, there was this magical thing that would happen. The energy of the poem would come through my body — I would *become* the poem.

And by becoming her poetry, she was becoming her blood, and by becoming her blood, her Ego was getting metamorphosed into someone able to "speak the unwanted and suppressed voices of the feminine."

Enactment: The Blood Tale*s*

Before long, Silver Moon moved into the Enactment phase, assisted by the always-needed and always-mysterious intervention of the Muse:

> After creating and touring my first performance of spoken-word poems, I received instruction from the Muse to create a show called *The Blood Tales*. Her instruction was to write all the poems from the space of the Blood. So for three consecutive moon cycles, I locked myself away and listened to what the Blood wanted me to say. Thirteen poems were born and so was *The Blood Tales* — a piece of art that started out as a spoken-word performance and has now become a full-scale theater production. This is a revolutionary piece in that it shifts the common perception of what the Blood is and offers the promise of a new paradigm as seen from the Moon.

Locking herself away for those three moon cycles was itself an ETC, a way of being She Who Becomes Her Blood, a way of crossing a threshold gifted her by the Muse. By crossing that threshold, her Ego was further shape-shifted, a Metamorphosis process and outcome. But the time with her Blood also gave birth to a public performance that was very much of the Enactment phase, in that it was conceived and offered as a way of gifting the world with her soul work, a way to shift her audience's perception of what the Blood is and to offer "the promise of a new paradigm as seen from the Moon."

Let's sharpen this distinction between Metamorphosis and Enactment. When in Metamorphosis, embodiments of mythopoetic identity (primarily through ETCs) are mainly for the purpose of shape-shifting the Ego (even if they might sometimes provide a service to others). During Enactment, in contrast, mythopoetic embodiments are focused on providing a service (even though they also contribute to the shape-shifting of the Ego). By the time we've reached Enactment, the Ego has been sufficiently reshaped to enable more meaningful and effective contributions.

Now consider the distinction between an Enactment-phase offering and a Wellspring-stage embodiment of a delivery system. In Enactment, we don't need a craft specifically honed, usually over many years, for delivering our soul gift. We only need a method that suffices for embodiment. This is the difference between merely skillful performance and soul-rooted art.

For Silver Moon, the mandate from her Muse to create *The Blood Tales* led to her choice to study theater as a delivery system:

> After touring *The Blood Tales* as a spoken-word performance in Europe and the US, I came across an experimental and way-off-the-wall theater school in Barcelona, called Laboratorio Escuela. When I saw the work that they were creating, I enrolled in a three-year course in corporally expressive theater-making, further deepening my ability to bring forth the essence of

my soul, and to do so onstage. The rare and unique methodology, developed by Jessica Walker, allowed me every day to explore the depths of my unconscious. I learned how the unconscious holds so much of our erotic life force. That which has been banished to the shadows is the source of our creative genius. The daily rigorous training expanded my emotional and expressive capacity in ways I never imagined possible. I fell in love with the freedom of the stage, the freedom to say and do things that in normal life are just not possible — to bring the shadow to the light. I became more and more aware of my soul essence, the fierce and wildly erotic feminine, and less and less ashamed to be seen in this taboo and repressed face of the feminine soul.

Three things are happening here: Metamorphosis (the shape-shifting of the Ego), Enactment (the embodiment of soul work in a way that serves or impacts others), and the start of the *stage* of the Wellspring (when delivery systems are learned and honed — theater, for Silver Moon).

Soul Initiation and the Wellspring: Red Waves of Divinity

Silver Moon was in the process of leaving the Cocoon and entering the Wellspring as an Apprentice to Soul. Looking back at this interval, she recalls one particular day that epitomizes this life passage of Soul Initiation — when our center of gravity shifts from the exploration of the mysteries of Soul to the embodiment of those mysteries in a life of service:

I had a bodywork session during which I was taken by one of the biggest griefs of my life, an opening of a place in my body where I had been hiding the deep knowing I had on a soul level of my connection to something much bigger than me. By opening this space, I knew there was no denying anymore. That which my soul knew all along, my ego was now ready to accept and welcome in. I grieved the loss of my old story, and yet everything I had been through on a soul level — the immense suffering, all the confusion, loneliness, rejection — all now made sense. I was never meant to belong to a culture that was sick at its roots. The gift of being the shadow seer, an edge dweller, was for a reason. I saw the pieces I always knew were missing, and I'd come to help create a new culture based on this knowing.

Later, at sunset that day, I sat and wept — I mean howled — for a few hours. I found myself whispering the words, "It's all been for you," speaking to the Mystery. Every painstaking, soul-shaping piece of my journey had been for the Mystery, and it was then affirmed that I needed to go about enacting that which was mine to enact. This led to my simultaneously stepping into apprenticeships to two delivery systems in addition to poetry:

theater-making and deep feminine facilitation. The added twist with the theater was that it allowed me to bring out of hiding that which is hidden. I got to create a theater performance where I could embody my soul, the Witch.

During the Wellspring, in the course of developing our delivery system(s), three processes unfold concurrently: We continue to learn about our mythopoetic identities (this might include additional soul encounters), our Egos continue to shape-shift (Metamorphosis), and we discover deeper layers of our soul work, the mythopoetic deep structure of our delivery systems (the task of the Wellspring). For Silver Moon, it looked like this:

> While developing *The Blood Tales*, a process that took four years to complete, so much of the hidden nature of the poems was revealed to me. By giving my body to the words written through the Blood, I would receive revelation after revelation about the true nature of the mysteries of the Blood. I began to see that the Blood Mysteries hold the keys to women's empowerment. The blood mystery journey takes a woman into the depths of her innate connection to body, earth, and the mystery and, in this way, allows her to reclaim her erotic and wild nature.

Silver Moon's soul work — her visionary artistry — is disruptive of the egocentric, feminine-suppressing, nature-disconnected, dominator worldview, and it is richly contributing to the building of a contemporary Western version of an ecocentric and soulcentric partnership culture. This is true of the lives and works of all soul-initiated Adults in this time of the dying of life-destroying societies and the birth of life-enhancing cultures. This is how the deepest cultural renaissance happens. All soul work, at this time in the world, is countercultural and revolutionary, as well as evolutionary.

In an excerpt from Silver Moon's "Liquid Love," we can feel the thunderbolt of culture disruption as well as the germinating seed of culture regeneration:

> …This is love people
> Our love lies in the blood
> We have been shamed for our love
> We've been told to keep it hidden
> What if you were to bleed
> Your red waves of divinity
> All over the streets of corporate insanity.[7]

From Metamorphosis to the Wellspring

Just as Metamorphosis is the bridge between Soul Encounter and Enactment (between a vision and its embodiment), Enactment is the bridge between the *phase* of

Metamorphosis and the *life stage* of the Wellspring (between the fashioning of an Adult Ego and the full-on embodiment of that Ego).

Actually, it's a bit more complicated than that because it depends on which life stage you're in during the Enactment phase in question: Although your first Descent to Soul takes place while you're in the Cocoon stage, later Descents can take place not only in the Cocoon but also after reaching the Wellspring and even in the subsequent life stage, the Wild Orchard.[8] As a reminder, the Descent is neither a life stage nor a passage between stages but an experiential journey that can take place in at least three different stages. When a Descent takes place within the Cocoon, it contributes to the fulfillment of the tasks of that stage and in that way helps a person move toward or into the Wellspring. When a Descent occurs in the Wellspring, on the other hand, it supports a person to *deepen* into the Wellspring. (For more on these distinctions, see appendix 4, "The Enactment Phase during the Cocoon versus the Wellspring.")

What Causes Soul Initiation and What about You Changes?

Soul Initiation is what happens when Mystery decides you've completed enough of your Cocoon tasks. If you have the good fortune to have a rite of passage at this time, it will help you adjust to this new stage of the Wellspring while also informing your community that you've undergone this change. (To be effective, this rite would need to be designed specifically for people going through Soul Initiation.[9])

It is sometimes possible to leave Soul Canyon by choice (that is, to cut short a Descent — often an unfortunate move), but you can't leave the Cocoon (or any other life stage) just by deciding to. It is Mystery who moves you from one stage to the next — when you're ready.

As you enter the Wellspring, your center of gravity shifts to enthusiastic dedication to service. The principal archetype with which you resonate is no longer the Wanderer; now it's the Apprentice to Soul. You might try out a few potential delivery systems before you find one or two that are a good fit. Ultimately, in the Wellspring, you commit yourself to learning a particular art or discipline, a set of skills that will eventually become your primary delivery system. You become an Apprentice to that delivery system but often also to an adept of that discipline — a stage-six Artisan (second half of Adulthood) or a stage-seven Master (first half of Elderhood).

Matt's Journey from Pastor to Priest of the Wild

Matt, the Presbyterian pastor who apprenticed to Old Man Compost, became a soul-inspired composter of his own religious tradition. A (r)evolutionary. (See "The Metamorphosis of Matt," pages 293–96.) This is not something he could have imagined when, at age twenty-three, he was abducted into Soul Canyon during his "divine wounding" in a field above a lake near Seattle. It's not something he could have imagined even fourteen years later on his vision fast.

On his Descent, Matt experienced several soul encounters — by way of dreams, waking visions, soul-infused insights, childhood memories, self-designed ceremony, and deep imagination. At age thirty-nine, he entered the Enactment phase and began to show up in his everyday life as Compost Bridger of Worlds. This is the thread he follows.

At first Matt embodied his mythopoetic identity in the context of his existing job and established career of ministry and by using the familiar skills and knowledge of that job and career. This is common and understandable for people in Enactment and nearing the end of the Cocoon — to use resources they already possess as they experiment with the embodiment of their vision.

At the start of his Enactment phase, Matt described for me his calling and his early sense of how he would embody his mythos:

> I can now see what I could not see before my vision fast — that the image of a decomposing bridge is a thread that runs through my life, from early childhood experiences playing behind my home in the woods to my current understanding of my soul image.
>
> Our current world order is based on consumption. Ours is a culture of violence, a society estranged and exiled from the wild world — from what makes us most deeply human. I feel our dying world's grief. It is in the broader context of this collective grief that I feel called to be Compost Bridger, someone whose task is to build a bridge from a dying world to the fructifying darkness of the soul. For me, this is an apprenticeship to the mysteries of the world or of the state of consciousness that Christian texts refer to as "the kingdom." As a Christian pastor in my dayworld vocation, I want to help others confront the reality that we are now standing at the dying edge of Christendom. Everywhere I see pastors wringing their hands as their church membership declines. I see uninspired leadership and burnout. I see tragedies and fear in the congregations, and I see the pastors reacting and acting out from helplessly wounded places. I see church leaders tenaciously clinging to the strategies of ego and emphatically believing that if we just think hard enough, we can come up with a new strategy to save the sinking ship of Christianity.

The result of fully opening to his grief over the dying of the old culture and of his religious tradition was an intensified longing to serve his people as Compost Bridger of Worlds. In this way Matt allowed his heart to continue the metamorphosis of his Ego that had been initiated by his Soul. In his everyday setting as a pastor, he saw the need and opportunity to facilitate a type of therapy for the culture of the Christian church.

One way to embody vision while in Enactment — before, that is, the cultivation of a delivery system — is to collaborate with others who share a similar goal. Matt and a few other "social prophets and sacred priests" dreamed up a "Seminary of the Wild" — a new paradigm for spiritual leadership rooted in practices that help pastors develop greater wholeness, authenticity, imagination, and courage. They felt a pastor's ordination should derive from "the depths of the wild" — not be conferred by an institution. Their culture-therapy goal was to "reclaim the soul of the Church, the wild root of the Christian story."

During this time, Matt had two dreams that were soul encounters and that further revealed and fleshed out his mythopoetic identity.[10]

The first dream was of a massive cottonwood in the center of a forest. In awe, I am standing in a ravine near the great tree and notice a large root, about a foot in diameter, coming from the tree and plunging deep into the Earth. The root is alive and smooth like a snake. I draw close to touch it; I can feel magic energy flowing from the tree through the root, giving life to the whole forest.

Upon awakening, Matt knew that Snake Root was an additional core element of his mythopoetic identity, a numinous image informing his psycho-ecological niche. He enacted a ceremony to say yes to this image, making "a vow to the Deep World." When he did...

I felt the world itself respond to me. It felt like something unlocked and opened — something in me that desires to devise new forms of speech, a kind of magic that reaches out in serpent-like, mycelial fingers to find places in others and myself ready for transformation.

His second big dream came just a few weeks later:

I am driving down the freeway somewhere in the Pacific Northwest when I look off to the forested hillside and see, in a large opening, a Great White Tree. I am riveted, in utter awe, because I *know* this Tree, and I *know* this place and know it is *real* and it is *mine* — I *actually belong to it.* And I am in awe because my sense is that it has been waiting for me. As I am driving by, time slows to a near stop.

When I wake, all I can feel is ravaged by my relationship to this place. I have a disturbing sense that this place is real, not just in my dream, and it has called to me *through* my dream. The Great White Tree in this old-growth forest, with a creek cascading down from its roots, is the life source of the whole forest ecosystem — and it is in some sense *my* place, my unique way of serving the forest ecosystem, its life cycles.

This glimpse of mythopoetic identity underscores how soul purpose is fundamentally ecological, not cultural. Soul did not call Matt to be a pastor — or take on any other religious, social, or vocational role — but rather to inhabit a particular ecological niche, metaphorically that of the Great White Tree.

Together, these two nightworld encounters catalyzed an evolution in Matt's understanding of his mythos — both a deepening and an elaboration. He still recognized his soul task to be the composting and bridging of worlds but now he understood he is to do this by drawing on the powers of Snake Root and the psycho-ecological niche of the Great White Tree:

> I am Snake Root Medicine of the White Tree, whose taproot reaches down into the heart of the World. The White Tree's life-blood flows through me, both as the medicine of Bridger and as the toxin I deliver as Decomposer of Worlds. My ancestral and archetypal roots compost the dying myths and images of Western culture and religion that have enabled humanity to exploit and damage Earth. I am one root system participating in the rewiring of our collective psychospiritual synapses to facilitate ecological awakening, deeper participation in the more-than-human world, and an understanding of our place and purpose in the imagination of the Cosmos.
>
> My intention is to help others remember, reclaim, and reimagine the ancient and wild root at the heart of the Christian mythos. Many of its images — the wild vine, the world tree, the root — are already embedded in the ancient scriptures.
>
> Much of Christian theology has split us off from our nature-based or-igins — from soul, from the deep feminine — and mislabeled it as "pagan," in this way suppressing everything truly wild that embeds us in Earth pro-cesses and consciousness. As a wild priest and shaman from my ancestral lineage, I am called to help *re-paganize* the Christian tradition — to rewild the scriptures, practices, and sacraments, restoring their original psychoac-tive power as medicine.

Soon after these two dreams, Matt entered the passage of Soul Initiation, which felt like "an urgent shift in my energy, like a deeper power was now working through me. I feel I am now living in the place that had been waiting for me my whole life."

Having entered the Wellspring, Matt dedicated himself to the development of his delivery systems. One has been the creation of a "wild church," a community he calls the Church of Lost Walls. He offers daylong immersions and evening gather-ings for pastors, priests, and people who are spiritual but not religious. He embod-ies the role of a "priest of the Wild," employing consciousness-shifting practices to reclaim the "original psychoactive agency" of liturgy, sacrament, and prayer — and in this way help people commune more deeply with one another and with the land. "Church of Lost Walls," he says, "is my local compost where I bridge worlds."

In his roles of preacher, teacher, and writer, Matt composts the Christian tra-dition in a variety of ways. He uses some of the oldest images in Christianity — the animistic motifs of the ancient Hebrew prophets and mystics — to deconstruct the conventional religious scaffolding in which those images have become enshrined ("entombed," as he says). The contemporary church, for example, holds that humans were given "dominion" over the Earth. This perspective reinforces our separateness or alienation from the greater Earth community. One of the creation myths in Genesis, however, offers the image of Adam having been formed from the ground itself (*adamah*), in the same way as all other living things.

> The Human is planted in the mythic garden, to "cultivate and serve" the ground. This is our sacred vocation. Breaking down the anthropocentric images into their more chthonic "ground" frees us from the hubris that has led us to this moment of disaster — the desacralization of Earth, the "body of God," the first incarnation.

Another conventional motif of the mainstream Christian establishment is *imago dei*, the doctrine that humans, unlike the rest of Creation, were created in the image of God. Like a gardener working a compost pile, Matt takes such "dead images" and turns them over with "ancient images from oral animistic and even 'pagan' worldviews" — images like *adamah*, or that of another Hebrew word, *nephesh* (meaning "animate soul" or "sentience," a quality shared by all living creatures), or what the ancient Celts called the "big book of nature." These are wild images that, because of their danger to the establishment, were split off during the emergence of the Christian church.

When working with groups, Matt invokes these older, wilder images and then invites his participants to wander on the land of their own watersheds while engaged in practices rooted in these images. He also weaves these images into prayer, dreamwork, and deep-imagery journeys. Some participants find themselves resisting, while others experience intense grief, joy, or wonder. Both of these reactions, Matt notes, are signs of the start of a composting process: a conventional Christian image — like *imago dei* — breaking down as consciousness opens to "the wound of our collective 'exile' that is rooted in our own theological inheritance and Christian cultural history."

Matt is also creating, with his colleagues, a two-year nature-based training program to support religious leaders to "rewild" their churches and seminaries, to "reclaim the wild roots of the Christian story and cultivate a sacred relationship with Earth." This is the next phase of the Seminary of the Wild. Their intention is to create "true Sabbath spaces in the original sense: a way of being in relation to the wild land and the sacred seasonal rhythms." For Matt, this is a way to "create mycelial networks between communities" and "connect with the ancient root system and the primal medicine of soul."

The embodiment of mythopoetic identity is soul work and it is always visionary action, the work of cultural evolution. It is always difficult work — in addition to being joyous and fulfilling. When performed within an unhealthy, egocentric society like ours, the embodiment of mythopoetic identity supports cultural therapy and renaissance. It is risky in any society because it creates change, but it's especially risky in an egocentric society because it is, by definition, subversive to that society. In a time like ours when the old cultural forms are collapsing, soul work is countercultural because nature always introduces what is needed, what is missing. And Soul — as ecological niche — *is* nature.

Matt's soul work is clearly disrupting and composting in relation to the culture of Christianity as well as to conformist-consumer culture, more generally. It is equally visionary, evolutionary, and revolutionary in support of engendering a future healthy, ecocentric, life-enhancing culture. His work, like that of all soul-initiated Adults, has the potential to transform whole cultural systems.

Enactment: Embracing the Relationships Inherent in Our Ecological Niche

Inhabiting and enacting our unique eco-niche is an ecological undertaking more than a vocational one. It's a matter of acting and being in resonance with the set of relationships that *is* that niche. Living a soul-initiated life is not, of course, a matter of pursuing fame or fortune nor of strategically choosing our path in life independent of the larger world that makes our existence possible; rather, a soul-initiated life embraces the opportunities made possible by inhabiting our niche and fulfilling its imperatives. It's more a matter of allowing our niche to direct us than carving out a niche for ourself.

Matt works as a pastor in a church and as a trainer in a seminary, but his niche is Compost Bridger of Worlds who carries the Snake Root Medicine of the White Tree. His primary question is not, *What can or should a pastor do or a trainer accomplish?* but rather, *What are the opportunities and invitations that arise when I show up in any setting as Compost Bridger?* Silver Moon's foremost questions are not about how to make a big splash as an actress or a living as a poet but how to embody She Who Becomes Her Blood and how to respond when openings appear to evoke "the fierce and wildly erotic feminine" — in herself and others. The relationships she's attuned to concern, primarily, how the wild feminine manifests (or doesn't) in specific settings and individuals and in both the counterculture and the dominant/dominator overculture. *Where is the wild feminine suppressed? Where is it boldly embodied? Where is it just now emerging from the shadows? What can I do to coax it out, celebrate it, be it?*

The greatest opportunity and challenge for soul-initiated Adults and Elders is to get out of the way of the Mystery as it moves through them. Their eco-niche consists of a bundle of particular relationships with other beings and places — and the opportunities those relationships make possible, the avenues their niche propels or guides or eases them to rove. Soul-initiated Adults are constantly learning how to detect those opportunities and helping those opportunities become manifest by creatively performing their unique, innate roles in the Earth community. This is not the Adolescent hero striving for victory and prevailing against all odds. It is the Adult visionary artisan manifesting what the world has made possible by virtue of the psycho-ecological relationships inherent in their niche.

We might imagine, for example, that, after Soul Initiation, Yeats didn't awake in the morning and wonder what play or poem he could write that day that might appeal to current taste or style, but rather, what apples might appear that were ripe for the plucking.

Christie: Piercing the Deepest Unclaimed Territories of the Heart

Christie completed the Metamorphosis phase of her first Descent when she danced with her bow beneath a beloved maple and shot an arrow for the first time (see "Dancing with Mystery," pages 286–88). Two months later, Christie noticed, to her surprise, that her inner protectors seemed to have relaxed, apparently accepting her shift in identity:

> I awoke one morning last week and, in the midst of fixing coffee, found myself noticing an absence. It was the "sudden" lack of that persistent sense of resistance, confusion, overwhelm, and doubt that has been with me since glimpsing my soul identity two years ago on my vision fast. It is as if a simple relaxation into being has happened in the dreamtime rather than through any effortful surrender.

This "relaxation into being" freed her to more fully sink into, embody, and enact the eco-niche of Beautiful Huntress: She increasingly experienced herself as Huntress/Protectress and felt a natural impulse to engage the world from the compassion, heartbreak, and vulnerability inherent in her soul identity. Although her Ego was still changing shape, her center of gravity was migrating from Metamorphosis, with its steady alterations of the psyche, to Enactment, with its focus on world-engaging service. She sensed this had been made possible by a kind of self-inflicted wound that amplified her capacity to be present to the world in all its beauty and tragedy:

> I am getting a taste of my own medicine: I am experiencing what happens *after* the arrows "pierce to the deepest unclaimed territories of the heart" — in this case, my *own* heart. It is as if the altered structure of my heart can no longer defend or contain itself. I am left with a sensitivity that is challenging to carry, such is the extent of my perception of exquisite tenderness and beauty everywhere, and such is the extent of my heartbreak at the pervasiveness of hurt, carelessness, and desecration. It is a staggering level of vulnerability.

Getting a taste of our own Soul medicine occurs often toward the end of a Descent. Mystery arranges for us to be subject to the effect of our own Soul power. This appears to be an essential part of the apprenticeship. Christie's heart was pierced by her own arrows, which are "harbingers of truth" and catalysts for death-rebirth. For me, through the process of learning to guide vision fasts, I ended up weaving a cocoon for my own transformation. Silver Moon, having been shown that her place is to help women become their Blood, was then instructed by her Muse to lock herself away for three moon cycles in order to listen to what the Blood wants her to say. Jung had to confront his own unconscious before he could help others do it.

Christie's newly amplified heart sensitivity and vulnerability moved her to enact a ceremony in which she pledged herself to action in service to the Earth community (such service being the essence of the Enactment phase):

> This week on the news there was a report of someone on Vancouver Island killing a black bear with an overt and entire lack of respect for the magnificence of its being — harvesting parts of its body and discarding the rest without any apparent care or consideration. Fury found me first, with visions of myself as a vigilante patrolling the woods, leaping out at just the right moment to instill a clear lesson. Then deep grief. I feel obligated to do something, but what is my right action? I took a small first step yesterday. I held a ceremony to acknowledge the slain bear, offered a lament, and pledged my allegiance to the kin of this bear so that maybe somewhere in the fabric of things there will be a stitch in the tear.

With this pledge, Christie was not merely embodying Beautiful Huntress in a way that changed her Ego, as in Metamorphosis, but leaning toward Jegermeister-type action that would directly change the world, *action made possible by her altered identity and Ego*. The emphasis was shifting from Ego transformation to world transformation.

A couple of weeks later, Christie spoke at a live storytelling event — a big stretch for someone so shy. She had responded to a call for "Expressions of Intimacy." Beyond being a performance, this was an early initiative in her Enactment phase, which is to say, an embodiment of her vision for her people to see and be affected by. What makes this more than an ETC is that its intent was not primarily to reshape her Ego but to serve others by using the archetypal intentions and powers of Beautiful Huntress. She wanted to convey the idea that intimacy can include our human relationships with wild others and wild places. Here are her notes introducing her story of an enchanted interaction with a grasshopper:

> I want to speak of times so sacred I can scarcely find the language. You see, I think it is possible, necessary even, to restore a right relationship between Humans and the Wild Others. One where humans are not in the role of saviors, nor of forces of destruction, but instead in genuine

partnership — intimate companions, even. For us to be willing to reveal the peculiarities of our humanness and to offer back our attention, praise, and love for the Other is to begin a new kind of relationship. I am humbled and grateful for what I am learning from the Ones who appear in the times when I allow my presence to carry the vulnerability of longing for genuine connection, without expectation.

With this public storytelling, Christie embodied Beautiful Huntress in her community and felt the effects she has on others while in this role. Enactment actions further our shape-shifting but they also impact others and our shared community, supporting our collective world to come alive again. And they prepare us for the life passage of Soul Initiation.

The following February, Christie said her subpersonalities seemed to have adjusted to her mythos:

> I sense that I am now carrying an acceptance of my ecological niche; a greater understanding of what is being asked of me; and a deeper faith that learning how to live as Beautiful Huntress could indeed become a life-enhancing offering to the Earth community.

In Christie's story, we see a common pattern of what takes place during the phase shift from Metamorphosis to Enactment: As the Ego is reshaped, the subpersonalities (of all four directions) become increasingly alarmed and attempt to sabotage the transformation. This is why many people during Metamorphosis are plagued with self-doubts and sometimes a variety of distractions, addictions, anxieties and depressions, and projections and possessions. The Metamorphosis practices, then, bring about both progress and regression. But as the shape-shifting proceeds, the subs gradually become comfortable with what is for them a new identity, a new niche. Perhaps the subs become convinced that the Ego has new and more mature strategies for self-care and that their childhood survival strategies are not needed as much. Perhaps the subs also become resigned that the Ego has made an irreversible commitment.

As of this writing, Christie is still primarily in the Enactment phase of her first Descent, but she may also be nearing the passage of Soul Initiation, the transition from the Cocoon stage to the Wellspring. Her primary orientation is shifting from soul discovery to soul embodiment. Perhaps the easefulness she has enjoyed over the past year is a feature of the radical simplification that takes place following the commitment to Soul that is the primary sign of Soul Initiation.

What delivery system(s) will she be drawn to cultivate? Too soon to tell, but given the archetypal pairings of Bow and Bear, Arrow and Artemis, Protectress and Huntress, and Love and Death, she's likely to violate a cultural boundary or two and pierce some deep and unclaimed territories of the Western heart.

Elisabeth: Dancing Her Song into the World

Elisabeth, She Who Dances the Earth and Dreams Song to Feed the Longing, had a rather rough time during Metamorphosis (see "Elisabeth's Formidable Metamorphosis," pages 256–62), but through her wholing and Self-healing work, she recovered quite well, despite the unavailability in her Australian community of human Elders:

> By trusting that there are still true elders all around me — in the call of birds, in the touch of the wind, in the way that the ocean holds me — I was able to cultivate compassion rather than contempt for my culture and thus begin to find a way back in to my people.

Elisabeth's early Enactment activities included land restoration work and teaching restoration ecology at a college, work that's related to what she had done in her earlier vocation but now enacted as She Who Dances the Earth — the thread she follows:

> As I matured into a somatic way of knowing my mythopoetic, I found that I could be true to the Song of the Unseen Woman anywhere, anytime, as it was a way of being in the world more than anything. As I completed what seemed like one task offered by Mystery, the next would arrive and I found that the more I just focused on what was before me, tending that task from my mythopoetic way of being, the next would be another step toward Her.

As one example, Elisabeth now leads nature-based programs two days a week in her community, programs she designed with the Cornman's instructions in mind: "You must stand up for what is wrong with your people":

> I have sat with this instruction for many years and believe that the prime failure of my people is simply that we have forgotten the sacred, we have forgotten the language of love that weaves all things together in the true economy of reciprocity whether that is through praise, song, wonder, or actual gifting of time and work. One of the key components of these programs is awe and wonder for the mystery, the sanctity of life. Deep reverence for the world is a good place to start a relationship of kinship. This is one of the ways I dance Her song into the world.

Elisabeth was surprised she loved returning to her previous profession. But she has done so with a different perspective and motive — namely, "to serve life":

> I had a preconceived idea that the journey of soul initiation would mean my "career" would no longer be right or relevant and that I would be propelled to make a massive change into some other work. I now see that my professional roles were just too small — because *I* needed to become bigger, not because my career necessarily needed to change.

If you were to spend a few hours with Elisabeth, it would be evident from her infectious enthusiasm and her innovative projects that she is something rare in the world today — a visionary sowing seeds of cultural renewal, a revolutionary feeding our collective longing to re-member the sacred.

FeatherStone: A Tether between Dream and Earth

During the soul initiation journey of the river-restoration ecologist Kevin Lloyd Fetherston, he discovered that he has the soul power to understand, through dreams and visions, the land's needs and desires (see "FeatherStone: The Tethered Feather and the Fire Sand Mandala," pages 209–20). He learned, through a series of soul en-counters, that he is a conduit between dream (feather) and Earth (stone). By "teth-ering" or "grounding" the etheric or invisible — the images of the dreamtime — he serves as a channel of communication between invisible beings or processes and his people or place. This is his eco-niche. It is the thread he follows. Restoration ecology is not his eco-niche; it's his delivery system.

FeatherStone's soul power is made possible, in part, by his atypical neurology — his open sensory gating system. At age thirty, a psychiatrist told him that he had, essen-tially, a "broken brain," and he believed it as, tragically, most people do when they hear such things from someone who's supposed to know what they're talking about (see "FeatherStone's Descent to Hell," pages 215–17). What FeatherStone learned through his journey of soul initiation is that his brain, although it operates outside the norm, is not at all broken. Rather, his neurological makeup enables what he calls "a direct heart perception of the soul of the land, of the Earth community." A person with this capac-ity is a great boon to the more-than-human community. In a healthier culture, such a gift would be recognized in childhood and nurtured by parents, cultivated with the help of mentors, shaped and guided by the wisdom of Elders. FeatherStone recognized and developed his gift through a more challenging route but one that was nonetheless blessed by the guidance of Mystery, Soul, dreamworld teachers, the land and waters, and some better-late-than-never human friends and mentors.

Flooded by Wild Powers

For many years now, FeatherStone has embodied and enacted his mythopoetic iden-tity through his delivery system of forest and river ecology. He is a consultant to organizations and governmental agencies throughout the American West, including Alaska, as well as the East Coast. He has also taught and trained ecology students at the University of Washington's Stream Restoration Program — a program he helped create.

Much of FeatherStone's work has been rooted in a particular place, his spiritual homeland: the westside rivers of the Olympic Peninsula that flow from the Olympic peaks to the Pacific Ocean through ancient, old-growth rain forests. This is the setting of his Salmon Woman dream, which initiated his apprenticeship to the mythic caregiver for the salmon, the rivers, and the forests of the Pacific Northwest. Many years ago, the final field trip for his dissertation research was a weeklong float down one of those Olympic rivers, the Queets. At the end of the trip, after he and his colleague finished packing their gear in their truck, FeatherStone walked back down to the river alone.

> Looking up valley I bowed in gratitude and gave thanks to the spirits of the Queets River that had held me during the many years of my research. I vowed to care for and protect that valley the rest of my life. In that moment, with my feet rooted in river gravel, the Queets River roared through my being. It felt as if my body was being flooded by wild powers, unknown beings coursing through me. I knew there was no resisting. I could only blend with these overpowering forces in a way similar to what I had learned in the martial art of aikido. I felt my inner being aligning with these river energies and spirits pouring through me. It felt as if I was becoming a conduit between the ineffable world of the wild Queets River and my everyday world. The power and beauty of this wild place shook me to my core.

This moment of communion was a soul encounter, an initiation deeper into "the ecocosmological beauty of the Earth" that FeatherStone first glimpsed years earlier when his dreamworld elder, Grandfather of the Desert Night, taught him to carefully observe and feel the downward-flowing spiral of the Fire Sand Mandala, a template for observing and studying the natural patterns of the wild world. This was "a direct heart perception of the wild powers" of that river, its valley, and its ancient rain forests. In that moment, his psyche was aligned with and began to be altered *by* those wild powers. He experienced this as a gift from the Queets after his four years in the heart of her wild expanses, seeking to understand the ecological processes that create and sustain her valley forest landscape. FeatherStone heard and felt the invitation extended to him by the Queets — to become a conduit between the river and the everyday world — and he said yes. Being that conduit was one of his early Enactment practices.

Communiqué from a Glowing Cottonwood

FeatherStone has helped the Quinault Indian Nation develop and implement their visionary restoration of the Quinault, another westside river of the Olympics. The Quinault and its valley forest are home of the legendary blueback sockeye salmon, iconic to the Quinault people. Forest clear-cutting, starting in the early 1900s, had unraveled the river's channels, floodplains, and sloughs, causing the crash of the local salmon population.

FeatherStone recognized the request for collaboration with the Quinault Nation not only as an opportunity to exercise his skills as a forest ecologist but, more significantly, as an invitation to embody his heartfelt vow to care for and protect the forest communities of the western Olympics. At the same time, it was an opportunity to embody his mythopoetic identity as a tether between feather and stone, as a student of Grandfather and the Fire Sand Mandala, and as an apprentice to Salmon Woman. FeatherStone's work with the Quinault community is an example of how a soul-initiated life is not so much a matter of strategically and autonomously choosing what actions to take but of embracing the opportunities made possible by inhabiting one's niche and fulfilling its imperatives. He allowed his niche to direct him.

One dimension of FeatherStone's restoration work on the Quinault concerned its forests. There are now few cottonwoods in the upper river valley because the elk eat most of the seedlings. In earlier times, the elk population had been kept in ecological balance by the wolves that roamed the Olympics. After the extirpation of the Quinault wolves in the early twentieth century, the cottonwoods in the valley floodplains began to disappear. This has profoundly impacted the ecosystem because this tree is an essential member, providing eagle and osprey nesting sites, among many other ecological benefits.

During a recent winter, after a long day conducting forest surveys in Olympic National Park, FeatherStone was headed home. As he drove across the Upper Quinault River bridge, he looked up valley and saw, glowing in the waning light of sunset, a lone thirty-foot cottonwood emerging above a stand of young red alders on a midchannel island. Something about this cottonwood — felt by FeatherStone through direct heart perception — moved him to stop his truck midbridge. He got out. He waded across the river channel to the tree. There, on the island, in addition to the one glowing cottonwood were hundreds of others just three feet tall — a miniature forest that would grow no taller due to the browsing elk.

> I walked the island for a time gathering my feelings. What was cottonwood offering me? Then a burst of understanding came directly into my heart from my feelings for this glowing tree: We simply could not plant cottonwoods in open floodplain sites. I lived with this encounter for days considering its meaning, after which I changed my silviculture approach: This spring we will gather cottonwood seeds. We will grow seedlings in nursery beds and then plant them within logjams that we'll engineer and in other natural wood-jam sites the elk are wary to step into.

Other scientists and ecologists might have eventually come to the same conclusion, but FeatherStone arrived on that island when he did because he was captured by a glowing cottonwood. "It was like a tractor beam pulling me in." The cottonwood had called to him, he heard-felt the call, and he responded. His ability to receive that heart communication was made possible not only by a personal capacity — his wide-open sensory gating system — but also by the relationship he had formed over many years with that particular river valley. It was made possible also through his apprenticeship with Salmon Woman and by his soul powers that enable him to connect image (feather) to the land (stone) and to see the deep-structure mandala patterns of particular ecosystems.

Good Manners: Cultivating Relationships with Earth Communities

As a soul-initiated Adult, FeatherStone is able to interweave the use of his soul powers with his skills and knowledge as an ecological scientist, naturalist, and horticulturalist. He uses the "communiqués" he receives from the natural world to design the scientific studies that form the basis of his restoration projects. FeatherStone possesses a particular kind of genius that many other contemporary scientists, ecologists, and river engineers lack — or have not yet cultivated: the ability to participate with the Earth and to directly perceive nature through feeling and imagination (his "feminine" South and West windows of knowing), or what he calls "imaginal play."[11] This makes all the difference in his capacity to serve the more-than-human community, which includes, for example, the Quinault River, all the plants and animals of the Quinault watershed, and the Quinault Indian Nation.

FeatherStone *participates* with the Earth communities he serves. Through years of study and dwelling on, in, and with the land, he has cultivated relationships with these places; he is a participating member of these communities and is committed to their care. "It's quite simply good manners," he says. He begins his relationship with a place by introducing himself to the land and its creatures and then requesting guidance from them. As he proceeds, he makes formal, ceremonial commitments to the place. This enables him to access the "wild intelligences of a valley, a river, a forest." He cooperates with the land and its creatures to create and manifest restoration plans that maximize the ability of all beings to flourish. This is all part of his Wellspring apprenticeship with Salmon Woman, through which he has come to more deeply understand his soul gifts, "further dimensions of my nature as a conduit between the ineffable and the observed worlds I have dedicated my life to" — a thread between Feather and Stone.

Through scientific measurements as well as observations informed by his heart perceptions, FeatherStone learns how humans can best support the flourishing of life and the full natural biodiversity of a place.

> I *see* the Quinault River restoration as a living mandala made up of the entire Earth community of the valley — Quinault Indians, blueback salmon, upper valley timber community, mountain lions, osprey, elk, eagle, ancient rain forest, and the Olympic Mountains. I see this living mandala unfolding before my eyes as the regenerative coming together of the entire Earth

community of this place. As an ecologist — an Earth doctor — I see this as
the only way forward at this time of great ecological crisis.

Engaging as an ecologist with the Quinault mandala is, for FeatherStone, a way
of keeping faith with the teachings of the Fire Sand Mandala, as he described in his
original dream-vision:

> Together Grandfather and I study the currents and eddies. Slowly, carefully,
> he picks up small sticks and rocks…and places them into the river. The
> streaming currents shift and change with each set object.

Etiquette of the Wild

In his work, FeatherStone brings a new/old way of cultivating relationships between
the land, waters, and human communities — what Gary Snyder calls the "etiquette
of the wild." FeatherStone's unique way of articulating and manifesting this etiquette
was made possible by his courageous navigation of the journey of soul initiation.
With hindsight we can see the early manifestations of FeatherStone's genius in his
shape-shifting experiences as a boy wandering along the shores of Lake Michigan,
where "the Great Weather taught me that the boundaries of my skin were actually
fluid and porous to the energies of the great storms that would take me away." Although such experiences are possible for all of us, FeatherStone has much easier access than most, enabling his soul work of Earthcare in partnership with all members
of the web of life, including his fellow humans.

> My so-called "severe debilitating lifelong mental illness" is actually my gift,
> my soul power to contribute to the caring for the Earth. I have come to cel-
> ebrate my abilities to see and feel our other-than-human sisters and broth-
> ers. I have been called into their communities, into their lives in ways that
> seem fantastic to the boxes of the modern Western mind.

The cutting-edge, visionary work of soul-initiated ecologists like FeatherStone
embodies what we might suppose to be an essential thread of the dream of the
Earth — that we humans might once again learn, in FeatherStone's words, "to honor,
celebrate, and more closely align with the deeper ecological order of life, so that all
beings may thrive." Along with other innovative restoration ecologists (and perma-
culturalists, rewilders, and regenerative agriculturalists), FeatherStone is pioneering
new methods of learning from the land and of partnering with Earth to support her
dreaming. Doing so is foundational to cultural renewal, evolution, and revolution.

Joanna Macy's Delivery Systems: The Great Turning

Joanna Macy's two soul encounters inspired and made possible her soul work as an
international leader in cultural transformation and evolution (see "Joanna Macy:

The Great Turning Wheel and the Stone in the Bridge," pages 172–77). Her first vision — of the Great Turning Wheel — directly shifted her Ego by gifting her with two things: the somatic and psychospiritual experience of paired opposites as the essential structure "at the heart of reality," and a liberation from her fear of the hole inside her that had formed when, in her early twenties, she left Christianity. This hole, around which the Great Wheel turns, became for her a symbol of the necessary not-knowing at the center of the human psyche.

Her second vision endowed her with a core element of her mythopoetic identity — the image of a stone in a bridge "between the thoughtworlds of East and West, connecting the insights of the Buddha Dharma with the modern Western mind."

How did these two visions animate her eventual delivery systems?

Becoming the Stone

In 1969, after living in Asia and Africa for several years, Joanna and her family returned to the United States and settled in Washington, DC. This was at the time of the Vietnam War, and Joanna became active in the antiwar movement. She was forty. Three years after her Stone in the Bridge revelation and twelve years after her Great Turning Wheel vision, she was still in the Enactment phase of her Descent, not yet having identified or chosen a delivery system. She was seeking a cultural setting in which to embody what her soul encounters had moved in her. She began with a part-time job with a civil rights organization and became a speechwriter for a Black politician. These were Enactment projects: "The civil rights work and these antiwar actions helped me take even more seriously than before the mystical openings I had experienced."[12]

After a few years of actively living the question of how she might become a Stone in the Bridge, she decided, at forty-three, to enter graduate school in world religions with a focus on Buddhist philosophy. "Maybe I could find a way to translate the Buddha's understanding of self — or non-self — into a Western mode, to help my countrypeople come home to each other and play their part in building a world not based on fear."[13]

Early in her graduate studies, she noticed a core pattern in the work of certain progressive Western poets and thinkers:

> ...a loss of belief in that pillar of Western thought: the autonomy of the individual self....How delusory was the separate, Cartesian ego, and how imprisoning its pretensions. So I began to see my own response to the Buddha Dharma as part of a larger paradigmatic shift in the West, as an urge arising within the Western mind — the urge to reconnect.[14]

In particular, Joanna was tracking correspondences between the Buddha Dharma and the work of two Western writers: the American poet Theodore Roethke and the Argentinean novelist Jorge Luis Borges. Through this Enactment project, she was bridging East and West — and seeing that the Buddha possessed a more mature and expansive vision that could help the modern West take its next steps in understanding the nature of the self.

Joanna was in the process of choosing her first delivery system for her soul work, a way to be a Stone in the Bridge: She would become a scholar both of Buddhism and of the germinal Western urge to move beyond the delusion of an unembedded self and to reconnect with the world through a greater identity. Making this choice marked her passage of Soul Initiation.

During her second year of grad school, Joanna came across a Buddhist scripture that "broke into my life," altered her understanding of Buddhism, and eventually became the conceptual hub of her work. This is the teaching known as *Prajna Paramita*, or the Perfection of Wisdom, the core insight of dependent co-arising that, because of its pivotal position in Buddhism, has been personified as the Mother of all Buddhas:

> Wisdom is not about bits and pieces, she said, it's about relationship. It's about the compassion that comes when we realize our deep relatedness. In this fashion, she brought forth in new words the Buddha's central teaching: the dependent co-arising of all phenomena.[15]

This core insight of interbeing — or, as I like to express it, ecologically, everything is what it is by virtue of its relationships with everything else — became known as the Second Turning of the Wheel (of the Buddha Dharma). Likewise, in the evolution of Joanna's soul work, her discovery of *Prajna Paramita* was the second turning of the wheel that she first saw as a vision at her son's birth, some fifteen years earlier. This second turning was a pivotal event in her scholarly exploration of the fruitful resonance between Buddhist thought and contemporary Western science. Her intention, at the time, was to "make new translations of the Perfection of Wisdom scriptures and to write commentaries on them."[16]

A Third Soul Encounter: The Tree and the Neural Net (Systems Theory)

But then, while still in the early years of her Wellspring stage, Joanna experienced a third soul encounter that resulted in a significant modification in her work. In the fall of 1974, she asked for and received a blessing from a visiting Tibetan Buddhist sage, His Holiness Karmapa. While the Karmapa held her head in his hands, she felt an electric charge shoot through her. "That's all — except that I barely slept for the next three weeks." Each night, she sat awake as words, images, and thoughts resounded in her psyche, "a torrent of revelation":

> In shifting patterns of breathtaking elegance all that I had ever learned, from Descartes to Jesus to the Buddha Dharma — all I'd seen and known

and been — suddenly fit together.... The laws that governed the interplay of forms — bringing forth worlds and dissolving them — were comprehensible to me then, but all that I can now recall are the images. Two visual themes predominated. One was the tree, with its branching limbs and roots. The other was the neuron in the neural net, with its intricate dendrites and synaptic connections. In their continual self-transformations there wasn't one stable point, nothing to hang on to, but I felt no fear — just wonder and a kind of exultation."[17]

Toward the end of these weeks of sleepless nights, Joanna walked into a graduate seminar and first learned about general systems theory — a then-emerging field of Western science that describes patterns of energy, matter, and information that give rise to everything from cells to galaxies. "Almost immediately I saw that the systems view of reality fit the patterns that I had been seeing all those wakeful nights since the Karmapa's blessing."[18] Systems theory became a second essential strand of Joanna's first delivery system.

Joanna had previously thought hers was a one-way Bridge — from the ancient East to the modern West. But with systems theory, she saw the bestowal could go both ways. Each could illuminate the other. The West held something for the East. Systems theory, for example, could elucidate and expand on some aspects of Buddhism, as she demonstrated in her dissertation, later published in 1991 as *Mutual Causality in Buddhism and General Systems Theory: The Dharma of Natural Systems*. In this book, Joanna offers a fresh, Western interpretation of the Buddha's core teaching of dependent co-arising.

In 2019, Joanna told me she had begun to see an additional way the modern West can serve Buddhism: "The East needs to be freed of the patriarchy of the Buddha Dharma, freed where it adopted and perpetuated patriarchy."

Environmental Activism and the Work That Reconnects

A second delivery system for Joanna has been environmental activism, especially concerning the nuclear power and weapons industries. She has assisted citizens' legal interventions against nuclear polluters, participated in nonviolent occupations of reactor sites, and chaired conferences on environmental dangers and responses. Her dedication to this work came out of her deepening grief in the 1970s while discovering how industrial growth was rapidly devastating the living systems of Earth. Her vision of the Great Turning Wheel shifted and deepened her psyche in ways that enabled her to confront these horrors.

Later, in her Wild Orchard time (late Adulthood), Joanna envisioned and developed her own unique delivery system — the Work That Reconnects, a paradigm-shifting model and methodology for personal and social transformation for which she is now well known. Also called Despair and Empowerment Work, this is, as she describes it, "a form of group work designed to foster the desire and ability to take part in the healing of our world." Courtesy of her vision of the Great Turning Wheel, Joanna gained the confidence that she — and all of us — could survive our despair over the possible catastrophic end of earthly life through nuclear holocaust, climate disruption, or mass extinction. In the Work That Reconnects, Joanna and her colleagues support people to submerge into the depths of that despair and not only survive it but emerge ready and empowered to lend heart and hands to what Joanna calls the Great Turning — the shift from the "Industrial Growth Society" (another term for what I call the consumer-conformist culture) to a life-sustaining civilization. Joanna says the Great Turning is "the essential adventure of our time," the opportunity to offer the future "the biggest gift we can give."

> The most remarkable feature of this historical moment on Earth is not
> that we are on the way to destroying the world — we've actually been on
> the way for quite a while. It is that we are beginning to wake up, as from a
> millennia-long sleep, to a whole new relationship to our world, to ourselves
> and each other.[19]

Joanna has been a leading activist internationally for over fifty years. Her visionary work has infused and inspired a variety of cultural systems, including movements for peace, justice, a safe environment, and personal development. She has carried and dispersed many seeds for cultural renewal, evolution, and revolution.

Our most effective activism is both motivated and powered by our conscious connection to our unique ecological niche, our soul story or image, the thread we follow. Joanna's inspired life and work are luminous testaments to this principle.

Sabina's Metamorphosis, Soul Initiation, Wellspring, and Wild Orchard

The Swiss woman Sabina Wyss returned from her vision fast on a Colorado mountain with the soul task to bring her people "here" and to embody her mythopoetic identity of Spark Heart on Bear Path (see "Sabina: Spark Heart on Bear Path," pages 168–72). At the time, she had no understanding of where or what "here" was, or even, with any certainty, who her people were, or for that matter, what it meant to be Spark Heart on Bear Path. But her ecopoetic calling now lived in her somatic awareness and began reshaping her Ego.

During Metamorphosis, Sabina did not have the concept of Experimental Threshold Crossings — or any near equivalent — but she was convinced that, if she kept listening, Soul would guide her in her initial attempts at showing up as Spark Heart.

> I only knew it had something to do with inner work that cracks people
> open (like the Spark) and helps them go toward their essence (Soul). Those

were my only clues, so I went with them. I had a deep feeling-sensing-intuiting, not a cognitive understanding. I went for it in the way Bear taught me — steadfast, calm and deep, keep at it, keep going.

Sabina had been working as a homeopath. After her fast, she continued this vocation for a while, but as Spark Heart, she moved beyond simply administering remedies; she began to guide her clients on inner explorations that might "crack them open" and reveal the deeper cause of their physical symptoms. She started to lead small groups in depth-energy work and "nature-soul" walks. These were some of her Enactment practices, in which she employed the skills and knowledge she had developed before her Descent but now utilized to follow the thread of the Bear Path.

By age thirty-two, Sabina had passed through the gate of Soul Initiation, and her primary focus had become the lived question of the Wellspring: how best to embody her mythopoetic identity — her eco-niche. She was ready to choose and begin cultivating her first delivery system for embodying Spark Heart as a gift to her world.

Because she had experienced her primary soul encounter on a vision fast, she felt that this ancient ceremony might be the "here" she would bring her people to, at least in part and at first. She became an apprentice at Animas Valley Institute and, in time, began to guide soulcentric immersions. After a few years, she was guiding her own vision fasts — in the Sahara, in remote sites accessed by multiday camelback journeys.

During this period, Sabina discovered another delivery system for her soul work. She learned about the emerging professional field of life coaching and enrolled in a training program. Coaching became a second way for her to bring her people "here."

A Wellspring Soul Encounter: Silver and Golden Crosses

During this period, still early in her Wellspring, Sabina had an additional soul encounter, this time assisted by a sacred medicine, peyote, in a ceremony led by an experienced Western guide. During the ceremony, she had a vision of "balanced" crosses (with equal-length arms) made of gold or silver. Precious gemstones accented the four ends and the center. During the vision, she was shown that these crosses were to be placed in people's homes or on the front of their houses and that they were to be used "to direct the energy of the people toward the center (toward their next step on the journey toward Soul)."

At first, she took her vision literally: She believed she was being asked to fashion physical crosses for people she worked with. She just didn't see how she could do this without interrupting the work she had already committed to. So, she didn't. For a long time she felt guilty.

Years later she realized she had been manifesting her vision all along: These were symbolic crosses whose four cardinal points represented the four facets of innate human wholeness; they were to be put up on people's "*inner* walls." The crosses were resources to "direct the energy of the people," and as Spark Heart on Bear Path, her task was to help people find their direction by leading them down the spiral path into the center (their Soul). This, she realized, is what it means for her to "bring your people here," each one in their own way. Her role as a guide is to point people toward their next step:

> In my vision, the crosses had a wonderful, beautiful, shimmering flair as well as a fierceness. Love and fierceness. Being loving and fierce is living my mythopoetic identity: *Spark* comes with a *bam* — a clear, immediate, waking people up. *Heart* brings the huge love and tenderness people need on this path. *Bear/Path:* The crosses give people a map, a direction, the energy to go straight into the depth of Soul. In the vision, there was a very clear, almost demanding energy about the crosses, no new-age fluff. Fierce and loving. Like Bear.

At the Wellspring: Apprenticing to Her Soul Name

Sabina began the core Wellspring practice of living her mythopoetic identity at all times — for her, all four elements of Spark, Heart, Bear, and Path:

> Wherever I went, I started deep conversations with people. Everything else bored me. I spiraled down with them, with Bear in the lead, Sparking their curiosity to look deeper, and loving them (with my Heart) so they might trust their own depths.

It was not for many years, however, that it dawned on Sabina that the four directions of the pan-cultural wheel — the fourfold wholeness of the Self — are embedded in her name, and in the same order: E-Spark, S-Heart, W-Bear, N-Path.

· As the years unfolded, and it became increasingly clear to Sabina where the world was heading, she developed a growing sense of urgency, and she became, like Bear, fiercer with her clients. "This helped so much to get clients rolling quickly and deeply on their path."

She gradually came to see that she was developing a new profession she ended up calling "soulcentric coaching" — helping people uncover their deepest dreams or soul callings. This insight, with which her Muse was signaling a new and idiosyncratic life direction, suggested that Sabina was making the passage from the Wellspring stage (and the archetype of the Apprentice to Soul) to the Wild Orchard stage (and the archetype of the Artisan). In the Wild Orchard (stage six, late Adulthood), we find ourselves inspired and compelled to create our own never-before-seen delivery system — as a gift not only to individuals but also to the evolution of our culture. Sabina was forty at the time of this passage. She had been in the Wellspring approximately eight years.

Visionary Artistry: The Soulcentric Coaching School

A couple of years later, while Sabina was walking in the Swiss Alps, her Muse spoke to her and insisted she launch a new major life project. She heard the adamant voice as clearly as she would if someone had been standing next to her: *You need to start your own training program, your own school!* Just like that. Many people had been asking her to teach them how she works with people, but she had not taken the idea seriously. She asked her Muse to tell her more:

Do it now. It is high time. I asked when the actual training should start (hoping for two to three years to develop it). She said, *In a half year.* Fear and a quiet determination flooded me at the same time. It felt so right, even though I didn't have one word written about this school. But by now I knew that I didn't need to wait until it was all clear, that I could take active steps into the middle of not-knowing, that *this* is the way of growing into it. Spark Heart on Bear Path walks, trusting Bear (Soul) to guide her, spiraling down ever deeper toward the center.

When she got home, she covered her living room walls with flip-chart pages, grabbed some sticky notes, and sat down in the middle of the room and prayed. She asked her Muse to come through, to speak for Soul. Muse did:

Small tidbits, big chunks, concepts, ideas, different elements. It was one big mess. So much came flooding through me — for several days. There was a lot of meditation, love, enthusiasm, fear, disbelief, and everything else.

She organized all the ideas on her wall. This was the birth of her soulcentric coaching school. Then, a realization:

Oh, if Soul wants me to start in half a year, I need participants (duuhh). Oh, that means I need to tell people, invite them. *That* scared me. The syllabus was nowhere near done. I had only rough sketches.

So I took all my courage and created a one-page flyer and sent it to my rather small list of former coaching clients. I was so scared. I did not really know what I would teach. I was so afraid to promise something that I could not deliver. I did it anyway.

Within ten days, all twelve spaces in the first-ever soulcentric coaches training were filled.

So, Sabina began to write and design. She was in the flow. And despite her preference to have partners, she launched her school alone — well, at least without human colleagues. Later, she realized this had been necessary in order not to compromise her vision. In her dream-vision, after all, she is walking alone with Bear.

As of this writing, the Soulcentric Coaching School has been in operation, evolving, and expanding for nine years.[20] It's not an exaggeration to say that Sabina, her eventual colleagues, and her trainees have manifested a profession that had not previously existed, a new approach to coaching that not only employs unique concepts, perspectives, and practices, but more significantly, applies the fundamental intentions of coaching to a realm of human development very few in the Western world have yet to recognize — the journey of soul initiation.

All this began, twenty-six years earlier, with a young Swiss woman finding herself plummeting over the rim of Soul Canyon while she lay in bed amidst the rubble of her life. Within a couple of months, she was on a one-way flight to the "random" destination of Los Angeles, and then on a nine-month wander through the American Southwest and Central America. This is the way the journey unfolds — with mystery, psychospiritual and physical hazards, serendipity, intimate encounters with the land and its creatures, visions, spasms of profound self-doubt, loneliness and deep connection, allies and guides (both "inner" and "outer"), ceremony, joys, and ecstasies. And — if you have the faith and psychospiritual resources to stay the course and to follow the thread — the journey culminates in visionary artistry that endows your culture and the wider world with an essential piece of the human puzzle, a revolutionary piece needed to enable our species to once again become not only life-sustaining but life-enhancing evolutionary partners with the cosmos.

Jung's Enactment, Soul Initiation, Wellspring, and Wild Orchard

Near the end of his life, Carl Jung looked back on his Descent to Soul, begun fifty years earlier, and wrote:

> The knowledge I was concerned with, or was seeking, still could not be found in the science of those days. I myself had to undergo the original experience, and, moreover, try to plant the results of my experience in the soil of reality; otherwise they would have remained subjective assumptions without validity.[21]

Following Soul Encounter and Metamorphosis, what matters most is, in fact, to manifest our vision "in the soil of reality." Jung's first soul encounter, his channeling of the *Seven Sermons to the Dead*, was not something he could fully understand until he had dedicated many years to embodying it in his work, in his largest conversation with the world. This is the way it is for us all.

Jung's first Enactment project was his careful recordings of his deep-imagination journeys — reworking and redrafting them from his original journals (his "black books") into his folio-size *Red Book*, adding his commentaries and incorporating many of his paintings (see "Working with the Images," page 289). We can see this work as not only an ETC to support his Metamorphosis but also as a way to commence his service to others (Enactment). What was most important to him, after all, was to incorporate what he learned on his Descent into contemporary understandings of the human psyche. Before developing his delivery systems, what he had available to him were the skills and inclinations of an early-twentieth-century psychoanalyst: tending to and faithfully recording inner experience — his own as well as his patients'.

Jung's other actions during his Enactment phase included his founding, in 1916, of the Psychology Club (an association of his former patients and students), lectures he gave at the Psychology Club and elsewhere, his ongoing work with his patients, and several essays and books presenting his early ideas and concepts — efforts to translate some of the themes of the *Red Book* into the existing psychological language of his time.[22]

Soul Initiation: "The Great Work Begins"

Jung went through the passage of Soul Initiation in early 1922, when he was forty-six. Recall that Soul Initiation, the passage from the Cocoon to the Wellspring, occurs when we make "a promise it will kill us to break" and our center of gravity shifts from the discovery and exploration of Soul to the manifestation of Soul as a gift to others. At this turning of the trail, we get kicked out of the Mystery School of our late Adolescence and into our early Adult years of developing ways to deliver our soul work to the world.

This passage is what we see unfolding in the stunning conversation Jung had with his "soul" on January 5, 1922. His soul (by which, as a reminder, he means his anima or what I call the Guide to Soul or Muse) announced to him, "The great work begins." Jung didn't know what she meant. She elaborated, "The work that should now be undertaken. It is a great and difficult work. There is no time to sleep." Jung concurred and said he was ready. She told him it was time, then, to get busy manifesting his soul encounter (his "revelation," as she put it), in this way fiercely and effectively kicking him out of Mystery School:

> You should listen: to no longer be a Christian is easy. But what next? For more is yet to come. Everything is waiting for you. And you? You remain silent and have nothing to say. But you should speak. Why have you received the revelation? You should not hide it. You concern yourself with the form? Is the form important, when it is a matter of revelation?...I serve you and your calling.... Your calling comes first.[23]

Ye gods. This is as clear a demand for soul-infused action as I can imagine. But the fearful and hesitant Jung, perhaps making a last desperate attempt to play the innocent card, asked his "soul": "What is my calling?" Then the decisive reply: "The new religion and its proclamation." Boom. Just like that. This horrified Jung, as we might imagine. He felt woefully inadequate for such an undertaking — as every person at first feels about their soul work. But at least he understood that his Muse did not mean a literal new religion, not the proclaiming of a new prophetic revelation, but rather a new *psychology*, including its new way of understanding the nature of religion, religious experiences, and the making of religions.

Three days later, Jung's impatient soul/Muse *insisted* he begin the crafting of his delivery system. She told him, "You know everything that is to be known about the manifested revelation, but you do not yet live everything that is to be lived at this time."[24] Jung understood her admonishment and accepted it, but he complained he didn't know how. Soul/Muse responded with some vague but pivotal advice, "There is not much to say about this. It is not as rational as you are inclined to think. The way is symbolic." And with that, Jung was dragged through Soul Initiation and flung into the Wellspring. Now his task was to develop a delivery system for what he had learned and suffered during his long twelve years in the Cocoon (from 1909 to 1922; ages thirty-four to forty-six).

Delivery Systems: Gnosticism, Psychology, Alchemy, and Faust

To piece together his first delivery system, Jung did what most recent arrivals to the Wellspring do: He looked for existing systems — traditional or contemporary crafts, professional disciplines, or arts — that were resonant with his mythopoetic identity. In particular, he sought "evidence for the historical prefiguration of my inner experiences."[25] Without such evidence, he believed he could never validate his ideas about the psyche — ideas that sprang from his own Descent. The first thing he found was Gnosticism, an assemblage of religious ideas and traditions that originated in the first century CE among early Christian and Jewish sects. The Gnostics, like Jung, focused on personal spiritual knowledge rather than orthodox teachings and church authorities. Until 1926, Jung studied the Gnostic writers, but in the end found them to be of limited use for his purposes. Consequently, he turned back to the science and depth psychology of his day, which served as his primary delivery system for many years.

However, what Jung ultimately discovered to be most useful for the conceptual infrastructure of his work was alchemy, as a historical parallel, and Goethe's play *Faust*, as a literary one.

Through his study of alchemy, Jung illuminated the content of his own experiences as well as early-twentieth-century discoveries about the unconscious. He pored through a great number of medieval alchemical texts with their obscure and cryptic symbols, and eventually he started "a lexicon of key phrases with cross references."[26] He was ardently dedicated: "In the course of time I assembled several thousand such key phrases and words, and had volumes filled with excerpts." This kept him busy for more than a decade! Such is the devotion of an Apprentice in the Wellspring.

The experiences of the alchemists were, in a sense, my experiences, and their world was my world. This was, of course, a momentous discovery: I had stumbled upon the historical counterpart of my psychology of the unconscious.... When I pored over these old texts everything fell into place: the fantasy-images, the empirical material I had gathered in my [psychiatry] practice, and the conclusions I had drawn from it. I now began to understand what these psychic contents meant when seen in historical perspective.[27]

This is the sort of wild enthusiasm characteristic of a soul-initiated person who has found a resonant delivery system.

Jung also learned much about the psyche from *Faust*, which he had been studying since he was a teenager. Goethe provided him a second delivery system:

I regard my work on alchemy as a sign of my inner relationship to Goethe. Goethe's secret was that he was in the grip of that process of archetypal transformation which has gone on through the centuries.[28]

Jung, in other words, assembled his second Wellspring delivery system for his soul work by employing the historically existing achievements of another discipline (alchemy) and those of Goethe's magnum opus, *Faust*. He supplemented these with existing scholarship on mythology. For many years, these were his means for exploring the unconscious and identifying its patterns. While in the Wellspring, he acted as an alchemist, literary analyst, and mythologist as much as a psychologist, scientist, and physician.

At the Wellspring: "A First Inkling of My Personal Myth"

If I'm correct about the timing of Jung's entrance into the Wellspring — in 1922 — then his second soul encounter, his Liverpool dream in 1927, most likely also took place in the Wellspring (see "The Flowering Tree and the Sunlit Island at the Center," pages 183–85).

Out of his Liverpool dream, Jung tells us, "emerged a first inkling of my personal myth." His *first inkling*? This might seem surprising. Hadn't he been living his personal myth ever since the *Seven Sermons* in 1916? I believe so, but I take him to mean that this dream offered his first satisfying way of *cognitively grasping* his mythopoetic identity. He had been living it but not consciously comprehending it. The dream was perhaps more a completion of a process than its beginning — in something like the way we refer to a graduation as a commencement.

A major indicator that this was a watershed moment in Jung's initiatory journey is that, immediately after this dream, he stopped drawing mandalas. If the mandalas were one of Jung's core Metamorphosis practices, how interesting that he drew his first one immediately after his first soul encounter, adopted this as a regular routine for eleven years, and then suddenly ceased the practice altogether after his last soul encounter — as if the reshaping of his Ego was now sufficiently complete.

The very next year, in 1928, Richard Wilhelm, the German Sinologist, sent Jung his manuscript of *The Secret of the Golden Flower*, a presentation of an ancient Taoist text, which Jung understood as a "specimen of Chinese alchemy."[29] In contributing the foreword and an appendix to Wilhelm's book, Jung presented his first public exploration of the significance of the mandala. Jung was struck by the resonances between the images and ideas of Taoism and his own imagery journeys and paintings. He wrote to Wilhelm, "Fate appears to have given us the role of two bridge pillars which carry the bridge between East and West,"[30] an interesting comment in its own right but also intriguing given Joanna Macy's image of a similar bridge. (It's noteworthy, however, that the man saw himself as a pillar, while the woman was quite content to be a single stone.)

Dropping Fully into the Wellspring: Jung's "Confrontation with the World"

Reading and commenting on *The Golden Flower* led to Jung's decision to launch his in-depth study of alchemy. At the same time, he abruptly stopped working on his *Red Book*, no longer transcribing the text and never finishing the last full-page image. He later commented that this was when his "confrontation with the unconscious" drew to a close and his "confrontation with the world" began.[31] Interesting. This is, in other words, when he dropped fully into the Wellspring and dedicated himself wholly to the development of the delivery systems for his soul work. Jung, now fifty-three, entered the public world with a good measure of self-confidence and began to give frequent lectures.

Jung's Liverpool dream may very well have been the catalyst that ushered him into the passage of Induction, the threshold of the Wild Orchard stage (late Adulthood), when a person develops their own innovative delivery system. Jung's innovation — his revolution — was what the world now knows as Jungian psychology with its key concepts of the "self," the shadow, anima and animus, and the process of individuation. The 1930s and 1940s saw the full flowering of Jung's mature and distinctive soul work. Perhaps this was prefigured in 1928 when he published a small book, *The Relation between the Ego and the Unconscious*, in which he first wrote in any detail about the process of individuation. During the ensuing three decades, Jung wrote his major works,[32] developed his core methods of analytical psychology, and established practices for training analysts. His achievements influenced and shaped many cultural systems, including the fields of psychiatry, anthropology, archaeology, mythology, literature, philosophy, and religious studies.

The Wild Orchard: Planting (R)evolutionary Seeds in the Soil of Reality

The foundations and primary keys to Jung's lifework are rooted in his understanding of the unconscious and its relationship to the dead (as experienced through his first soul encounter, the *Seven Sermons*) and his understanding of the "self" as the center of the human psyche (as evoked by his second soul encounter, his Liverpool dream). This is to say: Without his Descent to Soul, Jung would never have become Jung.

He concurred. From his memoir, written at age eighty-five, in 1960:

Today I can say that I have never lost touch with my initial experiences. All my works, all my creative activity, has come from those initial fantasies and dreams which began in 1912, almost fifty years ago. Everything that I accomplished in later life was already contained in them, although at first only in the form of emotions and images.[33]

Perhaps Jung's foremost accomplishment "in later life" was that he initiated the transformation of how we in the Western world think about personal development. Before Jung's mature work — which is to say, before his Descent to Soul — psychotherapy was primarily understood as the treatment of psychopathology, the mitigation of "mental illness." (In most places today, it still is.) After his Descent — and, in particular, after he entered the Wild Orchard and developed his own innovative models and methods — psychotherapy, for him at least, became, as Sonu Shamdasani puts it, "a practice to enable the higher development of the individual through fostering the individuation process."[34] Psychotherapy now embraced the possibility of cultivating wholeness, not just the reduction of fragmentation or pathology.

The challenge to fully understanding what Jung had in mind, however, is that he was never precise or specific about what he meant by "individuation." The definition provided in the glossary of *Memories, Dreams, Reflections*, for example, is "the process by which a person becomes a psychological 'in-dividual,' that is, a separate, indivisible unity or 'whole.'"[35] Not very helpful, really. My own best guess of what Jung meant is a combination of what I would call the cultivation of the four facets of wholeness (what I mean by the Self and similar to what Jung meant by the "self" — see the glossary of *this* book) and the journey of soul initiation (what he called the search for a personal myth).[36] But Jung never developed his own map for the latter. We can, however, be sure of this: What Jung meant by individuation had everything to do with two psycho-ecological processes at the heart of his two soul encounters: opening the door to the unconscious and approaching the "self" as the center of the psyche and the "goal" of life.

❧

In the moment of soul encounter, nobody *really* understands what just happened or what good it is. Our Ego must first be shape-shifted in the Metamorphosis phase, and then, during Enactment, we must take our first tentative steps to embody and manifest our vision. The encounter with Soul is only a seed, although an invaluable and indispensable one, perhaps one that requires something akin to a forest fire before it can sprout. We learn what this seed will bloom into only by living it into the world. We discover the nature and value of its fruit about the same time others do. We might very well be as surprised as anyone else. We must, as Jung wrote, "plant the results of [our] experience in the soil of reality; otherwise they [remain] subjective assumptions without validity."

Soul-initiated Adults and Elders are and always have been the ones who carry and plant the seeds of true cultural evolution and revolution. We and all other beings on Earth need them now more than ever. Indeed, the Earth community needs you to take *your* next steps on the journey of soul initiation so that, in time, you'll take your place as a visionary cocreator of a life-enhancing future.

Coda

Awakening to the Dream of the Earth

...There's only one question:
how to love this world....

— MARY OLIVER

The Question

I agree with Mary Oliver: This *is* the question.

Our principal and most essential inquiry at this time on planet Earth is not, for example, how to create a sustainable society. That's a *good* question, an urgent one, but not the most essential.

How to create a life-*enhancing* society is closer to the mark, but still not it.

The most important question is not how to survive biodiversity loss, climate disruption, ecological degradation, pandemics, and fascism. It's not even: *Will* we survive?

It's this: What would it look like if we really loved this world, our more-than-human world — as fully as we're able, both individually and collectively?

If enough of us got good at living this question, we'd be well on our way to building a healthier society that is not only sustainable but life-enhancing. By getting better at loving this world, we'd also be doing all we can to foster species and human diversity, ecological health, climate stabilization, and life-enhancing governance.

The primary question, then, is not, *How do I take care of myself or my family or my community?* but, *How do I care for the world?* If this were the principal question enough of us lived — or the question most of us lived most of the time — we would, among other things, be doing what is best for ourselves, our family, and our community.

339

What does it mean to love the world?

For everyone, it means to intimately know, deeply care about, and actively care for a particular place on Earth — its creatures (including its humans of all races, ages, classes, creeds, and genders), landforms, waters, soils, and air; its health, integrity, and stories. For those who have been through the journey of soul initiation, however, the single most effective way to love this world is to embody what was discovered on the journey. When we are living the truth at the center of the image we were born with, we're making our greatest contribution to ecological vitality and cultural evolution — and, in a time of societal collapse, to cultural revolution and renaissance as well.

Mary Oliver's question cannot be answered well by a cognitive process of deduction. The ultimate answer is born with us. We are born *as* that answer. We embark upon the journey of soul initiation to uncover and become the answer that has always been waiting within us.

Inside or Outside?

While in one sense the answer is waiting within us, in another sense it's waiting "out there," in the world. If the most effective way for us to love the world is to embody our Soul, and if what we mean by Soul is our unique ecological niche, then is the answer inside or outside (within the private personal psyche or within our shared world)?

We could say that, primarily, the answer is "out there" because an eco-niche is not an "inner" experience; it's a feature of our shared world.

But what about the way we *discover* our eco-niche? Is this inner or outer — accessed through introspection or through perception? A soul encounter can be an experience of something tangible that happens in the world, like an encounter with Bear, but it can also be something that happens "inside," like a dream of Salmon Woman. The boundaries, however, are not so clear when we investigate further. Bear is in the world, but what happened "inside" Sabina was equally essential to her soul encounter; her meeting with Bear would not have been a soul encounter without the accompanying numinous image-feeling of Bear as spiritual ally, granting Sabina the steadfast courage to walk her own path. Bear encounters are rarely soul encounters (and vice versa). Similarly, although Salmon Woman appeared in FeatherStone's dream, she is an embodiment of an ecological relationship that has existed for millennia between the salmon, the land, and the people indigenous to that land.

So, how to love this world? The answer is both inside and outside. The answer is in the *relationship* between the person and the greater web of life. This, after all, is precisely what we mean by an ecological niche: the role occupied by a living thing within its community. A role consists of a set of relationships. To love the world most fully is to actualize the relationships with the world that only you can actualize.

When Sabina is loving the world most fully, she is guiding others in the sort of inner work that cracks them open like a Heart Spark and, with Bear showing the way, she is accompanying them down the spiral Path toward their Soul. Through these relationships with Heart, Spark, Bear, Path, other humans, and Soul, Sabina brings her people "here" and contributes to cultural regeneration.

FeatherStone's most effective way to love the world is by "tethering" or "grounding" the etheric or invisible — the images of the dreamtime — in a way that creates a channel of communication between invisible beings or processes and his people or place. FeatherStone manifests this relationship to the world through his delivery system of restoration ecology. If you were to watch him at work, you might say he is, for example, building logjams or planting seeds, but on the Soul level, you'd say the significance of what he is doing — the deep structure of his work — is that he is a feather revealing the secrets of stone, and he is a stone anchoring feather. If you knew him on the Soul level, *that* is what you'd actually see him doing when at work in forests and river valleys. You wouldn't come away saying you had watched someone planting seeds, any more than, after attending a virtuoso piano concerto, you'd say you had watched someone wildly pressing little white and black keys.

Soul and Meaning

Beyond or deeper than the question of inner or outer, there's another essential query. This one is about meaning. Our eco-niche is what provides us with our ultimate personal meaning, our truest identity. A vital question about meaning — any meaning — is whether we create it ourselves or whether it is discovered.

For sure, we create much of the meaning in our lives: our personal version of religious belief or spiritual perspective, the work we find engaging, how we experience a romantic relationship, or our interpretations of, well, anything — a dream, a work of art, a conversation, our own or someone else's behavior. The way we experience most things — including ourselves — depends on the meanings we assign them, whether consciously or unconsciously.

But not all meaning is relative, arbitrary, or created by us. Not all meaning is synthetic and constructed. Some meanings are "out there" — embedded in the more-than-human world. The examples most relevant to this book are implicit in the definition of Soul as eco-niche. The ultimate meaning of our individual lives — our Souls — is not inside us but "out there" in the world as a feature of the land. This is also true of our collective human meaning, our species' place in this world. Our ultimate meanings — our truest identities — have everything to do with the relationship to the world we were born (or evolved) to take. That relationship is not inside us; it's a reality of, an aspect of, the world. As I'm fond of saying, everything is what it is by virtue of its relationships with everything else. Some of those relationships are objective features of the world. The relationship between a tree and the soil in which it is rooted is a real thing independent of our interpretation of it or even our awareness of that relationship. Likewise with the relationship between Bear and Salmon or between Sun and Moon. Likewise with the relationship between a certain salmon and its spawning place or between a butterfly and its great-great-great-grandparents' birthplace. These relationships are real and functional, whether or not we ever interpret them, and they give meaning to our world. Likewise with that particular relationship between you and the world, the one you were born to embody and fulfill — your eco-niche.

Our ultimate meaning, our deepest identity, then, is not something we make up. We don't construct it. It's not a creation of our Egos. It exists in the world as an objective thing. The only questions are whether we'll find it, allow it to be what it is without trying to mold it, and let ourselves be transformed, remade, shaped by that meaning so that we become, for the rest of our lives, a conscious servant, steward, or handmaiden for it.

Soul, again, is all about relationships — relationships that exist independent of our Egos and the meanings we assign, relationships that are features of the world not created by our conscious human choices and decisions, relationships that exist before we were born, perhaps as a consequence of our conception, relationships that arise or evolve as threads in the fabric of the self-organizing "natural" world.

This is how the world works. The most important meanings derive from features of the world not constructed or manufactured by us.

It might be that only we humans are even capable of assigning meanings that are independent of the self-organizing world — or, too often, in opposition to it (such as an ever-expanding economy as the meaning of societal "success"). Our human liability to assign and believe unhitched meanings is the origin of our ability to destroy the world. Earth has her own inherent design, in which every species and individual has a meaning, its own objective, life-enhancing place in the Earth community. To ignore this design while painting the world with our egocentric and anthropocentric (and often androcentric and racist) meanings is to eventually and inevitably undermine the biological and ecological systems that support life. Domination. In contrast, partnership requires truly seeing the Others, appreciating how they fit in and how they embody meaning. It also requires us to appreciate the inherent ways we humans, too, belong to the whole — independent from and prior to our conscious strategizing.

To be an Adult human, a partner in the unfolding of Earth's story, is to be faithful to the facts of the world that provide us with our deepest meanings. Said another way: To be an Adult human is to hold the Earth as sacred, as an animate planet that has been generating her own meanings from the beginning. To become a mature species, we must grow cultures that support us to recognize and be faithful to the facts of the world, to the meanings generated by Earth. The journey of soul initiation is a vital feature of such a culture.

Vision Ecologies and Mythopoetic Infections

A society loves the world most effectively when that society is shaped primarily by its soul-initiated Adults and Elders in accordance with the meanings they've uncovered in the natural world.[1]

Living and working together, these Adults and Elders form a "vision ecology" — an ecology of visionary projects.

A visionary project is whatever a soul-initiated person does to deliver their soul gift to the world, whatever means they use to inhabit their eco-niche. In addition to observable creations and tangible services, a visionary project can simply be an Adult or Elder's way of being in the world, the soul-infused qualities they bring to their community, the events and transformations they catalyze by their presence.

Healthy, mature cultures arise and evolve organically through the intermingling of the visionary initiatives of Adults and Elders in the various domains of society — education, healthcare, science, the arts, governance, economics, environmental stewardship, human development. This intermingling takes the form of reciprocal aid and cooperation that includes a certain amount of healthy, mutually enhancing competition between projects. It also includes mutual inspiration and the borrowing of ideas, metaphors, techniques, and technologies. Often it involves the merging or integration of visionary projects.

Imagine what might happen if, for example, Joanna Macy's Despair and Empowerment Work were to intermingle and merge with FeatherStone's forest and river restoration work to foster a consciousness shift in the human element of a particular watershed, say one on the Olympic Peninsula. Or if Sabina's Spark Heart were to team up with Matt's Snake Root Medicine to create a hybrid between a seminary of the wild and a soulcentric coaching school.

Many of the programs I guide with my partner, Geneen Marie Haugen, were co-imagined through an intermingling of cocoon weaving with Geneen's mythopoetic genius of generating perception-expanding images and asking identity-destabilizing questions.

I think of such partnerships as being inspired and fueled by what we might call the Imaginal Exchange of Mythopoetic Dream Viruses — aka Mythopoetic Infections. This is what happens in a vision ecology: Never-before-seen, life-enhancing social forms and practices are naturally birthed through the Mythopoetic Infections made possible by soul-initiated humans living and working in close proximity to one another.

Adults and Elders as Imaginal Cells

Each mythos-infused human project arises from nature. After all, Soul as eco-niche is a feature of the natural, self-organizing world. Vision ecologies are the way nature operates through humans to enhance the web of life, the way we most effectively and fully participate, consciously and collectively, in evolution. Our soul-initiated Egos, working together, become synergistic agents of the natural world. As they should be. As they were evolved to be.

A healthy human culture is grown, not made or manufactured or built. A thriving, life-enhancing culture is much more like a self-organizing ecosystem than a machine or a hierarchically structured corporation; it's more like an organic mycelial network than an assembled apparatus or a strategically structured contraption. Soul-initiated Adults and Elders are the seeds of a living, growing culture. Their intermingling vision projects are its mature forests. The self-organizing more-than-human world of a particular place, along with the sacred stories that grow out of that place, makes up its soil. Evolution-driving Mystery (love) is its rain and sunshine.

Another way to say this is that soul-initiated Adults and Elders are the imaginal cells of a culture. They are the way a caterpillar society eventually becomes a butterfly society. Once there are enough true Adults and Elders in a human community, their visionary projects link up in such a way that the whole society goes through a developmental-evolutionary unfolding. In the Western world, we are now, as a society, in a Cocoon. Our sociocultural structures have been dissolving for quite some time. This Dissolution is a necessary phase in cultural transformation — just as it is in individual initiation.[2] What percentage of Adults and Elders, as imaginal cells, are needed in a given egocentric dominator society, as it decays and dissolves, before that society begins to metamorphose into a mature partnership society? Hopefully, we'll find out later this century or the next.

Just as the caterpillar's immune system resists its own imaginal cells — which it sees as a threat and consequently tries to kill — so an egocentric, caterpillar culture will do all it can to resist and eliminate its Adults and Elders. Indeed, this is what dominator societies have been doing for several thousand years. If the map presented in this book is effective and widely adopted, the egocentric dominator powers will do all they can to sabotage, censor, and suppress it.

Did Gaia Goof?

Many people have come to think of the human Ego as the most unfortunate and dangerous thing to ever appear on Earth. Ecocidal. They've got a point. But I believe the emergence of the human Ego was not a mistake, even if it was the start of a terribly risky experiment. When we as a species learn to take our natural place as a collective agent of the natural world — *if* we do — the power of human conscious self-awareness will be merged with the creative powers of evolution. This would put human consciousness back in alignment with Mystery (or enable this for the first time, depending on how you see it). This would support and amplify the dream of the Earth beyond what any of us could imagine. This alignment might be tantamount to the conscious awakening of our planet. The journey of soul initiation, widely implemented in most societies, is the way to reach that goal.[3]

Did Gaia goof by creating humans? No, I don't believe so, but she did take a big chance on us, one that could result in the destruction of most of the life-forms she has generated over the past 300 million years or so — or it might yet turn out to be an unprecedented accelerator of evolution. Humanity is in the midst of a profound initiation journey and, consequently, the Earth is as well. Will we make it through? It appears to be a cliffhanger. It all depends on the collective decisions we make and the actions we take this century. What a blessing and opportunity to be alive at this time!

The Next Evolutionary Step for Humanity

The vision of the conscious awakening of the planet might suggest answers to some of the questions seeded at the start of this book: What is the unique ecological niche of the human species? What is our next evolutionary step? What is our destination as a species that we can only partially understand — at best, and on a good day?

Along with all other species, we're still very much on an evolutionary adventure. Perhaps a new human species is in the process of emerging, and the new wrinkle is not in our visible anatomy but an alteration in our mode of consciousness. At the heart of this shift in human consciousness might be our expanded and amplified capacity for imagination.

To grasp the importance of an amped-up imagination, first recall that the human is, as far as we know, the only creature with the ability to imagine alternative futures — and create them, using symbolic language and opposable thumbs. This understanding of our forward-seeing imagination — and its implications — is explored and articulated in the work of philosopher and imagineer Geneen Marie Haugen.[4] She points out that this faculty now acquires a significance more pivotal than any previous development in Earth's evolution and, conceivably, in the universe's. In the twenty-first century, humanity has the opportunity to learn to use its forward-seeing imagination not only for its own sake but for the sake of all species. As Thomas Berry writes, "We now in large measure determine the earth process that once determined us. In a more integral way we could say that the earth that controlled itself directly in the former period now to an extensive degree controls itself through us."[5] For better or worse (and so far it is unmistakably for worse), humanity has become the dominant presence on this planet. "We have become a geological force," writes evolutionary cosmologist Brian Swimme. "Because of us, the ice caps are melting. Because of us, coral reefs the size of mountains are dying."[6]

For this reason, our capacity to imagine the numberless facets of a viable future has far greater consequences and opportunities than ever before. We are now imagining not only for ourselves but for all earthly creatures and habitats. A highly skilled and nuanced imagination — exercised by not just a few but the majority of humans — now acquires the most fundamental significance for survival. As a species, we must go beyond all previous functioning of our uniquely human imagination. As I explored in *Nature and the Human Soul*, this evolution in our human capacity of imagination is made possible by the lengthening and differentiation of our species' new life stage of Adolescence.[7]

"We cannot intentionally create unless we are able, first, to imagine," writes Geneen. "Imagination may be the most essential, uniquely human capacity — creating both the dead-end crises of our time and the doorway through them."[8] The dead-end crises are generated by the egocentric ambitions of uninitiated humans (those whose meanings are unhitched from nature). The doorways through (and beyond) are created by the delivery systems and vision ecologies of initiated Adults and Elders.

Geneen coined the appellation *Homo imaginans* many years ago to refer to our evolving consciousness, our way into the future. "*Homo, human,* and *humus* are thought to arise from a shared root — of the Earth. Thus, *Homo imaginans* might translate not only as the imagining human, but as the imagining Earth."

In 1988, Thomas Berry, too, suggested the possibility of a new species: "Because we are moving into a new mythic age, it is little wonder that a kind of mutation is taking place in the entire earth-human order. A new paradigm of what it is to be human emerges."[9]

Earth may be trying to imagine her own future through soul-initiated humans. We might imagine she is supporting us to evolve in order to help herself evolve. If humanity succeeds at what Joanna Macy refers to as the Great Turning, we will awaken, as a species, to what Thomas Berry calls the dream of the Earth.

We know that the geo-biological community of Earth excels in its ability to engender countless new forms and species to fill opportunities and needs within its constantly evolving and self-organizing web of life. This occurred, for example, two billion years ago when most terrestrial life took the form of primordial, single-celled, anaerobic bacteria (prokaryotes) living in the oceans. A by-product of their metabolism was oxygen, which, for them, was a poison. They generated such prodigious volumes of it that Earth's atmosphere became significantly altered and the prokaryotes began to suffocate in their own waste. Then a new form of life appeared — bacteria that fed on oxygen (eukaryotes). Without such a transformational moment, life on Earth might have ended right there.

Now we find ourselves at a similar juncture. We humans are creating so much toxicity and pollution — and radically altering Earth's atmosphere (and land and waters) — that our own survival is in question. If ever Earth, in its fecund generativity, were going to bring forth a new human species, now would be the time.

Homo imaginans might be that species — soul-initiated imagineers who serve as Earth's faculty of forward-seeing imagination, who see the possibilities that their unique eco-niche enables them to see. These future possibilities are not conceived by human Egos. Rather, Earth herself conceives them, and soul-initiated Egos serve as her midwives. The ultimate meanings are not synthesized by human Egos but discovered by them.

This kind of forward-seeing imagination is what the journey of soul initiation makes possible. Only in partnership with our Souls do we have the capacity to imagine in this way.

So, what is the unique ecological niche of the human species? The answer, I suspect, has everything to do with our conscious partnership with evolution, which is to say, in effect, with Mystery or God. I believe we're meant to partner with Earth by consciously supporting her to enhance life — its diversity, complexity, and resilience — and that our primary resource for this partnership are the vision ecologies of soul-initiated Adults and Elders.

As I suggested earlier, true Adults and Elders are the imaginal cells of emerging eco-soulcentric butterfly societies. Taking this idea a step further, we might imagine that these butterfly societies will eventually serve as the imaginal cells of the next phase of human evolution — from a caterpillar species to a butterfly species — and this might in turn result in the next major step in *Earth's* evolution. As a species, we are now in a Cocoon. What percentage of butterfly societies will be needed globally before Earth begins to transform into a butterfly planet?

If we do evolve into a human form of a butterfly species, this would be a soul revolution for both humanity and Earth. Our previous human revolutions — including the agricultural, scientific, industrial, and digital — were necessary earlier steps, steps that make possible a soul revolution but in no way guarantee it. Only if we wake up in time will it come to pass. All initiation journeys are dangerous opportunities.

A Wildly Imaginative Partnership with Earth

What does the possibility of such a soul revolution suggest about the specific ways the human Ego must now transform? How would such an evolutionary unfolding differ from what humanity has experienced in the past? And what might this suggest about how the journey of soul initiation and the Descent to Soul, as modeled in this book, are different from their indigenous precursors?

Here's another way to ask this, as I have in appendix 2: What would have to be true about a human Ego capable of imagining futures that are utterly unlike any previous human experience — futures that are so wildly divergent that the word *future* itself must be re-visioned?

I believe it has to do, at least in part, with how we experience time.

One of the things I've learned from Thomas Berry is that modern science and cosmology require us to think about the world as not only unfolding in ever-repeating cycles — as in the traditional, classic, and indigenous views — but also as a one-way, progressive, nonrepeating trajectory of evolution and transformation. Everything in the universe is steadily moving into entirely new terrain, entirely new sequences of development. There is a panoramic arc to our own existence as well as a replicating pattern. This is a relatively new idea on the human scene, and a revolutionary one. We didn't begin to think this way until Darwin's time. The older, ever-renewing-cycle model of indigenous peoples supports an experience of time in terms of the repeating rhythms of nature — the rhythms of the day, the Moon, the seasons, and the stages of plant, animal, and human growth. This perspective is essential to any healthy, ecocentric worldview. In contrast, the irreversible trajectory model — for example, that the universe originated in a big bang about fourteen billion years ago and is still expanding, and birds evolved from dinosaurs, humans from apes, and all life ultimately from primordial single-celled organisms — is the perspective we find in modern cosmology and biology. This view has become indispensable to our modern understanding of the universe and our human place in it. Thomas refers to the latter perspective as "the time-developmental model."[10] His larger point is that our approach to the development of anything must now embrace *both* models — both circle and arc (in a sense, both feminine and masculine), which together describe a spiral progression through space and time.

An Ego that can imagine a future using an integration of both kinds of time is a very different Ego than has existed in the past. The future it must be able to imagine is radically different because it is not a variation on the patterns or rhythms of ever-repeating circular time. It's not a new version of anything we've done in human history. And yet such an Ego must at the same time hold as sacred the repeating natural rhythms of the wild world. This is an Ego capable of a conscious, forward-seeing, wildly imaginative partnership with evolution, with Earth.

Will we ever achieve such a partnership with Earth? At the time of this writing — in 2020, in the midst of the Covid-19 viral pandemic and in the face of the much more dire crises of social injustice, mass extinction, ecosystem pollution and degradation, cultural collapse, and anthropogenic climate disruption — I must confess to some doubts. But if enough of us offer what we can to the fashioning of life-sustaining and eventually life-enhancing societies, we might just get there. This project will require the efforts of several generations — and even this may only lay the foundation. Cultural change this deep and radical takes time. Evolution can't be rushed. But let's place this in context: Earth needed 4.3 billion years of evolution to get to this point. And modern humans (*Homo sapiens*) have been around for only two, maybe three hundred thousand years. What's another five hundred years or so? The main uncertainty is whether we'll be so fortunate as to have that much time — which will require, this century, a global revolution that enables human life to thrive.

Or maybe this kind of partnership with evolution won't be realized on Earth until some far distant future and by some future species endowed and cursed, like us, with conscious self-awareness.

Cultural Therapy and the Dream of the Earth

Speaking bluntly, Thomas Berry, a lifelong student of world cultures, referred to the current, near-universal commitment to industrial progress, unlimited growth, and a consumer society as "the supreme pathology of all history."[11] A valid response to such a pathology, he says, must include remedial treatment:

> The entrancement with industrial civilization…must be considered as a profound cultural disorientation. It can be dealt with only by a corresponding deep cultural therapy.
>
> …At such a moment a new revelatory experience is needed, an experience wherein human consciousness awakens to the grandeur and sacred quality of the Earth process. This awakening is our human participation in the dream of the Earth.…We probably have not had such participation in the dream of the Earth since earlier shamanic times, but therein lies our hope for the future for ourselves and for the entire Earth community.[12]

I hear Thomas saying that the cultural therapy we need springs from revelatory or visionary experience, an awakening to the dream of the Earth. The Earth's dream is what Thomas describes as "a mutually-enhancing human-Earth presence." To realize this dream, he tells us, we must individually journey into the mysteries:

> More than any other of the human types concerned with the sacred, the shamanic personality journeys into the far reaches of the cosmic mystery and brings back the vision and the power needed by the human community at the most elementary level.…Not only is the shamanic type emerging in our society, but also the shamanic dimension of the psyche itself. In periods of significant cultural creativity, this aspect of the psyche takes on a pervasive role throughout the society and shows up in all the basic institutions and professions.[13]

What Thomas refers to as "the shamanic dimension of the psyche" is what I call the Dark Muse-Beloved, the West facet of the Self, the dimension of our psyche that revels in night, dreams, destiny, death, and the mysteries and qualities of the underworld. This is the facet of our human wholeness that guides us on the Descent to Soul — the facet also known as the Guide to Soul, Magician, or Psychopomp. As we explored in chapter 2, this "shamanic" dimension of the psyche is one of the two (along with the South facet) that are least developed in the contemporary world and that must be cultivated if the Descent is to be fruitful.

Given that our awakening to the dream of the Earth calls for a journey into the mysteries, our cultural healing requires a means to facilitate that journey. Thomas suspects we have not had such a methodology since "earlier shamanic times," but he is not advising us to return to or recapitulate the methods of older traditions but rather to generate our own contemporary ways. This, precisely, has been our goal at Animas Valley Institute: to create a never-before-seen Western and nature-based way to participate in the dream of the Earth by way of the Descent to Soul (and the journey of soul initiation, more generally).

I spent much of the first half of my adult life as a psychotherapist, but this book does not offer a new or old form of therapy, at least not for individuals. Rather, what I've introduced here is a form of what Thomas called a "deep cultural therapy" — for societies that have crumbled, folded into themselves, and become traumatized due to the loss of the practices and ceremonies that create true Adults and Elders.

The distinguished environmental lawyer Gus Speth, founder of the World Resources Institute, also spoke to the need of what amounts to a deep cultural therapy:

> I used to think the top environmental problems were biodiversity loss, ecosystem collapse, and climate change, I thought that with thirty years of good science we could address those problems. But I was wrong. The top environmental problems are selfishness, greed, and apathy...and to deal with those we need a spiritual and cultural transformation, and we scientists don't know how to do that.[14]

Mystery Schools, Threshold Gates, and the Reinvention of Culture

In the midst of our ominous and auspicious epoch of multiple planetary crises and evolutionary opportunities, there are three things of which I am most certain.

First, the survival of the entire Earth community of which we are a part requires the radical reinvention of contemporary human cultures — our economies, our energy- and food-producing methods, our social justice systems, our ways of raising children and supporting teens, and our ways of enacting education, healthcare, government, and religion. This is the Great Work that Thomas Berry so passionately urged. Everything must change. All our systems must be reimagined. Life-destroying behavior stems from life-destroying cultures — cultures that fail to provide for healthy individual development and psychospiritual maturity. Developmental failures result in self-destructive and world-harming activities, businesses, social systems, and cultural customs — ways of life concocted by people stuck in egocentric Adolescence. Conversely, developmental success gives rise to life-enhancing behaviors, resilient communities, regenerative societies and economies, and cultural evolution.

Second, for each one of us, our greatest personal fulfillment and our most meaningful service to the world are one and the same, and our path to our most fulfilling service unfolds in the three-part journey of soul encounter, Soul Initiation, and soul embodiment: (1) Soul encounter takes place during the Descent to Soul and results in the discovery of our mythopoetic identity (the way we understand our unique ecological niche in the more-than-human world). (2) Sometime later, we go through Soul Initiation, the now-rare major life passage when our center of psychospiritual gravity takes root in that mythopoetic identity and that unique eco-niche. (3) This passage, in time, blossoms into soul embodiment — a true Adulthood of inhabiting that niche, as we deliver our singular gift to the more-than-human world.

And here's the third thing of which I'm certain: The first two are so entwined that it's not possible to have one without the other. Mature, evolving human cultures are always and everywhere the organic, self-organizing outcome when true Adults (and Elders) individually carry as a gift to others what had previously been hidden in their Souls — and creatively collaborate through vision ecologies. In other words, the only path to a healthy, mature culture is by way of the journey of soul initiation undertaken by many. Conversely, the single greatest support for individual Soul Initiation is a healthy, mature culture as the social and spiritual context for that journey. Cultural evolution and individual initiation proceed hand-in-hand.

If I were to add a fourth certainty, it is this: During our current era of cultural collapse, we must create contemporary forms of mystery schools. When there is an absence or dearth of healthy, mature cultures to serve as the social and spiritual environment for the individual journey of soul initiation, we must create independent social and spiritual settings that serve as greenhouses for engendering and nurturing the seeds of cultural renaissance, seeds that emerge from revelatory experience. These mystery schools must be led by Adults and Elders who've been called by Mystery to serve as nature-based soul-initiation guides.

My foremost intention and hope for this book is that it might serve as a foundational resource for such mystery schools and for a new craft of soul-initiation guiding, a manual for both guides and initiates, a handbook for an emerging soul-craft with roots in ancient ecocentric traditions — and blossoming branches reaching toward an unforeseeable ecocentric future. May this field guide help unlock a threshold gate now beckoning from the hidden heart of the initiatory and evolutionary crises of our time. Crossing through that gate is the alluring and dangerous opportunity of this planetary moment.

Death, Love, and Soul

We are going to die, each one of us. There's no question about *that*.

What there *is* a question about is whether in this lifetime we will manage to contribute our unique, Soul-rooted gift to this world — or even discover the nature of that gift. In the implacable reality and lucid light of our mortality, what other question could hold greater relevance and urgency? This is ultimately about love, about love in its most expansive and most selfless form, a love for the world that has become rare, a love that is wild and mature. This form of love grows out of an identification with and a commitment to something bigger, much bigger, than our individual lives. If, while alive, we can offer ourselves fully to the world, there is, in a certain sense, nothing left of us when we die. By merging with this world before we leave it, we never really leave. If, through a life of Soul work, our Ego identity expands until it's as wide and deep as the world, there's nothing lost when we take our last breath. On the Soul level, we were never separate anyway because, as an ecological niche, our Soul is an integral element of this world — and it will continue to be so even after our body has returned to Earth and our Ego has been reabsorbed into a greater consciousness. To experience this love and live from it, we must first make peace with our mortality. Indeed, we must uncover our deep gratitude for our mortality, a mystical apprenticeship to Death not as something opposed to life but rather as an indivisible component of it, of the life we had once found much easier to love than death when we thought they were somehow separate.

As a child, I dreamed of a cemetery. Later in life, I began to dream of a contemporary path to initiation, a nature-based way to die and so to grow into a soul-rooted Adulthood and, eventually, Elderhood.

Are you willing and able to love this world even though your Ego is fated to leave it, even though this world *requires* your Ego to leave it? Long before your final breath, will you risk your current life and identity for the possibility of uncovering your most sacred of tasks, your unique Soul-infused service to this world?

Appendix One

The Lost Journey

How and Why the Journey Was Lost

I have suggested that one reason the journey of soul initiation (or its precursor) has been lost for so long is because it has become nearly impossible for people in ego-centric societies to even understand what it is: Once forgotten for a few generations, it's hard to later identify as having ever existed. But there are other, deeper reasons.

The loss has its roots in environmental and cultural changes that began six to ten thousand years ago, including climate change (the end of the last ice age), the advent of agriculture and private property, population growth, and the exploitation of people and resources.

Let's consider just one strand: With the development of agriculture, a new form of Adolescent pathology became possible, a pathology that begins with greed and eventuates in hoarding, domination, and violence. Before agriculture, there was little to hoard because there was little material surplus. Among hunter-gatherers, no one within the tribe was significantly wealthier (in a material sense) than anyone else. The tribe's survival depended primarily on cooperation among its members. However, with the advent of agriculture and farming — the domestication of selected animal and plant species — came, inevitably, the pathogenic notion of personal property and the inexorable outcome that some people would conclude that hoarding things for themselves is a good idea. In order to remain healthy, a tribe had to develop social, educational, and spiritual methods to assure that most of its members would grow into true Adulthood — and that the immature ones among them would never attain significant social or economic power. Some tribes succeeded at this and some did not.

Once a tribe produces a single individual determined to hoard and able and willing to use lethal force to do so, the cultural fabric of that society begins to unravel. To protect themselves, other individuals hoard as well. The tribe becomes increasingly materialistic, competitive, anthropocentric, and violent — and disconnected from the natural world in which everything shares freely with everything else and there is no waste. Economic-class structure and slavery soon follow.

Before long, the ruler of such a tribe (a patho-adolescent individual, most likely male) decides that raiding other tribes for *their* crops, animals, people, land, waters, and other "wealth" would be another good idea. This is the beginning of empire. As Andrew Schmookler explains in *The Parable of the Tribes*, the neighboring communities now have four options: Be exterminated, be conquered and assimilated, become aggressive and warring themselves, or flee.[1] That, in a nutshell, is the human cultural history of our planet over the past several thousand years.

By the twentieth century, most societies had come under the control of egocentric Adolescent leaders (tyrants, plutocrats, and oligarchs) who altered cultural traditions, social practices, and societal structures in ways that enhanced their ability to dominate and to accrue and hoard wealth. Among the alterations were (and are) an emphasis on hostile competition over cooperation; land "ownership"; suppression of nature-honoring and nature-based rituals; class stratification and slavery; racism; sexism (and heterosexism); militarism; anthropocentric, androcentric forms of religion; plutocratic forms of governance; the systematic murder of true Adults and Elders (shamans and other cultural and spiritual leaders); compulsory egocentric education and the resulting ecological illiteracy; and perhaps the ultimate modern subversion of healthy society: the creation of so-called "corporations" bestowed with the rights of persons. These are all features of what cultural historian Riane Eisler, in *The Chalice and the Blade*, refers to as "dominator societies," in contrast to "partnership societies."[2] Various combinations of these dominator features are found not only in societies with Western origins but in many from Asia, Africa, Oceania, and the Americas. Domination is a universal liability inherent in our human mode of consciousness, not something exclusively invented by Western civilization. Slavery, for example, goes back at least five thousand years and is found among many indigenous peoples globally, including some pre-Columbian Native Americans.

Historically, the single most devastating cultural disruption used by tyrants has been to undermine the traditions, knowledge, symbols, languages, and myths that support people to mature into true Adults and Elders. The practices and ceremonies for soul initiation were suppressed, outlawed, or brutally extinguished. Soul-initiation guides were murdered. Abolishing and eradicating the initiatory journey and those who guide it profoundly compromised human development for that society. This disruption of the natural course of human maturation was and still is a central aim of dominator societies for the simple reason that children and psychological early Adolescents (of any age) are much easier to control and dominate than Wanderers, Adults, and Elders.

In the last century, this process of cultural degradation and greed-rooted empire building reached its inevitable culmination, and in two ways. First, most societies in the world have now been assimilated within the modern dominator model of culture: the global industrial growth society, or what I call consumer-conformist culture. There are very few places left on Earth for healthy, partnership societies to live in peace. (There might be a few yet remaining in the most remote corners of the planet.) Second, consumer-conformist culture now threatens most species, including our own, with extinction.

In many societies, even healthy ones, greed is a common trait for lots of people — in early childhood, that is. If still present to any significant degree in middle childhood, it is a sign of developmental problems (and family dysfunction). If it persists into early Adolescence, it becomes a pathology that blocks further psychological and social maturation. What might begin as an ordinary feature of human childhood can eventually become, if embodied in a community leader or head of state, a societal crisis of the most dire sort. If that leader is not removed, his or her pathological greed and egotism become the ruin of that society, a result we are seeing all over the globe at the time of this writing — and potentially the ruin of the entire Earth. What's needed to prevent (or reverse) such scenarios are true Adults and Elders and the cultural practices and systems they provide for supporting the psychosocial maturation of all their people (including that of voters, a vital concern in a democratic society because politicians, on the whole, are no more mature than the people who vote for them).

It might not be too simplistic to say that greed is the challenge and love is the answer. As a species, we are now faced with the global opportunity and necessity to form compassionate partnerships with all beings (human and otherwise) with whom we share our small planet — or perish. Most importantly we must now re-invent maps and methods for the journey of soul initiation — so we'll have the Adults and Elders we need to guide us.

Examples of Where the Journey Still Exists

If the journey of soul initiation (or its forerunner) has been largely lost, where is the evidence it ever really existed? What forms did it take? We have countless examples of societies that incorporate a variety of rites of passage, but here I am asking something different: What is the evidence for traditions that incorporated the journey of soul initiation — or something like it?

Let me answer plainly: I don't have a lot of compelling examples for you. I don't know if anyone does. It's possible there really aren't a lot of good examples — either because the journey has been lost for so long or because it never actually existed in many or most places. All I really have are hints and glimmers, and even then I've had to look persistently for many years.

We might simply presume that certain older, nature-based, partnership traditions must have incorporated the journey of soul initiation simply because we have reason to believe (or imagine) their societies were healthier than ours today —

psychologically, socially, and ecologically. But of the many features that made them healthier, did these include maps and methods specifically for the journey of soul initiation (and its core component, the Descent to Soul)? Good question.

We know of myths from peoples all over the world that sound and feel like they incorporate and express many dynamics of the Descent — Inanna (Sumerian), Beowulf (Anglo-Saxon), Persephone (Greek), Psyche and Eros (Greek), Jumping Mouse (Native American). But in which societies are these myths still embodied in actual initiatory journeys? Or what evidence is there they ever were?

These are difficult questions to definitively answer because, as sketched above, Western and other dominator cultures have damaged or destroyed partnership cultures everywhere in this world. Few, if any, have survived intact. There's a kind of Heisenberg uncertainty principle when it comes to healthier cultures: If they've been discovered ("contacted") by a Western or other egocentric observer, they have already been altered in such a way that they are no longer intact — or soon won't be. If someone who cares about cultural health stumbles upon an unscathed, traditional partnership society, perhaps the only ethical course is to say nothing about them — or do everything possible to protect them from the corporate and governmental ravages of consumer-conformist societies. We do, however, have many well-publicized accounts of relatively intact traditional cultures. In each case, we might ask if we see evidence, specifically, for a living, functioning embodiment of the journey of soul initiation.

A second dimension of the difficulty here is this: If it's true the journey has been lost so widely and for so long, then it's likely there have been very few people asking the questions I'm asking here. Whether you're a cultural anthropologist, ethnologist, mythologist, ecopsychologist, journalist, novelist, or spiritual seeker — if you don't have a clear conception of the journey of soul initiation, you won't find it in other cultures simply because you won't look for it. Even if you stumbled upon it, you wouldn't realize it. And if you did, you wouldn't have the language to describe it, at least at first. Further, whoever read your account would have trouble understanding the distinctions you're making because they'd be so foreign to your readers' worldview — which, of course, is precisely the challenge I face in writing this book. In short, it's possible that one reason I have only hints and glimmers is that there have been so few people looking for evidence.

Gregory Cajete, however, is someone who *has* looked, and what he tells us appears to be credible evidence. A Native American (Tewa) educator who has authored several books on indigenous education and native science, he is one of the indigenous scholars who maintain that while every indigenous culture has their own unique worldview and perspective on human development, they all share common themes. One theme is that the purpose of education is to "find one's face, find one's heart."[3] This is a phrase Dr. Cajete attributes to the Nahuatl-speaking Aztec people of Mexico. To find your face, he writes, is to "develop and express [your] innate character and potential"; to find your heart is to "search out and express [your] inner passion." To do this, a person needs to "access knowledge from primary sources deep within themselves and the natural world." (Note: *both* "inner" and "outer.") This is accomplished through a "process of questing." What we seek may be "a special song, an animal, a plant, a person, a place, a feeling, a wisdom, a dream," all of which are "expressions of vision, that innately human calling to search for higher levels of meaning. To find that special thing, we have to explore the boundaries of our world and beyond. We have to expand our consciousness and paradoxically go outside ourselves to find that special something inside ourselves." He adds: "Visions are essential: they are integral to individual and communal success, and they are a foundation of conscious evolution and human development." Dr. Cajete feels that young indigenous people today need to develop "a vision that guides them toward fulfillment of themselves as complete human beings. This is exactly what the context and process of dreaming and visioning were able to accomplish for Indian people in the past. Visioning continues to do this today for those tribes and those individuals who have the remnants of this once-great and highly effective educative process."

I'm not aware of any indigenous cultures that describe the journey of soul initiation or map the Descent to Soul in the same way I do in this book, but Dr. Cajete's characterizations of indigenous education, although not descriptions of specific initiatory ceremonies and methods, suggest some meaningful overlap.

A compelling contemporary indigenous account of an initiatory process that seems similar in many ways to what I describe as the Descent to Soul is offered by Malidoma Somé — a shaman, teacher, and elder of the Dagara people of what is now Burkina Faso in West Africa. In his book *Of Water and the Spirit*, he describes his own initiation.[4] Malidoma's account is first-person reporting by a Dagara native, not anthropological observation. But he is able to describe his experiences in language we have a chance of understanding because he was thoroughly educated in Western languages and worldviews. He holds, for example, three master's degrees and two doctorates from the Sorbonne and Brandeis University.

Malidoma recounts in generous detail the six weeks of initiatory practices he and other Dagara boys went through in the 1970s.[5] Many of these practices involved austere and grueling "missions" or "exercises" that a few of the boys did not survive. One of Malidoma's missions, for example, involved an all-night self-guided journey to a distant mountain range, and then a precipitous ascent in darkness toward a particular cave Malidoma had been told earlier was his to enter. On the way to the cave, he encountered a rabbit who explained to him where Malidoma was going and why. After some time in the cave, Malidoma realized he was in the "underworld," a realm as extensive and differentiated as his Dagara Village world. He ended up living there for what felt like several years and had many strange and harrowing adventures that changed him to the core, including getting married to a woman warrior, having children, being sentenced to death, and getting pushed into a black hole.

The intense and hazardous features of the Dagara initiation activities do not, of course, prove they were soul-initiation practices. But his experiences and the way his elders (his guides) described the journey to him suggest they were. Below, for example, Malidoma tells us what the Dagara elders said to him and the other boys at the beginning of their initiation ordeals.

> He who does not know where he came from cannot know why he came here and what he came to this place to do. There is no reason to live if you forget what you're here for.... You chose to be born within a particular family because that made your purpose easier to fulfill.... When you do not know who you are, you follow the knowledge of the wind.
>
> There are details about your identity that you alone will have to discover, and that's why you have come to initiation to go and find out.[6]

Phrases like "why [you] came here," "what [you] came to this place to do," and "who you are" have a strong resonance with that ecological realm, unique to each individual, that I call Soul, our innate eco-niche.

Malidoma came away from what he calls the "Dagara initiation process" with an understanding of his life purpose expressed in a way that suggests Soul Initiation. He describes his purpose, in other words, not as a social role or vocation but, rather, as what I consider a mythopoetic identity: namely, to "make friends with the stranger or enemy." This is what he has done ever since — in relation to us strangers/enemies of the Western world. His delivery systems include writing books and offering workshops, ceremonies, and trainings.

Malidoma concludes:

> [A] person who lives in denial of who he really is must have a hard time living, because he would have to invent meaning and purpose from the ground up. No one can tell us who we are or how we must live. That knowledge can be found only within.[7]

A second good example of twentieth-century soul-initiation ceremonies as practiced by an indigenous community — in this case the Tzutujil Maya of what is now Guatemala — can be found in Martín Prechtel's eloquent *Long Life, Honey in the Heart*.[8]

Similar initiatory themes also seem to be reflected in the practices of Siberian peoples, the indigenous Sami people of northern Europe, and the Basque people of the Pyrenees, and in the walkabout rituals of the Australian Aboriginals, to name a few.

Beyond these similarities, however, I suspect there are significant differences between the initiatory practices of most indigenous peoples and my models of and practices for both the Descent to Soul and the more extensive journey of soul initiation. I explore these differences in appendix 2.

If we look carefully, we can also find signs that the journey of soul initiation — or a forerunner — may have existed for millennia in our own Western traditions. We might carefully investigate the nature of Moses's time on Mt. Sinai, Jesus's forty days in the desert, or Muhammad's time in the cave near Mecca. Something like the Descent to Soul might be detected, if you know how to look, in such Western habitats as Greek myth and rites (the Eleusinian mysteries, for example), the Arthurian legends, the sacred mythologies of the Celtic-speaking peoples, and the mysteries and occult processes of the medieval alchemists. While you're at it, examine closely the written works of the fourteenth-century Italian Dante Alighieri, the nineteenth-century Englishman William Blake, or his German contemporary Johann Wolfgang von Goethe. More recently, consider the "confrontation with the unconscious" identified and solo-navigated by Carl Jung or the descent to the goddess portrayed by Jungian therapist Sylvia Brinton Perera.[9] Reflect on "the descent into our pre-rational, our instinctive resources" that Thomas Berry urged, or his concept of "in-scendence" as the alternative now needed to transcendence.[10] Consider, too, the works of authors D. H. Lawrence, Herman Hesse, and Ursula Le Guin (especially her Earthsea Cycle); poets Coleridge, Wordsworth, Rilke, Yeats, Eliot, Manley Hopkins, William Stafford, Mary Oliver, and David Whyte; psychologists, in addition to Jung, such as Robert Johnson, James Hillman, Marion Woodman, Jean Houston, James Hollis, and Clarissa Pinkola Estés; and contemporary mythologists such as Michael Meade and Martin Shaw.

With each instance, however, I encourage you to ask: Does this really involve *soul-initiation* practices and experiences? Does it encompass some version or variation of the five-phase process I describe as the Descent to Soul? Or is it something with only intriguing similarities? With the written works, do they offer mere allusions to or an intimation of or a theoretical reference to soul initiation or the Descent, or do they describe actual living enactments of initiatory practices? Does this experience, tradition, legend, or treatise provide both a detailed map of the Descent *and* a set of specific practices for navigating it? Or even just one or the other? This book can help you frame these questions meaningfully — and perhaps find some answers.

Although not definitive, even collectively, the above examples from across time and around the world suggest to me that what I call the journey of soul initiation — or something like it, or an ancestor of it — had at one time been a core element of most or all cultures. On the other hand, I believe the initiatory practices we need now for cultural renaissance and human evolution are in vital ways unprecedented, something never-before-seen — different in structure and destination as well as in methods. (See appendix 2.) We must re-vision the journey of soul initiation in ways that fit who we are now and the threshold upon which we find ourselves standing.

Appendix Two

The Descent to Soul Compared to Rites of Passage, the Hero's Journey, and Indigenous Practices

The five phases of the Descent to Soul are both more in number and different in kind and name than the more familiar three phases popularized by the Dutch-German-French ethnographer Arnold van Gennep and the American comparative mythologist Joseph Campbell. Van Gennep's area of study was rites of passage, ceremonies enacted in all cultures to mark the major transitions of life, such as birth, puberty, marriage, and death. He was, in fact, the very person who, in 1908, coined the phrase *les rites de passage* in his book of that title and identified their three phases as *separation, transition,* and *incorporation.*[1] Campbell, whose topic of investigation was not rites of passage but the archetypal hero's journey as found in myths throughout the world, named the three phases of that journey *departure, initiation,* and *return.* In contrast, the book you hold in your hands (or see on your screen) maps the Descent to Soul, which is neither a rite of passage nor a myth, and on that account alone there should be no surprise that the phases (Preparation, Dissolution, Soul Encounter, Metamorphosis, and Enactment) are different in number, kind, and name.

Let's further unpack these differences. First, a rite of passage, as described by van Gennep, marks and supports a major life passage, which is an event, a moment in a person's life, such as puberty, pregnancy, marriage, induction into a secret society, the ordination of a priest, or the enthroning of a king. For van Gennep, these are passages between socially defined roles or statuses rather than between psychospiritual life stages. Rites of passage of these kinds are generally brief — often only a couple of hours, rarely more than a few days. The Descent to Soul, in contrast, is an extended process, a spiritual adventure that unfolds over a number of months or years and results in a radical alteration in consciousness as well as a shift in life stage — not merely or simply a change in social role.

A Descent might include a variety of ceremonies and rituals along the way, but it's much more than a rite. A Descent is a major feature or dimension of the life stage of the Cocoon and is the primary catalyst of the eventual passage (Soul Initiation) that carries a person into the next stage, the Wellspring (early Adulthood). A Descent may bring about a life passage but is entirely distinct from that passage.

Campbell, in his classic text *The Hero with a Thousand Faces*, based his understanding of the hero's journey on van Gennep's template: "The standard path of the mythological adventure of the hero is a magnification of the formula represented in the rites of passage: *separation — initiation — return*."[2] Notice, however, that two of the three terms he uses here for the phases are not those used by van Gennep (*separation — transition — incorporation*) and also that one term is different from his own sequence (*departure — initiation — return*). Campbell includes van Gennep in his bibliography and in one endnote,[3] but he doesn't mention him anywhere in the main text of the book. Nonetheless, Campbell apparently framed the hero's journey using van Gennep's model.

When I began my work as a guide, in 1980, I assumed the Descent to Soul would unfold in accord with both van Gennep's and Campbell's models, that it was both a rite of passage and a hero's journey. Only very gradually did I discover that neither model adequately informs or illuminates the experience. These models do not at all match up with the phases of the Descent to Soul: The phase of Preparation is entirely missing from the two older models; Dissolution is different from and much more than *separation* or *departure*; soul encounter is not among the kinds of *transitions* considered by van Gennep or among the array of possible experiences Campbell identified as *initiation*; and although Metamorphosis and Enactment each have some similarities to van Gennep's *incorporation* and Campbell's *return*, they are very different and much more complex.

I believe the reason Preparation is missing from both of the two older models is largely because the goals of this first phase of the Descent are dimensions of human development that take place as a matter of course in a healthy culture. I added Preparation to my model because my work has been with contemporary people who have not enjoyed the benefits of such a culture and who usually need much preliminary work before the commencement of their first Descent. So, the absence of Preparation does not suggest to me a defect in the other two models as much as a deficiency in contemporary societies.

With the second phase, Dissolution, my model diverges significantly from the other two. Unlike van Gennep's *separation* or Campbell's *departure*, Dissolution is not a mere social or vocational severance or leave-taking from everyday Village life. Rather, it's the complete and conclusive undoing of one's former psychological and social identity and the definitive ending of one's belief that any and all identities rooted in social life could ever again be fundamental to who one really is. Although the words *separation* and *departure* work well to designate a distinct phase in a rite, they do not suggest the total unmaking of an identity and life story in the way this occurs in the Dissolution phase of a Descent.

The third phase, Soul Encounter, brings about a change in consciousness and a psychospiritual shift in identity that is not primarily or necessarily social, whereas the shifts marked by most rites of passage are changes in social status — boy to young man, single to married, inductee to member, novice to priest, princess to queen. Soul Encounter for sure sets in motion a type of *transition* or *initiation* (into a Soul-infused and nature-based identity), but this isn't at all the sort of social-role transition with which van Gennep was concerned nor the kind of existential shift Campbell was tracking. Campbell summarizes his understanding of the middle phase ("initiation") of the hero's journey:

> When [the hero] arrives at the nadir of the mythological round, he undergoes a supreme ordeal and gains his reward. The triumph may be represented as the hero's sexual union with the goddess-mother of the world (sacred marriage), his recognition by the father-creator (father atonement), his own divination (apotheosis), or again — if the powers have remained unfriendly to him — his theft of the boon he came to gain (bride-theft, fire-theft); intrinsically it is an expansion of consciousness and therewith of being (illumination, transfiguration, freedom).[4]

Soul Encounter does not match any of these Campbellian images of "rewards." Indeed, Soul Encounter would not properly be deemed a "triumph" at all. It's more akin to a defeat (of the Ego), but a defeat that makes it possible for the initiate to merge with Soul and serve the world in the deepest possible way. The performance of *that* service and the fulfillment that comes with it will be the initiate's eventual reward — and it is everything one could hope for. "Triumph" is more of an early-Adolescent hero's fantasy (rescuing the damsel in distress, slaying the monster, retrieving the treasure, saving the world). Soul Encounter, moreover, is not anything like a sacred marriage with the goddess-mother of the world, nor is it father atonement or apotheosis. Those are Adolescent spiritual daydreams in which the hero is divinized — Ego inflation. Soul Encounter rewards the initiate with the opportunity to be a servant of the sacred, not a monarch or a god. Although we could say a boon is received during Soul Encounter, it is not stolen; it is the retrieval and claiming of *the identity one was born with*. When we merge with something inherently and innately our own, this is not theft. Neither is Soul Encounter an *expansion* of consciousness, as in enlightenment or illumination or any other variety of transcendent or upperworld experience,[5] but a *focusing* of consciousness through the specific Soul powers of a unique ecological niche. My definition of Soul as eco-niche and my identification of Soul Encounter as the centerpiece of the journey are probably the single biggest differences between a Campbellian hero's journey and the Descent to Soul.

The fourth Descent phase, Metamorphosis, reveals another major difference between a rite of passage and the Descent to Soul, namely the radical transformation that occurs in the structure of an initiate's psyche, not merely to their social role or status. This might explain why van Gennep didn't include such a phase, but it's unclear why Campbell didn't incorporate the dynamics inherent in Metamorphosis. It might have been because his topic was myth and not the actual experience of the Descent — even though some myths appear to be road maps for the Descent, as explored elsewhere in this book. Or Campbell might have simply overlooked this thread of the mythological pattern due to his focus on Freudian themes and on the goal of spiritual transcendence or divine union as espoused by Eastern spiritualities.[6] Metamorphosis is the phase of the Descent when the Ego is actually shape-shifted into something useful to the world, a dynamic Campbell neglected.

The final phase of the Descent, Enactment, is made possible primarily by the metamorphosis of the Ego, not by a change in social status, as in a rite of passage, and not by the mere possession of a boon or gift, as in Campbell's reading of the universal "monomyth" of the hero's journey. What is enacted is also not what Campbell refers to as "illumination," the hero as "perfected, unspecific, universal man," or "the knowledge of...unity in multiplicity."[7] Rather, it is the unique and specific genius and singular Soul gift of the initiated woman or man. The transcendent goal and outcome of Campbell's hero's journey — enlightenment, universality, or unity — is in stark contrast to the goal and outcome of the Descent to Soul: the unique, nature-based, and world-serving embodiment of mythopoetic identity.

Although van Gennep's and Campbell's models do not at all match up with the phases of the Descent to Soul, they do accord with my understanding of the journey of soul initiation (JoSI), but only in terms of overall structure: JoSI begins with a *separation* or *departure*, in this case from the life stage of early Adolescence, enters a long period of *transition* or *initiation* corresponding to the entire life stage of the Cocoon, and ends with an *incorporation* into the life stage of the Wellspring. But, as we've seen, JoSI is a far cry from a rite of passage, not the least difference being the duration — several years or more for JoSI compared to a few days at most for nearly all rites of passage. More generally, JoSI is a complex developmental sequence, while a rite of passage is the marking of a single transition from one life stage to the next (or, in other instances, from one social status to another).

Although JoSI can be understood as a version of Campbell's hero's journey (*departure — initiation — return*), the core feature of JoSI, the Descent with its encounter with Soul, is not, as we saw above, among the array of possible experiences in what Campbell understood as the myth of "the hero with a thousand faces."

Let's also consider how this book's models of the Descent to Soul and of JoSI might compare and contrast — in terms of methods, structure, and outcome — with the initiatory processes of earlier and current indigenous traditions. I can't offer a definitive comparison here simply because I'm not aware of any explicit analyses of either the structure or outcome of indigenous versions of the Descent or of·the larger journey of soul initiation. I've read and heard intriguing accounts of indigenous initiatory practices (some are noted in appendix 1), but not structural analyses. Respectful questions and speculation are nonetheless possible.

First, the structure of the Descent may or may not be different from indigenous models in the four ways noted above with regard to Campbell's and van Gennep's models. When making comparisons between a particular indigenous practice and the models in this book, we might ask: (1) Does it include a Dissolution phase and is that phase "only" a social or vocational severance or leave-taking from everyday Village life, or is it, as in my model, a complete and conclusive undoing of one's former psychological and social identity and the definitive ending of one's belief that any and all identities rooted in social life could ever again be fundamental to who one really is? (2) Does it include a Soul Encounter phase, and does this involve not a union with Spirit or the discovery or gaining of a new social role but a revelation of one's unique place in the greater web of life? (3) Does it include a Metamorphosis phase of significant duration that brings about a change in consciousness and a psychospiritual shift in identity that is not primarily or necessarily social? (4) Does it include an Enactment phase, in which the initiate gradually learns to embody their new identity in their human community?

If there turns out to be significant differences between the indigenous practice in question and the Descent as modeled here, this would not render either as "better" than the other — only as something different.

What about the methods used — the particular techniques, practices, and ceremonies? How much overlap is there with those described in this and my earlier books?

What about the outcome of the practice? Within a given indigenous tradition, does their version of what might be the Descent result in a discovery that corresponds to what I name mythopoetic identity, and is this identity a way of fathoming what I refer to as a person's unique psycho-ecological niche? (In other words, do they have a similar concept of *soul*?) In addition to the mere discovery of this identity, does the Descent result in a transformation of the structure and nature of the Ego — such that it becomes capable of serving the more-than-human world as an agent of or handmaiden for Soul?

My speculation is that most indigenous initiatory practices (those that result in initiated Adulthood) have some similarities to but also significant differences from the model of the Descent presented here — in terms of methods, structure, and/or outcome. I make no claim that the model and practices described in this book are more effective or better than any indigenous traditions, past or present — only that they are likely different and necessarily so; each culture must fashion its own unique, authentic, and always-evolving methods for supporting the maturation of its people.

Second, considering the larger journey of soul initiation, does the indigenous culture in question differentiate between two distinct stages of Adolescence and the ways both stages are different from Adulthood? (See chapter 1 and *Nature and the Human Soul.*) Does this culture understand developmental tasks as one of the core features of a developmental stage? If so, how do they describe the tasks of childhood and adolescence? In their developmental journey from childhood to adulthood, are there two additional major life passages *after puberty*? Do these passages correspond in some way to those I name Confirmation and Soul Initiation? As for the outcome of the journey, what is the indigenous understanding of or definition of initiated adulthood? How does this compare with the definition in this book of Adulthood? What are the various methods used for supporting the process of maturation?

I suspect that my model of the journey of soul initiation, with its three distinct life stages and two passages (after puberty), involves a conception of adolescence you'll not find in indigenous traditions. First, my model has two stages of Adolescence, and indigenous traditions may have only one — and possibly none at all if the individual, as a result of the journey, is understood to transition directly from childhood to adulthood. In *Nature and the Human Soul*, I discuss how Adolescence itself, as I understand it, may be an evolutionary advance that has become apparent only in the last few centuries and may never have existed before in the human story. I also discuss how the potentials inherent in this advance (which have to do with the higher development of human imagination) have not yet been realized, although the necessary structures of psyche are already in place.

As I explore in the Coda, the kind of Ego that results from the contemporary journey of soul initiation may be one that has not appeared before in human evolution, an Ego capable of imagining futures that are so different from any previous human experience that the word *future* itself must be re-visioned.

Appendix Three

Additional Dissolution Practices

A long with the ten dissolution strategies described in chapter 4, there are many other practices for supporting the unraveling of identity, the deconstruction of the old story, and our courageous crossing into the unknown. Some are employed within the context of group process or ceremony. Others, such as soulcentric dreamwork, are best facilitated by a soul-initiation guide. Yet others would be too complex to describe in these pages.

Dissolution practices not mentioned in chapter 4 but that you can use without a guide include these: praising out loud the other-than-human beings of our world; walks and talks with Death as your companion; memorizing poems that assist you to access underworld consciousness; composing your own poetry — or any other form of writing by which you slip into the underworld of meaning, symbol, and significance (the dreamtime); extreme physical exertion; extended solo times in the dark (especially in wild places); and wandering in wild or semi-wild terrain, seeking particular spots in which you experience a thinning of the boundaries between the mundane and the sacred, between the civilized and the wild, between you and not-you — I call these spots "portals" — and then spending time in these spots, letting them do their work on you.

Also, here is a list of Dissolution practices described in my previous books, *Soulcraft, Nature and the Human Soul,* and *Wild Mind.* As noted below, some of these are related to practices described in chapter 4:

- Honing the Skills of Self-Reliance (physical, social, psychological, and spiritual; *Soulcraft,* page 81)
- Relinquishing Attachment to Your Former Identity (*Soulcraft,* page 85; has an effect similar to the practices, in this book, of "The One-Way Portal Ceremony," pages 104–5, and "Unplugging from the Matrix," pages 105–7)
- The Death Lodge (a ceremony for making peace with your past; *Soulcraft,* page 105, and *Nature and the Human Soul,* page 264; this ceremony can

support "The One-Way Portal Ceremony," pages 104–5, and "Unplugging from the Matrix," pages 105–7)

- The Art of Disidentification through Meditation (to help you loosen your grip on your former identity, which you are going to lose during Dissolution; *Soulcraft*, page 109, and *Nature and the Human Soul*, page 266; this practice, also, can support "The One-Way Portal Ceremony," pages 104–5, and "Unplugging from the Matrix," pages 105–7)
- Sacred Speech (communicating what has meaning and value and what deepens your journey) and Ritual Silence (*Soulcraft*, page 159)
- Trance Drumming and Rhythms, and Trance Dance (methods for entering trance states, opening the door to the underworld, and unearthing what lies beneath your surface life; *Soulcraft*, page 160)
- Ceremonial Sweats and Saunas (practices for altering consciousness, communing with the Others, and entering the underworld; *Soulcraft*, page 165)
- Talking Across the Species Boundaries (dialogues with other-than-humans; *Soulcraft*, page 167)
- Self-Designed Ceremony (those that amplify Dissolution; *Soulcraft*, page 183; in this book, see "The One-Way Portal Ceremony," pages 104–5, "The Mandorla," pages 107–9, and "Self-Designed Ceremonies," page 276)
- The Fire Ceremony (a way of relinquishing attachment to your former identity; *Soulcraft*, page 185; this can support "The One-Way Portal Ceremony," pages 104–5 of this book, and "Unplugging from the Matrix," pages 105–7)
- Body Practices for Altering Consciousness (for bridging the inner and outer, the seen and unseen, and making the unconscious conscious; *Soulcraft*, page 208)
- The Art of Solitude (to help you discover what truly brings you alive and what doesn't; *Soulcraft*, page 233, and *Nature and the Human Soul*, page 276)
- Wandering in Wild Places (to deepen your connection with the wild world, which is the realm of Soul, and to cultivate a sensibility of wonder and surprise; *Soulcraft*, page 241, and *Nature and the Human Soul*, page 278; this practice is related to and supplements "Romancing the World and Dwelling in the Wild," pages 100–103)
- The Art of Being Lost (to cultivate nonattachment to your former life goals; *Soulcraft*, page 247; in this book, related to "Relinquishing Attachment to Outcomes," page 100, "The One-Way Portal Ceremony," pages 104–5, and "Unplugging from the Matrix," pages 105–7)
- The Art of Soulful Romance (to further destabilize the Ego; *Soulcraft*, page 280; in this book, related to "Romancing the World," pages 100–103)

- Befriending the Dark (a ceremony for cultivating your comfort and intimacy with the unknown; *Soulcraft*, page 253; this practice can support "Grief Work," pages 98–99 in this book, "Full-Bodied Experience of All Emotions," page 99, "Surrendering to Your Deepest Longing," pages 99–100, and "The Obstacle Threshold," pages 109–11)
- Confronting Your Own Death, Inviting Death as an Advisor, and Writing Your Eulogy (practices for cultivating nonattachment to your former identity; *Soulcraft*, page 263, and *Nature and the Human Soul*, page 280; these practices, also, can support "The One-Way Portal Ceremony," pages 104–5, and "Unplugging from the Matrix," pages 105–7)

Appendix Four

The Enactment Phase during the Cocoon versus the Wellspring

This appendix explores the differences in how Enactment is experienced depending on the life stage you're in at the time. While you're reading this appendix, it might be helpful to look at the diagrams of the Descent to Soul (page 21) and the Eco-Soulcentric Developmental Wheel (page 34). It would also be good to keep in mind that the Descent to Soul has *phases*, while the Eco-Soulcentric Wheel has *stages* — this will help you distinguish the spiritual adventure of the Descent from the developmental progression of life stages.

The Enactment Phase during the Cocoon

The transition from *phase* four to *phase* five of the Descent (from Metamorphosis to Enactment) is not at all the same as the passage from *life stage* four to *life stage* five (from the Cocoon to the Wellspring). When you're in an Enactment phase of a Descent while in the Cocoon stage (a phase five in stage four), you're still in the mystery school that is the Cocoon; you haven't yet "graduated," which is to say you've not yet gone through Soul Initiation. But you *are* consciously embodying your mythopoetic identity for your people to see. It's just that you're doing this through actions and projects that do not require a true delivery system. Rather, you're embodying your mythopoetic identity through everyday endeavors or the skills of your earlier vocation — embodiments that serve others or the world. You're getting invaluable practice inhabiting your unique ecological niche. Doing this is part of your Cocoon-stage Enactment phase, which supports further Ego reshaping and helps bring about your eventual Soul Initiation, your passage into the Wellspring. Although your Experimental Threshold Crossings during the prior phase (Metamorphosis) will probably have no obvious relation to the Big Life Project to which you'll dedicate your Adult years, your Enactment activities just might be fledgling versions thereof.

The Enactment Phase during the Wellspring

When you're in an Enactment phase of a Descent while you're in the Wellspring stage (phase five, stage five), you're no longer in the mystery school of the Cocoon. You've been through the life passage of Soul Initiation and you've probably been honing a delivery system for a while. But because you're in the Enactment phase of a Descent, you're now consciously embodying a "new" (perhaps deeper) dimension of your mythopoetic identity, something you discovered during the Soul Encounter phase of this Descent, an embodiment made possible by its Metamorphosis phase. Being in this stage-five Enactment enables you to practice weaving this new dimension of your mythopoetic identity into your existing delivery system, thereby modifying that delivery system — or, perhaps, discovering through your Enactment activities that you need to identify and cultivate an entirely new delivery system. For example: When Joanna Macy was in the Wellspring, she received a blessing from a Buddhist sage, an experience that led to her third soul encounter — a series of visions of neural nets and of branching tree limbs and roots. These visions in turn reshaped her psyche in such a way that when she was introduced to general systems theory during a university course, she recognized it immediately as a way to understand the patterns in her recent visions. General systems theory became a second essential strand of her first delivery system for being a stone in the bridge between the ancient East and the modern West (see "A Third Soul Encounter," pages 325–26).

During an Enactment phase that takes place early in the Wellspring stage, you'll most likely be asking these questions: Will my prior or current vocation, craft, career, and/or skill set be useful in my future delivery systems? If so, in what ways, and in what ways not? Before your first soul encounter, your career or craft was merely your job or hobby. You didn't yet have a delivery system because you had no awareness or understanding of what was yours to deliver — and your Ego had not yet been refashioned in a way that made delivery possible. Then, following your first soul encounter, you have this question, for the first time in your life, about future delivery systems.

Perhaps the skills and knowledge you developed before your first Descent will be relevant to your Wellspring delivery system. Maybe they won't. In any case, you'll need to develop skills and acquire knowledge you do not yet possess. Maybe you'll be able to deliver your soul gifts within the context of your previous vocation, job, or career, but if so, it's likely you'll need to develop a new delivery system within that context. Or maybe an entirely different job or social role would be more suited to your mythopoetic identity. You might continue, however, to operate within your former role until you're ready to move to or develop a new one. After all, you need a survival dance as well as a sacred dance.

Although Descents may be much less common during the Wild Orchard (life stage six), they do occur. Given that we never entirely complete the tasks of any earlier life stage, we might find ourselves descending into Soul Canyon while in the Wild Orchard in order to address an incomplete task of the Cocoon, namely the encounter with Soul. There's always more to discover about Soul, and additional ways that Soul wants to transform the Ego. The only difference in an Enactment phase while in the Wild Orchard compared to the Wellspring is that the delivery system you're now modifying is a unique, never-before-seen craft or art that you've been developing ever since you entered the Wild Orchard.

Glossary

In this book (and my others), I use many common words and expressions in uncommon ways. I also use some not-so-common phrases and even personally coined neologisms. In this glossary, I specify my meanings. Some psychologists say many of these terms cannot be usefully defined. Saying so confuses the realm of meaning with the realm of facts. What we mean by a word is nonempirical — and, in particular, *pre*empirical. In order to meaningfully discover what the facts are (the empirical goal), we must first be clear what subject matter we intend to investigate (the preempirical requirement); we must first be able to say, as clearly as possible, what it is we're intending to study or research. (I'm not referring here to so-called "operational definitions," which are not real definitions.) Otherwise, we wouldn't know if what we discovered had anything to do with what we thought or merely claimed we were studying. Any "findings" about "soul," for example, are indeterminate or meaningless unless we can, before beginning our research, be explicit and clear about what it is we mean by "soul." Otherwise, we might have thought we were researching soul, when it turns out we were actually investigating something else entirely — the anima, perhaps, or the collective unconscious, vocational purpose, morality, the Ego, or even the brain.

For an explanation of why I capitalize some words and not others, see the Author's Note (page xiii).

All bolded words below are defined in this glossary.

Adolescence: Not a chronological age range (our teen years) but a psychosocial life stage, divided into early and late Adolescence. Early Adolescence has one **ecocentric** version (**the Oasis**) and several **egocentric** versions (such as **Conforming and Rebelling**). Late Adolescence has only an ecocentric version (**the Cocoon**). (For more specific definitions of Adolescence, see the **Oasis**, the **Cocoon**, and **Conforming and Rebelling**. Also see diagram, page 34.)

Adulthood: Also known as true or **ecocentric** Adulthood, this is the life stage whose central feature is the conscious inhabiting of the unique **eco-niche** a person was born to inhabit, during which they deliver their singular gift to the **more-than-human world**. An Adult is someone who experiences themself, first and foremost, as a member of the Earth community, who has had one or more revelatory experiences of their unique place in that ecological community, and who is embodying that unique place as a gift to their people and to the Earth community. Doing so makes them an agent of evolution — and, in an **egocentric, patho-adolescent** society like ours, an agent of revolution. All Adults are visionary artisans of cultural evolution. (See diagram, page 34.)

anima/animus: Jung's terms for, respectively, the feminine "personality" within a man, and the masculine "personality" within a woman, both generally unconscious, according to Jung. In its healthy form, the anima is often a version of what I call the **Dark Muse-Beloved** (the West facet of wholeness) of people of any gender. (Jung's "negative anima" and "negative animus" are subpersonalities, not facets of wholeness.)

center of gravity: The hub of a person's life, the priorities and focus that their day-to-day existence revolves around. For example, in early **Adolescence**, center of gravity is peer group, sex, and society. In late Adolescence, it's the **underworld**, or the mysteries of nature and psyche. And in early **Adulthood**, it's the depths of one's culture (the *embodied* mysteries of nature and psyche). Center of gravity illuminates the deep structure of a life stage, helping us understand what people in that stage find most compelling. The way you can tell a person is about to move into the next stage is that their center of gravity begins to shift in that direction. (See diagram, page 34.)

Cocoon: Ecocentric late **Adolescence**, the fourth of eight life stages in the **Eco-Soulcentric Developmental Wheel**, in which the **Descent to Soul** first becomes possible. The human archetype of this stage is the **Wanderer**. The culture-oriented task is leaving home (departing from the early-Adolescent identity). The nature-oriented task is exploring the mysteries of nature and psyche. The psychospiritual **center of gravity** is the **underworld** (the mysteries of nature and psyche). The trajectory of this stage is toward the experiential encounter with **Soul**. (See diagram, page 34.)

Confirmation: The life passage between the stage of the **Oasis** and the stage of the **Cocoon**, the passage during which the **center of gravity** shifts from peer group, sex, and society to the mysteries of nature and psyche. What is confirmed are the adequate completion of the tasks of the Oasis (the adequate completion of an early-**Adolescent** personality, one that is both authentic and socially accepted) and the readiness to embark upon the **journey of soul initiation**. (See diagram, page 34.)

Conforming and Rebelling: An **egocentric** version of early **Adolescence** in which people either conform to or rebel against mainstream egocentric society; a way of life that emphasizes social acceptability, materialism, self-centered individualism, and superficial security rather than authenticity, intimate relationships, soul-infused individual service, and creative risk and adventure (as in the **ecocentric** early-**Adolescent** stage of the **Oasis**).

Core Wound: A psychospiritual wounding so distressing we form our primary childhood survival strategies in reaction to it, so hurtful that much of our personal style and sensitivities have their roots there. Unlike the ordinary hurts and injuries of everyday life, our Core Wound arises from the convergence of a preexisting innate vulnerability or sensitivity and one or more wounding events. The Core Wound, which is not healable, holds secrets of our **Soul**. When we experientially reenter our Core Wound during the **journey of soul initiation**, our **Ego** is shifted toward Soul, and the Core Wound becomes a Sacred Wound.

Dark Muse-Beloved: The West facet of the **Self** (see page 48).

delivery system: A role, craft, trade, profession, style, or art for enacting your **Soul**'s desires — your **eco-niche** — within your particular culture, time, and place.

Descent to Soul: A psychospiritual expedition into one particular precinct of the **underworld** — the precinct I call **Soul Canyon** — and, if fortunate, the eventual emergence from those depths having been radically transformed by an encounter with **Soul**. The Descent is the most significant element of the **journey of soul initiation**. A Descent can, however, also occur one or more times after the journey of soul initiation. The Descent to Soul has five phases: Preparation, **Dissolution**, **Soul Encounter**, **Metamorphosis**, and **Enactment**. (See diagram, page 21.)

Dissolution: The second phase of a **Descent to Soul**. What occurs in this phase is the dismemberment of who you believed you were, the unconditional disintegration of everything you believed the world was, the definitive end of the story you have been living, everything that enabled you to get the things done that you thought essential to who you were and who you could become. (See diagram, page 21.)

Eco-awakening: The transition from **egocentrism** to **ecocentrism** — the major life passage from egocentric early **Adolescence** (such as the stage of **Conforming and Rebelling**) to the ecocentric early-Adolescent life stage of the **Oasis**. Eco-awakening occurs when someone has their first conscious and embodied experience of their innate membership in the Earth community.

ecocentrism: Holding the greater Earth community (the ecosphere) as central in importance; contrasts with both **egocentrism** (holding the individual conscious self as central) and anthropocentrism (humanity as central).

ecological niche (eco-niche): A person or thing's unique place, role, or function in a particular ecosystem. See **Soul**.

Applying it to humans, I refer to this sometimes as our *psycho*-ecological niche. By adding the *psycho*, I am highlighting that our human niche in the **more-than-human world** has an intrinsic psychological dimension. Our eco-niche is not just a matter of where we fit in the food chain. More important is what we bring to the evolution of the *anima mundi*, the soul of the world, the way we're able to enhance and enrich the relational net made up of and shared by all living things. A distinguishing characteristic of our human eco-niche is something psychological or noetic: our particular mode of consciousness, namely our conscious self-awareness.

Eco-Soulcentric Developmental Wheel: A model of human development rooted in the cycles and qualities of the natural world. It describes what the stages of human development look like when we grow with nature and **Soul** as our primary guides: We take root in a childhood of innocence and wonder; sprout into an **Adolescence** of creative fire and mystery-probing adventures; blossom into an authentic **Adulthood** of cultural artistry and visionary leadership; and finally ripen into a seed-scattering **Elderhood** of wisdom, grace, and the holistic tending of the **more-than-human world**. (See diagram, page 34.)

Ego: The conscious self; the locus, or seat, of conscious self-awareness within the human **psyche**, the "I"; a fragment of the psyche observing the rest of itself from a psychological distance. (See also **3-D Ego**.)

egocentrism: Holding the **Ego** — the individual conscious self — as the most important element of the human **psyche** and as the center of personal existence. Contrasts with **ecocentrism**.

Elder: Someone who, following their years of true **Adulthood**, now occupies their **ecological niche** without effort, freeing them for the Elder task of caring for the **Soul** of the **more-than-human world**, an endeavor with even greater scope, depth, and fulfillment than that of Adulthood. An Elder cares for the Soul of the world by defending and nurturing the innocence and wonder of children, mentoring early **Adolescents**, guiding late Adolescents on the **journey of soul initiation**, mentoring Adults in their soul work, supporting the evolution of the culture, and maintaining the balance between the **Village** and the greater Earth community. A true Elder contrasts with an "older," an aging uninitiated person. True Elders have become rare in our world. (See diagram, page 34.)

Enactment: The fifth and final phase of the **Descent to Soul**, when you begin to embody your **mythopoetic identity** through acts of service to your community — when you launch your giveaway, the wholehearted performance of your **vision**. (See diagram, page 21.)

Experimental Threshold Crossings (ETCs): Practices for embodying your **mythopoetic identity** before you're ready for **Enactment** or to choose or develop a **delivery system** — practices that reshape your **Ego** to be a channel for that identity. ETCs are your primary activities during **Metamorphosis** for bridging between the experience of **soul encounter** and the eventual cultivation of a delivery system to embody your **Soul** as a gift to others.

inner protectors: See **subpersonalities**.

Innocent/Sage: The East facet of the **Self** (see page 48).

journey of soul initiation (JoSI): The extended developmental process of searching for **Soul**, encountering Soul, and being shape-shifted by that encounter. JoSI takes you from the end of one particular life stage (the **Oasis, ecocentric** early **Adolescence**), across the passage of **Confirmation** into a second stage (the **Cocoon**, ecocentric late Adolescence), through the Cocoon and then across the next passage of **Soul Initiation**, which is the start of the life stage of the **Wellspring** (early **Adulthood**). Using a bigger lens, the journey of soul initiation could be understood as starting as early as conception or birth and ending with death. (See diagram, page 34.)

Mandorla: Literally, the almond shape formed at the center of two partly overlapping circles — *mandorla* being the Italian word for "almond." The Mandorla symbolizes the interplay of opposites and the inherent tension between them, the interaction and interdependence between apparent contraries.

The Mandorla Practice is a way to amplify the tension of a pair of opposites within your **psyche** in order to crack yourself open and quicken your plummet toward **Soul**. (See pages 107–9.)

Metamorphosis: The fourth phase of a **Descent to Soul**, in which the **Ego** is shape-shifted in light of and in accordance with the revelation or **vision** in the previous phase of **Soul Encounter**. (See diagram, page 21.)

middleworld: Our everyday, waking identity and state of consciousness — the personal and interpersonal world of **Ego**. This is the domain of family, friends, school, work, business, politics, community, and the natural environment in which we exist. It includes the practical embodiment of our soul work.

molting: A significant change in a person's social, vocational, geographical, religious, therapeutic, or other **middleworld** circumstances, especially when it occurs in psychological early **Adolescence** (in either the **ecocentric Oasis** or in an **egocentric**

stage such as **Conforming and Rebelling**). Not to be confused with the **Metamorphosis** phase of the **Descent to Soul**.

more-than-human world: Cultural ecologist David Abram's term for our larger world that includes the human realm as one element or subset; in other words, the not *merely* human world. Not to be confused with the *other*-than-human world, the self-organizing world beyond the human **Village** or outside the walls of our homes. Synonyms: the Earth Community; the greater web of life.

Muse: See **Dark Muse-Beloved**.

Mystery: The universal consciousness, intelligence, psyche, or vast imagination that animates the cosmos and everything in it, including us, and in which the **psyche** of each person participates. Common synonyms include Spirit, God, and the nondual. When consciously attuned to Mystery, we experience a profound connectedness with all things — the "oneness" of Mystery. The manner in which Mystery manifests itself or unfolds has been called, to cite just three examples, evolution's trajectory, the Tao (the way of life), or the Universe story.

mythopoetic identity: The way we consciously identify and experience the nature of **Soul** — namely, through metaphor in the form of poetic or mythic images or patterns. Since it's not possible to directly describe our **eco-niche** in everyday descriptive language, we comprehend and appreciate it mythopoetically. Essentially what Carl Jung meant by "personal myth."

Nature-Based Map of the Human Psyche: A map of psychological wholeness — a nonarbitrary and comprehensive map because it uses the template of nature's own map of wholeness. It serves as a guide to becoming fully human by cultivating the four facets of the **Self** and discovering both the limitations and the gifts of the four groups of our wounded, fragmented, and shadowed **subpersonalities**. It maps all these elements of the **psyche** onto the qualities of the natural world that we observe in the cardinal directions as well as the characteristics of the four seasons and the four times of day: dawn, noon, dusk, and midnight.

Nurturing Generative Adult: The North facet of the **Self** (see page 47).

Oasis: Ecocentric early **Adolescence**, the third of eight life stages in the **Eco-Soulcentric Developmental Wheel**, the stage that follows the passage of puberty; the time of foundational social individuation. The human archetype of this stage is the Thespian. The culture-oriented task in the Oasis is the creation of a secure and socially accepted personality. The nature-oriented task is the cultivation of social authenticity. The psychospiritual **center of gravity** is peer group, sex, and society. The goal of the Oasis is to find a genuine way of belonging and a group to be faithful to. When successful, the Adolescent gradually differentiates a persona, a personality, an individuality, one that has an endorsed place in the social world — a place that is respected and deemed worthy by both self and others in a peer group or community. This results in an **Ego** ready for the **journey of soul initiation**, which begins in the next stage, the **Cocoon**. (See diagram, page 34.)

patho-adolescence: A pathological version of **Conforming and Rebelling**; often a life centered in greed, self-centeredness, shame, addiction, and, for some, violence; the effect **egocentric** society inflicts on many of its citizens; not normal for humans.

psyche: Our capacity or faculty to experience, both consciously and unconsciously — including through dreams, thoughts, perceptions, imaginings, memories, and feelings. Most people use the word *psyche* as if it refers to a nonphysical structure or thing (a "mind") or even equate it with the physical brain (a dreadful conceptual error), but psyche is actually a capacity, attribute, or characteristic of all sentient beings, such as humans, bears, birds, or trees. Each being has unique qualities of psyche.

psycho-ecological niche: See **ecological niche**.

psychospiritual center of gravity: See **center of gravity**.

rite of passage: A ceremony or other event that marks and supports (1) a major life passage, such as birth, puberty, **Confirmation**, or **Soul Initiation**, or (2) a passage between socially defined roles or statuses, as with school graduation; induction into a social, vocational, or military group; completion of a personal growth program; ordination; or marriage.

Sacred Wound: See **Core Wound**.

Self: A bundle of innate resources all humans have in common, an integral whole that holds all the original capacities of our core humanness. The Self incorporates the four facets of our "horizontal" wholeness, which exist at birth but only as possibilities that we may or may not learn to access, actualize, and embody. The four facets of the Self (the **Nurturing Generative Adult**, the **Innocent/Sage**, the **Wild Indigenous One**, and the **Dark Muse-Beloved**) can be described in terms of archetypes — universal patterns of human behavior and character found in all cultures and in myths, dreams, art, and literature. The **Nature-Based Map of the Human Psyche** maps the four facets onto the qualities of the natural world. The Self contains all the resources we need to meaningfully contribute to our **more-than-human world**; to live a mature, fulfilling, creative human life; to effectively manifest our **Soul**'s desires; and to align ourselves with **Spirit**'s unfolding.

The Self is similar to but different than Carl Jung's concept of the "self." Jung described the "self" as "the totality of the personality": "The self is not only the center but also the whole circumference which embraces both conscious and unconscious;

it is the center of this totality, just as the ego is the center of consciousness" (Jung, *Memories, Dreams, Reflections,* 398). Jung and I both refer to a totality that encompasses both conscious and unconscious elements, but I mean something less than Jung — but more focused. For me, the Self is our "horizontal" wholeness (the four facets) but not our "vertical" wholeness (Soul and Spirit) and not the **Ego**. For Jung, the "self" is the totality of the **psyche**; presumably, this would include what I mean by Soul, Spirit, Ego, and **subpersonalities,** and in this sense, I mean a smaller totality than Jung. Paradoxically and perplexingly, however, Jung also says that the "self" is the center of the psyche. For Jung, the "self" includes the ego. For me, the Self and the Ego are separate, but the Ego can have some degree of conscious access to the Self. (In fact, what I call the cultivation of wholeness is the process of the Ego developing conscious access to the Self.) For me, the Self and the Ego are categorically different kinds of things: The Self is a set of resources, while the Ego is the seat of conscious self-awareness; the Self does not have its own separate consciousness the way the Ego does. For me, by defining the Self as something less than Jung's "self," it's easier to describe a variety of psychological phenomena, and it avoids the paradox of something being both the totality and the center. In another sense, however, my concept of the Self is more than Jung's "self" in that I have more fully differentiated it by specifically describing its four facets (in addition to its four **windows of knowing**).

Self-healing: The process of healing our psychological woundedness by embracing our **subpersonalities**. Self-healing utilizes the compassionate perspective of the Self to cultivate acceptance of our subpersonalities. The goal is also to hone our ability to continue functioning from the Self when one of our subpersonalities tries to take over. In this way, we gradually cultivate a mature **Ego** that can act and speak for our subpersonalities rather than from them.

Shadow: Elements of our own psyches that are unknown to the Ego *and* incompatible with the Ego's beliefs about itself. The Shadow (as I mean it) is not what we know about ourselves, don't like, and keep hidden; rather, the Shadow is what is true about us that we don't know — don't know at all — and, if accused of, would adamantly and sincerely deny. The repression (rendering unconscious) of our characteristics and desires unacceptable or inconceivable to our **Ego** is one of the ways our **psyche** tries to keep us safe. (The Shadow corresponds to the West **subpersonality**.) Shadow characteristics can be either "negative/sinister" (what the Ego would consider morally "beneath" it) or "positive/golden" (what the Ego would consider "above" it and out of reach).

Soul: A person or thing's unique, innate niche in the Earth community. To discover our unique **eco-niche**, we must go through an initiatory process if and when we are developmentally prepared to do so. We become conscious of our Soul — if we ever do — through metaphor, through poetic or mythic images or patterns that I call **mythopoetic identity**. For me, *Soul* is an ecological concept, not a psychological one, and not a spiritual or religious one.

My definition of Soul is distinct from both Carl Jung's and James Hillman's. Jung wrote mostly in German, and the German word *Seele* means both "psyche" and "soul." But Jung was careful to define both of these English words: "I have been compelled, in my investigations into the structure of the unconscious, to make a conceptual distinction between *soul* and *psyche*. By *psyche*, I understand the totality of all psychic processes, conscious as well as unconscious. By *soul*, on the other hand, I understand a clearly demarcated functional complex that can best be described as a 'personality'" (Jung, *Psychological Types*, def. 48, par. 797). More specifically, Jung used the word *soul* to refer to the **anima**.

Hillman, in *The Soul's Code*, employs a great variety of terms for something similar or related to what I mean by Soul or mythopoetic identity — including "soul," "innate image," "acorn," "calling," "character," "daimon," "genius," and "destiny." It turns out, however, that what he's referring to, primarily, is an image we access in childhood of what we'll be doing later in life; for Hillman, this is not mythopoetically identified but rather described in everyday terms of vocation, craft, social role, and so on. Hillman, for example, understood Judy Garland's acorn or image to be her singing, Thomas Wolfe's as book writing, and the calling of the famous Spaniard Manolete as bullfighting. So, by "soul," Hillman is referring to what I would call a **delivery system** for Soul, not mythopoetic identity and not eco-niche.

Soul Canyon: A metaphorical image for the psychospiritual terrain of the middle three phases of the **Descent to Soul**. (See **underworld**.)

soulcentric: Holding the **Soul** as most important and the center of individual existence. Contrasts with **egocentrism**.

soulcentric dreamwork: An approach that does not interpret dream images or seek meanings or messages from dreams but, rather, ushers the dreamer back into the full experience of the dream so that the dream can do its transformative work on the dreamer's **Ego**. Soulcentric dreamwork is divergent from most other contemporary Western methods, which seek to mine the dream, to extract from it information, messages, or guidance for use in the dreamer's everyday **middleworld** life; this is the Ego doing its interpretive work on the dream rather than allowing the dream to do its transformative work on the Ego.

Soulcraft: A contemporary, Western, and nature-rooted path to the *terra mysterium* of **Soul Initiation**. Soulcraft has been shaped and influenced by wilderness rites and writers, the theories and practices of depth- and eco-psychologies, the poetic tradition, perspectives and practices common to current and earlier traditions of animism and Earth-honoring, the lived experiences of thousands of contemporary people, and the wild Earth herself. Soulcraft practices include dreamwork and deep-imagery journeys, solo ceremonies and exercises while wandering on the land, trance dancing and drumming, council work, storytelling, vision fasts, symbolic artwork, soul-oriented poetry, **Shadow** work, and communicating with birds, trees, the winds, and the land and waters.

Soul Encounter/soul encounter: When capitalized, this refers to the third and central phase of the **Descent to Soul**, a phase in which soul encounters occur. (See diagram, page 21.) Not to be confused with **Soul Initiation**.

When lowercase, *soul encounter* refers to the **vision** or revelation itself, an experience of a **Soul** image, symbol, or story — something numinous or sacred at the very core of a person's individual life, and which mythopoetically communicates something of their unique, innate **ecological niche**.

Soul Initiation: The life passage from the **Cocoon** (ecocentric late **Adolescence**) to the **Wellspring** (early **Adulthood**), the passage that consummates the **journey of soul initiation**. This is the moment when our life becomes firmly rooted in the desires of our **Soul**, when the embodiment of Soul becomes our highest priority. (See diagram, page 34.)

Soul Initiation is not to be confused with either **Soul Encounter** or **soul encounter**. Soul Encounter is a phase of the **Descent to Soul**; a soul encounter is a type of experience; and Soul Initiation is the transition between two specific developmental stages.

soul powers: The powers that enable us to successfully occupy and embody our unique **eco-niche**, to take our ultimate place in the world, to manifest our **Soul**. Soul powers consist of the particular abilities, knowledge, and values that are especially easy for us to develop or acquire and that we're able to hone to exceptional degrees. We need these powers to fulfill our eco-niche, but having these powers is not the same as having that niche. It's possible for some other people to have and develop those powers without having that niche. And it's possible to have that eco-niche (and know it) without yet having honed those powers, the powers necessary to successfully occupy that niche.

Spirit: See **Mystery**.

subpersonalities ("subs"): The sometimes hidden fragments of our human psyches — such as our Victim, Rebel, Critic, Tyrant, Addict, or Shadow — each of which attempts to protect us from further injury using childhood survival strategies. Also known as our inner protectors, our subs are constellations of feelings, images, and behaviors that operate more or less independently from one another and often independently of our conscious selves (**Egos**). Subpersonalities form in childhood, with the enduring purpose of protecting us from physical, psychological, and social harm. Often they succeed, but in the process they invariably create a great variety of other problems — for others as well as ourselves. Our subs are the source or instigators of what Western psychology understands to be our psychological symptoms and illnesses.

3-D Ego: A three-dimensional **Ego** — an Ego blessed with some degree of conscious communion and integration with **Self**, **Soul**, and **Spirit**; a mature Ego. It's "3-D" if you imagine Self as the horizontal plane with its four cardinal directions; Soul as the downward direction; and Spirit as the upward direction.

trauma: *Not* the occurrence of deeply distressing or overwhelming experiences but, rather, what we do within our psyches to protect ourselves — mostly unconsciously — from the psychological, social, and physical impact of those experiences. Our protective measures are specifically our **subpersonality** survival strategies. The trauma is created and sustained not by the original disturbing experience but by the reactions of our subpersonalities — most often without our awareness of what our subs are up to or why. The primary way we protect ourselves is our Escapists' (East) strategy of disconnecting us from the affective and somatic dimensions of these experiences (our emotions, body feelings, and gut instincts). We numb out and tune out — the principal symptoms of trauma.

underworld: Transpersonal states of consciousness and identity characterized by depth, darkness, demons, the daemon, death and the dead, dreams (the "nightworld"), the subconscious, sacred woundings, **Shadow**, the unknown or not-yet-known, and visions of personal and cultural destiny; the realm in which the **Ego** is deepened and matured; the realm of the **Soul** (until it becomes conscious).

upperworld: Transpersonal states of consciousness and identity associated with **Spirit** and characterized by unity (or nonduality), grace, bliss, transcendence, emptiness, light, enlightenment (such as Buddha mind, nirvana, satori, or Self-realization), the celestial realm, and pure awareness (consciousness without an object). During upperworld experiences, consciousness communes with or merges with Spirit, in this way disidentifying from all personal and cultural beliefs, goals, desires, and attachments. Meditation, prayer, contemplation, and yoga are common practices for cultivating a relationship with the upperworld.

Village: A human community, or, better, the human element of the greater Earth community.

vision: An experiential encounter with **Soul** in which you glimpse some feature of the image you were born with, a revelation of your **mythopoetic identity**, something that is unique to you — not on the level of personality, social role, or vocation but in the particular way you belong to the Earth community. A vision is your discovery about or your waking up to your particular thread of the dream of the Earth.

Wanderer: The primary archetype of someone in the **Cocoon** stage; someone roving through the mysteries of nature and psyche in search of **Soul**.

Wellspring: Early **Adulthood**, the fifth of eight life stages in the **Eco-Soulcentric Developmental Wheel**, the stage that follows the passage of **Soul Initiation**; the period of soul-rooted individuation. The human archetype of this stage is the Apprentice to Soul. The task of this stage is to learn to embody **Soul** in culture — acquiring and implementing **delivery systems** (the culture component of the task) for soul qualities (the nature component). The psychospiritual **center of gravity** is the depths of one's culture (the *embodied* mysteries of nature and **psyche**). Newly initiated Adults dwell at a kind of wellspring, tend to it, apprentice there. Having discovered in the **Cocoon** the **underworld** source of their one true life, they now reside where that underground gift surfaces, where it becomes visible and valuable to their people. They abide at the interface between the mysteries and the manifest in order to decipher the manner in which the transformational enigmas emerge into form. In the course of their exploration, they become a wellspring themselves. In apprenticing to Soul, they learn to embody in everyday enterprises subterranean secrets in service to the Earth community. (See diagram, page 34.)

wholing: The cultivation of wholeness — all four facets of the **Self**.

Wild Indigenous One: The South facet of the **Self** (see pages 47–48).

windows of knowing: Psychologist Eligio Stephen Gallegos's term for the four modalities or faculties — feeling, imagining, sensing, and thinking — through which we learn about self and world. Each of the four is of equal power and importance in living a balanced and creative life. Each is a distinct faculty not reducible to any of the other three.

Acknowledgments

This field guide was made possible by what my colleagues and I learned while accompanying thousands of people on the Descent to Soul, women and men who bravely immersed themselves in the mysteries of nature and psyche and returned carrying life-enhancing gifts for our precious and fragile world in need.

I am especially grateful for the lives, time, patience, and psychospiritual depths of the people whose stories are told in these pages and who worked with me for months, in some cases years, to shape their complex, nuanced, and mythic stories into forms that can be expressed, if only partially, through the written word — even while we knew their stories might have been better sung or danced or painted. More important than telling their stories, of course, is how they are living them every day as visionary and revolutionary offerings to our transforming world. With gratitude, I bow to Christie D., Dan Dolquist, Elisabeth Nicolson, Joanna Macy, Kate Joyner, Kent Dobson, Kevin Lloyd Fetherston, Marty Miller, Matt Syrdal, Sabina Wyss, and Tracy Rekart. In drafting these narratives, I strove for accuracy as my foremost intention and guideline. Multiple drafts were sent back and forth until we were sufficiently satisfied with the fidelity of the telling.

I am grateful, also, to the many others who generously contributed strands of their stories, through written narratives and interviews: Alejandra Balcázar, Belle Lovelock, Ben Bont, Cathy Toldi, Chris Henrikson, Dave Bingham, Dianne Monroe, Erica Jones, Georgia Wingfield-Hayes, Hilary Leighton, Iris Garthwaite, Jan Garrett, Jerry Derstine, Joe Powell, John Lynch, Laura Page, Mary Marsden, Nicholas Triolo, Randy Morris, Rhonda Brandrick, Sage Magdalene, Sara McFarland, Sheila Murray, Susanne Moser, and Wendy Robertson Fyfe.

Many ideas and images that flesh out the map offered here were sparked or generously offered by Julian Norris, Geneen Marie Haugen, Sabina Wyss, Palika Benton, and Laura Page. Each of these colleagues graciously reviewed and commented on one or more chapters or, in the case of Geneen and Sabina, all of them. I want to thank Julian, especially, for several conversations that rearranged my understanding of cultural evolution and of older indigenous traditions in comparison to the model presented in this book. Julian also offered invaluable help as I pondered how best to articulate the essential nature of the five phases of the Descent, and while we mused on the best words to name them. My beloved partner, Geneen, has mentored me for many years in the art of writing, including word choice and the craft of shaping sentences, chapters, and books. (I only wish I had been a better student.) Moreover, many of the ideas and images in this book have been seeded or shaped by Geneen through what I learned while designing and guiding with her a variety of experiential group immersions and through the hazardous adventure of our countless conversations. I am also indebted to Jack Wieland, Brian Stafford, Randy Morris, Daniel Maté, Greg Cajete, and John Loudon for vital input offered along the way. As an element of her dissertation research, Laura Page conducted deeply perceptive interviews with more than two dozen people who have undertaken the Descent, focusing especially on the phase of Metamorphosis. With permission of the interviewees, Laura generously shared with me the transcripts of these insightful conversations, several strands of which found their way into these pages.

New World Library editorial director Georgia Hughes has been an indispensable ally and companion on all four of my books. With this project, she dedicated untold brave hours reviewing and editing each chapter, some more than once, and offered the most insightful suggestions of where to trim, rearrange, and reframe. In more ways than one, this book would not have been possible without her. Likewise, my tenacious and multitalented literary agent, Anne Depue, edited every chapter and offered discerning advice on more pages than not.

I am grateful for Animas guide and graphic artist extraordinaire Doug Van Houten, who created the intricate and imaginative collage for this book's cover.

So much of the model presented in this book, and the practices as well, I learned from or created alongside many of the other Animas guides. I am grateful for their brilliance, creativity, and warm companionship over many years: Geneen Marie Haugen, Sabina Wyss, Jeffrey Allen, Mary Marsden, Sage Magdalene, Nate Bacon, Rebecca Wildbear, Gene Dilworth, Doug Van Houten, Sheila Belanger, Peter Scanlan, Jade Sherer, Dianne Timberlake, Pete Fonken, Brian Stafford, and Laura Gunion.

I am grateful to the Animas operations staff, who have expertly kept the institute functioning smoothly, efficiently, and in good cheer during the five years of this book project: Becky Maloney, Jess Gellings, Donna Medeiros, Jeanine Surber, and Kristin McKinnen. And to the Animas Board of Directors, whose deep imagination, love, dedication, and sense of humor have, over these five years, deepened the roots and grown the proliferating branches of the institute: Julian Norris, Laura Page, Brian Stafford, Barbara Ford, Nate Bacon, and Betsy Fields.

Special thanks to Roger Strachan, Steven and Jessica Zeller, Aryeh Margolis, Michael Thunder, Deborah Demme, Louden Kiracofe, Jamie Reaser, Dave Abram, Rebecca Lambert, Richard Rohr, Terry and Anne Symens-Bucher, Michael DeMaria,

Ann Roberts, Peggy Dulany, Christina Stout, Suzannah Bacon, Wendell Bacon, Keith Watts, and Lisa Varga.

I offer my eternal gratitude to the Monk and the Butterfly — and my Muse — for having faith in me (my Ego) as a potential agent for Cocoon Weaver.

As always, and daily, I thank the Cosmos for existing with such utterly breathtaking and imaginative inventiveness, and for the animate Earth for giving birth so generously and wildly to all her species and habitats. May we humans become life-enhancing partners with both Earth and Cosmos. Soon.

Notes

Book epigraph: Thomas Berry, *The Great Work: Our Way into the Future* (New York: Bell Tower, 1999), 173–74.

Preface

Epigraph: Rainer Maria Rilke, *Rilke's Book of Hours: Love Poems to God*, trans. Anita Barrows and Joanna Macy (New York: Riverhead, 1996), 88.

1. Mainstream Western science believes we are psychologically shaped by only two factors, "nature and nurture": nature in the form of genetics and hormones, and nurture in the form of family, culture, education, and early experiences. From a soulcentric perspective, however, there's a third realm of guidance and influence that is at least as important, an intrapsychic realm that includes dreams and the denizens of the deep imagination. This is the primary realm through which the Soul acts. James Hillman articulates a similar perspective in *The Soul's Code*.

Introduction

Epigraph: From Johann Wolfgang von Goethe, "The Holy Longing," trans. Robert Bly, in *News of the Universe: Poems of Twofold Consciousness* (San Francisco: Sierra Club, 1980), 61, and tweaked by David Whyte (personal communication), who changed Bly's phrase "the massman" to the more easily comprehended "those who do not understand."

1. Although Elders and Adults share the qualities identified in this paragraph, they are quite different in other ways — as different as Adults are from Adolescents. Elders have a role in their more-than-human community that Adults are not yet developmentally prepared for, a role that is essential to the health of the Earth community as well as the human Village within it. See *Elder* in the glossary.

2. I write "remember" here because some myths suggest that before birth we know our individual destiny, but the gods see to it that we forget — perhaps to make possible a normal childhood rooted in family and community. Years later, when it's time for soul initiation, we must undergo a journey that makes it possible to remember.

3. Thomas Berry, *The Dream of the Earth* (San Francisco: Sierra Club Books, 1988), 207–8.

4. See Bill Plotkin, "Inscendence — The Key to the Great Work of Our Time: A Soulcentric View of Thomas Berry's Work," in *Thomas Berry, Dreamer of the Earth*, eds. Ervin Laszlo and Allan Combs (Rochester, VT: Inner Traditions, 2011), 42–71.

5. Cocoon Weaver, personal communication.

6. One person who *has* said it is Robert Bly in *The Sibling Society* (New York: Vintage, 1997). There are many authors who decry the loss or absence of elderhood, but I have seen little on the loss of adulthood.

7. Many descriptive labels have been coined for contemporary cultures in order to contrast them with more traditional societies. Kavoly's "Industrial Growth Society" is often used. Other distinguishing adjectives include *postindustrial, techno-capitalistic, materialistic, dominator, imperial, mass, global, information,* and *synthetic.* To add to the fray, I've often used *egocentric* and *patho-adolescent.* In this book I use *conformist-consumer culture* in order to emphasize a primary activity (producing and buying things, much of it not needed) and a value (owning stuff) but also to name a dominant social and psychological pattern of conforming to consumer trends — a society in which most people are hypervigilant about current fads, trends, and gadgets; are concerned not to be left behind; and tend to look outside themselves for how to be and what to do. Even though our contemporary society might be as individualistic as any ever, too many people's choices and "creativity" amount at best to idiosyncratic variations on what is in vogue.

8. Geneen Marie Haugen, personal communication.

9. The reader might wonder if these statements about adolescents, adults, and elders are true for traditional, indigenous cultures known to the West. See appendix 1, "The Lost Journey."

10. Others we might note: Jane Goodall, Maya Angelou, Martin Luther King Jr., Buckminster Fuller, Crazy Horse, Gandhi, Jesus, Mother Teresa, Hildegard von Bingen, Vandana Shiva, and the Buddha.

11. There's a categorical difference between life stages and life passages. Passages are relatively brief transitions between stages. The journey of soul initiation is not a passage and is not brought about by or contained within a rite of passage. Rather, it is an extended process that unfolds during a life stage I call the Cocoon. Ideally, it begins and ends with a rite of passage but is, itself, not one. Although a rite of passage does not bring about a transition from one stage of life to the next, it is invaluable nonetheless. It celebrates a profound milestone for the individual and family, informs the community that there is one among them who has undergone a radical shift (and could use some support), and assists that person in the challenges of adjusting to their new stage, their new responsibilities, opportunities, and powers; see Bill Plotkin, *Nature and the Human Soul* (Novato, CA: New World Library, 2008), 66. But not all rites of passage serve the individual or their community. Rites enacted by egocentric leaders or for egocentric purposes can end up confirming and reinforcing isolation, superficial belonging, self-centeredness, or social and ecological roles that are harmful to self, others, and the greater web of life. (Consider the incorporation rites for racist organizations or terrorist cults.) Rites of passage can, alas, be harnessed for shallow or damaging ends, whether consciously or unconsciously.

12. Many groups that identify themselves, at least in part, as rites-of-passage organizations nevertheless provide support for personal development beyond passages between life stages. Outstanding examples in the United States include the Stepping Stones Project, Springhouse Community School, Rites of Passage Journeys, Youth Passageways, Illuman, and the School of Lost Borders.

13. The now indispensable phrase "more-than-human world" was originally coined by ecophilosopher David Abram in his brilliant and landmark work *The Spell of the*

Sensuous: Perception and Language in a More-Than-Human World (New York: Vintage Books, 1996).

14. I've found one near exception: Although he doesn't use the word *soul* in this context, the contemporary Earth poet and bardic naturalist Stephen Harrod Buhner offers the closest thing I've yet seen to my definition of *Soul* when he observes that we humans "are expressed as a unique ecological communication when we are born." See his extraordinary *Plant Intelligence and the Imaginal Realm: Beyond the Doors of Perception Into the Dreaming of Earth* (Rochester, VT: Bear & Company), 232.

15. This way of understanding Soul could transform the new field of ecopsychology, and psychology more generally. It makes possible a complete ecopsychology — an eco-depth psychology.

16. "Unique eco-niche" is, to me, such an obviously fitting definition for *soul* that I've wondered why Western people hadn't seen it earlier. I suspect psychologists were generating psychological definitions and theologians theological ones; neither discipline was thinking ecologically. Now, with the emergence of ecopsychology and ecospirituality, both groups can and ought to be thinking this way. We all must now learn to think, feel, imagine, and act ecologically in everything we do. The survival of the Earth community depends on it.

17. In many spiritual circles, "the ego" is thought to be the primary problem, public enemy number one, something to rid oneself of. But without an Ego, we're not human. The actual problem is not Egos but *immature* Egos (egocentric or self-centered Egos), by far the most common kind in the Western world today. The goal is not to get rid of the Ego but to mature it through wholing and Self-healing (see chapter 2), and deepen it by rooting it in Soul (by way of the journey of soul initiation).

18. Diane di Prima, "Rant," in *Pieces of a Song* (San Francisco: City Lights Books, 1990), 159.

19. Gary Snyder, *Back on the Fire* (Berkeley, CA: Shoemaker and Hoard, 2007), 160.

20. Although this model has five phases, an alternative would be to have three, with a prephase (Preparation) and a postphase (Enactment). With the five-phase model, the middle three are the liminal phases, those in which the initiate is set apart from the everyday life of the Village.

21. For caterpillars, Dissolution is the result of a kind of autoimmune shock. An immune response is triggered by the inability of the final caterpillar skin to stretch any further (no more molting is possible) and by the presence within the body of the imaginal cells, which the immune system sees as invaders. The caterpillar body melts down in response to the unfamiliarity of its own potential — a fertile metaphor on many levels. It's as if our middleworld selves are allergic to the seeds of Soul.

Chapter One: Phase One: Preparation for the Descent — Part 1

Epigraph: Adrienne Rich, "Prospective Immigrants Please Note," in *The Fact of a Doorframe: Poems 1950–2001* (New York: Norton, 2002), 24–25.

1. The stages of the *egocentric* developmental wheel, too, are presented and described in detail in *Nature and the Human Soul*.

2. In a healthy, ecocentric culture, the two stages of childhood and the stage of early Adolescence are what I name, as shown in the diagram, the Innocent in the Nest, the Explorer in the Garden, and the Thespian at the Oasis, respectively. But in a psychospiritually challenged society, young people, tragically, have very different experiences;

they go through a sequence of *egocentric* stages I name Obedience and Entitlement Training (early childhood), Primary Socioeconomic Training (late childhood), and Conforming and Rebelling (the first substage of egocentric early Adolescence). All these stages are described in detail in *Nature and the Human Soul*.

3. James Hollis, *The Middle Passage: From Misery to Meaning in Midlife* (Toronto: Inner City Books, 1993).

4. What I call Eco-awakening has been noted and discussed, in other terms, by a number of authors. The Norwegian ecophilosopher and founder of deep ecology Arne Naess, for example, introduced the notion of an "ecological self" — our identification with "the larger community of all living beings." See John Seed, Joanna Macy, Pat Fleming, and Arne Naess, *Thinking Like a Mountain: Towards a Council of All Beings* (Santa Cruz, CA: New Society Publishers, 1988), 20. And the environmental activist and scholar of Buddhism Joanna Macy has written of "the greening of the self" — the expansion of our experienced circle of identity. See her chapter of that title in Llewellyn Vaughan-Lee, ed., *Spiritual Ecology: The Cry of the Earth* (Point Reyes, CA: The Golden Sufi Center), 145–56; see also Joanna Macy, *World as Self, World as Lover* (Berkeley, CA: Parallax Press, 1991).

5. In the stage of Conforming and Rebelling, in which the Ego is experienced as if it were at the center of everything, people tend to have two predominant emotions: fear of not belonging, which leads to a life priority of conforming to the social expectations of one's group; and anger about others trying to shove them into boxes, which results in a life priority of rebelling against parents, authorities, and social expectations (especially those of the mainstream). In both emotional atmospheres, authenticity is neglected because people are either trying to be what others expect or doing their best to be subversive, or a convoluted mixture of both.

6. The neglect of these two developmental tasks is precisely what results in a child's disconnect from the natural world, which, in turn, diverts children from the healthy, ecocentric stages of the Nest and the Garden and into the unhealthy, egocentric stages.

7. In the Eco-Soulcentric Developmental Wheel, each life stage has two developmental tasks unique to each stage, and these two tasks correspond to two sets of everyday opportunities for individual development or growth. One of the two tasks is culture oriented, the other nature oriented. Movement from one stage to the next requires significant success with (not completion of) both tasks. In our conformist-consumer culture, both tasks of both childhood stages tend to be poorly addressed, but the nature-oriented tasks are especially neglected. Consequently, in this chapter, I emphasize the nature-oriented tasks and opportunities, the ones we have most strayed from as a culture and most need to return to. See *Nature and the Human Soul* for a description of the culture-oriented tasks as well as a more in-depth discussion of the nature-oriented tasks.

8. See *Nature and the Human Soul*, chapter 4, for a more thorough discussion.

9. See *Nature and the Human Soul*, pp. 106–8, for a more complete description of these practices. See also my 2015 essay, "A Short Introduction to the Eco-Soulcentric Developmental Wheel: Stages of Life, Rites of Passage, and Cultural Transformation," https://www.animas.org/wp-content/uploads/Intro-to-ESDW-for-Animas-website.pdf.

10. Cultivating our ability to surrender to wonder and rapture and to fall in love with the other-than-human world — a stage-two task — rests upon our stage-one foundational capacities of innocence, present-centeredness, and relationality.

11. For practices you can undertake on your own to awaken and deepen your innate,

childlike sense of wonder in nature, see *Nature and the Human Soul*, pp. 161–63. For a variety of other approaches to nature connection, see David Abram's *Becoming Animal*, Jon Young's *Coyote Guide*, Robin Wall Kimmerer's *Braiding Sweetgrass*, Stephen Buhner's *The Secret Teachings of Plants*, and Sandra Ingerman's *Speaking with Nature*. For perspectives on ecotherapy, see Linda Buzzell and Craig Chalquist, eds., *Ecotherapy: Healing with Nature in Mind*.

12. This difficulty is compounded by a number of pathogenic features of mainstream conformist-consumer culture: pervasive egocentric competition, resulting in people looking out primarily for themselves and hesitant to trust others; the challenge of making an adequate living combined with the cultural belief that only "losers" fail economically, resulting in low self-esteem; psychologically unhealthy parents unable to instill positive self-esteem in their children, a self-perpetuating syndrome from one generation to the next; the oppression of minorities and marginalized groups; and the underdevelopment of empathy and compassion. These and other elements of cultural decay result in widespread shame, defeat, addiction, and depression.

13. Social self-design is difficult if you had insufficient success with the nature-oriented tasks of childhood. It's hard to be authentic when you have trouble being present (an early-childhood accomplishment), presence being the prerequisite for empathy and compassion — including self-compassion. Likewise, authenticity is much more difficult when you don't feel at home in the more-than-human world (a middle-childhood task), nature connection being the evolutionary and psychological foundation for feeling at home in any other context, including a peer group. As we see repeatedly, most challenges in human development stem from the cultural disconnect from the greater Earth community — a collective eco-attachment disorder. Conversely (and positively), our single greatest collective opportunity now is Eco-awakening.

14. Psychological, social, and/or ecological belonging, in addition to being what most Western people mean by *soul*, is also what they mean, oftentimes, by *heart* — namely, the experience of loving connection or communion with self, other, and the greater Earth community. Beginning in the Cocoon, however, the meanings of *heart* and *Soul* diverge: *heart* implies intimacy, love, and communion, while *Soul* refers to ecological identity. With these stage-four meanings, heart and Soul can at times be in tension with each other, even in opposition. For example, we often must risk or lose relationships with some people, places, or social roles we love in order to move toward or say yes to our Soul as ecological identity.

15. Every healthy life stage, starting with the first, is the best stage to be in while you're in it. Later stages are not better than earlier ones. It's not hierarchical. People in each of the eight ecocentric stages are essential to shaping a healthy culture. People in each stage possess a unique gift for their community, a gift not carried as fully by people in both later and earlier stages. Although each stage incorporates the capacities of the earlier ones, people in later stages cannot manifest the particular flair of earlier stages as well as they could when they were in that stage. As an example, Thespians in the Oasis are the best we humans ever get at social innovation, at generating new styles and memes in fashion, music, dance, language, games, sex, business, and sports. A Thespian — someone in a healthy psychological early Adolescence — brings a fresh perspective and is endowed with an enormous unquenchable desire. She shakes things up, like a hyperactive critic from a strange and exotic discipline; she has a new outlook and she's going to share it with you whether you ask for it or not. And god knows she can show you some things you wouldn't have seen otherwise, because maybe you've become a bit

overinvested in one particular way of being alive. She keeps social life fresh, new, safe from calcification. She reminds you that, as important as essence is, style matters, too. She's in your face, holding up a mirror to your social forms, showing you where you've begun to take yourself too seriously, showing you where you've forgotten to grow in style. People in later stages — true Adults and Elders — are not nearly so capable and effective at critiquing current social styles and generating new ones (nor should they be; they have other fish to fry).

Chapter Two: Phase One: Preparation for the Descent — Part 2

Epigraph: Pesha Joyce Gertler, "The Healing Time," in *The Healing Time: Finally on My Way to Yes* (Columbus, OH: Pudding House Publications, 2008), 7.

1. Many traditions from around the world have, of course, used the four (or seven) directions template. The particular elements on my map of human wholeness, however, and my specific understandings of the four directions themselves do not fully correspond to any tradition of which I'm aware. Indeed, I don't know of any two maps from any times or places that are identical. It may be that every nature-honoring society in every epoch employs the archetypes of the seven directions to fashion their own map that reflects the unique features of their cosmology, mythology, and ecosystem.

2. Eligio Stephen Gallegos, *Animals of the Four Windows: Integrating Thinking, Sensing, Feeling, and Imagery* (Santa Fe, NM: Moon Bear Press, 1991). Gallegos understands thinking, feeling, and sensing much the way Carl Jung did, but where Jung wrote of intuition as the fourth "function of consciousness," Gallegos offers the insight that the fourth function is actually imagination. Gallegos explains that intuition is our ability to know things "beyond the present moment and circumstance and for which there is no immediate evidence" (p. 6). Intuition, he notes, can operate by means of any of the four windows, although for any given person it tends to operate primarily through one in particular. In other words, for some people, intuitions arrive through the imagination — say, an image of a loved one's face just before that person walks in the door. Other people intuit by way of a thought or a voice "out of nowhere" that enables them to understand more deeply something happening in the moment. Some people intuit by way of a feeling or emotion — for example, a feeling-sense of a place being welcoming or dangerous. A fourth group experiences intuition primarily through sensory perception — say, the appearance of a certain bird, breeze, or blossom that suggests some specific event (perhaps a birth or a death) has just happened or is about to happen. Jung's own intuition, as it turns out, operated primarily through his imagination, which likely led him to identify the fourth function as simply "intuition."

3. See Stephen Harrod Buhner, *Ensouling Language: On the Art of Nonfiction and the Writer's Life* (Rochester, VT: Inner Traditions, 2010), especially chapter 5.

4. Here I am blending the acute sensing of the East with the embodied sensuousness of the South. The East and South naturally work together in this way: the South's sensuousness bestows emotion, feeling, and eroticism to what the East purely perceives through the five senses.

5. Consider, for example, the activist group Extinction Rebellion: https://rebellion.earth (accessed January 9, 2020).

6. James Hillman and Michael Ventura, *We've Had a Hundred Years of Psychotherapy — and the World's Getting Worse* (San Francisco: Harper, 1993).

7. Gabor Maté, *In the Realm of Hungry Ghosts: Close Encounters with Addiction* (Berkeley,

CA: North Atlantic Books, 2010) and *The Myth of Normal: Illness and Health in an Insane Culture* (forthcoming).

Chapter Three: Phase Two: Dissolution — Part 1

Epigraph: Rainer Maria Rilke, *Rilke's Book of Hours: Love Poems to God,* trans. Anita Barrows and Joanna Macy (New York: Riverhead Books, 1996), 95–96.

1. See "The Journey of Soul Initiation versus the Descent to Soul," page 20; diagram, page 34; "Success with the Two Tasks of the Oasis," pages 39–41; and *Nature and the Human Soul,* chapter 6.

2. All quotes in this paragraph are from C. G. Jung, *The Red Book: Liber Novus,* ed. Sonu Shamdasani (New York: Norton, 2009), 230–36.

3. James Hillman, *The Force of Character and the Lasting Life* (New York: Random House, 1999).

4. In nature-based traditions, sacred medicines themselves do not bring about soul encounters. They are only one element in ceremonies and initiatory practices that can be quite elaborate. In *any* tradition or society, the psychedelic agent itself can be psychologically dangerous when used by unprepared people without support from experienced guides. But even when participants are psychologically prepared and expertly guided, sacred medicine ceremonies are unlikely to result in soul encounters unless the participants have reached the Cocoon stage of human development or later. Western psychologists rightly focus on the importance of both "set and setting," but developmental stage is an equally significant consideration with psychedelic experience. Even for people in the Cocoon or later, a soul encounter without follow-through practices or follow-up guidance is likely to become a relic, not an experience that reshapes the Ego — an essential phase of the Descent, as explored in chapter 9. Soul encounter is the appearance of a kind of spiritual doorway. If we don't walk through the door — because we don't recognize it as a door or don't know how to walk through — it becomes a missed opportunity.

5. From W. B. Yeats, "The Song of Wandering Aengus," *The Collected Poems of W. B. Yeats,* ed. Richard J. Finneran (New York: Scribner, 1996), 59–60.

6. See "Tree Lore" at Druidry.org: http://www.druidry.org/library/trees/tree-lore-hazel (accessed January 20, 2016).

7. Dan points out that the words "he descended into hell" are not from the gospels but from an early church statement of belief called "The Apostles' Creed."

8. Stanislav Grof and Christina Grof, *Holotropic Breathwork: A New Approach to Self-Exploration and Therapy* (Albany, NY: Excelsior Editions, 2010).

9. For soulcentric dreamwork methods, see Robert Bosnak, *Tracks in the Wilderness of Dreaming* (New York: Delta, 1997), *A Little Course in Dreams* (Boston: Shambhala, 1998), and *Embodiment* (New York: Routledge, 2007); Jill Mellick, *The Art of Dreaming* (Berkeley, CA: Conari Press, 1996); and Stephen Aizenstat, *Dream Tending* (New Orleans: Spring Journal Press, 2011). Or join us on one of the five-day Soulcentric Dreamwork intensives offered by Animas Valley Institute: www.animas.org. For the best theory or conceptual perspective on soulcentric dreamwork, see James Hillman, *The Dream and the Underworld* (New York: Harper and Row, 1979).

10. Seven years might seem like a long time between Confirmation (the commencement of the Cocoon) and the start of the first Descent, but I've found this to in fact be common when there is little awareness or understanding of the Descent and no Elders

or initiators available as guides. Perhaps the greater wonder is that so many Western people (perhaps as much as 15 percent) reach the Cocoon stage at all. That said, I do believe that in a more mature and soulcentric future culture, the first Descent, for most people, would occur earlier in the Cocoon and probably during the late teens or early twenties.

11. T. S. Eliot, "Little Gidding," in *Four Quartets* (New York: Harcourt, Brace, and World, 1943), 58–59.
12. Barbara Hannah, *Jung: His Life and Work* (New York: Perigee, 1976), 129.
13. T. S. Eliot, "East Coker," in *Four Quartets*, 28.

Chapter Four: Phase Two: Dissolution — Part 2

Epigraph: From "Trail Sign," unpublished poem by Geneen Marie Haugen.
1. See Francis Weller, *The Wild Edge of Sorrow: Rituals of Renewal and the Sacred Work of Grief* (Berkeley, CA: North Atlantic Books, 2015); and Joanna Macy and Molly Brown, *Coming Back to Life: The Updated Guide to the Work That Reconnects* (Gabriola Island, BC, Canada: New Society Publishers, 2014).
2. Rainer Maria Rilke, "The First Elegy," in *In Praise of Mortality*, trans. and eds. Anita Barrows and Joanna Macy (New York: Riverhead Books, 2005), 31.
3. Rilke, "The Ninth Elegy," in *In Praise*, 60.
4. See Jon Young, Evan McGown, and Ellen Haas, *Coyote's Guide to Connecting with Nature* (Shelton, WA: Owlink Media, 2010).
5. My use of the term *mandorla* corresponds, at least loosely, to that of Jungian analyst Robert Johnson. See his *Owning Your Own Shadow: Understanding the Dark Side of the Psyche* (San Francisco: HarperSanFrancisco, 1994).

Chapter Five: Jung's Preparation and Dissolution

Epigraph: C. G. Jung, *Memories, Dreams, Reflections* (New York: Vintage, 1965), 199.
1. To enter the Cocoon, a person needs to have gone through the life passage of Confirmation. To do *that*, they must have been in the Oasis stage, and that means that sometime earlier they had gone through the life passage I call Eco-awakening. Is there evidence Jung went through Eco-awakening? Yes. In fact, there are suggestions of something more: Jung may have been one of the rare Western people who actually didn't need to go through Eco-awakening because as a child he might never have lost his innate connection with the wild world. Recalling his boyhood, he wrote, "Nature seemed to me full of wonders, and I wanted to steep myself in them. Every stone, every plant, every single thing seemed alive and indescribably marvelous. I immersed myself in nature, crawled, as it were, into the very essence of nature and away from the whole human world" (Jung, *Memories*, 32). A pattern I've found among people I've guided on vision fasts is that those most likely to have soul encounters are the ones who, like Jung, had frequent nature immersions in childhood. For more on Jung's childhood nature-connection experiences, see in *Memories*, pp. 22, 34, 45, 68, 76, 85, and 143.
2. Jung, *Red Book*, 231–32.
3. Like virtually all Westerners who undergo the passage of Confirmation (a small minority), Jung did not have the benefit of a ceremonial rite of passage on his way into

the Cocoon. The possibility of Confirmation — even its existence — was not and is still not recognized in the West.

4. It's important to note the significant difference in how Jung and I use the word *soul* (see also the glossary). While I mean a person's unique and innate psycho-ecological niche, Jung means, most of the time, his anima, a feminine dimension of his psyche. Jung's *anima* is what I refer to as the West facet of the Self, namely the Dark Muse-Beloved or the Guide to Soul. At other times, Jung appears to use the word *soul* to mean the psyche in a more general sense, especially the greater portion of the psyche that is unconscious. But Jung's two uses of *soul* are related: For him, the anima is the guide to the depths of the psyche — and these depths are generally unconscious (until they are entered by the Ego). So, sometimes *soul*, for Jung, refers to the mysterious depths of the psyche, but more often to the facet of the psyche (the anima) that guided him to explore those very depths and be changed and initiated by them. My use of the word *Soul* broadly correlates with Jung's "personal myth." More precisely, the way a person understands their unique ecological niche is in terms of a personal myth, or what I call a mythopoetic story. For both Jung and me, this mysterious realm — his "personal myth," my "mythopoetic identity" — is one which a person has no conscious awareness until sometime after they begin to "confront the unconscious" (Jung) or embark upon the journey of soul initiation (me). This myth-infused realm, for both of us, is a significant element of the depths of the human psyche, perchance the single most vital element.

Jung	Plotkin
soul or anima	Guide to Soul / Dark Muse-Beloved
soul	psyche
personal myth	mythopoetic identity
spirit of the times	middleworld
spirit of the depths	underworld/Soul
the image of God	upperworld/Spirit

5. Jung, *Red Book*, 229–30.
6. Jung, *Memories*, 163, 164.
7. Ibid., 167–69.
8. Ibid., 170.
9. Ibid., 171.
10. The quotes in this paragraph come from Hannah, *Jung*, 104, 117, 118.
11. "Nekyia" is the title of the eleventh book of the *Odyssey*, which describes Odysseus's descent to Hades to ask the dead about the means to return home to Ithaca.
12. This was not Jung's first extramarital affair. From 1905 to 1911, he was romantically involved with Sabina Spielrein, who was at first his patient and then his research assistant and doctoral student.
13. Jung quotes from *Memories*, 165.
14. Ibid.

15. In his preface to his 1952 revision of *Symbols of Transformation* (Princeton, NJ: Princeton University Press, 1956), Jung wrote, concerning his confrontation with the unconscious, "I took it upon myself to get to know 'my' myth and I regarded this as the task of tasks" (p. xxix).
16. Jung, *Memories*, 166.
17. Ibid., 171–72.
18. Hillman, *The Dream*, 130.
19. Ibid., 122–23.
20. Jung, *Memories*, 172.
21. Ibid., 173.
22. Ibid.
23. Ibid.
24. Rainer Maria Rilke, "The Man Watching," in *Selected Poems of Rainer Maria Rilke*, trans. Robert Bly (New York: Harper and Row, 1981) 105.
25. Jung, *Memories*, 174–75.
26. Ibid., 183.
27. Ibid., 176.
28. Ibid.
29. Ibid., 176–77.
30. Ibid., 193–94.
31. Ibid., 194.
32. Ibid., 177.
33. Ibid., 189.
34. Ibid., 177.
35. Ibid., 181.
36. Ibid.
37. Jung, *Red Book*, 245–46.
38. Jung, *Memories*, 182.
39. Jung, *Red Book*, 245.
40. Jung, *Memories*, 182.
41. Whether this division would be true in a more mature and healthy culture is debatable; for sure, in *any* culture, both male-bodied and female-bodied people, in order to fully mature, must cultivate both sets of resources. Jung understood this himself.
42. Jung, *Red Book*, 248.
43. The quotes in this paragraph are from ibid.
44. Ibid., 252.
45. Ibid., 254.
46. Ibid.
47. Ibid., p. 247, footnote 164.
48. Ibid., 247.
49. Jung, *Memories*, 180.
50. Jung, *Red Book*, 259.
51. Ibid.
52. Quotes in this paragraph from ibid., 260, 261.
53. Quotes in this paragraph from ibid., 266.
54. Ibid., 272–73.
55. Ibid., 279.
56. Ibid., 280.

57. Ibid., 290.
58. Ibid., 295.
59. Ibid., 298.
60. Ibid.
61. Ibid., 307.
62. Jung, *Memories*, 182, and Jung, *Red Book*, 312.
63. Jung, *Memories*, 184.
64. First two quotes: Jung, *Memories*, 185; third: Jung, *Red Book*, 306, footnote 232. Sonu Shamdasani, who edited the *Red Book*, notes in the latter footnote that Ka first appeared to Jung in a fantasy on October 22, 1917, which is more than a year after the end of the experiences recorded in the *Red Book*, including his first soul encounter. Jung discusses Ka in one of his black book journals, not in the *Red Book*.
65. Jung, *Memories*, 183.
66. Ibid., 183–84.
67. Jung, *Red Book*, 318.
68. Ibid., 322, 323.
69. Quotes in this paragraph from ibid., 323.
70. Ibid., 324.
71. Ibid., 202. Here Shamdasani seems to use the word *soul* to refer to the human psyche in general — in contrast to meaning the anima, which was Jung's most common use of the word.
72. Jung's accompaniment of Christiana Morgan on her Descent might be one of the exceptions. See his "Visions Seminar": C. G. Jung, *Visions: Notes of the Seminar Given in 1930–1934*, ed. Claire Douglas (Princeton, NJ: Princeton University Press, 1997).
73. The training of depth psychologists tends to be heavily focused on theory, history, and technique and not so much on personal transformation — and virtually never on guiding in wilderness settings.
74. James Hillman writes, "Jung was not primarily concerned with psychotherapy. He was a medical psychiatrist, and he had his patients, but he was interested in exploring the psyche and finding ways to make those explorations more transparent to his patients. But that is not what therapy has since become." Sonu Shamdasani adds, "It's not for nothing that in the 1920s and '30s Jung recommended that people had psychotherapy *before* they came to him, and that they needed a preparation that should be gotten elsewhere." My understanding is that what Jung was doing when he was helping his patients "explore the psyche" was primarily what I call the cultivation of wholeness, which contrasts with the healing work that psychotherapy has largely become — but it also contrasts with the Descent to Soul. I elaborate on this in chapter 11. Quotes above are from James Hillman and Sonu Shamdasani, *Lament of the Dead: Psychology After Jung's Red Book* (New York: Norton, 2013), 165.

Chapter Six: Phase Three: Soul Encounter — Part 1

Epigraph: From Yeats, "The Song of Wandering Aengus," 59–60.
1. In his *Memoirs* (New York: Macmillan, 1973), Yeats writes of his first meeting with Maud and how she had "a complexion like the blossom of apples" (p. 40). And in his *Autobiographies* (New York: Scribner, 1999), he writes, "Her complexion was luminous, like that of apple-blossom through which the light falls, and I remember her standing that first day by a great heap of such blossoms in the window" (p. 120).

2. Jung, *Memories*, 178.
3. Ibid., 181.
4. Ibid., 190.
5. Jung's colleague Cary de Angulo (later Baynes) discussed this episode with Jung, and she later sent him her notes, which include, "Of course I knew you were the fisherman in your son's picture and you told me so, but the boy didn't know it" (Jung, *Red Book*, 205).
6. This is reminiscent of Rilke's "now you must go out into your heart as onto a vast plain." It also resonates with Kevin Fetherston's experience in his senior year of high school when all he wanted was to "experience this larger, amazing world."
7. When I speak of your "mythopoetic identity," we could also use phrases such as: your soul-rooted destiny, your innate image, your mystical calling, your unique genius, the gift you're meant to bring to the world, your one true life, your bigger story, your particular way of belonging to the Earth community, the largest conversation you can have with the world, your unique psycho-ecological niche in the web of life, or your ultimate place in the world. Each of these phrases refers — whether explicitly or implicitly — to an identity that can be described only in terms of your relationship to the Earth community, a relationship that is both mystical and ecological.
8. When I write of "visions" or "revelations," I mean an experiential encounter with Soul in which you glimpse some feature of the image you were born with, a revelation of your mythopoetic identity. This is the Soul speaking. We could equally well say this is the world speaking, or the wild; after all, the Soul, as ecological niche, is a feature of the natural world. A third alternative is to say that a vision is Mystery speaking to you. In whichever way you prefer to think of the speaker, the subject matter is the same, namely something that is unique about you — not on the level of personality, social role, or vocation but in the particular way you belong to the cosmos. A vision, in this sense, is your discovery about or your waking up to your particular piece of the dream of the Earth.
9. David Whyte, from "The Soul Lives Contented," in *Fire in the Earth* (Langley, WA: Many Rivers Press, 1992), 31.
10. I have not conducted formal research on experiences with psychedelics (also known as plant allies, sacred medicines, or entheogens), but it seems that soul encounters during these journeys are rare among contemporary Westerners — unless, that is, the person is in the Cocoon stage or later. This again underscores the critical importance of developmental stage for psychological and spiritual growth. What can happen for a person on a spiritual retreat, on a path of study, or during a psychedelic session depends at least as much on the stage of the individual as it does on the quality of the practice or the mastery of the teacher.

    Nearly all of the many hundreds of accounts I've heard or read of Westerners' high-dose entheogenic journeys are either healing experiences (whether psychological, spiritual, or physical) or transcendent (experiences of unity, light, God, or the absence of a self). Although these experiences are profound for the journeyer, they are not soul encounters. My speculation is that soul encounters with entheogens are much more common among members of societies in which the plant ally is used as a sacrament in a ceremonial manner. The larger ceremony that holds and frames the experience is a factor as important as the plant ally or medicine itself. And the developmental stage, psychological state, and cultural background of the person are equally significant. Elisabeth was well into her Cocoon stage when she drank ayahuasca and had had several previous encounters with Soul.

11. The Ego is born during the fourth year of life, at the passage of Naming, not at the time of our physical birth. We have no Ego at birth. Between birth and Naming, our Ego gestates within the womb of family and culture.

12. The more-than-human world (the greater Earth community) is the progenitor not only of each individual soul-initiated human but also of each healthy and mature human culture. Egos are healthiest when they gestate within such nature-rooted cultures.

13. David Byrne, *Bicycle Diaries* (New York: Viking Adult, 2009), 194.

14. Although soul encounters can take place in just a few moments, it's not uncommon for them to unfold more gradually over a few hours or even over several days. Note, too, that although soul encounters during vision-fast ceremonies usually occur during the solo time, they can also happen before or after the solo. Many if not most modern vision fasters, however, don't have soul encounters at all; for this experience to occur, the faster must be in the Cocoon or later and be psychospiritually prepared for the Descent. A final point here: Vision fasts are not, of course, necessary for soul encounters; there are many other practices and circumstances that can be equally or more effective, as the stories in this book amply illustrate.

15. Somewhere between the ages of twenty-seven to thirty, we have our first "Saturn return," which is when the planet Saturn comes back for the first time to the place in the sky it was when we were born. Astrologers say this is when we have our first major crisis of identity, when big existential questions loom about what we will do and who we will be in our life. This transit shakes the tectonic plates of our psychic depths. Major changes in life course are common at this time. I've noticed that first soul encounters often occur in this age range — if, that is, the person has reached the Cocoon. You'll see this phenomenon in many of the stories in this book. Joanna's first Saturn return was likely a significant factor in why her first soul encounter occurred when it did.

16. Joanna Macy, *Widening Circles: A Memoir* (Gabriola Island, BC: New Society Publishers, 2000), 74.

17. Ibid., 75.

18. Ibid., 76.

19. Ibid., 51.

20. This is a version of the old Greek idea of enantiodromia, which was introduced into modern psychology by Jung, who defined it as "the emergence of the unconscious opposite in the course of time. This characteristic phenomenon practically always occurs when an extreme, one-sided tendency dominates conscious life; in time an equally powerful counterposition is built up, which first inhibits the conscious performance and subsequently breaks through the conscious control" (C.G. Jung, *Psychological Types* [Princeton, NJ: Princeton University Press, 1971], 426).

21. Macy, *Widening Circles*, 91.

22. Ibid., 105.

23. Ibid., 106.

Chapter Seven: Jung's Soul Encounters

Epigraphs: Jung, *Memories*, 192; and David Whyte, "What to Remember When Waking," in *The House of Belonging* (Langley, WA: Many Rivers Press, 1997), 27.

1. All quotes in this paragraph are from Jung, *Memories*, 190.

2. Ibid., 190–91.

3. Ten evenings is how the timeframe appears in the *Red Book*, but in *Memories* (p. 191), Jung remembers his writing of the *Sermons* as even speedier, as only three evenings.

4. Jung, *Memories*, 191.
5. As Aniela Jaffé (Jung's friend, colleague, and editor of *Memories, Dreams, Reflections*) comments, this was "a deliberate game of mystification" (ibid., 378). Basilides was an apt choice for an alias because the *Sermons* borrow many ideas from the Gnostics (for example, that the psyche consists of paired opposites) and some of their terminology (for example, God as Abraxas).
6. In the *Red Book* version, there are several sections that are not in the original; these are Jung's commentaries couched as conversations between Jung and Philemon about the preceding sermon.
7. Jung, *Memories*, 191.
8. Ibid.
9. Ibid., 191–92.
10. Ibid., 192.
11. Ibid.
12. Ibid., 198.
13. Ibid., 198–99.
14. Ibid., 199.
15. Ibid., 196.
16. Quote by Sonu Shamdasani from Jung, *Red Book*, 217.
17. Jung, *Memories*, 199.
18. Ibid., 195.

Chapter Eight: Phase Three: Soul Encounter — Part 2

Epigraph: From Whyte, "What to Remember When Waking," 27.
1. Jean Houston offers a brilliant perspective on the Sacred Wound in her book *The Search for the Beloved: Journeys in Mythology and Sacred Psychology* (Los Angeles: Tarcher, 1987).
2. For more on Core Wound work, see Bill Plotkin, *Wild Mind* (Novato, CA: New World Library, 2013), 176–80.
3. Houston, *Search for the Beloved*, 105.
4. See Animas Valley Institute's Depth Council Intensive at www.animas.org.
5. The form of this question is borrowed from David Whyte's poem "Self-Portrait," in *Fire in the Earth* (Langley, WA: Many Rivers Press, 1992), 10.
6. Jal al-din Rumi, *The Essential Rumi*, trans. Coleman Barks (San Francisco: Harper, 1995), 103.
7. From Rilke, "The Man Watching," 105 and 107.
8. However, our parents, grandparents, and other family members — if they are soul initiated — might have great interest and capacity to muse about us in this way.
9. "The pattern that connects" is one of the seminal ideas of Gregory Bateson. See his books *Steps to an Ecology of Mind* (New York: Ballantine, 1972) and *Mind and Nature: A Necessary Unity* (New York: Bantam Books, 1979).
10. Sources for these quotes and terms are from the following: Thomas Berry, foreword to Plotkin, *Soulcraft*, xiii; Rupert Sheldrake, *The Presence of the Past: Morphic Resonance and the Habits of Nature* (London: Fontana/HarperCollins, 1989); David Bohm, *Wholeness and the Implicate Order* (London: Ark Paperbacks, 1984); R. Buckminster Fuller, *Synergetics: Explorations in the Geometry of Thinking*, vols. 1 and 2 (New York: Macmillan, 1975, 1979); and Robert A. Johnson, *Inner Work* (San Francisco: Harper and Row, 1986), 7.

11. The quotes in this section are from Johnson, *Inner Work*, 219–20, 221.
12. Christie's use of "quiver" here — a quote out of her journal at the time — is of interest because, as she notes, it was not a word or image she knew herself to use and because, six months later, the bow and arrow became prominent mythopoetic images as well as physical realities in her life.
13. From Lorna Crozier, "A Murder of Crows," in Lorna Crozier and Ian McAllister, *Voices from the Forest and Sea: The Wild in You* (Berkeley, CA: Greystone Books, 2015), 62.
14. The way I prefer to say it is that the Muse speaks on behalf of the Soul. Jung's version was that his "soul" (by which he meant his anima — essentially his Muse) revealed to him his "personal myth."
15. Image-precipitated-by-emotion was true for Jung: Recall, for example, the emotionally explosive events preceding his channeling of the *Seven Sermons*. More generally, Jung's exploration of his unconscious, he tells us, was a matter of "translating" his emotions into images. The images, he said, were "concealed in the emotions" (Jung, *Memories*, 177).
16. From Whyte, "What to Remember When Waking," 28.

Chapter Nine: Phase Four: Metamorphosis — Part 1

Epigraph: From David Whyte, "Revelation Must Be Terrible," in *Fire in the Earth* (Langley, WA: Many Rivers Press, 1992), 32.
1. Joseph Campbell, *The Hero with a Thousand Faces*, 3rd ed. (original edition, Bollingen Foundation, 1949; repr., Novato, CA: New World Library, 2008), 167. Citations refer to New World Library edition.
2. Plotkin, *Soulcraft*, xxvii.
3. Ibid., xxvii, xxix.
4. From Robert MacLean's poem "Nass River," which starts with a swoon: "Tent tethered among jackpine and blue- / bells. Lacewings rise from rock / incubators. Wild geese flying north. / And I can't remember who I'm supposed / to be." See Robert MacLean, *Heartwood* (Silverton, CO: Way of the Mountain Center, 1985), 10.
5. I learned the importance and methods of the Council of Elders in 1985 from my teachers Steven Foster and Meredith Little of the School of Lost Borders.
6. Geneen Marie Haugen, "The Return," in *Written River: Journal of Eco-Poetics* 4, no. 2 (winter 2013): 11.

Chapter Ten: Phase Four: Metamorphosis — Part 2

Epigraph: Antonio Machado, in *The Soul Is Here for Its Own Joy*, ed. and trans. Robert Bly (New York: Ecco, 1999), 248.
1. Mary Oliver, "Hunter's Moon — Eating the Bear," in *Twelve Moons* (Boston: Little, Brown, 1979), 50.
2. Ibid.
3. Jung, *Memories*, 192–93.
4. Ibid., 188, from Aniela Jaffé's footnote.
5. Hillman and Shamdasani, *Lament of the Dead*, 63.
6. Quotes in this paragraph from Jung, *Memories*, 195, 196.
7. Ibid., 196.

8. Ibid.
9. Ibid., 223.
10. Ibid., 225.
11. Jung, *Red Book*, 247.
12. Jung, *Memories*, 199.
13. Ibid., 209.

Chapter Eleven: Phase Five: Enactment

Epigraph: From William Stafford, "The Way It Is," in *The Way It Is: New and Selected Poems* (Saint Paul, MN: Graywolf Press, 1998), 42.

1. Berry, *Dream of the Earth*.
2. In the early 1970s, I studied *A Vision* indirectly as it was a primary foundation for a new astrological understanding of the moon phases, as developed by my teacher Dorothy Wergin and her two colleagues. See Marilyn Busteed, Richard Tiffany, and Dorothy Wergin, *Phases of the Moon: A Guide to Evolving Human Nature* (Berkeley, CA: Shambhala, 1974). Their book was one of the influences in the shaping of the Eco-Soulcentric Developmental Wheel as introduced in my book *Nature and the Human Soul*.
3. Whyte, "What to Remember When Waking," 28.
4. To learn more about Animas Valley Institute's mission and why we say it's distinct from the offerings of others, including many who use the word *soul* but in quite different ways, see "What We Do" at the Animas Valley website (http://www.animas.org /about-us/our-organization/what-we-do).
5. John G. Neihardt, *Black Elk Speaks* (Lincoln: University of Nebraska Press, 1961), 204.
6. These lines have been attributed to sources as diverse as Chief Seattle, Winston Churchill, and anonymous.
7. Silver Moon's unpublished poem "Liquid Love" is part of *The Blood Tales*; see www.thebloodtales.com.
8. We can't rule out the possibility that Descents could also happen in the two stages of Elderhood, but I'm not aware of any instances. Also, it's not clear what the point would be: In Elderhood, as I understand it, it is time to move beyond any striving to embody our individual vision and toward the tending of the collective Soul of the Earth community. From this perspective, it's not evident why Mystery would, in Elderhood, support a deeper revelation of our mythopoetic identity. The time for that was in late Adolescence and the two stages of Adulthood.
9. See Plotkin, *Nature and the Human Soul*, 309.
10. During a Descent, a person can be, as noted earlier, in more than one phase at a time. While Matt was in a Metamorphosis phase brought about by his earlier soul encounters, he was also having additional encounters with visionary images. After a first Descent, a person can have soul encounters without having to first go through another Dissolution. A soul encounter, in fact, can amplify a previous dissolution of identity as well as initiate the next step of a Metamorphosis as well as generate new possibilities for Enactment.
11. These abilities are the very ones that make possible Goethian or Gaian science. Goethe, for example, employed what he called "exact sensorial imagination." See Stephen Harrod Buhner's *Plant Intelligence and the Imaginal Realm: Beyond the Doors of Perception Into the Dreaming of the Earth* (Rochester, VT: Bear & Co., 2014) and Stephan Harding's *Animate Earth: Science, Intuition and Gaia* (Cambridge, UK: Green Books, 2009).

12. Macy, *Widening Circles*, 128.

13. Ibid.

14. Ibid., 132–33.

15. Ibid., 135.

16. Ibid., 140.

17. Ibid., 141–42.

18. Ibid., 142.

19. From the film *Joanna Macy and the Great Turning*, produced by Landry Communications (2014), www.joannamacyfilm.org.

20. Sabina's Soulcentric Coaching School is located in Switzerland. The trainings are conducted in German. You can learn more about Ausbildung Seelenzentriertes Coaching at www.seelenzentriert.ch.

21. Jung, *Memories*, 192.

22. In 1916, for example, Jung wrote an essay entitled "The Relations between the Ego and the Unconscious." And for a few years he studied the relationship between consciousness, personality, and the world, which culminated in his 1921 publication of *Psychological Types*.

23. All quotes from January 5, 1922, from Jung, *Red Book*, 211.

24. Ibid.

25. Jung, *Memories*, 200.

26. Ibid., 205

27. Ibid. In this quote, Jung makes it clear that for him the alchemists' texts constituted a map of the "psychic contents" of his and his patients' fantasy-images — *not* a map of the Descent itself (its structure or phases).

28. ·Ibid., 206.

29. Ibid., 204.

30. Jung, *Red Book*, 218.

31. This quote and details in this paragraph from ibid., 218, 219.

32. Jung's books published in these years include *Modern Man in Search of a Soul* (1933), *Psychology and Religion* (1938), *Aion: Researches into the Phenomenology of the Self* (1951), *Answer to Job* (1954), and *Animus and Anima* (1957).

33. Jung, *Memories*, 192.

34. Jung, *Red Book*, 215.

35. Jung, *Memories*, 395.

36. However, as noted elsewhere in this book, I suspect that the services provided by most Jungian analysts and therapists are some combination of psychotherapy (treating psychopathology) and the cultivation of one or more of what I call the four facets of wholeness. Few seem to guide or even understand the journey of soul initiation. It's likely also that few of their clients are psychologically prepared for the journey, in any case, a circumstance for which the practitioner is not, of course, primarily responsible.

Coda

Epigraph: From Mary Oliver, "Spring," in *House of Light* (Boston: Beacon Press, 1990), 6.

1. In addition to being embodied through the soul work of Adults and Elders, these nature-rooted meanings are also assimilated and incorporated into the sacred stories, myths, rituals, and practices of their culture.

2. Joanna Macy makes this point about cultural transformation by saying that the Great

Unraveling (a dissolution) is a necessary component of the Great Turning (a metamorphosis). See Macy and Brown, *Coming Back to Life.*

3. To fully embrace and facilitate the journey of soul initiation, a society must first have enough true Adults and Elders to support all its children and Adolescents to grow whole — because only healthy Adolescents are prepared to embark on the journey (see *Nature and the Human Soul*).

4. See Geneen Marie Haugen, *Awakening Planetary Imagination: A Theory and Practice* (San Francisco: California Institute of Integral Studies, ProQuest/UMI, 2015) and Geneen Marie Haugen, "Council of the Wild Gods," *Kosmos Journal* (spring 2019), https://www.kosmosjournal.org/kj_article/council-of-the-wild-gods.

5. Berry, *Dream of the Earth*, 133.

6. Brian Thomas Swimme and Mary Evelyn Tucker, *Journey of the Universe* (New Haven, CT: Yale University Press, 2011), 102.

7. The word *adolescence* itself was not used to refer to a stage of human development until the early twentieth century. The word, in fact, was coined in 1900 by Stanley Hall, the first American to earn a doctorate in psychology. I believe modern adolescence represents a potential evolutionary advance, but one we have not yet begun to fulfill. Microbiologists tell us that our genetic coding is 98.6 percent identical to that of chimpanzees and that the other 1.4 percent mostly dictates the duration (specifically, the slowness) of our juvenile development (neoteny). In other words, a core feature of what differentiates humans from other primates is the relatively long, pre-adult phase of our individual development. It appears that adolescence is a recently emerged and still very much evolving stage of growth, a stage gradually distinguishing itself from both childhood and adulthood. As the millennia unfold, we humans are maturing slower and, on the average, living longer. Rather than a sign of psychological regression or biological error, modern adolescence might be evidence of an evolutionary trajectory, a momentous advantage we've not yet benefited from — and are just beginning to understand. Longer juvenility makes possible, but does not compel, fuller maturation.

8. Quotes here and below from personal conversations with Geneen Marie Haugen, but these points are also made in *Awakening Planetary Imagination.*

9. Berry, *Dream of the Earth*, 132–33.

10. See, for example, Thomas Berry, *The Great Work: Our Way into the Future* (New York: Bell Tower, 1999), 162–63, 198–99.

11. Berry, *Dream of the Earth*, 206.

12. Berry, *Great Work*, 165.

13. Berry, *Dream of the Earth*, 211–12.

14. Steve Curwood interview with Gus Speth, "'We Scientists Don't Know How to Do That'…What a Commentary!" Winewaterwatch.org, May 5, 2016, http://winewater watch.org/2016/05/we-scientists-dont-know-how-to-do-that-what-a-commentary.

Appendix One

1. Andrew Schmookler, *The Parable of the Tribes: The Problem of Power in Social Evolution* (Albany: State University of New York Press, 1995).

2. Riane Eisler, *The Chalice and the Blade: Our History, Our Future* (New York: Harper and Row, 1987). Eisler differentiates cultures organized around the principle of domination from those organized around the principle of partnership. The dominator model

glorifies "the lethal power of the blade," while the older (original) partnership model reveres the chalice, "the life-generating and nurturing powers of the universe" (p. xvii).

3. The quotes in this paragraph are from Gregory Cajete, *Look to the Mountain: An Ecology of Indigenous Education* (Durango, CO: Kivakí Press, 1994), 35, 40, 71, 145, 148.

4. See Malidoma Somé, *Of Water and the Spirit: Ritual, Magic, and Initiation in the Life of an African Shaman* (New York: Penguin/Arkana, 1994).

5. From the age of four, Malidoma had been raised away from his village by Jesuits. At nineteen, he escaped and returned home. The initiation of Dagara boys is normally undertaken when they are thirteen or fourteen. Malidoma was twenty.

6. Somé, *Of Water and the Spirit*, 252–53.

7. Ibid., 297.

8. Martín Prechtel, *Long Life, Honey in the Heart: A Story of Initiation and Eloquence from the Shores of a Mayan Lake* (New York: Tarcher, 1999). Martín was raised on a Pueblo Indian reservation in New Mexico. As a young man, he traveled to Guatemala and eventually became a shaman and leader in the Mayan village of Santiago Atitlan.

9. Sylvia Brinton Perera, *Descent to the Goddess: A Way of Initiation for Women* (Toronto: Inner City Books, 1981).

10. Berry, *Dream of the Earth*, 207–8.

Appendix Two

1. Arnold van Gennep, *The Rites of Passage* (Chicago: University of Chicago Press, 1960).

2. Campbell, *Hero with a Thousand Faces*, 23.

3. Ibid., 6, 342.

4. Ibid., 211.

5. Campbell asserts, "The goal of the [mono]myth is…a reconciliation of the individual consciousness with the universal will" (ibid., 205–6).

6. In *Hero with a Thousand Faces*, see the top of p. 15 and the bottom of p. 31, and dozens of other passages throughout the book, especially "The Ultimate Boon" section, for examples of Campbell's fixation on enlightenment, illumination, and transcendence as the (upperworld) goal of the hero's journey.

7. Quotes in this sentence come from ibid., 15, 31, 211.

Index

abduction, 93–94, 97, 114, 116. *See also* Dissolution phase

Aborigines (Australia), 70, 219, 358

Abram, David, 380, 392n13, 395n11

acceptance, social, 39, 40–41, 54. *See also* Oasis stage

accomplishment, 108–9

active imagination method, 122, 129–35, 138, 166–67, 180, 198. *See also* deep imagination; Jung, Carl

Adam, 313

Addicts, 58, 59, 201. *See also* inner protectors

Adolescence: and Confirmation, 41–42; in Dissolution phase, 71; and eco-niche, 16, 27; in Eco-Soulcentric Developmental Wheel, 33; and Ego, preparation of, 161; and evolutionary potential, 9, 10, 13, 346, 366; and hero's journey, 363; human stagnation in, 11; in journey of soul initiation, 13, 32; Jung's departure from, 123; in Metamorphosis phase, 23, 244; and molting vs. Dissolution, 42–43; peer group as center of, 162; usage of term, 35, 408n7. *See also* Cocoon stage; Oasis stage

Adulthood: Artisans in, 309; and Cocoon stage, 43; definitions of, 11; Descent to Soul as path to, 3; and eco-niche, 11, 301,

314–15; in Eco-Soulcentric Developmental Wheel, 33, 35; vs. Elderhood, 391n1; importance of, 2; in journey of soul initiation, xxix, 2, 13; and Metamorphosis phase, 23, 244; and partnership with Earth, 342; and pollinating vs. consuming, 44; and rites of passage, 14–15; scarcity of true, 11–13; as soul embodiment, 7, 18, 350–51; and soul encounters, 148; and Soul Initiation, 148, 162; and vision ecologies, 343–44, 347; Wellspring stage, 20

Aengus, 71–72, 149, 245. *See also* Yeats, William Butler

agriculture, 353–54

alchemy, 122, 146, 333–34, 335, 359

Alighieri, Dante, 118, 359

analytical psychology, 115, 335. *See also* Jung, Carl

ancestors, 182, 210, 211, 220

Angulo, Cary de, 402n5

Anima/Animus, 48, 56–57, 130. *See also* West facet of Self

animal tracking, 198

anima mundi, 16, 20, 75, 196, 214

Animas Quests, 154

Animas Valley Institute, 3, 4–5, 8, 216–17, 350, 406n4

411

outcomes of, 309; and Descent to Soul, 362; and Enactment phase, 317; and facets of wholeness, 183; importance of, 350–51; of Joanna Macy, 325; of Jung, 332–33; of Matt Syrdal, 312; and Metamorphosis phase, 243–44; overview, 20, 302, 332; of Sabina Wyss, 328; of Silver Moon, 307–8; and Soul vs. social purpose, 27; and true Adulthood, 148, 162

soul-initiation guides, 77–80, 122, 278–79, 351, 354

soul names, 155, 156–57, 172, 233–35, 291–93, 329

South facet of Self (Wild Indigenous One): contemporary need for, 188; cultivation of, 53; on Descent to Soul, 54–55; and Dissolution phase, 99, 125; and East facet, 396n4; and ETCs, 265; and femininity, 131, 188, 400n41; and full-bodied feeling, 49–50, 52; of Jung, 130–31, 138–39, 140, 142; and Metamorphosis phase, 252, 258, 261; overview, 47–48, 51; in romancing the world, 103; and soul encounters, 153, 203

species boundaries, dialogue across, 109–11, 164–65, 195, 198, 222–33, 283–86, 319–23. *See also* Others and other-than-human-world

sperm, 194

Speth, Gus, 350

Spielrien, Sabina, 399n12

Spirit. *See* Mystery; upperworld

Stafford, William, 299, 359

St. Francis, 84

St. John of the Cross, 84

stories, 17–19, 25–26. *See also* mythopoetic identity

storms, 155, 170, 212, 323

Stream Restoration Program, 319

stress, 91, 92

subpersonalities (subs). *See* inner protectors

Sufism, xx

suicide, 256

Sun, 221–22, 245, 300–301

survival of the fittest, 6. *See also* evolution

survival strategies, 58, 63, 142. *See also* inner protectors

sweats and saunas, 199, 368

Swimme, Brian, 345

Syrdal, Matt, 82–86, 163–68, 234, 235, 293–96, 309–14

systems theory, 176, 325–26, 372

Taoism, 335

Telegraph Cove, 225–26, 271, 283, 286

terrorism, 52

Thespian at the Oasis, 35, 37, 128–29, 393n2, 395n15

thinking, 48–50, 396n2

three-worlds model, 115–17. *See also* middle-world; underworld; upperworld

threshold crossings. *See* Experimental Threshold Crossings; one-way portal ceremonies

time, 347–48

tomb, xxii, 244

Tower, 290–91

trance dances, 154, 199, 368

trance visions, 233, 234–35

transcendence, 9–10

transcendent function, 118, 232

transformation. *See* Dissolution phase; Metamorphosis phase

transpersonal dedications, 87–88, 120, 223

Trappist monks, 209

trauma, 62–64, 191, 259

Trickster, 53, 56, 77. *See also* East facet of Self

Tzutujil Maya, 358

uncertainty principle, 356

underworld: and becoming one's Blood, 195–96; in Celtic lore, 72; in Christian myth, 76; and Dagara initiation, 357; and Dan's eco-niche, 204, 205, 206; and Dissolution phase, 68, 82, 85, 95–96, 367–68; and East facet of Self, 55–56; and Elisabeth Nicolson, 258, 259, 260; and Enactment phase, 315; and ETCs, 292; in Greek myth, 73, 93–94; and inner protectors, recognition of, 200; Jung's experience of, 113, 114, 119, 124, 133, 143–44, 181–82, 289; and Kevin's eco-niche, 92, 217, 219, 319, 341; and Metamorphosis phase, 294; and mythopoetic identity, 20; and North facet of Self, 53–54; and self-sacrifice, 135; in

About the Author

Bill Plotkin, PhD, is an eco-depth psychologist, wilderness guide, and agent of cultural regeneration. As founder of southwest Colorado's Animas Valley Institute, he has, since 1980, guided thousands of women and men on the journey of soul initiation. He's also been a research psychologist (studying nonordinary states of consciousness), rock musician, and white-water river guide. In 1979, on a solo winter ascent of an Adirondack peak, Bill experienced a "call to spiritual adventure," leading him to abandon academia in search of his true calling. His previous books are *Soulcraft: Crossing into the Mysteries of Nature and Psyche* (an experiential guidebook), *Nature and the Human Soul: Cultivating Wholeness and Community in a Fragmented World* (a nature-based stage model of human development), and *Wild Mind: A Field Guide to the Human Psyche* (a nature-based map of the psyche). His doctorate in psychology is from the University of Colorado at Boulder. Visit him online at www.animas.org.

About Animas Valley Institute

A nimas Valley Institute, founded in 1980, offers a diverse set of journeys into the mysteries of nature and psyche, including Soulcraft™ intensives, contemporary vision fasts, and training programs for soul-initiation guides and other nature-based human development facilitators.

Soulcraft skills and practices evoke the world-shifting experience of soul encounter — the revelation of our unique mythopoetic identity, an identity expressed through symbol and metaphor, image and dream, archetype and myth, an identity embodied in a mysterious story that whispers to us in moments of expanded awareness and exquisite aliveness. The shape and rhythm of this story reveals the hidden treasure that each of us carries for the world — a world longing for the transformative contributions of visionary leaders and artisans of cultural renaissance.

> Individually and collectively, we launch into an uncertain future — at once both perilous and saturated with possibility. Our accustomed, culturally determined roles and identities are inadequate for navigating the sea change of our time. Our collective journey requires a radical shift in the human relationship with the community of all life — a cultural transformation so profound that future humans might regard it as an evolution of consciousness. Safe passage requires each of us to offer our full magnificence to the world. Popular culture cannot help us uncover our singular gifts; contemporary institutions do not invite their expression. Our particular genius can be discovered only in an initiatory journey — an accidental or intentional descent into the mysteries of Soul. Guiding the *intentional* descent to Soul has been the unfolding work of Animas Valley Institute for over forty years.
>
> — GENEEN MARIE HAUGEN, author and Animas guide

Soulcraft has been shaped and influenced by many sources, including wilderness rites and writers, the theories and practices of depth- and eco-psychologies, the poetic tradition, perspectives and practices common to current and earlier traditions of animism and Earth-honoring from across the human family, the lived experiences of thousands of contemporary people during Animas immersions, and the wild Earth herself. Soulcraft is the emergence of a contemporary, Western, and nature-rooted path to the *terra mysterium* of Soul Initiation.

The descent into the mysteries of nature and psyche is where the husk of outgrown ego-identity is shed; is where tricksters, demons, and perhaps angels are encountered; and is the experience from which a new self emerges as a vessel for one's distinctive genius and world-transforming gifts. Although the institute's work evokes nonordinary perception and ways of knowing, it is not shamanism or rites of passage, nor is it primarily wilderness-based psychotherapy or emotional healing. Animas immersions are not designed to transcend the Ego, solve everyday personal problems, or help people better adjust to — or be happier in — the flatland of contemporary Western culture. Rather, the intent is a deep-structure shift that matures the Ego and elicits each person's most creative, soul-rooted response to our critical, liminal moment in the unfolding of the world's story — on the threshold of a future shaped by those who can see beyond our own time.

Animas Valley Institute's twenty guides lead multiday experiential explorations into wild landscapes and into the wilds of Soul. They also offer online programs, organizational consulting, programs in partnership with other organizations, and individual mentoring and guiding. Each year, the institute guides approximately seventy programs in various locations and ecosystems in North America, South America, Europe, Australia, and New Zealand.

Animas offers two multiyear professional training programs: one for soul-initiation guides (the Soulcraft Apprenticeship and Initiation Program) and one for professional human-development guides, including psychotherapists, ecotherapists, life coaches, religious leaders, and educators (the Wild Mind Training Program).

To learn more about Animas programs, trainings, and guides, contact:

Animas Valley Institute
PO Box 1020
Durango, CO 81302 USA
970-259-0585
www.animas.org
soulcraft@animas.org